Consumer Lending

Sixth Edition

AMERICAN
BANKERS
ASSOCIATION ®

This publication is designed to provide accurate and authoritative information in regard to the subject matter covered. It is sold with the understanding that the publisher is not engaged in rendering legal, accounting, or other professional service. If legal advice or other expert assistance is required, the services of a competent professional person should be sought.

From a Declaration of Principles jointly adopted by a Committee of the American Bar Association and a Committee of Publishers and Associations.

The American Bankers Association is committed to providing innovative, high-quality products and services that are responsive to its members' critical needs.

To comment about this product, or to learn more about the American Bankers Association and the many products and services it offers, please call **1-800-BANKERS** or visit us at our website: **www.aba.com**.

This textbook has been approved by the American Institute of Banking for use in courses for which AIB certificates or diplomas are granted. The American Institute of Banking is the professional development and training affiliate of the American Bankers Association. Instructional materials endorsed by AIB have been developed by bankers for bankers.

American Institute *of* Banking

AMERICAN **BANKERS** ASSOCIATION ®

© 2009 by the American Bankers Association
Sixth Edition

All rights reserved. No part of this publication may be reproduced, stored in a retrieval system, or transmitted in any form or by any means—electronic, mechanical, photocopying, recording, or otherwise—without prior written permission from the American Bankers Association.

Printed in the United States of America

10 9 8 7 6 5 4 3 2 1

Catalog Number: 3005095   ISBN:0-89982-630-X

Contents

LIST OF EXHIBITS   xv

PREFACE   xix

ABOUT THE AUTHORS   xxv

ACKNOWLEDGMENTS   xxvii

CHAPTER 1   INTRODUCTION TO CONSUMER LENDING

LEARNING OBJECTIVES   1

INTRODUCTION   2

CONSUMER LENDING DEFINED   2

HISTORY OF CONSUMER LENDING   4

    Credit in the Early Colonies   4

    Shaping Consumer Finance in the 1900s   5

    The Great Depression   5

    After World War II   6

    Economic and Social Change in the 1960s and 1970s   6

    Lending in the Late Twentieth Century   7

    Lending in the Twenty-first Century   8

LENDING AND RETAIL BANKING   12

FEDERAL AND STATE REGULATIONS   14

    The Regulators   15

    Laws and Regulations   16

    Consumer Lending Compliance Programs   20

SUMMARY   21

END NOTES   22

SELF-CHECK AND REVIEW   23

ADDITIONAL RESOURCES   23

APPENDIX 1—GALAXY FINANCIAL BANK COMPLIANCE POLICY   25

CHAPTER 2   THE CONSUMER LENDING MARKET

LEARNING OBJECTIVES   31

INTRODUCTION   32

LOANS OUTSTANDING   32

    Closed-end and Open-End Loans   33

Product Life Cycle   34

Direct and Indirect Lending   35

LOAN VOLUME   36

Sociodemographic Environment   36

Economic Environment   40

Natural, Seasonal, and Geographic Issues   40

The Regulatory Environment   41

Technology   41

Competitive Environment   41

LAWS AND REGULATIONS   43

Community Reinvestment Act   44

Home Mortgage Disclosure Act   45

Fair Lending   46

SUMMARY   48

END NOTES   49

SELF-CHECK AND REVIEW   49

ADDITIONAL RESOURCES   50

CHAPTER 3   DIRECT LENDING

LEARNING OBJECTIVES   51

INTRODUCTION   52

DIRECT LENDING DEFINED   52

ORGANIZING DIRECT LENDING   53

The Centralized Approach   53

The Decentralized Approach   53

DIRECT LENDING AND THE BANK   54

Advantages   54

Disadvantages   55

DIRECT LENDING AND THE CONSUMER   55

Advantages   56

Disadvantages   57

SECURED AND UNSECURED LOANS   57

Secured Loans   57

Unsecured Loans   61

LOAN GUARANTEES   62

Cosigned and Personally Guaranteed Loans   62

Government-Guaranteed Loan Programs   62

LAWS AND REGULATIONS   66

Credit Practices Rule   66

Privacy Provisions   67

Subprime Lending Guidelines   68

SUMMARY   71

SELF-CHECK AND REVIEW   72

ADDITIONAL RESOURCES   73

CHAPTER 4   INDIRECT LENDING

LEARNING OBJECTIVES   75

INTRODUCTION   76

INDIRECT LENDING DEFINED   76

The Indirect Lending Market   76

The Indirect Lending Relationship   77

THE DEALER RELATIONSHIP   78

Establishing a Dealer Relationship   79

Types of Goods Sold   79

Identifying the Dealers   79

The Dealer Agreement   79

Processing Loan Applications   80

THE BANK'S PERSPECTIVE   81

Advantages   81

Disadvantages   84

THE DEALER'S PERSPECTIVE   86

Closing Deals Quickly   86

Monthly Payment Terms   86

Increased Profit   86

THE CONSUMER'S PERSPECTIVE   87

Advantages   88

Disadvantages   88

FLOORPLAN FINANCING   89

LEASING   90

THE FUTURE OF INDIRECT LENDING   93

Purchasing Expensive Items   93

Choices in Loan Sources   93

LAWS AND REGULATIONS   94

Restrictions on Insider Lending (FRS Regulation O)   94

Holder in Due Course Rule: UCC Article 3 vs. FTC Rule   96

Consumer Leasing Act   96

SUMMARY	97
SELF-CHECK AND REVIEW	99
ADDITIONAL RESOURCES	100

CHAPTER 5   OPEN-END, REVOLVING CREDIT PRODUCTS

LEARNING OBJECTIVES	101
INTRODUCTION	102
OPEN-END CREDIT FEATURES	102
OPEN-END CREDIT PRODUCTS	103
Credit Cards	103
Check Overdraft Lines of Credit	107
Unsecured Lines of Credit	108
Secured Lines of Credit	108
Related Products	111
OPEN-END CREDIT PROCESS	113
Documentation	113
BANK BENEFITS AND CHALLENGES	113
Benefits to the Bank	114
Challenges for the Bank	116
CONSUMER BENEFITS AND CHALLENGES	118
Benefits to the Consumer	118
Challenges for the Consumer	119
LAWS AND REGULATIONS	121
Fair Credit Reporting Act	121
Truth in Lending	123
SUMMARY	127
END NOTES	129
SELF-CHECK AND REVIEW	129
ADDITIONAL RESOURCES	130

CHAPTER 6   FORMULATING A CONSUMER LOAN POLICY

LEARNING OBJECTIVES	133
INTRODUCTION	134
THE CONSUMER LOAN POLICY	134
What a Loan Policy Does	135
COMPONENTS OF A LOAN POLICY	139
Statement of the Bank's Objectives	140
Responsibilities of the Directors, Management, and Staff	141

Geographic Limits of the Market Area 141

Pricing Guidelines 141

Types of Loans Desired 142

Loans to Insiders and Employees 143

Lending Authority 143

Credit Criteria—General Terms 144

Loan Documentation 144

Compliance and Loan Review 145

Collection and Charge-Off 145

Corporate Responsibility and Ethics 146

LOAN POLICY AND CREDIT CRITERIA 147

Credit History 147

Capacity and Decision-Making Systems 147

Collateral 148

KEYS TO AN EFFECTIVE LOAN POLICY 149

Unambiguous Loan Standards 150

Communication 151

Procedures 151

Exceptions 152

LAWS AND REGULATIONS 152

Regulating Purpose Credit 152

Transactions with Affiliates 153

Financial Institutions Reform, Recovery, and Enforcement Act 154

SUMMARY 154

END NOTE 155

SELF-CHECK AND REVIEW 155

ADDITIONAL RESOURCES 156

APPENDIX II—GALAXY BANK LOAN POLICY 157

CHAPTER 7   GENERATING LOAN APPLICATIONS

LEARNING OBJECTIVES 165

INTRODUCTION 166

THE CONSUMER LENDING PROCESS 166

APPLICATION PROCESS OBJECTIVES 166

Generate Applications 167

Get Information for a Decision 167

Ensure Compliance with the Law 168

Respond Promptly 168

Earn Applicant Goodwill   169

LOAN PRODUCT CONSIDERATIONS   169

    Direct Lending   169

    Indirect Lending   170

    Open-End Loan Products   171

MARKETING PROGRAMS   171

    Define Objectives   172

    Select Target Markets   172

    Select Promotion Channels   174

    Implement the Plan   176

    Measure Results   177

TAKING APPLICATIONS   177

    In-Person Applications   177

    Telephone Applications   180

    Direct Mail Applications   180

    Electronic Applications   180

    Challenges   180

LAWS AND REGULATIONS   182

    Truth in Lending Act   182

    Real Estate Settlement Procedures Act   186

    Telemarketing and Consumer Protection   187

    CAN-SPAM Act   188

SUMMARY   189

END NOTES   191

SELF-CHECK AND REVIEW   191

ADDITIONAL RESOURCES   191

CHAPTER 8   CREDIT INVESTIGATION

LEARNING OBJECTIVES   193

INTRODUCTION   194

CREDIT INVESTIGATION DEFINED   194

    Credit Investigation Objectives   195

    The Credit Investigation Process   196

TYPES OF CREDIT INFORMATION   198

    Credit History   198

    Income   199

    Employment   201

    Residence   203

Collateral	204
SOURCES OF CREDIT INFORMATION	205
Credit Reporting Agencies	205
Personal Financial Statements	207
Personal Tax Returns	207
Warning Signs	210
Open-End Loan Product Considerations	216
LAWS AND REGULATIONS	216
Fair Credit Reporting Act	217
FACT Act	218
SUMMARY	220
SELF-CHECK AND REVIEW	222
ADDITIONAL RESOURCES	223
APPENDIX III–SAMPLE CREDIT REPORT	225

CHAPTER 9   CREDIT EVALUATION AND DECISION MAKING

LEARNING OBJECTIVES	233
INTRODUCTION	234
EVALUATION AND DECISION-MAKING OBJECTIVES	234
Make the Best Loan	234
Comply with Regulations and Bank Policy	236
Retain the Consumer's Goodwill	237
Ensure that the Risk Is Acceptable	237
THE JUDGMENTAL APPROACH	238
Character	238
Capacity	242
Capital	246
Collateral	249
Conditions	250
Making a Judgmental Decision	250
CREDIT SCORING	252
Credit Score Variables	252
Credit Scores and the Cs of Credit	254
Credit Scoring Advantages	254
Credit Scoring Disadvantages	256
Credit Scoring with Judgmental Elements	256
DECLINING A LOAN	257
Retain Consumer's Goodwill	257

Legal and Regulatory Compliance 257

EQUAL CREDIT OPPORTUNITY ACT 257

Evaluation Criteria 257

Credit Scoring 259

Notifications 259

Appraisal Notices 260

SUMMARY 262

SELF-CHECK AND REVIEW 264

ADDITIONAL RESOURCES 264

CHAPTER 10   LOAN PRICING AND PROFITABILITY

LEARNING OBJECTIVES 267

INTRODUCTION 268

THE COST TO BORROW 268

Calculating Interest 268

Interest Rates 269

Payment Protection 272

Loan Terms 274

LOAN PRICING 275

Regulatory Environment 275

Competitive Environment 275

Economic Conditions 276

The Bank's Internal Environment 276

Other Factors 276

LOAN PROFITABILITY 278

The Bank's Cost 278

Evaluating Loan Profitability 280

Product Line Profitability 283

LAWS AND REGULATIONS 283

Legal Lending Limits 284

Debt Cancellation Contracts and Debt Suspension Agreements 285

SUMMARY 286

SELF-CHECK AND REVIEW 288

ADDITIONAL RESOURCES 289

APPENDIX IV—GALAXY BANK FINANCIAL CASE STUDY 290

CHAPTER 11   SELLING AND LOAN STRUCTURING

LEARNING OBJECTIVES	301
INTRODUCTION	302
MARKET-DRIVEN SELLING	302
Consultative Selling	303
Cross-Selling	303
THE SALES-ORIENTED BANK	303
Establishing a Sales Culture	303
Effective Selling Skills	304
The Selling Process	306
LOAN STRUCTURING	308
Meeting Sales Objectives	308
Loan Structuring by Product Line	310
Loan Structuring Variables	311
LAWS AND REGULATIONS	317
Home Ownership and Equity Protection Act	317
Higher-priced Mortgage Loans	319
SUMMARY	319
END NOTE	321
SELF-CHECK AND REVIEW	321
ADDITIONAL RESOURCES	321

CHAPTER 12   LOAN DOCUMENTATION AND CLOSING

LEARNING OBJECTIVES	323
INTRODUCTION	324
DOCUMENTATION AND CLOSING OBJECTIVES	324
Completing the Documents	324
Efficient and Accurate Document Preparation	325
Compliance with the Law and the Loan Policy	325
Making Sure the Customer Understands the Terms	326
Creating the Best Image for the Bank	327
Selling Other Bank Services and Asking for Referrals	327
TYPES OF DOCUMENTATION	327
Fixed-Rate Closed-End Loans	328
Variable-Rate Loans	330
Open-End Loan Accounts	331
ESTABLISHING A SECURITY INTEREST	331
Creating a Valid Lien—Attachment	332

Giving Notice—Perfection   333

Possession of Collateral   334

LOAN CLOSING   335

LOAN REVIEW   335

Ensure Compliance with the Law   336

Examine Documents and Resolve Errors   336

Expedite Booking New Loans   336

Record and Report   337

Obtain Lien and Insurance Documents   337

LAWS AND REGULATIONS   337

Insurance Sales Disclosures   337

Flood Disaster Protection   338

Unfair or Deceptive Acts or Practices   338

SUMMARY   339

END NOTES   340

SELF-CHECK AND REVIEW   340

ADDITIONAL RESOURCES   340

CHAPTER 13   COLLECTION AND RECOVERY

LEARNING OBJECTIVES   343

INTRODUCTION   344

OBJECTIVES OF COLLECTION AND RECOVERY   344

Keep Delinquency Levels Acceptable   345

Keep Loan Loss Levels Acceptable   346

Generate Loss Recoveries   346

Counsel Customers Experiencing Difficulty   346

Ensure Consistency with Bank Objectives   347

Manage Collection and Recovery Costs   348

CAUSES OF DELINQUENCY   348

Unexpected Changes in Financial Situation   349

Economic Downturn   349

Excessive Debt   349

Poor Money Management   349

Marital Problems   350

Carelessness and Changing Attitudes   350

Irresponsible Lending   350

Fraud or Intentional Default   350

Substance Abuse and Gambling   350

THE COLLECTION AND RECOVERY FUNCTIONS   351
    The Collection Function   351
    Recovery Operations   351
THE COLLECTION CYCLE   352
    Early Stage   353
    Personal Contact Stage   354
    Serious Delinquency   356
    Charge-Offs   357
BANKRUPTCY   358
    Chapter 7, Liquidation   359
    Chapter 13, Adjustment of Debts   360
    Bankruptcy and Banks   360
LAWS AND REGULATIONS   361
    Fair Debt Collection Practices Act   361
    Servicemembers Civil Relief Act   362
    Bankruptcy Abuse Prevention and Consumer Protection Act   363
SUMMARY   365
END NOTES   366
SELF-CHECK AND REVIEW   367
ADDITIONAL RESOURCES   367

ANSWERS TO SITUATIONS AND SELF-CHECK AND
    REVIEW QUESTIONS   369
ANSWERS TO GALAXY BANK FINANCIAL CASE STUDY QUESTIONS   413
GLOSSARY   417
INDEX   435

List of Exhibits

CHAPTER 1

1.1	Consumer Credit Categories	3
1.2	Net Interest Margin	7
1.3	The Financial Crisis of 2008	11
1.4	The Evolution of Consumer Credit	12
1.5	Consumer Credit Outstanding: Major Holders	13
1.6	Consumer Credit Outstanding: Major Holders by Type of Credit	14
1.7	Federal Banking Regulators and the Institutions They Supervise	15
1.8	Major Consumer Lending Laws and Regulations	17
1.9	Federal Reserve System Regulations	18
1.10	Federal Box Disclosures	19

CHAPTER 2

2.1	Consumer Loans Outstanding	33
2.2	Product Life Cycle	34
2.3	Life Cycle of Two Loan Products	35
2.4	Sample Portfolio Distribution of Closed-End Loan Volume	37
2.5	Life-Cycle Stage and Credit Use	38
2.6	Information Reported on an HDMA LAR	46

CHAPTER 3

3.1	Depreciating Value Collateral	58
3.2	Fluctuating Value Collateral	59
3.3	Stable Value Collateral	60
3.4	Appreciating Value Collateral	61
3.5	Federally Guaranteed Student Loan Programs	63
3.6	Sample Notice to Cosigners	67
3.7	Sample Privacy Notice	69

CHAPTER 4

4.1	Indirect Lending Flow Chart	77
4.2	Sample Percentages of Loans Outstanding in Selected Dealer Plans	83
4.3	Dealer Income from a Retail Contract	87
4.4	How Banks Pay for Dealer Reserves	87

4.5	Sample Questions on Floorplan and Indirect Lending	91
4.6	Leasing vs. Buying a Vehicle	92
4.7	Holder Notice on Promissory Note	96

CHAPTER 5

5.1	Comparison of Three Credit Card Plans	105
5.2	Home Equity Line of Credit Assets at Commercial Banks	109
5.3	Sample Home Equity Line of Credit Portfolios	110
5.4	Potential Revolving Credit Debt	117
5.5	Holiday Advice to Credit Card Customers— Use Your Credit Wisely	121
5.6	Safeguarding Financial Information	122
5.7	Risks to Earnings or Capital in Credit Card Lending	123
5.8	Sample Disclosure Table for Credit Card Applications and Solicitations	125
5.9	Notice of Right to Rescind	126

CHAPTER 6

6.1	Signs that a Loan Policy Needs a Tune-Up	136
6.2	Risk Areas in Banking	137
6.3	Contents of a Typical Bank Code of Conduct	140
6.4	Sample Consumer Lending Authority Schedule	144
6.5	Sample Loan Charge-off Policy	146
6.6	Automobile Loan Policy	149
6.7	Sample Marine Loan Policy	149
6.8	Sample Home Equity Line of Credit Policy	150
6.9	Restricted Transactions Between Affiliates	153

CHAPTER 7

7.1	The Lending Process	167
7.2	Loan Application Sources	170
7.3	Open-end Credit Product and Application Sources	171
7.4	Consumer Tips: Avoiding Predatory Lending Scams	179
7.5	Sample of Charges Included in the Finance Charge	183
7.6	Sample Truth in Lending Triggering Terms in Advertisements	184
7.7	FTC and FCC Telemarketing Rules	187

CHAPTER 8

8.1	Information Verified in Credit Investigations	195
8.2	Sources for Valuing Collateral	198

8.3	Red Flags	201
8.4A	Sample Loan Application	208
8.4B	Sample Personal Financial Statement	209
8.4C	Sample 1040 Statement	211
8.4D	Sample Schedule A	213
8.4E	Sample Schedule B	214
8.4F	Credit Report for Frank Dunten	215
8.5	Prescreen and Preapproval Process	217

CHAPTER 9

9.1	Application for a Joint Loan	235
9.2	Sample Credit Report	241
9.3	Sample Credit Report for a Heavy User of Revolving Credit	242
9.4	Debt-to-Income Ratio Table	243
9.5	Personal Financial Statement	247
9.6	The Five Cs of Credit—Sample Elements	251
9.7	Hypothetical Credit-Scoring System	253
9.8	Credit Scores Held by Percent of U.S. Population	254
9.9	Adverse Action Flow Chart	260
9.10	Notice of Adverse Action	261

CHAPTER 10

10.1	Depreciating Value Collateral with Extended Loan Maturity	272
10.2	Effect of Loan Term on Monthly Payments	274
10.3	Sample Pricing Schedules	277
10.4	Time Value of Money: Present and Future Value	278
10.5	Profitability Analysis—Effect of Loan Term	281
10.6	Profitability Analysis—Rate Effect	281
10.7	Breakeven Analysis for Loan Amount	282
10.8	Interest Accrual on Simple-Interest Loans	283
10.9	Product Line Profitability	283
10.10	Bank Income on Two Dealer Contracts	284
10.11	DCC Short Form Disclosure Sample	287

CHAPTER 11

11.1	Purchase Cycle	307
11.2	Loan Size Relative to Interest Income—Closed-End Loans	313
11.3	Term, Rate, and Monthly Payment Comparisons	314
11.4	Loan Structuring	316

11.5   Credit Insurance Sales: Effect on Loan Payments
and Bank Income   317

CHAPTER 12

12.1   The Lending Process   328

12.2   Documentation Required for Certain Loan Products   329

12.3   Sample Open-end Credit Statements and Notifications   332

12.4   Methods of Perfecting a Security Interest   334

CHAPTER 13

13.1   Consumer Credit Delinquency Percent Delinquent—
National Averages   345

13.2   Residential and Consumer Credit Charge-Offs—
Commercial Banks, 4th Quarter   347

13.3   Collection Cycle   353

13.4   Percentage of Accounts Delinquent   353

13.5   Loan-Loss Reserve Account   358

13.6   Nonbusiness Bankruptcy Petitions   359

13.7   U.S. Bankruptcy Laws Timeline   364

13.8   Provisions of the Bankruptcy Abuse Prevention and
Consumer Protection Act of 2005   365

Preface

This sixth edition of *Consumer Lending* is a revision of the textbook originally written by Paul R. Beares, who guided it through the third edition. Richard E Beck, Jr. and Susan M. Siegel wrote the fourth edition. For the fifth edition, Mr. Beck served as subject matter expert, and for the sixth edition, he is a co-author with Kathlyn L. Farrell.

Like its predecessors, the sixth edition introduces students to the process of lending, to its importance to the bank and consumers, and to the environment in which it functions. The textbook takes a practical approach to the fundamentals of lending. It addresses contemporary issues and developments important to understanding consumer lending today.

It is not the intent of this textbook to make the readers seasoned lenders. That will come in due time. Rather, the American Bankers Association hopes to spark an interest in consumer lending and to encourage students and other readers to pursue further studies and embark on careers in this challenging field.

OBJECTIVES OF THIS BOOK

- Define consumer lending and discuss its evolution to meet the financial needs of consumers.
- Identify loan product life cycles and discuss the benefits of consumer lending for banks.
- List characteristics, benefits, and disadvantages of direct lending and discuss the categories of collateral value.
- Explain the advantages and disadvantages of indirect lending from the perspectives of the bank, the dealer, and the consumer.
- Explain leasing as an alternative to a consumer loan.
- Describe the characteristics, benefits, and challenges of open-end credit products.
- Explain the objectives and components of a bank loan policy.
- State the objectives of the loan application process and discuss how banks generate applications through marketing and different delivery channels.
- Describe the sources of consumer loan information and the steps in the credit investigation process.
- Explain how the five Cs of credit are used in credit evaluation and decision making in both the judgmental and credit-scoring approaches.
- Describe the factors that affect loan pricing and the methods used to calculate profitability.

- Identify structuring options for different loan products and describe how these options achieve sales objectives.
- Describe the documentation needed for different loan types, the loan closing process, and the loan review function.
- Discuss causes of consumer loan delinquencies and identify the objectives and processes of the collection and recovery functions.
- Describe the laws and regulations that affect consumer lending and identify the regulatory agencies that supervise the banking industry.

CHANGES IN THIS EDITION

In addressing these objectives, this text updates the material in the previous edition of *Consumer Lending*. Throughout, the book incorporates lessons learned from the financial crisis of 2008 and new laws and regulations that relate to chapter topics. Some of the new information presented in this book:

- an explanation of the Financial Crisis of 2008 and its effect on the banking industry, the economy, and consumers
- information about federal legislation and regulations that were a response to subprime lending developments
- content on government support for Fannie Mae and Freddie Mac
- a revision to the discussion on cosigned loans and personal guarantees
- content on the factors in managing an indirect lending portfolio to expand the business relationship and develop new opportunities
- emerging consumer options in indirect lending, such as automobile brokerage
- discussion of the unbanked and financial literacy programs
- discussion of the ever-more-important issue of risk and incorporating risk management into bank loan policy
- an explanation of the CAMELS system and the role of bank directors, management, and staff in creating and implementing bank policy and underwriting standards
- discussion of how the financial crisis effected changes in loan policies
- an explanation of what banks can do and should not do to turn rate shoppers into customers
- discussion of red flags during the application, credit investigation, and credit evaluation processes, with special attention to identity theft red flags
- an explanation of overrides and the disadvantages of the credit scoring system

- a discussion of regulatory changes related to subprime lending, identity theft, practices on certain home loans, such as higher-priced loans, unfair clauses in loan and security agreements, and sales of insurance
- updates on loan documentation requirements for certain loans
- new or revised discussion on the following laws and regulations:
  - Bankruptcy Abuse Prevention and Consumer Protection Act
  - Fair and Accurate Credit Transactions Act
  - Fair Credit Reporting Act, and FRS Regulations V and FF
  - Federal Reserve System Regulation AA, Unfair or Deceptive Acts or Practices
  - Gramm-Leach-Bliley Act
  - Holder in Due Course Rule, Uniform Commercial Code Article 3, and the Federal Trade Commission Rule
  - Real Estate Settlement Procedures Act
  - Subprime lending guidelines
  - Truth in Lending Act
  - Unfair Practices on Certain Home Loans

Thirty-nine exhibits were revised and the following were added:
- Timeline on the Financial Crisis of 2008
- Holiday Advice to Credit Card Customers
- Red Flags in applications and credit reports, and for identity theft
- Sample Disclosure Table for credit card applications and solicitations
- Sample Truth in Lending Triggering Terms in Advertisements

Many glossary terms, information in sidebars, additional resources, review questions, and appendixes were revised and added. A sample credit report appears after chapter 8.

TEXT ORGANIZATION

The text is organized as it was in the fifth edition. Chapter 1 describes the legal and regulatory environment for lending. All chapters have a section on laws and regulations important to consumer lending. The text is typeset in a single column, with sidebars that highlight especially relevant information. Graphics visually enhance the reading and learning experience. The appendixes have been moved from the back of the book to follow the related chapters. Instructional design features are:

- learning objectives at the beginning of the chapter
- an introduction that sets the stage for topics covered in the chapter

- sidebars, charts, exhibits, and "by the numbers" and "did you know?" callouts that supplement chapter content
- definitions in sidebars for terms bolded in the text
- situations with questions that test the reader's understanding of concepts and principles
- a summary that reviews each chapter's main points
- self-check and review questions for testing comprehension of chapter content
- a list of additional resources, such as publications and Web sites, that contain material related to chapter content
- sections at the back of the book with answers to chapter self-check and review questions and the situations
- appendixes that include a compliance policy statement, a consumer loan policy statement, and a case study with questions and answers
- a glossary that defines terms used in the text
- an index that can be used to locate content

The first two chapters present an overview of consumer lending: The Introduction sets the scene for what follows. Chapter 1 presents a historical perspective on consumer lending, establishes foundational issues, and explains the regulatory environment in which consumer lenders operate. Chapter 2 deals with the dynamics of the consumer loan market and its evolution.

The next three chapters introduce today's consumer lending products and services: Chapter 3 looks at how the direct lending function has changed over the years and how technology affects the delivery of loan products. Chapter 4 addresses the traditional function of indirect lending, changes in the market, and the effects of technology. Chapter 5 discusses the ever-changing consumer lending product line, open-end credit.

Chapter 6 looks at the process of drafting a consumer loan policy, its importance to all involved in the lending process, how it is created, its features and benefits, and how compliance with it can be ensured.

The next five chapters deal with the actual process of making a loan. Chapter 7 looks at how the loan application process and interviews are conducted. It also discusses the challenge of generating quality loan applications, an issue for all lending institutions. Chapter 8, which discusses the credit investigation function, highlights the importance of conducting rapid yet thorough investigations. Chapter 9 covers the evaluation and decision-making phases of the process, suggesting methods for efficient and effective evaluations and quick decisions. Chapter 10 delves into the joint issues of loan pricing and loan profitability and the importance of balancing both while making consumer loans. Finally, Chapter 11 tackles selling and how lenders use loan structuring to find the most appropriate loan for the borrower while at the same time building consumer relationships.

Consumer Lending concludes with a discussion of other areas of consumer loan administration. Chapter 12 discusses the importance of loan documentation and proper loan closings. This chapter presents lists of typical documents required for different types of loans, the process for establishing a security interest, and related legal essentials. Chapter 13, the final chapter, addresses the world of collections and recovery. It discusses how banks approach collection and the importance of monitoring and following up on delinquent loans; it also deals with bankruptcy.

The appendixes at the end of the chapters are additional readings intended to enhance the learning experience. They are examples of a compliance policy, a loan policy, a sample credit report, and a case study. Appendix 4, The Galaxy Bank Financial Case Study, is an example of a bank's experience with many of the content points covered in this textbook, supplemented by questions and answers for the student.

About the Authors

The American Bankers Association extends its gratitude to Richard E. Beck, Jr. and Kathlyn L. Farrell, who co-authored this textbook.

Richard Beck has been in the financial services industry for more than 35 years. Although he has worked in many areas of the bank, from retail through corporate and training to private banking, for most of his career, he has been in consumer finance. He also has taught future bankers and career bankers at such venues as the American Institute of Banking, the Indiana Bankers Association, the American Bankers Association, the North Dakota and South Dakota Schools of Banking, the Kansas-Nebraska Schools of Banking, and the Kentucky Bankers Association. His expertise led to his teaching a summer session in marketing at Concordia's International University in Estonia.

Mr. Beck holds an M.B.A. from Indiana Wesleyan University and a B.A. in political science from Ball State University in Muncie, Indiana. He is currently Senior Vice-President and Corporate Sales Manager for STAR Financial Bank in Fort Wayne, Indiana.

Kathlyn Farrell, CRCM, CAMS, AMLP is the National Director of Risk Management Services for Sheshunoff Consulting + Solutions, a bank consulting and software company based in Austin, Texas. She has more than 30 years' experience in the banking industry, which includes having been in-house counsel for medium and large banks. Her experience encompasses federal and state regulatory compliance, secured lending transactions, and management of loans in litigation and bankruptcy. She also has worked in the legal division of General Electric Capital Corporation.

Ms. Farrell is a frequent speaker at bank-related conferences and conducts compliance seminars, including Internet-based compliance training for Office of Thrift Supervision examiners. She is the author of *Law and Banking,* 6th edition, the *Reference Guide for Regulatory Compliance*, 19th edition, and co-author of the first edition of the *Compliance Audit Manual,* all published by the American Bankers Association. She has served as an instructor for the National Intermediate Compliance School and faculty advisor for the National Compliance School. Ms. Farrell is a Certified Regulatory Compliance Manager, a Certified Anti-Moneylaundering Specialist, and an Anti-Money Laundering Professional. She received her undergraduate degree from Texas A&M University and her law degree from the University of Houston.

Acknowledgments

The American Bankers Association thanks Trans Union LLC for permission to reprint pages from the *TransUnion Credit Report User Guide* for Appendix 3 in this textbook.

The Association also extends sincere thanks to the task force members who reviewed and commented on this or the previous edition of the *Consumer Lending* textbook. They provided valuable guidance on both content and presentation.

Theresa Cavanaugh
Vice President
Consumer Credit Product
Manager
STAR Financial Bank
Indianapolis, IN

Debbie Clayborn, CRCM, CTA
Vice President
Compliance and CRA Officer
Independence Bank of Kentucky
Owensboro, KY

Steven E. Doan, CFA
Senior Vice President
Treasurer
SWM, Senior Investment Officer
STAR Financial Bank
Fort Wayne, IN

Amy G Greene, CRCM
Vice President
Compliance and BSA
The Hardin County Bank
Savannah, TN

Ed Hanashiro, CRCM
Vice President
Consumer Lending Compliance
Manager
Bank of Hawaii
Honolulu, HI

Katrina G. Hightower, CRCM
Mortgage Compliance
CRA Officer
First National Bank
Fort Collins, CO

Pauline Ikawa, CRCM
Vice President
Community Development
TD Bank, N.A.
Bedford, NH

Steven J. Manderscheid, CRCM
Compliance Officer
Johnson Financial Group
Racine, WI

Patricia Mills, CRCM
Vice President
CRA-Fair Lending Officer
Webster Bank, N.A.
Hartford, CT

Christopher G. Poor, CRCM
Vice President
Compliance Officer
Citigroup, Inc.
Baltimore, MD

Introduction to Consumer Lending

1

Learning Objectives

After completing this chapter, you should be able to

- define consumer lending
- describe the evolution of consumer lending
- identify the four basic consumer financial management needs
- describe the relationship between laws, regulations, and bank policies
- identify the government banking regulatory agencies
- identify laws and regulations that affect consumer lending
- define the terms that appear in bold type in the text

Introduction

Amid rapid changes in the economy, the banking industry is managing its consumer lending business by responding to changing consumer needs and purchasing behavior and by continuously improving its processes. Consumer lending law, policies, and practices are evolving along with the market. Consumer lending is crucial to a bank's ability to increase profits and serve diversified financial markets.

An effective consumer lender needs knowledge, skills, and common sense. Lenders must have the education, training, and experience to meet both the challenges of their markets and official requirements for bank policies, lending products, and systems. They must be able to sell, communicate well, provide quality customer service, adhere to ethical standards, and comply with the law. These abilities are not bestowed by magic. They are learned through study, practice, and the accumulation of experience.

CONSUMER LENDING DEFINED

The legal definition of consumer lending varies from state to state. All definitions, however, rely on two basic concepts—**consumer** and **consumer credit**.

One source for a definition of consumer lending is the Consumer Credit Protection Act, passed by Congress in 1968. This law defines a consumer as a natural person who is primarily or secondarily liable on a credit contract—in other words, the person who is responsible for repaying the loan.

The Consumer Credit Protection Act contained several individual laws at the time of enactment, including the Truth in Lending Act (TILA); in 1975, the Equal Credit Opportunity Act (ECOA) was added. The purpose of ECOA is to ensure that all consumers have equal access to credit. ECOA refined the definition of *consumer* to be "any person who is or may be contractually liable for an extension of credit, or a guarantor, surety, endorser, or a similar secondarily liable party."

Title One of the Consumer Credit Protection Act, also known as the TILA, defined *consumer credit* as borrowed funds of $25,000 or less used for personal, family, household, or agricultural use—not for commercial or business purposes. A loan to purchase an automobile or furniture for a home, for example, fits in this category. A loan to start a business does not.

consumer—The person who buys and uses goods and services for family or personal use. In lending, the person ultimately responsible for repaying a consumer loan.

consumer credit—Credit extended to consumers, either individually or jointly, primarily for buying goods and services for personal use.

Therefore, consumer lending is credit extended to consumers, either individually or jointly, primarily for the purpose of buying goods and services for personal use.

Consumer credit may be open-end or closed-end, and it may be secured by collateral or unsecured (see exhibit 1.1). It includes the following loan types:

- installment loans repaid in two or more periodic payments
- single-payment loans (demand loans or loans with a specific payment date)
- credit cards
- home equity lines of credit
- loans to purchase cars, boats, planes, and recreational vehicles
- loans for bill consolidation, vacations, and home improvements
- loans for other services and durable goods used by the consumer
- home equity loans (second mortgages)
- student loans

Situation

The Rileys own a small business selling garden plants. ABC Bank has long financed their plant inventory. The business has been successful, and when the Rileys purchased their home five years ago, ABC Bank provided the mortgage loan. When the Rileys wanted to buy furniture and did not want to use their savings to pay for it, they applied for a credit card from ABC Bank. Later, when they wanted to build an addition to their home, they obtained a home equity loan from ABC Bank.

Are all these loans the same?

Exhibit 1.1 Consumer Credit Categories		OPEN-END	CLOSED-END
		A credit arrangement that allows the borrower to make purchases and take cash advances up to a previously agreed limit. Once payments are made, the loan can be advanced again as long as the balance does not go over the limit.	A credit arrangement in which the borrower and the lender agree on the total amount being loaned and the number, size, and due dates of each payment
SECURED	A loan requiring the borrower to pledge specific assets that become the property of the lender if the loan is not repaid	*Open-end Secured* • home equity lines of credit • personal lines of credit (secured)	*Closed-end Secured* • home equity loans • auto loans • RV loans • boat loans
UNSECURED	A loan made on the basis of a borrower's credit history and ability to repay, not on the requirement of pledging assets to the lender	*Open-end Unsecured* • credit cards • personal lines of credit (unsecured)	*Closed-end Unsecured* • personal loans

purchase-money mortgage—A loan the proceeds of which are used to purchase real property, which also secures the loan.

lease—A contractual arrangement through which the owner of property, such as automobiles or equipment, rents the property to someone else.

chattel mortgage—A loan secured by a pledge of personal property.

Did You Know ...

Debt was common in the eighteenth and nineteenth centuries. People owed the grocer or the butcher or family members. Pawnbrokers were major lenders. In fact the children's song "Pop Goes the Weasel" is about pawn transactions. In England, "pop" meant "to pawn," and "weasel" is an expression for "coat." Although pawnbrokers still exist, most people prefer to use the credit products offered by banks.

Although they are not included in the text definition, people may consider home mortgages and leases for individual use, not business purposes, as forms of consumer lending. Home mortgages, technically **purchase-money mortgages**, differ from other forms of consumer lending in that the loan proceeds are used to purchase a residence and the amounts are usually greater than $25,000. The purchaser signs a mortgage pledging the home as collateral for the money borrowed. A specialized unit or bank affiliate usually handles mortgage loans. A **lease** for consumer purposes is usually for an amount up to $25,000 and for a term of four months or more. Although different laws apply, the consumer lending department may manage leases for consumers.

HISTORY OF CONSUMER LENDING

Using credit to obtain goods and services is deeply rooted in our culture. Many current practices, philosophies, and attitudes toward credit have evolved over hundreds of years.

Throughout history, lenders and merchants have extended credit. The Romans were among the first to add provisions to standard loan contracts to reduce their risk and increase the likelihood that they would be repaid. They asked for premium terms for high-risk loans, such as for shipping. They sold other services, such as credit life insurance, along with credit—a practice known today as cross-selling. This Roman practice was the basis for current credit insurance concepts. Not only did insurance help protect lenders' investments and produce additional income from the credit transaction, it also helped protect borrowers and their estates.

CREDIT IN THE EARLY COLONIES

Among Benjamin Franklin's many talents—statesman, entrepreneur, inventor—was his skillful use of credit. In his book-selling and printing business he extended credit liberally to others. His personal records show that he also extended **chattel mortgages** to borrowers. Typically, the goods purchased with the proceeds were used as collateral.

During the Industrial Revolution in the late eighteenth and early nineteenth centuries, advances in technology made it possible for consumer goods to be mass-produced. This fueled demand for consumer lending from both merchants

Situation

Jacob, a farmer in colonial America, has just moved his family. With winter approaching, he is in a hurry to buy a larger cast-iron wood-burning stove so that the family remains warm and healthy. Because he does not yet have a crop to sell for cash, he must take out a loan to pay for the stove. Jacob turns to an unscrupulous "lender," who lends him the money at an exorbitant rate of interest. The loan is due in full, interest included, after the fall harvest. Jacob knows that if he has no money to repay the loan, the lender will use harsh tactics to collect. He is afraid for himself and his family but feels he has no choice and must take the risk.
Could this happen today?

and consumers. For mass production to succeed, it needed a large base of consumers to purchase the increased quantity of goods. Consumer lending programs also were needed to help consumers buy more expensive goods.

However, consumers were wary of debt. Many borrowers had been victimized by unscrupulous lenders—"loan sharks"—who charged usurious rates. In an economy without the benefit of banking regulation, borrowers often were subjected to heavy-handed collection tactics. It is not surprising that consumers were hesitant to borrow.

SHAPING CONSUMER FINANCE IN THE 1900S
Unethical lenders and shady practices greatly concerned the public, legitimate financial institutions, and legislative bodies. This concern led in the early 1900s to the emergence of a formal consumer finance market.

Legislators enacted laws to regulate consumer lending, control unfair or illegal lending practices, and provide rules for conducting a lending business on a sound and responsible basis.

At the same time, new credit opportunities became available to consumers. In 1910 finance companies and **Morris Plan banks** introduced credit plans for consumers that made small- and medium-sized loans available to any consumer who could find two other people to cosign the note. Until then most banks made loans only to businesses.

In 1916 the Russell Sage Foundation, a charitable institution dedicated to improving social and living conditions in the United States, devised the Uniform Small Loan Law. This provided for licensing consumer lenders and established guidelines to improve lender credibility.

Simultaneously, **installment loan** programs were introduced. The installment loan innovation, fueled by mass production of automobiles, gave banks the opportunity for substantial growth in consumer lending.

THE GREAT DEPRESSION
The 1920s was a period of national prosperity. As the stock market soared, investors who did not have funds to invest in stocks borrowed from banks to do so, using the purchased stock as collateral. **Buying on margin** was common.

On October 28, 1929, the stock market crashed. Stock values plunged by $14 billion. The crash triggered the most severe economic depression this country had experienced. The Great Depression lasted more than 10 years, pushing unemployment in the United States to 25 percent. Unable to collect on loans, banks suffered losses and bankruptcy; by 1933 about half the nation's banks had failed.

Among the factors that contributed to bank failures were poor securities underwriting practices, inadequate margin requirements, and insufficient liquidity. Banks could both underwrite securities issues and lend money to borrowers to purchase the underwritten stock. In theory, the bank could make money on both the loan interest and the securities sale. More cautious banks required high

Did You Know ...

As early as 1462 Italian Franciscan friars set up "banks of pity" (*mont de pietes*) to make small, secured loans to the needy.

Morris Plan bank—A financial institution of the type established in 1910 by Arthur J. Morris to make small and medium-sized unsecured loans to consumers who could secure two cosigners. Because most banks at that time made loans only to businesses, Morris Plan banks were among the earliest institutions to provide consumer credit.

installment loan—A loan repaid in two or more periodic payments of fixed amounts.

buying on margin— The use of borrowed funds, plus some equity, to purchase assets such as securities. The difference between the amount of equity and the amount of the loan is the margin.

margins; others did not, exposing themselves to more risk. Stringent rules prevented the Federal Reserve from making loans to banks to keep them liquid and solvent.

Congress set out to correct the situation. The Banking Act of 1933 (the Glass-Steagall Act) among other things created the Federal Deposit Insurance Corporation (FDIC) and prohibited banks from underwriting securities. The Securities and Exchange Act allowed the Federal Reserve to set margin requirements for loans secured by purchased securities. The Banking Act of 1935 strengthened the authority of the FDIC so that it could, for example, reduce the potential for troubled banks to fail.

AFTER WORLD WAR II

The advent of World War II brought the end of the depression and put the nation into a wartime economy. When the war ended in 1945, the consumer lending market was still relatively small. The Federal Reserve estimated consumer installment debt outstanding to be $2.1 billion. However, major growth was just around the corner.

After 1945 the U.S. economy, which had been geared for wartime, shifted to a consumer-based economy. Pent-up consumer demand for goods and services was insatiable. Movement to the suburbs, economic and social stability, job security, and the availability of consumer goods all fueled explosive growth in the consumer market. By the end of 1949, consumer debt had jumped 750 percent, to $15.5 billion, and by the end of the 1950s it had risen another 291 percent, to $45.1 billion.

ECONOMIC AND SOCIAL CHANGE IN THE 1960S AND 1970S

By the late 1960s strong economic growth, aggressive monetary and fiscal policies, and shortages in such resources as oil added to inflationary pressures, which affected the profitability of consumer lending. Because banks had to pay more to attract deposits, acquiring funds to lend became more expensive—but the rates banks could charge for loans were capped. Laws limiting the amount of interest banks could charge for loans had been imposed in response to the **usurious** practices of the past. Consequently, banks rarely were able to raise rates enough to match the higher cost of deposits.

On another front, a major consumer movement in the 1960s culminated in the enactment of numerous state and federal consumer protection laws in the late 1960s and throughout the 1970s. Legislative concern to protect consumers continues today. Although the laws imposed disclosure requirements and procedural changes on lenders, they also allowed lenders to create new consumer lending products. They could make larger loans, offer longer repayment periods, and charge rates that were fairer to the lending business. At the time, most long-term loans were fixed-rate.

Did You Know ...

In his 14th century book, *The Divine Comedy*, author Dante Alighieri placed usurers in the inner ring of the seventh circle of hell, where they suffered in a desert of flaming sand with rains of fire from the sky (Cantos XIV through XVII).

usury—Charging interest rates that are higher than the law allows on money borrowed.

LENDING IN THE LATE TWENTIETH CENTURY

Dramatic regulatory, economic, and technological changes characterized the last decades of the twentieth century. In 1979, the Federal Reserve made a significant policy change, allowing interest rates in the marketplace to float freely. The rates banks were allowed to pay on deposits were deregulated. Banks could charge more for loans and pay more for deposits.

Several events had a significant influence on consumer lending. Among these were disintermediation, narrowing net interest margins, the Consumer Credit Restraint Program, a dramatic rise in personal consumption, and the savings and loan crisis.

Disintermediation

From the 1960s through the 1980s more competition for deposit dollars arose from nonbank sources that paid higher rates. While banks were at the time not allowed to raise the interest paid on deposits, less-regulated sources like brokerage firms could offer consumers higher returns. Not surprisingly, consumers took their deposit dollars out of banks and invested them in higher-paying securities and mutual funds. For banks, the most damaging effect of **disintermediation** was that funds necessary to support the lending function became more expensive and harder to attract.

Narrowing Net Interest Margins

Banks carried into the 1980s large portfolios of fixed-rate loans from the earlier price-regulated era. As the cost of core deposits soared, so did the **cost of funds**. The difference between the cost of funds and the yield from loans—the **net interest margin (NIM)**—diminished. As long as the rate on loans was fixed and the rate on savings was increasing the profitability of loan portfolios was in jeopardy. For example, if the loan portfolio yield is 10 percent and the cost of funds is 6 percent, the NIM is 4 percent. As the gap narrows, perhaps because the cost of funds rises to 8 percent, the lender makes less money. Exhibit 1.2 illustrates the effect on the NIM when fixed-rate loans are funded with variable-rate sources of funds.

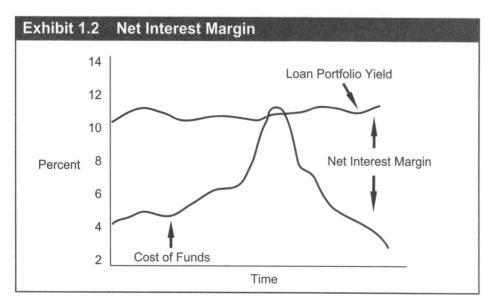

Exhibit 1.2   Net Interest Margin

Did You Know ...

By 1979 the prime rate had risen to 21 percent and certificates of deposits with terms of six months had yields greater than 16 percent.

disintermediation— The flow of funds out of depository institutions, such as banks, and into alternative sources, such as mutual funds, that pay higher rates.

cost of funds—What the bank pays to secure the money it uses to lend, usually in terms of interest on deposits or funds borrowed from investors.

net interest margin (NIM)—The difference between the percentage yield on the loan portfolio and the cost of funds to the lender.

Consumer Credit Restraint Program

Another significant event during this period was the creation in 1980 of the federal Consumer Credit Restraint Program. The program was intended to stem consumer demand for credit, particularly unsecured credit card loans, by imposing penalties on institutions that increased their unsecured loan portfolios. It induced banks to significantly change their lending policies, and thus their portfolios. They discontinued credit accommodations for marginal consumers, restricted offers for new credit cards, stopped making loans to consumers who were not already customers, and discontinued many unsecured loan programs. Where possible, banks relocated consumer lending operations to states with more favorable interest rate ceilings.

Because of the restrictions, banks persuaded state legislatures to provide relief from interest rate caps and to allow them to sell a wider variety of loan products and add features to meet changing market demands.

Consumer Consumption

In the 1980s it became common for consumers to use credit for instant gratification in the purchase of goods and services. Consumption rose dramatically and demand, fueled by easily accessible credit, spurred another growth cycle. Consumers, businesses, and even government increased their use of credit. The United States, once the world's largest creditor nation, became the largest debtor nation.

The Savings and Loan Crisis

Eventually the pace of spiraling debt and consumption had to take its toll on the economy. It did so in the late 1980s and early 1990s, bringing down many savings and loans and some commercial banks. Among the leading causes for the savings and loan crisis were long-term fixed-rate mortgages that unbalanced loan portfolios in an inflationary period and narrowed net interest margins. Put simply, credit practices were not sound. The crisis ultimately cost taxpayers billions of dollars, and the total number of savings banks and savings and loan associations was halved. Regulatory controls tightened, and lending policies became more conservative.

LENDING IN THE TWENTY-FIRST CENTURY

At the outset of the twenty-first century the consumer lending industry faced many opportunities but also intense competition. The convergence of technological advances, deregulation, and an influx of new players into the financial services market changed the lending landscape. Banks could never again take the consumer lending market for granted.

Banks became more aware of the markets they served. Competitor nonbank lenders took high risks to reap the rewards of the nontraditional loan products they offered to diversified groups of consumers. Market share and earnings pressures were intense, forcing many commercial banks to increase their customer bases quickly, adopt new marketing strategies to reach ever newer groups of customers, modify product offerings, encourage account usage, revise credit standards, and revise their lending processes to accept more risk.

The Financial Crisis of 2008

Then, in 2008 the United States became embroiled in a world-wide financial crisis, perhaps the worst since the Great Depression. The crisis significantly changed the landscape for commercial and investment banking.

Questions about and investigations into the root causes for the crisis abounded. Banking regulators, other federal agencies, and Congressional subcommittees analyzed and responded both in unison and independently to the urgent needs in the financial markets. Just as in past economic crises, keeping the financial markets functioning was the critical goal.

The financial crisis manifested itself first with the bursting of the housing bubble in the United States. The push to fulfill the American dream to own a home was driven from a variety of points in both the public and private sectors. When rates dropped in the early 2000s, mortgage payments seemed to be affordable for many. Unfortunately, the use of adjustable rate mortgages and nontraditional credit practices would lead to financial trouble for many. Buyers overextended themselves financially to make the home purchase.[1]

Even after defaults and delinquencies increased at a noticeable rate, the lending did not end. More new lending products, securitization of mortgages, and hedge fund investment instruments were created. The market was too hot. Taking on higher-risk lending became known as subprime lending.

Federal Reserve Chairman Ben S. Bernanke summarized these events succinctly in December 2008:

> This extraordinary period of financial turbulence is now well into its second year. Triggered by the contraction of the U.S. housing market that began in 2006 and the associated rise in delinquencies on subprime mortgages, the crisis has become global and is now affecting a wide range of financial institutions, asset classes, and markets. Constraints on credit availability and slumping asset values have in turn helped to generate a substantial slowing in economic activity.[2]

By June 2007 the financial problems were significant, evident, and spreading. Two hedge funds owned by Bear Stearns, which had invested heavily in subprime credit, collapsed. That was just the beginning. As time went on more investment banks discovered that the investments they had made were comprised of defaulting subprime loans. Repricing of many adjustable rate mortgages pushed up the monthly payments of already strapped homebuyers, who defaulted, resulting in foreclosures throughout the country. Tightening credit led to a decline in housing prices, and it was not long before prime mortgages began to default as the values of the homes plummeted below the mortgage balances.

The nation's economy felt the effect of the spiral on all fronts, from Wall Street and other global exchange markets to bank balance sheets to homeowners and other consumers not just in the United States but throughout the world. Chairman Bernanke explained the developments in his speech:

> Many traditional funding sources for financial institutions and markets have dried up, and banks and other lenders have found their ability to securitize mortgages, auto loans, credit card receivables, student loans, and other forms of credit greatly curtailed.[3]

Ultimately governments in both major and developing markets throughout the world had to step in to apply emergency resources and powers to forestall a total collapse of their economies and world trade. Exhibit 1.3 lists in chronological order major events that occurred from the onset of the financial crisis through December 2008. National and internationally coordinated intervention efforts to stabilize and invigorate the global economy continue.[4]

Lessons Learned

What can the commercial banking industry learn from the financial and economic crises of the early twenty-first century?

Most bankers agree on the necessity of getting back to basics. To lend effectively, to maintain and grow their consumer lending customer relationships, banks must continue to

- serve an increasing number of customers through new business opportunities
- adopt new marketing strategies to attract customers and core depositors
- formulate products for a diversity of consumer groups
- adapt products to meet changing consumer needs
- strengthen relationships with customers through cross-selling
- encourage customers to open nontransaction accounts, such as savings accounts

Bankers must do all these things responsibly, ethically, and mindful of the importance of bank safety and soundness. They must

- avoid unnecessary risks with investment portfolios
- remember the relationship of risk and interest rate
- make the loan only if the risk makes sound business sense
- safeguard the quality of the loan portfolio

Sales, marketing, quality service, and relationship-building are all still important to consumer lending. Nevertheless, as always, sound business practices and adherence to quality lending standards are just as important. Exhibit 1.4 (see page 12) summarizes the evolution of consumer credit.

Exhibit 1.3	The Financial Crisis of 2008
April 2007	Credit losses associated with nontraditional mortgages are reported. Estimates of losses are in the billions of dollars.
July 2007	Bear Stearns hedge funds collapse.
Third Quarter 2007	More problems with nontraditional mortgages surface in other investment banks.
March 2008	Federal Reserve facilitates the sale of Bear Stearns to JP Morgan Chase.
September 7, 2008	The U.S. Department of the Treasury announces the Government takeover of Freddie Mac and Fannie Mae.
September 12, 2008	Government talks with the company fail to prevent Lehman Brothers from filing bankruptcy.
September 15, 2008	Merrill Lynch is sold to Bank of America to avoid bankruptcy.
September 16, 2008	The federal government rescues American International Group Insurance Co., which was on the verge of bankruptcy.
September 18, 2008	U.S. Treasury Secretary Henry Paulson announces a $700 billion plan to buy troubled assets from the nation's largest lenders in order to shore up balances and restore confidence.
October 3, 2008	President George W. Bush signs the rescue bill into law as the " Emergency Economic Stabilization Act of 2008."
October 8, 2008	Central banks in the U. S., Europe, and Asia simultaneously cut interest rates.
October 12, 2008	European and U.S. government officials announce coordinated actions to take equity positions in major banks operating within their territories.
October 14, 2008	The U.S. Department of the Treasury announces the voluntary $250 billion Capital Purchase Program that allows it to purchase investments, primarily preferred stock, in banks. The program is intended to encourage financial institutions to build capital and increase lending to U.S. businesses and consumers to support the economy.
October 14, 2008	The Federal Deposit Insurance Corporation announces the Temporary Liquidity Guarantee Program to build confidence and encourage liquidity in the banking system by guaranteeing newly issued senior unsecured debt of banks, thrifts, and certain holding companies, and by providing full coverage of non-interest-bearing deposit transaction accounts regardless of dollar amount.
November 25, 2008	The Federal Reserve announces the Term Asset-Backed Securities Loan Facility to use $800 billion to help market participants meet the credit needs of households and small businesses by supporting the issuance of asset-backed securities collateralized by student loans, auto loans, credit card loans, and loans guaranteed by the Small Business Administration.
December 1, 2008	The National Bureau of Economic Research officially declares that the United States is in a recession.

Exhibit 1.4   The Evolution of Consumer Credit

1700s	Colonial America saw the beginnings of the chattel mortgage and excessive lending and collection tactics.
Late 1700s	The Industrial Revolution fueled the demand for consumer lending through the 1800s.
Early 1900s	Credit opportunities were provided by Morris Plan Banks; then the Uniform Small Loan Law and the introduction of installment loans provided the basis for a new loan industry.
Post-World War II	A booming consumer market, fueled by pent-up demand, built up consumer debt outstanding.
1960s and 1970s	Economic and social pressures contributed to strong demand for credit, which resulted in laws emphasizing consumer protection and fair lending.
1979	Federal Reserve policy and regulatory changes squeezed bank profit margins, leading to significant structural changes in the consumer lending market.
1980s	The consumer lending environment was affected significantly by disintermediation, narrowing net interest margins, the Consumer Credit Restraint Program, and the savings and loan crisis.
1990s– 2000s	Innovations in communications technology, such as telephone and mobile phone banking, Internet access to accounts, and consumer use of the Internet to make loan applications and pay bills, changed the way consumers access financial services. Consumer demand for open-end facilities like credit cards and home equity lines of credit continues to lead the way. The Gramm-Leach-Bliley Act changed the regulations on products and services that can be offered.
2008	The financial crisis and related recession initiated federal legislation designed to stabilize the financial industry and the real economy, protect homeowners and other consumers, and initiate programs to increase employment and grow the economy.

Did You Know ...

On October 3, 2008, President George W. Bush signed into law the Emergency Economic Stabilization Act of 2008. Its purpose is to restore liquidity and stability to the U.S. financial system; to protect home values, college funds, retirement accounts, and life savings; and to preserve homeownership and promote jobs and economic growth.

LENDING AND RETAIL BANKING

Consumers need financial management services that go well beyond credit. The retail banking function in most banks attempts to meet these needs with a full line of products and services. The way each bank approaches the retail function normally depends both on its size and philosophy and on the marketplace. Larger regional banks may take a transactional approach, looking at the profit generated from each transaction or product line. Smaller community banks tend to focus more on relationships, selling a range of services tailored for selected market segments to capture a high percentage of each customer's financial activities.

Core consumer financial needs do not change. What do change—rapidly— are the strategies banks use to meet them. There are in fact four basic consumer financial management needs:

A method of exchange	Consumers want products that help them make purchases easily, such as checking accounts, debit cards, and stored-value cards. They also want access to technologies that deliver services, such as telephone banking, secured Internet banking, retail Web sites, mobile banking, and alternative methods of bill payment.

A means of preserving and accumulating wealth

Consumers want financial products that enable them to save and grow their money, such as savings accounts, mutual funds, and other investment vehicles. Since passage of the Gramm-Leach-Bliley Act in late 1999, banks may affiliate with investment banks and create subsidiaries to engage in a wide range of financial activities, such as selling mutual funds, other investments, and insurance.

A way to increase purchasing power

Consumers want products that help them make large purchases without waiting until they have saved the entire purchase price, such as credit services that enable them to pay for goods and services over time.

Assurance of security and safety

Consumers want to know their money is safe from theft, mismanagement, or economic downturns, and they want deposit protection like that provided by the Federal Deposit Insurance Corporation (FDIC).

The core financial needs of consumers may remain the same, but the alternatives available to them to satisfy those needs vary. Banks continually innovate to deal with the ever-changing marketplace. Exhibit 1.5 illustrates the consumer lending market share held by banks relative to the competition, and exhibit 1.6 (next page) breaks this down by share of revolving and nonrevolving credit.

Situation

The Thompsons, a dual-income couple that is doing fairly well, have been investing in mutual funds through a nonbank financial institution. They also have a variety of insurance products they bought from an insurance agent. The Thompsons use their bank for savings and checking accounts, a mortgage loan, and most recently a home equity loan. In a casual conversation with their lender, Paul Baselton, they expressed frustration over having their financial business so fragmented. They were surprised when Paul referred them to a financial planner in the bank to discuss consolidating all their financial activities.

When did banks become true full-service providers?

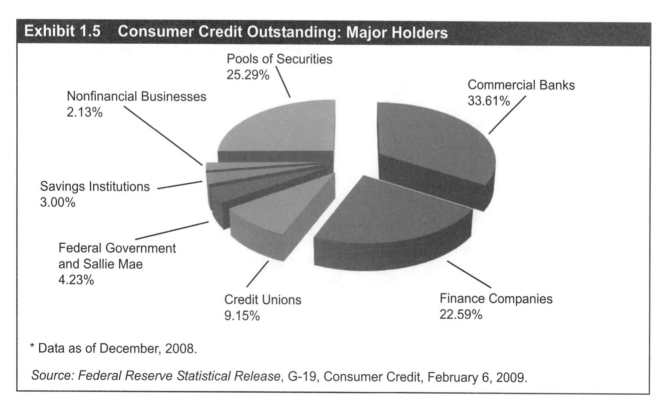

Exhibit 1.5   Consumer Credit Outstanding: Major Holders

Pools of Securities 25.29%

Commercial Banks 33.61%

Nonfinancial Businesses 2.13%

Savings Institutions 3.00%

Federal Government and Sallie Mae 4.23%

Credit Unions 9.15%

Finance Companies 22.59%

* Data as of December, 2008.

Source: Federal Reserve Statistical Release, G-19, Consumer Credit, February 6, 2009.

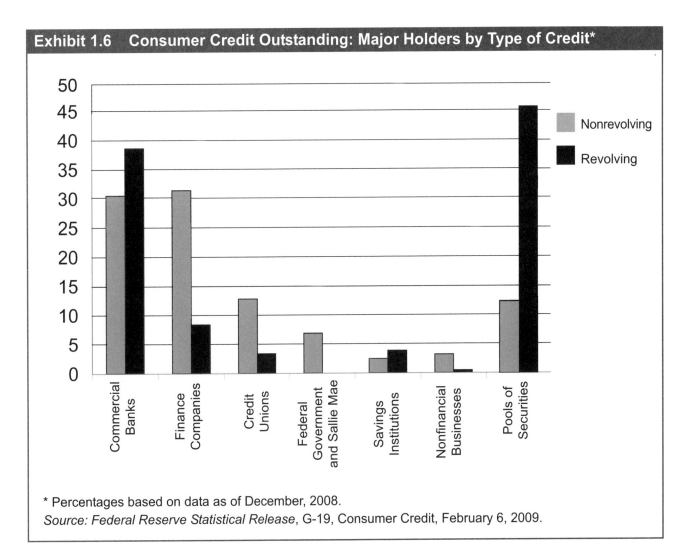

Exhibit 1.6   Consumer Credit Outstanding: Major Holders by Type of Credit*

Legend: Nonrevolving, Revolving

Categories: Commercial Banks, Finance Companies, Credit Unions, Federal Government and Sallie Mae, Savings Institutions, Nonfinancial Businesses, Pools of Securities

* Percentages based on data as of December, 2008.
Source: Federal Reserve Statistical Release, G-19, Consumer Credit, February 6, 2009.

FEDERAL AND STATE REGULATIONS

Federal and state regulatory roles

Federal
- consumer protection
- consumer awareness
- access to credit

State
- types of loans
- loan rates
- contract terms
- fees and maturities
- unfair and deceptive practices
- add-on products like credit insurance

State and federal laws attempt to ensure fair trade practices and provide for equitable distribution of credit. They also attempt to facilitate a relationship of trust between consumers and financial institutions, foster market acceptance of consumer lending products, and encourage the responsible extension and use of credit.

Federal laws are enacted by the U.S. Congress and state laws by state legislatures. State lending laws tend to protect consumers by specifying permissible types of loans, interest rates, fees and maturities, add-on products like credit life insurance, and certain contract terms, such as warranties. They often prohibit unfair or deceptive credit practices. Federal laws usually focus more on other consumer protection concerns, such as keeping the public informed through required disclosures and ensuring access to credit.

Federal legislative and regulatory action related to consumer lending was relatively limited until the 1960s, when the civil rights movement focused attention on issues of equality and fair treatment. What followed was a series of federal government programs, such as President Johnson's Great Society program, and federal consumer lending laws primarily designed to

- require consistent and uniform disclosures of credit features
- provide credit on an equal basis to all qualified borrowers

Laws provide the legal framework for an activity, such as consumer lending. Banks abide by laws by complying with the regulations that implement them and the regulators that interpret them.

THE REGULATORS

Regulatory authority may be state or federal. Federal agencies regulate national banks, state and national banks that are members of the Federal Reserve system, banks with deposits insured by the FDIC, and federal and many state-chartered savings institutions. State banking authorities regulate state-chartered banks for compliance with state law and state-chartered banks that are not members of the Federal Reserve for compliance with all laws (see exhibit 1.7).

Regulatory agencies are responsible for issuing and enforcing regulations required by law. For some banking laws, all agencies use regulations issued by the Federal Reserve. For example, the Home Mortgage Disclosure Act is implemented by the Federal Reserve's Regulation C. However, federal bank regulators may issue their own regulations for some laws. These can be found in the Code of Federal Regulations (CFR). For example, the Federal Reserve implements the Community Reinvestment Act (CRA) for member banks under 12 CFR 228, also known as FRS Regulation BB. For national banks the Office of the Comptroller of the Currency (OCC) implements CRA under 12 CFR 25. For state banks that are not members of the Federal Reserve System, the FDIC implements CRA under 12 CFR 345. And for savings and loans regulated by the Office of Thrift Supervision (OTS), OTS implements CRA under 12 CFR 563e.

The Code of Federal Regulations (CFR) codifies federal rules by title and chapter numbers so that rules can be referenced easily. The CFR has 50 titles. Title 12 consists of federal agency rules that affect banks.

regulatory agency— A government entity responsible for interpreting legislation and formulating and enforcing regulations.

Exhibit 1.7 Federal Banking Regulators and the Institutions They Supervise	
PRIMARY FEDERAL REGULATOR	**INSTITUTIONS SUPERVISED***
Office of the Comptroller of the Currency (OCC)	National banks
Federal Reserve Board (FRB)	Bank holding companies and state-chartered banks (members of the Federal Reserve System)
Federal Deposit Insurance Corporation (FDIC)	State-chartered banks (not members of the Federal Reserve) and state-chartered savings associations
Office of Thrift Supervision (OTS)	Savings banks and savings and loan associations
National Credit Union Administration (NCUA)	Federal credit unions
Federal Trade Commission (FTC)	Consumer finance companies, mortgage bankers, and certain other creditors

*All institutions listed, except finance companies, are assumed to be insured.

---

functional regulation system—A principle incorporated in the Gramm-Leach-Bliley Act that places certain authorized banking activities under the authority of federal and state regulators other than the principal federal bank regulators.

applicant—A person who requests or receives credit from a lender, including anyone who is to be liable contractually on the debt.

prohibited basis—Under ECOA, a characteristic of the applicant that cannot be considered when a creditor makes a decision on a consumer credit application.

ECOA prohibited bases

- race
- color
- religion
- national origin
- sex
- marital status*
- age*
- receipt of public income assistance
- exercise of rights under the Consumer Protection Act

* Age and marital information can be obtained in cases where this information affects a loan's legality or is a pertinent element of creditworthiness.

Regulatory agencies monitor banks for compliance with the law. Violations and lesser problems may be resolved administratively or they may require court intervention. Some nonbanking federal agencies enforce laws that affect banking activities. For example, the regulation implementing the Real Estate Settlement Procedures Act (RESPA) is issued by the Department of Housing and Urban Development as HUD Regulation X. The Gramm-Leach-Bliley Act established a **functional regulation system** for oversight of the new powers given to banks. For example, banks that choose to open subsidiaries to sell securities must register with the Securities and Exchange Commission (SEC) and accept SEC rules and oversight.

LAWS AND REGULATIONS

Consumer protection laws have had a dramatic effect on lending since the first was passed in 1968. Although most have been amended as new protections became necessary, their basic intent has remained constant. Exhibit 1.8 lists consumer lending laws and exhibit 1.9 (on page 18) lists the Federal Reserve System (FRS) regulations.

The Equal Credit Opportunity Act

Congress passed the Equal Credit Opportunity Act (ECOA) in 1974 as an amendment to the Consumer Credit Protection Act. The act, implemented by FRS Regulation B, covers both consumer and business credit. ECOA is an antidiscrimination law that was passed in response to a history of denial of credit to **applicants** based on factors other than their creditworthiness.

ECOA prohibits lenders from treating one borrower or prospective borrower more or less favorably than another in any aspect of a credit transaction if the treatment is founded on a **prohibited basis**. Prohibited bases are listed in the law. Among other things, they include personal characteristics, such as a person's race or sex, receipt of income from a public assistance program, or good faith exercise of rights under the Consumer Credit Protection Act.

ECOA affects all aspects of consumer credit and some business transactions, including

- bank procedures for taking loan applications
- criteria for credit evaluation
- notifications of adverse action
- record-keeping requirements

Truth in Lending Act

The purpose of the Truth in Lending Act of 1968 (TILA) is to ensure uniform and detailed disclosure of credit terms and costs. It has been revised significantly since it was first passed.

Exhibit 1.8　Major Consumer Lending Laws and Regulations

1934　Securities and Exchange Act, FRS Regulations T, U, X

1968　Truth in Lending Act (TILA), FRS Regulation Z
Fair Housing Act

1971　Fair Credit Reporting Act (amended by the FACT Act, 2003)

1973　Flood Disaster Protection Act

1974　Real Estate Settlement Procedures Act (RESPA), HUD Regulation X
Fair Credit Billing Act
Equal Credit Opportunity Act, FRS Regulation B

1975　Home Mortgage Disclosure Act (HMDA), FRS Regulation C

1976　Consumer Leasing Act, FRS Regulation M

1977　Fair Debt Collection Practices Act
Community Reinvestment Act (CRA), FRS Regulation BB

1978　Financial Institutions Regulatory and Interest Rate Control Act, FRS Regulation O

1982　Garn-St Germain Depository Institutions Act

1985　Credit Practices Rule, FRS Regulation AA

1988　Fair Credit and Charge Card Disclosure Act

1990　Americans with Disabilities Act (ADA)

1991　Telephone Consumer Protection Act

1994　Riegle Community Development and Regulatory Improvement Act
Home Ownership and Equity Protection Act
Telemarketing and Consumer Abuse Protection Act

1995　OCC Rules on Lending Limits

1996　Economic Growth and Regulatory Paperwork Reduction Act

1999　Gramm-Leach-Bliley Act (GLBA)
Agency Advisories on Sub-Prime Lending (1999, 2001, 2004)

2001　Uniting and Strengthening America by Providing Appropriate Tools Required to Intercept and
Obstruct Terrorism Act (USA PATRIOT Act)

2003　Fair and Accurate Credit Transactions (FACT) Act, FRS Regulations V and FF
Transactions with Affiliates, FRS Regulation W
Servicemembers Civil Relief Act
OCC Rules for Debt Cancellation Contracts and Debt Suspension Agreements

2004　Controlling the Assault of Non-solicited Pornography and Marketing Act (CAN-SPAM Act)

2005　Bankruptcy Abuse Prevention and Consumer Protection Act

2008　Emergency Economic Stabilization Act

Exhibit 1.9 Federal Reserve System Regulations

A	Extensions of Credit by Federal Reserve Banks
B	Equal Credit Opportunity
C	Home Mortgage Disclosure
D	Reserve Requirements of Depository Institutions
E	Electronic Fund Transfers
F	Limitations on Interbank Liabilities
G	Disclosure and Reporting of CRA-Related Agreements
H	Membership of State Banking Institutions in the Federal Reserve System
I	Issue and Cancellation of Federal Reserve Bank Capital Stock
J	Collection of Checks and Other Items by Federal Reserve Banks and Funds Transfers through Fedwire
K	International Banking Operations
L	Management Official Interlocks
M	Consumer Leasing
N	Relations with Foreign Banks and Bankers
O	Loans to Executive Officers, Directors, and Principal Shareholders of Member Banks
P	Privacy of Consumer Financial Information
Q	Prohibition Against Payment of Interest on Demand Deposits
R	Exceptions for Banks from the Definition of Brokers under the Securities and Exchange Act of 1934
S	Reimbursement to Financial Institutions for Providing Financial Records; Recordkeeping Requirements for Certain Financial Records
T	Credit by Brokers and Dealers
U	Credit by Banks and Persons Other than Brokers or Dealers for the Purpose of Purchasing or Carrying Margin Stocks
V	Fair Credit Reporting
W	Transactions Between Member Banks and Their Affiliates
X	Borrowers of Securities Credit
Y	Bank Holding Companies and Change in Bank Control
Z	Truth in Lending
AA	Unfair or Deceptive Acts or Practices
BB	Community Reinvestment
CC	Availability of Funds and Collection of Checks
DD	Truth in Savings
EE	Netting Eligibility for Financial Institutions
FF	Obtaining and Using Medical Information in Connection with Credit

Source: Federal Reserve Board of Governors, www.federalreserve.gov/regulations/default.htm.

Implemented by FRS Regulation Z the TILA protects consumers borrowing $25,000 or less primarily for personal, family, or household use. It also covers loans for any amount made to a consumer if the loan is secured by real property. It emphasizes the importance of disclosures that allow consumers to determine the cost of a credit transaction and to compare rates and other credit costs to make informed decisions.

The TILA and FRS Regulation Z stipulate how the **annual percentage rate, finance charge**, and other fees and costs are to be disclosed to borrowers (see exhibit 1.10). It also requires certain disclosures about closed- and open-end loans and variable-rate loans. The act gives consumers the right to cancel (**right of rescission**) certain real estate transactions within a certain period after a loan is consummated. It also has special rules for high-cost mortgage loans.

Fair Credit Reporting Act

Effective since 1971, the Fair Credit Reporting Act (FCRA) is directed primarily at consumer reports and most often is associated with consumer reporting agencies. However, the law also affects other types of reports, including those about a consumer's medical history. FCRA has four primary objectives; it

- establishes acceptable purposes for which a consumer credit report may be obtained
- defines consumers' rights regarding credit reports, emphasizing their rights to request and receive their reports and the necessity of a procedure for correcting inaccurate information
- establishes requirements for handling an adverse credit decision that resulted in whole or in part from information contained in a credit report
- defines the responsibilities of a consumer reporting agency

The FCRA was updated in 2003 to add more privacy provisions and requirements that help prevent identity theft.

annual percentage rate (APR)—The interest and other finance charges on a loan expressed as an annual rate.

finance charge—The borrower's cost for a loan in dollars and cents. It includes any charge payable directly or indirectly by the consumer and imposed directly or indirectly by the creditor as an incident to or a condition of the extension of credit. It does not include any charge of a type payable in a comparable cash transaction.

right of rescission—The right of a customer to cancel a legally binding agreement within a specified period, such as three days after a contract is signed. This right is available for consumer credit agreements that give the creditor a security interest in the consumer's primary residence for a purpose other than to purchase the home.

Consumer reporting agency. Any organization or company that regularly assembles or evaluates the credit histories of consumers (other than its own experience with the consumer) for the purpose of furnishing credit reports to third parties. *Also known as* credit reporting agency.

Exhibit 1.10	Federal Box Disclosures		
ANNUAL PERCENTAGE RATE	**FINANCE CHARGE**	**AMOUNT FINANCED**	**TOTAL OF PAYMENTS**
The cost of your credit as a yearly rate	The dollar amount the credit will cost you	The amount of credit provided to you or on your behalf	The amount you will pay after you have made all scheduled payments
6.750%	$33,351.60	$56,400.00	$89,751.60

Community Reinvestment Act

The Community Reinvestment Act (CRA), enacted in 1977, has no direct effect on individual loan requests or decisions, but it does affect bank lending strategies, marketing efforts, and lending policies. Through regulations and periodic examinations, regulators encourage FDIC-insured depository institutions, such as banks and savings associations, to lend to their entire community, including low- and moderate-income groups.

FDIC-insured depository institutions are examined for their CRA performance and given a public evaluation, including a CRA rating of outstanding, satisfactory, needs to improve, or substantial noncompliance.

CRA directs the supervisory agencies to take a bank's CRA performance into account when considering whether to approve any application for a deposit-taking facility, such as a new branch, or for acquisition of or merger with another bank or bank holding company. In practice, CRA reinforces the special relationship banks have with their communities and underscores the importance of serving the credit needs of local businesses and individual consumers.

CONSUMER LENDING COMPLIANCE PROGRAMS

The complexity of many regulations makes the reporting and record retention requirements costly. Regulators emphasize compliance as part of their regular bank examinations. Banks have responded by putting in place self-auditing compliance programs to address the full range of compliance issues, including employee training, documentation, and internal controls. Compliance programs are designed to achieve a variety of objectives, such as

- improving customer service by specifying procedures to resolve inquiries and problems efficiently
- increasing bank efficiency by standardizing some tasks and providing clear direction about actions to be taken
- ensuring compliance with all regulations
- avoiding costly penalties and litigation resulting from violations of regulations

The regulatory compliance audit function often reports directly to the chief executive officer, board of directors, or special audit committee. Compliance, however, is everyone's responsibility—from the directors to tellers and customer service representatives. A regulatory compliance program should

- document bank policies
- draft formal procedures to ensure compliance
- train lenders and support personnel in the requirements of t the law
- conduct internal audits

Situation

As a busy lender, Matt barely has time for lunch, let alone attend another four-hour compliance training program; but the notice on his desk does not give him a choice. He will have to be in the training room at 9:00 a.m. on Thursday morning. What could have changed in the six months since his last compliance training session? Then he remembers how valuable that last session was—how he learned procedures for resolving customer inquiries.

In what ways do Matt, his customers, and his bank benefit from regular compliance training?

Such a program uses periodic formal reviews to help the bank in compliance. If the review detects an inadvertent error or violation, the bank can correct it before a problem becomes major (see appendix 1 for an example of a bank compliance policy that addresses the regulations banks consider when setting compliance policies).

Compliance training ensures that lenders learn how to give the customer the best service possible within the law. Regulations are often amended. Regulatory examinations and bank audits can raise issues that have not been covered by the bank previously. Regular compliance training ensures prudent and legal lending practices.

Did You Know ...

The consumer lending function has experienced more regulatory changes in the last 45 years than in the preceding 100.

SUMMARY

- Consumer lending is credit extended to consumers, either individually or jointly, primarily for buying goods and services for personal use. Consumer credit may be open-end or closed-end, secured by collateral or unsecured. Typical consumer lending products are installment loans, credit cards, and home equity lines of credit.

- Many of the values and practices associated with contemporary consumer lending reflect the history in which they are rooted. Unscrupulous and unsafe lending practices over time have shaped the regulatory structure within which consumer lending operates today. Economic conditions and technological advances have given rise to a multitude of contemporary consumer lending products.

- Acceptance and growth of consumer lending in the United States were fueled by several events, including mass production of consumer products, greater purchasing power that allowed consumers to buy the products, greater economic stability in jobs and income, and growth of disposable personal income. At the same time there evolved a system of regulators and a willingness on the part of banks to lend money in this environment.

- Banks and other financial institutions have experienced the rewards and the fall-out of the business cycles. With every upturn and downturn governments relax, increase, or refine laws and regulations to promote or protect the financial services industry, consumers, and the economy. The most recent example of a major downturn was in 2008. Manifested by the bursting of the housing bubble and increasing numbers of home mortgage defaults and foreclosures, the downturn turned into a financial crisis affecting the U.S. and world economies. In response, government leaders and central banks used a variety of programs to support the financial system and direct the economy toward stability and growth.

- Retail bankers recognize that consumers have financial concerns beyond a need for loans. They need financial services to provide a method of exchange or payment, a way to preserve and accumulate wealth, a means to increase purchasing power, and an assurance of security and safety. Management must stay current with the marketplace and manage the consumer lending function to adapt to economic changes while fulfilling the primary fiduciary obligation of meeting safety and soundness goals.

- Consumer lending is highly regulated. Since 1968 federal laws have been directed at protecting consumers in the credit market. These laws focus primarily on the need for uniform disclosure to consumers of key credit features and on ensuring that credit is provided to all qualified consumers on an equal basis. Bank regulators interpret the laws and issue regulations that different types of lending institutions must follow. These laws and regulations have brought about significant changes in industry policies, procedures, and practices. Compliance with the law is enforced by a variety of regulatory agencies and by banks themselves. Examples of such laws are the Equal Credit Opportunity Act (ECOA), the Truth in Lending Act (TILA), the Fair Credit Reporting Act (FCRA), and the Community Reinvestment Act (CRA).

- To comply with consumer regulations and effectively administer their compliance efforts, most banks have implemented consumer lending compliance programs.

END NOTES

[1] For more information about the housing market see "2007 HMDA Data," Federal Reserve Bulletin, No. 94 (December 2008), page 107, www.federalreserve.gov/pubs/bulletin/2008/pdf/hmda07final.pdf. The article explains declining conditions from 2006 through 2007 and lists nonbank mortgage lenders that closed in 2007.

[2] Ben S. Bernanke, Federal Reserve Chairman, "Federal Reserve Policies in the Financial Crisis," speech delivered at the Greater Austin Chamber of Commerce, Austin, Texas, December 1, 2008, www.federalreserve.gov/newseventsspeechberhanke20081201a.htm.

[3] Ibid.

[4] For more information about the economic recession and recovery, visit the Web site of the American Bankers Association, www.aba.com, which also has links to resources provided by federal agencies.

SELF-CHECK AND REVIEW

Learning Check

1. What is consumer lending? What types of loans made to consumers are not included in this definition? Why not?

2. What effect did the consumer movement in the 1960s and 1970s have on the consumer lending industry?

3. What short- and long-term effects did deregulation of the banking industry during the 1980s through early 2000s have on bank consumer lending programs?

4. What are the four basic consumer financial management needs? Which specifically apply to consumer lending?

5. How has technology changed the way banks compete for consumer loans?

6. How are banking laws made and implemented? What are the primary federal agencies that regulate banks?

7. What is the functional regulation system? What is the source of this concept?

8. What are the purposes of the Equal Credit Opportunity Act (ECOA) and Truth in Lending Act (TILA)? Name the bases on which a provider of credit may not discriminate.

9. What should be the primary objectives of most bank consumer lending compliance programs?

ADDITIONAL RESOURCES

Resources

"2007 HMDA Data," *Federal Reserve Bulletin*, No. 94 (December 2008), p. 107, www.federalreserve.gov/pubs/bulletin/2008/pdf/hmda07final.pdf.

ABA Bank Compliance Magazine, Washington: American Bankers Association, bimonthly periodical.

ABA Banking Journal, New York: Simmons-Boardman Publishing Corp., monthly periodical.

ABA Banking News, Washington: American Bankers Association, biweekly newspaper.

American Bankers Association, **www.aba.com**.

Banking and Finance Terminology, 5th edition, Washington: American Bankers Association, 2005.

Bernanke, Ben S., Federal Reserve Chairman, "Federal Reserve Policies in the Financial Crisis," speech delivered at the Greater Austin Chamber of Commerce, Austin, Texas, December 1, 2008, www.federalreserve.gov/newseventsspeechberhanke20081201a.htm.

Comptroller of the Currency, www.occ.treas.gov.

Federal Deposit Insurance Corporation, www.fdic.gov.

Federal Financial Institutions Examination Council, www.ffiec.gov.

Federal Reserve Bank of Atlanta, www.frbatlanta.org.

Federal Reserve Bank of Boston, www.bos.frb.org.

Federal Reserve Bank of Chicago, www.chicagofed.org.

Federal Reserve Bank of Cleveland, www.clevelandfed.org.

Federal Reserve Bank of Dallas, www.dallasfed.org.

Federal Reserve Bank of Kansas City, www.kc.frb.org.

Federal Reserve Bank of Minneapolis, www.minneapolisfed.org.

Federal Reserve Bank of New York, www.newyorkfed.org.

Federal Reserve Bank of Philadelphia, www.phil.frb.org.

Federal Reserve Bank of Richmond, www.rich.frb.org.

Federal Reserve Bank of St. Louis, www.stls.frb.org.

Federal Reserve Bank of San Francisco, www.frbsf.org.

Federal Reserve Board of Governors, www.fedreralreserve.gov.

Federal Reserve Board of Governors, G-19 Consumer Credit, www.federalreserve.gov/releases/g19.

FindLaw.com, www.findlaw.com.

Government Printing Office, www.access.gpo.gov/.

Office of the Comptroller of the Currency, www.occ.treas.gov.

Office of Thrift Supervision, www.ots.treas.gov.

Reference Guide to Regulatory Compliance, Washington: American Bankers Association, published annually.

Securities and Exchange Commission, www.sec.gov.

APPENDIX 1

Galaxy Financial Bank Compliance Policy

POLICY STATEMENT

The board of directors of Galaxy Financial Bank is committed to serving the public on a fair and nondiscriminatory basis and to being a major force in the development of the bank's local community.

To achieve this, it is necessary that the bank be in compliance with all consumer protection laws at all times. Therefore, the board of directors has established a compliance committee to supervise the bank's compliance activities and appointed Robert Seaton as compliance officer. The members of the compliance committee are Dorothy Burch, Sally Clark, Ralph Crittendon, Heather Nichols, Jonathon Mason, Candi Boyens, John Schultz, and Nancy Lowry. The compliance officer will serve as chair of the committee.

As chair of the compliance committee, the compliance officer is responsible for the implementation and oversight of the bank's compliance efforts. This carries with it the authority to call meetings of the committee, establish a written agenda for meetings, delegate responsibilities to other committee members, and devote sufficient bank time and resources to maintain compliance. The committee will meet at least quarterly and has the authority to call on outside advisors for assistance when needed. The secretary will record minutes of the meetings and forward the minutes to the compliance officer, who will forward them to the bank's executive committee.

Compliance Committee Responsibilities

The compliance committee is responsible for overall bank compliance with consumer protection statutes. Specifically, the compliance committee is responsible for

- maintaining current copies of compliance statutes, regulations, and interpretations
- maintaining proficient knowledge of compliance statutes, regulations, and interpretations
- formulating and updating bank policies and procedures to maintain bank compliance with statutes, regulations, and interpretations
- coordinating the training of bank personnel on compliance policies and procedures
- monitoring the resolution of written consumer complaints
- continuously reviewing bank compliance

The compliance committee is responsible for ensuring that the bank is in compliance with the following regulations and any new or amended compliance laws and regulations:

- Laws and regulations affecting lending:
    — Truth in Lending Act (Regulation Z)
    — Equal Credit Opportunity Act (ECOA) (Regulation B)
    — Regulation AA (Credit Practices Rule)
    — Fair Credit Reporting Act (FACT Act)
    — Fair Debt Collection Practices Act
    — Servicemembers Civil Relief Act
- Laws and regulations affecting securities lending:
    — Regulation U

- Laws and regulations affecting real estate lending:
  — Flood Disaster Protection Act
  — Real Estate Settlement Procedures Act (RESPA) (Department of Housing and Urban Development's Regulation X)
  — Fair Housing Act
  — Real estate appraisal requirements
  — Home Mortgage Disclosure Act (HMDA) (Regulation C)
  — Private Mortgage Insurance (PMI) disclosures

- Laws and regulations affecting deposit accounts:
  — Interest on deposits and reserve requirements (Regulations Q and D)
  — Expedited Funds Availability Act (EFAA) (Regulation CC)
  — Check 21
  — Electronic Fund Transfer Act (EFTA) (Regulation E)
  — Truth in Savings Act (Regulation DD)

- Laws and regulations affecting cash transactions:
  — Bank Secrecy Act (BSA)
  — Anti-Money Laundering
  — USA PATRIOT Act
  — Office of Foreign Assets Control

- Laws affecting the sale of insurance:
  — Consumer Protection in Sales of Insurance

- Laws and regulations affecting customer privacy:
  — Right to Financial Privacy Act
  — Privacy of Consumer Financial Information (Regulation P)

- Laws and regulations affecting bank insiders:
  — Insider lending (Regulation O)
  — Insider transactions (Sections 23A and 23B)

- Community reinvestment:
  — Community Reinvestment Act (CRA)

- Other laws and regulations:
  — Federal Trade Commission (FTC) trade regulations

Galaxy Financial Bank Compliance Policy

Members of the compliance committee are responsible for overseeing compliance in their functional area. This responsibility includes

- maintaining knowledge of the laws and regulations affecting their area

- drafting policies and procedures to implement those laws and regulations

- seeing that the policies and procedures are followed

The areas of responsibility for the members of the committee are:

Lending regulations

- Laws and regulations:
    — Truth in Lending Act
    — Equal Credit Opportunity Act
    — Fair Credit Reporting Act (FACT ACT)
    — Fair Debt Collection Practices Act
    — Regulation AA
    — Regulation U
    — Servicemember's Civil Relief Act
- Persons responsible: Robert Seaton and Sally Clark

Additional lending regulations for real estate loans

- Laws and regulations:
    — Flood Disaster Protection Act
    — Real Estate Settlement Procedures Act
    — Fair Housing Act
    — Real estate appraisal requirements
    — Community Reinvestment Act
    — Home Mortgage Disclosure Act
    — Private Mortgage Insurance (PMI) disclosures
- Persons responsible: Robert Seaton and Sally Clark

Operations

- Laws and regulations:
  — Regulation D
  — Regulation E
  — Regulation CC
  — Regulation DD
- Person responsible: Jonathon Mason

New accounts

- Laws and regulations:
  — Regulation CC
  — Regulation E
  — Regulation D
  — Regulation DD
- Person responsible: Jonathon Mason

Advertising

- Laws and regulations:
  — Regulation DD
  — Regulation Z
  — Fair Housing Act
- Person responsible: Candi Boyens

Insider transactions

- Laws and regulations:
  — Regulation O
  — Sections 23A and 23B of the Federal Reserve Act
- Person responsible: Robert Seaton

Other laws and regulations

- Bank Secrecy Act
  — Persons responsible: Dorothy Burch and Robert Seaton

- Right to Financial Privacy Act
  - — Persons responsible: Jonathon Mason and Dorothy Burch
- Privacy of Consumer Financial Information
  - — Person responsible: John Schultz
- Community Reinvestment Act
  - — Persons responsible: Sally Clark and Robert Seaton
- Consumer Protection in Sales of Insurance
  - — Persons responsible: Sally Clark and Robert Seaton
- Bank Protection Act
  - — Person responsible: John Schultz

The compliance committee is responsible for implementing procedures for compliance with new consumer protection statutes and regulations and changes to laws and regulations. To achieve this, all correspondence from regulatory agencies and other sources regarding compliance will be directed to the compliance officer. The compliance committee will review and analyze this correspondence to determine what action, if any, is required of the bank. If changes are required, the committee will implement the required changes, including a training program for affected bank personnel. New procedures will be reviewed with the personnel affected at one or more meetings. Attendance rosters of all such meetings will be retained and submitted to the committee. If the compliance committee determines that meetings are not necessary, a memorandum concerning the new procedure will be circulated to the personnel affected and a record of receipt will be obtained.

Compliance Training Program

The compliance committee will develop a training program on all new regulations and changes to current regulations to ensure compliance. The committee also will coordinate the training of bank personnel to correct violations found as a result of examinations and consultant reviews.

The training director, Patricia Porto, and the employees' immediate supervisor will coordinate training of new personnel in the necessary compliance areas. The training director will be responsible for ensuring continuing compliance training of all bank personnel.

Continuous Review Program

The compliance committee is responsible for maintaining continuous reviews of bank compliance. The compliance officer will develop a schedule of areas to be covered by each review. Results of the reviews will be sent to the compliance committee and the board of directors.

The board of directors approved and adopted this policy on _____.

The Consumer Lending Market

Learning Objectives

After completing this chapter, you should be able to

- describe lending measures: loans outstanding and loan volume
- distinguish between credit product categories: closed-end and open-end loans (revolving lines of credit)
- distinguish between lending delivery channels: direct and indirect
- identify the stages in the consumer loan product life cycle
- describe factors affecting consumer demand for credit
- identify principal consumer lending competitors
- explain the Community Reinvestment Act, the Home Mortgage Disclosure Act, and fair lending laws
- define the terms that appear in bold type in the text

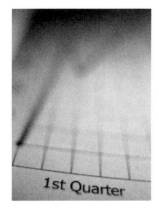

1st Quarter

I ntroduction

Although new banking powers have expanded the product and service horizon of most banks, lending is still one of the important ways banks earn income. Beyond the dollar measurements, lending to consumers has the wide-reaching effect of meeting the needs of consumers, banks, the local community, and the national economy. Laws and the regulations that implement them help ensure that consumer, community, and national needs are met.

As the lending market constantly changes, so do the ways banks respond to the market. Many factors, such as the economy and customer demographics, influence the selection of products offered and the dollar value of loan portfolios; among them are loans outstanding and loan volume. This ever-changing prism of interrelated causes and effects in the marketplace is part of the consumer lending dynamic.

loans outstanding— Interest-earning assets that represent the total amount of money owed to a bank from its borrowers.

credit risk—The probability, which exists with any loan, that the debtor cannot or will not repay the debt.

loan loss reserve—An amount set aside to cover undetermined potential losses from borrowers who default on their loans. The amount is built from deductions to net income and funds counted in the bank's capital.

reputation risk— The risk that negative publicity will affect the bank in a damaging way, such as by making it difficult to attract or retain customers or raise capital; causing a loss of revenue; or leading to litigation.

LOANS OUTSTANDING

The consumer lending market grew significantly in the years leading up to 2008. With the advent of the financial crisis in 2008 and the recession, the market began a period of adjustment. **Loans outstanding** and loan volume are used to assess the size of a bank's share of the consumer lending market.

On a bank balance sheet loans outstanding are assets. The interest the loans earn is reported as interest income on the profit-and-loss statement, and the bank earns the interest until the loans are fully repaid. Increasing loans outstanding is a strategic planning goal for many banks. It represents growth in earning assets.

The banking industry faces many types of risks but the major concerns are credit, market, and operational risk. Market risk refers to the value of a bank asset in the marketplace at any given time; operational risk refers to potential losses derived from the normal operations of the bank; but the chief risk for loan portfolios is **credit risk**: Will borrowers repay their loans? Many factors weigh on credit risk, such as changes in the economy and the borrower's own credit-worthiness. That is why, as a safety and soundness measure, banks maintain a **loan loss reserve**.

Reputation risk also matters because of the central role public confidence plays in the success of a bank. Also, because banking is a regulated industry, regulatory risk must be considered. That is why, although regulatory changes may be profound, they usually are made carefully, with draft regulations issued for industry and public comment before they are made final. In this way, the likely effects are known.

CLOSED-END AND OPEN-END LOANS

Closed-end loans and **open-end loans**, which are revolving lines of credit, are the two major categories of loans outstanding.

Closed-end loans may have a fixed or a variable interest rate. They may be demand loans or single payment loans, or they may **amortize** over the loan term with repayments made in installments. For example, a $10,000 48-month home improvement loan with monthly payments of $248.80 is a closed-end loan. It is for a fixed amount ($10,000) and a specified period (48 months); it has installment payments ($248.80 per month); and, once paid, its principal cannot be advanced again for the same loan account.

An open-end loan may be secured or unsecured, attached to a checking account, a stand-alone credit, or accessed through a credit card. Outstanding balances on open-end loans that are carried forward from month to month are subject to an interest or finance charge.

These revolving lines of credit have been the fastest-growing segment of the consumer lending market for the last several decades, primarily because of their ease and convenience. Once the initial loan is approved, the customer may use the funds as needed without returning to the bank for more credit. As long as the minimum payments are made and other loan requirements are met, the customer may continue to use the credit up to the stated limit. This arrangement gives customers more flexibility and control over finances than closed-end loans do.

Exhibit 2.1 shows the dollar amount of consumer installment loans outstanding at the end of selected years for open-end (revolving) and closed-end (non-revolving) credit.

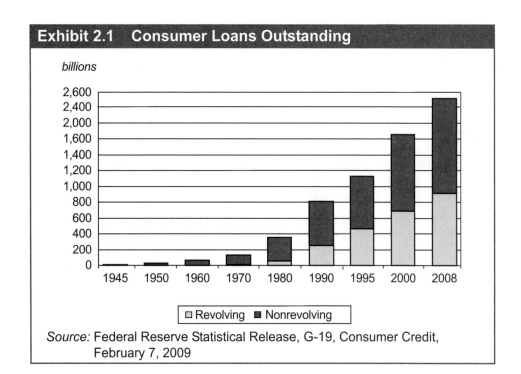

Exhibit 2.1   Consumer Loans Outstanding

billions

Source: Federal Reserve Statistical Release, G-19, Consumer Credit, February 7, 2009

closed-end loan—A loan for a specific purpose and for a fixed amount that is established at the beginning of the transaction, to be repaid in one or more regular payments over a set term.

open-end loan—A specified amount of credit available for use at the customer's discretion; repayment ranges from interest only through minimum stated amounts to a percentage specified in the contract.

amortization—Periodic repayment of the principal amount due on a term loan until the entire balance is paid.

Did You Know ...

"Stroke-of-the-pen risks" are changes in policy, regulation, or accounting that address issues outside the financial services industry that can result in risks to banks. Because these changes are often political, they cannot be predicted. The risks that result from tax law reforms and international agreements on farm subsidies are two examples. *Source*: FDIC Outlook, October 2005

product life cycle—
The successive stages of a product's sales and profits. The four stages, which vary in length from product to product, are introduction (low sales and losses likely); growth (sales growth and profit gains); maturity (slower sales and reduced profits); and decline.

PRODUCT LIFE CYCLE

Demand for specific loan types changes over time. For example, the demand for open-end credit is fast replacing the demand for closed-end credit. Consumer lending products—like all other products—move through a **product life cycle** from the time they are introduced to their eventual disappearance from the market. Although some products last longer than others, all eventually move through the cycle illustrated in exhibit 2.2. The phases of the cycle are

Introduction	When a new loan product enters the market, sales often are slow and the bank may initially lose money due to the expense of creating and introducing the product.
Growth	Sales accelerate as consumers become aware of and seek the loan product. Increased sales also attract competitors.
Maturity	With the entry of new competitors, sales growth slows because many purchasers already have the product. The heavy advertising and promotional expenses needed to maintain sales reduce profits.
Decline	Sales take a downturn. Fewer banks offer the product, it takes fewer forms, and promotion lags. Exhibit 2.3 demonstrates the relationship of closed-end and open-end credit life cycles.

Because they are aware of the product life cycle, banks regularly de-emphasize or totally excise less profitable products in favor of products that better meet the changing needs of the marketplace.

Upfront expenses for product introduction:

- research and development
- setting up the delivery system
- advertising
- sales training

Factors in product decline:

- new products as replacements
- technological innovations
- laws and regulations
- social change and consumer preference

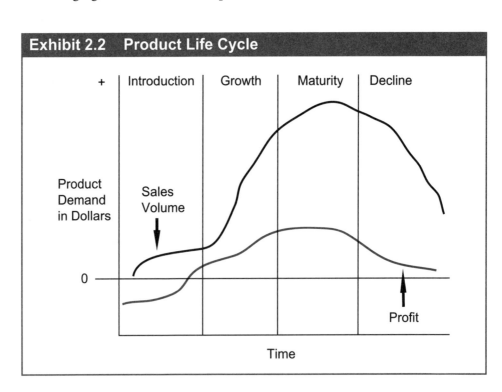

Exhibit 2.2 Product Life Cycle

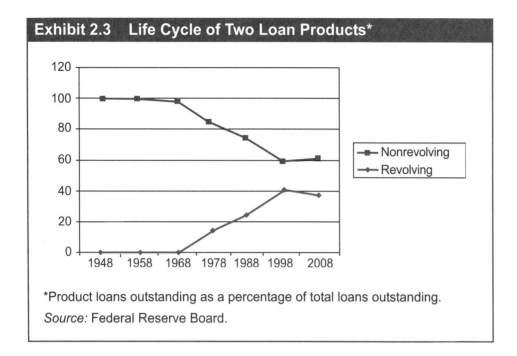

Exhibit 2.3   Life Cycle of Two Loan Products*

Legend: Nonrevolving, Revolving

*Product loans outstanding as a percentage of total loans outstanding.
Source: Federal Reserve Board.

DIRECT AND INDIRECT LENDING

The portfolio of loans outstanding also categorizes loans by the major delivery systems—**direct lending** and **indirect lending**.

In direct lending, whether open-end or closed-end, bankers make loans to consumers without any intermediary—hence "direct." Although demand for direct lending from banks declined in the past three decades because consumers had access to other lending sources, credit cards and home equity lines of credit continued to be the bank direct lending products of choice. Meanwhile, captive finance companies, such as those owned by automobile manufacturers, increased their market share, another trend banks monitored to mitigate losses and take advantage of opportunities. Today, due to the financial crisis of 2008, many nonbank competitors have closed shop, and bank direct lending is making a steady comeback.

Indirect lending can be a viable alternative. In indirect lending, a third party arranges financing for the borrower. However, the indirect lending market is highly competitive, and it has been difficult for banks to be viable sources of credit. In what also is known as dealer financing, customers obtain credit from a dealer or retail outlet, which then sells the loan to the bank. The dealer's customer becomes the bank's borrower. Automobile financing is perhaps the best-known example of a bank indirect lending relationship.

Many banks organize their consumer lending departments around direct and indirect lending to accommodate the requirements of the delivery systems and the loans that are made through them.

direct lending—
Lending that is straight from bank to consumer.

indirect lending—
Lending in which a third party, such as a retailer, arranges financing for the borrower and by prior arrangement sells the loan to the bank.

Situation

When Ellen graduated from college, she received gifts of money from friends and relatives. She has enough now for the down payment on a new automobile and plans on financing the balance. Ellen assumes that, once she finds the auto she wants to purchase, she will have to go to her bank for a loan. This is her first auto purchase, and she does not know the dealer offers financing.
How can the dealer do that?

loan consummation—
The point at which the consumer signs the loan contract and becomes liable on a credit transaction.

loan volume—The number and dollar amounts of new loans made or advanced during a given period, such as a month or a year.

Factors affecting consumer demand for credit:

- sociodemographic environment
- consumer financial needs life cycle
- economic environment
- seasonal or geographic issues
- regulatory environment
- technology
- competitive environment

Did You Know ...

Activated debit cards reached 3 billion worldwide in 2007 and should top 5.2 billion by 2012. *Source*: Global Industry Analysts Inc., www.strategyr.com.

Each department has separate lending officers and support staff. Other banks centralize the lending function: the retail locations (branch or dealer) generate applications and send them electronically to a central location for analysis. When the analysis is complete, the decision and documentation are sent back to the retail location, where the loan is **consummated**.

LOAN VOLUME

Bank management closely monitors loan volume because it reflects both the marketplace and the effectiveness of the bank's lending strategy. Exhibit 2.4 illustrates average **loan volume** over the years for different types of closed-end loans.

In the recent past there was a general downward trend for direct loan products that require consumers to apply at a bank branch. Although consumers want a branch close by, it usually is not for lending purposes. At the same time, demand increased for open-end loan products in response to consumers' need for control and flexibility.

Many factors affect consumer demand for credit, and thus ultimately loan volume, including the sociodemographic environment, the consumer financial needs life cycle, the economic environment, seasonal or geographic issues, the regulatory environment, technology, and competition.

Sociodemographic Environment

Whether to keep up with the Joneses or out of actual need, consumers tend to be driven by consumption. As consumption increases, inventories are reduced, which drives up the cost of the goods and services that satisfy consumer demand. The sociodemographic environment reflects consumer attitudes toward credit, which in turn affect demand.

As of the second half of the twentieth century, in addition to large-dollar items, consumers used credit for luxury items, basic everyday living items, and emergency needs. Early lenders could not have envisioned consumers buying groceries with a credit card, but consumers have come to embrace the use of credit for any purpose.

Many consumers who financed luxury items through high-interest credit cards became burdened with large payment obligations and heavy debt. In the low-interest-rate environment of the early 2000s, consumers refinanced mortgages to lower their payments or to take out extra money to pay off or consolidate credit-card balances.

Banks also responded to the need for more affordable credit with the now-common home equity line of credit. Rather than refinancing existing loans, borrowers use the equity in their homes to secure loans for many purposes, including paying off credit-card debt. Usually the interest paid on home equity lines of credit is tax-deductible. Also, more consumers are using debit cards for payments. By 2006, debit card payments were closing in on the position held by credit cards, with an annual growth rate of 17.5 percent between 2003 and 2006.[1]

Exhibit 2.4 Sample Portfolio Distribution of Closed-End Loan Volume*

	2000 % Distribution		2005 % Distribution		2009 % Distribution		2009
	Based on Number %	Based on Amount %	Based on Number %	Based on Amount %	Based on Number %	Based on Amount %	Average Amount per loan $
Personal—secured	4.9	4.8	5.4	5.8	8.9	6.9	15,900
Personal—unsecured	12.0	5.6	22.9	11.9	11.9	7.6	12,500
Automobile—direct	11.2	10.8	12.2	10.4	13.6	12.1	19,455
Automobile—indirect	46.2	58.1	29.9	47.8	47.3	47.8	21,756
Property improvement, own plan and FHA Title 1, direct and indirect	2.3	4.6	1.2	1.1	1.8	1.8	35,566
Mobile home, direct and indirect	0.4	0.7	0.6	1.3	1.2	1.3	36,450
Recreational vehicle, direct	0.5	0.4	0.4	0.3	1.5	1.5	15,575
Recreational vehicle, indirect	2.9	3.3	2.4	4.1	4.8	5.8	42,367
Marine financing, direct and indirect	1.0	2.0	1.7	2.9	4.6	11.1	81,235
Education lending, Federal Family Education Loan Program (FFELP)	14.9	3.4	14.7	3.7	1.1	0.3	3,509
Education lending, non-FFELP	**	**	2.4	0.7	0.8	0.6	1,809
Airplane, direct and indirect	**	0.1	**	0.1	n.a.	n.a.	n.a.
Debt consolidation, secured other than by real estate	0.3	0.2	n.a.	n.a.	n.a.	n.a.	n.a.
Debt consolidation, unsecured	**	**	n.a.	n.a.	n.a.	n.a.	n.a.
Other, direct	2.9	5.7	5.6	9.6	2.4	3.0	24,678
Other, indirect	0.5	0.3	0.6	0.3	0.1	0.2	29,675
Total	100.0	100.0	100.0	100.0	100.0	100.0	32,673

* Excluding floor plan and open-end credit.
** Less than 0.05%

Situation

John and Susan Miller both turned 35 in 2009. John recently was promoted and Susan re-entered the work force after their youngest child started school. After the lean years of living on only John's income and the expenses associated with starting a family, John and Susan were anxious to experience a few of life's luxuries. With confidence that their combined monthly income could absorb some debt payment for the next few years, John and Susan took out a loan to fund a vacation, a new automobile, and new living room furniture.

Is this typical behavior?

Did You Know ...

It has been predicted that today's high school graduates will have seven to nine jobs and three different careers in their lifetimes. Lenders need to keep this in mind as they evaluate credit applications and look at time on one job as a stability factor.

Consumer Financial Needs Life Cycle

As consumers go through life, their need for financial products changes dramatically. Exhibit 2.5 illustrates the high and low points in credit use. The following are typical life stages for consumers:

Early development
Typically characterized by low income and high borrowing. The need for life's essentials and a few luxuries often is not matched by beginning careers and salaries.

Family growth
Incomes rise along with financial responsibilities, such as the number of children. With more stable jobs and credit history, households often are able to borrow more.

Midlife
High household expenses and education of children make credit demand highest in these years.

Empty nest
The focus shifts from borrowing to investing as incomes exceed obligations. Loan demand declines. Consumers want to get out of debt before retirement and have acquired most of the things they want. The majority of the baby boom generation, the largest age group in the United States, has reached this level.

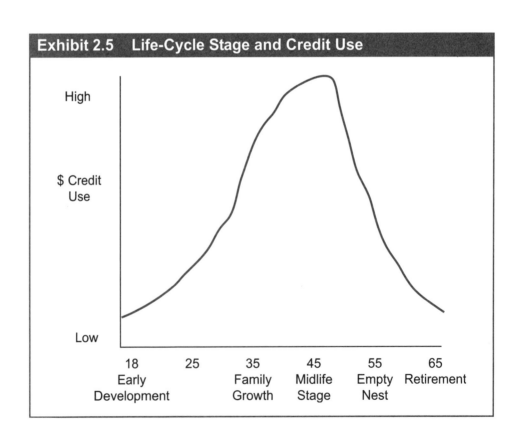

Exhibit 2.5   Life-Cycle Stage and Credit Use

Retirement	Loan demand is at its lowest as retirees live off investment income and accumulated wealth. The baby boom generation is now entering this stage and in a few more years, this will be the largest group.

Other Sociodemographic Factors

Among other demographic factors that consumer lenders monitor to see if they will affect growth of loans outstanding and loan volume are population shifts, education levels, household composition, and the population mix.

Population shifts	Since the 1950s the trend of income-producing populations moving out of the city to the suburbs required banks to build new branches and find new ways of providing services, such as through automated teller machines (ATMs), the telephone, and now the Internet. Although some urban centers, such as Washington, D.C., are experiencing a movement back to the city, the general trend remains outward.
Education	Rising levels of education and the wide availability of information through the Internet and television allow consumers to be better shoppers for credit and better users of financial products and services.
Household makeup	Adults are living longer and having fewer children. Many retirees are returning to work. The household of today may consist of a single parent with children or two unmarried individuals, of the same or different sexes, with or without children.
Population mix	The population is increasingly multicultural, incorporating racial, ethnic, national, and religious groups that mirror the global environment. Hispanics are now the second largest population group in the United States.

Much research has been done on the behavior and buying patterns of consumers in different life stages and sociodemographic groups. Banks use this research to design and market products to meet the specific needs of each group. Loan volume is affected by the choices a bank makes in targeting products to various groups.

Consumer lenders have been far more successful thinking in terms of the financial needs of customers based on their life cycle and demographic makeup than in terms of their general credit need.

Did You Know ...

More retirees are returning to work, for many reasons: job changes, the economy, employer decisions that affected pension and retirement plans, longer life expectancy, the need to take care of parents or children or grandchildren, and the desire and ability to remain active.

Generational Groups

Mature: born between 1925 and 1944
Boomers: born between 1945 and 1965
Generation X: born between 1966 and 1985
Millennials: born between 1986 and the present

Federal Funds Rate

The interest rate charged on short-term loans made by one bank to another through the Federal Reserve System. *Also known as* the Fed funds rate.

Federal Reserve Discount Rate

The interest rate charged by the Federal Reserve to member banks for loans from its reserves made to banks to finance temporary liquidity, and seasonal or emergency needs.

ECONOMIC ENVIRONMENT

The economic environment has a tremendous effect on loan volume. Business cycles, changes in disposable income, inflation, fluctuations in interest rates, stock market performance, unemployment rates, and the availability of raw materials all affect the market, and thus consumers.

Consumers are generally more willing and able to take on debt when they expect to have steady or rising income throughout the loan repayment period. In a weak economy where job security is threatened, they borrow less. In a strong economy, they will use a loan to finance purchases because they are confident they can repay.

Inflation and interest rates also affect borrowing. As prices rise in an inflationary economy, consumers may be more inclined to "buy now before prices rise," fueling more inflation. To stem inflation the Federal Reserve may raise the federal funds rate or the bank discount rate, making credit more expensive. As credit becomes more expensive, fewer consumers use it.

Low interest rates, like those of the early 2000s, gave consumers opportunities to buy homes, seek larger home loans, and refinance current home loans. Banks promoting refinancing could barely keep up with the volume. New mortgages with interest income, points, and fee income increased loan volume. Still, banks needed to monitor upward trends as carefully as they monitor downward trends.

Banks have little direct control over the economy. Understanding and anticipating what the economy will do next is critical to their solvency. Good economic times and consumer confidence in job and income stability increase demand for credit. Although lenders reap the benefits of a growing economy with low inflation, they also must plan for a time when the trend will reverse.

In 2006 the U.S. economy began to show signs of weakening and the fault lines created by previous risky financial practices of primarily nonbank lenders—loose credit standards, wide use of subprime lending, poorly analyzed and rated asset-backed securities, derivative instruments built on other derivative instruments—began to spread and infect the general economy, business and consumer financial positions alike. The result was a credit crunch and an economic contraction that resulted in business bankruptcies and closures and consumer job losses, loan defaults, and foreclosures. Through the efforts of the federal government, the financial industry, and the U.S. taxpayer, measures were taken in 2008 and since to stabilize the economy and create a climate for growth built on more solid ground. Front and center in this effort are the thousands of U.S. banks willing to make loans while emphasizing credit fundamentals as a pillar of bank safety and soundness.

NATURAL, SEASONAL, AND GEOGRAPHIC ISSUES

Any market is affected by natural, seasonal, and geographic issues. Loan volume will therefore vary by bank location and the primary industry of the region. Consumer lenders need to be aware of the effect such factors will have on the marketplace.

Natural	The environment can create situations, such as natural disasters, to which banks must respond. In the last several years, hurricanes in the Gulf states left millions of people homeless. Coordinating with government agencies, banks began offering special financing options for repairs and infrastructure building.
Seasonal	The need for consumer loans may vary by season; winter holidays and spring renovation projects increase demand for certain types of loans.
Geography	In heavily industrial or agricultural areas the strength of local and regional economies affects consumer spending and borrowing.

THE REGULATORY ENVIRONMENT

The regulatory environment can either encourage or discourage borrowing and lending. Both the states and the federal government enact consumer lending laws. State laws define usury rates, types of products offered, and many loan terms. Federal laws focus more on consumer protection and fairness.

In addition to their effects on product, pricing, and distribution strategies, laws and regulations also affect advertising. Interstate banking requires bank holding companies and their banks to adjust to larger geographic market areas and accommodate a variety of both federal and state laws.

TECHNOLOGY

Technology, a new factor influencing loan volume, has made credit more accessible to consumers. The proliferation of computers and cell phones with access to the Internet has stimulated banks to create new products and new delivery strategies. Through the Internet consumers can access product information, apply for loans, and monitor their deposit and loan balances.

At the same time, technology has expanded both the types of products banks can offer and their profitability. To stay profitable, banks have turned to technology to streamline nearly all aspects of loan processing, from application and approval through documentation and closing, thereby reducing the time, and often the cost, of generating and maintaining loans.

COMPETITIVE ENVIRONMENT

Well into the twentieth century banks faced little competition for consumer lending. Then, in the second half of the century the market began to bulge with new competitors, which had a negative effect on bank loan volume. Competition for consumer loan dollars comes from many sources—banks, finance companies, credit unions, savings institutions, other nonbank companies, Internet-based banks, and loan brokers.

Did You Know ...

Thirty years ago banks provided about 60 percent of all credit. Today traditional bank products consist of less than 30 percent. Yet in response to demand during the recession that began in 2008 banks actually increased their lending. In the last quarter of 2008, business loans expanded by 12 percent and consumer loans by 9 percent; in contrast, in the six previous recessions median business loans declined by 0.7 percent and consumer loans by 5.1 percent. *Source: The Impact of the Capital Purchase Program and Bank Lending*, American Bankers Association, February 9, 2009.

Ahmed is a teacher. He takes care of most of his financial business through the credit union, which is available only to school-system employees. Although he has other choices, the credit union offers the most competitive rates on savings, loans, and other products. Several years ago, Ahmed received in the mail a credit-card solicitation from the captive finance company of a major automobile manufacturer. By using this card, he could earn credit toward the purchase of a new automobile. Knowing the time was not far off when he would need an automobile, Ahmed applied for the card. He used this card almost exclusively for his card-based transactions. When he was ready to purchase his automobile, he went to the dealer and discovered that he also could finance the automobile purchase through the manufacturer's captive finance company at an even lower rate than his credit union's auto loan rate offer.

Could Ahmed have gotten these services from a bank?

Consumer Lending Competitors

- commercial banks
- finance companies
- credit unions
- savings institutions
- other nonbank competitors

Banks

Although how much an individual bank emphasizes consumer lending varies, banks generally do enjoy several advantages: a more positive image than many competitors, a large base of retail consumers, networks of convenient branches, expanding Internet and other electronic resources, and personal relationships with customers. Often viewed as experts in personal finance, banks have credibility as reliable resources for loans.

But commercial banks cannot rely solely on past advantages of reputation and personal contact. The Internet and other electronic resources are also available to competitors as consumers seek speed, convenience, and access to credit.

Finance Companies

Finance companies specialize in making small- to medium-sized loans to consumers and small businesses. The most common are personal and captive finance companies.

Personal finance companies have been in the consumer lending business for years. Their market has been high-risk borrowers with a negative credit history, although they also have some customers who might qualify for a loan from a bank. Because most of their customers presented more risk, personal finance companies charged them higher rates. Formerly big players in the indirect lending business, personal finance companies no longer enjoy the market share they once had.

Captive finance companies are subsidiaries of manufacturing companies. They were formed to help the companies sell the goods they produced. In recent years, however, most of these companies have expanded their consumer lending and have been aggressive and formidable competitors in terms of interest rates and terms.

Credit Unions

Credit unions are financial institutions that serve individuals with a common bond—a profession, a religion, or an employer, for example. Although most credit unions do not yet offer the full range of services provided by banks, they are expanding their offerings. They have access to relatively low-cost funds, obtained primarily from member savings accounts. Because credit unions have some regulatory and tax advantages over banks, they now have a significant market share. Most credit unions are not required to comply with some regulations that banks are, such as the Community Reinvestment Act.[2]

Savings Institutions

Savings institutions historically were known for deposit accounts and residential mortgages only. Before 1980, savings and loan associations (S&Ls) and mutual savings banks were permitted to invest only a small percentage of their assets in consumer loans. With the expanded opportunities deregulation gave them, they have become one of the fastest-growing groups in the consumer lending market. They benefit from having a large base of retail customers to whom they can market loan products.

Other Nonbank Competitors

Nonbank institutions with access to a large consumer base have ventured into consumer lending. They mostly come from the world of insurance, retail, and investments. Many nonbank competitors have expanded their corporate holdings to include bank affiliates or subsidiaries. Examples are State Farm Federal Savings Bank and Nordstrom Bank, a federally chartered savings bank.

Internet Banks and Loan Brokers

Other players in the consumer lending arena are Internet-only banks and Internet loan brokers. Internet-only banks exist in cyberspace without a bricks-and-mortar facility. The potential for Internet-only banks will increase as more consumers go online for financial services and transactions and as technology, security, and regulatory issues are resolved. These banks can meet nearly all a consumer's banking needs without the consumer ever leaving home.

Loans are available over the Internet from every conceivable source. Because of their low overhead, many Internet sources can offer interest rates below those of less high-tech competitors. Some Web sites provide toll-free numbers where borrowers may call in an application 24 hours a day, seven days a week. Others claim to make a loan decision in 30 seconds and to send a check within seven days. Loan brokers claim to provide offers from many different banks within seconds of the consumer submitting an application.

LAWS AND REGULATIONS

Among the laws that demonstrate the federal government's commitment to opening the market to lending are the Community Reinvestment Act, the related Home Mortgage Disclosure Act, and fair lending laws. Economic and political factors are usually the drivers for new regulatory initiatives. For example, in the 1960s increased consumer demand for credit and the demonstrated need to protect consumer transactions prompted passage of such laws as the Truth in Lending Act. A rise in identity theft in a growing electronic banking era was a factor in enactment of the Fair and Accurate Credit Transactions Act of 2003. The financial crisis in late 2008 has spurred a whole spate of government action. Although most traditional banks were not involved in the types of transactions that spawned the crisis, the legislation in response to it will certainly have an effect on all financial institutions.

Sample Captive Finance Companies*

Ford Credit
John Deere Credit
G.E. Money
* As of February 2009.

Did You Know …

State Farm Bank, F.S.B., received formal approval for a thrift charter from the Office of Thrift Supervision in 1998. Its focus is on consumer-oriented financial products. It is a nontraditional financial institution that does not have branch offices. Most direct customer interaction and product assistance is provided by the insurance company agents, a telephone call center, and the Internet. *Source*: State Farm Bank, www.statefarm.com/bank/bank.asp.

Did You Know ...

Competition is not limited by geography. A bank may lose a customer's auto loan to a bank down the street or to a financial institution in another time zone that offers loans nationally through automobile dealerships.

assessment area—
Under the Community Reinvestment Act, the geographical area a bank designates as the community it will serve. Generally, this will be the area where the bank has branches, from which the bank receives most of its deposits, and in which the bank makes the majority of its loans.

COMMUNITY REINVESTMENT ACT

To emphasize bank responsibilities to meet credit needs in the communities where they are located, Congress passed the Community Reinvestment Act (CRA) in 1977. Of critical interest to bank regulators is how well a bank reinvests a community's deposited funds back into that community. It also covers small farm and business loans.

CRA gives regulators the authority to assess a financial institution's record in meeting the needs of its entire community. It mandates that a bank should meet the needs of its community by making credit available, making investments that benefit low- or moderate-income (LMI) consumers, and providing services that benefit such consumers. The institution's record is then considered in evaluating future applications for mergers, acquisitions, branches, or a national charter. Banks thus must demonstrate that they are lending actively in their communities, including LMI neighborhoods. CRA applies to all FDIC-insured institutions.

General Requirements

Although CRA performance standards vary according to the size of a bank's assets,[3] some general requirements apply to all banks.

Assessment area

The bank must delineate its **assessment area** for CRA evaluation. This area covers all the communities the bank serves. It may consist of one or more metropolitan statistical areas (MSAs) or one or more contiguous political subdivisions, such as a town, city, or county. The assessment area should include the places where the bank has its main office, branches, and deposit-taking ATMs, and surrounding areas where it originates most of its loans.

CRA notice

The bank must post a CRA notice in the public lobby of its main office and in each branch. The notice informs the public that CRA information is available and that the public has a right to participate in the CRA process.

Public file

The bank must maintain a CRA public file at its main office that contains information relating to its compliance with CRA. The file must be available to the public for inspection upon request and at no cost. The file should contain

- written correspondence between members of the public and the bank specific to bank performance in meeting community credit needs

- a copy of the public section of the bank's most recent CRA performance evaluation

- a list of branches, their street addresses, and geographies (also known as census tracts), including branches recently opened or closed

- a list of services generally offered at the branches and descriptions of significant differences in the availability or cost of services at any particular branch

- a map of each assessment area

Larger banks have more requirements, including the responsibility to collect data on all small business and small farm loans. They also have a responsibility to make community development loans, which provide a benefit to low- or moderate- income consumers.

HOME MORTGAGE DISCLOSURE ACT

The Home Mortgage Disclosure Act (HMDA) passed in 1975 requires commercial banks and S&Ls to publicly disclose certain information about their mortgage and home improvement loans. HMDA is implemented through the Federal Reserve's Regulation C, Home Mortgage Disclosure, and requires banks and other lenders to report where and to whom they make loans. It does not prohibit any activities or require banks to make certain kinds of loans.

HMDA data give the public information about how banks are serving the housing credit needs of their neighborhoods and communities, reveal possible discriminatory lending patterns, and enforce fair lending laws by requiring the collection and disclosure of certain applicant data, such as characteristics. Information is compiled on a Loan Application Register (LAR) of all eligible applications, loans originated, and loans purchased.

Exhibit 2.6 lists information that must be reported on the LAR. The following loan types are reported:

- home purchase loans, which are loans secured by and made for purchasing a dwelling, such as a condominium, mobile home, cooperative, and single- or multifamily dwelling

- home improvement loans, such as loans to remodel, repair, or rehabilitate a dwelling, including a multifamily dwelling

- home equity lines of credit, which are reportable only at the bank's option

- refinancing of any loan secured by residential real property

- applications for preapprovals of home purchase loans that are denied, or approved but not accepted by the applicant

If not provided by the applicant, the loan officer must collect information about race or national origin, sex, and income by visual observation and note that the information was taken in a face-to-face interview. If the application is taken by telephone, mail, or Internet, the information must be requested, but the bank does not have to provide the information if the applicant does not supply it.

Using the LAR, the Federal Financial Institutions Examination Council (FFIEC) prepares a mortgage loan disclosure statement, which is then made

Community Development Loans Under CRA

- loans that are for affordable housing for low- or moderate-income persons
- loans that promote economic development by financing
  – small businesses
  – farms
  – community or tribal child care
  – educational, health, or social services in low- or moderate-income areas

Home Ownership and Equity Protection Act (HOEPA)

HOEPA was enacted in 1994 in response to consumer complaints about unfair and deceptive lending practices in home equity lending, particularly with regard to loans offered to the elderly and minorities. These high-cost, home-secured credit products had high upfront fees and repayment amounts and schedules based on the home's equity, not the borrower's ability to repay.

Exhibit 2.6   Information Reported on an HMDA LAR

- type of loan—conventional, FHA, VA, or FMHA

- purpose of loan—home purchase, home improvement, or refinancing

- property status—one-to-four-family residence, mobile home, or multi-family dwelling

- whether the owner occupies the property

- amount of loan or application request

- date and type of action taken by the lender (approved or denied)

- reason for denial (optional except for national banks and federal savings institutions)

- location of property by metropolitan statistical area, state, county, and census tract if the lender has an office within that metropolitan area

- ethnicity, race, and sex of the applicant or borrower and the income relied on in processing the loan application

- type of entity purchasing the loan, if applicable

- whether the loan is subject to the Home Ownership and Equity Protection Act (HOEPA)

- the rate spread on higher-priced mortgage loans, showing the difference between the average prime offer rate and the rate on the loan

available at the home office and in a branch in each metropolitan area. Within three days after receiving the FFIEC statement, the bank must make it available in its CRA public file.

FAIR LENDING

By law banks must treat everyone who applies for credit equally and fairly, regardless of race, sex, religion, national origin, age, or any other protected personal characteristic. Discrimination is expressly prohibited by two fair lending laws: the Equal Credit Opportunity Act (ECOA) and the Fair Housing Act (FHA). ECOA requirements are implemented by Federal Reserve Regulation B.

ECOA, enacted in 1974, prohibits discrimination in all types of credit, consumer and commercial. It also requires notification to loan applicants that their application has either been granted or denied. FHA, enacted in 1968 as part of the Civil Rights Act, prohibits discrimination in housing transactions based on race, color, national origin, sex, religion, handicap, or family status. It applies to any person whose business engages in residential real estate-related transactions—not only lenders but also appraisers, real estate agents, landlords, and others in the housing market.

Since ECOA and FHA were enacted there have been other initiatives to discourage discriminatory lending. The federal regulatory agencies issued a

Joint Policy Statement on Fair Lending in 1992 that gave guidelines on factors used to determine whether lending is discriminatory.

The Americans with Disabilities Act (ADA) also applies to fair lending. Banks are obligated to reasonably accommodate individuals with disabilities throughout the lending process.

Laws like the Community Reinvestment Act and the Home Mortgage Disclosure Act are closely related to fair lending, although their purpose is not specifically to prohibit discrimination. Still, CRA encourages lenders to be active in marketing and lending to all segments of their communities, especially low- or moderate-income consumers, small businesses, and small farms. LMI neighborhoods often have large numbers of protected classes such as minorities, women, and the elderly. HMDA encourages regulatory monitoring by requiring disclosures of home loan applications received each year.

Evidence of Discrimination

To determine whether a lender is illegally discriminating, the regulatory agencies look for evidence of overt discrimination, disparate treatment, and disparate impact.

Evidence of overt discrimination	Blatant and open discrimination against an individual or a class of persons, such as by expressing a preference for illegal activities even if the lender never acts on the statement.
Evidence of disparate treatment	Treating people or classes of people differently based on a prohibited basis; no proof of actual intent to discriminate is required. This generally occurs where a lender has discretion. Lenders have the burden of proving that the treatment has no prohibited basis.
Evidence of disparate impact	A policy or practice that is applied to all applicants but has a disproportionately negative impact on one group; no intent to discriminate is necessary.

A policy or practice adversely affecting a protected group may not be illegal if it is justified by a business necessity and a less discriminatory alternative is not available.

Americans with Disabilities Act

An average person can perform major life activities, such as walking, breathing, seeing, hearing, speaking, learning, and working, with little or no difficulty. A person with a disability has a physical or mental impairment limiting one or more major life activities or has a record of or is regarded as having an impairment. The

Situation

Roberto is Spanish; English is his second language. He lives in a community that is predominantly Spanish-speaking. When he went to his bank, EFG Bank, to inquire about a personal loan and asked to speak to a loan officer, the customer service representative told him, in an unfriendly tone of voice, that no one was available. She handed him a brochure, printed in English, and told him to read it and call back with any questions. She did not offer to make an appointment for him, although this is a common practice at EFG Bank.

Because Roberto did not understand the brochure fully, he went across the street to XYZ Bank, which advertised Spanish language assistance. The XYZ customer service representative did not speak Spanish either, but she found a loan officer who did. Roberto applied and received his loan. He also transferred his deposit accounts, totaling $50,000, to XYZ Bank.

What form of discrimination does this situation exemplify?

reasonable accommodation—
Under the Americans with Disabilities Act, an accommodation of a disabled person's limitations that can be made without undue financial hardship to the business making the accommodation.

Americans with Disabilities Act (ADA), enacted in 1990, prohibits discrimination against persons with disabilities.

Of the five titles in ADA, Title III applies to bank lending. It states that businesses considered "public accommodations" may not discriminate against persons with disabilities in the enjoyment of goods, services, facilities, privileges, or access. A bank is considered a public accommodation. The Department of Justice enforces Title III. As places of public accommodation, banks must make an effort to **reasonably accommodate** persons with disabilities, for example by offering special assistance, such as reading to customers who have sight impairments; allowing service animals into the branch; and removing architectural barriers, as by installing ramps.

Sample Reasonable Accommodations

- printing bank documents in large type
- having documents transcribed onto audiotape
- having employees read documents to customers who have impaired eyesight
- allowing service animals in the bank
- allowing a disabled customer to complete transactions at a desk, if a bank does not have a wheelchair-accessible teller window
- allowing a customer to sign documents using a drive-up window
- installing ramps
- making curb cuts in sidewalks
- rearranging tables, chairs, display racks, and other furniture
- installing flashing alarm lights
- widening doors
- installing text telephone (TTY) services
- putting Braille instructions on ATMs

SUMMARY

- The size of a bank's consumer lending market is measured by the growth of loans outstanding (the total dollar amount of money owed to the bank as credit obligations) and loan volume (the amount of money borrowed by consumers during a specific period). These measurements are divided further by loan type (closed-end and open-end) and delivery channel (direct and indirect). Like all financial services products, loan products go through a product life cycle in which they grow to maturity and then decline.

- Consumer loan demand is affected by such factors as the sociodemographic environment; the financial needs of the stages of the consumer life cycle; the economic environment; natural, seasonal, and geographic issues; the regulatory environment; technology; and the competitive environment. Banks need to be aware of how all these factors interact to affect the marketplace in which they operate. Consumer behavior has affected the types of loans outstanding over the years. Both direct and indirect consumer lending by regulated financial institutions has been declining. Open-end credit has become the consumer's credit product of choice from banks. The financial crisis that began in 2008 will affect consumer loan demand and choices as well as bank lending programs.

- Competition for consumer loan dollars comes from many sources. Among the competitors are commercial banks, finance companies, credit unions, savings institutions, nonbank institutions, and Internet-only banks or Internet-delivered services, such as loan brokerage. The financial crisis that began in 2008 is reshaping the competitive landscape.

- At least two sets of laws affect the consumer lending market place: those associated with the Community Reinvestment Act and the related Home Mortgage Disclosure Act; and the fair lending laws, among them the Equal Credit Opportunity Act, the Fair Housing Act, the Americans with Disabilities Act, and regulatory agency statements such as the 1992 Joint Policy Statement on Fair Lending.

END NOTES

[1] "Recent Payment Trends in the United States," *Federal Reserve Bulletin*, Vol. 94, 2008, www.federalreserve.gov/pubs/bulletin/2008/articles/payments/default.htm.

[2] Only state-chartered credit unions in Massachusetts and state-chartered community bond credit unions in Connecticut are required to abide by CRA rules.

[3] The three asset classes for CRA evaluation standards are small bank, intermediate small bank, and large bank. The asset thresholds are adjusted annually.

SELF-CHECK AND REVIEW

Learning Check

1. What is the difference between loan volume and loans outstanding? Why are these numbers important?

2. What is the difference between closed-end and open-end loans? Referring to exhibits 2.1 and 2.3, what has been the trend of closed-end and open-end loans over time?

3. What is the difference between direct and indirect lending? What are some examples of each?

4. What are the most important factors determining the position of a product in the product life cycle?

5. What are the five stages in the consumer financial needs life cycle? Which products are most appropriate for each stage?

6. What advantages and disadvantages do commercial banks have in the consumer lending market?

7. Why do captive finance companies offer credit to their customers? How has their share of the credit market fared?

8. Which type of discrimination is each of the following according to the fair lending laws?

    a. a bank loan policy that unsecured credit is not to be extended to single women because they generally have only one source of income

    b. a policy that loans will not be made below a certain amount, when there is no objective business reason for that policy

    c. a statement by a loan officer to a disabled applicant that the bank does not like to make construction loans to persons with physical handicaps

    d. quotation of more favorable conditions for a loan for a Caucasian male than an African-American male with the same credit rating

9. What are some examples of accommodations for customers with disabilities under Americans with Disabilities Act?

Resources

ADDITIONAL RESOURCES

"Activated Debit Cards to Reach 5.2 Billion Worldwide by 2012," *ATM & Debit News*, Vol. 9 #18, March 20, 2008.

American Bankers Association, **www.aba.com**.

ATM & Debit News, http://www.accessmylibrary.com/coms2/browse_JJ_A236.

Community Reinvestment Act Regulation, joint final rule effective September, 2005, www.federalreserve.gov/BoardDocs/Press/bcreg/2005/20050719/attachment.pdf.

Economics: Fundamentals for Financial Services Providers, Washington: American Bankers Association, 2006.

FDIC Regional Economic Data, customized reports, www2.fdic.gov/recon/index.asp.

FDIC Reports of Condition and Income and Thrift Financial Reports, www2.fdic.gov/Call_TFR_Rpts/.

FDIC State Profiles, a quarterly summary of state banking and economic conditions, www.fdic.gov/bank/analytical/stateprofile/index.html.

Federal Reserve Release G19, www.federalreserve.gov/Releases/G19/Current/g19.htm.

FFIEC Uniform Bank Performance Report (UBPR), Financial Institutions Examination Council, www.ffiec.gov/UBPR.htm.

Law and Banking, Washington: American Bankers Association, 2008.

Marketing Financial Services, Washington: American Bankers Association, 2009.

Nordstrom Bank, www.Nordstrombank.com.

Recent Payment Trends in the United States, Federal Reserve Bulletin, Vol. 94, 2008, www.federalreserve.gov/pubs/bulletin/2008/articles/payments/default.htm.

Reference Guide to Regulatory Compliance, Washington: American Bankers Association, updated annually.

Senior Loan Officer Opinion Survey on Bank Lending Practices, www.federalreserve.gov/boarddocs/SnLoanSurvey.

StateFarm Bank, www.statefarm.com/bank/bank.asp.

Workplace Spanish, Washington: Workplace Spanish Inc., available through the American Bankers Association, www.aba.com.

Direct Lending

Learning Objectives

After completing this chapter, you should be able to

- describe centralized and decentralized direct-lending approaches
- discuss the advantages and disadvantages of direct lending for banks and consumers
- describe four categories of collateral for secured loans and their risks
- discuss loan guarantees used in direct lending
- explain the Credit Practices Rule, the privacy provisions of FRS Regulation P, and subprime lending guidelines
- define the terms that appear in bold type in the text

Introduction

The universe of consumer lending products and services banks offer is constantly expanding. In the past, banks looked to commercial loans to bring in profit. Now consumer loans are prominent in their portfolio of financial services—producing interest income and providing fee income.

Direct lending to the consumer has been a mainstay of banking. Traditionally, most consumers visited their local bank branch to discuss loan options that would fulfill personal credit needs. Today the consumer need not go near an office. Loans can be made directly to the consumer through the bank's Web site. Nevertheless, both the bank and the consumer benefit from direct lending options that allow for personalized service.

To meet the credit needs of a variety of consumers and expand loan portfolios, banks seek ways to offer a variety of loan products while managing collateral risk and limiting credit risk. By careful selection of the types of acceptable collateral and adhering strictly to their valuation policies, banks manage collateral risk. By obtaining guarantees from cosigners or government agencies, banks may limit credit risk. In turn, lawmakers and regulators monitor consumer lending and give banks guidance in an effort to protect consumers, the banking industry, and the nation's economy.

Did You Know ...

As of June 4, 2009, there were 8,227 FDIC-insured institutions with average assets of $13,594,359 and average deposits of $8,981,871.
Source: FDIC, Institution Directory, www2.fdic.gov/idasp/index.asp.

DIRECT LENDING DEFINED

Direct lending generally involves only the bank and the borrower. Convenient branch locations were traditionally the driving force behind successful direct lending programs. Before computer technology increased access to banking services, the branch was the most available option for consumers wishing to inquire about, apply for, and close a loan. Today more than ever branches offer a full range of services to consumers seeking sophisticated financial products.

As technology improves to provide more convenient service delivery, consumers tend to gravitate to institutions that offer a variety of direct lending delivery channels. Years ago, banks responded to consumer demands for expedient service by providing drive-through and walk-up windows. Next came telephone banking, ATMs, and access cards. Lending institutions now take loan applications through telephone call centers, direct mail, the Internet, and supermarket branches. Consumers choosing these options may never enter a branch until the loan is closed, and sometimes not even then, which means that bankers have less opportunity for direct contact with them. Thus, although technology gives banks opportunities, it also has presented challenges to direct lending through branches.

ORGANIZING DIRECT LENDING

Many factors influence the organization of the direct lending function, including bank asset size, the relative importance of consumer credit in the portfolio, corporate structure, lenders' skills, and the bank's objectives and strategy.

THE CENTRALIZED APPROACH

Many large banks use a centralized approach in which applications taken at branches or through other sources, such as the Internet, are forwarded electronically to a centralized credit approval area. This area underwrites the loan by investigating the applicant's creditworthiness, doing the financial analysis, and making the loan decision. The lender at the branch or the consumer applying through the Internet is notified of the decision and, if it was approved, the process for closing the loan. Any loan documents that must be signed are sent to the nearest branch, usually electronically. The customer meets with a branch representative to close the loan.

This process is convenient and efficient if the bank has enough staff available to review applications promptly. Banks are competing with automated responses from Internet and other loan application channels; customers want to know quickly if they have been approved for a loan.

Lending software can be complex, with all underwriting guidelines built into the program, or it can be simple, allowing only data entry for application information and requests for credit reports. Even where underwriting is centralized, preparation of the loan documents may take place at the branch, particularly for simple loan transactions. Information technology used by the credit approval area gives lenders immediate access to the bank's internal electronic files containing customer information, credit reports, and other information critical to the loan decision. Armed with information from the applicant and these additional verifications, lenders can make a credit decision quickly.

THE DECENTRALIZED APPROACH

In many small banks, the direct lending function is decentralized entirely because this is appropriate for their smaller loan volumes. Each branch is responsible for issuing loan applications, making credit decisions, closing loans, and even collecting payments or handling delinquencies. This organizational approach has implications for staff training, loan quality control, and marketing programs—issues addressed in the bank loan policy and loan strategy. Although the decentralized approach

> ### *Situation*
>
> The Rodriguezes have chosen a contractor to remodel their kitchen. The contractor will finance the new kitchen on what appear to be reasonable terms. On the way home from the contractor's office, they stop at their bank branch to cash a check. While talking to Gina, a teller they have known for years, they mention their plans. Gina suggests they talk to Hannah Katz, the loan officer, to compare the costs of a bank loan with the loan offered by the contractor. After discussing loan options with Hannah, they decide to apply. Hannah takes their application, and after pressing several keys on the computer, tells the Rodriguezes they will have their answer in a few minutes.
> *How can this be done so fast?*

Deciding Factors in Direct Lending:

- bank size
- importance of consumer credit in the bank portfolio
- bank corporate structure
- skills of bank personnel
- bank objectives and business strategy

can be labor-intensive and costly, it is more customer-friendly. Applicants usually work directly with the decision-maker.

Today technological advances have encouraged many banks to combine decentralized and centralized approaches, allowing personal-computer–driven automation to assist lenders and reduce credit risk. Banks may use centralized lending for some loans and functions, such as documentation, and they may use decentralized lending for loan sales, financial counseling, taking applications, and loan closings.

DIRECT LENDING AND THE BANK

Despite certain disadvantages, banks continue to use direct lending, with good reason. It helps build customer relationships and gives the bank a visible presence in the community.

Decentralized Functions

- application-taking
- closings

Centralized Functions

- review
- booking
- loss recovery
- collections
- payment processing

ADVANTAGES

Direct lending offers banks the advantages of a high degree of control over the loan process, personal contact with the customer, and loan structuring and cross-selling opportunities. It also ensures compliance with laws and regulations and bank policy.

Controlling the Loan Process

Direct lending usually brings the customer into contact with bankers who can answer inquiries about credit products, take applications, communicate the credit decision, and handle the loan closing. Bankers can be taught how to handle each loan function in a customer-oriented and efficient way. This control usually results in a higher-quality loan decision, enhanced profit opportunities, and reduced credit risk.

Personal Contact

The opportunity to establish a personal relationship with the customer is an important benefit of direct lending. Many bankers have a following of customers who are loyal not just to the bank but to them personally. This relationship, which evolves from providing high-quality service to customers over time, is a factor in building the retail banking market. When the bank offers high-quality personal service in its direct lending program, it enhances the total retail banking effort.

Loan Structuring and Cross-Selling Opportunities

Applications generated through direct lending provide a wealth of information about the applicant, making it possible for the lender to recommend a variety of borrowing structures. In reviewing the application, the lender may think of a loan structure that would be more beneficial to both the borrower and to the bank and so recommend a different type of loan or amount than what was requested.

Direct lending also gives the bank the opportunity to build a total banking relationship with the customer. Information from the loan application and personal financial statement may be used to target cross-selling efforts—the lender can help the customer find beneficial solutions for other financial needs.

Compliance with Laws, Regulations, and Bank Policy

Another advantage of direct lending is the control the bank has over the forms and the process. This allows banks to more effectively ensure the loan complies with laws, regulations, and bank policy. In contrast, loans obtained through indirect lending transactions or other application channels may risk regulatory violations because there is less control over individual transactions.

DISADVANTAGES

Historically, the primary disadvantage for banks offering loans through direct lending has been the high cost of doing business. The process is labor-intensive and relies primarily on skilled lenders and attractive branch locations, which can pose operational challenges. Banks meet these challenges through such cost-saving measures as

- automating or centralizing much of the loan process
- emphasizing open-end credit products to reduce the costs of handling future borrowing needs
- using alternative methods for taking applications, such as telephone and direct mail applications, supermarket branches, and the Internet

Another disadvantage for banks may be an inability to make the most of the direct-lending opportunity. To be successful, direct lending must be supported by a strong sales culture and management commitment to enhancing the product knowledge and sales skills of bank personnel. This can be difficult given personnel turnover and the variety and complexity of shifting bank priorities. Within this ever-changing environment, direct lenders keep striving to learn more about banking and financial services, and banks have training programs in product knowledge and sales skills so that lenders may offer other services to customers.

DIRECT LENDING AND THE CONSUMER

With all the choices available for sources of credit, credit products, and product delivery methods, many consumers still want branches nearby and still want to talk to their bankers. Yet many other consumers, particularly those in the younger generations, have never talked to a banker personally because they are more

Automated Loan Support Systems

In addition to laptop computers and secured bank Web sites, automated loan support systems are used to

- take applications
- order credit reports
- underwrite loans
- process originating documents
- track the process
- report on the loan for management and regulatory compliance
- prepare closing documents
- send information to loan offices, accounting systems, and the parties to the loan

Using streamlined automated loan processing systems

- saves time for bank, banker, and customer
- standardizes the loan decision process
- reduces training costs
- increases volume
- improves loan quality
- improves efficiency

adept at using the Internet and point-of-sale methods to access their financial relationships. Contrasts in consumer preferences reflect the advantages and disadvantages of direct lending for consumers.

ADVANTAGES

Consumers benefit from direct lending through personal financial counseling, the potential for lower costs, and the customization associated with flexible loan structuring.

Financial Counseling

The financial counseling provided in connection with the lending process can help consumers better manage their personal finances. Personal interaction with the banker gives consumers the opportunity to learn about the broad range of financing options available that they might not otherwise know. A lender may offer suggestions about a particular loan or advise on debt structuring or other services to build savings and accumulate wealth. Effective counseling requires product knowledge, communication skills, a customer service orientation, and relationship sales skills.

It is helpful for a consumer to be acquainted with a banker so that, when a need arises, the relationship is already established. Consumers who use financial products obtained through channels where no relationship is established, such as through captive finance companies or the Internet, usually have no relationship to rely on when their needs are more complex. By allowing a banker to assess their situation fully, customers are more likely to achieve financial success.

Creative Loan Structuring

The flexibility to structure loans that the direct lending process allows can benefit the consumer. The lender's ability to structure often makes it possible for the loan to be approved rather than rejected. Benefits to the consumer may include

- lower monthly payments by consolidating outstanding loans
- reduction in the number of debts
- lower interest rates on loans
- increased borrowing flexibility in the future through versatile open-end credit programs
- a shorter term for a slightly higher payment
- matching loan term to purpose of proceeds

Situation

Loan officer Hannah Katz knows the Rodriguezes. They are long-time customers and visit the branch often to make deposits and open savings accounts for their children. The information on their loan application, along with bank files and credit history reports that Hannah requested electronically, suggest that the Rodriguezes may have other options. Hannah notes that they own their home and have several outstanding loans in addition to their mortgage. She demonstrates that, by taking out a home equity loan, the Rodriguezes can pay off all existing debt, pay for the new kitchen, and reduce their overall monthly payments.

Should Hannah Katz suggest this option to the Rodriguezes or should she process their original request for a personal loan?

DISADVANTAGES

The disadvantages to the consumer stem more from the convenience of other forms of lending than from problems with direct lending itself. For many consumers, coming to the bank during business hours to apply for a loan is less convenient than, for example, applying for a loan at a dealership where the dealer arranges financing through its network of lenders, or applying through loan brokers on the Internet. Banks are meeting this challenge by offering easier ways to apply for loans, such as through the bank's own Web site, and using technology, such as e-mail, to keep in personal touch with the consumer throughout the loan process. Many institutions accept electronic applications and then follow through by asking the borrower to go to a branch for the loan closing.

SECURED AND UNSECURED LOANS

Although the major consumer loan categories are open-end and closed-end, consumer loans are classified also as unsecured and secured, and, if secured, by type of collateral. This system has worked well for banks because most have lending policies and procedures that specifically address the types of collateral the bank is willing to accept to secure loans.

SECURED LOANS

Collateral is required for secured consumer loans to reduce credit risk. If a customer is unable or unwilling to repay a secured loan according to the terms of the contract, the lender may choose to take possession of the collateral. If the loan contract and security agreement allow it, the lender then may sell the collateral to satisfy the debt.

Secured loans can be grouped into four categories according to how the value of the collateral is likely to change over time: depreciating value, fluctuating value, stable value, and appreciating value. Each category has unique considerations that a bank addresses in its lending policies and procedures.

Depreciating Value Collateral

The bank accepts **collateral risk** when a loan is secured by **depreciating value collateral**. Automobiles, boats, trucks, airplanes, recreational vehicles, mobile homes, motorcycles, and equipment are examples of collateral that declines in value over time, often faster than the balance of the loan. If it is necessary to repossess such goods, even early in the loan the bank may not be able to recover the full amount of the loan by selling them. That is why many banks require that such collateral be protected by insurance. Furthermore, there is inherent risk that banks must take into consideration when collateral can be moved easily from one location to another, making it difficult to retrieve.

secured loan—A loan for which an asset (collateral) has been pledged as a source of debt repayment if the borrower defaults.

collateral risk—The financial risk to a bank that the value of collateral will not cover the principal balance on a loan.

depreciating value collateral—An asset pledged for a loan that declines in value over time, such as a standard automobiles.

Situation

Colum O'Neill takes out a four-year loan for $18,000 to buy a $20,000 automobile. After a year, Colum stops making payments and defaults on the loan, leaving a principal balance of $13,500. The bank takes possession of the collateral, the automobile, and turns it over to an agent for sale. The agent sells the automobile for the market value of $12,000. After paying the agent's fees and other costs associated with the default, the bank receives $11,000 for the automobile.

How much is the bank losing?

Exhibit 3.1 illustrates the relationship between the collateral value of goods that depreciate and the balance on the loan they secure. The gap between collateral value and loan balance is the collateral risk on the loan. The difference represents an unsecured portion of the debt, a deficiency balance.

A bank's lending policy may require that each application be reviewed for both credit risk and collateral risk. However, when securing a loan with depreciating value collateral, it is important for the bank to consider

The value of the collateral at loan closing	Value guides, such as the *National Automobile Dealers Association (NADA) Used Car Guide*, will assist in this process. Many of these guides are available on the Internet. Inspection or appraisal services also are available.
The rate of collateral depreciation the collateral risk.	The rate of depreciation depends on the type, brand, location, and use of each item. The more rapidly an item depreciates, the greater
The market for the collateral	Lenders must determine if there is a market for the collateral and how easy or difficult it would be to sell if repossessed.

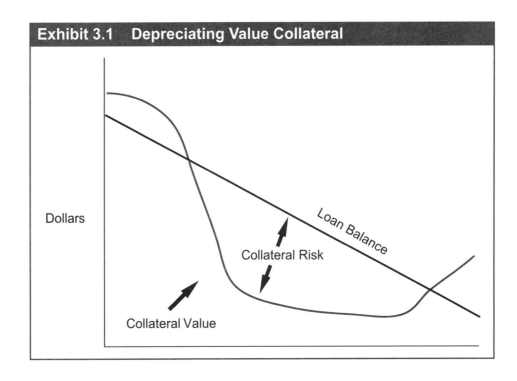

Exhibit 3.1   Depreciating Value Collateral

The bank's experience with the type of collateral   A bank may have experience in selling repossessed automobiles but not fine art.

Fluctuating Value Collateral

Stocks, bonds, and other types of marketable securities are examples of collateral whose value rises and falls over time (see exhibit 3.2). By increasing collateral risk, these fluctuations may make risk management difficult. Before accepting **fluctuating value collateral**, banks have to assess the risk. For example, the value of the stock of a well-established blue-chip company with solid earnings usually is more predictable than that of a small company with a limited earnings record.

Banks have a variety of policy guidelines about what fluctuating value collateral is acceptable. Many lenders do not accept it for consumer loans, or lend only a percentage of its value and monitor it for changes. Some banks accept securities only as collateral for demand loans; if the collateral value begins to fall, the bank can require that the loan be repaid. Other banks require additional collateral if the value of the original collateral decreases beyond a certain point. Alternatively, the bank may require the customer to pay down the loan balance to bring it in line with margin requirements for the loan.

Stable Value Collateral

Unlike depreciating or fluctuating value collateral, **stable value collateral** carries much less risk: savings accounts, certificates of deposit, and cash-value life insurance are examples. The collateral account is often in the lender's possession. The value is determined directly from the account record, CD, savings account statement, or insurance policy.

fluctuating value collateral—An asset pledged for a loan that rises and falls in value over time, such as a share of stock.

stable value collateral—An asset pledged for a loan that has a definite value throughout the loan term, such as a certificate of deposit.

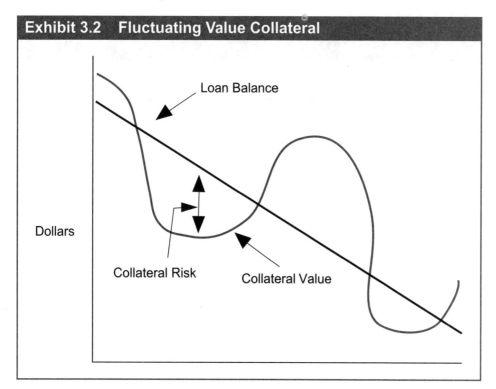

Exhibit 3.2   Fluctuating Value Collateral

Loan Balance

Dollars

Collateral Risk

Collateral Value

Situation

Raji Turner is a loan officer in a small community bank. One of his more affluent customers has submitted a loan application for $25,000 to buy a valuable oil painting. The loan will be secured by the painting. To his knowledge, this is the first time a customer has asked to use art as collateral. His bank does not have experience in valuing art, and he wonders whether its use as collateral is consistent with bank loan policy.

What steps should Raji take to determine whether this loan should be made?

appreciating value collateral—An asset pledged for a loan that increases in value over time, such as real estate.

Loans secured by stable value collateral generally are regarded as risk-free, although losses sometimes do occur because of improper documentation, operational errors, or legal disputes. If a hold on a savings account serving as collateral is released accidentally, the customer may take advantage of the opportunity to remove the funds, leaving the bank unsecured.

Barring operational errors, however, these loans have low risk and therefore carry lower interest rates. Exhibit 3.3 illustrates the relationship between loan balance and stable value collateral.

Appreciating Value Collateral

Some collateral actually appreciates—increases in value—over time. For example, real estate values normally appreciate. Unlike mass-produced automobiles used for daily transportation, classic automobiles usually appreciate. In theory, loans made using **appreciating value collateral** would show the relationship to the loan balance illustrated in exhibit 3.4. If the lender has built in a small margin of protection up front, the collateral risk should be negligible.

Yet at times the value of residential property or classic automobiles may decrease. Real property may depreciate due to neglect, a decline in the surrounding community, natural or manmade disasters, or the general state of the local economy. A classic automobile may be neglected or damaged. Even well-maintained collateral in strong economies may sell for less than full value in an auction or foreclosure.

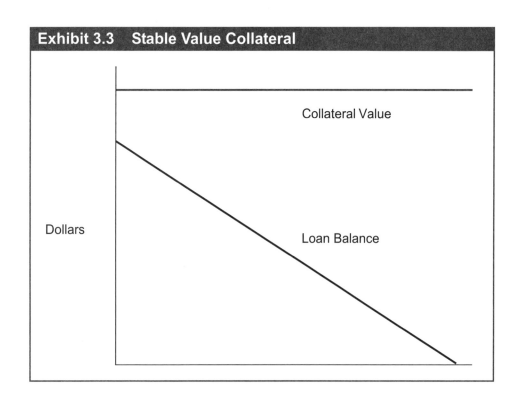

Exhibit 3.3   Stable Value Collateral

Collateral Value

Dollars

Loan Balance

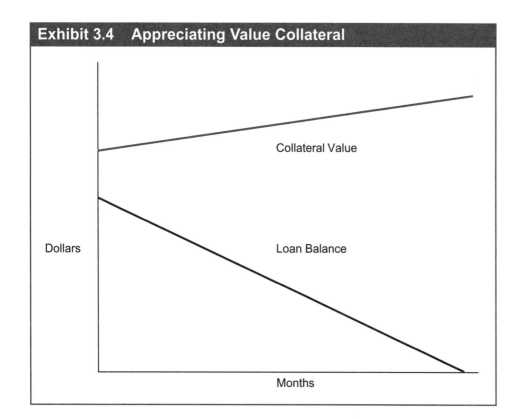

Exhibit 3.4 Appreciating Value Collateral

Collateral Value

Dollars

Loan Balance

Months

Did You Know ...

Appraisal fraud is a risk for both lenders and consumers. It involves an appraisal of property that has tweaked the numbers to satisfy either a lender's or a consumer's financing needs, unbeknownst to the other party.

To avoid this situation, bank lenders and consumers should obtain independent appraisals of the property from an ethical and state-certified or licensed appraiser who provides references that can be verified.

Knowledge, experience, and prudent practices are required to manage portfolios secured by residential properties and specialty collateral. A qualified appraiser usually is consulted to set a value on real property or a classic automobile.

Other Considerations

The first line of defense against loss is a well-written credit policy that is communicated to employees and followed throughout the bank. Among critical elements of an effective credit policy are a requirement to document the borrower's capacity to repay the debt, collateral valuation guidelines, and loan and collateral documentation policies. Although other elements of the loan process also are considered, if the lien on collateral is not properly executed, the bank may find it has no recourse for a loan in default. The loan, in effect, would become unsecured.

UNSECURED LOANS

Because **unsecured loans** lack collateral, conservative bank direct lending programs will make unsecured closed-end loans only to highly qualified customers. Less risk-averse banks extend unsecured loans to a broader range of consumers. Credit cards are an example of unsecured open-end or revolving credit.

Unsecured loans sometimes are called personal loans because the creditworthiness of the customer is very important, as is effective risk management. Banks

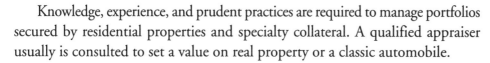

Situation

John Matsuda has always dreamed of buying a sporty two-seater. Now that the children have grown and the family budget is less strained, he has found the model automobile of his dreams. Instead of raiding the family savings, he plans to take out a loan with the automobile as collateral, make monthly payments, and own the automobile within three years. Ashanti Daniels is the loan officer who has accepted John's application.

What type of collateral value has John offered to secure the loan?

unsecured loan—A loan for which no collateral is offered or required.

must balance customer creditworthiness with the profit potential of the loan. The making of an unsecured loan is based on intangible factors, such as trust in the honesty, integrity, and character of the customer. As always, the lender must be able to properly evaluate the risk associated with the loan request and, if necessary, work with the customer to reduce it. Yet bankers cannot personally know the character of every loan applicant. For that reason, they use credit-scoring models that rely on aggregated historical information to help predict the likelihood an applicant will repay the loan.

As with all loans, customers pledge to repay unsecured loans under the terms of a loan agreement. When they cannot make payments as they come due, the loans are in default. The bank then must work with the customers to resolve their problems, because there is no collateral to help repay the debt. Because unsecured loans have higher risk, they normally have higher interest rates and shorter maturities than other loan types.

LOAN GUARANTEES

Loans made through direct lending, whether closed-end or open-end, secured or unsecured, may fall into other categories, depending on such credit enhancements as cosigners (sometimes called comakers) or guarantors, including government agencies. A loan may fall into more than one category. For example, it is possible to have a closed-end guaranteed loan. Obtaining guarantors is one way to reduce credit risk.

COSIGNED AND PERSONALLY GUARANTEED LOANS

A **cosigner** is an additional party who signs the promissory note and can be held liable for repaying the loan. The cosigner's agreement to repay lowers the credit risk. Similarly, another person who signs a guarantee agreement and not the promissory note may guarantee a loan. The guaranty agreement may reference one loan specifically or it may cover all debts of the borrower.

Often, when an applicant does not qualify for a loan, the bank will grant the credit if there is a creditworthy cosigner or guarantor. A cosigner is sometimes necessary when the applicant is a minor or has not yet established credit. Cosigners and guarantors must go through the application process like the applicant, even though they typically receive no benefit from the loan. A cosigner and a guarantor are contractually bound to repay the loan if the original applicant defaults.

GOVERNMENT-GUARANTEED LOAN PROGRAMS

National, state, and local governments support some bank loan programs. A government agency commits to reimburse the bank if the borrower defaults on a guaranteed loan. Because the loans are made to applicants who meet the

cosigner—A natural person who assumes liability for the obligation of another person without receiving goods, services, or money in return or, in the case of an open-end credit obligation, without receiving the contractual right to obtain extensions of credit on the account. A cosigner signs the promissory note or other evidence of debt.

requirements of the guaranteeing agency, guaranteed loan programs are handled by the lending area within the bank that has the most expertise in similar lending. These loans usually have minimal credit risk for the bank as long as the underwriting and maintenance requirements of the guaranteeing agency have been met. Arrangements that provide only partial guarantees carry some risk for the bank.

Exhibit 3.5 describes federally guaranteed student loan programs. One of the largest government-guaranteed loan programs is the Department of Education Federal Family Education Loan (FFEL) Program. The consumer lending area usually manages the version of the program that is coordinated through banks. Other government programs are the USDA Rural Development, Department of Housing and Urban Development, and Small Business Administration loan programs. These loans may be managed by other bank lending areas, such as real estate lending, commercial lending, or small business development.

Federal Family Education Loan Program

The largest student loan program, the FFEL Program, provides low-cost loans for eligible college students. The program, which is coordinated through state agencies, is available to banks that meet certain qualifications. The loans are guaranteed up to the full amount advanced so long as the lender has complied with FFEL requirements.

Did You Know ...

Private student loans from lending institutions are becoming popular to fill the gap between the student's loan need and the annual maximum of a traditional student loan. These usually have long-term fixed rates and affordable repayment plans. Nontraditional schools such as beauty colleges or bartending schools usually qualify.

Exhibit 3.5	Federally Guaranteed Student Loan Programs
LOAN	**FEATURES**
FDLP or FDSLP: William D. Ford Federal Direct Student Loan Program	Offered directly by the government through selected colleges and universities; covers Stafford and PLUS loans.
Federal Perkins Loans	Low-interest (5%) loans for undergraduate and graduate students with exceptional financial need. The school is the lender, and the loans are funded by the government with a share contributed by the school. The loan is repaid to the school.
FFELP: Federal Family Education Loan Program	Loans are funded by private lenders, such as banks, guaranteed by guarantors, and reinsured by the federal government. The programs are Federal Stafford, Federal PLUS, Federal SLS, and Federal Consolidation Loans.
Federal Stafford Loans	The most common education loan, available to both graduate and undergraduate students. May be either subsidized or unsubsidized. *Subsidized* loans are need-based; the government pays the interest while the student is in school and during a grace period before repayment must begin. *Unsubsidized* loans are not need-based. The borrower is responsible for the interest as soon as the loan is made.
PLUS: Federal Parent Loans for Undergraduate Students	A federally insured loan for parents of dependent students. Parents can fund the entire cost of their child's education (less other financial aid).
Federal Consolidation Loan	A debt management tool used to ease the burden of repaying education loans. Borrowers may combine all eligible variable-rate college loans into a single extended-term loan with a low fixed interest rate.

Source: Sallie Mae, www.salliemae.com.

Did You Know ...

Sallie Mae offers tips and tools to help graduates begin to repay student loans and build a healthy credit history. Among the tips and tools are:

• Set up an automatic debit for monthly payments.

• Use Sallie Mae's loan repayment calculator to estimate the monthly payment and total costs for different repayment plans.

• Notify the student loan servicer of any change in name, address, telephone number, employer, or Social Security number.

• Prepay or pay extra whenever possible to lower the overall cost.

Source: Sallie Mae, wwwsalliemae.com.

The FFEL program is open to both colleges or universities and financial institutions. The William D. Ford Federal Direct Student Loan Program (FDLP or FDSLP) is coordinated through colleges and universities, the Federal Family Education Loan Program (FFEL) through financial institutions.

Lenders have the option of either servicing the loans themselves or selling the guaranteed loans in the secondary market through Sallie Mae. Sallie Mae was created in 1972 as a government-sponsored entity (GSE). The company was privatized in 2004, having terminated its ties to the federal government. Sallie Mae is the leading financial intermediary for higher education and the largest single source of funds for education loans. Federally chartered but stockholder-owned, Sallie Mae provides a variety of financial products and services to the education market.

USDA Rural Development Loans

The USDA Rural Development mission is to help improve the economy and the quality of life in rural America. As one of its programs, the agency promotes economic development by supporting loans to businesses through banks and community-managed lending pools. Other programs support rural family housing and community development. The following are some examples of programs offered:

Business programs	Business programs help fund projects that create or preserve quality jobs, promote a clean rural environment, or both. The financial resources are used with those of other public and private lenders to meet credit needs in underserved areas. Recipients may be individuals, corporations, partnerships, cooperatives, public bodies, nonprofit corporations, Indian tribes, or private companies.
Single-family housing guaranteed loans	These loans, made through approved lenders, help low-income individuals or households to buy homes in rural areas. Funds may be used to build, repair, renovate, or relocate a home or to purchase and prepare sites, including providing water and sewage facilities.
Community Facilities Loan Program	These loans are made through approved financial institutions to public entities, such as municipalities, counties, special-purpose districts, nonprofit corporations, and tribal governments. Loan funds are used to construct, enlarge, or improve community facilities for health care, public safety, and public services.

Housing and Urban Development Loans

The Department of Housing and Urban Development (HUD) is the federal government agency responsible for administering government housing and urban development programs. It offers loan and mortgage insurance for single-family homes, multifamily homes, and special-purpose programs. Most loans under a HUD program may be sold as mortgage-backed securities in the secondary markets operated by the government-sponsored enterprises—Federal National Mortgage Association (Fannie Mae), Federal Home Loan Mortgage Corporation (Freddie Mac), or Government National Mortgage Association (Ginnie Mae).

Federal National Mortgage Association (Fannie Mae)	Chartered by Congress in 1938, Fannie Mae is a private shareholder-owned company that works with lenders to ensure that they have funds for home mortgages. Fannie Mae operates exclusively in the secondary mortgage market, buying mortgages from lenders and issuing **mortgage-backed securities (MBS)**.
Federal Home Loan Mortgage Corporation (Freddie Mac)	Congress chartered Freddie Mac in 1970 to keep money flowing to mortgage lenders in support of homeownership and rental housing. Freddie Mac buys single-family and multifamily residential mortgages and mortgage-related securities, which it finances primarily by issuing mortgage pass-through securities and debt instruments.

mortgage-backed security (MBS)—
A security that represents an undivided interest in a pool of mortgages. An MBS commonly is referred to as a "pass-through" certificate because the principal and interest of the underlying loans are passed through to investors. The interest rate on the security is lower than the interest rate on the underlying loans to cover payment of servicing and guaranty fees.

The Rescue of Fannie Mae and Freddie Mac

On September 7, 2008, the U. S. Department of the Treasury and the Federal Housing Finance Agency (FHFA) announced a detailed plan to rescue Fannie Mae and Freddie Mac, whose stability had been threatened by the default of many of their mortgages.

The two government-sponsored enterprises were put into conservatorship. Among other things, the plan called for the U.S. Treasury to purchase mortgage-backed securities guaranteed by Fannie Mae and Freddie Mac, provide a secured lending credit facility for the two government-sponsored enterprises and inject capital to bolster their ability to attract investors and continue funding mortgages.

Fannie Mae and Freddie Mac buy mortgages from banks and other lenders to generate more cash for those lenders to make more home loans. Together they hold or guarantee trillions of U.S. dollars in mortgages— about half the home loans outstanding in the United States. Because of their important role, the U.S. Treasury stepped in to stabilize the housing market and ultimately benefit consumers, financial institutions, and the U.S. economy.

The FHFA removed the boards of directors and appointed new CEOs. Fannie and Freddie continue to operate as usual— buying mortgages from lenders and securitizing them for sale or to hold in their own portfolios. They also continue to raise funding in the marketplace through bond offerings.

The U.S. Treasury purchased $1 billion of senior preferred stock in each company and exercised warrants for the purchase of 79.9 percent of each company's common stock. The U.S. Treasury also created a credit facility for short-term borrowing by Fannie, Freddie, and the Federal Home Loan banks, to be repaid with interest.

Source: ABA News to Use, September 2008.

Government National Mortgage Association (Ginnie Mae)	Chartered in 1968, Ginnie Mae is a government-owned corporation within HUD. Ginnie Mae mortgage-backed securities offer the full faith and credit guarantee of the United States government.

Small Business Administration Loans

The Small Business Administration (SBA) was created to promote small businesses by guaranteeing loans. Small-business lending usually is housed in the commercial loan or small business development area of a bank, although in some banks it is in the consumer loan area. The SBA guarantees a significant percentage of the loan principal, within certain maximums and guidelines. The agency has programs for business, economic injury, and special-purpose loans.

LAWS AND REGULATIONS

Most of the laws that apply to consumer lending apply to direct lending. The three that will be discussed here are the Credit Practices Rule, privacy provisions, and subprime lending guidelines.

CREDIT PRACTICES RULE

pyramiding late charges—The accumulation of charges by assessing a late charge against an amount that includes an unpaid late charge; the practice is prohibited by the Credit Practices Rule.

In 1985, the Federal Trade Commission (FTC) adopted the Credit Practices Trade Regulation Rule to define and prevent unfair or deceptive acts or practices in credit transactions. Although the FTC regulates many creditors, it does not regulate banks, but the Federal Reserve Board has adopted a similar rule for insured financial institutions. FRS Regulation AA, Unfair or Deceptive Acts or Practices, also is known as the Credit Practices Rule.

The rule applies only to consumers seeking or acquiring goods (other than real property), services, or money for personal, family, or household use. The purpose of the rule is to protect consumers from unfair practices such as **pyramiding late charges** and unfair clauses in loan agreements. It also prescribes a notice for cosigners to loan agreements.

Contract provisions prohibited by the Credit Practices Rule include confessions of judgment, waivers of exemption, assignment of wages, and security interests in household goods (unless it is a purchase money loan).

Confessions of judgment	Clauses that allow a creditor to file suit against a customer and take a judgment without notifying the customer
Waivers of exemption	Clauses in which a customer waives property exemption rights provided by state law

Assignment of wages	Clauses giving the lender access to a borrower's wages if the loan is in default. These are prohibited unless the customer can revoke them or they apply only to wages already earned at the time of contract.
Security interest in household goods	Prohibited unless it is a purchase-money security interest. Household goods include most household possessions, except works of art, antiques, jewelry (except wedding rings), and electronic equipment (except one television and one radio).

Did You Know ...

Clauses allowing preauthorized deductions from payroll for loan payments are allowed in loan agreements, as are clauses for garnishment of wages.

Creditors notify cosigners of their liability to repay the loan if the borrower defaults. This notice is given before the loan agreement is signed. Cosigners include guarantors and others who may not be labeled as such in a credit document. The notice may be either separate from or part of the document evidencing the debt (see exhibit 3.6).

PRIVACY PROVISIONS

The 1999 Gramm-Leach-Bliley Act gives consumers privacy protection, which is implemented for Federal Reserve member banks by FRS Regulation P, Privacy of Consumer Financial Information. Other bank regulators have similar regulations. FRS Regulation P requires banks

- to provide initial and annual notices of their privacy policies to all customers

- to keep confidential and not disclose certain information considered private—nonpublic personal information—to nonaffiliated third parties, unless the customer has been given a privacy notice and an opportunity to opt out, and has not opted out

---

Exhibit 3.6   Sample Notice to Cosigners

You are being asked to guarantee this debt. Think carefully before you do. If the borrower doesn't pay the debt, you will have to. Be sure you can afford to pay it if you have to, and that you want to accept this responsibility.

You may have to pay up to the full amount of the debt if the borrower does not pay.

You may also have to pay late fees or collection costs, which increases this amount.

The bank can collect this debt from you without first trying to collect from the borrower.

The bank can use the same collection methods against you that can be used against the borrower, such as suing you or garnishing your wages, and so forth. If this debt is ever in default, that fact may become a part of *your* credit record.

This notice is not the contract that makes you liable for the debt.

Source: FRS Regulation AA, Unfair or Deceptive Acts or Practices.

Nonpublic personal information includes account balance information, payment history, debit card purchase information, or information on a credit report. Public information is that obtained from federal, state, or local government records or from widely distributed media, such as a telephone book.

Banks are required by law to annually disclose through **privacy notices** to all customers their policies and procedures for protecting personal information (see exhibit 3.7). They must disclose their policies and practices for disclosure of information to both nonaffiliated third parties and affiliated entities. Furthermore, they must ensure that they have taken reasonable precautions against the illegal activity of **pretext calling**.

SUBPRIME LENDING GUIDELINES

In a subprime loan, the lender structures the credit for a customer with a flawed or no credit history and receives higher fees or interest rate as compensation for assuming the additional credit risk. Properly administered, subprime lending enables first-time borrowers to build a credit record and allows repeat borrowers to rehabilitate blemished credit histories. **Subprime lending** also can be a means for low-income borrowers to purchase homes. Government bank regulators—the Office of the Comptroller of the Currency (OCC), Federal Reserve (the Fed), Federal Deposit Insurance Corporation (FDIC), and the Office of Thrift Supervision (OTS)— have provided considerable guidance for those engaging in subprime lending:

1999 *Interagency Guidance on Subprime Lending*, issued jointly by the Fed, FDIC, OCC, and OTS	The guidance • recommends the amount of capital a bank should have to support subprime lending • describes the components of a risk management program for these loans • advises bank boards of directors and management to ensure subprime lending is consistent with bank strategy and within risk tolerances • advocates that bank lending policies specify underwriting parameters to comply with consumer protection laws
2001 *Guidance* expanded	The guidance was expanded to require • more capital for subprime lending (Allowance for Loan and Lease Losses, ALLL) • regulatory examination of subprime activities • classification of risk • documentation on re-aging, renewing, or extending delinquent accounts

privacy notice—A notice the law requires to be given to customers explaining a bank's policies and practices related to disclosure of nonpublic personal information.

pretext calling—The practice of obtaining consumer account information over the telephone by fraudulent means, such as by pretending to be the account holder or an authorized signer on the account.

subprime lending—Lending to borrowers who do not qualify for prime rates or conventional loans. Because of the higher risk, these loans have higher interest rates and fees than other loans.

Information Disclosure

Under the privacy regulations, disclosure of nonpublic information (outside of situations listed in the regulation that are exempt) is allowed only when the consumer has been given
• an initial privacy notice
• an opt-out notice
• a reasonable opportunity to opt out of the disclosure, and has not opted out

Exhibit 3.7   Sample Privacy Notice

For an institution that does not have affiliates, does not disclose information outside of the opt-out exceptions, and has no joint marketing agreements.

SAMPLE PRIVACY NOTICE

Protecting your privacy is important to [institution name] and our employees. We want you to understand what information we collect and how we use it. In order to provide our customers with a broad range of financial products and services as effectively and conveniently as possible, we use technology to manage and maintain customer information. The following policy serves as a standard for all [institution name] employees for collection, use, retention, and security of nonpublic personal information.

What Information We Collect

We may collect "nonpublic personal information" about you from the following sources:

- Information we receive from you on applications or other loan and account forms;
- Information about your transactions with us or others; and
- Information we receive from third parties, such as credit bureaus.

"Nonpublic personal information" is nonpublic information about you that we obtain in connection with providing a financial product or service to you. For example, nonpublic personal information includes information regarding your account balance, payment history, and overdraft history.

What Information We Disclose

In certain circumstances, we are permitted by law to disclose nonpublic personal information about you to third parties. For example, we may disclose nonpublic personal information about you to third parties to assist us in servicing your loan or account with us, to government entities in response to subpoenas, and to credit bureaus. We do not disclose any nonpublic personal information about you to anyone except as permitted by law.

If you decide to close your account(s) or become an inactive customer, we will continue to adhere to the privacy policies and practices described in this notice.

Our Security Procedures

We also take steps to safeguard customer information. We restrict access to your personal and account information to those employees who need to know that information to provide products or services to you. Employees who violate these standards will be subject to disciplinary measures. We maintain physical, electronic, and procedural safeguards that comply with federal standards to guard your nonpublic personal information.

Source: FRS Regulation P, Privacy of Consumer Financial Information.

2003 OCC guidance for national banks	The guidance advised that banks should • avoid predatory lending practices, such as **equity stripping** and **loan flipping** • exercise due diligence when making or purchasing loans originated through mortgage brokers or other intermediaries to ensure that they do not use predatory or abusive practices	**equity stripping—** Requiring and financing so many fees that the borrower's equity in the property is substantially lessened. **loan flipping—**Frequent refinancing with no benefit to the borrower.

Predatory Lending Practices

- high-pressure sales
- fraudulent marketing tactics
- excessive fees and interest rates
- fees for unnecessary products
- prepayment penalties that may cause foreclosure
- balloon payments that may cause foreclosure
- frequent refinancing with new fees for the new loan

2003	OCC advisory letter to national banks on brokered or purchased loans	Banks should • avoid abusive lending practices in brokered or purchased loans • avoid encouraging the market for predatory loans, especially those made without regard to the borrower's creditworthiness • refuse to purchase predatory loans or assist brokers that deal in them • have policies and procedures to prevent involvement in these lending practices • perform due diligence before entering into a relationship with a broker or loan seller
2004	OCC rules on federal preemption of state law and the agency's powers	National banks may not make any consumer loans—mortgage, automobile, or student—based mostly on the collateral's foreclosure or liquidation value and not the borrower's creditworthiness.
2006	*Interagency Guidance* on non-traditional mortgage loans	• Guidance issued in response to softening real estate market and looming problems with subprime loans. • Loans covered include interest-only loans and other loans with payment options that run the risk the loan will negatively amortize. • Guidance addressed loan terms, underwriting standards, risk management policies and practices, communications, and promotional materials.

Although the lending practices of most commercial banks were prudent and the majority never made any subprime loans, nonregulated lenders and brokers helped to fuel the overheated housing market early in the decade.

2006	Housing market begins to soften.
2007	Foreclosure rates spike, affecting most subprime loans, which were packaged in mortgage-backed securities.
2007-2008	Lending institutions that heavily invested in subprime loans and related mortgage-backed securities began to fail, fueling a crisis in confidence in the financial industry that eventually spread beyond securities dealers.

2008, fourth quarter   The federal government took extraordinary measures to calm the financial markets and restore order to the investment banking system, including enactment of the Emergency Economic Stabilization Act.

Did You Know ...

SUMMARY

- Direct lending is a transaction between banker and borrower: direct loans typically are made within a branch, although other sources, such as the Internet, telephone call centers, or direct mail also can be direct lending. The direct lending function can be either centralized or decentralized. Cost considerations have caused more banks to adopt a centralized system. However, technological advances are allowing more banks to use a combination of decentralized and centralized lending, depending on the loan product and the lending function.

- Banks benefit from direct lending because it gives them more control over the loan process, encourages personal contact with customers that promotes cross-selling opportunities, and allows them to be flexible with loan structuring and selling opportunities. Historically direct lending has been labor-intensive and costly because it relies on skilled lenders and convenient branch locations. For direct lending to be successful, the bank must have a strong sales culture and management that is committed to building the product knowledge, lending, and sales skills of its lenders.

- Consumers benefit from direct lending because they get personal financial counseling, loan costs may be lower, and flexible loan structuring allows loan products to be customized to their needs. The disadvantages stem more from the convenience of other forms of lending, such as dealer financing or Internet loan brokers, than from problems with direct lending through bank branches.

- The major consumer loan categories are open- and closed-end credit. Consumer loans also are classified as unsecured and secured, and if secured, by the type of risk related to collateral value: depreciating, fluctuating, stable, or appreciating value. Banks that make unsecured loans must apply careful risk management—balancing the creditworthiness of the customer against the loan return.

- Loans made through direct lending, whether closed- or open-end, secured or unsecured, may fall into other categories depending on whether another party is liable, such as a cosigner, personal guarantor, or a government agency guarantor. Guarantors on a loan reduce the credit risk.

Banks saved the city of Frederick, Maryland, during the Civil War. In September 1862 General Jubal Early and his 18,000 Confederate soldiers were on their way to Washington, D.C., crossing into Maryland by way of the Monocacy River.. Early threatened to destroy the city and take the movable property if the city did not come up with ransom money. The four banks in Frederick, including Farmers and Mechanics and Fredericktown Savings, supplied the cash to pay the ransom in the form of a long-term loan to the city. To repay the loan, the city issued renewable municipal bonds at 4 percent interest that were finally paid off—despite repeated unfulfilled petitions to the Federal Government to pay the debt—in 1951.

Source: PNC Bank brochure and 1914 New York Times article.

- Loans guaranteed by the federal government normally have the least credit risk for banks. Among the largest government-guaranteed loan programs are the Federal Family Education Loan (FFEL) Program and the USDA Rural Development, Housing and Urban Development (HUD), and Small Business Administration (SBA) loan programs.

- Most of the laws that apply to consumer lending generally apply to direct lending. Three of these are the Credit Practices Rule, privacy provisions, and subprime lending guidelines. The Credit Practices Rule is designed to protect consumers from such practices as pyramiding late charges and writing unfair clauses into loan agreements, and to require that loan agreements contain a prescribed notice for cosigners.

- For insured banks, FRS Regulation P, Privacy of Consumer Financial Information, and identical regulations issued by the other agencies implement the privacy protection provisions of the 1999 Gramm-Leach-Bliley Act. The act requires banks to formulate policies and procedures to protect nonpublic customer information and to deliver privacy notices to customers about these policies, including policies about disclosures to third parties of information considered private.

- Bank regulators in 1999 issued the *Interagency Guidance on Subprime Lending*, which recommended a structured risk management program for this type of lending, related policies and procedures, and compliance with consumer protection laws. Beginning in 2003, the federal banking regulators issued more guidance to help regulate lending and business practices related to subprime lending. Nevertheless, due to the drop in real estate markets across the country, mortgage defaults and foreclosures increased dramatically. The federal government then intervened to help both borrowers and banks to withstand the severe market downturn.

Learning Check

SELF-CHECK and REVIEW

1. What is the difference between centralized and decentralized approaches to organizing the direct lending function?

2. What are the advantages and disadvantages of direct lending for the bank? How are banks reducing the effect of the disadvantages?

3. What are the advantages and disadvantages of direct lending for the consumer? What can banks do to limit the disadvantages?

4. What are four categories of collateral value for secured loans? How does each affect credit risk?

5. What intangible factors does unsecured lending depend on?

6. Why do federally guaranteed loans usually have the least risk for banks? List some popular guaranteed loan programs.

7. What federal law protects cosigners on a loan agreement? What is the bank required to do? What other protections are included in this law?

ADDITIONAL RESOURCES

Resources

ABA Banking Journal, Washington: American Bankers Association, monthly periodical.

American Bankers Association, **www.aba.com**.

Banking and Finance Terminology, Washington: American Bankers Association, 2009.

Board of Governors of the Federal Reserve, www.federalreserve.gov.

BUC boat guides, BUC International Corp, www.buc.com.

Emergency Economic Stabilization Act, http://frwebgate.access.gpo.gov/cgi-bin/getdoc.cgi?dbname=110_cong_bills&docid=f:h1424enr.txt.pdf.

Fact Sheet: Government-Sponsored Enterprise Credit Facility, U.S. Department of the Treasury, September 7, 2008, www.ustreas.gov/press/releases/reports/gsecf_factsheet_090708.pdf.

Fact Sheet: Questions and Answers About Conservatorships, Federal Housing Finance Agency, September, 2008, www.ofheo.gov/media/pdf/FHFACONSERVQA.pdf.

Federal Home Loan Mortgage Corporation (Freddie Mac), www.freddiemac.com.

Federal National Mortgage Association (Fannie Mae), www.fanniemae.com.

Federal Trade Commission (FTC), www.ftc.gov.

Government National Mortgage Association (Ginnie Mae), www.ginniemae.gov.

Interagency Guidelines Establishing Information Security Standards, www.federalreserve.gov/boarddocs/press/bcreg/2005/20051214/attachment.pdf.

It all Adds Up, PNC Bank brochure, https://www.pnc.com/webapp/unsec/Requester?resource=/wcm/resources/file/eb190108aebd98e/FrederickMag_Nov2007.pdf.

Law and Banking, Washington: American Bankers Association, 2008.

NADA vehicle guides, www.nadaguides.com.

National Automobile Dealers Association, www.nada.org.

Office of the Comptroller of the Currency (OCC), www.occ.treas.gov.

Office of Thrift Supervision (OTS), www.ots.treas.gov.

Paulson, Henry M., Jr., Statement of the Secretary on Treasury and Federal Housing Finance Agency Action to Protect Financial Markets and Taxpayers, U.S. Department of the Treasury Press Release, H-1129, www.treas.gov/press/releases/hp1129.htm.

Reference Guide to Regulatory Compliance, Washington: American Bankers Association, annual publication.

Sallie Mae, www.salliemae.com.

Small Business Administration (SBA), www.sba.gov.

U.S. Department of Agriculture, www.usda.gov.

U.S. Department of Education, www.ed.gov.

U.S. Department of Housing and Urban Development, www.hud.gov.

USDA Rural Development, www.rurdev.usda.gov/rd/index.html.

Vote $200,000 War Claim, New York Times, April 5, 1914, http://query.nytimes.com/gst/abstract.html?res=9A04E3DB163AE633A25756 C0A9629C946596D6CF.

Indirect Lending

Learning Objectives ——————

After completing this chapter, you should be able to

- explain bank and dealer relationships and agreement terms
- describe the advantages of indirect lending for banks, dealers, and consumers
- discuss the disadvantages of indirect lending for banks and consumers
- describe floorplan financing for dealers
- explain leasing as an alternative to a consumer loan
- explain FRS Regulation O, loans to insiders, the Holder in Due Course Rule, and FRS Regulation M, consumer leasing
- define the terms that appear in bold type in the text

Introduction

Loans outstanding can be classified as open-end and closed-end, secured and unsecured, and by delivery channels: direct and indirect. Indirect lending offers banks additional opportunities to grow loan portfolios and expand their customer base to sell more bank products and services. Bank programs supporting indirect lending benefit banks, retailers, consumers, and the communities they serve.

The market, consumer behavior, and the credit environment are continually changing. Lending programs also continually adjust as lenders compete for market share. Although the opportunities are compelling, indirect lending, like all banking activities, must be conducted carefully, with an eye to avoiding risk and complying with the law. While working to grow their loan portfolios, banks also must concern themselves with safety and soundness. Careful management of business relationships loan standards, policies, and procedures, and adherence to the laws and regulations that govern indirect lending are all important for a successful program.

INDIRECT LENDING DEFINED

There are three parties to indirect lending—the *consumer*, who obtains financing from a *dealer*, who then sells the loan to a *bank*. Since 1916, when the Guaranty Securities Corporation announced the first national dealer plan, indirect lending has been part of the consumer lending business. Indirect lending was developed to help third-party retailers—**dealers**—increase their sales by giving their customers a convenient source of credit and to help lenders make credit readily available to consumers who could not be served as effectively by direct lending.

THE INDIRECT LENDING MARKET

Automobile, boat, recreational vehicle, and mobile home retailers have been the primary dealers in indirect lending. Home improvement contractors often seek financing for their customers through indirect lending programs. Merchants selling large appliances and furniture also offer these programs, although many purchases from these merchants are now handled conveniently with credit cards.

Banks seek indirect lending arrangements because most cannot compete effectively for these types of loans on a direct-lending basis. Fewer consumers now go to bank branches to apply directly for loans for automobiles, boats, and similar consumer goods or services. Also, competition from **captive finance companies** has cut into the market for bank products. Indirect lending gives banks an opportunity to retain a share of this market.

dealer—An individual or firm that buys, holds inventory, and resells goods or securities for profit.

captive finance company—A subsidiary of a large corporation the primary business of which is to perform credit operations and finance consumer purchases of the parent corporation's products.

THE INDIRECT LENDING RELATIONSHIP

Unlike direct lending, where the loan relationship is with the consumer, in an indirect lending program the bank has two customers: the dealer and the consumer. The bank must compete with other lenders first for the dealer's business and then for the consumer's business.

The relationship begins when lender and dealer execute an agreement (a contract). At that point, the dealer may offer the lender's credit services to consumers. Exhibit 4.1 illustrates this indirect lending process.

Essentially, indirect lending allows consumers to purchase goods and arrange for credit at the same time and location. When a consumer wants to finance a portion of the purchase price of a product, the dealership's finance manager accepts credit information from the prospective buyer and submits the application to the lender. Dealers may send the loan application to a number of competing lenders, usually by fax or other electronic means.

The lender reviews the terms of the sale—signers, amount, rate, maturity, and down payment—and makes a decision within those constraints. The lender may approve the application as submitted, decline the loan, or condition an approval on a change, such as a larger down payment or a shorter loan term.

Unlike a direct lending transaction, however, the lender cannot offer this consumer other loan products, such as a bill consolidation loan, at this time. The dealer will assign the sales contract to the lender that makes the best offer. Best offers have contract terms that meet the consumer's needs and an acceptable **buy rate** for the contract. Often the contract will be assigned to the lending source that was the first to respond with an approval or for another reason not related to price.

buy rate—The rate of interest a lender will charge a dealer of consumer goods or services for the purchase of retail contracts originated by the dealer. *Also known as* retention rate.

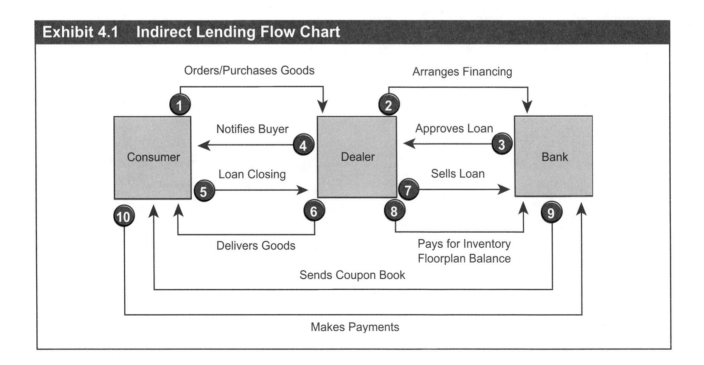

Exhibit 4.1   Indirect Lending Flow Chart

Situation

The Krandalls have retired. They want to buy an RV so they can see the country in comfort. They have found the perfect RV at a local dealership and met with the dealer to arrange financing. They would like to put 10 percent down and have a four-year term on the loan. The dealer has them complete an application, asks a few questions, and faxes the information to several banks.

Fifteen minutes later, the dealer receives one bank's reply and says he can make the loan if the Krandalls either make a slightly larger down payment or increase the term to five years. According to the bank, the Krandalls' income cannot quite support the monthly payments for the loan requested but could support a loan with a slight change in terms.

Who sent the fax that promoted the counteroffer of different terms?

The lender does not have direct contact with the consumer until after the loan has been made. In fact, the consumer often does not know which lender is making the loan. The first contact the lender has with the consumer may be when a billing statement or a coupon book is mailed.

Although many banks have stopped or are reconsidering their indirect lending programs, those that remain seek to build closer relationships with customers who come to them through this channel. These banks actively manage their indirect lending portfolios for marketing opportunities to expand relationships with the new customers. The bank must keep in mind the average maturities of these loans, their profitability, and the opportunities for new business development:

Average maturities of loan types	With this knowledge, the bank will know the distribution of all indirect loan customers. They will know when these customers may be ready to make other purchases.
Loan profitability	Knowing the profitability breakeven points for different loan structures helps banks decide which loan product types to keep, which to restructure, and which to eliminate.
Customer profitability	Knowing the profiles of the customer groups that contribute to the portfolio's profit also helps banks determine which customer base to build on and the expected growth rates.
Opportunities for new business development	Knowledge of portfolio, loan, and customer profitability helps banks plan marketing programs targeted to particular customer groups. This knowledge helps banks manage their loan portfolio objectives.

THE DEALER RELATIONSHIP

Indirect lending relationships begin when the bank and the dealer negotiate and execute a contract for the business relationship. With this contract the relationship is established formally and legally, and the bank may accept applications from the dealer.

ESTABLISHING A DEALER RELATIONSHIP

Bank personnel build indirect lending relationships through direct sales efforts with dealers and manufacturers. A bank normally structures its indirect lending programs by types of goods sold (brands), dealer reputation, and the bank's objectives for the product line.

TYPES OF GOODS SOLD

Banks first determine the types of goods they are interested in financing. This decision should be based on their knowledge, skill, and experience with the product being considered. Banks generally do not participate in lending programs where they have no expertise. Failure to understand the dealer's business and the products or services sold and financed likely will result in loan losses that will affect profitability.

Once banks determine the products to be financed, they create strategies to attract and retain the desired dealer relationships. Banks may seek to diversify their loan portfolios by targeting dealers who handle different types of products, such as automobiles, recreational vehicles, and boats. They also may seek dealers who handle particular brands of those products, such as Volvo or Mercedes-Benz or Ford automobiles.

Banks also consider the quality of the goods being sold. One manufacturer's product line may range from top-of-the-line to the most basic models. The general rule about lending only in market areas where the bank has expertise also applies to dealer products and relationships.

IDENTIFYING THE DEALERS

After a product line is researched, analyzed, and selected, banks identify specific dealers for a possible indirect lending relationship. They solicit only those dealers who will produce the kinds of loans they want in their portfolios. The dealers must maintain an acceptable image, reputation, and sales practice, and they must be creditworthy.

The number of dealers, as well as the product types, that a bank will work with varies depending on its size, objectives, and capabilities; the dealers in the area near the bank; and what the competition is doing. With expanding technological efficiency, banks are now engaging in indirect as well as direct lending outside the geographic boundaries of their own branch locations.

THE DEALER AGREEMENT

A successful sales effort results in a formal business agreement. The contract defines the terms of the relationship and covers the specific services the bank will provide to the dealer. For indirect loans, the contract often is known as the dealer plan of operation, or simply the **dealer agreement**.

The dealer agreement covers a wide range of topics relating to the business relationship, including the bank's loan rates, maturities, and down payment

---

In evaluating dealer-relationship risk, ask:

Systemic Risk. Does the product or service perform in the manner for which it is advertised and sold?

Collateral Risk. If the borrower defaults on the obligation, can the bank take possession of the collateral and sell it to repay the outstanding debt?

Reputation Risk. If the dealer is involved in fraudulent or other criminal activity that affects the product sold, is the bank liable? Would the bank be a party to a lawsuit against the dealer? Even if not liable or involved in a lawsuit, would the publicity harm the bank?

---

dealer agreement—
A business contract that describes the rates, terms, and other requirements on which a bank will buy loans from a dealer.

Dealer agreement plans include the

- buy rate (retention rate)
- maximum rate the dealer can charge consumers
- maximum loan term
- down payment requirement
- dealer recourse and dealer reserve options
- dealer recourse account details
- add-ons or aftermarket products

shotgunning—The practice by which a dealer sends a loan application by fax or other electronic means to many lenders at one time.

warranty—A guarantee made by a seller of the quality or suitability of the product or service for sale. It is often required for loans secured by used vehicles.

aftermarket product—An additional product added to a loan, such as credit insurance or warranty services. *Also known as* add-on.

requirements. It details how the terms will be maintained, changed, or communicated; how the dealer's earned income from the loan interest will be paid; and the dealer's rights and responsibilities.

The interest rates that may be charged are based on the agreed dealer-pricing plan and are subject to a maximum rate set by state law. Some agreements also set maximum rates dealers may charge consumers over the buy rate. The agreements also explain how add-ons or aftermarket products, such as credit insurance or warranties, will be covered in the loan agreements.

Dealers usually have agreements with more than one lender. The lender that establishes the closest relationship with the dealer by responding the fastest to loan applications, or by offering the lowest rates or the most liberal credit terms, is likely to obtain most of the dealer's business.

PROCESSING LOAN APPLICATIONS

Once the agreement is signed, the dealer may begin directing business to the bank. The dealer takes applications in the normal course of business and sends them to potential lenders. Usually these applications are transmitted by fax or other electronic means so that the dealer can send the application to a number of lenders in a matter of minutes. This practice is known as **shotgunning**. Dealers want quick responses; the bank that responds first with a good rate usually will get the loan contract.

Most banks use applications transmitted electronically by computer for both direct and indirect applications. Generally, within the bank a centralized credit department that specializes in indirect lending processes the applications. The application information is verified and lenders immediately make a credit decision, which is then communicated by telephone or computer to the dealer.

Given the competition in indirect lending, some banks guarantee a decision within minutes of receiving the application. If more than one lender approves the application, the dealer decides which will get the loan—normally, the lender with the lowest buy rate.

The dealer prepares the sales contract for all approved loans. Most of these documents are completed automatically by computer. In small-volume dealerships a sales representative or the office manager may prepare the documents manually for the loan closing. In most dealerships, the business manager or the finance and insurance specialist will close the loan.

The dealer who closes the loan usually attempts to cross-sell credit insurance and **warranty** services as part of the loan. The sale of these services usually provides an additional source of income for both dealer and salesperson, who may be paid commission. These extra products typically are referred to as add-ons or **aftermarket products**. The lender must have in place a policy stating how these products are to be handled. If they are added to the amount financed, the total may be more than the amount the bank has approved. Some banks may decide not to offer financing for aftermarket products, such as extended warranties, finish protection, or maintenance agreements. The dealer agreement defines the choices.

Next, the dealer sends the completed documents—the loan agreement, original application, and contract—to the bank. At this time, the dealer also processes the documents required to obtain the title and record the lender's lien. Bank personnel review the loan agreement to ensure it is executed properly and the loan complies with the conditions for approval noted on bank records and the dealer agreement.

Finally, the bank books the loan and disburses the proceeds to the dealer. It then sends a coupon book or billing statement to the consumer, who is now a bank customer. At this point the bank may begin direct contact with the customer and cross-sell other products to expand the relationship.

THE BANK'S PERSPECTIVE

Banks pursue different strategies for indirect lending. Some large banks have a broad base of dealers and actively compete for this business. As a service in the mature stage of its life cycle, indirect lending is subject to heavy competition and is price-sensitive. Consumers choose their loan based almost exclusively on the lowest price. Some banks are unable to make the desired return on their investment with indirect lending or find that it is not compatible with their strategy. Those that stay in the market have a larger market share, but they also must meet the challenges of achieving acceptable loan quality and profitability.

To improve efficiency, most banks have centralized their indirect lending function, usually combining it with the direct lending function. Lenders reviewing loan requests from direct lending branches also review applications from dealers. The same lenders can process a loan request and get back to either a dealer or a branch banker quickly. Banks involved in indirect lending always seek to maximize opportunities while maintaining credit standards.

ADVANTAGES

Having the dealer sell the bank's credit services is the most important benefit to the bank. Although indirect lending programs help dealers sell products, they also may reduce the bank's operating costs and generate loan volume.

Selling Bank Services

The dealer base can be a powerful extension of the bank's own sales force. Dealers enable the bank to reach consumers in geographic markets that may be out of reach of any of its branches. The dealer base also helps banks reach desired types of customers. A Mercedes-Benz dealer likely has high-net-worth customers who would benefit from a wide range of specialized bank products and services. Another dealer may prefer to generate sales and loans from young adults just beginning to establish households. In either case, the dealer can generate customers and loan volume for the bank.

Did You Know ...

Dealer shotgunning of applications could result in several inquiries on a consumer's credit report, first from the dealership and then by all the financing sources. Indirect credit scoring models recognize this practice, so the consumer is not penalized.

Dealers handle some of the functions in the lending process. They also may accept some liability for loan performance. The dealer takes the application, prepares loan documents, and closes the loan. Having the dealer assume these responsibilities allows the bank to process more applications with a smaller staff and possibly increase productivity.

Dealer Recourse

The bank may reduce the risk of indirect lending if the dealer is willing to accept some responsibility for loan performance through **dealer recourse**, for which banks usually set up a special dealer recourse account.

The dealer recourse account is usually a bank-controlled account in which funds are set aside to cover loan loss payments. A dealer will set up a separate recourse deposit account, which can be debited by the bank directly or drawn on by the dealer's check payable to the bank for the recourse amount. Alternatively, a bank may use the dealer reserve account for this purpose; this account holds the dealer's interest earnings. When a recourse situation occurs, the bank debits the account for the required amount for a net settlement result.

There are four basic dealer recourse options:

Nonrecourse or no liability	The dealer has no responsibility beyond normal warranties and recording the lien.
Full recourse or recourse	The dealer is responsible for reimbursing the bank for the full amount of any losses on loans made.
Repurchase recourse	The dealer is responsible for the full amount of any losses if the bank returns the collateral to the dealer. There may be certain time constraints on when the bank must make the claim for reimbursement, such as within 90 days of when the loan becomes delinquent.
Limited recourse	The dealer may agree to reimburse the bank for a flat dollar amount, $1,000 for example, or for a specific period, such as the first 12 months. The bank absorbs any loss suffered above the dollar amount or beyond the agreed time. This option may be used selectively.

In recent years, due to competitive pressures there has been a trend away from options other than nonrecourse. When nonrecourse is the only option, the bank's exposure to loan losses through indirect lending increases. Exhibit 4.2 illustrates loans outstanding by dealer plans for banks of different asset sizes.

---

dealer recourse—The right of the bank to collect from the dealer full or partial payment of a loan on which a consumer defaults.

Did You Know ...

The dealer-to-bank process can be reversed with special computer software programs. The programs let consumers determine the price of the auto they want and then submit a request to the bank for a loan quote. When the loan is approved, the bank submits a complete financing package to a network of auto dealers. This arrangement also requires a formal business relationship between bank and dealers.

Exhibit 4.2 Sample Percentages of Loans Outstanding in Selected Dealer Plans

	BANK ASSETS (In Millions of Dollars)		
	Bank 1 Less than $300	Bank 2 $300 to $999	Bank 3 $1,000 and more
Recourse or repurchase			
Dealer loss reserve held	1%	2%	4%
No dealer loss reserve held	5%	*	*
Limited recourse or repurchase	*	10%	*
Nonrecourse	85%	88%	96%
Other	9%	n/a	n/a

*Less than 0.5%.

The value of a recourse plan depends on, among other factors, the dealer's financial strength and reliability. If the dealer has no regard for contract obligations, or if the business fails, the bank can incur losses even with a full recourse agreement. At best, dealer recourse can help the bank minimize loan losses and allow it to make loans to customers who carry more risk. At worst, dealer recourse can lull the lender into a false sense of security, to the point where unexpected loan losses or unacceptably high delinquencies may threaten portfolio quality and profitability.

Both dealer and bank benefit when the bank monitors a dealer's financial exposure due to recourse loans. The more recourse loans there are, the more potential there is for **contingent liability** for the dealer. Contingent liability can be a factor when ownership of a dealership changes. It usually is addressed in the dealer agreement.

contingent liability—
A liability that may exist if a specific event occurs that is out of the control of the borrower or the lender.

Increasing Loan Volume

Indirect lending enables banks to adjust loan volume quickly. Dealers, particularly high-volume auto dealers, can generate hundreds of loans and millions of dollars in loan volume in a short time. This volume can help banks invest more funds quickly to generate earning assets.

If necessary, banks may slow loan volume from dealers. They may strengthen credit standards or even withdraw financing plans from certain dealerships.

Consistent policy is fundamental to managing indirect lending. The policy should ensure that buying habits, loan structures, and interest rates are consistent over time. Banks without a sound and clear strategy and a prudent lending policy are likely to have difficulty retaining quality dealer relationships.

DISADVANTAGES

Banks must be careful to avoid the pitfalls inherent in indirect lending, especially reduced profitability, shifting loyalties, marginal loan pressure, and improper or fraudulent dealer practices.

Declining Profitability

One disadvantage for banks is that the profitability of indirect lending has come under pressure. As the product line matures, competition reduces lender profits by

- reducing the spread between the bank's cost of funds and the dealer buy rates
- forcing lenders to relinquish recourse protection
- compelling lenders to loosen credit requirements to remain competitive

Because of these changes, many banks have withdrawn from the market and sold their indirect lending portfolios. Indirect lending is then highly concentrated in a smaller base of lenders, usually larger banks. However, as the market changes, so do the participants, and banks of all sizes still constantly explore different approaches to indirect lending.

Shifting Loyalties

The indirect lending market often is characterized by rapidly shifting loyalties. Dealers will shift business from one loan source to another at the slightest reduction in the dealer buy rate or change in buying practices. Lenders will relax or tighten their credit standards to increase or decrease loan volume. The interest subsidy programs of captive finance companies are also highly competitive. Captive finance companies offer the public below-market-rate loans in an effort to boost sales of a particular automobile model or brand name. When first introduced, interest subsidy programs slashed domestic new-automobile loan volume for many banks and forced them to reassess their indirect lending programs. Captive finance companies are still the major competitor in the indirect lending market.

Marginal Loan Pressure

Problems associated with indirect lending sometimes result from improper or fraudulent dealer practices. A problem unique to indirect lending is dealer pressure on banks to make **marginal loans**. Dealers that send a significant volume of business to a bank sometimes expect the bank to take a few customers who represent nonstandard credit risk. This is especially true when the dealer accepts some recourse on the loans.

It is not good risk management for banks to compromise credit standards. Instead they may temper dealer pressure to accept marginal credit risk loans by

- requiring a higher authority for approval of nonstandard credit risks
- requiring dealer recourse endorsements on high-risk applicants

marginal loan—A loan considered to be a borderline credit risk.

- discontinuing relationships with dealers who continue to send, and expect the bank to approve, nonstandard credit risk loans

Unacceptable Dealer Sales Practices

Problems may develop for a bank because of the high-pressure, deceptive, or otherwise unacceptable sales practices of some dealers. In some cases, these may cause the bank to suffer credit losses. Banks need to determine that each dealer's sales practices are acceptable before establishing a relationship, and they should monitor the relationship continually. When problems arise, such as consumer complaints, failure to correct documentation problems, high delinquency on the dealer's loans, and discrepancies between terms disclosed in loan documents and information provided by the dealer, the bank should carefully review and correct each situation.

Dealer Fraud

Banks sometimes experience serious problems with their indirect lending programs because of dealer fraud. Fictitious loans, double financing, misrepresentation of terms, and straw purchases may occur if a dealer is under financial strain. Because the sales representative's commission may depend on loan approval, there is pressure to enhance the application. The bank then makes credit decisions based on inaccurate information. Although fraud often is detected quickly, it still can result in considerable losses for a bank.

Dealers may submit fictitious loans from applications and contracts for nonexistent individuals or for people who did not in fact enter into a contract with the dealer. Sound investigative practices can detect this type of fraud by verifying the existence of the consumer and using audit confirmation programs, which detect discrepancies in loan contracts.

Applications and contracts also may be submitted to and approved by more than one lender, so that the dealer is paid more than once for the same sale. The fraud of **double financing** usually is revealed quickly because consumers receive more than one loan statement. Banks must correct the situation quickly when customers complain.

Dealer sales personnel may misrepresent some of the information on a loan application to make it appear acceptable. Selling prices, down payments, or other terms may be misrepresented so that the consumer appears to have invested more in the sale than the dealer actually received. To minimize this problem, banks rely on valuation guides to determine the amount the bank may lend on various types of collateral. Random audits to verify loan terms also help curb misrepresentation.

Another fraudulent practice is the **straw purchaser** who signs the loan documents for another and does not receive a direct benefit from the loan. This practice arises when the actual purchaser of the goods does not qualify for a loan due to a negative credit history or other significant factor. Unlike a cosigner,

Did You Know ...

The purchase of an average-priced new vehicle in the second quarter of 2008 took 23.1 weeks of median family income, down from 27 weeks in 2005. Including finance charges, the total cost of an average-priced light vehicle was $27,704 in the second quarter, down $1,496 from 2005. Because of high gasoline prices, consumers were purchasing less expensive and more fuel-efficient models.
Source: Comerica Bank Auto Affordability Index, August 7, 2008.

double financing—The fraudulent practice in which a dealer applies for and receives loans for the same consumer from two different sources.

straw purchaser—A lending scenario where one party's name and credit strength are used by another person to borrow money and receive the benefit of the financed goods.

Situation

John Rossini works for a Ford dealership. Alice Field is shopping for a Taurus. She would like the high-end model with leather seats, moon roof, and other amenities, but it is beyond her budget. Alice settles on a base model, trades in her current automobile, and asks for a 36-month loan for the balance. John works out some figures. He explains to Alice that by extending the loan term to 48 months, she can buy the more expensive model while keeping her payments the same as for the cheaper model on a 36-month term.

How do the dealer and the consumer both benefit from this offer?

a straw purchaser often does not pay a loan if the borrower defaults. Nevertheless, the straw purchaser is obligated by law to repay and there are options available to banks to recover the loan amount.

THE DEALER'S PERSPECTIVE

An indirect lending program helps dealers close sales on the spot, enables them to offer reasonable monthly payments to customers who do not have funds for the full purchase price, and increases dealer profits.

CLOSING DEALS QUICKLY

By closing purchase transactions quickly, dealers avoid losing customers to other businesses or customers who might otherwise postpone their decision. This is one reason why fast loan approvals are so important in indirect lending.

MONTHLY PAYMENT TERMS

Loan programs allow the dealer to offer monthly payments that can bring the purchase of large-ticket items within the reach of more consumers. Thus, instead of trying to sell a new automobile for $27,000, the dealer can sell it, with the trade-in value of the customer's old auto, for $530 per month—which sounds more affordable.

INCREASED PROFIT

The extra profit earned from credit sales, such as income from loans and insurance, is important to dealers. Banks pay dealers a portion of the interest on the loans they generate. The payments compensate the dealers for the tasks they perform in taking the application and closing the loan. The dealer portion of the interest income is the difference between the rate charged to the consumer and the bank buy rate. For example, if the dealer charges the buyer 7.5 percent and the bank buy rate is 6.5 percent, the dealer earns the difference—1 percent—over the term of the loan.

The dealer's share of the finance income is deposited to the **dealer reserve account**. As new loans are booked, funds are added to the account during the month and are disbursed to the dealer at the end of the month. Two basic schedules generally are used:

dealer reserve account—
A deposit reserve account set up by a bank containing the interest rate differential that accrues to dealers when they sell or discount installment loan contracts to a bank.

Earn as bank earns   Dealer receives income the same way the bank does: As payments are made, the interest income is split between the bank and the dealer according to the agreed percentage.

Reserves paid upfront Dealer receives its full share of finance charge income for loans booked the previous month. This amount is reduced by income on prior loans that must be rebated when any loan is paid off early, such as a 48-month loan that pays off in 24 months. The bank and the dealer will not earn all the interest anticipated on these loans. The dealer must refund the unearned portion that has been paid.

Exhibit 4.3 illustrates the income a dealer might receive from a retail contract—$864.84 in this sample transaction. Exhibit 4.4 illustrates how banks of different asset sizes pay on average for dealer reserves.

Exhibit 4.3   Dealer Income from a Retail Contract*

	CONTRACT TERMS	DEALER INCOME
Amount financed	$20,000.00	
Bank retention rate	6.50%	
Consumer rate	7.50%	
Total finance charge	$3,211.84	
Bank's retention	$2,766.40	
Dealer share of finance charge		$445.44
Life insurance premium	$144.00	
Dealer commission: 32%		$46.08
Accident and health premium	$276.00	
Dealer commission: 32%		$88.32
Warranty policy	$585.00	
Cost to dealer	$300.00	
Dealer profit on warranty		$285.00
Total dealer earnings on this retail contract		$864.84

*Consumer is purchasing a new sedan, 48-month term.
Note: Dealer also will include profit on the automobile itself, with all the add-ons.

Exhibit 4.4   How Banks Pay for Dealer Reserves

	BANK ASSETS (in Millions of Dollars)		
	Bank 1 Less than $300	Bank 2 $300 to $999	Bank 3 $1,000 and more
Means of Payment			
Up front	71%	83%	73%
As earned	21%	**	16%
Other	8%	17%	11%

*Less than .05%.

Did You Know ...

Consumers can arrange their own financing for an automobile through the Internet, even while the dealer is seeking financing through its indirect lending network. The Internet is accessed through personal computers at home, laptop and notebook computers, and some cell phones.

THE CONSUMER'S PERSPECTIVE

Consumers are, of course, vital to the indirect lending relationship. Both dealers and lenders must address their needs as purchasers and borrowers. The indirect lending program offers consumers both advantages and disadvantages.

ADVANTAGES

The main benefits consumers derive from indirect lending are convenience, flexibility, and more liberal qualification requirements.

Convenience

Convenience is becoming increasingly important to consumers, who have long working days, tight schedules, and less time for their families and leisure. Many consumers place a high value on convenience, and some are willing to pay extra for it. To buy a product and arrange financing at the same time is a definite benefit that indirect lending programs have emphasized. In fact, high-volume dealers often sell vehicles, close loans, and send satisfied customers on their way before getting final approval on the loan from the bank.

Flexibility

More flexible terms are another benefit. Dealers often offer loans for longer terms with lower down payments than the bank offers through direct lending. They can do this because competitive pressures and dealer recourse often lead banks to use more liberal credit standards in indirect lending.

Liberal Credit Requirements

Consumers who lack the solid credit record required for many loans often are able to obtain financing through a dealer. Automobile dealers may offer a "first-time buyer" plan or advertise "credit available to everyone, even if you have had credit problems in the past." These marketing programs usually are arranged with the cooperation of a lender. The consumer benefit arises primarily from either the dealer's willingness to accept some credit risk on the loan, thereby reducing the bank's risk, or from the pressure dealers exert on the bank to accept nonstandard, marginal, or high-credit-risk applications.

DISADVANTAGES

Consumers can be at a disadvantage in an indirect lending situation because there is no opportunity for financial counseling from the banker; they may not be able to compare loans to get the best price; and they may be the target of unfair or deceptive practices.

No Financial Counseling

When a consumer's total financial needs are considered, a loan through indirect lending may not be the best choice. Because each loan request must stand on its own, and there is no provision for restructuring the consumer's existing debts, creating the best loan for the customer is difficult. The lender cannot give the consumer any financial counseling. Although the dealer's finance and insurance representatives may give the consumer some information, they are concerned primarily with making a sale rather than making the best loan for the consumer or building a full financial relationship.

No Loan Comparisons

Another drawback is that, in the interest of convenience, the consumer may not have compared products and credit options. The result is often an impulse purchase that the consumer may regret later. A familiar story is that of an automobile shopper desiring a particular automobile and wanting to take it home immediately. Salespeople are trained to recognize these strong urges and to help consumers realize their dreams without delay. These decisions may come under closer scrutiny after it is too late, such as when the buyers have paid too much for an automobile, or bought features they really did not want or need.

Deceptive Dealer Practices

Unfair or deceptive dealer selling practices harm consumers. High-pressure sales approaches, deals packed with unnecessary credit insurance or warranty policies, and unclear loan terms are sales practices that may surface only after the contract is signed and the customer has gone home. Consumers sometimes are told that the bank requires them to take the insurance or that the bank sets the rate on the loan. Worse, consumers occasionally sign blank or incomplete contracts, only to be surprised later about the unfavorable terms. These problems show why banks must be careful in selecting dealer relationships.

FLOORPLAN FINANCING

Banks often provide **floorplan lines of credit** to retailers as part of an indirect lending program. Banks that extend floorplan lines of credit generally have close relationships with the dealers. The relationship, in turn, enhances the possibility of obtaining other business from the dealers and usually gives the banks first priority on the dealers' consumer loans.

Although it is a commercial loan product, floorplan financing is discussed here because of its effect on the success of an indirect lending program. The bank's ability to extend a wholesale line of credit can help its effort to attract business from the dealer. The more financial services the bank can provide to the dealer—checking and savings deposits, investments, and cash management services—the more valuable the relationship is to both parties. Dealers generally give priority to their floorplan bank when deciding which lender will receive preference on their consumer contracts. This explains why a large percentage of new automobiles are financed through captive finance companies. The dealer may have a floorplan financing agreement with the captive finance company that requires certain sales contract volumes.

floorplan line of credit— A commercial line of credit in which the bank finances the dealer's inventory. When the goods are sold, the bank is repaid. *Also known as* inventory financing or wholesale line of credit program.

Situation

Sally has a new job with a high monthly income and prospects for continued advancement. She wants to buy a new auto but does not have enough in her savings account for a down payment. Because she is upwardly mobile, she plans to get a new auto every two years. Frank, the dealer, suggests she might be interested in leasing instead of buying. Frank refers Sally to the dealer's leasing agent for more information.

How is the bank involved in this leasing arrangement between Frank, the dealer, and Sally, the consumer?

leasing—A financing program in which a lessor (a bank or dealer) agrees to allow the use of the collateral (goods to be leased) by a lessee (the consumer renting the goods) for a specified period and monthly payment.

residual value—The estimated value of an asset at the conclusion of a lease agreement.

Dealers also benefit from floorplan financing. When shopping for automobiles, boats, and appliances, consumers usually want immediate delivery of their purchase. If the exact item the consumer wants is in inventory, a dealer may close the sale quickly. Floorplan financing enables dealers to keep a well-stocked inventory and therefore make more sales. Although banks may reduce the amount of financing for older inventory, the reduction usually is consistent with the reduced value of the older inventory. Nevertheless, a floorplan line of credit allows the dealer to use its funds elsewhere in the business rather than in inventory.

Carefully structuring the floorplan and indirect lending arrangement and monitoring the portfolio are important. Exhibit 4.5 lists questions examiners ask when reviewing indirect lending portfolios.

LEASING

Leasing programs compete directly with traditional direct and indirect lending programs. The most common example is automobile **leasing**, where the bank or dealer owns the automobile and leases it to the consumer for a period of years.

Leasing is popular in the automobile market and its availability and use continue to spread. It is not restricted to new vehicles; some markets offer leases on used vehicles as well. Consumers who are indifferent about whether they own or rent a product or who can realize some benefits that leasing plans offer may be persuaded to lease rather than obtain a loan to purchase the auto.

Benefits consumers seek through leasing include the ability to drive a new-model automobile; lack of worry about the service issues that owners have; the ability (in some situations) to walk away at the end of the lease; and sometimes the ability to write off the cost as a business expense.

The benefits of leasing vary depending on how the lease is structured. It is important for consumers to read leasing documents closely to understand the commitment. Monthly payments may not cover the estimated **residual value** of the collateral at the end of the lease term. Despite the apparent benefits, leasing may be more expensive to consumers in the long run, as in the case of an automobile lease, charges for mileage and wear.

Banks may offer leasing programs on a direct or indirect lending basis. The bank either offers the lease directly to the consumer or underwrites a leasing company that offers the lease to the consumer. In underwriting, it actually does not enter into a lease contract. Instead, it gives the company a line of credit for the leases the company initiates, and the leasing company is responsible for the consumer's repayment of the lease. Due to the complexity of computing the transactions, a specialized unit within the bank generally handles leasing programs.

Exhibit 4.5   Sample Questions on Floorplan and Indirect Lending

Lending Policies

- Has the board of directors, consistent with its duties and responsibilities, adopted written floorplan and indirect lending policies that
    - establish procedures for reviewing loan applications?
    - define qualified borrowers?
    - establish minimum standards for documentation?
- What management tools are in place to manage any negative trends that surface with a dealer relationship?
- Are lending policies reviewed at least annually to determine if they are compatible with changing market conditions?
- What has been the rejection rate for referrals of indirect loans for each dealer?
- Are underwriting policies, procedures, and controls adequate to prevent unsafe and unsound lending practices?
- Does management possess the expertise necessary to underwrite this type of lending?

Collateral

- Are surprise physical inventories conducted at least monthly?
- Are physical inventories more frequent if the dealer is experiencing financial difficulties?
- Are the individuals who perform these checks rotated?
- Do inventory inspections include, as a minimum, the following: serial number verification, inventory of equipment and furnishings, condition and location of asset, and accounting for assets sold out of trust or rented?
- Are trade-ins inspected and appraised for reasonableness of value?
- Is the quality and sufficiency of the loan collateral and the volume and rate of inventory turnover adequate?

Loan Administration

- Is the loan administration process adequate regarding
    - credit and financial analysis?
    - collateral policies and procedures?
    - enforcement of curtailment and buyback agreements?
    - segregation of duties for authorizing and funding disbursements?
- Is purchased retail paper subject to thorough underwriting review and confirmation with borrowers?

Although many banks are leaving the leasing business, others have adjusted their requirements for down payments and monthly payments. Some banks contact lease customers in advance of lease maturity and offer special financing options so that they may keep the goods instead of returning them. By changing practices, these banks have kept satisfactory profits. Exhibit 4.6 on the next page compares leasing to buying an automobile.

Consumer Benefits in Leasing

- access to a new model
- no worries about service
- perhaps walk away from the lease

Exhibit 4.6   Leasing vs. Buying a Vehicle

	LEASING	BUYING
Ownership	Consumer does not own the vehicle. Consumer may use it, but must return it at the end of the lease unless he or she chooses to buy it.	The consumer can own the vehicle and obtain clear title to it at the end of the financing period.
Upfront costs	Upfront costs may include the first month's payment, a refundable security deposit, a capitalized cost reduction (like a down payment), taxes, registration and other fees, and other charges.	Upfront costs include the cash price or a down payment, taxes, registration and other fees, and other charges.
Monthly payments	Monthly lease payments usually are lower than monthly loan payments because the consumer pays only for the vehicle's depreciation during the lease term, plus rent charges (like interest), taxes, and fees.	Monthly loan payments usually are higher than monthly lease payments because the consumer pays for the entire purchase price of the vehicle, plus interest and other finance charges, taxes, and fees.
Early termination	Consumer is responsible for early termination charges if the lease ends early.	Consumer is responsible for any pay-off charge if the loan is paid off early.
Vehicle return	Consumer may return the vehicle at lease end, pay any end-of-lease costs, and walk away.	The vehicle may have to be sold or traded when the consumer wants a different vehicle.
Future value	The lessor has the risk of the future market value of the vehicle.	The consumer has the risk of the vehicle's market value when it is traded or sold.
Mileage	Most leases limit the number of miles a consumer may drive, such as 12,000 to 15,000 per year. The consumer can negotiate a higher mileage limit and pay a higher monthly payment. The consumer may have to pay charges for exceeding those limits if the vehicle is returned.	The consumer may drive unlimited miles, but higher mileage will lower the vehicle's trade-in or resale value.
Excess wear	Most leases limit wear to the vehicle during the lease term. Consumers will likely have to pay extra charges for exceeding those limits if the vehicle is returned.	There are no limits or charges for excessive wear to the vehicle, but excessive wear will lower the vehicle's trade-in or resale value.
End of term	At the end of the lease, typically two to four years, the consumer may have to make a new payment either to finance the purchase of the current vehicle or to lease another vehicle.	At the end of the loan term, typically four to six years, the consumer has no further loan payments.

Source: Primarily from "Keys to Vehicle Leasing," Federal Reserve, www.federalreserve.gov/pubs/leasing/.

THE FUTURE OF INDIRECT LENDING

The future of indirect lending will be determined by how consumers purchase goods and the alternatives they use for lending sources.

PURCHASING EXPENSIVE ITEMS

How consumers will purchase expensive retail items in the future is open to speculation, but two practices today that may foretell the future are locate-to-order and automobile brokerage.

Locate-to-order is a consumer-driven process in which dealers trade with other dealers to get the vehicle the consumer wants. The Internet has enhanced this method of automobile purchase. The consumer locates the vehicle for purchase from a dealer at a distant location and then asks a local dealer to make a **dealer trade** for the vehicle. In return, the local dealer offers the nonlocal dealer a vehicle. Most dealers would rather sell their own inventory than participate in a dealer trade, but a direct sale is an opportunity to earn additional revenue on the vehicle. Dealer trading reduces a dealer's inventory, and helps the dealer earn a return on the traded vehicle. Also, by reducing inventory, the interest expense on the floorplan line of credit is reduced.

Brokerage has long been a common practice in the real estate market for agents and brokers who work on behalf of buyer and seller to negotiate a sales transaction. The same practice occurs on a limited basis in the automobile market. The business arrangement is based on the premise that buying autos from dealers is a stressful transaction. For a fee brokers help consumers determine which vehicles are best suited for their needs, locate the vehicles, and negotiate the transactions. The broker then informs the consumer of the closing dates to sign the contract and other documents and take possession of the vehicle. Dealers have accepted this arrangement as an opportunity to attract another consumer market segment.

In the past, the auto industry led the indirect lending industry for automobiles. Banks had to be aware of any direction that industry explored. However, the two business practices—locate-to-order and automobile brokerage—are driven by consumers, not the industry. These practices represent a significant change in strategy for automobile sales and indirect lending.

CHOICES IN LOAN SOURCES

As consumers become more comfortable with the Internet and related technology, the indirect lending business must find more ways to respond to consumer needs. Numerous Web sites allow consumers to apply for a loan before or during the purchase of an automobile. Technology has made the retail market a buyer's world, and the buying practices of that world are changing. Two online lending alternatives illustrate indirect lending situations from the perspective of the loan broker and the dealer.

> **dealer trade**—A product exchange process whereby two dealers trade similar products, such as vehicles, without a monetary exchange. The trade typically is used when a consumer has located a desired high-ticket product at another dealership. This practice is prevalent in the automobile market.

Loan broker Web site	This is primarily a loan application site: The consumer selects the loan type and answers a few simple questions. The preliminary application is forwarded to several participating banks; usually the applicant receives up to four loan offers, selects the best, and closes the loan—all in one day. The strategy is to make the application process simple and put the consumer in control as much as possible.
Dealer Web site	Automobile purchases and indirect lending processes are moved to the dealer's Web site, which guides the consumer through the purchase, offering information and search programs to select the vehicle, get price quotes, calculate payments, and order the automobile or auto parts. The Web site provides the loan application and assistance, usually with a direct connection to a sales representative. When the consumer selects the vehicle, finance options are selected as well and the approval process begins.

LAWS AND REGULATIONS

Indirect loans made to consumers have the same regulatory requirements as direct loans. Some of these rules were discussed in previous chapters and others will be covered in later chapters. For example, restrictions on insider lending (FRS Regulation O) apply to both types of loans. The holder-in-due-course rule of the Federal Trade Commission (FTC) applies to loans sold by dealers to financial institutions. However, leasing has its own law, the Consumer Leasing Act, and regulation, FRS Regulation M.

RESTRICTIONS ON INSIDER LENDING (FRS REGULATION O)

insider—As defined by FRS Regulation O, an executive officer, director, or principal shareholder, and any related interest of such a person.

Some U.S. bank failures in the past were traced to loans made to **insiders**. In the 1970s, there were some well-publicized cases of banks providing beneficial lending arrangements to their own executives and directors. The practices that were discovered were considered abusive.

Although Federal Reserve Act restrictions on Reserve member bank lending to insiders date from the 1930s, changes to the restrictions in the Financial Institutions Regulatory and Interest Rate Control Act (FIRA) in 1978 form the basis for FRS Regulation O, Loans to Executive Officers, Directors, and Principal Shareholders of Member Banks.

FRS Regulation O applies to extensions of credit by a member bank to an executive officer, a director, or a principal shareholder of that bank, a bank holding company of which the member bank is a subsidiary, and any other subsidiary of that bank holding company. The rules also apply to any **related interest** of the executive officer or director. A related interest is any entity that is controlled by the insider. When considering indirect lending relationships, banks should carefully review the dealer's business organization and ownership to determine if the dealer is a related interest of a bank insider.

Insiders are considered to have control over another company if they own a large percentage of the stock, if they are an officer or director, or if they control the company's management in some other way.

FRS Regulation O Requirements

FRS Regulation O prohibits preferential lending to insiders, requires prior board approval for certain amounts of credit to insiders, limits overdraft payments to insiders, and sets insider lending limits.

Preferential lending	Insiders cannot receive loans that have terms more generous than those for noninsiders.
Prior board approval	The board of directors must approve in advance large amounts of credit extended to an insider.
Overdrafts	A bank cannot pay an executive officer's or director's overdraft unless the insider has a credit plan or agrees in writing to a transfer agreement.
Lending limits	FRS Regulation O has special lending limits for insiders in addition to the bank's legal lending limit. The most stringent limits are for executive officers.

Disclosure and Recordkeeping

FRS Regulation O has disclosure and recordkeeping requirements. Executive officers must report to their boards of directors all credit received from other institutions if it is more than they could borrow from the bank. Upon written request, a bank must disclose the name of an insider when aggregate borrowings require prior board approval. Specific amounts of credit do not have to be disclosed. Banks must survey insiders every year, or use another effective method, to to identify insider-related interests. Finally, banks must keep records of the amounts and terms of all loans made to insiders.

related interest—
As defined by FRS Regulation O, an entity controlled by an insider, such as an executive officer, director, or principal shareholder.

"Extension of Credit" Under FRS Regulation O
An extension of credit includes "any . . . transaction as a result of which a person becomes obligated to pay money, or its equivalent, to a bank, whether the obligation arises directly or indirectly, or because of an endorsement on an obligation or otherwise, or by any means whatsoever."

HOLDER IN DUE COURSE RULE: UCC ARTICLE 3 VS. FTC RULE

The **Uniform Commercial Code** (UCC) governs most commercial transactions. UCC Article 3 states that a person (or entity) obtaining a negotiable instrument—such as by purchasing a promissory note—becomes a holder in good faith, without any knowledge of any claims against the right to collect it, and thus is a **holder in due course** and not subject to claims the borrower could have brought against the original holder.

Therefore, in the sale of goods, when the seller finances the purchase and sells the promissory note to a holder in due course, the borrower cannot refuse to make payment if the goods turn out to be defective. The holder in due course is protected from such claims.

However, the Federal Trade Commission (FTC) Holder In Due Course Rule, 16 CFR 433, issued in 1976, changed the rule for consumer transactions. The FTC rule applies to banks and is enforced by bank regulators. It states that a purchaser of a consumer credit contract for the sale of goods continues to be subject to claims the consumer can make against the original seller—such as a claim against warranties or a claim that the goods are defective.

Consumer credit contracts sold by a retailer, such as an automobile dealer, to a bank must contain a notice in the legend that states this rule. The notice discloses to consumers that they still may exercise their rights to stop making payments, if the goods turn out to be defective. Exhibit 4.7 illustrates the notice.

CONSUMER LEASING ACT

In 1976, Congress passed the Consumer Leasing Act to provide consumers with uniform meaningful disclosures of financial terms when they lease consumer property. FRS Regulation M defines a consumer lease as a lease of personal property for a term of four months or more for which the consumer's total obligation will not exceed $25,000. The Consumer Leasing Act does not cover leases for agricultural, business, or commercial purposes.

Uniform Commercial Code (UCC)—A set of laws adopted by states to govern commercial and financial transactions between parties. Many states add their own amendments to the basic code.

holder in due course—A purchaser of a negotiable instrument, such as a check or a promissory note, that buys the instrument in good faith, for value, and without knowledge of any claims or defenses the maker has against the original holder.

Exhibit 4.7   Holder Notice on Promissory Note
NOTICE
ANY HOLDER OF THIS CONSUMER CREDIT CONTRACT IS SUBJECT TO ALL CLAIMS AND DEFENSES WHICH THE DEBTOR COULD ASSERT AGAINST THE SELLER OF GOODS OR SERVICES OBTAINED PURSUANT HERETO OR WITH THE PROCEEDS HEREOF. RECOVERY HEREUNDER BY THE DEBTOR SHALL NOT EXCEED AMOUNTS PAID BY THE DEBTOR HEREUNDER.
Source: Federal Trade Commission, Holder in Due Course Rule, 16 CFR 433.

Lessors must make certain disclosures in advance of any consumer lease transaction. The required disclosures, similar to those in FRS Regulation Z, are:

- a description of the leased property
- the number, amount, and due dates of the payments
- the total amount to be paid under the lease
- an itemized list of charges
- the amount for which the lessee will be liable at the end of the term
- insurance costs
- the party responsible for maintaining the property
- late charges
- standards for wear and tear, if any
- information about the amount the lessee may owe at lease termination
- a statement of limitations on the amount the lessee will owe at lease termination

The law also regulates the advertising of consumer lease arrangements. For example, the lessor must furnish more complete information if certain terms are used in advertisements, such as the amount of a payment, the number of payments, or that a down payment is not required. Other terms of the lease to be advertised are the total amount of the security deposits, the amount and schedule of lease payments, whether the leased property can be purchased and the price, and the amount, or method of determining the amount, the lessee must pay when the lease ends.

SUMMARY

- Indirect lending has three parties: the consumer, the dealer (retailer), and the bank. The bank has two customers: the dealer and the consumer.

- All kinds of goods and services may involve a dealer and indirect lending arrangements. However, the most common are those for large-ticket items such as vehicles, mobile homes, boats, and home improvements. Banks begin by identifying the types of products and the dealers they wish to support through indirect lending. Choices vary depending on the bank's asset size, objectives and capabilities; the market; and the competition.

- The contract between the bank and dealer—the dealer agreement—defines the terms of the business relationship. It includes the bank's loan rates, maturities, and down payment requirements; how the contract terms will be maintained, changed, or communicated; how the dealer's earned income from loan interest is to be paid; the dealer's rights and responsibilities; and whether the loan can finance add-ons or after-market products.

- This is the customary lending process: The consumer arranges to finance the purchase through the dealer. The dealer takes the initial application and sends it to several lenders, a process known as shotgunning. Each lender investigates and reviews the application and returns a decision, often within minutes. Then the dealer selects, from the lenders who responded, the loan with the best terms for both consumer and dealer. The lender is notified and the loan documents are prepared either at the dealer site or by the lender and then delivered electronically. The consumer signs a loan agreement, which is sent to the lender. At this point, the bank may contact the consumer about other bank products and services.

- Indirect lending has advantages for banks, consumers, and dealers. For banks, the advantages are that loan volume is increased, more bank services can be sold, the dealer handles such tasks as taking the application and closing the loan, and the dealer may assume some loan risk, depending on the dealer recourse option. There are four types of dealer recourse: non-recourse (no liability), full recourse (recourse), repurchase recourse, and limited recourse. The benefits consumers enjoy are convenience, flexibility, and more liberal credit.

- For the dealer, the advantages are that deals close quickly, monthly payment terms are better, and profits increase. The dealer earns that portion of the interest income that is the difference between the rate charged to the consumer and the bank's buy rate, an amount that is deposited into a dealer reserve account. Dealers are paid either on an "earn as the bank earns" or a "reserves paid up front" basis.

- Indirect lending may have disadvantages for both banks and consumers. Banks must avoid such pitfalls as reduced profitability, shifting loyalties, and improper or fraudulent dealer practices, such as double financing and straw purchasers. Consumers miss out on the financial counseling that occurs in direct lending; they are not able to compare loan terms directly; and some dealers may use deceptive sales practices, such as requiring unneeded credit insurance or warranty policies.

- Banks often provide floorplan lines of credit to retailers as part of an indirect lending program. Banks that extend floorplan lines of credit generally have closer relationships with the dealers. The relationship in turn enhances the opportunity for more business from the dealers and usually gives the banks first priority on the dealer's consumer loans.

- Leasing programs compete directly with lending programs. The most common example is vehicle leasing, where the bank or dealer owns the vehicle and leases it to the consumer for a period of years. The benefits of leasing vary depending on how the lease is structured. Monthly payments may not cover the residual value of the collateral at the end of the lease term. The bank either offers the lease directly to the consumer or underwrites a leasing company that offers the lease to the consumer.

- In the future, traditional indirect lending may be replaced by expanding choices for sales of expensive items such as automobiles and for loans. More consumers may use locate-to-order and product broker programs. The automobile and real estate markets offer examples of these processes. Thanks to advancing Internet technology, loan sources also are changing the process. Loan broker and dealer Web sites offer consumers flexibility in the choice of process, product, and seller.

- Loans made to consumers through indirect lending have the same regulatory requirements as loans made through direct lending. For example, the restrictions on insider lending in FRS Regulation O apply to loans however they are made. The Federal Trade Commission Holder In Due Course Rule applies to all consumer contracts that are sold to a bank. Consumer leasing has its own law, the Consumer Leasing Act, implemented by FRS Regulation M.

SELF-CHECK AND REVIEW

Learning Check

1. In what ways may a bank reduce its risk on a loan made through indirect lending?

2. At what point in the indirect lending process does the bank have direct contact with the consumer?

3. How does dealer recourse reduce a bank's risk on a loan made through indirect lending? Why have nonrecourse arrangements become more common?

4. How do dealers benefit financially from indirect lending, other than being able to make the sale? Explain.

5. Why may a loan to purchase a new auto through indirect lending not be the best loan alternative for a consumer?

6. What is leasing? Explain how banks can offer leases on either a direct or an indirect basis.

7. What is a floorplan line of credit and how does it enhance a dealer relationship?

8. What does FRS Regulation O address and why should it be considered when a bank establishes a dealer relationship?

9. What change to the UCC Article 3 holder-in-due-course concept did the Federal Trade Commission (FTC) make in situations such as bank purchases of promissory notes from dealers and subsequent responsibilities to consumers?

Resources

ADDITIONAL RESOURCES

American Bankers Association, **www.aba.com**.

American Bankers Association Education Foundation, for consumer information on credit, www.aba.com.

Association of Consumer Vehicle Lessors, www.acvl.com.

Automobiles.com, a division of Classified Ventures, LLC™, www.automobiles.com.

Comerica Auto Affordability Index, www.comerica.com/Comerica_Content/ Corporate_Communications/Docs/Auto_Affordability_Index_Q22008.pdf.

DealerTrack, www.dealertrack.com.

Federal Deposit Insurance Corporation, "The Changing Landscape of Indirect Automobile Lending, Supervisory Insights," www.fdic.gov/regulations/examinations/supervisory/insights/sisum05/ article04_auto_lending.html.

Federal Reserve Board of Governors, "G.19 Consumer Credit Historical Data," www.federalreserve.gov/releases/G19/ hist/.

Federal Reserve Board of Governors, "Keys to Vehicle Leasing," www.federalreserve.gov/pubs/leasing.

"In Focus This Quarter: The U.S. Consumer Sector," FDIC Outlook, www.fdic.gov/bank/analytical/regional/ro20044q/na/2004winter_04.html.

Law and Banking, Washington: American Bankers Association, 2008.

National Automobile Dealers Association, www.nada.org.

National Vehicle Leasing Association, www.nvla.org.

Office of Thrift Supervision, *Asset Quality, Floor Plan and Indirect Lending Program, Regulatory Handbook,* www.ots.treas.gov/docs/4/429047.pdf.

RouteOne, www.routeone.com.

Open-End, Revolving Credit Products

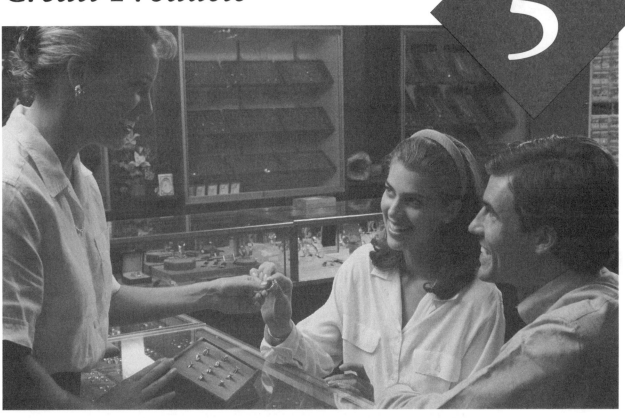

Learning Objectives

After completing this chapter, you should be able to

- describe the characteristics of open-end credit products
- describe credit, debit, and stored-value card services
- explain the open-end credit application and documentation process
- discuss the benefits and challenges of open-end credit for banks and consumers
- explain how the Fair Credit Reporting Act (FCRA) and the Truth in Lending Act (TILA) apply to open-end credit
- define the terms that appear in bold type in the text

Introduction

Open-end or revolving lines of credit have been the fastest-growing form of lending to consumers since the mid-1970s. Starting as retail store and gasoline company credit, these accounts were intended to help increase the sale of specific goods and services and to encourage consumers to shop in specific retail stores and service stations.

As Americans became more mobile and the number of retail stores proliferated, so did the need for more flexible credit. When national credit cards first appeared in the late 1950s, they gained rapid acceptance. Banks went on to expand open-end products to include check credit or overdraft lines of credit, stand-alone unsecured revolving lines, and home equity lines of credit. Open-end credit expanded both the borrowing power of consumers and the convenience of credit. With open-end credit, lenders can offer more credit services to more consumers.

The introduction of different kinds of plastic access cards has continued over the years; they now include check, or debit, cards and stored-value cards. Each meets a different type of consumer payment need.

OPEN-END CREDIT FEATURES

Open-end credit accounts usually remain open as long as the consumer handles the account in an acceptable manner and the lender wishes to offer the product.

Bank credit card programs are a form of open-end credit. Although bank credit card accounts usually have an expiration date, most are renewed automatically. The expiration date is simply a control point to help reduce delinquency, losses, and unauthorized use. It also provides a logical point for increasing marketing efforts, revising credit limits, and cross-selling other services. Many banks also have periodic reconfirmation features that require consumers to update their financial information, and they review the cardholder's credit record with home equity and other high-dollar lines of credit. The intention is to keep the account open but also manage credit risk and identify additional marketing opportunities.

Some lines of credit do have expiration dates, however. Today, most home equity lines of credit typically expire five years after the credit line is opened. At that time, the customer must pay off the balance or refinance the line of credit. Because these are high-dollar lines, banks need to ensure that the committed funds are not idle but are being used and earning the bank income.

Most open-end credit accounts have a specific **credit limit**. The bank, which establishes the customer's credit limit when the account is opened, bases

credit limit—The maximum allowable unpaid balance on open-end credit accounts, such as credit cards or lines of credit.

the amount on the type of product, the customer's credit capacity, and the bank's policy on debt-to-income ratios. For example, the credit limits on a regular bankcard account may range from $500 to $5,000, on a premium card account from $5,000 to $10,000, and on a home equity line of credit from $5,000 to $100,000 or more.

The bank, at its option or in response to a consumer's request, may increase the limit on unsecured lines of credit and credit cards. In fact, for creditworthy customers banks may do so without a request, to encourage them to use the bank's credit services rather than a competitor's service. Credit limit increases on home equity and other secured lines of credit are more complicated. They generally require that new disclosures be made and new documents signed. Conversely, when credit is tight, banks may decrease the limit on credit card accounts to help control their risks.

Once an open-end credit account is established, the credit is easy to access. Consumers have the freedom and control to use the line of credit as they wish up to the maximum credit limit. There is no waiting for loan approvals, and no one needs to know the consumer is borrowing money. As payments are made, the amount of credit available is replenished. The available credit represents future borrowing power for the consumer.

OPEN-END CREDIT PRODUCTS

The open-end credit product line includes credit cards, check credit (overdraft) lines, stand-alone unsecured lines, and secured lines, which are primarily home equity lines of credit. Credit cards constitute the largest share of the market, although home equity is taking a growing share. Each product has a special role in the consumer lending market as a whole.

CREDIT CARDS

Consumers use a wide variety of plastic cards, among them retail private label cards, national and international bankcards, travel and entertainment cards, and cobranded, affinity, and special value cards. Each has unique characteristics and markets.

Retail Private Label Credit Cards

Many retailers offer private-label cards to be used for purchases only from the issuing retailer. Making credit available enables consumers to purchase more goods, which ties them to the retailer. Many consumers prefer to shop at stores where they have an established credit relationship. Major national retailers maintain large credit card customer bases, as do regional department store chains and specialty stores. These retailers place a high value on building customer loyalty. Indeed, retailers often advertise special sales offers only for their private-label cardholders.

Open-End Credit vs. Closed-End Credit

Open-end credit:
A specified amount of credit available for use at the consumer's discretion, of which a minimum repayment amount or percentage is specified in the contract.

Closed-end credit:
A fixed amount of credit for a specific purpose established at the beginning of the transaction, to be repaid in one or more regular payments over a set term.

Types of Credit Cards

- retail private label cards
- national credit cards
- international credit cards
- travel and entertainment (T&E) cards
- cobranded cards
- affinity cards
- special value cards

Although retailers issue the credit cards, they often use a bank credit-card system that brands the card with the retailer's name. This arrangement is more cost-effective than setting up a separate system.

National and International Credit Cards

Although they did not experience major growth until the late 1960s, Visa and Mastercard trace their roots to the 1950s. Mass marketing of both national cards began in the mid-1960s as many banks, recognizing the significant potential of credit cards, rushed to gain a competitive advantage in what was to become a high-growth, high-profit market. Internationally, Visa, Mastercard, and the Japanese JCB card have gained wide acceptance.

National credit-card programs became segmented when prestige versions, such as gold and platinum cards, were introduced to compete with travel and entertainment cards. Targeted to high-income and high-net-worth customers, these cards offer higher credit limits, travel services, free travel accident insurance, frequent flier mileage award credit, and product warranties. Lenders whose credit cards have value-added features expect to increase their customer base and card usage and thus to generate higher revenues. Exhibit 5.1 illustrates various credit card offers.

Travel and Entertainment Cards

Travel and entertainment cards (T&E cards) traditionally have been different from credit cards because they are primarily transaction cards that act as an alternative to cash and personal checks. Cardholders use a T&E card to purchase goods and services for which they are charged during the next billing cycle. The balance usually is due in full and is not subject to finance charges if paid by the due date. Some T&E cards now permit consumers, under certain circumstances, to repay the balance over a number of months, but usually the interest rate is higher than the rate for bank credit cards.

The T&E category includes American Express and Diners Club and some cards issued by travel-related companies. Some T&E cards impose membership fees and offer different membership levels. Some have expanded their lines of both credit and noncredit products beyond that of traditional cards.

T&E cards, generally marketed to consumers in higher socioeconomic groups, rarely have stated credit limits. Marketing themes, annual fees, and product features all tend to create an image of exclusivity and high value. For example, Diners Club offers a special concierge program to assist members with hotel reservations and accommodations, including finding the room with the best view.

Affinity Cards

One popular and successful credit-card marketing strategy is for a lender to offer a group of consumers with a common interest a credit-card product customized for and available only to members of the group. These programs are particularly popular for large national associations, such as the AARP, and for special-interest groups, such as alumni of a particular college or hobby group. Generally, the

travel and entertainment (T&E) card—A transaction card that serves as an alternative to cash and personal checks. American Express and Diners Club are examples.

Exhibit 5.1 Comparison of Three Credit Card Plans

FEATURE	CARD A COLLEGE	CARD B REGULAR	CARD C PREMIUM/FLYER
What are the APRs?	0% for six months, then	0% for six months, then	0% for six months, then
Purchases	17%	10%	13%
Cash advances	22	22	22
Balance transfers	17	10	13
Late payments	30	30	30
What type of interest does the card have?	Variable US prime rate as published in the *Wall Street Journal*, plus percentage	Variable US prime rate as published in the *Wall Street Journal*, plus percentage	Variable US prime rate as published in the *Wall Street Journal*, plus percentage
Tiered by balance	No	No	No
How long is the grace period?	15 days	15 days	15 days
Balance carryover	N/A	N/A	N/A
Balance paid monthly	New minimum balance must be paid monthly.	New minimum balance must be paid monthly.	New minimum balance must be paid monthly.
Cash advances	N/A	N/A	N/A
How is the finance charge calculated?			
Cycles (one or two?)	One	One	One
New purchases (included or excluded?)	Includes new purchases	Includes new purchases	Includes new purchases
Average or adjusted	Average daily	Average daily	Average daily
Minimum finance charge	$0.50	$0.50	$0.50
What are the fees?			
Annual	None	None	$65
Late payment	$10 on balances up to $100	$10 on balances up to $100	$10 on balances up to $100
	$25 on balances of $100 to $2,000	$25 on balances of $100 to $2,000	$25 on balances of $100 to $2,000
	$40 on balances of $2,000 or more	$40 on balances of $2,000 or more	$40 on balances of $2,000 or more
Over the credit limit	$30	$30	None
Set up	None	None	None
Other:	2.5% for amount of purchases made in foreign currency after conversion to U.S. currency	2.5% for amount of purchases made in foreign currency after conversion to U.S. currency	2.5% for amount of purchases made in foreign currency after conversion to U.S. currency

Continued on next page

Exhibit 5.1   Comparison of Three Credit Card Plans, *continued*

What are the cash advance features?

Transaction fees	2.5% of amount	2.5% of amount	2.5% of amount
Limits	$10 minimum	$10 minimum	$10 minimum
How much is the credit limit?	Minimum $500	Minimum $500	Minimum $2,500
What kind of card is it?	Regular with rewards	Regular without rewards	Premium level, regular with rewards
Does the card offer other features?			
Rebates/rewards	Yes, up to $1,500 annually and they expire; percent varies for necessary purchases v. other purchases. May be used towards car purchase/lease/service or on special purchases.	None	Yes, up to $250,000 annually with no expiration; points for spending on purchases or frequent flyer miles.
Frequent flier miles	No	No	Yes
Insurance	No	No	Lost luggage
Online services	Account balance and bill payment	Account balance and bill payment	Account balance and bill payment
Other	$0 liability for unauthorized purchases	$0 liability for unauthorized purchases	$0 liability for unauthorized purchases

Source: Federal Reserve Board, *Choosing a Credit Card,* www.federalreserve.gov/pubs/shop/.

---

affinity card—A card product offered by a bank in conjunction with a partner and targeted to a group of like-minded individuals brought together by a common interest, such as a profession, university affiliation, or cause.

cobranded card—A bankcard issued with a commercial partner, such as an airline, telephone company, or retailer, to promote loyalty through value-added incentives, such as discounts, rewards, and other consumer benefits.

lender shares revenues from the program with the participating group. **Affinity cards** also have a philanthropic purpose because they can provide a source of income for nonprofit organizations.

Cobranded Credit Cards

Like affinity programs, **cobranded card** programs, such as the Chase-Disney Visa credit card, represent strategic alliances between a lender and another organization. These alliances can help build a stronger relationship between the consumer and the organization offering the cobranded product. The better designed and administered programs often translate into higher sales volume and revenues for the participants while offering benefits for the consumer.

Reward Cards

Reward cards are not tied to a particular card type or branded relationship. Rewards may be rebates on purchases made, frequent flyer miles, deposits into checking or savings accounts, or savings toward the purchase of an automobile or other high-price goods. Two examples are the Volkswagen Platinum Visa card with rewards and the World Perks Visa Platinum Card.

Special Value Credit Cards

Taken together, affinity, reward, and cobranded cards have created a new category, the **special value card**, that has achieved significant transaction volume. Theses cards have a large consumer base with higher than average spending amounts and frequency of use. The Internet is fast evolving as the new market for special value cards.

CHECK OVERDRAFT LINES OF CREDIT

One of the first forms of open-end credit offered by banks was the check overdraft line of credit. This credit line offers qualified checking account customers a line of credit to be used at their discretion. The line of credit protects consumers against overdraft charges and helps them avoid the embarrassment and inconvenience associated with returned checks. Banks benefit because of reduced check-return costs and increased customer goodwill.

Overdraft lines of credit are cross-sold to consumers who are opening new checking accounts or to current checking account customers through special marketing programs and branch sales efforts. If approved, the customer is given a specific credit limit that is accessed simply by writing a check in an amount greater than the checking account balance. Some banks also provide special checks that will access the credit directly without affecting the customer's checking account balance.

These simple line of credit programs not only offer customers convenience and peace of mind, they also offer the bank an additional source of revenue from a product that customers value.

Credit limits on overdraft lines of credit are generally small, ranging from $300 to $10,000, with most under $2,000. The lower limits restrict credit line use to relatively small amounts and short-term cash-flow requirements, such as borrowing until payday. Check overdraft lines of credit also have relatively low usage because most consumers use them only as a short-term or emergency source of credit. Generally, dollar usage is less than 50 percent of the available credit, with average balances around $1,000.

Banks often charge a higher rate of interest for overdraft lines of credit than for other types of credit. As with all loans, there is an important relationship between rate and risk, and banks price loans accordingly. A secured, closed-end loan, for example, likely will have a lower interest rate than an overdraft line of credit, because the risk of default usually is lower.

Overdraft Lines of Credit vs. Overdraft Protection

Check credit or overdraft lines of credit should not be confused with overdraft protection services. Overdraft protection is marketed also as "bounced-check protection" or "courtesy overdraft protection." A customer writes a check for more than the funds available in the deposit account up to an overdraft limit. Whether the check is paid (if within the limit) or not (amount is above the limit), a fee is charged to the customer's transaction deposit account. There is no line of credit attached to the transaction deposit account.

> **special value card**—A category of credit cards that includes affinity, cobranded, and reward cards. These cards have features that are especially important to the consumer.

Overdraft Lines of Credit vs. Payday Loans

Payday loans should not be confused with overdraft lines of credit or overdraft protection services. Payday loans are small-dollar, short-term, unsecured loans that consumers promise to repay out of their next paycheck. These loans are priced at a fixed-dollar fee representing the finance charge. Typically, the customer gives the creditor a debit authorization or a check for the loan amount plus the fee, which the creditor holds until the customer's payday. On payday, the creditor may cash the check or the customer pays the loan amount plus fee to the lender.

UNSECURED LINES OF CREDIT

The popularity of revolving credit programs encouraged banks to create and market accounts that would be more valuable to consumers as an alternative method of borrowing.

Banks seeking to reach beyond their own deposit account customer base to attract desirable market segments began offering stand-alone **unsecured lines of credit** to a broader base of consumers. Although some of these programs are marketed directly and exclusively to executives and professionals, others are marketed as an alternative to closed-end loans for consumers who meet the bank's requirements.

To enhance the value of these accounts, credit limits generally are high, for example from $3,000 to $25,000, or even up to $100,000 in some circumstances. These high limits encourage many additional borrowing uses and make the programs more attractive. Consumers who qualify may use the unsecured line of credit for any legal purpose, such as paying medical bills, buying an automobile, or making major home improvements. Customers access the account with special checks.

SECURED LINES OF CREDIT

Banks did not offer secured lines of credit to any significant degree until the early 1980s, when home equity lines of credit came on the market. Most secured-line-of-credit programs are based on the value of real estate collateral, usually the consumer's primary residence. The credit limits on these lines tend to be the highest on any type of consumer loan. Some secured line of credit programs rely on fluctuating value collateral, such as stocks and bonds, but they require sophisticated operational support to monitor continually the value of the collateral. Consumers may access their accounts in a number of ways, such as through use of special checks and, in some states, by credit card.

Home Equity Lines of Credit

Home equity lines of credit (HELOCs), the most common form of secured revolving credit, allow consumers to borrow against the equity in their homes. The amount of each individual credit line varies with the market value of the home, the

unsecured line of credit—A line of credit not secured by collateral. The borrower may use the available credit, repay the loan, and withdraw again. *Also known as* unsecured revolving line of credit.

Home Equity Line of Credit Features

- high credit limits
- higher than average balances
- high levels of account and dollar use
- lower levels of delinquency and loss

Exhibit 5.2 Home Equity Line of Credit Assets at Commercial Banks*

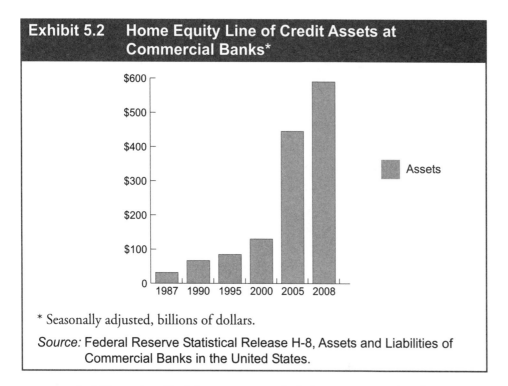

* Seasonally adjusted, billions of dollars.

Source: Federal Reserve Statistical Release H-8, Assets and Liabilities of Commercial Banks in the United States.

consumer's ability to handle debt repayment, the balance on any related mortgages, and the bank's policy about the amount that can be financed.

Home equity lines of credit were not permitted in most states before the 1980s. Since then, however, they generally have been a growth product. The only exception has been when mortgage interest rates have fallen sufficiently to entice consumers to refinance HELOC balances into new closed-end mortgage loans. See exhibit 5.2 for the changes in HELOC loans outstanding at commercial banks.

Some products allow for credit lines equal to 100 percent or more of the **equity** in the consumer's home. Other banks limit the credit line to a lower percentage of the equity, usually 75 to 80 percent. The maximum credit line a consumer may borrow is determined by calculating the **loan-to-value ratio (LTV)**. In markets with falling real estate prices, financial institutions are more conservative in setting the LTV ratio.

Credit lines of $30,000 and more can accommodate most borrowing needs. In fact, the credit line can replace or consolidate most of the consumer's outstanding debt, an attractive feature because of the potential tax deductibility of the interest. The high average loan balance illustrates that consumers use these lines to cover major expenses, such as college tuition, home improvements, and automobile purchases.

equity—The interest or value an owner has in the property less the amounts of liens on it.

loan-to-value ratio (LTV)—The ratio used to calculate the maximum amount a consumer can borrow based on an appraised value of the collateral and the maximum percentage of this value that the bank will lend.

By The Numbers

Calculating HELOC Loan to Value (LTV)
Suppose a consumer's residence is valued at $150,000, and the bank will lend up to 80 percent LTV.

$150,000 x .80 = $120,000

If the consumer has a $75,000 first mortgage balance, the maximum available on a home equity line of credit would be $45,000:

$120,000 – $75,000 = $45,000

If the bank's program allows the consumer to borrow up to 100 percent LTV, the consumer would have access to a $75,000 credit line.

$150,000 – $75,000 = $75,000

Situation

Alan Fredricks is starting college in the fall. His parents have some savings for his tuition but only enough to cover about half the cost. They also have some credit card debt that they carry over from month to month and they have another year to pay on an automobile loan. They are thinking about taking out a new loan to cover the rest of the tuition. Their banker, Tom Wilson, recommends that they consider a home equity line of credit and describes the features and benefits. The credit line is appealing to the Fredricks because they are not exactly sure how much they will need.

How does a HELOC benefit the Fredricks and the bank?

Home Equity Line of Credit Benefits

To the consumer:
- access to substantial amounts of credit
- possible tax deduction
- lower rates

To the bank:
- consumers with higher credit quality
- sound collateral
- higher levels of account and dollar use
- lower levels of delinquency and loss

Home equity lines of credit offer benefits to both consumers and banks. Consumers gain all the benefits of revolving credit, plus access to substantial amounts of credit, a possible tax deduction, and generally lower rates than those available on other consumer credit products. In fact, some banks offer HELOCs with low monthly payments or interest-only payments to their creditworthy customers.

Banks may use these credit line programs to attract a base of consumers who have better than average credit characteristics and collateral that is sound. Through HELOCs, banks may optimize profits and achieve the operational efficiencies associated with revolving credit accounts, large average limits, and longer repayment periods.

Exhibit 5.3 illustrates the average statistics for bank HELOC portfolios by total loans outstanding. These figures represent the percentage of active accounts in the portfolio and the percentage of dollars outstanding compared to the total credit available.

Reverse Mortgages

Home equity lines of credit should not be confused with a related loan product, the reverse mortgage. With a reverse mortgage, elderly homeowners seek a line of credit or monthly payments from a bank, secured by the equity in their homes. The loan is repaid from the sale of the home once it is permanently vacated; the homeowner does not have to make any payments while still residing in the home.

Exhibit 5.3	**Sample Home Equity Line of Credit Portfolios**		
	PORTFOLIO SIZE		
	Bank 1 **Less than** **$10 Million**	**Bank 2** **$10 to $99** **Million**	**Bank 3** **$100 Million** **or More**
Number of accounts			
Total committed lines	100	691	10,771
Lines with outstanding balances	77	550	8,511
Dollar amounts (in $000s)			
Total committed lines	$3,067	$32,275	$729,379
Lines with outstanding balances	$1,801	$20,854	$411,394
Percent outstanding	59%	65%	56%

There are some concerns with this product. If the market value of a home declines, the homeowner may have no equity, or in severe cases may lose the home. In addition, irresponsible credit use can strain family budgets significantly. Sound bank loan policies and consumer education can help minimize these problems.

The Home Equity Loan Market

The autumn of 1986 ushered in a frenzy of activity in the consumer lending market. Congress had approved tax legislation that would phase out the deduction for the interest paid on most consumer loans—but it did preserve the interest deduction on most loans secured by the consumer's residence. Bank promotional campaigns stressed the attractiveness of the home equity line of credit tax feature. Promotional strategies of the time included

- reduced introductory rates
- payment or rebates of some or all closing costs
- applications by phone or fax
- shortened application forms
- conditional approval, pending verification and documentation of the value of the collateral and the credit and income information

HELOCs signaled a shift in the way many consumers met their future credit needs. Now that they are common, consumers often apply for these products through the Internet and may use brokers and other third parties to obtain them. Features and access methods for these products are as varied as state laws allow.

RELATED PRODUCTS

Some payment services are related to open-end products. These include check or debit cards and stored-value, or smart, cards.

Check or Debit Cards

Unlike a credit card transaction, a check card or **debit card** transaction draws funds directly from the consumer's checking account. The check card is a convenient **access device** to the checking account and replaces a standard check. To access funds in their checking accounts, consumers have the choice of using the debit card or writing a check; they may also pay in cash, use a credit card, or write a convenience check to access a standalone or overdraft protection line of credit. These products give the consumer more choices and more control over the source of funds and the means to access those funds.

There are two types of check or debit cards. The standard proprietary card at first was used primarily to access funds through an automated teller machine (ATM). Over time, more point-of-sale terminals at merchant locations, such as gas stations, accepted the cards as well. The cards use ATM interchange networks, such as NYCE Payments Network, LLC, and the STAR Network.

Did You Know ...

Home equity lines of credit assets at commercial banks in December 2008 were $587.5 billion. Just three years before, in 2005, these loans outstanding were $435.1 billion.

Source: Federal Reserve Statistical Release, H.8.

debit card—A plastic card similar to a credit card that enables the cardholder to withdraw cash or purchase goods or services, the cost of which is charged immediately to the cardholder's bank deposit account. It may be activated at point-of-sale terminals. On-line settlement requires a personal identification number (PIN).

access device—A card, code, or other means of access to a consumer's account, or any combination thereof, that may be used by the consumer to initiate electronic funds transfers.

stored-value card—
A prepaid plastic wallet-size card that stores a predetermined amount of money to be used for purchases or specific transactions, such as telephone calls or public transit fares. As the card is used, the amount is deducted from the card until the balance is depleted. Some cards, also known as smart cards, may be replenished with a new balance.

Did You Know ...

By Spring 2007, the number of payments with debit cards exceeded the number of payments with checks. The estimated number of total debit card payments increased 19.0 percent annually between 2004 and 2007, and the value of total debit card payments increased 20.3 percent annually.[1] Changes in payment behavior are due to technology, preferences, costs, and the regulations, policies, and practices that govern the payments system.[2]

Source: Federal Reserve System

The other type, the now prevalent check-card plan, is associated with the networks of major credit card associations, such as Visa and Mastercard. With cobranded cards, consumers may access their deposit accounts repeatedly through ATMs, point-of-sale terminals, and the Internet, or by an in-store signature-based transaction. Attaching the credit card relationship adds value to the card because it then may be used anywhere Visa or Mastercard is accepted.

Many banks provide a direct link between the check card and a line of credit. Under this arrangement, if consumers attempt debit card transactions that would overdraw their checking accounts, funds will be taken first from the balances that remain in their checking accounts and then any additional amounts will be drawn against the lines of credit.

Stored-Value Cards

Stored-value cards hold a specific value or amount of funds; when the card is used, the transaction amount is deducted. With stored-value cards, consumers make purchases much as they would with a credit or debit card. The card is usable with a compatible card reader.

Some stored-value cards are set up for one-time use and discarded when the balance is drawn down completely. Others can be reloaded once the stored funds are used. These smart cards have embedded computer chips that can store vast amounts of data about the user. For example, they can hold a medical history, personal identification, and even a credit report stating account balances and credit availability.

One-time-use cards tend to be sold as gift cards. Most retailers, from hotels to department stores, sell them. It is even common to see display stands in grocery stores selling a variety of retail gift cards. Now American Express, Visa, and Mastercard sell stored-value cards, often for use as gifts so that the recipient may use the card wherever the issuer's card is accepted.

Reusable stored-value cards often are available through payroll offices, federal or state benefit agencies, or mass transit systems. For smart cards used in mass transit systems, the consumer usually uses cash or a credit or debit card to establish an initial balance in the card account, up to as much as $500. To pay for the bus ride, the commuter scans the card on a card-reader attached to the bus fare box. The amount of the fare is deducted from the balance and the new balance is recorded on the card. Deposits can be made to increase the balance. Some transit systems allow commuters to do this by depositing cash in a bus fare box, and the card reader adds the value to the card.

Situation

When Alan Fredricks gets to college, he immediately opens a checking account at the local bank. He applies for and receives a debit card tied to his new account. Like all students at his college, Alan also gets a University Express card. This card can be used like a check for many purposes, including paying for books, food, and laundry—providing he has enough money on the card. When Alan runs out of money on his University Express card, he can replenish it.

What kind of card is this?

OPEN-END CREDIT PROCESS

Consumers may apply for an open-end credit account just as they apply for a closed-end loan: they complete the application form and wait for a credit decision. This is the most common way to acquire home equity and check overdraft lines of credit.

Another common way for consumers to obtain an open-end credit account is to accept a **preapproved credit offer** in which the lender makes a commitment to extend a specified amount of credit based on a prescreening credit investigation program and receipt of a properly executed acceptance agreement.

Prospect names, obtained from a variety of sources, are run through consumer reporting agency programs to identify consumers who meet the bank's criteria, such as credit history and geographic location. **Prescreening** allows lenders to screen out obvious high-risk consumers, select those that clearly meet their criteria, and investigate others further. Creditors are prohibited from issuing unsolicited credit cards.

For lender-initiated preapproved credit offerings, the consumer signs the acceptance form; and furnishes some basic information, such as current employer, income, and address verification; and returns the form to the bank to open the account. This approach often is used in marketing credit cards to obtain higher response rates. For consumers who do not qualify for preapproval or for other types of accounts, the lender will ask the consumer to furnish more information, usually on an application form.

DOCUMENTATION

Once the consumer's application is approved and the legal documents are signed, the account is opened and the consumer receives an access device for the credit line. The most common access devices are special checks and plastic cards for use at merchant locations and in ATMs. Access devices and the restrictions on their use are matters of bank policy, state law, and type of account opened. Some states, for example, allow consumers to access a HELOC with a credit card; others do not.

Once the line is established and the access device is delivered, the consumer has control over how the credit is used, as long as the account is handled satisfactorily.

BANK BENEFITS AND CHALLENGES

There are many reasons why open-end credit is so popular among both banks and consumers. Nevertheless, for both, open-end credit also poses challenges.

---

preapproved credit offer—An offer in which the lender makes a commitment to extend a specified amount of credit based on a preliminary credit analysis and receipt of a properly executed acceptance agreement. *Also known as* preselected credit offer.

prescreening—The practice of examining consumer credit reports to identify individuals who meet certain requirements in order to offer them credit opportunities.

Situation

Janice has had the same credit card for several years. Hoping to find a better deal, she decided to compare the terms of her card to other plans. For the next month, Janice saves the credit card solicitations that arrive in the mail. Each states that she has been preapproved for credit and needs only to return an enclosed form. By the end of the month, Janice has received six or seven of these notices. She can now compare the costs and features of these cards with each other and with her current card.

How did all these banks find Janice?

Benefits:
- increased profits
- broader market area
- high consumer acceptance
- adapts easily to technological improvements
- operational efficiencies
- more liquid portfolios

Challenges:
- possible use of all potential debt
- lower consumer payment priority
- fraud

netting—The process of valuing the payment obligations for both sides of a transaction and having the party that pays more transfer only the difference to the other.

convenience user—A credit account customer who uses the account and pays the balance in full each month, thereby avoiding finance charges.

BENEFITS TO THE BANK

Open-end credit accounts are attractive to banks because they can increase profits, broaden the market, achieve high consumer acceptance, connect well with technological developments, offer operational efficiencies, and add liquidity to portfolios.

Increased Profits

The profitability of revolving loan products varies depending on state law, type of product, competitive conditions, loan quality, loan volume, loans outstanding, and the efficiency of the lending operation. Credit card programs, for example, contributed substantially to the banking industry's profits during most of the 1980s, and they continue to provide income for many banks today.

Most of the income from a credit card program comes from finance charges—the interest and other charges consumers pay on what they owe. State law governs the fees permitted on a credit card account. Other potential sources of income are

Interchange fees	Fees charged by national credit card companies and member banks for using a credit card network. A bank receives fee income when cardholders with accounts at other banks buy goods and services from merchants for whom the bank processes credit card transactions; similarly, the bank is charged a fee when its own cardholders buy goods and services from another bank's merchants. Interchange income and expense fees are **netted out** to determine whether the bank has earned income or incurred expense.
Annual fees	Fees that allow banks to recoup the cost of servicing and renewing accounts, especially those of occasional and **convenience users**
Credit card registration plans	Plans that protect consumers if a card is lost, stolen, or used fraudulently. For this protection, the consumer pays a monthly or annual fee.
Credit insurance	Arrangements to repay the monthly outstanding balance if the consumer dies or is disabled. The fee charged usually is a percentage of the balance.
Merchant discount fees	Fees for processing credit card sales transactions that cover the cost of handling the account. The charge is based chiefly on the merchant's monthly sales volume and the average ticket price.
Late and overlimit charges	Fees charged to offset specific actions by an account holder to discourage their recurrence

Broader Market Area

Revolving loan products are highly attractive to banks because most may be marketed outside the bank's geographic market area. Many companies, banks and nonbanks, routinely market credit cards nationally. In the 1980s, Delaware and South Dakota became havens for credit card issuers from around the country because they have favorable laws for rate ceilings, fee structures, and tax provisions. Consumers generally show little concern about where their credit cards come from as long as the features and benefits are acceptable.

Unsecured lines of credit also may be offered beyond the bank's primary market area and state borders. They can be especially valuable when the bank is trying to enter a new market or reach attractive loan markets beyond those served by its branches and indirect lending dealer network. Although these programs often are targeted to current customers, banks use direct mail to market more broadly.

Secured lines of credit, particularly home equity lines of credit, generally are limited to the bank's primary market area. HELOCs usually are opened at bank branches because appraisers and other support personnel are needed in processing the applications. Some banks, however, have opened loan production offices in other states to market these lines of credit, and others use third-party loan brokers to attract out-of-market-area applications. Always, however, a bank must meet all state legal requirements.

Consumer Acceptance

Excellent consumer acceptance is driving the expansion of open-end credit products. Consumers accept the products because they are flexible, convenient, and offer personal credit control. The acceptance of access devices by major markets is commonplace. Today fast food restaurants, doctors' offices, grocery stores, movie theaters, and even state and federal tax departments accept credit cards. In addition to broader acceptance, reward programs have motivated consumer acceptance of open-end credit products.

Tie-Ins with Technological Development

The flexibility of open-end credit programs gives them a natural tie-in with the industry's efforts to expand its ATM programs, merchant payment systems, and Internet-delivered banking products. Credit lines packaged with other consumer banking products create unique product offerings targeted to selected market segments. Some banks, for example, offer cash management accounts that combine deposit, loan, and brokerage services for qualified consumers.

Operational Efficiencies

Compared with closed-end loan programs, open-end credit products offer operational efficiencies. It is only necessary to go through a complete application and documentation

Did You Know ...

As the use of cell phones and personal digital assistants increases worldwide, these devices and bankcards are converging for "cardless" bankcard transactions. Consumers can enjoy the convenience of making purchases at the point of sale using their wireless devices and having the transaction posted to their bankcard account.

Variables that Affect Profit

- state law requirements
- product type
- competitive conditions
- loan quality
- loan volume
- loans outstanding
- operational efficiencies

liquidity—The speed and ease with which an asset may be converted to cash without loss in value.

premium—The amount or percentage above the face or stated value at which securities are bought or sold; the opposite of discount.

securitization—The packaging of loans as a unit to be sold to outside investors. The loans are no longer assets of the bank, although the bank may continue to service them for investors.

process once. Applications often are handled by mail, telephone, or the Internet, saving the bank the relatively high cost of conducting in-person loan interviews and the need for branch offices.

Open-end credit products lend themselves to centralized processing, which is helpful in handling high-volume products, such as credit cards, or products requiring specialized knowledge, such as HELOCs, which require appraisals and property reports. Banks have been able to achieve economies of scale and improve productivity and credit quality by centralizing open-end credit functions.

Portfolio Liquidity

Liquidity is important to banks, particularly in a dynamic or troubled economic environment. Portfolios of revolving credit, particularly credit cards, have proven very attractive from this perspective because they are easier to expand and contract than closed-end products.

Selling the portfolio and securitization are two strategies for raising cash from open-end credit portfolios. Some banks put their entire portfolio, or large portions of it, up for sale to the highest bidder, for which they are able to obtain a significant **premium**.

Securitization involves packaging a group of loan accounts for sale in increments to investors. The loans outstanding are removed from the bank's balance sheet, although the accounts usually continue to be serviced by the originating bank. Earnings from the portfolio pay the yield to investors and provide servicing income to the bank. The sale often is transparent to the bank's customers.

CHALLENGES FOR THE BANK

Because revolving credit products give consumers more control over how they use credit, there always is a need to refine credit controls. Unsecured revolving products, particularly credit cards, historically have been associated with higher losses than traditional loan products. To reduce losses, control programs are used to detect fraud, review accounts, and handle exceptions, such as delinquencies, deteriorating credit conditions, and overlimits.

The aggressive marketing of many open-end credit products contributes to the higher credit risk. As banks send out preapproved solicitations to expand their market areas beyond their traditional boundaries, their control over risk declines. Personal bankruptcy numbers often increase because consumers mismanage credit card debt. Nevertheless, banks have been able to justify higher losses because of the higher gross yields and economies of scale associated with most open-end credit accounts.

Potential Debt

The wide availability of revolving credit also raises the issue of "potential debt." The consumer example in exhibit 5.4 has many open revolving credit accounts that have limited use. Although currently using only $1,700 of the available

Exhibit 5.4 Potential Revolving Credit Debt

LENDER	CREDIT LIMIT	BALANCE	POTENTIAL ADDITIONAL DEBT
Bank card	$3,000	$1,000	$2,000
Bank card	5,000	500	4,500
Store card	1,000	200	800
Store card	5,000	0	5,000
Bank card	2,500	0	2,500
TOTAL	$16,500	$1,700	$14,800

credit, if the consumer were to fully use the lines (potential debt), the debt would increase by $14,800. That clearly would affect the perceived risk and financial position of the consumer. Lenders address the issue of potential debt in their credit decision-making policy. Although consumers may use potential debt fully, lenders realize, through portfolio maintenance and analysis, that most consumers demonstrate consistent behavior patterns as light, medium, or heavy users of credit.

Control Tools

The need to balance aggressive marketing with prudent credit judgment has given rise to services that help banks achieve these sometimes divergent objectives. Consumer reporting agencies and credit-scoring vendors, working with banks, have built computerized control tools. The software automates the gathering and analysis of applicant credit histories and applies both bank loan policy and statistically relevant credit criteria to help lenders process decisions faster and more consistently.

Another important tool is a bankruptcy predictor model. This model may be used before a credit offer is extended, or on an existing portfolio, to identify consumers with characteristics that flag the likelihood of a future bankruptcy filing. High-credit-risk consumers can be monitored closely, eliminated from new credit offerings, or offered less credit.

Payment Priorities

The fact that most open-end products are unsecured increases credit risk. Credit card and unsecured line of credit programs tend to rank low on the typical consumer's list of bills to pay, especially when financial problems arise.

This means higher delinquencies and losses are likely on credit cards and on unsecured lines of credit than on home equity lines of credit. When considering repayment priorities, the lender keeps in mind that certain essentials, such as food, utilities, and clothing, must be factored into the equation. Lenders should take into account potential drains on the family budget.

Did You Know ...

A typical priority list for bills paid by a person having financial difficulties is
1. mortgage or rent
2. home equity or second mortgage
3. automobile loan
4. other secured loans
5. credit cards
6. other unsecured loans

Fraud

Fraud is another major area of risk posed by open-end credit products, particularly credit cards. Sources of fraud are lost or stolen credit cards or credit access checks, counterfeit cards, and dishonest merchants, cardholders, and bank employees.

The fraud risk is being addressed in a number of ways. Credit card providers are refining operations to improve credit card security at the point of purchase. Holograms on cards and point-of-sale verification terminals, which verify every credit-card transaction, make fraud more difficult. So does biometric technology that includes embedding the customer's personal identifying characteristics, such as iris image, thumbprint, or handprint in the access card. Credit approval and account opening procedures are being refined to detect fraudulent applications.

Consumer reporting agencies have increasingly sophisticated systems for catching fake addresses, mail-drop locations, inaccurate Social Security numbers, and the use of a deceased person's name and credit file. Issuers also have implemented sophisticated programs that alert them if a transaction falls outside the normal usage pattern for the customer. The issuer then calls the consumer to ensure the activity is legitimate. Finally, efforts are being made to catch fraud soon after accounts have been opened by distributing data on stolen cards regularly.

CONSUMER BENEFITS AND CHALLENGES

Consumers, like banks, enjoy the benefits and must deal with the challenges of open-end credit. Financial control, flexibility, and potentially positive credit histories are all benefits to consumers who will use credit throughout their lives. The challenges to consumers are to manage their debt wisely and to ward off the threats of fraudulent use of their accounts and identity theft.

BENEFITS TO THE CONSUMER

In a society that values the material goods and services associated with "the good life," anything that makes it easier to buy those goods and services is likely to be popular with consumers. Consumers have embraced revolving credit products because having credit readily available allows them to make impulse purchases, take advantage of unexpected opportunities, and make planned purchases with relative ease. Because most merchants accept credit cards, checks, and debit cards, consumers have greater purchasing power.

Financial Control

Most consumers want to feel they are in control of their lives and their finances. For example, automobiles give consumers control over where, when, and how they travel, and DVDs give them control over what they see on their television sets. Revolving credit products give them control over when, where, and for what purposes they use credit. Such products may be used to meet short-term cash flow needs. Check overdraft lines of credit, for example, help consumers avoid the risk of an embarrassing and expensive overdraft. Large credit lines allow consumers to reduce the number of credit accounts they use and sometimes to reduce the amount of interest and monthly payments on their debts.

Flexibility

Flexibility in payment options is attractive. Many open-end credit lines give the account holder the option of

- paying a minimum monthly payment
- paying more than the minimum, with the excess amount applied to the outstanding balance
- paying the balance in full
- making "interest only" payments

As the balance is reduced, the consumer rebuilds credit availability for future use, and the available credit becomes accessible immediately.

Account History

Finally, the required monthly billing statement provides a ready history of account activity. This is helpful information for managing personal finances and preparing for future borrowing needs.

CHALLENGES FOR THE CONSUMER

With every advance in financial services for consumers come the challenges of using the services wisely and safely. Managing personal debt and protecting personal finances and financial information from fraud are challenges for today's consumer.

Managing Personal Debt

Most consumers manage revolving credit obligations rather well. A percentage, however, lack discipline or financial knowledge and have too much credit available, causing them to be overextended.

It is sometimes necessary to rescue overextended consumers by consolidating their loans into a closed-end loan, preferably one secured by collateral. However, this approach effectively opens up the consumer's available credit, unless steps are taken to close revolving accounts. Although difficult, failure to limit a problem loan customer's access to credit could mean more serious account problems in the future.

Did You Know ...

A survey of early participants in the FDIC Money Smart program noted positive results. Immediately after completing the course, 69 percent of respondents reported an increase in their savings, 53 percent reported a decrease in debt, and 58 percent stated they were more likely to comparison shop. Also 55 percent of respondents indicated they "always" pay bills on time.

As of 2008, more than a million consumers had been to a Money Smart class.

Source: Federal Deposit Insurance Corporation

There is a sector of the market consisting of consumers who do not have bank accounts, often referred to as the "unbanked." Some customers do not use bank accounts for the following reasons:

They had accounts but did not manage them well.	Because most banks report unsatisfactory account handling, these consumers no longer have access to bank accounts and must seek alternative ways to transact their personal financial business.
Their family or culture has not used bank accounts.	These consumers may distrust banks or may not understand how to use bank accounts.
They lack financial literacy.	Many young people are not taught how to handle money, prepare a budget, or buy insurance. They need tools to be able to handle their finances in a prudent manner.

Banks and other government and community organizations have recognized the seriousness of the unbanked population and the lack of financial literacy and have dedicated resources to educating consumers about personal finances. Banks often provide financial literacy programs for both children and adults in their communities. For society as a whole, financial education promotes consumers who can more successfully handle their financial matters throughout their lifetimes. According to the National Endowment for Financial Education, only 10 hours of financial education can help consumers manage their money better. Some states require high school students to take a personal finance course.[3] Others have enacted requirements and will implement them soon.

Exhibit 5.5 illustrates simple reminders for managing finances that can be shared with bank customers during the holiday season.

Fraud

Consumers are very much concerned about protecting their financial information. Though fraud is not a new phenomenon, it has taken on new dimensions with advances in technology.

The Internet gives thieves easy access to information. Thieves also use "dumpster diving" to retrieve financial statements from commercial and residential trash cans. The theft of account information often leads to **identity theft**.

identity theft—A crime involving the possession of identifying information not belonging to the person using it, or the attempt to access the financial resources of another person by using illegally obtained identifying information.

Today there is a concerted effort to combat identity theft. Laws, such as the Fair and Accurate Credit Transactions Act (FACT Act), have been enacted to ensure private companies and organizations housing personal financial information have systems in place to protect personal information and monitor for identity theft.

Identity theft is a crime. The criminal justice system processes consumer complaints, follows cases, shares information, and tracks down thieves. However, the first line of defense still consists of the knowledgeable consumer and the

Exhibit 5.5	**Holiday Advice to Credit Card Customers—Use Your Credit Wisely**

Create a budget.	Before you start your shopping, develop a realistic budget. Be as detailed as possible. Look at past banking and credit card statements and receipts from last year to gauge your holiday spending.
Be thrifty.	The fewer lines of credit you have, the easier it is to keep track of bills and pay off debt on time. Be cautious about applying for additional cards.
Be alert to fraud.	Beware of fraudsters or suspicious offers for products. Do not enter your credit card number unless you are certain a Web site is trustworthy. Keep receipts and billing statements to check for unauthorized charges. Shred documents that contain personal information. If you think you could be vulnerable to fraud or identity theft, notify the consumer reporting agencies to refuse to provide your credit report unless you approve.
Know your terms.	Understand the terms of your credit card. Credit cards are great financial tools when used with care.
Fight temptation.	Holiday shopping can be overwhelming, and items on sale can make it difficult to say no. Resist impulse shopping and stick to your budget.

Source: Adapted from the ABA Educational Foundation and ABA News Release, November 2008.

vigilant bank employee who follows bank policies and responds to inconsistencies that represent red flags in transactions or customer behavior. Exhibit 5.6 (next page) outlines some measures consumers may take to safeguard their information.

LAWS AND REGULATIONS

Many of the laws and regulations addressed in other chapters of this book also apply to open-end credit. However, due to the unique nature of open-end credit, some rules have added importance. The Fair Credit Reporting Act (FCRA) has provisions on prescreening, which is popular for credit card solicitations. The FACT Act, which amended FCRA, addresses protections against identity theft. Finally, the Truth in Lending Act (TILA) has special provisions that apply to open-end credit.

FAIR CREDIT REPORTING ACT

Enacted in 1971, FCRA is directed primarily at the collection and reporting of information by consumer reporting agencies. However, it also has some requirements for users of credit reports, such as financial institutions.

Prescreening

Prescreening consumers for credit cards may lead to fraudulently issued credit cards. The practice also may lower a consumer's credit score due to the number of inquiries on the account. Therefore the federal government regulates this practice through the Federal Trade Commission (FTC). The FTC rules require lenders to explain in advance their criteria and to make "firm offers of credit" to

Exhibit 5.6　Safeguarding Financial Information

- Check your credit card and other statements immediately upon receipt. Make sure you made all listed transactions.
- Keep your receipts to check against the statement.
- Tear up or shred receipts, bank statements, and unused credit card offers before throwing them away.
- Memorize your personal identification number (PIN). Never store the PIN with your bank ATM or debit card.
- Secure your Internet transactions. When submitting financial information to a Web site, look for the padlock or key icon at the bottom of your browser, and make sure the Internet address begins with "http."
- Use a combination of letters, numbers, and symbols for your passwords and change them periodically.
- Consider placing passwords on credit card, bank, and phone accounts.
- Secure personal information in your home.
- Know your cash advance limit and your purchase or credit limit.
- To ensure accuracy, order copies of your credit report once a year.
- Watch out for people with cell phones who stand near you by point-of-sale or ATM terminals. Cell phones that can take pictures may capture your password as you enter it.
- Do not give your Social Security number or other personal credit information to anyone who calls you.
- Do not carry your Social Security card with you. Memorize the number.
- Check for any missing mail, such as monthly bills.
- Deposit outgoing mail at the Post Office or other secure mailbox location.
- Do not open e-mail from unknown sources; use virus detection software.
- Never give out personal financial information in response to an unsolicited phone call, fax, or e-mail, no matter how official it may seem.
- Do not respond to e-mail that may warn of dire consequences unless you validate your information immediately.
- If you have responded to such e-mail, contact your bank immediately so it can protect your account and your identity.
- If your card is lost, stolen, or used fraudulently, immediately contact your bank, the police Fraud Unit, and consumer reporting agencies.
- Choose to do business with reputable companies, particularly when buying online.
- Ask about information security practices at your workplace, businesses, doctors' offices, and other locations that collect your personal information.
- When ordering checks, pick them up rather than have them mailed to you.
- Be careful not to leave your debit or credit card behind at hotels or retail establishments. Your personal information may be recorded in the card's magnetic strip.
- Report suspicious activity to the Internet Fraud Complaint Center (www.ic3.gov), a partnership between the FBI and the National White Collar Crime Center (www.nw3c.org).

Source: Primarily the ABA Educational Foundation, American Bankers Association.

consumers that meet the criteria. Consumers may opt out of the prescreening process and not receive such offers.

Preapproved credit card lending also carries risks for banks, among them credit, transaction, liquidity, strategic, reputation, and compliance risks. Exhibit 5.7 explains the risks to earnings or capital.

Exhibit 5.7   Risks to Earnings or Capital in Credit Card Lending

Credit risk	Arises when borrowers may fail to meet the terms of any contract with the bank or otherwise fail to perform as agreed. Aggressive solicitation programs may increase the bank's credit risk if the resulting credit card accounts experience higher than projected delinquencies and losses.
Transaction risk	Arises from problems with service or product delivery. An influx of new accounts from a solicitation may increase risk if a bank is unable to process the responses in an accurate or timely manner.
Liquidity risk	Arises from a bank's inability to meet its obligations when they come due without incurring unacceptable losses, including the inability to manage unplanned decreases or changes in funding sources. For example, higher than anticipated delinquencies or losses in securitized pools may lead to market pressure on the bank to provide additional support to the pool.
Strategic risk	Arises from adverse business decisions or improper implementation of those decisions. Failure to adequately test a new market, analyze test results, and refine subsequent solicitation offers may result in unsuccessful marketing efforts or accounts that do not perform as anticipated.
Reputation risk	Arises from the possibility of negative public opinion. Poorly underwritten or performing receivables can affect a bank's reputation as issuer of credit cards and underwriter of credit card securitizations. Future credit enhancements for securitizing credit card receivables may be more costly, reduced, or not available. If a bank's reputation as an underwriter is impaired, future access to financial markets may be limited or cost more.
Compliance risk	Arises from the possibility that preapproved solicitations do not comply with the FFIEC Interagency Policy Statement on Prescreening by Financial Institutions and the Fair Credit Reporting Act (FCRA). The FCRA, the Truth in Lending Act, and other consumer protection laws carry civil and sometimes criminal liability for negligent and willful noncompliance.

Source: Credit Card Pre-approved Solicitations, OCC Advisory Letter (AL96-97).

The FACT Act and Identity Theft

The FACT Act of 2003 was enacted primarily to prevent identity theft. Financial institutions and consumer reporting agencies are required to implement systems to detect identity theft red flags and alert consumers when their personal information has been stolen or their credit records are damaged due to fraudulent transactions.

TRUTH IN LENDING

TILA requires lenders to give consumers clear and meaningful disclosures about the terms of a loan so that consumers may shop effectively for the best terms. FRS Regulation Z implements the law's disclosure requirements and establishes procedures for timely resolution of open-end credit billing disputes. TILA also prohibits certain types of activity, including issuance of unsolicited credit cards to consumers.

Initial Disclosures

TILA requires that initial disclosures of all information related to an account, such as the annual percentage rate (APR), the periodic rate, and finance charge information, be given to a consumer before the first transaction. If the interest rate is variable, this fact also must be disclosed, along with an example of how the rate can change. Consumers who do not like the terms may cancel their accounts

Personal Information Used in Identity Theft

- name
- address
- date of birth
- mother's maiden name
- Social Security number
- financial account numbers
- name of bank
- place of employment
- children's names
- driver's license number

periodic rate—The rate that the creditor applies to the account balance for a day, week, month, or other subdivision of a year. For example, for an APR of 18 percent, the periodic monthly rate is 1.5 percent (18 divided by 12).

grace period—The period during which no interest accrues on a credit card; the time between the date a credit card transaction is posted to a cardholder's account and the date when the payment is due.

variable-rate loan—A loan with an interest rate that may fluctuate. The rate usually is tied to an index that reflects changes in the market rates of interest. A fluctuation in the interest rate causes changes in either the payments or the loan term. Limits may be placed on how much the interest rate or the payments will vary.

before incurring any expense. As of 2009, the most important information must be set out in a table in the initial disclosures so that the terms are clear to the customer when the account is opened. Exhibit 5.8 illustrates the disclosure table required by FRS Regulation Z.

The required initial disclosures for open-end loans must include, for example, each **periodic rate** used, rates that apply to different types of transactions, the **grace period**, the method used to determine the balance, the date the finance charge will begin to accrue and how it is determined, and how the consumer may resolve billing errors.

Periodic Statement Disclosures

TILA requires that other disclosures be given to the consumer after the account is opened. Periodic statements (monthly billing statements) must be provided to the consumer for each billing cycle in which there is activity on the account or a balance remaining. The statement must disclose the balance at the beginning of the cycle as well as all transactions that occurred.

As of 2009 the arrangement of the information, as well as terms, such as the balance computation, promotional rate, and payment information, were changed to make these disclosures easier for consumers to understand. Periodic statements must include a notice that making minimum payments will increase the time it takes to repay. An example must be given, along with a toll-free telephone number the consumer may call for an estimate of the time it will take to repay the balance.

Monthly periodic billing statements must disclose the late payment fee that will be imposed for failure to make the minimum payment by the due date. The disclosure must state the date when the payment is due or, if different, the earliest date on which a late payment fee may be charged, and the amount of the fee.

Change in Terms Disclosures

When account terms are being changed, a notice must be sent to the customer before the change takes effect. Changes in the finance charge or another term required for the table in the initial disclosure must be disclosed in the notice and mailed before the effective date; generally, 15 days before for home equity lines of credit and 45 days for unsecured credit lines. If the notice is included with the periodic statement, the terms that are changed must be in a table on the front page of the statement. Customers may pay off the balance on the account under the old terms if they are unwilling to accept the changes.

Variable Rate Disclosures

TILA also requires disclosure statements for **variable rate loans**. These disclosures must explain how the rate is determined and when it may change. The customer should be given an example that demonstrates how the loan terms may change if the rate increases. Because there are different variable rate loan programs, one disclosure usually cannot cover all of them.

Exhibit 5.8 Sample Disclosure Table for Credit Card Applications and Solicitations

Annual percentage rate (APR) for purchases	2.9% until 11/01/XX, after that 14.0%
Other APRs	Balance transfer APR: 15.9% Cash advance APR: 15.9% Penalty APR: 23.9%. See explanation below.*
Variable-rate information	The rate for purchase transactions is determined by adding 5.9% to the prime rate.**
Grace period for repayment of balances for purchases	25 days on average
Method of computing the balance for purchases	Average daily balances, excluding new purchases.
Annual fees	None
Transaction fee for purchases	$.50
Transaction fee for cash advances	3%
Balance transfer fee	3%
Late-payment fee	$25
Over-the-credit-limit fee	$25

* The penalty APR may be applied to your account if you make a late payment or go over your credit limit.

** The variable rate for this account is the prime rate as it appears in the *Wall Street Journal* at the end of every calendar month plus 5%.

Source: FRS Regulation Z, Truth in Lending, G-10(A) —Applications and Solicitations Model Form (Credit Cards).

Right of Rescission

TILA protects consumers who use the equity in their primary residence as collateral for loans or lines of credit. A lender must disclose the security interest and its potential consequences and provide for a period in which the loan may be rescinded (canceled) after the loan closing. The **Notice of Right to Rescind** (see exhibit 5.9, next page) is given to the customer when the loan is closed. Customers have until midnight of the third business day (including Saturday) after the loan closing date or the date the customer receives the final disclosures, whichever is later, to rescind the loan agreement.

If the consumer rescinds the transaction, the lender must void the transaction, refund all amounts paid, and cancel the lien or security interest. Under some very limited circumstances, the consumer may waive the right to rescind the loan. An incorrectly performed rescission cannot be corrected and allows the consumer to extend the rescission period for up to three years.

Notice of Right to Rescind—The notice that establishes the right of a customer to cancel a contract or legally binding agreement within a specified period, usually three business days after signing the contract. This right is available for consumer credit agreements that give the creditor a security interest in the consumer's primary residence. If after that period the consumer has not canceled the contract, the loan proceeds are disbursed.

Exhibit 5.9   Notice of Right to Rescind

Notice of Right to Rescind

Customer   Amount   Security

_____

NOTICE TO CUSTOMER REQUIRED BY FEDERAL LAW

Today, __(date)__, you have entered into a transaction which may result in a lien, mortgage or other security interest on your home. Federal law provides you with the right to cancel this transaction, if you so desire, without any penalty or obligation at any time within three business days from the above date or the date on which all material disclosures required under the Truth in Lending Act have been given to you. By canceling this transaction, any lien, mortgage or other security interest on your home resulting from this transaction is automatically void. Any down payment or other consideration you may have tendered on entering this transaction must be refunded to you in the event you cancel. If you desire to cancel this transaction, you may do so by notifying the following party:

_____

Name

_____

Address

by mail or by telegram sent by midnight ___(date)___, or by any other form of written notice delivered to the above address no later than midnight _____(date)_____.

Unauthorized Use

TILA has some requirements that are specific to credit card transactions. One of these involves the cardholder's liability for **unauthorized use**. Credit cards may be issued to consumers only in response to an application or request or as a renewal of a card already issued. A customer's liability for unauthorized use is the lesser of $50 or the amount of credit obtained with the card before the customer notified the issuer. The lender must disclose this potential liability and the issuer must give notice of the customer's potential liability and the process for reporting any unauthorized use.

unauthorized use—The use of a credit or debit card by a person other than the cardholder when such person does not have actual, implied, or apparent authority to use the card and from which use the cardholder receives no benefit.

Payment Disputes

In some cases, a consumer may withhold credit card payments when purchases made with the card are unsatisfactory. TILA requires the consumer to make a good-faith attempt to resolve the dispute with the merchant. If that cannot be done, the consumer may notify the card issuer of the dispute and, in most cases, may withhold payment for the transaction from the issuer until the dispute is resolved. During the dispute, the card issuer cannot report the customer as delinquent in making payments on the account. Instructions on the process for dispute resolution and payment are in the customer Statement of Billing Rights, which must be mailed at least annually.

Solicitation Disclosures

Amendments to TILA in 2005 and to FRS Regulation Z in 2009 revised the disclosures to be given to consumers in solicitations. Consumers are now given more information so they may make better credit decisions and thus avoid excessive debt and bankruptcy. The required information is meant to help consumers understand the debt they are undertaking and to stay within their ability to repay. Some terms must be in bold type.

Promotional rates must be accurate as of a certain period before the solicitation and the permanent rates that will apply must be set out near the introductory rate. If the lender may revoke the temporary rate for reasons other than the end of the introductory period, that must be disclosed on or with the application or solicitation, The disclosure must include a description of the reasons and the rate, fixed or variable, that will then apply.

Solicitations made through the Internet must make the credit card application and solicitation disclosures easily accessible.

Account Termination

This rule applies to convenience users of credit cards. An open-end account cannot be terminated before its expiration date solely because the consumer did not incur finance charges, but it may be closed if it is inactive for three or more consecutive months.

Did You Know ...

In 2008, as a result of the economic downturn and financial crisis, the trend to increase credit card limits began to reverse. Nearly 60 percent of bank respondents indicated that they had tightened lending standards on credit card and other consumer loans.

Source: Federal Reserve Board of Governors

SUMMARY

- Open-end credit expanded both the borrowing power of consumers and the convenience of the credit services available. With open-end credit, lenders can offer more services with more options to more consumers. Open-end credit accounts generally remain open as long as the consumer handles the account in an acceptable manner and the lender wishes to offer the product. Although bank credit cards usually have an expiration date, the overwhelming majority are renewed automatically.

- Most open-end credit accounts have a specific credit limit. The bank, at its option or in response to the consumer's request, may increase the limit on unsecured lines and credit cards. Once an open-end account is established, credit is accessed easily, and consumers have the freedom and control to use the line of credit as they wish up to the limit.

- Credit cards, which are the most widely used revolving credit products, include retail private label cards, national and international cards, travel and entertainment cards, and special value cards, such as affinity and cobranded cards. Home equity lines of credit (HELOCs) have been one of the fastest-growing products since the 1980s. Along with check overdraft and stand-alone secured or unsecured lines of credit, these products have given banks a vehicle for reaching beyond their traditional markets to serve additional consumer market segments. They also have given consumers alternatives to traditional closed-end credit products. It is clear that open-end credit has changed the way consumers meet their borrowing needs, and the way lenders serve them.

- Other payment devices, such as stored-value cards, which substitute for cash, and debit cards, which access deposit accounts, evolved from the technology of credit card programs.

- Consumers may apply for an open-end credit account just as they would for a closed-end loan, by completing an application and waiting for a decision. They also may receive a preapproved offer of a credit card, in which the lender makes a commitment to extend a specified amount of credit based on a prescreening credit investigation program and receipt of a properly executed acceptance agreement. For HELOCs, consumers may receive conditional approval pending receipt of a complete application or more information. Once the application is approved and the legal documents are signed, the account is opened and the consumer receives an access device, such as special checks, for the credit line.

- Bankers and consumers both benefit from open-end credit. Banks gain increased profits, access to a larger market, and consumer acceptance; open-end credit adapts well to technological improvements and offers the potential for operational efficiencies and more liquid portfolios. Consumers gain more control over their finances and have flexible credit and payment options. They also may establish favorable credit histories for future use. However, among the challenges for banks are potential consumer debt overloads and changes in consumer payment priorities. Banks and consumers must be alert for misuse and unauthorized use of credit, including fraud schemes and identity theft.

- Banks often take the lead in providing financial literacy programs for both children and adults in their communities. For society as a whole, financial education promotes consumers who can handle their financial matters more successfully throughout their lifetimes.

- Two laws among the many that apply to open-end credit are the Fair Credit Reporting Act (FCRA) and the Truth in Lending Act (TILA). Although the FCRA is most often associated with consumer reporting agencies, it also has requirements for credit report users, such as banks. It has been amended to add rules on credit prescreening. The act details conditions for using prescreened lists, including the requirements that creditworthiness criteria be defined in advance and that those who meet the requirements be given "firm offers of credit." The FACT Act amendments to FCRA address identity theft red flags.

- TILA, implemented by FRS Regulation Z, requires lenders to give consumers clear and meaningful initial disclosures about the terms of the loan being offered, so that they may shop effectively for the best loan, and to give consumers periodic disclosures about open-end credit. The act requires notices for changes in terms on the credit account and special disclosures for variable rate loans. It provides for the right of rescission of home equity loans and lines of credit. The act establishes rules for unauthorized use of an open-end credit account. It also prohibits issuance of unsolicited credit cards to consumers, provides procedures for resolving payment disputes, and requires special disclosures in solicitations about minimum payments and introductory rates. TILA also has rules on what information must be included in the periodic statement, including the minimum payment, its effect on loan repayment, and information on late payments and penalties. The act prohibits closing the accounts of convenience users but does allow banks to close accounts that are inactive for three or more months.

END NOTES

[1] *The Depository Institutions Payments Study, A Survey of Depository Institutions for the 2007 Federal Reserve Payments Study*, 2008, www.frbservices.org/files/communications/pdf/research/2007_depository_institutions_payments_study.pdf.

[2] *Recent Payment Trends in the United States*, Federal Reserve Board of Governors, October 2008, www.federalreserve.gov/pubs/bulletin/2008/pdf/payments08.pdf.

[3] According to the ABA Education Foundation, some states require a personal finance course for high school graduation, including Alabama, Georgia, Idaho, Illinois, Kentucky, New York, and Utah.

SELF-CHECK AND REVIEW

1. Why have open-end credit products had the highest rate of growth of any form of consumer credit in recent years?

2. What are four different types of open-end credit products? Describe each..

3. What is the difference between a check, or debit, card and a stored-value card?

Learning Check

4. What is a preapproved open-end credit offer? Why do banks make such offers?

5. In today's consumer credit environment, what primary advantages do home equity lines of credit offer to banks? To consumers?

6 What are the types of income a bank may derive from a credit card program? Which is the most important?

7. What protections for consumers are provided in the Fair Credit Reporting Act as revised by the FACT Act?

8. What are some protections the TILA gives against unauthorized use of open-end credit?

Resources

ADDITIONAL RESOURCES

A Longitudinal Evaluation of the Intermediate-term Impact of the Money Smart Financial Education Curriculum upon Consumers' Behavior and Confidence, Federal Deposit Insurance Corporation, April 2007, www.fdic.gov/consumers/consumer/moneysmart/pubs/ms070424.pdf.

AARP, www.aarp.org.

ABA Education Foundation, www.aba.com/ABAEF/default.htm.

ABA Guide to Credit Cards, www.aba.com/aba/documents/press/ccguide_62207.pdf.

American Bankers Association, **www.aba.com**.

American Express Corporation, www.americanexpress.com.

Assets and Liabilities of Commercial Banks in the United States, Federal Reserve Statistical Release, H.8, www.federalreserve.gov/releases/h8.

Choosing a Credit Card, Federal Reserve Board of Governors, www.federalreserve.gov/pubs/shop/.

Credit Card Comparison Chart, e-wisdom.com, www.e-wisdom.com/credit_cards/chart.html.

Equifax, www.equifax.com.

Experian, www.experian.com.

Federal Financial Institutions Examination Council, www.ffiec.gov.

Federal Trade Commission, www.FTC.gov.

Federal Trade Commission Resources on Credit, www.ftc.gov/bcp/menu-credit.htm.

Get Smart About Credit, ABA Education Foundation, http://aba.com/abaef/gsac.htm.

International Card Manufacturers Association, www.icma.com.

JCB International Credit Card Co., Ltd., www.jcb-global.com/english/index.html.

Mastercard International, www.Mastercard.com.

National Endowment for Financial Education, www.nefe.org.

NYCE Corporation, www.nyce.net.

Office of the Comptroller of the Currency Anti-Fraud Resources, www.occ.treas.gov/fraudresources.htm.

Office of the Comptroller of the Currency, Credit Card Preapproved Solicitations, OCC Advisory Letter (AL 96-7), www.ffiec.gov/ffiecinfobase/resources/retail/occ-al-96-7_c_card_preapp_solicit.pdf.

Senior Loan Officer Opinion Survey on Bank Lending Practices, Federal Reserve Board of Governors, January 2009, www.federalreserve.gov/boarddocs/SnLoanSurvey/200902/default.htm.

STAR Systems, Inc., www.star-system.com.

TransUnion, www.transunion.com.

Visa International, www.Visa.com.

When Your Home Is on the Line: What You Should Know About Home Equity Lines of Credit, Federal Reserve Board of Governors, www.federalreserve.gov/pubs/HomeLine.

Formulating a Consumer Loan Policy

Learning Objectives

After completing this chapter, you should be able to

- explain the importance of having a consumer loan policy
- describe the components of a loan policy
- discuss how the loan policy defines the bank's criteria for credit
- explain the key features of an effective loan policy
- discuss the Financial Institutions Reform, Recovery, and Enforcement Act (FIRREA)
- discuss the laws and regulations relating to purpose loans and transactions with affiliates
- define the terms that appear in bold type in the text

Introduction

Historically the success and stability of banks have been linked to how well they managed risk. The Great Depression of the 1930s, the savings and loan crisis of the 1980s, and the financial crisis of 2008 are all examples of economic cycles that required banks to have sound loan policies and practices for survival and growth. Likewise, in competitive economic environments, it is critical that a bank's board of directors approve a written loan policy, and that bank officers and employees adhere to it in order to prevent excessively risky behavior.

Because regulators are responsible for ensuring the safety and soundness of the banking industry, they have examinations and written guidelines on bank loan policy to cover the standards for operational and management controls; insider lending; information and audit systems; loan documentation; credit scoring; credit underwriting; interest rate exposure; asset growth; and lender compensation, fees, and benefits.

THE CONSUMER LOAN POLICY

A well-managed consumer lending department depends on the use of a clear and complete lending policy. A consumer **loan policy** takes into account bank size, loan portfolio objectives, core competencies, the product lines, and the markets where the bank operates. Therefore, bank loan policies should, and do, vary.

A consumer loan policy is a written guideline to help bank employees make sound and consistent decisions in all aspects of the lending process. A sound policy defines the level of risk the bank is willing to accept. It affirms corporate responsibility and ethical standards for business operations. Informed and consistent decisions are the foundation of a sound, efficient, legally compliant, and profitable operation.

The bank's lending policy is the result of a dynamic rather than a static process. It is a living document. It reflects and evolves with the bank's strategy and objectives and must be responsive to the rapidly changing competitive, economic, regulatory, and sociodemographic environment. The board of directors sets broad policy goals, and the bank's executives set policies to achieve those goals. Loan policies may change as the environment and the bank's objectives change.

An effectively written and implemented loan policy

- helps the bank serve the legitimate credit needs of its market area and meet its Community Reinvestment Act (CRA) compliance requirements

loan policy—A written statement of the goals, guidelines, standards, and procedures for lending set forth by the board of directors and executive officers. It helps employees make decisions at every stage of the lending process.

- establishes guidelines for the bank's lending staff for granting loans on a sound, consistent, and profitable basis
- helps ensure operational efficiency
- helps manage risk
- accomplishes consumer lending portfolio objectives—loans outstanding, growth, volume, profits, asset quality, and portfolio diversification
- helps ensure compliance with laws and regulations
- helps ensure corporate responsibility
- helps ensure ethical practices

What happens when banks do not have well-written and strictly enforced loan policies? Lack of clear direction for loan officers exposes the bank to a host of potential pitfalls in such areas as loans offered, the market, loan processing, customers served, and policy compliance:

Loan types	Uncertainty about the types of loans that can be made results in arbitrary or time-consuming loan decisions.
Market	Uncertainty about the types of business the bank is seeking could result in applications being taken for unacceptable loans.
Loan processing	Confusion over policy and process leads to delays in all phases of the loan process, from application taking to loan closing and booking.
Customers served	Lender bias, intentional or not, against people with certain characteristics or who are employed in certain jobs results in discrimination and violation of fair lending laws.
Policy	Lack of awareness of policy changes results in continued reliance on outdated guidelines.

Exhibit 6.1 (next page), which lists common warning signs that a loan policy needs to be updated, was published by the Federal Deposit Insurance Corporation (FDIC) in a communication about bank examinations.

WHAT A LOAN POLICY DOES

Adherence to a formal loan policy enables the bank to serve the needs of the market, establish guidelines for lending staff, ensure operational efficiency and consistency, manage risks, accomplish lending objectives, ensure compliance with the law, and ensure corporate responsibility and ethical practices.

Loan Policy Objectives

- serve the needs of the market
- establish guidelines for lending staff
- ensure operational efficiency
- manage risks
- accomplish lending objectives
- ensure regulatory compliance
- ensure corporate responsibility
- ensure ethical practices

Exhibit 6.1   Signs that a Loan Policy Needs a Tune-Up
• The policy has not been revised or reapproved in more than a year.

- The policy has not been revised or reapproved in more than a year.
- Multiple versions of the policy are in circulation.
- The table of contents is not accurate.
- The policy is disorganized or contains addendums from years past that have never been incorporated into the body of the policy.
- The policy contains misspellings, typos, and grammatical errors.
- Officers and directors who no longer serve are listed, or new ones are not listed.
- The designated trade territory includes areas no longer served, or new areas are omitted.
- Discontinued products are included, or new products are not addressed.
- New regulations are not addressed.
- In reviewing lending decisions there are departures from loan policy, such as
  - Actual lending practices vary significantly from those outlined in the policy.
  - Numerous exceptions to policy requirements have been approved.
  - Policy limits are being ignored.

Source: The Importance of a Loan Policy "Tune-Up," Supervisory Insights, Federal Deposit Insurance Corporation.

Serve the Needs of the Market

Banks, unlike some of their consumer lending competitors, have a responsibility to meet the credit needs of their primary market areas. This obligation, required by the Community Reinvestment Act (CRA), also is sound business practice. Banks should want to make all the good-quality loans they can. The loan policy stipulates how the bank will make these loans and thereby fulfill its CRA obligations. A firm loan policy can help ensure that the bank's CRA program is profitable as well as effective.

Establish Guidelines for Lending Staff

Giving the lending staff guidelines is vital to a sound loan portfolio. Banks want to ensure that loan decisions are sound, consistent, and profitable. By stating the guidelines clearly, the loan policy helps lenders structure loans that are consistent with bank policy. Loans that cannot be made in conformity with policy must be rejected; those that comply should be made.

Banks also want a diverse loan portfolio that conforms to their strategic goals. Guidance for sound and consistent lending decisions is achieved by having a clearly written policy and by regular monitoring to ensure that lenders are complying with the policy.

Ensure Operational Efficiency

If a loan policy is poorly written, loan decision making and processing are more time-consuming. Today, when quick turnaround can make the difference in whether the consumer will apply for a loan, lenders can ill afford extra investigation time. Having consistent policies and procedures for each loan type can reduce the time for loan evaluation, decision making, documentation, and closing. Management can ensure operational efficiency by clearly stating requirements and standardizing the approach to making loan decisions.

Manage Risks

Every business has risks, but the risks of banking are critical. Because banks are fiduciaries and have a central role in the nation's economy, taking excessive risks can affect more than just banks.

Risk analysis in banking is a dynamic function. The list of risks is evolving as new areas are identified, such as risks in technology and the payments system. Exhibit 6.2 outlines risk areas the Office of the Comptroller of the Currency (OCC) has identified as important for national banks. The senior officers of the bank manage these risk areas, with the approval of the board of directors.

Did You Know ...

The aggregate efficiency ratio for commercial banks was 61.93 percent in the first quarter of 2006. This means that banks spent about 62 cents to generate one dollar of revenue— a ratio that was 3.5 percentage points lower than in 1994. Although it does not identify risks, the efficiency ratio does address one of the more important measurements of bank performance.

Source: Federal Reserve Bulletin, April 2007.

Exhibit 6.2   Risk Areas in Banking

Generally, the major categories of risk are credit, market, and operational risks. The Office of the Comptroller of the Currency (OCC) has identified nine risk management areas for national banks:

Strategic risk	A risk from adverse business decisions or improper implementation of decisions.
Reputation risk	A risk from negative public opinion, affecting the bank's ability to retain existing or establish new relationships.
Credit risk	The risk to earnings or capital that comes from a borrower's failure to meet the terms of a loan contract.
Interest rate risk	A risk from movements in interest rates. The focus is on the sensitivity of interest rates to change and the timing of changes.
Liquidity risk	A risk to earnings and capital dependent on the bank's ability to meet obligations as they come due as well as unplanned decreases or changes in funding sources.
Price risk	A risk arising from the value changes of loans and investments.
Foreign exchange risk	A risk due to the movement of foreign exchange rates (applicable, for example, to credit card advances or purchases in foreign countries).
Transaction risk	The risk associated with service problems or product delivery problems. It is related to the major category of operational risk, regarding internal controls, information systems, employee integrity, and operating processes.
Compliance risk	A risk stemming from violations or nonconformance to laws and regulations. Banks are exposed to fines, civil money penalties, payment of damages, and voided contracts.

Source: Appendix H, Bank Supervision Process, Comptroller's Handbook, September 2007, Office of the Comptroller of the Currency.

Collateral risk. The financial risk to the bank that the value of the collateral will not be sufficient to cover the remaining balance on a defaulted loan.

The major risk areas for banks in general, and the consumer lending function in particular, are credit and operational risks. Related to these major risk areas for lending functions are collateral and interest rate risks. Consumer loan policies must address the management of risk areas to ensure bank safety and soundness as well as the growth and stability of loan portfolios.

Federal and state bank examiners evaluate banks for safety, soundness, and risk management. They examine banks for a series of factors known by the acronym CAMELS, which stands for capital adequacy, asset quality, management quality, earnings, liquidity, and sensitivity to market risk. Numerical ratings from one to five are assigned to each factor. Banks receive a single composite CAMEL rating, with a rating of one being the highest. Factors that can affect a CAMELS analysis are market risk, credit risk, reputation risk, interest rate risk, liquidity risk, price risk, transaction risk, the risk of crime against the bank, risks in information technology and other systems, and compliance risks. Bank regulators note that the elements of bank risk management are corporate governance, effective policies and procedures, management reports, and internal controls.

Accomplish Loan Portfolio Objectives

The bank coordinates its loan policy with its asset and liability program to achieve portfolio objectives for loans outstanding, growth, volume, profits, asset quality, and portfolio diversification.

When the bank's goals change, the loan policy should be revised to conform to the new goals. For example, relatively lax lending policies are out of place when a bank is trying to reduce delinquencies and losses or is responding to negative economic trends, such as recessions. Similarly, tight credit policies do not complement an aggressive loan growth objective. If the bank is in an aggressive growth environment, for example, loan policy might allow 100 percent financing on automobile loans. If it moves to a more conservative objective, the policy might require a 25 to 30 percent down payment.

An example of this fluctuation between aggressive and conservative loan policies occurred with the economic downturn of 2008. By not changing their installment loan credit standards, even as demand weakened most banks signaled their willingness to make consumer installment loans. However, a few banks across the country did tighten credit standards for both credit cards and other types of consumer loans in anticipation of a much slower economy.

Diversifying the loan portfolio with different types and sizes of loans helps to spread the credit risk and reduce the bank's exposure to downturns in a single industry. To diversify its lending portfolio bank management must clearly communicate its goals and specific objectives for each branch and department. Well-written loan policies are useful for this purpose. The loan policy example in appendix 2 that follows this chapter, states that Galaxy Bank has given the chief executive officer (CEO) the duty of setting portfolio goals and instituting procedures to implement the policy. The policy lists goals for the loan portfolio, for example that 30 percent of the portfolio should consist of installment and consumer loans. Other loan product groups, such as personal loans and credit cards, have their own goals, expressed as a percentage. Furthermore, each bank region or branch must contribute to total loan volume and loans outstanding based on its market and its annual budget or strategic plan. The external environment must be monitored continually and closely so that the bank may make timely and educated decisions to maintain an acceptable risk level within its loan portfolio concentrations.

Ensure Compliance with Laws and Regulations

Well-conceived and consistently applied lending policies keep the bank within the law. Sound loan policies reduce the opportunity for employees, whether willfully or unknowingly, to violate regulations. Combined with sound loan review procedures, loan policies help bankers identify inadvertent compliance violations and ensure timely correction of errors. Indeed, when defending itself against claims of violations, or during regulatory audits, the bank may offer its loan policy as evidence of its intent to comply with all regulations.

Ensure Corporate Responsibility and Ethical Practices

Closely related to ensuring regulatory compliance and giving guidance to lenders is the policy objective of ensuring corporate responsibility and ethical practices. Because of their central role in the nation's financial system, banks must maintain stricter accounting controls, greater financial transparency, higher ethical standards, and greater corporate accountability than other businesses.

Corporate **ethics** have a clear business purpose because bank employees handle the financial assets of both the bank and its customers. Bankers are required by law to tell the truth, act ethically, and avoid criminal activity. They must avoid any arrangement that may lead to a **conflict of interest**. Today, many banks incorporate in their loan policy their **code of conduct**, in full or by reference to a separate code of conduct that applies to all employees. Exhibit 6.3 (next page) illustrates some of the topics often covered in a code of conduct.

COMPONENTS OF A LOAN POLICY

The bank's policy statement can be brief or extensive, depending on the size and complexity of the organization, the types of products offered, and management preference for detail. Banks may want separate loan policies for such topics as loan administration; loan categories; environmental risk; collections, charge-offs, and recoveries; loan review and grading; loan loss reserves; and fair lending.[1]

Regardless of the format or extent, most consumer loan policies address the following topics to some degree:

- bank objectives
- responsibilities of the Board of Directors, senior management, and lending staff
- geographic limits

ethics—Principles of conduct and judgment that affect business practices.

conflict of interest—An action taken by a person in an official capacity that may benefit that person personally to the detriment of the employer.

code of conduct—A formal set of guidelines that represents a company's policies for corporate responsibility and individual conduct.

Did You Know ...

A result of the financial crisis of 2008 was the federal regulatory agency affirmation of "the crucial role that prudent bank lending practices play in promoting the nation's economic welfare… Banking organizations … [should] continue to ensure that they consider new lending opportunities on the basis of realistic asset valuations and a balanced assessment of borrowers' repayment capacities."

Source: Joint Press Release, "Interagency Statement on Meeting the Needs of Creditworthy Borrowers," November 12, 2008.

- pricing guidelines
- types of loans
- loans to insiders and employees
- lending authority
- credit and collateral criteria
- general underwriting standards
- loan documentation
- compliance and loan review
- collection and charge-offs
- corporate responsibility and ethics

STATEMENT OF THE BANK'S OBJECTIVES

The loan policy opens with a statement of the bank's objectives and how these objectives are supported by the lending function. The policy statement clearly expresses the bank's commitment to complying with the law, in addition to stating its objectives for the loan portfolio. For example, Galaxy Bank states in its loan policy:

> The management of the Bank believes that sound loans represent a desirable and profitable means of employing the Bank's funds. All such loans and extensions of credit shall be consistent with sound and prudent banking practices and in full conformity with applicable laws, regulations, rulings, and interpretations thereof, and shall be made without regard to race, sex, or national origin, or any other prohibited basis.

Exhibit 6.3 Contents of a Typical Bank Code of Conduct

- Corporate creed or letter from the senior executive
- Organization principles and values
- General statement of compliance with laws and regulations
- Equal Employment Opportunity statement
- Fair Lending or Community Reinvestment statement
- Environmental laws
- Conflict of interest
- Criminal activity
- Confidential information
- Insider trading
- Purchasing defaulted property
- Relationship with the investment community
- Financial accountability and internal controls
- Integrity of accounting and financial information

- Money laundering and transaction structuring
- Embezzlement, theft, and misapplication of funds
- Use of corporate name and letterhead
- Relationship with the media
- Things offered *to* employees
- Things offered *by* employees
- Estate matters
- Outside activities
- Sound personal finances
- Employment of relatives or persons having close personal relationships
- Safety
- Disclosure and recordkeeping
- Acknowledgment
- Code of conduct violations

RESPONSIBILITIES OF THE DIRECTORS,
MANAGEMENT, AND STAFF

When it comes to the bank's loan policy the role of the board of directors typically is limited to approval of the policy itself. The board depends on management reports, including internal and external audit reports, to keep informed about the bank's compliance with the policy.

Management's role is more direct. Senior management usually formulates the policy based on the strategic direction of the bank, hires staff to implement procedures to carry out the policy, and monitors compliance with the policy through reports and direct contact with staff and customers.

Bank employees carry out management's policy directives. In loan documentation, review, and audit areas, employees monitor and report to senior management the bank's practices so that procedures may be adjusted to ensure compliance.

GEOGRAPHIC LIMITS OF THE MARKET AREA

The lending policy defines the bank's primary lending area, for example, the state where the bank is headquartered, and sometimes a secondary lending area, such as areas in nearby states that relate economically to the primary area. The policy also defines procedures for handling loan requests outside these areas. A bank's primary lending area for consumer credit products may vary with the type of product but generally mirrors its branch network. Direct loans generally are confined to a specific geographic area because they are made through branch offices; indirect loans and revolving credit products may extend over a wider geographic area.

The Community Reinvestment Act, which requires that banks serve the credit needs of their communities, should be kept in the foreground when this part of the loan policy is drafted. Galaxy Bank's loan policy addresses this point as follows:

> One of the goals of the Bank's lending policy is to meet the legitimate credit needs (as may be defined from time to time by the Bank) of the community it serves. Generally, that community includes all the metropolitan City X MSA area and those towns where the Bank's branches are located, as further designated in the Bank's CRA map in the public file. Effective ability to lend in varying geographic areas is a function of servicing requirements, credit risks, economies of scale in relation to transaction size, and incremental profitability of the credit transaction.

PRICING GUIDELINES

The loan policy presents the criteria upon which pricing decisions are made. For example, it may stipulate the average number of basis points over the marginal cost of funds that each type of loan is supposed to achieve. The policy may define how often lenders should receive reports of current rates, terms, and conditions, and the cost of funds. Some policies are more explicit than others. The sample Galaxy Bank loan policy gives authority to the CEO in coordination with the

asset and liability committee (ALCO)—
The bank committee that monitors the costs of deposits and the income from loans, reviews the matching of term and interest rates of deposits and loans, and otherwise manages the bank's assets and liabilities to maximize long-term wealth for bank shareholders.

Loan Types Usually Covered in a Loan Policy

- *Closed-end loans*
  — automobile
  — home equity or second mortgage
  — recreational vehicle
  — unsecured

- *Indirect*
  — automobile
  — marine
  — recreational vehicles
  — motorcycles

- *Revolving*
  — credit cards
  — check credit lines
  — home equity lines of credit
  — unsecured lines of credit

asset and liability committee to devise a pricing policy consistent with the bank's objectives. The committee comprises bank lending and finance officers.

One of the many factors banks take into consideration when pricing loans is the cost of recording a loan, commonly known as "booking the loan." Banks also consider the pricing of their competitors. The policy articulates the conditions necessary for a bank to maintain consistent quality standards and prices.

Pricing loans fairly is an important part of fair lending compliance. Because consistency in loan pricing is one of the factors bank examiners consider in a fair lending examination, the loan policy should give loan officers both specific guidance and flexibility to respond to market conditions. Exceptions to policy requirements should be addressed in the policy itself. The loan policy should state who has the authority to make or approve exceptions and how the exceptions should be documented. Effective policy also requires that exceptions be reported to senior management so that this activity can be monitored and managed. The frequency of such reports depends on the bank's risk tolerance for exceptions.

TYPES OF LOANS DESIRED

The loan policy indicates which types of loans the bank wishes to emphasize. Assuming the bank wants to promote its open-end credit products, the policy would encourage lenders to sell those types of loans more aggressively than closed-end products. The bank might price its open-end products lower or might even elect to use less stringent debt-to-income and credit history requirements.

Policy statements vary on how they present the types of loans to pursue. Some simply itemize types of loans desired based on the needs of the community, expertise of lending officers, and product lines offered. Galaxy Bank has done this in its loan policy. It says, for example: "Loans to individuals for consumer purposes are considered to be a desirable segment of the Bank's lending activities. These loans are to be made in accordance with generally accepted principles of installment lending." The policy also stipulates terms and maximum limit for different loan types, such as "Personal loans: Maximum amount — $25,000; maximum term — 60 months."

Loan policies do not simply address the types of consumer loans that may be made. It is equally important that they address loans that may not be made. Management carefully identifies loans it does not want in the portfolio. Generally, loans that present high credit risk may be handled more appropriately by the commercial loan area or may be of a type for which the bank lacks core competence. Loans fitting this description might be

- loans for speculative purposes, such as investments or new businesses
- loans to corporations or partnerships
- home equity loans secured by investment properties
- loans referred by loan brokers

Situation

Elton works for State National Bank. He and his wife are remodeling their home and Elton inquires about his bank's home equity loan program. Other State National Bank employees have applied for loans, and there is a special loan officer who handles their requests. Elton meets with this loan officer and receives a document that outlines the bank's policy for loans to employees.

How will Elton's loan request be handled compared with other customers of State National Bank?

LOANS TO INSIDERS AND EMPLOYEES

The bank should state clearly its policy on loans to officers, directors, and employees of the bank. Federal Reserve Regulation O restricts loans to insiders, such as members of the board of directors and senior management of the bank—the president and executive officers. Galaxy Bank has this statement about loans to insiders: "It is the policy of the Bank to encourage extensions of credit to its officers and directors or their interests provided that such extensions conform to this policy."

There are no special restrictions on loans to other bank employees; indeed, many banks view their own employees as an attractive market for loan products. The policy statement might define which employees are eligible, what the underwriting requirements are, and who will have the authority to approve employee loan requests. Many banks create separate committees to review employee loans.

LENDING AUTHORITY

The policy statement sets forth the bank's **lending authority** system and decision-making guidelines. The power to grant lending authority is vested with the board of directors. The directors establish the lending limits for each lender or loan committee and monitor employee performance.

The policy statement also specifies the procedures for approving loans. The loan approval system may consist of individual lending authorities, loan committees, or a combination thereof. The sample lending authority structure depicted in exhibit 6.4 (next page) is a model framework for handling loan decisions.

Loan committees generally are not used for consumer lending decisions, which usually require quick response times and involve lower dollar amounts and a high volume of applications, but they are sometimes necessary to review large consumer loan requests, such as airplane and boat loans over $150,000.

Another option for handling larger or special loan requests is to allow lenders to combine their loan authorities, and to ensure that at least two lenders have reviewed a large loan request or an adverse credit decision. When the loan policy allows it, lenders may combine their authority to approve an applicant's request that is larger than either lender's individual authority.

Did You Know ...

Some banks do not lend to insiders, having decided that the monitoring and recordkeeping requirements are too much trouble.

Regulations Governing Loans to Insiders

Federal Reserve:	FRS Regulation O
OCC:	12 CFR 31
FDIC:	12 CFR 337.3, 349
OTS:	12 CFR 563.43

States also may have laws that restrict loans to insiders. These may be stricter than the federal law. State banks should be aware of the laws of the states where they operate.

lending authority— The maximum dollar amount of a loan that an individual lender or group of loan officers can make without referring the loan to the bank's loan committee.

Exhibit 6.4   Sample Consumer Lending Authority Schedule

LEVEL	UNSECURED	SECURED	MINIMUM LENDER QUALIFICATIONS
I	$2,500	$7,500	Must complete the bank's credit training program and have one year of experience.
II	$5,000	$15,000	Must complete the bank's advanced lender training and have one year of experience and a satisfactory lending record.
III	$25,000	$50,000	Must have three years satisfactory lending record and complete the consumer credit review course.
IV	$50,000	$100,000	Senior Consumer Loan Division officers only

Note: Loans over the lender's authority are referred to an officer with the required authority level. Level IV officers may combine their authorities to approve unsecured loans up to $75,000 and secured loans up to $150,000. Loans over those amounts must be submitted to the consumer loan committee for final approval. Two lenders must sign off on all rejected closed-end loans.

CREDIT CRITERIA—GENERAL TERMS

The loan policy describes the system, such as a credit scoring or a judgmental system, that the bank uses to determine the consumer's capacity to repay and sets general conditions for credit history, collateral, and other aspects crucial to the lending decision. For example, Galaxy Bank emphasizes credit investigation; its policy states, among other criteria, that

Positive identification of each applicant is required. An investigation through an outside consumer reporting agency and such other investigation as is deemed necessary should provide a history of satisfactory payments. A review of the Bank's previous credit history with the applicant is required.

Underwriting standards are an important part of each bank's loan policy. They may include factors such as minimum credit score, acceptable debt–to–income ratios, loan-to-value ratios on secured loans, such as real estate loans, and standards for financing purchases of new and used vehicles.

LOAN DOCUMENTATION

Loan documentation is very important to the lending function and often is critical in addressing credit or regulatory compliance risk. The loan policy specifies the type of documentation required for

Situation

A customer of TBF Bank loan officer David Mertz is seeking a $50,000 unsecured consumer loan. Because David's individual lending authority is only $25,000 for this type of loan, he cannot make the decision to grant the loan on his own. He calls on Ethyl Rich, whose lending authority is also $25,000, to review the application jointly with him.

Can they make the loan decision together?

various types of loans. Loans secured by collateral, for example, will require different documentation than an open-end credit loan. The policy may stipulate that the following documentation is required for an automobile loan:

- consumer credit note and disclosure statement
- security agreement
- copy of insurance policy naming bank as loss payee
- certificate of title or lien recording
- copy of the bill of sale

COMPLIANCE AND LOAN REVIEW

The loan policy establishes the bank's responsibility for loan compliance and **loan review** functions. It specifically addresses the regulations that govern consumer lending. For example, the policy will have a statement about bank policies and practices related to the CRA, the Equal Credit Opportunity Act (ECOA), and the Truth in Lending Act (TILA). Specifics of each of these may not be in the loan policy itself but may be in a comprehensive compliance policy or in separate policies devoted to specific laws and regulations.

Galaxy Bank emphasizes the importance of **compliance officers** in ensuring that bank loans conform to the law:

> The Compliance Officer of the Bank will review and ensure the adequacy of compliance by the Bank with all laws and regulations relative to lending, extension of credit, and all other pertinent compliance areas. . . . The Compliance Officer shall draft a Compliance Plan to be approved by the Bank's Board of Directors. Administration of the plan shall be the responsibility of the Compliance Officer, who shall report on the status of those responsibilities at least annually to the Board of Directors.

The loan review function of the loan operations department is charged with reviewing loan applications—both rejected and approved—for compliance, completeness, and accuracy of all documents. This may mean reviewing every application or (more likely) reviewing a random selection of a certain percentage of applications. Typically, the loan review staff will

- check all documents for accuracy and completeness
- verify conformity with all loan policies
- review all rejected applications for compliance and proper documentation
- verify that the lending authority level is appropriate
- verify the loan rate

COLLECTION AND CHARGE-OFF

As part of management's strategy for meeting the bank's loan quality objectives, the loan policy defines an acceptable level of delinquency and loan losses.

loan review—The function of examining loan documents to ensure accuracy, completeness, and conformity with bank loan policies and regulatory requirements. It also monitors long-term documentation and loan status.

compliance officer— The bank employee charged with establishing controls to ensure compliance with banking regulations and bank policies.

Ethical Business Conduct

- cultivates strong teamwork and productivity
- promotes a positive public image
- improves society
- maintains a moral course during difficult times
- helps avoid losses to the bank

Banks with very conservative delinquency and loss goals are determined to minimize risk. Their loan policies may require higher down payments, use lower debt-to-income ratios, and screen out applicants with weak credit scores or minor derogatory information on their credit reports. In contrast, a bank that has more liberal delinquency and loss objectives, or aggressive sales goals, may accept lower down payments, use higher debt-to-income ratios, and excuse some negative information.

Specific loan policies must be consistent with the bank's portfolio objectives. It would be inconsistent, for example, to expect high consumer loan sales while at the same time raising credit requirements to eliminate marginal applications.

The loan policy defines the bank's practices for handling delinquent accounts and charge-offs. It specifically defines the point at which delinquent accounts will be charged off as a loss to the bank. Those responsible for collecting delinquent accounts must be thoroughly familiar with the collection department's policies and procedures. Exhibit 6.5 illustrates a sample loan charge-off policy statement.

CORPORATE RESPONSIBILITY AND ETHICS

It is essential to success in banking that employees embrace the bank's organizational values. Yet sometimes unofficial or unethical norms of behavior exist even when official stated principles prescribe otherwise. Today, more than ever, banks expect their employees and operations to comply with the law. Because compliance and ethical behavior are important to retain the trust of the bank's customers and community, policy statements and codes of conduct must be stated, reinforced, and above all followed by all bank employees.

Ethical dilemmas appear daily in the workplace. Loan policy statements on credit guidelines, conflicts of interest, and loan review help keep lenders' behavior ethical. Business and community relationship codes of ethics focus on rules and guidelines for the treatment of employees, customers, and vendors.

Exhibit 6.5 Sample Loan Charge-off Policy	
Closed-end loans	Loans will be charged off when payments are 120 days past due, unless one of the following conditions exists: • The collateral securing the loan will be sold within the next 30 days, resulting in a full recovery of the balance due. • Firm arrangements have been made with the customer to bring the account current or pay off the balance within the next 30 days.
Open-end loans	Accounts will be charged off when payments are 180 days past due unless the line is secured and one of the conditions noted above applies.

Galaxy Bank emphasizes ethical behavior in its policy on loans to insiders:

> Officers and directors shall conduct their business affairs with such standards of integrity that no conflict of interest exists or could be construed to exist. Each officer and director must be alert to the potential for conflicts of interest where personal profit or gain might arise from relationships with consumers that might tend to interfere with the exercise of independent judgment in the handling of business for the Bank.

LOAN POLICY AND CREDIT CRITERIA

The loan policy defines the criteria for credit, such as how the bank measures an applicant's character and capacity, collateral risk, and the quantifiable measures used.

CREDIT HISTORY

An applicant's credit history is one of the most important variables in predicting future behavior. Interpreting credit history is not always easy. The lending policy usually focuses on those factors in an applicant's credit history that lead to automatic rejection of the application.

Bankruptcies, repossessions, judgments, foreclosures, charge-offs, and delinquent installment loan accounts of 90 days or more often are cited as reasons for rejecting a loan. If such conditions will lead to automatic rejection, the loan policy must clearly communicate that standard.

If there are to be exceptions to these standards, the loan policy must define the reasons for them and define the approval method for each exception. Some lenders, for example, will make an exception for applicants who have gone bankrupt if the bankruptcy was due to a medical crisis. Similarly, exceptions may be made for those who have had small judgments against them, delinquencies on department store accounts, or voluntary repossessions that did not result in a loss. When making exceptions bank employees must be consistent.

CAPACITY AND DECISION-MAKING SYSTEMS

The policy will state the actual decision-making system the bank uses. This could be a judgmental system based on the five Cs of credit, a credit-scoring system, or some combination of the two.

Credit-scoring systems offer a more scientific and consistent approach to lending than judgmental systems, which are often subjective. For banks using a credit-scoring system, the policy may define the minimum score, such as 150 points, and the procedures for addressing exceptions to the policy. **Overrides**, which are exceptions to a credit score standard, should be documented and the loan policy should define the standard for documentation.

Situation

Danny is a good friend of Marty Paulson, a loan officer at ABC Bank. Danny is unable to get an auto loan due to his negative credit history. Marty has known Danny for a long time and is aware of how his recent divorce changed his financial situation. He also knows that Danny has a new job that pays well. Marty decides to loan Danny enough money from his personal funds at a low rate of interest.

Could Marty's personal loan to Danny be considered an unethical transaction?

The Five Cs of Credit

- character
- capacity
- capital
- collateral
- conditions

override—In reference to a credit score, when the decision to make or deny an application does not conform to the bank's stated policy on the minimum qualifying credit score. A "high-side override" occurs when an applicant with a credit score that meets the bank's policy is denied for another reason. A "low-side override" occurs when an applicant with a credit score below the minimum is approved for another reason.

By The Numbers

Calculating Debt

An applicant has a $10,000 line of credit with a $500 balance at another bank; the minimum monthly payment on the line is 5 percent of the current balance. To calculate the debt portion of the debt-to-income ratio, the loan policy would stipulate whether the minimum payment would be based on the current balance or on the full credit line.

Using current balance:
5% X $500 = $25

Using full credit line:
5% X $10,000 = $500

Capacity to make loan payments is a crucial aspect of evaluating credit risk in a judgmental system. The income figure may be calculated based on gross or net income; there can be a significant difference between the two.

The policy may require that the applicant's debt-to-income ratio not exceed 40 percent of gross monthly income—income before taxes, insurance, and other deductions. Thus, if the applicant's gross monthly income is $2,500, the maximum acceptable amount of monthly debt payments, including the new loan payment, is $1,000.

The consumer loan policy dictates how both "income" and "debt" are to be determined for calculating the debt-to-income ratio. The debt portion, especially for open-end loans, is defined in the loan policy. Although closed-end loans have set monthly payments, open-end line of credit payments vary directly with use. Thus, the policy must state whether the debt figure for open-end lines of credit is based on the current balance or on the total line amount, which takes into account potential debt. Likewise, variable rate debt is calculated either at its current interest rate or at a higher level to allow for possible interest rate and monthly payment increases.

COLLATERAL

Collateral requirements are spelled out in a lending policy. The types of acceptable collateral, the method of establishing the collateral's value, and the amount that may be borrowed against different types of collateral are detailed.

For example, a loan policy may stipulate the following criteria for automobiles used as collateral:

- Automobiles more than seven years old are not eligible.

- All vehicles must have physical damage and liability insurance coverage with a $250 maximum deductible.

- The bank must have the first lien on all vehicle loans.

- The suggested down payment on all automobile loans is 10 to 20 percent, but the lender may grant an exception as long as the total advance is less than the maximum advance as determined by the debt-to-income ratio.

The policy in exhibit 6.6 sets guidelines for the collateral, maximum loan advance, and maximum loan term for automobile loans. Note that the lender has flexibility on the required down payment.

Exhibit 6.6　Automobile Loan Policy

CATEGORY	MAXIMUM ADVANCE	MAXIMUM TERM
New automobiles	100% of dealer invoice	Loans up to $20,000—48 months Loans over $20,000—60 months
Used automobiles	100% of NADA average loan value	Current model—48 months 1–2 years old—42 months 3–4 years old—30 months 5–7 years old—24 months

KEYS TO AN EFFECTIVE LOAN POLICY

For a consumer loan policy to be effective, the standards must be unambiguous, communicated to the lending staff, and accompanied by implementing procedures. If exceptions to the policy are allowed, this fact should be stated in the policy, along with the procedure for approving exceptions.

The policy statement shown in exhibit 6.7 is not intended to be complete but it illustrates unique considerations that should be taken into account when making a marine loan. The abbreviated policy statement shown in exhibit 6.8 (next page) gives all lenders guidance about the collateral requirements for a home equity line of credit.

Exhibit 6.7　Sample Marine Loan Policy

Eligible collateral: All boats titled in Maryland or Virginia or documented with the U.S. Coast Guard. Outboard motors and trailers may be financed if they are purchased with the boat.

Ineligible collateral: Wooden vessels, boats to be used for charter, and vessels used for business purposes.

CATEGORY	MAXIMUM ADVANCE	MAXIMUM TERM
New	100% of dealer cost	180 months
Used		
1–5 years old	80% of high BUC book	Advance > $15,000—180 months 12 months per $1,000
6–10 years old	75% of high BUC book	Advance > $15,000—120 months 12 months per $1,000

Rates

New boats: Fixed rate: ___% for loans up to 120 months only
Variable rate: Prime plus __%

Used boats: Fixed rate: ___% for loans up to 84 months
Variable rate: Prime plus __%

Marine survey: A marine survey (appraisal) is required to establish the value of all boats more than five years old or when the loan advance is more than $15,000.

Federal documentation: Required on all loans with a cash advance greater than $35,000, on all vessels displacing five tons or more, or when the boat will be operated outside the state. All other boats must be titled in Maryland or Virginia.

Exhibit 6.8	Sample Home Equity Line of Credit Policy

Eligible collateral:	Owner-occupied homes located in Maryland, Virginia, or the District of Columbia.
Lien position:	The bank must have either a first or second mortgage position.
Maximum advance:	100 percent of the appraised value of the home, minus the first mortgage balance.
Rate:	Prime plus 2 percent
Other requirements:	• Property must be appraised by a certified appraiser as per FIRREA.
	• Property must be the applicant's primary residence.
	• Property must not be used for commercial purposes.
	• Properties located in a flood zone must be covered by flood insurance.
	• The three-day rescission period may not be waived under any circumstances.
	• The bank must be named as loss payee on the homeowner's insurance policy.

UNAMBIGUOUS LOAN STANDARDS

The elements of a loan policy should not be open to interpretation. The requirements must be expressed in clear terms that have the same meaning for every loan officer. When the requirements are incorporated into the bank's loan policy, decisions of all lenders are consistent. Any terms that may be ambiguous, such as character, complete application, or positive trait, should be defined either within the policy or in a separate "Definitions" section. Examples of clearly written lending requirements are:

- The maximum term for a new automobile loan is 60 months.
- The minimum down payment requirement is 20 percent of the selling price.
- The maximum debt-to-income ratio is 45 percent of gross monthly income.
- A loan may not be made to an applicant who has declared bankruptcy in the past seven years.
- A minimum acceptable credit score is 190 points.

Unclear policy statements that are open to interpretation add risk to approved loans and the lending process. The following are some examples.

Do not make loans to applicants who have been at their address less than one year, unless there are offsetting positive attributes.	This statement needs a definition of "positive attributes."
Decline loan requests from applicants who have major derogatory credit histories.	This statement needs a definition of "major derogatory credit history."

Do not make bill consolidation loans unless the applicant has been cross-sold a loan with a higher amount.

The intent of this statement is unclear, arbitrary, and unethical.

COMMUNICATION

The best-conceived and best-written loan policy cannot be effective unless its contents are communicated fully and regularly to the lending staff. Communication goes beyond ensuring that each loan officer has a copy of the policy. Training programs and meetings should supplement the policy and there should be regular updates to highlight its contents. Loan officers must be trained to use the guide as a constant reference source. It is particularly important to keep the lending staff apprised of changes and updates. Lenders who are unaware that the bank has loosened its credit standards might deny loans to applicants who now qualify.

Frequent updates also help lenders keep up with new bank products or legislation. For example, the issues of privacy and information protection have to be reviewed often because new technology and fraud techniques require consistent and vigilant protections. Galaxy Bank has included in its loan policy an extended description of its privacy rules, emphasizing the importance of maintaining the customer's trust.

> Whereas Galaxy Bank recognizes its customers' expectations of financial privacy and whereas preserving our customers' trust is one of the core values of the Bank and the broader banking community, we therefore resolve to abide by the following guidelines for the responsible use and protection of our customers' information.

Emerging issues underlie the need for keeping loan policy statements and procedures current. Updates also are essential for staff changes, branch additions, changes in business strategies, mergers and acquisitions, new loan products, changes in rates and terms, changes in regulations, and economic changes.

PROCEDURES

It is helpful to supplement loan policies with a **procedures manual** that provides guidance about proper preparation and handling of all loan documents. Detailed procedures, for example, may explain how to get a lien on an automobile title and how to verify insurance coverage before the loan is made. Policies and procedures often are presented together in a single manual that answers most questions lenders have. Whether the bank provides a printed manual or an online resource on its Intranet, lenders are able to make frequent use of the resource.

> ### Situation
> Maria Alonso is a loan officer. On Thursday morning, the chairman of the loan committee calls her into a meeting. The loan policy has been revised to refine the policy on maintaining consumer financial privacy. The chairman explains the change to all the loan officers. Maria asks several questions, as do some of the other loan officers. By the end of the meeting, she is confident that she understands the policy. Later that day, Maria receives an updated consumer loan policy and procedures manual with a cover memo highlighting the changes and additions. She also receives an e-mail from the bank's president emphasizing the importance of the change.
>
> *Why is this much communication regarding changes to the loan policy important?*

procedures manual—
A written statement of how tasks are to be accomplished within the bank to comply with bank policy.

exception—Part of the loan policy that details what policies can be waived and under what circumstances.

purpose loan—A loan backed by securities and used for purchasing securities or for carrying securities (maintaining, reducing, or retiring debt incurred for obtaining securities).

margin—The difference or spread between the market value of securities used as collateral for a loan and the amount of loan granted.

FRS Regulations Related to Margin Loans

FRS Regulation T, Credit by Brokers and Dealers

FRS Regulation U, Credit by Banks and Persons other than Brokers or Dealers for the Purpose of Purchasing or Carrying Margin Stocks

FRS Regulation X, Borrowers of Securities Credit

EXCEPTIONS

Although loan policies provide clear guidelines, they usually are flexible to allow for identifying and handling situations that justify an **exception** to the standard policy. For example, although an applicant may fail to meet the bank's credit-score requirements, the loan may merit an exception if it will be secured by a savings account with the bank. In this case, the bank may want to make an exception contingent on the applicant's having an acceptable credit history and meeting the bank's debt-to-income ratio. The policy notes what criteria may be waived and the circumstances. Exceptions must be consistent to comply with fair lending laws, and they must be documented in the loan file.

The Galaxy Bank loan policy represents much of what is standard in loan policies, but it does not include all the features discussed in this chapter, and it may not reflect other banks' loan policies. Prudent lenders should review their bank's loan policies.

LAWS AND REGULATIONS

Laws and regulations that apply to consumer lending are referenced in the loan policy. It also may reference the bank's compliance program. The policy may include, for example, laws and implementing regulations for **purpose loans**, transactions with affiliates, and certain specific situations, such as appraisals of real estate. It also may describe penalties for violating specific legal requirements. For example, the Financial Institutions Reform, Recovery, and Enforcement Act (FIRREA) sets out penalties banks and bankers may incur for violating federal banking laws.

REGULATING PURPOSE CREDIT

One of the causes of the 1929 market crash that led to the Great Depression was the excessive extension of credit for buying or carrying securities. A purpose loan to purchase margin stock allows investors to buy the stock even if they do not have enough cash on hand. A purpose loan to carry margin stock enables the borrower to maintain, reduce, or retire debt previously incurred to purchase margin stock. These loans are risky because the value of the collateral, the securities, fluctuates.

To curb excessive speculation in the securities market by limiting how much credit a lender can extend for buying or carrying securities, the Securities Exchange Act of 1934 authorized the Federal Reserve to set **margin** requirements. The act has been amended over time, and Federal Reserve Regulations T, U, and X address margin requirements for different groups.

The margin requirement, set periodically by the Federal Reserve under FRS Regulation U, is the maximum spread of the stock's value and the purpose loan amount expressed as a percentage. For example, if FRS Regulation U sets the margin at 50 percent, the bank may lend only 50 percent of the market value of the stock being purchased. The market value is measured on the day the loan is made. Regulation U prohibits lenders from extending any purpose loan, secured directly or indirectly by margin stock, in an amount exceeding the maximum loan value of the collateral.

Galaxy Bank, in its sample loan policy, is cautious about making loans for securities speculation; included in the list of loans not desired by the bank are "Loans for speculative purposes, particularly to enable the consumer to speculate in the futures, securities, or commodities market."

TRANSACTIONS WITH AFFILIATES

Many banks failed during the Great Depression because they engaged in complex transactions with affiliated companies. The Banking Act of 1933 (the Glass-Steagall Act) addressed this weakness by adding section 23A to the Federal Reserve Act. Section 23A limits individual and aggregate transactions between a member bank and its affiliates to set percentages of the bank's capital stock and surplus. It also imposes certain transaction requirements, such as specifications for the quantity and quality of the collateral securing the transaction.

Section 23B, enacted as part of the Competitive Equality Banking Act of 1987, complements section 23A by ensuring that permissible transactions between member banks and affiliates are carried out on market terms and conditions ("on an arm's-length basis").

In 2003 the Federal Reserve issued FRS Regulation W, Transactions Between Member Banks and Their Affiliates, to make it easier for banks to comply with sections 23A and 23B. FRS Regulation W specifies criteria for determining whether a company is an affiliate and lists exceptions, such as certain operating subsidiaries. Restricted transactions include the transfer of **low-quality assets** between affiliates. Exhibit 6.9 lists transactions covered by FRS Regulation W.

Under FRS Regulation W, an affiliate may

- control the bank.
- be owned by the same parent company
- have an interlocking directorate with the member bank.
- be either a depository or a financial subsidiary of the bank.
- be a partnership in which the member bank or an employee or director serves as a general partner.

low-quality asset— An asset that examiners so classify, is on a nonaccrual status, is more than 30 days past due, or has been renegotiated due to the borrower's deteriorating financial condition.

Exhibit 6.9 Restricted Transactions Between Affiliates	
Section 23A restricted transactions	• Extensions of credit • Purchases of, or investments in, securities issued by the affiliate • Purchases of an asset from the affiliate, including an asset subject to recourse or an agreement to repurchase, except as specifically exempted by the Federal Reserve • Acceptances of a security issued by the affiliate as collateral for an extension of credit to any person or company • Issuance of a guarantee on behalf of an affiliate
Section 23B restricted transactions	• All restricted transactions under 23A, *plus* • Sales of assets by member banks to their affiliates • Payments of money or furnishing of services by member banks to their affiliates • Transactions in which an affiliate acts as an agent or broker for the member bank or the member bank is a participant • Transactions by a member bank with third parties, if an affiliate has a financial interest in the third party or is a participant in the transaction

Galaxy Bank addresses affiliate relations in its policy statement on concentrations of credit. It later directs the loan review committee to review these loans regularly.

> Concentrations of credit are defined as obligations, direct or indirect, of the same or affiliated interests that represent 25 percent or more of the Bank's total equity, capital, and reserves.

FINANCIAL INSTITUTIONS REFORM, RECOVERY, AND ENFORCEMENT ACT

The savings and loan failures of the 1980s cost taxpayers billions of dollars. Many of the failures were due to insider abuse. The Financial Institutions Reform, Recovery, and Enforcement Act (FIRREA) of 1989 gave bank regulators more enforcement authority over directors, officers, bank employees, controlling stockholders, independent contractors, and in some cases, former employees. Officers and directors found guilty of misusing bank assets may be required to make restitution to the bank or indemnify, or guarantee, it against loss.

FIRREA increased civil money penalties for regulatory violations. It also created a three-tiered system of violations and related penalties:

- unintentional violations
- knowing or reckless violations with minimal loss
- knowing or reckless violations with substantial loss

Because overvalued real estate pledged as collateral contributed to loan losses during the 1980s, FIRREA overhauled the regulations governing appraisals. Lenders must have appraisals on real estate collateral securing loans for more than $250,000. The appraisals must be current, performed by state-certified or state-licensed appraisers, and conform to the Uniform Standards of Professional Appraisal Practice. A bank must ensure the independence of appraiser selection and of the entire process when an appraisal is conducted within the bank.

The financial crisis of 2008 and subsequent economic downturn generated scrutiny of all financial institutions and their lending functions. As in past crises, it is likely that additional laws and regulations will result.

SUMMARY

- An effective consumer lending operation depends on a sound policy for guiding loan decisions. Loan policies vary among banks and are dynamic, evolving as a bank's environment, strategy, and objectives change. A clearly communicated loan policy helps ensure uniform decision-making and operational efficiency. Adherence to a formal loan policy enables the bank to serve the needs of the market, establish guidelines for lending staff, ensure operational efficiency, manage risks, accomplish lending objectives, ensure compliance with the law, and ensure corporate responsibility and ethical practices.

- Consumer loan policies usually include a statement of the bank's objectives; geographic limits of the lending market; pricing guidelines; types of loans desired; guidelines on loans made to insiders and employees; lending authority; general terms and conditions, such as credit criteria and collateral requirements; credit underwriting standards; compliance and loan review; collection and charge-offs; and corporate responsibility and ethics.

- The loan policy for credit criteria may describe the system, usually a credit scoring or judgmental system, that the bank uses to determine the consumer's capacity to repay, and sets general terms for credit history, collateral, and other factors crucial to the lending decision.

- To be effective a consumer loan policy must contain unambiguous loan standards; it must be communicated to the lending staff; and it must be accompanied by procedures for implementation. In addition, the policy should describe clearly the allowed policy exceptions and the exception process.

- The loan policy references the laws and regulations that apply to consumer lending and sometimes the bank's compliance program. It should specify laws and implementing regulations for purpose credit and transactions with affiliates as well as FIRREA provisions such as those for appraisals of real estate.

END NOTE

[1] For additional information on loan policy guidelines for bank boards of directors, see *Insights for Bank Board of Directors*, St. Louis Federal Reserve, www.stlouisfed.org/col/director/reference_view.htm.

SELF-CHECK AND REVIEW

Learning Check

1. Why is loan policy creation a dynamic rather than a static process?
2. In what way does a formal lending policy help curb regulatory violations?
3. What is lending authority and how is it granted?
4. How does the loan policy help lenders judge an applicant's character?
5. Why does the loan policy need to clarify how "debt" and "income" are calculated for use in the debt-to-income ratio?
6. What information would help the following ambiguous loan policy statements become clear and unambiguous?

    Statement 1: Do not make loans to applicants who have been at their address less than one year, unless there are offsetting positive attributes.

    Statement 2: Decline loan requests from applicants who have major derogatory credit histories.

7. Why does the federal government restrict purpose loans?

ADDITIONAL RESOURCES

ABA Bank Compliance Magazine, Washington: American Bankers Association, periodical.

American Bankers Association, **www.aba.com**.

Appendix H, *Bank Supervision Process, Comptroller's Handbook*, September 2007, Office of the Comptroller of the Currency, www.occ.treas.gov/handbook/banksup.pdf.

Appraisal Subcommittee, www.asc.gov.

Banking and Finance Terminology, Washington: American Bankers Association, 2005.

Federal Deposit Insurance Corporation, www.FDIC.gov.

Federal Reserve, www.federalreserve.gov.

Insights for Bank Boards of Directors, St. Louis Federal Reserve, www.stlouisfed.org/col/director/reference_view.htm.

Interagency Guidelines Establishing Standards for Safety and Soundness, www.fdic.gov/news/news/financial/1995/fil9549.html.

Interagency Guidelines for Real Estate Lending Policies, 2000 FDIC Rules and Regulations, www.fdic.gov/regulations/laws/rules/2000-8700.html#2000appendixatopart365.

Interagency Statement on Meeting the Needs of Creditworthy Borrowers, Joint Press Release, November 12, 2008, www.federalreserve.gov/newsevents/press/bcreg/20081112a.htm.

Office of the Comptroller of the Currency, www.occ.treas.gov.

Office of Thrift Supervision, www.ots.treas.gov.

Reference Guide to Regulatory Compliance, Washington: American Bankers Association, annual publication.

The Importance of a Loan Policy "Tune-Up," Supervisory Insights, Federal Deposit Insurance Corporation, 2004, www.fdic.gov/regulations/examinations/supervisory/insights/siwin04/policy_tune_up.html.

"What Is Liquidity Risk?," FRBSF Economic Letter 2008-33; October 24, 2008, Federal Reserve Bank of San Francisco, www.frbsf.org/publications/economics/letter/2008/el2008-33.html.

APPENDIX II

Galaxy Bank Loan Policy

The officers of the Galaxy Bank, N.A. (Bank), in making loans, and in their direction of other Bank personnel engaged in the preparation, administration, and safekeeping of loan documents, shall be guided by this policy as amended by the Board of Directors at its regular meeting on July 5, 20XX.

I. BANK OBJECTIVES

A. The management of the Bank believes that sound loans represent a desirable and profitable means of employing the Bank's funds. All such loans and extensions of credit shall be consistent with sound and prudent banking practices and in full conformity with applicable laws, regulations, rulings, and interpretations thereof, and shall be made without regard to race, sex, or national origin or any other prohibited basis. This policy clearly enforces adherence to the Equal Credit Opportunity Act.

   1. Authorized Bank employees are expected to make, and seek to develop, all such loans that opportunity affords and the resources of the Bank allocated for that purpose permit.

   2. The allocation of resources available for making loans shall be determined by the senior management of the Bank in consultation with Galaxy Bankshares, provided, however, that the decisions of the Board of Directors shall be consistent with the maintenance of a sound capital structure, adequate liquidity, and appropriate profitability standards. In the allocation of resources available for loans, primary consideration will be given to current and potential consumers within the areas defined in the Bank's Community Reinvestment Act (CRA) statement.

B. The Bank recognizes that the lending of money necessarily includes reasonable business risks. Some losses are to be expected in the lending program.

   1. It is the policy of the Bank to maintain a reserve for future loan losses consistent with the policy set forth by Galaxy Bankshares, provided, however, that the Board of Directors shall review quarterly, or as often as the board deems proper, such reserve to determine its adequacy to meet possible loan losses.

   2. Loans may be charged off with the concurrence of the Chief Executive Officer. The amount charged off shall be the amount of exposure on the loan that the Bank has identified as uncollectible. The loss shall be taken at the end of the month in which the loss is identified. All loans charged off shall be reported to the Board of Directors at its next scheduled meeting.

II. DETERMINATION AND ADMINISTRATION OF LOAN POLICY

A. The Board of Directors shall be delegated the responsibility to review regularly (generally at the monthly meeting) the administration of lending activities. As part of its regular responsibilities, and at its regular meeting, the Board of Directors shall

   1. Review all approvals of and extensions of credit to any obligated party of the Bank, either directly or indirectly, where the total indebtedness exceeds $75,000. Participation loans in any amount also will be reviewed and approved.

   2. Review all delinquent loans above $25,000, including those in the commercial, correspondent, installment, and mortgage divisions. (Delinquent loans shall include all those so defined by the regulations of the FDIC or the State Banking Department.)

   3. Review all loans determined by the Bank through its loan review process or by any regulatory authority as possessing unwarranted or more than normal risk.

   4. Approve recommendations of the Chief Executive Officer, as described above, for loans to be charged off.

   5. Review reports and exceptions that may be brought to its attention by the Loan Review Department of Galaxy Bankshares.

   6. Review exceptions to and interpretations of this loan policy.

7. Review all exceptions to compliance with laws and regulations as may be brought to its attention from time to time by the Compliance Officer of the Bank or others.

8. Review concentrations of credit where the obligations of the same or an affiliated interest exceeds 25 percent of the Bank's equity, capital, and reserves. Concentrations of credit are further defined in Section VII.A.

B. The Officers Loan Committee shall meet each Wednesday and shall be composed of the Chief Executive Officer, Chief Operating Officer, and Senior Loan Officer. A quorum shall consist of two voting members. Other officers of the Bank who have been delegated lending authority as hereinafter described may attend meetings of this committee as nonvoting members. Responsibilities of this committee are as follows:

1. To approve all authorizations for and extensions of credit above an individual officer's lending authority.

2. To discuss and evaluate the recommendations of any officer who wants the Officers Loan Committee as a forum for discussion of loans of a new or unusual nature that may involve an interpretation of this policy, or where there is no existing credit approval.

3. To review all transactions in the commercial, installment, or mortgage divisions that exceed $100,000 and represent new loans or renewals since the preceding meeting.

4. To review all maturing notes at an appropriate interval before maturity so as to enable the responsible officer to share with the Officers Loan Committee the disposition of such notes and the rates to be charged on any renewals or extensions.

5. To provide a forum for the determination, analysis, and examination of pricing policies and strategies for the lending areas.

6. To provide a forum for communication among the lending officers of subjects such as marketing, changes in laws and regulations, changes in economic conditions, review of the current asset and liability administration policies in effect at the Bank, ascertaining the effort put forth by the lending groups to comply with the Bank's CRA Statement, and for other purposes that officers may feel appropriate for discussion within the lending areas.

7. To review all loans determined by the Bank's loan review process or by any regulatory authority to possess unwarranted or more than normal credit risks. It shall be the responsibility of any officer to report any loan under his or her administration that develops such risks and add it to the list of such loans.

C. Administration of the Bank's lending activity shall be supervised by the Chief Executive Officer (CEO) of the Bank (who shall be appointed by the Board of Directors), who shall follow the policies set forth herein. The CEO shall seek the advice and counsel of the Board of Directors when in doubt as to credit decisions or questions involving the interpretation or application of loan policies. The CEO shall be responsible for the development and administration of procedures to implement this policy. Such procedures shall be communicated clearly to members of the Officers Loan Committee in writing, forming a procedures manual, which shall be used as a supplement to implement the requirements of this policy.

III. LENDING AUTHORITIES

A. Although ultimate authority for all lending activities is vested in the Board of Directors, the Board hereby delegates the administration of these responsibilities to the Officers Loan Committee and further delegates responsibilities for execution of the lending policy to loan officers by the establishment of lending authorities.

— A loan authority is the amount that an individual officer may extend to any one obligor and it shall include all direct loans, unfunded commitments, overdrafts, liabilities under letters of credit, and contingent liabilities that may be described as "all direct and indirect liabilities."

— Specifically excepted from this delegation of responsibility are all loans or credits to insiders or their interests (defined as executive officers, directors, principal shareholders, or any of their interests) where the amount of credit extended by the Bank to such insider or interest would result in an aggregate loan or commitment exceeding $25,000. Such extensions of credit to insiders or their interests are covered specifically in Section IX of this policy. Pursuant to the Board's right to delegate authority, lending limits are delegated as follows:

1. Chief Executive Officer—legal lending limit of the Bank

2. Officers Loan Committee (acting as a committee)—legal lending limit of the Bank

3. Credit approval authority for individual officers may be designated by the CEO up to $75,000. Such designations must be reported to the Board of Directors in writing at its next regularly scheduled meeting. In addition, any new consumer whose aggregate loan amount is $50,000 or more must have the approval of a quorum of the Officers Loan Committee.

4. Lending officers may not combine their lending authority with that of another lending officer. A lending officer who does not have sufficient authority to approve a loan must seek the additional approval of an officer with sufficient authority or refer the loan to the Officers Loan Committee.

5. All loans requested as part of the Bank's CRA programs for minorities and loans being made in low- to moderate-income census tracts as defined by the CRA map may be approved in the normal lending process. Such loans shall be reported to the Officers Loan Committee at its next regularly scheduled meeting. All such loans that are being declined must first be reviewed by the Officers Loan Committee and, if requested, by the Executive Committee before a final decision is made.

B. One of the purposes of this policy is to provide a privilege of responsibilities under which each officer with lending authority may operate in the performance of his or her function as a lending representative of the Bank. All lending authorities granted herein, to any and all officers, will be accepted as a great responsibility to be exercised wisely. Even though loans are made or committed within the individual loan officer's authority, such authorizations and extensions of credit shall be reviewed by the Officers Loan Committee at its next regularly scheduled meeting.

C. Each officer shall initial all notes evidencing loans approved and administered by such officer. Where the requisite lending authority requires the initials of two officers, the officer primarily responsible for the lending relationship shall initial above the officer joining him or her. No note will be accepted for processing by the Loan Operations division of the Bank unless appropriately initialed.

IV. LENDING AND MARKET AREAS TO BE SERVED

A. One of the goals of the Bank's lending policy is to meet the legitimate credit needs (as may be defined from time to time by the Bank) of the community it serves. Generally, that community includes all the metropolitan City X MSA area and those towns where the Bank's branches are located, as further defined in the Bank's CRA map in the public file.

B. Effective ability to lend in various geographic areas is a function of servicing requirements, credit risks, economies of scale in relation to transaction size, and incremental profitability of the credit transaction. Accordingly, various loan types will have, because of their inherent nature, different constraints.

1. Loans for consumer purposes will be made primarily in the metropolitan City X MSA area and in those political subdivisions where Bank branch offices are located.

2. Real estate loans will be made primarily in the metropolitan City X MSA area and in those political subdivisions where Bank branches are located.

3. Any secured loan (a secured loan is defined as a loan that is fully secured by readily marketable securities, passbooks, or similar deposit products, or cash surrender value of life insurance) that involves primary collateral relied upon as the basis for making a loan may be made outside the normal lending area.

V. PRICING

A. Pricing policy will be formulated by the CEO and coordinated with the Galaxy Bankshares Asset and Liability Committee to ensure that the profitability objectives of both the Bank and Galaxy Bankshares are met in conformity with one another.

VI. BASIS OF CONSUMER LENDING

A. It is expected that the Bank will offer consumer loans of various types to meet the specific needs of communities in its trading area. Unless secured by the equivalent of cash collateral (passbooks, stocks, bonds, certificates of deposit) these loans are to be considered unsecured. Secured consumer loans normally should not exceed terms of 60 months and the collateral requirements are the same as for business lending.

B. Unsecured consumer loans shall be made under normal consumer credit lending practices. A minimum term of 12 months and a minimum amount of $1,000 have been established for installment loans. Requests for terms less than these minimums will be considered under the Bank's Revolving Credit program. Consumer installment loans will comply with the following additional guidelines:

1. Personal loans: Maximum amount—$25,000; maximum term—60 months

2. New automobiles: Maximum amount—90 percent of dealer cost; maximum term—60 months, except that if the amount financed is in excess of $25,000 and is for an "exotic" vehicle, terms of up to 84 months may be offered

3. Used automobiles: Based on model year

    a. Current or immediately previous model year: Maximum amount—80 percent NADA retail value; maximum term—48 months

    b. Models 2, 3, or 4 years old: Maximum amount—100 percent NADA loan value; maximum term—36 months

    c. Models 5 years and older: Maximum amount—100 percent NADA loan value; maximum term—24 months

4. Home improvements (unsecured): Maximum amount—$25,000; maximum term—84 months (amounts or terms in excess of the above must be secured by either a first or second mortgage on the owner-occupied building.)

5. Dealer-originated auto loans: Same requirements as for new and used automobiles on a direct loan

6. Mobile homes

    a. New: Maximum amount—90 percent of cost; maximum term—180 months

    b. Used: Maximum amount—75 percent of cost; maximum term—84 months

7. Recreational vehicles and boats: Same requirements as for new and used automobiles

8. Exceptions or requests not covered must be referred to the Officers Loan Committee for approval.

9. Loans may be made against the cash surrender value of life insurance.

10. Loans may be secured by savings accounts, certificates of deposit in the Bank or other banks, or accounts in federally insured savings and loan associations.

11. Loans to individuals for consumer purposes are considered to be a desirable segment of the Bank's lending activities. These loans are to be made in accordance with generally accepted principles of installment lending. Although the collateral available is an important part of the lending decision, the general principal source of repayment is recognized to be the availability of income flow to repay the loan. Generally, the following criteria are to be met:

a. Positive identification of each applicant is required. An investigation through an outside consumer reporting agency and such other investigation as is deemed necessary should provide a history of satisfactory payments. A review of the Bank's previous credit history with the applicant is required.

b. Both the amount and the source of the applicant's income must be verified and analyzed to assist in the evaluation of ability to repay.

c. Stability is revealed by the nature and tenure of the applicant's employment and occupation and by such personal characteristics as financial reputation, bill-paying habits, and the amount and type of assets accumulated.

d. Willingness to pay shall be determined by past payment records. Any record of significant collection difficulties should be considered a reason to decline the application.

e. In some instances, the loan must be supported by the collateral offered. In those instances, an adequate loan-to-value margin shall be a condition precedent to the granting of the loan.

f. The rights of each applicant must be thoroughly reviewed and all pertinent rules and regulations complied with.

g. Loans of the following types are not considered desirable loans for the purposes of this Bank and will ordinarily be declined unless they are specifically approved as an exception to this policy:

- real estate mortgage loans secured by property out of the Bank's recognized trade area, subject to the exceptions outlined elsewhere

- loans secured by stock in closely held corporations that have no ready market value

- loans for speculative purposes, particularly to enable the consumer to speculate in the futures, securities, or commodities market

- loans secured by unimproved land

C. Revolving Credit is an open-end credit program that may be accessed either by overdrawing a regular checking account in the Bank or through special checks issued to accounts that have no checking account with the Bank. These loans will be made under normal consumer loan lending practices. Credit lines have a minimum amount of $1,000 and a maximum amount of $25,000 in increments of $500.

VII. CONCENTRATION OF CREDIT

A. A diversification of the loan portfolio is practical to the extent that it minimizes risk without adversely affecting sound credit opportunities and the legitimate credit needs of the community. Concentrations of credits to a particular industry and credits supported by the same or similar types of collateral (including, but not limited to, real estate within a small geographic area and a large percentage of the dealer automobile loan portfolio of one dealer) shall be reviewed by the CEO. Our objective will be to structure the Bank's loan portfolio as follows:

- Installment and consumer loans—30%

- Commercial loans—40%

- Agricultural loans—10%

- Real estate loans—20%

B. Concentrations of credit are defined as obligations, direct or indirect, of the same or affiliated interests that represent 25 percent or more of the Bank's total equity, capital, and reserves. The Board of Directors will review these concentrations of credit at least annually.

VIII. FINANCIAL GUIDELINES

A. In the interest of sound and prudent banking practices and to ensure adequate liquidity and appropriate profitability, the CEO shall recommend loan portfolio policy guidelines to the Board of Directors and be responsible for the administration thereof. Included in such recommendations will be the relationship of risk-based assets and commitments to capital as defined by the Federal Reserve Board (8 percent is the acceptable minimum); loans as a percentage of deposits (generally not to exceed 70 percent); and loans that have been rated by any regulatory authority to contain more than normal risk (generally not to exceed 20 percent of capital).

B. These recommendations shall be communicated to the Galaxy Bankshares Asset and Liability Management Committee to ensure that they are consistent at all times with the goals and objectives of that committee.

IX. INSIDER TRANSACTIONS

A. It is the policy of the Bank to encourage extensions of credit to its officers and directors or their interests provided that such extensions conform to this policy. Officers and directors shall conduct their business affairs with such standards of integrity that no conflict of interest exists or could reasonably be construed to exist. Each officer and director must be alert to the potential for conflicts of interest where personal profit or gain might arise from relationships with consumers that might tend to interfere with the exercise of independent judgment in the handling of business for the Bank.

X. LOAN REVIEW

A. The loan review officers are responsible for reviewing the credit risk inherent in the lending activities of the Bank. The Loan Review Department of Galaxy Bankshares shall be relied upon for advice as needed. Any policies set forth by the Loan Review Department of Galaxy Bankshares shall be carried out by the loan officers. Any reviews made by Galaxy Bankshares of the Loan Department will be furnished to the Board of Directors, with copies made available to the CEO.

B. A loan review shall be conducted on a continuing basis for all loans made by the originating officer. Generally it is the policy of the Bank that the originating officer shall be responsible for collecting all loans originated by him or her and shall follow such loans after they have been charged-off until all reasonable efforts at recovery have been exhausted. The CEO may assign additional officers to assist in collection activities as may be necessary.

C. Loans previously charged off shall be reviewed within the Loan Department continuously and by the Officers Loan Committee every six months until there is no longer any possibility of recovery.

XI. COMPLIANCE

A. The Compliance Officer of the Bank will review and ensure the adequacy of compliance by the Bank with all laws and regulations relative to lending, extension of credit, and all other pertinent compliance areas. The Compliance Officer shall be appointed annually by the Board of Directors.

B. The Compliance Officer shall draw up a Compliance Plan to be approved by the Bank's Board of Directors. Administration of the plan shall be the responsibility of the Compliance Officer, who shall report on the status of those responsibilities at least annually to the Board of Directors.

XII. EXCEPTIONS TO POLICY

A. In appropriately meeting the legitimate business needs of the community, there will be loan requests received which, if granted, would represent exceptions, in whole or in part, to this policy. It is recognized that some of these exceptions will be warranted. The system of organization and responsibilities herein established provides for the approval of such exceptions.

B. Each exception must be specifically recognized as an exception to policy and be specifically reviewed and approved by the appropriate committee.

C. It is the responsibility of the loan officer to recognize, document, justify, and advocate for those exceptions that he or she feels are warranted to properly meet the legitimate credit needs of the community within the framework of sound and prudent banking.

XIII. CONSUMER PRIVACY POLICY

A. Whereas Galaxy Bank recognizes its customers' expectations of financial privacy, and whereas preserving our customers' trust is one of the core values of the Bank and the broader banking community, we therefore resolve to abide by the following guidelines for the responsible use and protection of our customers' information:

1. We will always value the trust of our customers and the importance of keeping their personal financial information confidential.

2. We will provide our customers with our policy on using their personal financial information responsibly and protecting it.

3. We will hold our employees to the highest standard of conduct in ensuring the confidentiality of customer information.

4. We will hold any personal medical information about our customers sacred and will NOT use it for marketing purposes or in making credit decisions.

5. We will use information responsibly in order to provide our customers with significant benefits, including fraud prevention and improved products and services, and to comply with laws.

6. We will establish procedures to maintain accurate information and respond in a timely manner to our customers' requests to change or correct information.

7. We will use a combination of safeguards to protect our customers against the criminal use of their confidential information and to prevent unauthorized access to it.

8. We will offer our customers the option of restricting information shared with third parties for marketing purposes and will honor their preferences.

9. We will require the companies we do business with to abide by our privacy policy to maintain the confidentiality of our customers' information.

10. We will not provide account numbers to companies outside our family of companies for marketing purposes.

Generating Loan Applications

7

Learning Objectives _____

After completing this chapter, you should be able to

- explain the five primary objectives of the loan application process
- discuss how banks generate applications for direct lending, indirect lending, and open-end credit products
- describe the elements of effective consumer loan marketing programs
- discuss considerations involved in taking loan applications in person
- review telemarketing, direct mail, and electronic application options
- explain the provisions of the Truth in Lending Act, the Real Estate Settlement Procedures Act, FTC and FCC rules on telemarketing, and the CAN-SPAM Act that relate to marketing and disclosures
- define the terms that appear in bold type in the text

Introduction

"If you make a product good enough, even though you live in the depths of the forest the public will make a path to your door, says the philosopher. But if you want the public in sufficient numbers, you would better construct a highway." So said William Randolph Hearst (1863–1951), an American newspaper publisher. This statement applies to most business efforts, including banking in general and consumer lending in particular.

Banks that have "good enough" products and desire "the public in sufficient numbers" continually seek ways to communicate effectively their product offerings to consumers. As businesses with an eye to the future, they want to generate applications for their loan products in volumes that build loan portfolios, reach bank asset and liability management goals, serve their communities well, and ultimately keep the nation's economy growing. To that end, the upfront efforts of marketing and application generation are very important steps in the consumer lending process.

THE CONSUMER LENDING PROCESS

The consumer lending process comprises a series of logical steps that begins with generating **applications** and continues with credit investigation, evaluation and decision making, loan structuring, documentation and booking, and finally account servicing until the loan is paid off (see exhibit 7.1). Sometimes, when an application is declined after the credit investigation reveals the applicant to be a poor risk, the loan process ends there. Other times, the application proceeds through the investigative, **underwriting**, and approval stages. The loan is then booked on the loan system, and the consumer may be cross-sold other retail banking services.

The consumer loan application process may vary for different loan products and delivery channels. As consumer loans become a major component of a bank's mix of assets, generating applications from a wide variety of sources is important, if not critical, to the bank's success. Effective marketing is essential for the bank to generate a sufficient number of consumer loan applications.

APPLICATION PROCESS OBJECTIVES

The bank's consumer loan application process has five primary objectives: to generate a flow of applications, to obtain enough information for a decision, to ensure compliance with the law, to ensure a prompt response to the consumer's request, and to earn applicant goodwill.

application—An oral or written request for an extension of credit that is made according to the procedures established by a lender for the type of credit requested.

underwrite—To analyze credit quality and determine whether the bank should assume the risk of making a loan. The term also is used in the insurance and securities industries.

Exhibit 7.1   The Lending Process

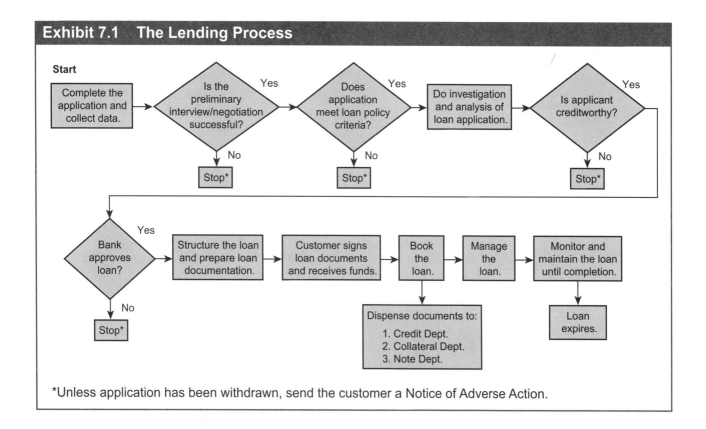

*Unless application has been withdrawn, send the customer a Notice of Adverse Action.

GENERATE APPLICATIONS

The first challenge is to generate applications. Without an adequate number of qualified applications, the bank will not make enough loans to meet its objectives for loans outstanding, volume, portfolio diversification, asset quantity and quality, and profitability.

The bank must attract qualified applicants who will meet its underwriting standards and can be approved for a loan. Bankers face a dilemma that is not common to other businesses—they must promote their product and then refuse to sell it to some customers. Imagine a hardware store that advertises lawn mowers but refuses to sell them to consumers who have very small lawns!

GET INFORMATION FOR A DECISION

When a consumer requests a loan, the bank must obtain sufficient information to make a sound loan decision. This process starts with the loan application. The bank will need to obtain certain types of information about the applicant. The type and amount of information requested depends on many variables, such as the amount of the loan request, whether or not the loan will be secured, and the loan's risk to the bank. Bank policy normally dictates the types of applicant information required for different types of loans and loan terms.

That is why the extent of the information requested on loan applications varies. Consumers who receive preapproved credit-card applications may take only a few minutes to complete the application. A closed-end loan application generally requires more information.

Objectives of the application process are to

- generate a flow of applications
- obtain information for a decision
- ensure compliance with the law
- ensure a prompt response to consumer requests
- obtain applicant's goodwill

ENSURE COMPLIANCE WITH THE LAW

Laws and implementing regulations address the loan request and requirements for loan applications in detail, including the types of information that cannot be solicited. Banks must ensure that the application generation process complies with federal laws, such as the following:

Equal Credit Opportunity Act (ECOA), FRS Regulation B	Restricts the types of information that may be asked during the loan application process. It also defines an application and thereby determines when an application is made.
Truth in Lending Act (TILA), FRS Regulation Z	Mandates the type of disclosures lenders must make in advertisements as well as at the time a loan application is taken. Helps consumers compare credit offers by requiring that credit information be presented uniformly.
Real Estate Settlement Procedures Act (RESPA), HUD Regulation X	Requires application disclosures on the settlement process and costs associated with it, which are required for certain loans secured by residential real estate. Early disclosures must accurately reflect closing costs or, in certain cases, the bank must reimburse the borrower.
Community Reinvestment Act (CRA), FRS Regulation BB	Assesses the extent to which the bank addresses the credit needs of consumers residing in its primary market area, including low- and moderate-income borrowers.
Home Mortgage Disclosure Act (HMDA), FRS Regulation B	Requires mortgage lenders to report certain information to help regulators evaluate whether a bank is complying with fair lending laws and the CRA.

RESPOND PROMPTLY

The bank's application process must meet consumer expectations and need for a timely decision. Although different products have different timing requirements, the guiding principle should be to reach a decision and to communicate it as rapidly as possible. Today, technology makes it possible to render many decisions within minutes of the bank receiving completed applications. Timely decisions help convert applications into loans. Delayed decisions may result in good applications being lost to competitors.

Quick turnaround is an excellent marketing tool. Consumers may be more interested in applying for a loan at a bank that makes decisions quickly than at another bank whose lengthy underwriting procedure slows its responsiveness.

Earn Applicant Goodwill

The final objective of the application process is to cultivate the consumer's goodwill. The programs used to generate applications must attract potential borrowers by offering something of value. They also must create interest in the bank's products and motivate consumers to respond.

As part of its effort to foster consumer goodwill, the bank should make the application process as convenient and pleasant as possible. Banks that take applications over the telephone or over the Internet, for example, offer greater convenience for their customers than those that require the applicant to go to a branch to apply.

Banks must work with applicants in a way that builds customer goodwill and loyalty. This is true at every stage of the loan process, but especially during the loan interview, loan selling, and loan structuring stages.

LOAN PRODUCT CONSIDERATIONS

The bank's efforts to attract loan applications will be different for each type of consumer loan product offered. Marketing strategies will differ for loans generated through direct lending, indirect lending, and open-end product delivery channels.

Direct Lending

Banks try to attract customers to their direct lending programs in creative ways. Generating applications for direct lending primarily depends on having enough branch locations with convenient hours, as well as having alternate delivery systems. Direct lending itself depends on personal relationships with customers. Bankers must understand their customers' needs and objectives and give them the products and services that best meet them.

Finally, generating direct lending applications demands an active process. It is not enough to sit back and wait for loan applicants to walk into the branch. In the most effective lending programs, bankers actively pursue applicants. The fundamentals for building a direct lending portfolio are

- establishing the bank's image and market share in the community
- building a consumer franchise, starting with current bank customers
- communicating to customers that the bank has a robust lending program
- actively seeking consumer loan applicants
- offering competitive rates, terms, and products
- maintaining sound and efficient systems for processing applications
- training staff in product knowledge, customer service, and sales techniques

> ## *Situation*
>
> Nina wants to purchase a used auto from a neighbor. She must come up with the money quickly or the neighbor will sell it to someone else. She immediately calls several banks in her area. One requires her to come to the bank during business hours, complete an application, and wait three days for a response. At a second, she can apply at a loan terminal in the bank lobby and have her response in 24 hours. The third bank directs Nina to its Web site, where she can submit an application online this evening from her home computer and get her response in the morning at the latest.
>
> *At which bank is Nina likely to choose to apply for her loan? Why?*

As illustrated in exhibit 7.2, applications for some consumer loans may be drawn from other sources in addition to the bank's customer base.

Turning Rate Shoppers into Customers

Sometimes bankers miss an opportunity to solicit a loan application when quoting interest rates. It can be a mistake to answer a rate inquiry simply by quoting the annual percentage rate (APR). Often a caller would respond to help from the banker with the loan application process. By using the opportunity to turn an interest rate inquiry into an application, the banker provides real value and worth to the consumer, and the banker can forge a relationship and make the applicant a loyal customer.

Bankers should be cautious, however. A conversation with a potential applicant may result in a denied application if the consumer provides enough information to allow the bank to make a loan decision. When an oral application is made and then denied by the bank, the Equal Credit Opportunity Act requires the bank to send the consumer a Notice of Adverse Action.

INDIRECT LENDING

Strategies for attracting indirect lending applications differ from those for direct lending. The key to generating indirect lending applications is a strong dealer network. Except for building their relationships with dealers, lenders cannot do much to stimulate the generation of indirect applications because they have no direct contact with applicants. The dealer represents the lender in these transactions. Banks may encourage applications for indirect lending by offering dealers competitive interest rates and quick loan decisions. Once the indirect lending applicant becomes a customer, the lender has the opportunity to broaden the banking relationship by anticipating the customer's banking needs and marketing products that meet those needs.

Exhibit 7.2   Loan Application Sources

TYPE OF LOAN	POSSIBLE APPLICATION SOURCES
Home equity loans	Home improvement contractors, accountants, home shows, and loan brokers
Other personal loans	Referrals from trust and commercial officers, attorneys, and accountants
Marine and recreational vehicle (RV) loans	Marine dealers, RV dealers, sport and vacation shows, boat and RV shows
Education loans	College fairs, financial aid personnel, government guarantee agencies
Most loans	Automated systems, Web sites, telephone call centers, faxes, and employee referrals

---

OPEN-END LOAN PRODUCTS

Applications for open-end loan products are generated in many of the same ways as those for direct lending, but they also can be obtained from a larger market area. Marketing strategies for open-end credit products, such as credit cards and home equity lines of credit (HELOCs), include the branch network, but they also include direct mail and the Internet, with follow-up calls or e-mail as permitted to maximize response.

In generating open-end applications, it is important for lenders to recognize when such a credit product may be useful to a customer. As exhibit 7.3 demonstrates, there are many opportunities for cross-selling open-end credit products.

MARKETING PROGRAMS

Banks whose marketing programs are effective can generate applications even in a saturated market. Sophisticated marketing programs, based on an understanding of market segments and consumer purchasing behaviors, focus on consumer wants, needs, and preferences. By harnessing the power of information technology and statistical analysis, marketers can help lenders to offer attractive loan products for selected market segments and then create effective promotion programs to reach those consumers.

Successful marketing programs define objectives, select target markets, select promotion channels, implement the plan, and measure the results.

Did You Know ...

The Pareto principle was named after economist Vilfredo Federico Damaso Pareto (1848–1923). It specifies an unequal relationship between inputs and outputs: In many situations, 20% of invested input is responsible for 80% of the results obtained, and 80% of consequences stem from 20% of causes. This also is referred to as the "80/20 rule."

Exhibit 7.3   Open-end Credit Product and Application Sources

PRODUCT	APPLICANT SOURCES
Check overdraft line of credit	Current checking account customers
	Consumers opening new checking accounts
	Customers who have overdrawn their accounts
Home equity line of credit	Consumers applying for any type of loan who own or are buying their home, have equity to qualify, and may have future borrowing needs; loan brokers; and home improvement contractors
Credit cards	Any consumer likely to meet minimum requirements
Unsecured line of credit	Established consumers in targeted market segments, such as doctors, lawyers, and other professionals
Secured line of credit	Consumers with other assets to pledge (stocks, bonds, or savings) who are considering a large purchase
Most lines of credit	Automated systems, Web sites, telephone call centers, faxes, and employee referrals

---

In designing a marketing plan, banks

- define objectives
- select target markets
- select promotion channels
- implement the plan
- measure results

DEFINE OBJECTIVES

Clear objectives are essential for a quality marketing program. They will set the tone and give direction to the marketing effort. Using a marketing program for a HELOC, the following illustrates how objectives are defined.

Product to be promoted	Anytown Bank's Home Equity Line of Credit
Number of applications, loans, and dollar volume to be generated	• Generate 1,000 loan applications April through June. • Book 600 new customers. • Achieve $19.2 million in new credit lines. • Achieve $9.6 million in loans outstanding.
Portfolio profitability	Achieve a 2.15 percent return on assets.
Quantifiable loan quality goals	Maintain a 0.5 percent portfolio delinquency rate.

SELECT TARGET MARKETS

A bank begins the process of selecting its target markets by defining its niche in the marketplace. Once the bank understands what it does best and which related products it will offer, it can select the groups of consumers to target.

Market Segmentation

market segmentation— The process of dividing the market into relatively homogeneous groups to more effectively market products and services.

Sophisticated **market segmentation** strategies are used to identify specific consumer segments to which certain loan types may be marketed successfully. Markets may be segmented in a number of different ways. The five principal alternatives are geographic, demographic, psychographic, volume, and benefit.

Geographic segmentation	Divides the market according to geographic units. A bank may decide, for example, to market low-limit credit cards to a marketplace with a college and a large concentration of adults in their twenties
Demographic segmentation	Categorizes the market in terms of population characteristics, such as age, sex, income, occupation, and position in the life cycle. A bank that markets a HELOC aimed at homeowners with incomes of $35,000 or more is targeting a specific demographic segment.
Psychographic segmentation	Classifies the market in behavioral terms according to lifestyle, social class, or personality profile. A bank may identify the "fast-track young professional" as a prime market segment for credit card sales.

Volume segmentation	Distinguishes heavy, medium, and light users of a product. Using the Pareto principle (80 percent of the profits are generated by 20 percent of the customers), banks determine the common characteristics of customers in the 20 percent group and then focus marketing efforts toward attracting more like them.
Benefit segmentation	Categorizes the market in terms of the product-related benefits different groups seek. One bank may base its approach on convenience and fair value; another may be distinguished by an approach based on high levels of service and personal assistance.

Market segmentation and other tools have improved greatly. Banks now target advertising to market segments through a variety of promotion channels.

Marketing Customer Information File (MCIF)

Often, prime prospect lists identified through market segmentation can be narrowed further by using sophisticated tools, such as a **marketing customer information file (MCIF)**. The MCIF is a system for organizing and sorting information. As a data bank, the MCIF contains information that is generated both internally, such as account information from the bank's customer information system (CIS), and externally, such as geocoding and psychographic information.

Banks use the MCIF for a process called **data mining**. The market researcher will analyze information in the MCIF to create profiles of the bank's entire customer base. The same profiles would be used to get lists of prospects from the marketplace, such as those obtained from consumer reporting agencies.

For example, a bank on a quest to generate HELOC applications might select the target market using the following process:

Analyze current users of the product.	Determine their age, income, geographic location, and credit characteristics. Home ownership is clearly a prerequisite.
Correlate characteristics with demand.	Those characteristics may include older neighborhoods (geographic), families with college-age children (demographic), or midlife consumers who use credit for life-style enhancements (psychographic).

The bank may find that its current home equity customers are concentrated in the 30- to 55-year-old age group, have household incomes of $80,000 or more, and have owned their homes for five or more years.

marketing customer information file (MCIF)—An internal bank database containing detailed demographic information about customers and prospects.

data mining—Using specialized software to locate patterns and relationships within a database, such as locating customers with common interests.

Once the target market is identified, the bank searches its MCIF for prospects, buys a list of customers meeting its criteria from a consumer reporting agency, and starts a marketing promotion. Branch lenders may have access to this information online so that they can produce lists of customers for direct mail, telephone solicitations, and other promotional strategies for their own markets.

SELECT PROMOTION CHANNELS

In addition to advertising in the media, such as television, radio, billboards, and posters, banks have other promotional options, among them direct mail, telemarketing, e-mail marketing and text messaging, bank Internet Web sites, banker incentives, and consumer incentives, such as special offers. Many banks now advertise electronically by placing banner lines and tag lines on Web sites. ATMs also offer advertising opportunities.

Banks evaluate the **promotion channels** they use to judge their effectiveness. The results of previous marketing programs, and the goals and costs of the proposed plan, are among the factors considered in the selection of a promotion channel.

Direct Mail

Direct mail has been used heavily to promote credit card and line-of-credit products. Credit card and unsecured line-of-credit products can be offered to a broader consumer market than products closely tied to a branch distribution system. Open-end credit products therefore benefit from direct mail campaigns. These marketing campaigns are highly refined and targeted to control costs and optimize response rates. (Banks screen their lists against internal Do-Not-Mail lists first.) To promote their services, banks also use such direct mail sales materials as statement stuffers sent with customer account statements.

Preapproved credit offers are a direct mail promotion technique. Individuals whose names have been prescreened against consumer reporting agency files are sent preapproved credit offers. The bank commits to extending a specified amount of credit upon receipt of a properly executed "acceptance agreement." The consumer need only sign the acceptance form; furnish some basic information, such as current employer, income, and address verification; and return the agreement to the bank to open the account. Preapproved credit offers are used mostly for credit cards and generally draw high response rates. It is common for consumers to receive preapproved credit offers from a variety of sources as often as monthly or even weekly.

Telemarketing

Banks have used proactive telephone sales to generate a wide range of retail business. Working from targeted prospect lists and a flexible sales script, telemarketing sales representatives extend credit offers on a range of products.

Telephone calls often are used to follow up on a direct mail program to increase sales. Coordinated telemarketing calls to the list of customers receiving a direct mail piece can increase the response rate dramatically. However, marketers

promotion channel— A method a bank uses to communicate with consumers, such as advertising, direct mail, and direct selling.

Did You Know ...

The six top promotion channels for banks are
- cross-selling within the bank
- community newspaper advertisements
- direct mail
- brochures [take one]
- employee incentives
- the Internet

must ensure that the lists have been compared to the national and state do-not-call lists and internal do-not-call and do-not-mail lists.

Branches and bank call centers may use telemarketing to attract loan applications from current and former customers. Call center activity may be reactive or proactive. Reactive call centers respond to customer contacts, such as inquiries. Proactive call centers initiate the contact with the bank's customer or prospect. Done in a professional manner, a telemarketing call may be received by the consumer as if from the bank. A script or discussion guide helps the telemarketer become comfortable with the call's purpose and ensures that the customer is presented with all relevant information.

Sometimes simply calling good customers and asking if they could use help with a current borrowing need, or reminding them to think of the bank if they have a need in the future, may generate applications. Well-handled calls also produce goodwill for the bank.

E-mail Marketing and Text Messaging

E-mail has many benefits. It is timely: messages are created and distributed quickly. It is content-rich: messages can include graphics. It is shared: messages can be passed along to many other people. It is targeted: it can be sent to specific market segments.

Although potentially effective, the proliferation of e-mail **spam** has caused many consumers to ignore e-mail marketing messages. However, laws like the CAN-SPAM law are clearing e-mail as a channel of communication for legitimate marketing. It is important that a bank conduct e-mail marketing in a manner that both complies with the law and is effective.

Text messaging has become the communication of choice for younger consumers. Banks use text messaging for many types of communication with their customers, including information about loan products.

The Internet

A bank's Web site provides a public window to the bank, its corporate mission, and its community service focus as well as its products and services. The majority of banks offer Internet banking services through their Web sites. Customers may use Internet banking to get information about their accounts or use the bank's bill payment service. With check imaging, customers can see actual images of checks that have cleared their account.

Banks also use the Internet to promote new products. Banners on other Web sites, such as search engines, serve as links back to bank product promotion Web sites. With more people accessing the Internet and online banking, the Internet is now an ideal platform to promote products, communicate with consumers, and generate applications. Its use as a promotion channel likely will increase.

Situation

The Kangs moved into their new home five years ago. Not wanting to wait to furnish the house, they financed their furniture purchases with credit cards and personal loans. They thought they could handle the payments but miscalculated how much the interest charges would be over time. Just when they were wondering what options were available to them, they received a phone call from the bank that holds their mortgage. The pleasant voice on the other end described a home equity line of credit with no closing costs and a much lower interest rate than they are paying on their credit cards.

How did this banker know they were looking for a new plan?

---

spam—Unwanted e-mail messages, intended to sell something, that clog e-mail inboxes.

Banker Incentives

Promotion strategies are designed to motivate lenders to sell loans and consumers to apply for them. Incentive programs often are used to motivate bank staff, who may receive cash or other awards for each application taken or for meeting branch consumer loan objectives. Including consumer loan objectives in the evaluation and reward systems for branch bankers emphasizes the importance of loan products.

By providing incentives to attract loan applications that meet quality standards, such as delinquency and loss minimization, banks can enhance the volume and quality of their loan portfolios.

Consumer Incentive Programs

Another strategy for generating applications is through special offers and incentives for consumers. For example, banks may

- advertise special loan programs, with lower rates during peak borrowing months
- offer special rates and terms at consumer-oriented trade shows, such as boat, RV, auto, and home shows
- offer closing-cost rebates on HELOCs
- waive credit card fees for the first year
- offer incentives to transfer balances from current credit cards
- allow one month when no payment is due (a payment "holiday")
- guarantee replacement of lost or stolen merchandise purchased with a credit card
- offer reduced pricing on packages of services

Consumers are exposed daily to advertising messages. To be successful, the bank's marketing program has to stand out by reaching the right people, carrying the right incentives, and being presented in a way that motivates consumers to act. The most successful programs target different offers to different market segments.

IMPLEMENT THE PLAN

A product promotion should be planned thoroughly, and the bank must be able to effectively handle the response generated. Although a promotion may generate a high volume of applications, it will fail if the bank cannot handle the response efficiently. All appropriate personnel in the bank must be aware of the promotion before consumers start responding. Once the promotion is designed, all bank employees who work in areas related to the promotion should be fully trained on the products being promoted. Promotions should be staggered and contingency plans drafted to handle marketing successes.

MEASURE RESULTS

Measuring the results of marketing programs determines the effectiveness of the materials, the targeted mailing lists, the product offering, and the timing. Only by measuring the results of a promotion can banks improve future promotions. Success is measured against the objectives established for the promotion at the beginning. In the home equity line-of-credit example, the bank would determine

- how many loan applications were actually generated from April through June
- how many new loans were booked
- loans outstanding
- portfolio delinquency rate
- net interest margin
- income from add-on services

These results would be judged against the objectives. Successful marketing programs will generate enough new applications to meet loan objectives and still maintain the quality of the loan portfolio. It is important to meet these goals at the lowest possible cost if the bank is to maximize its profit.

TAKING APPLICATIONS

Applications are received in four ways: in person, by telephone, electronically by fax or the Internet, and by mail. In-person and telephone applications involve personal contact between consumer and banker; mail-in and electronic applications initially do not.

IN-PERSON APPLICATIONS

Many lenders prefer to take applications face-to-face because they believe that gives them the best opportunity to obtain the information needed for both the underwriting decision and the bank's customer identification program. The lender can ensure that all necessary information has been entered on the application and that identification documentation is reviewed and recorded. The lender also has the opportunity to understand the consumer's financial situation. Follow-up questions can be asked to elicit information not covered on the application.

To be effective in a face-to-face interview, the lender must be well prepared and knowledgeable. All loan interviewers should

- understand the parts of the loan application form
- know the regulations governing loan interviews
- know the bank's direct lending policies

Techniques for Taking In-Person Applications

- Smile and greet the customer.
- Use the customer's full name.
- Set the customer at ease.
- Create a comfortable environment.
- Use a conversational approach.
- Use both open-end and closed-end questions.
- Practice active listening.
- Close the interview politely.

- exercise discretion when dealing with the applicant
- know the complete lending operation, including collection procedures

Techniques the lender can use to make the in-person loan application process successful for both consumer and lender are smiling and greeting the customer, using the customer's name, setting the customer at ease, creating a comfortable environment, using a conversational approach, using both open-end and closed-end questions, practicing active listening, and closing the interview politely.

Smile and Greet the Customer

A smile projects many things to people—friendliness, warmth, confidence, and caring. A smile helps convey a good first impression not only of the lender but also of the bank. This is as important for loan interviewers as it is for tellers and other bank sales representatives.

Use the Customer's Name

Calling the customer by name is a personal touch, but it should be at the proper level of formality for the situation. Although some customers want to be called by their given name, their title and surname should be used at the outset.

Set the Customer at Ease

Some general conversation is helpful in putting the applicant at ease before beginning the more formal application steps. Empathy with the applicant during the loan interview also is important. It is up to the interviewer to establish a relaxed, positive approach and to soothe any anxieties the applicant may have.

Situation

Dora Blanca, who is 22, applied for her first loan to cover the cost of college. She was very nervous about meeting with the loan officer, Ms. Johnson. When Ms. Johnson came out to the lobby to greet Dora, she smiled and shook Dora's hand. Ms. Johnson's small talk about the weather on the way to her office helped put Dora at ease, and she welcomed the offer of a cup of coffee. She also was flattered that Ms. Johnson called her "Ms. Blanca." It made her feel respected. Dora soon relaxed as the interview became more like a conversation with a friend than a trip to the principal's office.

Why is Dora's experience no longer a unique customer experience? What did Ms. Johnson do to encourage the relationship with Dora?

Create a Comfortable Environment

Applications are best taken in a setting that gives the customer privacy to discuss nonpublic personal information. The customer being asked personal questions may be understandably reluctant to share information that might be overheard. Privacy requires a reasonable space, appropriate voice levels, and projection of respect for confidentiality.

Use a Conversational Approach

Once the loan interview begins, a conversational approach usually is the most effective way to gather enough information to facilitate a sound credit decision and elicit the customer's goodwill. The conversational approach involves asking questions and responding to the customer with consideration and objectivity.

Use Both Open-end and Closed-end Questions

Open-end questions or statements do not limit the way the customer responds. They encourage detailed responses and are appropriate when the lender is trying to understand the customer's financial situation and loan purpose.

Closed-end questions require shorter answers. They are appropriate when the lender is seeking specific information for the application and toward the end of an interview to steer the conversation to other areas.

Practice Active Listening

Listening well is not an inherent skill, but it can be acquired. Tuning in to what the applicant is really saying involves paying close attention and giving responsive feedback.

Close the Interview Politely

The loan officer politely explains the next steps in the lending process, when the decision will be made, and what additional documents may be needed. It is very important to tell customers when they will get a decision—and to keep that commitment.

Treating all customers with equal respect and consideration is very important for business. Doing so facilitates compliance with fair lending laws and encourages customer trust in the bank—a vital component of successful banking. It is important to offer all customers an equal level of assistance with their banking transactions, particularly loan applications. Because new fraud schemes always are emerging and predatory lending scams are in the news, cultivating customer trust is an objective bankers strive for daily. In fact, many banks serve their customers by giving them information on how to protect their accounts and avoid predatory lending scams (see exhibit 7.4).

Sample open-end questions:

"Tell me something about your job."
"What credit experience do you have?"

Sample closed-end questions:

"Where do you work?"
"How long have you worked for that company?"
"Do you have any credit card accounts in your name?"

Exhibit 7.4 Consumer Tips: Avoiding Predatory Lending Scams

- Consult your local banks first when you look for a loan. Local bankers understand your needs as a consumer.
- Be wary of telemarketers or door-to-door salespeople who contact you offering unsolicited bargain loans and claiming that your credit history is no problem. Most legitimate lenders do not do business this way.
- Take time to shop around. Compare interest rates and total costs for loans. High up-front fees and points can cost you more over the long run.
- Get references and check them out.
- Do not act under pressure. Beware of telephone lenders who offer fast approval or guaranteed low-interest loans paid the same day if you will apply over the telephone.
- Ask questions about any fees, terms, and conditions you do not understand.
- Do not sign any loan documents until you have the facts you need—and you understand them. You have the right to know the total cost of the loan, annual percentage rate (APR), amount of monthly payments, and the term, length of time, you have to pay back the loan.
- Avoid "balloon" payments. The monthly payment may be small, but the big balloon—the last payment— could be beyond your means.
- You can change your mind. By law, you can change your mind for any reason within three days of signing a contract when your home is offered as security.
- Ask for help from someone you trust. Have someone who understands loan terms—banker, financial advisor, tax expert, or friend with borrowing experience—review the loan documents to make sure that all is in order.
- Report predatory lenders. If you have been a victim of predatory lending, let others know—you may prevent others from becoming victims, too. Report your experience to your county consumer affairs office or your state Attorney General's office (listed in the government section of your telephone book).

Source: American Bankers Association.

Telephone Applications

Taking applications over the telephone is efficient and effective for both consumer and banker. Telephone applications usually take less time than in-person interviews because much of the general conversation is eliminated. By arranging to call the applicant back after-hours or at a convenient time during the day, bankers can fit the call into the day's schedule—a significant advantage. Many direct banking centers take telephone applications for consumer loans. A centralized lending unit offers efficiency and allows highly trained specialists to handle applications.

Direct Mail Applications

Direct mail applications often are used because they are convenient for consumers. However, because the consumers do not come to the bank, there is less opportunity for the banker to cross-sell products that also may benefit them.

Mail-in applications, which are generally less complex than in-person applications, are used only for certain consumer loan products. Although brevity and simplicity encourage consumers to complete the form, many applications are completed incorrectly or only partially. Banks have different policies about how to handle incomplete applications. Some return them for the additional information; others call the consumer.

The Equal Credit Opportunity Act requires that when the bank receives an incomplete application it either notify the applicant of the items required to complete it or make a decision (approve or deny the application) with the information provided. This law also requires lenders to exercise reasonable diligence to collect information to complete the application.

Electronic Applications

electronic application— An application for a bankservice or product that is completed and sent through a fax machine or over the Internet.

Electronic applications, such as those taken through bank Internet Web sites, are increasing as more consumers become comfortable with using the Internet and with bank security systems.

Banks and nonbank entities alike offer loan options through the Internet. Consumers may apply for automobile financing, mortgages, and other types of loans by providing information online. In return, they get information about loan terms and a quick reply. Loan application availability through the Internet appeals to time-conscious consumers and to lenders who want optimal efficiency. Internet loan applications tend to be relatively brief and easy to complete.

Challenges

Taking loan applications has certain challenges, especially in the areas of competition, establishing the consumer's identity, limiting exposure to fraud, and determining when an inquiry actually becomes an application.

Increased Competition

Access to loan information from many lenders at once has increased competition and made consumers more knowledgeable about their options. Gathering information is faster and more convenient for consumers than visiting or calling individual banks or scanning newspaper ads. The Internet has changed consumer credit markets. Consumers are more price-conscious, less loyal, and better informed.

Nonbank entities are also taking advantage of this trend. Various e-commerce loan companies offer to "shop the world" to find the applicant the best interest rate, selling consumers the convenience of doing the comparison-shopping for them.

Establishing Identity

Because the lender may never meet the applicant, it is all the more important to verify the applicant's identity. However, when the applicant is in a distant location communicating through cyberspace and there is competitive pressure to make loans quickly, establishing identity is more difficult for both consumer and banker.

Loan application fraud is made easier by technology, which allows the applicant to make the application remotely. Banks are taking the initiative, and are required by law, to implement policies, procedures, and security measures to prevent application fraud.

Lenders must be watchful for indicators that the applicants are not using their own identity when applying. The identity theft red flag rules for the Fair Credit Reporting Act require lenders to establish procedures to detect red flags. When taking loan applications the lender should compare identification information against databases like those from consumer reporting agencies to determine whether applicants are in fact who they claim to be. If red flags are detected, the lender should investigate further.

Lenders must provide excellent and timely service, meet bank guidelines for loan quality, comply with the law, and reduce the risk from fraud—all at the same time. This is a daily challenge. Lenders meet these competing objectives by following their bank's loan and compliance policies. By doing so, they are assured that they are adhering to their bank's security measures, the regulations, and the requirements for different loan types. Although doing so does not guarantee full protection, it does reduce risk.

Determining When an Inquiry Is an Application

Customers make inquiries about loan products in order to decide if they should apply. They may simply want general information, such as the bank's interest rate on an automobile loan, or they may pose more complicated questions specific to their situation.

Yet even quoting interest rates properly can be complicated. The Truth in Lending Act (TILA), implemented by FRS Regulation Z, requires that a loan rate be quoted as an annual percentage rate (APR). Banks now provide loan rates as APRs on the rate sheets they

loan application fraud— The attempt by criminals to use loan applications to obtain bank funds dishonestly, such as by using another person's identity.

Situation

Ryan wants to refurbish for his elderly in-laws an apartment that is on top of the garage attached to his home. He has a deposit account at Meadow Lark Bank. One evening, he reviewed the bank's Web site for loan information. Then he decided to check other banks in his community. When he calls Adams Mill Bank, customer service representative Tracy answers the phone. Ryan asks Tracy about the bank's rate on home improvement loans.

What should Tracy do?

distribute as memos or on bank Intranets, with examples where necessary. The following example is a variable rate quoted for a home equity line of credit:

Anytown Bank's Low Home Equity Credit Line: The fully indexed annual percentage rate (APR) on variable rate home equity lines of credit as of 7/15/09 is 5.49 percent. The APR on variable rate lines is determined by adding a margin to an index. For example, if we assume a prime rate index of 5.75 percent and a margin of minus 0.26 percent, the resulting daily periodic rate will be 0.0150411percent, or 5.49 percent APR. The APR on variable rate lines may increase or decrease but is not to exceed 25 percent.

Regulation Z allows the bank to include the interest rate as well as the APR. In addition, if the bank knows that prepaid finance charges, such as loan origination fees or points, will affect the APR, an example of the how the finance charges will increase the rate should be provided with the quote. For example, Anytown Bank charges a 1 percent prepaid finance charge on home equity loans. Currently the interest rate is 5 percent. The banker quoting the rate could say, "Our current interest rate on home equity loans is 5 percent with a 1 percent prepaid finance charge. On a $50,000 loan for 3 years, with a 5 percent interest rate and a 1 percent prepaid fee, the annual percentage rate would be 5.67 percent."

Consumers often shop for a loan and do not want to make a formal application. They may request rate and standard loan terms but also may offer specific information to get an idea if an application would be approved. In such circumstances, bankers should either provide only the general product information and refrain from asking qualifying questions, or encourage the consumer to complete an application. When the consumer is ready to apply, the inquiry becomes an application and the loan interview may begin.

LAWS AND REGULATIONS

Fair lending laws, such as the Equal Credit Opportunity Act (FRS Regulation B) and the Fair Housing Act, and related laws, such as the Americans with Disabilities, Community Reinvestment, and Home Mortgage Disclosure Acts, all relate to the application generation process because they provide consumer protections against discrimination and ensure access to credit in all communities. These laws and related regulations were discussed earlier in this book.

TILA and the Real Estate Settlement Procedures Act (RESPA) apply to disclosures at time of application. In addition to TILA, other laws pertain to the marketing of consumer loans, such as those setting up the National Do Not Call list for telemarketing and the CAN-SPAM Act.

TRUTH IN LENDING ACT

Implemented by FRS Regulation Z, TILA requires certain standard disclosures, uniform terminology, standard computation of costs, and simplified explanations of loan terms in lending documents.

Did You Know ...

Although TILA covers a consumer's loan to purchase a principal dwelling regardless of the amount, it does not cover an automobile loan for $50,000 because the amount is greater than $25,000 and is not secured by real estate.

TILA applies only if the loan involves consumer credit for personal, family, or household purposes. It covers consumer loans for amounts up to $25,000 and all consumer loans secured by real estate regardless of the dollar amount.

The law also requires additional disclosures for high-interest rate and high-fee loans where the consumer's home equity secures the loan. In 2008, the Federal Reserve modified FRS Regulation Z to expand protections for high-cost loans as well as for all loans that are secured by the borrower's principal dwelling. The regulation prohibits certain unfair practices in connection with these loans.

Disclosures

Certain disclosures must be made for open-end loans, including the finance charge and the APR, at the time of application and periodically thereafter, and for closed-end loans at the time of loan consummation.[1] Closed-end credit disclosures place the amount financed and the total of payments in a section called the federal box. In either case, if a loan that is not a purchase money loan is secured by the consumer's principal dwelling, the consumer must receive a notice of the right to rescind the transaction before the loan closing date.

The finance charge for a loan consists of all the charges a customer pays in connection with the loan: interest, points, and loan origination fees, and sometimes service charges, transaction charges, and certain insurance premiums (see exhibit 7.5). Some charges may be calculated into the finance charge even when the lender receives no benefit, such as a brokerage fee for a real estate loan.

Right of rescission

The right of a customer to cancel a legally binding agreement within a specified period, such as three days after a contract is signed. This right is available for consumer credit agreements that give the creditor a security interest in the consumer's primary residence for a purpose other than to purchase the home.

Exhibit 7.5   Sample of Charges Included in the Finance Charge

- Interest, time price differential, and any amount payable under an add-on or discount system of additional charges

- Service, transaction, activity, and carrying charges, including any charge imposed on a transaction account up to where the charge exceeds the amount charged for a similar account without a credit feature

- Points, loan fees, assumption fees, finder's fees, and similar charges

- Appraisal, investigation, and credit report fees

- Premiums or other charges for any guarantee or insurance protecting the creditor against the consumer's default or other credit loss

- Charges imposed on a creditor by another person for purchasing or accepting a consumer's obligation, if the consumer is required to pay the charges in cash, as an addition to the obligation, or as a deduction from the proceeds of the obligation

- Premiums or other charges for credit life, accident, health, or loss-of-income insurance, written in connection with a credit transaction

- Premiums or other charges for insurance against loss of or damage to property, or against liability arising out of the ownership or use of property, written in connection with a credit transaction

- Discounts for the purpose of inducing payment by a means other than the use of credit

- Debt cancellation fees: charges or premiums paid for debt cancellation coverage written in connection with a credit transaction, whether or not the coverage is insurance under the law

Source: Truth in Lending Act, FRS Regulation Z.

TILA requires banks to disclose the APR in both open- and closed-end credit transactions. How to calculate the APR is defined in FRS Regulation Z. Whenever there is a charge besides interest, the APR is greater than the loan's basic interest rate.

Other Closed-End Disclosure Requirements

Banks must make TILA disclosures for closed-end loan products before the loan is consummated. In addition to the disclosures in the federal box, FRS Regulation Z gives the customer the option of receiving a detailed explanation of the items included in the amount financed. The bank must detail the payment schedule, describe the property given as security, and explain late charges that may be applied and whether a penalty will be imposed if the loan is prepaid.

When the loan is not a purchase money loan and is secured by the consumer's principal dwelling and the interest rate or fees are high, FRS Regulation Z requires disclosure of the APR, the payment amount, variable rate information, and the total amount borrowed, including any credit insurance. This disclosure must be provided at least three days before the loan closing date.

triggering term—
A phrase or figure used in advertising that will require regulatory disclosures. For example, the following terms require further disclosure on closed-end credit: payment period, payment amount, down payment amount, and finance charge.

Advertising

TILA requires disclosure in advertising of consumer credit costs in uniform and understandable terms. The content of an advertisement is up to the bank unless it contains **triggering terms** that require further disclosures. Exhibit 7.6 lists triggering terms and the accompanying disclosures that must be made for closed-end and open-end loans.

Exhibit 7.6 Sample Truth in Lending Triggering Terms in Advertisements	
TRIGGERING TERM	**REQUIRED DISCLOSURE**
Closed-end loans	
• number of payments or period of repayment • amount of any payment • amount of any charge included in the finance charge	• terms of repayment, including any balloon payment • the annual percentage rate (APR), and whether it can be increased after loan consummation
• Loan may exceed the fair market value of the .property	• The amount exceeding fair market value may not be tax deductible, and borrower should consult a tax advisor.
Open-end loans	
• annual percentage rate (APR • fees and finance charges • security interest	• any periodic rate expressed as an APR • the maximum APR that may be charged • any loan fee that is a percentage of the credit limit • an estimate of other fees for opening the account
• a promotional rate that is lower than the permanent rate for the loan	• length of time the promotional rate will be in effect and a reasonably current rate charged for the loan
• minimum payments required under the plan	• if the minimum would result in a balloon payment

In 2009, the Federal Reserve added restrictions on the word "fixed" in advertisements describing loan products with rates that may vary. For example, in an advertisement for both variable and nonvariable rate loan products, the term "adjustable rate mortgage," "ARM," or "variable rate mortgage" must be as prominent as the terms "fixed" or "fixed rate mortgage." Whenever the word "fixed" applies to a payment or a rate, there must be a statement, equally prominent and placed nearby, about the period during which the payment is fixed and that the payment will increase after that period.

Here is an example of Anytown Bank's newspaper advertisement:

> Anytown Bank's home equity line of credit allows you to access credit up to $100,000, even if your home is worth less. We offer a promotional rate of 3.5% APR for the first six months. After that time, the rate reverts to our posted rate of the prime rate plus 4% (currently the posted rate is 5.5%). After the end of the promotional period, all rates will be subject to change at any time without notice and may be higher or lower than the rate currently advertised here. Depending on the value of your home, not all interest may be tax-deductible. See your tax advisor for advice on the deductibility of interest. Fees on this plan include a $25 late fee for payments received after the due date, a $30 over-the-limit fee, and a $50 annual fee. Minimum payments of $100 are required on this line of credit. Payment of the minimum payment could result in a balloon payment.

Unfair Practices on Certain Home Loans

In 2008, the Federal Reserve amended Regulation Z to add prohibitions on consumer loans secured by a consumer's principal dwelling and for high-cost or high-fee home loans. These rules apply only to closed-end credit.

For loans secured by a consumer's principal dwelling, lenders are prohibited from coercing or influencing an appraiser. The objective is to prevent artificial inflation of a home's value in order to increase the loan amount. Also, lenders must credit payments on a consumer dwelling loan as of the date received. They may not pyramid late fees on these loans.

If a dwelling-secured loan has high fees or an APR that is higher than the Federal Reserve annual threshold, other restrictions against onerous loan terms apply. For example, high-rate loans cannot have a balloon payment unless the term is more than five years. In general, such loans should not amortize negatively, apply prepayment penalties, or have a demand clause. The lender and assignee may not refinance a high-rate loan within one year after consummation, unless doing so benefits the customer. Lenders must use consumer-favorable rebate methods if the loan is paid off early. Finally, lenders must base the loan decision on the consumer's ability to repay, not the collateral, and then must verify the consumer's income and assets.

Loans where the rate is higher than the average rate, also known as the **average prime offer rate**, are subject to the prepayment penalty restriction and suitability requirements of high-rate loans and have an additional requirement: When these loans are secured by a first lien, the lender must establish an escrow account for taxes and insurance.

Finance charge:
The borrower's cost for a loan in dollars and cents. It includes any charge the consumer pays directly or indirectly, or the creditor imposes directly or indirectly, as an incident to or a condition of the extension of credit.

Annual percentage rate (APR):
A measure of the cost of credit, expressed as a yearly rate, that relates the amount and timing of value received by the consumer to the amount and timing of payments made. It is the interest and other finance charges on a loan expressed as an annual rate.

average prime offer rate—A rate published by the Federal Reserve that represents the average of offer rates for the lowest-risk prime mortgages. It is used to set reporting thresholds for first-lien and subordinate lien loans and to require other lender actions, such as the establishment of escrow accounts.

REAL ESTATE SETTLEMENT PROCEDURES ACT

Enacted in 1974 and amended most recently in 2009, RESPA is implemented by the Department of Housing and Urban Development (HUD Regulation X). RESPA covers loans secured by a lien on residential property on which there is located or will be constructed a one- to four-family residence. Also covered are loans secured by condominiums or mobile homes situated on real property. RESPA applies to first liens and subordinate liens. Similar disclosures for home equity lines of credit are covered under TILA and FRS Regulation Z.

RESPA has numerous requirements for disclosure at the time of application that may include a servicing disclosure statement, settlement costs booklet, **good faith estimate** of settlement costs, and an **affiliated business arrangement** disclosure.[2] At or before loan closing, the customer must be given the HUD-1 or HUD-1A settlement statement. These disclosures are designed to give consumers a better understanding of the costs associated with loan transactions for which their homes are used as collateral.

Servicing Disclosure Statement

The servicing disclosure statement tells the applicant whether the bank plans to sell the loan after the loan closing. The disclosure helps consumers decide whether to continue the application process if they have a personal preference to have a local institution service the loan. This disclosure must be given to the consumer within three days of the bank's receipt of the application if the loan is secured by a first lien.

Settlement Costs Booklet

Published by HUD, the booklet "Buying Your Home: Settlement Costs and Information" describes the settlement process and costs the borrower will pay at closing. For first lien transactions, banks must give consumers the booklet within three business days of receiving the application. It is not required for loans to refinance and loans with subordinate liens for consumer purposes. However, under FRS Regulation Z, HELOC applicants must receive a similar booklet titled "What You Should Know about Home Equity Lines of Credit," published by the Federal Reserve.

Good Faith Estimate of Closing Costs

The good faith estimate must be given to consumers within three business days of the bank's receipt of the application. In 2009, HUD amended Regulation X. All lenders must use HUD's good faith estimate form and they must state the date through which the estimated fees are valid. Most estimated costs must be good for at least 10 days from the time the lender provides the disclosures.

The good faith estimate describes details of the loan, including interest rate, payments, prepayment penalties, and escrow requirements. It also describes by category all settlement costs that will be required at closing and states whether the borrower can choose the service provider or whether the lender will choose

good faith estimate— The disclosure statement provided to an applicant for a mortgage loan within three business days of the application. It describes the proposed loan, the types and amounts of charges payable at the closing of the loan, and the tolerances within which each category of closing costs may change before closing.

affiliated business arrangement—An ownership interest of more than 1 percent in a business connected to a federally regulated mortgage transaction.

or identify one. The good faith estimate also describes settlement costs that may change at closing, those that can change within a 10 percent tolerance, and those that cannot change.

Affiliated Business Arrangement Disclosure

If the bank has a controlling interest in a service provider to which it refers borrowers, it must give the affiliated business arrangement disclosure to the applicant with the good faith estimate. Applicants are not required to use a service provider the bank controls, except for an attorney, consumer reporting agency, or real estate appraiser.

HUD-1 or HUD-1A Settlement Statement

The settlement statement is a document that specifies what each party pays at closing and to whom all sales, loan proceeds, and settlement costs are paid. Every person or entity that receives funds must be listed. The simplified version, HUD-1A, is provided when there is no seller, as with home equity loans. The amended HUD-1 form provides a comparison table where the lender lists the charges from the good faith estimate alongside the updated charges for the HUD-1 form. The borrower may determine whether changes to estimates meet the required tolerances.

Did You Know ...

The 2009 amendment to HUD Regulation X requires that lender-controlled fees, such as points and origination fees, may not change from those disclosed on the good faith estimate except under very limited circumstances. If the fees change, the lender must reimburse the customer for any excess amount.

TELEMARKETING AND CONSUMER PROTECTION

With telemarketing, consumers are sought in their own homes or offices, an approach that raises questions of privacy and full disclosure. As illustrated in exhibit 7.7, these issues have been the subject of rulemaking by both the Federal

Exhibit 7.7	FTC and FCC Telemarketing Rules	
	FEDERAL TRADE COMMISSION (FTC)	**FEDERAL COMMUNICATIONS COMMISSION (FCC)**
Law	Telemarketing and Consumer Abuse Protection Act (TCAPA)	Telephone Consumer Protection Act (TCPA)
Date	1994	1991
Rules	Telemarketing sales rule (TSR) implements TCAPA. Banks are exempt, but it does apply to hired telemarketers.	Applies only to unsolicited advertising through use of the telephone (not e-mail or the Internet). Applies to banks.
Do Not Call Program	National Do Not Call Registry (2003). Consumers register in advance to not receive telemarketing calls. Applies to interstate calls made by certain businesses. Exceptions are charities, political parties, and, technically, banks.	Requires sellers such as banks to keep internal lists of customers who request no solicitation calls. Names must be kept indefinitely. Applies to consumer residential and personal wireless (cell or mobile) numbers only. In 2003, the FCC agreed to joint enforcement of the FTC National Do Not Call Registry. Under the FCC, the Registry's rules apply to banks. FCC covers both interstate and intrastate calls.
Established business relationship exception	Businesses may call customers with whom they have an established relationship for up to 18 months after the end of the relationship.	Banks may call customers with whom they have an established relationship up to 18 months after the end of the relationship. However, if the customer asks to be placed on the bank's internal do not call list, no solicitation calls can be made.

Trade Commission (FTC) and the Federal Communications Commission (FCC). Although the FTC does not have authority to regulate banks directly, it does have authority over third-party telemarketing firms hired by banks. Because the FCC has authority over electronic and telephonic communications, its rules do apply to banks that use these systems.

National Do Not Call Registry

The National Do Not Call Registry, activated in 2003 by amendments to the FTC's Telemarketing Sales Rule, contains the telephone numbers of consumers who do not wish to be disturbed by unwanted phone calls from sellers of products and services. It was immediately successful. The FCC then adopted similar rules and jointly enforces the registry with the FTC.

The Do-Not-Call Rules

A bank conducting a telemarketing promotion is considered a seller under do-not-call rules and must comply with those rules whether it uses its own call center staff or outside telemarketers. Unless an exception applies, such as an established business relationship with the consumer, it is a violation of the do-not-call prohibition to initiate a telemarketing call to a residential or personal wireless (also known as mobile or cell) telephone number listed on the National Do Not Call Registry.

Established Business Relationship

A bank may call a consumer listed on the National Do Not Call Registry with whom it has an **established business relationship**. This is a person who has conducted a financial transaction with the bank within the 18 months immediately preceding the telemarketing call or who has inquired about or applied for a product or service offered by the bank within the 3 months immediately preceding the call.

A bank that does telemarketing only to its own customers is not required to check the National Do-Not-Call Registry. However, the established business relationship usually does not extend to the bank's affiliates. Furthermore, if the customer asks to be placed on the bank's internal do-not-call list, no solicitation calls can be made.

Caller Identification

A bank telemarketing to a consumer, or a telemarketer calling on the bank's behalf, must give the consumer the name of the actual caller, the name of the bank, and a no-charge telephone number to contact the bank.

CAN-SPAM Act

The Controlling the Assault of Non-Solicited Pornography and Marketing Act of 2003 (known as the CAN-SPAM Act) establishes requirements for use of electronic mail to advertise or promote a commercial product or service.

established business relationship—A relationship where the consumer has conducted a financial transaction with a company, such as a bank, within the 18 months immediately preceding a telemarketing call, or the consumer has inquired about, or applied for, a product or service offered by the company within the 3 months immediately preceding a telemarketing call.

E-mail that facilitates a transaction or provides information to a customer in an established business relationship may not contain false or misleading routing information but otherwise is exempt from most CAN-SPAM Act provisions. For example, the restrictions do not apply to e-mail used to complete or confirm a transaction, such as a loan document; nor do the restrictions apply to e-mail used to change the terms or features of an account or loan.

Anti-Spam Requirements

When banks do use commercial e-mail to advertise their products and services, the CAN-SPAM Act

- bans false or misleading header information
- prohibits deceptive subject lines
- requires senders to give recipients an opt-out method
- requires senders to respond to opt-out requests
- requires commercial e-mail to be identified as an advertisement

The CAN-SPAM act also prohibits anti-consumer practices: harvesting e-mail addresses, using dictionary attacks, scripting, relaying, and phishing.

SUMMARY

- Generating applications is normally the first step in a consumer lending process that also involves, among other tasks, credit investigation, loan evaluation and decision making, loan structuring, documentation, booking, and account monitoring. The application process may differ for different products and delivery channels. Effective marketing is essential for generating applications.

- Generating consumer loan applications in an increasingly competitive environment is a major challenge. Lenders must meet the following objectives: generate a flow of consumer loan applications, obtain enough information for a sound credit decision, ensure regulatory compliance, ensure a timely response, and earn the applicant's goodwill.

- In recent years, competition has motivated banks to pursue different product strategies and find new ways of promoting loan products. Strategies will differ for loans generated through direct lending, indirect lending, and open-end product delivery channels. For direct lending the strategy is to: establish the bank's image and market share in the community; build a consumer franchise starting with current bank customers; communicate to customers that the bank has a robust lending program; actively seek consumer loan applicants; offer competitive rates, terms, and products; maintain sound and efficient systems for processing applications;

and train staff in product knowledge, customer service, and sales techniques. For indirect lending, banks must build good dealer relationships and offer competitive interest rates with quick decisions. For open-end products such as credit cards, strategies vary. Banks use all delivery channels and tools, such as preapproved credit offers.

- Successful marketing programs define objectives, select target markets, select promotional channels, implement the promotion, and measure the results. Objectives may be number of applications, loans booked, dollar volume generated, portfolio profitability, a desired loan quality, or all or some combination of these. Using such tools as the Marketing Customer Information File to segment consumer markets by geography, demographics, psychographics, user characteristics (volume), and benefits, bankers fine-tune marketing promotions and communications to reach selected groups.

- Promotion channels used by bankers include general media advertising, such as television, radio, billboards, posters, and Internet banners, and also direct mail, telemarketing, e-mail marketing, bank Web sites, banker incentives, and consumer incentives, such as special offers. Carefully planned promotions ensure that bank staff and systems can support anticipated volume surges. The results of promotions are evaluated so that successes can be repeated and future promotions improved.

- Applications are received in person, over the telephone, through the mail, and through the Internet. Taking applications through alternative channels like the Internet has challenges, such as increased consumer access to competitive information, establishing the consumer's identity, and, as with in-person situations, determining when an inquiry has become an application according to the Equal Credit Opportunity Act.

- Many laws and implementing regulations affect the application generation process. The fair lending laws, such as the Equal Credit Opportunity Act, Fair Housing Act, and Americans with Disabilities Act, protect consumers from discrimination in obtaining credit. Laws such as the Community Reinvestment Act and the Home Mortgage Disclosure Act protect communities' rights of access to credit.

- Other lending laws, such as the Truth in Lending Act (TILA) and the Real Estate Settlement Procedures Act, require certain disclosures to consumers at the time of application. TILA also has rules on disclosures in advertisements as well as requirements and restrictions on high-rate and high-fee dwelling-secured loans. There are other laws that affect marketing efforts, notably those governing the National Do Not Call Registry for telemarketing and the CAN-SPAM Act for e-mail marketing efforts.

END NOTES

[1] Truth in Lending Act disclosures for open-end and variable-rate products are covered in chapter 5.

[2] The Housing and Urban Development forms referenced in the section covering RESPA may be found on the Web sites noted in the additional resources section for this chapter.

SELF-CHECK AND REVIEW

Learning Check

1. What are the five primary objectives of the loan application process? Describe each objective.

2. Does the type of loan and delivery channel have any effect on the effort to generate loans? Discuss in terms of direct lending, indirect lending, and open-end loan products.

3. What are the elements of a consumer loan marketing program? Give examples of how marketing techniques are used to optimize results.

4. What are some techniques that may make the in-person loan application process successful?

5. What advantages do electronic (including the Internet), telephone, and mail-in applications have over traditional in-person applications? What are some challenges for lenders taking loan applications in person and through other channels?

6. What is an established business relationship, and may banks use telemarketing to promote products and services to their own customers?

ADDITIONAL RESOURCES

ABA Bank Compliance Magazine, Washington: American Bankers Association, periodical.

ABA Bank Marketing Magazine, Washington: American Bankers Association, periodical.

ABA Marketing Network, www.aba.com/MarketingNetwork/default.htm.

Advertising and Marketing on the Internet: Rules of the Road, Federal Trade Commission Facts for Businesses, www.ftc.gov/bcp/edu/pubs/business/ecommerce/bus28.shtm.

Affiliated Business Arrangement Disclosure, U.S. Department of Housing and Urban Development, www.hud.gov/offices/hsg/ramh/res/resappd.cfm.

American Bankers Association, **www.aba.com**.

Resources

Authentication in an Internet Banking Environment, a Guidance from the Federal Financial Institutions Examination Council, www.ffiec.gov/pdf/authentication_guidance.pdf.

Buying Your Home: Settlement Costs and Information, U.S. Department of Housing and Urban Development, www.hud.gov/offices/hsg/sfh/res/stcosts.pdf.

Do You Know How to Put Your Identity Back Together Again?, Federal Trade Commission, www.ftc.gov/opa/2006/01/idtquiz.htm.

Dot Com Disclosures, Federal Trade Commission Facts for Businesses, www.ftc.gov/bcp/edu/pubs/business/ecommerce/bus41.pdf.

Federal Communications Commission, www.fcc.gov.

Federal Trade Commission, for consumer information on credit, www.ftc.gov.

Fighting Back Against Identity Theft, Federal Trade Commission, www.ftc.gov/bcp/edu/pubs/consumer/idtheft/idt01.shtm.

Good Faith Estimate, U.S. Department of Housing and Urban Development, www.hud.gov/offices/hsg/ramh/res/gfestimate.pdf.

HUD-1 Settlement Statement, U.S. Department of Housing and Urban Development, www.hud.gov/offices/hsg/ramh/res/hud1.pdf.

HUD-1A, U.S. Department of Housing and Urban Development, www.hud.gov/offices/hsg/ramh/res/hud1-a.pdf.

Interagency Guidelines Establishing Information Security Standards, www.federalreserve.gov/boarddocs/press/bcreg/2005/20051214/attachment.pdf.

Internet Crime Complaint Center, http://www.ic3.gov/default.aspx.

Internet Pirates Are Trying to Steal Your Personal Financial Information. Here's the Good News: You Have the Power to Stop Them, Office of the Comptroller of the Currency, www.occ.gov/Consumer/phishing.htm.

Marketing Financial Services, Washington: American Bankers Association, 2009.

National Fraud Information Center, www.fraud.org.

Putting Your Home on the Loan Line Is Risky Business, www.federalreserve.gov/pubs/riskyhomeloans/default.htm.

Reference Guide to Regulatory Compliance, Washington: American Bankers Association, annual publication.

U.S. Department of Housing and Urban Development, www.hud.gov.

What You Should Know About Home Equity Lines of Credit, Federal Reserve Board, www.federalreserve.gov/pubs/equity/equity_english.htm.

When Internet Scam Artists Go "Phishing," Don't Take the Bait, Federal Deposit Insurance Corporation, www.fdic.gov/consumers/consumer/news/cnwin0304/phishing.html.

Credit Investigation

8

Learning Objectives

After completing this chapter, you should be able to

- describe the objectives of and steps in a credit investigation
- explain the types of information obtained in a credit investigation
- identify credit investigation information sources and warning signs
- explain the Fair Credit Reporting Act and the FACT Act rules that apply to credit investigation
- define the terms that appear in bold type in the text

Introduction

In the country's early days, and even in many rural communities today, men and women gathered at markets to exchange the farm products, crafts, tools, and animals needed to sustain themselves and the community. Often at these marketplaces, sales and loans would be made with oral promises and a handshake. People knew each other, their families, their occupations, and their reputations. The transactions were based on first-hand knowledge and mutual trust.

Today the market is much more complex. Knowing the customer is not so easy. Although handshakes may occur at loan closings, much has transpired beforehand to establish mutual trust, and a legal contract confirms the relationship.

Of all the steps taken in the loan process, credit investigation is one of the most important. It ensures that the loan decision is made with information that is fair and valid for both the consumer and the bank.

CREDIT INVESTIGATION DEFINED

credit investigation— The process of verifying information provided by a loan applicant to determine the applicant's ability to repay a loan.

account monitoring— Analyzing the status and behavior pattern of current loan customers to guide decisions on whether to change or continue credit limits or to terminate lines of credit.

After the application is complete, the **credit investigation** begins. A lender initiates the investigation upon receipt of a loan application or for a risk analysis of an existing account.

Credit investigation practices have changed significantly over the years, driven by improvements in technology and analytical techniques. Closed-end loan applications are investigated as they are received. Prospective open-end credit customers may have their credit history reviewed before they apply through a prescreening process. In other cases, open-end credit applicants may be investigated at the time of application. Borrowers may be investigated periodically during the life of the account, which is a process known as **account monitoring**.

Lenders rely on a variety of direct and indirect sources to verify applicant information, including the bank's own account records, other creditors, consumer reporting agencies, and employers. The extent of the investigation depends on the type of loan requested, the bank's loan policies, and the individual characteristics of each application.

Thorough credit investigations help the bank make sound credit decisions, avoid weak or marginal credit-risk consumers, and limit open-end credit use by applicants who are having financial difficulties. Generally, the greater the risk associated with the loan, the more thorough the investigation.

CREDIT INVESTIGATION OBJECTIVES

The primary objectives of the credit investigation process are to verify the accuracy and completeness of the data supplied on the application; conduct the investigation in an efficient, cost-effective manner; identify negative trends or potential problems that may affect the creditworthiness of a consumer; and acquire enough information to make a sound credit decision.

Verify Application Accuracy and Completeness

The bank's loan policy identifies the information to be verified. Some data are accepted as given by the applicant, but others are too important to the soundness of the loan decision to be left unverified. Exhibit 8.1 lists the types of information that may be in the loan policy, including the kinds of data often accepted as given, data customarily verified by the bank's credit investigators, and data customarily verified through a consumer reporting agency.

Conduct Investigation Efficiently

It is neither necessary nor desirable to verify all data on the application. Experience has shown that most people are honest. The investigator, therefore, usually focuses attention on a few key areas.

Many banks establish a deadline for completing the credit process. Because each loan product is unique, the product typically sets the time objectives. A 30-minute turnaround from receipt of an application to final credit decision might be standard for indirect loans, but a home equity line of credit may take five days because documentation from other sources may be necessary. Because the decisions on many uncomplicated loan products are based primarily on credit scores, it is possible to make the decision quickly. For other loans, generally those for larger amounts that are based at least partially on the value of collateral, a

Credit Investigation Objectives

- Verify that the application is accurate and complete.
- Conduct the investigation efficiently.
- Identify negative trends or potential problems.

Sources to Verify Applicant Information

- the bank's own account records
- other creditors
- consumer reporting agencies
- employers

Exhibit 8.1	Information Verified in Credit Investigations
Data accepted as given	• length of time at current address • number of dependents • previous address • previous job • checking and savings account information with another bank
Data verified by the credit investigator	• current employer • income—amount, frequency, and type (salary or commission) • other sources of income (source and amount) • current home address • value of collateral to secure the loan
Data verified through the consumer reporting agency	• credit references • name and address • Social Security number • public records

red flag—An indicator that something could be wrong. Examples include information uncovered during a credit investigation that appears suspicious or requires further action to verify, or an indicator during the credit process or in the bank's record systems that there has been an incident of identity theft.

Credit Investigation Process

- Review the application for information warranting immediate rejection.
- Check bank credit files for the applicant's account history.
- Obtain credit agency reports.
- Contact employers and other creditors for references.
- Verify the value of any collateral securing the loan.

decision will take longer. Even with short deadlines, lenders must gather the information necessary to underwrite the loan. Sound loans are major assets of most banks. Therefore, policy governing credit investigations and loan underwriting decisions reflects the importance of loan assets in bank portfolios.

Identify Potential Problems

A thorough investigation either substantiates the applicant's creditworthiness or uncovers problems or factors that suggest the risk may be unacceptable. If the investigation uncovers inconsistent or inaccurate information, or information that cannot be verified by a reliable source, the bank will need to investigate further. Any inconsistency or questionable incident may be an indicator of credit problems—a red flag for credit quality. Inconsistent or inaccurate information in a credit report may be a red flag for identity theft as well. **Red flags** for credit quality and for identity theft do not necessarily indicate a serious problem but they do warrant further investigation.

Acquire Information to Support a Sound Decision

Once the investigation is complete, the applicant's file is given to the loan officer or other decision maker for a decision. Credit decisions are sound only if they are based on good information. Lenders must be assured that the information obtained on the application and verified during the investigation is accurate and complete. Because lenders have reduced to the basics the information that is needed, it is important that they have all essential information.

Missing or inaccurate information may delay the lending process or cause lenders to make loans that do not meet bank requirements. In some cases, the loan might be approved provided the consumer verifies data that the bank could not verify directly. The applicant may need to bring to the closing a recent pay stub to verify income and employment, for example.

THE CREDIT INVESTIGATION PROCESS

The basic steps in the credit investigation process are reviewing the application for information that warrants immediate rejection, checking bank files to determine applicant's account history, obtaining a credit report, contacting employers and creditors for references, and verifying the value of the collateral securing the loan.

Review the Application for Information Warranting Rejection

Any application that does not meet the bank's policy requirements should be reviewed to determine if the bank would make an exception to policy or the application should be rejected without further delay or expense. If, for example, the applicant requests an automobile loan with no down payment, and the bank's stated policy calls for a 20 percent down payment, the lender may make a counteroffer with a different loan structure, request more or better quality collateral, or reject the application. This also would be the case if the applicant does not meet the bank's minimum income requirement or is not of legal borrowing age. In these cases, the lender may choose to request a cosigner rather than reject the application.

Banks may make exceptions to policy where doing so benefits the bank. For example, if the applicant has a low credit score but keeps a large deposit account at the bank, it is likely to make an exception to policy requirements, accommodate the customer, and make the loan. The reason for the exception should be noted in the file.

Check Bank Files for Applicant's Account History

The bank's own records are a convenient, inexpensive, and reliable source of credit information. Information from past or current accounts demonstrates whether the bank has had a satisfactory credit experience with the consumer. If the relationship is satisfactory or the consumer has no experience with the bank, the investigation proceeds to the next step. If previous experience with the consumer has not been satisfactory, the investigation may end and the loan request denied. This process saves both time and money.

Obtain Credit Agency Reports

In the past banks waited until the end of the credit investigation process to order credit reports. Now, however, the cost of most credit reports is minimal and with automated equipment the reports can be obtained in seconds. Many banks therefore examine credit reports early in the process to reduce or eliminate the need for further investigation. Often this is the most efficient and least costly way to proceed.

Contact Employers and Creditors for References

Direct references may be necessary to verify some information. At this point, the credit investigator contacts employers, creditors, and other sources. If these sources are unable or unwilling to provide the necessary information, the investigator will turn to indirect sources, such as the applicant's most recent pay stub to verify employment. If to this point the information has been favorable, the credit investigation process continues.

Verify Collateral Value

The value of collateral must be verified as part of the investigation, and there are many resources available to do so. Exhibit 8.2 (next page) lists common sources.

Outside **appraisals** may cause the greatest delay, particularly on real estate, boat, and airplane loans. Rather than wait until the appraisal is complete, banks usually inform the applicant that the loan request is approved subject to determination of collateral value. The loan amount may need to be adjusted after the value is verified.

Did You Know ...

Before 1960, lenders commonly mailed account confirmation forms to other lenders, a practice still used in mortgage lending. Then banks moved to telephoned and faxed confirmations. Today automated processing systems link application tracking systems with online consumer reporting agencies that transmit credit reports. The application is scored on the bank's internal credit-scoring system and a decision may be made within minutes. In the meantime, the lender may cross-sell the consumer other bank services.

appraisal—The valuation of property. The value determined on a specific date is known as the appraised value.

Exhibit 8.2	Sources for Valuing Collateral
New car, boat, recreational vehicle	Dealer invoice or new product price guides
Used car	Physical inspection by authorized person, NADA (National Automobile Dealers Association) or Kelly Blue Book valuation guides
Used boats	Marine survey, BUC Used Boat Guide
Stocks, bonds	Current stock quote from broker, or newspaper such as the *Wall Street Journal*
Savings accounts	Current account statement
Home	Certified real estate appraiser

Note: Many of the printed price and valuation resources are now available on the Internet.

Types of Credit Information

- credit history
- income
- employment
- residence
- collateral value

TYPES OF CREDIT INFORMATION

The investigator may access many types of credit information. Again, the extent to which any one of these is pursued depends on the type, size, and risk of the loan. Most credit investigations review the applicant's credit history, income, employment, residence, and collateral value.

CREDIT HISTORY

Because past behavior tends to be a reliable predictor of future behavior, credit history is one of the most important decision-making variables. It provides data about the applicant's character, capacity to pay debts, and credit behavior. It is often the best indicator of the probability of repayment. In evaluating credit history, the lender wants to know

- from whom the applicant has borrowed
- what types of accounts the consumer has used and now has available
- how long the accounts have been open
- how accounts have been paid
- current obligations and potential credit exposure (available credit on open-end credit accounts)

Credit history information is available from the application, the bank's files, other financial institutions, consumer reporting agencies, and public records.

Bank Files

Factual data in the bank's credit files should be the most reliable and accurate. Direct references from other lenders also may produce current and accurate credit information about the applicant, although in practice they are rare.

Consumer Reporting Agencies

Incomplete information is a common problem on credit reports. Some lenders do not send their credit histories to all local consumer reporting agencies. Without complete reports, confirming information is difficult and all lenders are exposed to more risk. If the applicant does not disclose all debts on the application, and if the undisclosed debts are not shown on the credit report, the loan risk might be greater than it appears.

Credit repair clinics pose another problem. Although there are legitimate free credit counseling services that work with consumers and lenders to help consumers restore their finances, credit repair clinics often try to pressure lenders into changing negative credit report information. They may threaten legal action or offer payment on a previous loss. Many credit repair clinics have been involved in fraud. Credit reports that no longer reflect charged-off accounts expose lenders to greater credit risk.

Public Records

Information about judgments, bankruptcies, and liens usually is available from consumer reporting agencies, but in some cases, it may be obtained directly from court records. Because of time and expense, court records generally are checked only on loans secured by real property or goods that are recorded by filing a **financing statement**. Filings are listed in the name of the borrower.

INCOME

Income, a principal indicator of the applicant's capacity to repay the loan, is a crucial variable in any credit evaluation. Consumer loans most often are repaid monthly from recurring weekly or monthly income. The major elements of income that lenders investigate are its source, reliability, frequency, and probable continuity over the term of the loan.

credit repair clinic—
A firm that advertises fee-based services to consumers for the purpose of improving credit ratings and resolving bad debts. Some clinics are illegitimate and have been involved in scams.

financing statement—
A document that contains basic information about certain collateral pledged by a borrower on a loan. It is filed in local or state public records.

Income is investigated for
- source
- reliability
- frequency
- probable continuity

Situation

Chip, 28, is a software developer for a new high-tech company. He has worked for four companies since he graduated from college at 21. Although this is typical in the high-technology arena, his father is concerned that being a job-hopper on paper will keep Chip from getting the consumer loan he is seeking.

Will changing jobs so often prevent Chip from getting a loan?

The reliability of the applicant's primary source of income depends on the market, the local economy, and the employer's business and employee salary structures. Because both employment information and income source determine reliability, weakness in either area is cause for concern. A short time on the job, frequent job changes, seasonal disruptions, and payments by commission or bonuses rather than salary may indicate income instability. Confronted with information on frequent job changes, the credit investigator needs to do more research.

Situation

Brenda is conducting a credit investigation on Carlene Smith, who has applied for a $20,000 personal loan. Smith wants to convert a room in her home to a children's playroom. The money will be used for shelving, carpeting, furniture, and lighting. Because of a policy of confidentiality, Smith's employer will verify that she works for the company but will not verify current income or earnings history. Without this verification, Brenda cannot approve the loan.

What should Brenda do?

direct verification—
A credit investigation procedure that involves direct contact with creditors, employers, and landlords to verify information on an application.

personal tax return—
The tax form individuals file with federal and state agencies.

Sources for Income Information

- employers
- pay stubs
- W-2 forms
- tax returns
- direct payroll deposit records
- legal documents

To verify income, credit investigators may contact employers directly or may rely on information from pay stubs, W-2 forms, tax returns, legal documents, and direct payroll deposits.

Employer Verification

Direct references from employers are the best way to verify income; they provide the most current information and may allow the investigator to verify job classification and time on the job. Many employers are reluctant, however, to provide **direct verification**, or will verify only that the applicant is employed. In these cases, lenders must rely on indirect sources to verify income.

Pay Stub

A recent pay stub may be an excellent alternative to direct verification. A pay stub gives the lender some insight into payroll deductions and overtime income, and therefore a better understanding of the applicant's gross and net income. The pay stub should be examined closely to ensure that it is valid, is complete, and has not been altered. Unscrupulous individuals can forge pay stubs. The date on the pay stub should be checked to ensure it is recent—an old pay stub may indicate a problem.

W-2 Forms

The Wage and Tax Statement, the W-2 form, is a record of the applicant's past income. An accurate W-2 shows the names and addresses of the employer and applicant and the amount of income paid to the applicant during the reported year. However, anyone can obtain a blank W-2 form and falsify the income. Because W-2s do not show present income, they are a weak method of verification. However, if the income amount seems reasonable and the applicant's employment can be confirmed, most lenders are comfortable using W-2s to verify income.

Personal Tax Returns

Personal tax returns, like W-2 forms, relate past, not current, income information but they do contain substantial information about the applicant's financial behavior. Tax returns generally are the only reliable way to verify income for self-employed consumers. Lenders usually review tax returns only when they are considering large loan requests from self-employed consumers and requests for large open-end lines of credit. To reduce the risk of fraud, tax returns used for a loan request should be signed and dated by the consumer.

Legal Documents

Legal documents, such as divorce decrees, separation agreements, and public assistance notices, often are necessary to verify nonwage income. Pension receipts also may be used to verify income. It is important to review these documents carefully to determine the amount of income, the benefit period, continuity, and any limitations that may apply to these sources of income.

Although lenders may not ask applicants about their income from alimony or child support, if an applicant volunteers information about such income, the lender may request documentation of its amount and reliability.

EMPLOYMENT

The major elements of employment to investigate are type of job, time on the job, employer's business and stability, and applicant's employment history. Any inconsistencies in these areas may raise red flags, which must be investigated further. See exhibit 8.3 for a list of red flags that may arise at different stages of a credit investigation.

Type of Job

The type of job gives insight into relative level of income, job mobility, continuity of income, and level of education. Titles, however, tell only part of the story. One title does not describe the same job in different locations. For example, not

Exhibit 8.3 Red Flags	
Red flags from employment and residence verification	• the same address for home and business • addresses not consistent with local street patterns • home or business address that is a post office box or mail drop • home address that is a hotel or motel • variations in phone numbers • questionable persons giving references • telephone calls answered in an unusual manner, such as for a business where customer service is important
Red flags on credit reports	• all credit less than 12 months old • no credit history for applicants over 21 • heavy recent inquiries or applications for credit with other lenders • all credit references with unknown or small companies • all references that are closed accounts • warning flags on the credit report • undisclosed creditors • heavy use of open-end credit accounts • excessive debt in relation to income • pyramiding of debts • adequate income but chronic delinquency

Identity theft red flags	• fraud or active-duty alerts included with a consumer report
	• consumer reporting agency provides a notice of credit freeze in response to a request for a consumer report
	• agency provides a notice of address discrepancy
	• report indicates a pattern of activity that is inconsistent with the history and usual pattern of activity of an applicant or customer, including:
	   — recent and significant increase in the volume of inquiries
	   — unusual number of recently established credit relationships
	   — material change in the use of credit, especially with respect to recently established credit relationships
	   — accounts that were closed for cause or identified for abuse of account privileges by a financial institution or creditor

all bank vice presidents have the same responsibilities or income. In addition, jobs with different titles might be similar, such as "new accounts advisor" and "customer service representative." The applicant's responsibilities and income are more important than the job title. Under the Equal Credit Opportunity Act, lenders may not treat income from part-time employment less favorably than from other sources. Income from part-time jobs must be evaluated the same as all other types of income.

Time on Job

Time on the job indicates the stability of an applicant's income. If the employer will not verify this information, the credit investigator may accept the information supplied by the applicant or the information on the credit report, assuming the applicant's place of employment is verifiable.

Required Employment Information

- type of job
- time on job
- employer's business
- employer's stability
- applicant's employment history

Employer's Business and Stability

Lenders should know the general market conditions and stability of the major employers in the market area. Corporate downsizing or weak local economic conditions may signal increased risk. The type of business also makes a difference. For example, the airline business has been subject to bankruptcies, mergers, and reorganizations for several decades.

Employees who have been on the job for a short time may be more of a credit risk than those who have a long, stable employment history. However, income sources subject to seasonal disruptions, as in the construction industry, make it difficult to predict reliability. Commissions and bonuses are other income sources that may not be steady and may therefore affect reliability.

Employment History

The final concern is the applicant's employment history. Employment history may present issues that require more investigation and informed consideration, especially when the applicant has worked for many different employers but with gaps in employment. When an applicant has been at the current job for only a short time, the loan officer should check previous employment. Frequent job changes may not signal instability; it is possible that a recent job change is a positive rather than a negative change. Today's employees will have many jobs and different careers in their lifetimes, especially those in rapidly growing fields.

Verifying Information

To verify employment references, investigators should obtain the employer's phone number from an independent source, such as a telephone directory or directory assistance. Differences in phone numbers may mean a third party is on standby to give a false reference, the company is out of business, or the applicant does not work at the address listed.

Most investigators obtain the identity and title of the person they contact for a reference. This eliminates asking an unqualified or inappropriate person for an important reference. It is unusual for a secretary, for example, to verify a manager's salary or for an employee to verify the income of the owner of the business. Although these people may verify employment, it is better to confirm income from a tax return or pay stub.

RESIDENCE

Residence information can provide evidence of an applicant's stability and character. Investigators review the application for information on type of residence, time at residence, and previous residence. Although this information may reveal a great deal about the applicant's lifestyle and financial condition, it should serve only as a general indicator of stability rather than as a major determinant of credit risk. Loan officers must avoid discriminatory practices, such as **redlining**, in which applicants are denied access to credit based solely on the location of their residence.

> **redlining**—An illegal practice in which certain areas of a community are eliminated from eligibility for mortgages or other loans, either intentionally or unintentionally, allegedly because the geographic area is considered a poor investment risk. In effect, a red line is drawn around the eliminated area on a map.

Type of Residence

The applicant's current residence is a measure of stability and may indicate financial strength. The credit investigator must determine if the applicant owns or is buying a home, rents, lives with relatives, or has some other arrangement. Homeownership normally demonstrates greater stability and financial strength because the applicant has an asset of significant value and is less likely to leave the area unexpectedly. Renting and other residence status, such as living with parents or in temporary housing, are not regarded as demonstrating the same stability as homeownership. Despite the importance of this variable, residence type often is accepted as given, unless the place of residence will be used to secure the loan. The residence must be verified if it will be collateral for the loan.

Time at Address

Time at an address, a measure of stability, is analyzed in relation to the applicant's age and lifecycle stage. Frequent address changes usually are a negative factor that requires further investigation, but young applicants may have only recently established a household. If the address can be verified, banks usually accept the applicant's time-at-address information.

Previous Residence

Information about previous addresses usually is requested but often not investigated. It is helpful for obtaining accurate credit reports, particularly when the applicant is new to the area, and in evaluating the applicant's stability, but verifying previous residence may be expensive and difficult.

Verifying Residence

Residence information can be verified directly with landlords, mortgage holders, public records, and consumer reporting agency records.

As with verifying employment information, investigators should obtain the phone number from an independent source. Again, differences in phone numbers may mean a third party is on standby to give a phony reference. The home may be abandoned, the apartment building may not exist, or the applicant may not live at the address listed.

Landlords and mortgage holders are the best sources for residence information, if they are willing and able to provide the data quickly. Many mortgage holders give references only in writing, making verification rare for consumer loan requests.

Public records, such as for deeds or taxes, may be used to verify address and residence information. Although consumer reporting agency information may not be current, it usually is sufficient to verify residence unless conflicting information materializes elsewhere in the investigation. If the reporting agency or another lender had a different address, for example, the investigator would need direct verification.

COLLATERAL

When a secured loan is requested, the credit investigator and lender identify the terms of any purchase-money secured loans and determine the ownership of the collateral. The lender, or in some cases a credit investigator, determines the value.

On **purchase-money secured loans** the lender must have details about the terms of the sale to evaluate the collateral risk. A bill of sale, invoice, or purchase order should reveal the actual cash selling price, the amount and composition of any down payment, and a complete description of the item being purchased. Consumers are asked to supply this information when they apply for a loan or when they come to the closing.

In analyzing the terms of a purchase, the investigator looks at the **cash selling price** of an item, the consumer's **down payment**, and the **cash value** of any trade-in. To determine the amount financed, the down payment amount is deducted from the cash selling price.

Collateral Value

The amount financed is based on the value of the collateral. Simply relying on the down payment may result in advancing too much credit and increasing risk for the lender. The credit investigator should consult valuation guidebooks or take other steps, such as obtaining appraisals, to determine the value. The Internet has legitimate valuation Web sites that provide lenders with valuations for different types of property.

Collateral Ownership

Ownership of the property offered as collateral should be verified to ensure that the bank nay obtain a lien that can be perfected. For collateral in the consumer's possession, examination of the ownership document, such as a deed or a title,

---

purchase-money secured loan—A loan the proceeds of which are used to purchase the goods securing the loan.

cash selling price—The actual price the consumer is paying for an item, including the full price plus any sales tax.

down payment—A partial payment made at the time of purchase, with the balance to be paid later; the consumer's initial investment in the goods.

cash value—The book or fair market value of an asset on the day it is sold.

---

can serve as verification. Ownership of goods to be purchased may be verified directly with the seller or by examining bill-of-sale documents. To secure the loan, all owners of the collateral must execute loan documents.

Collateral Identification

Except for new vehicles, boats, and airplanes purchased from reputable dealers, many lenders require collateral be inspected before loan approval. Verifying the identity of the collateral, such as by serial number, and its condition is essential for determining loan value. Automobile titles, for example, may be inspected to determine if the auto was salvaged from a wreck and is therefore of lower value.

SOURCES OF CREDIT INFORMATION

Among the sources banks use for credit information, consumer reporting agencies and the applicant's personal financial statements and tax returns provide the most comprehensive information.

CONSUMER REPORTING AGENCIES

Consumer reporting agencies are the largest providers of credit information to the banking industry. Since the early 1900s, they have been an important means of exchanging information on consumer credit history. **Consumer reporting agencies** receive information from participating lenders and from public records, such as bankruptcy court filings. Credit reporting is voluntary; the same information may not be available from all agencies serving a market area.

Consumer reporting agencies have streamlined the lending process by eliminating the need for banks to contact each of the applicant's credit references directly. They have made it possible for lenders to conduct effective investigations by providing a central source to help uncover information that was not disclosed in the application.

Consumer reporting agencies offer banks more than historical credit data on consumers. Their integrated systems, which are similar to bank internal credit scoring systems, help lenders make loan decisions. Their loss and bankruptcy predictor models use basic consumer credit information to predict the likelihood that a loan to a specific applicant could result in a loss to the bank. After receiving a request from a member bank, the reporting agency releases to the bank the information requested on a credit report.

Credit reports contain a wealth of information gathered from lenders, public files, and other sources, including consumer identifying information, **trade lines**, **inquiries**, and public record and collection information, such as judgments, tax liens, and bankruptcy. The credit report does not include information about the consumer's checking or savings accounts, bankruptcies that are more than 10 years old, debts charged-off or placed for collection that are more than 7 years old, gender, ethnicity, religion, political affiliation, medical history, or criminal records. The credit score that may be generated from the information in the

---

Information Commonly Found on Credit Reports

- information that identifies the consumer
- trade lines
- inquiries
- public record information
- collection information

---

consumer reporting agency—An organization or company that assembles or evaluates the credit histories of consumers for purposes of furnishing credit reports to third parties. *Also known as* credit reporting agency, credit bureau.

trade line—Detailed information about credit accounts found on a credit report, including the name of the creditor, type of loan, loan amount, account balance, payment terms, cosigners, and the consumer's payment history.

inquiry—A notation on a credit report that indicates the applicant has applied for credit from a specific organization or that an updated report was ordered.

Did You Know ...

The USA PATRIOT Act requires banks to have a written customer identification program (CIP). The goal is to stop terrorists from using the U.S. financial system to finance their crimes. The CIP must have procedures to
• collect information, such as name, birth date, address, and an identifying number, such as a Social Security number
• document customer identification
• determine if a customer appears on any government lists of known or suspected terrorists
• maintain records of information used to verify a customer's identity

credit report is not part of the report itself. Appendix 3 to this chapter provides an example of a credit report and descriptions of the data provided.

There are three national consumer reporting agencies. In some cases, only one or two of them may serve a particular community. Because they may gather information from different sources, reports received from competing agencies may vary. It is essential that lenders evaluate these differences and periodically test each to see which agency provides the best service and the most accurate information. This can be done by requesting a credit report on a consumer from each agency serving the bank's community, then comparing the reports to determine which has the most complete information.

Consumer's Identifying Information

To prevent intentional fraud and accidental misidentification and to thwart identity theft, properly identifying the applicant is essential. Identity theft is, unfortunately, a fast-growing form of fraud that claims thousands of victims a year. Banks often suffer losses from this type of fraud. Inconsistent information on a credit report can be an identity theft red flag.

Equally important for a valid credit report is an accurate date of birth, name variations, Social Security number, and residence. Most identification problems arise because the bank did not obtain correct information from the applicant. Some banks require a driver's license or other valid photo ID to verify identity.

Age should be verified to ensure that the applicant is old enough to sign a legal contract or meets the age requirement for payment protection insurance.

Occasionally consumers obtain credit under a variety of names. A common example is a married woman who maintains credit in both her married and maiden names. Another example is inconsistency in the use of initials. For example, J. Donald Jones, Joseph D. Jones, and J.D. Jones may all be the same person. Generation designations (such as Sr. and Jr.) often cause considerable confusion, making it difficult to verify the consumer's identity. In an effort to identify situations in which variations on a name have been used, some banks specifically ask applicants to list all names under which they have obtained credit.

Social Security numbers are used to identify people. Some consumer reporting agencies use the numbers to identify matches within their report files, and some banks use them as additional identification in conjunction with consumer account numbers. Variations in Social Security numbers usually are flagged in credit reports. They might be typographical errors but they also might indicate fraud. Criminals often use the identity of a deceased person to obtain credit. Consumer reporting agencies flag Social Security numbers for deceased persons in their reports. They also have devices to detect fraudulent use of Social Security numbers.

Trade Lines

Trade lines are the accounts consumers have with banks, retailers, credit-card issuers, utility companies, and other lenders. The accounts may be in the consumer's name as the owner, or the consumer may be listed as an authorized user. The accounts are listed by type of loan, such as revolving credit or installment loan; date the consumer opened the account; credit limit or loan amount; account balance; payment terms; any cosigners of the loan; and the consumer's payment pattern over the past two years. Closed or inactive accounts may stay on the report up to eleven years from the last activity date.

Inquiries

The inquiries section of a credit report lists the names of those who have obtained copies of the consumer's credit report within the past year (two years for employment purposes). An inquiry is recorded whenever another party requests a copy of the report.

Public Record and Collection Information

Public record information lists court records on bankruptcy, tax liens, or monetary judgments, such as overdue child support. Nonmonetary judgments may be listed as well. These may remain on the record for seven years.

PERSONAL FINANCIAL STATEMENTS

The bank's loan policy may stipulate when a **personal financial statement** is required as part of the loan application process. Exhibits 8.4-A and 8.4-B on the next two pages show a sample loan application and a personal financial statement. Note the details on assets, liabilities, and net worth. For business loans, some banks use detailed personal financial statements, which should reflect a recent date. A personal financial statement often is compiled as of year-end, although the lender may require a more current statement. By signing and dating it, the applicant attests to the information in the document and certifies its accuracy. This is particularly important where there has been a bankruptcy.

The personal financial statement allows the credit investigator to analyze the applicant's liquidity and ability to meet current financial needs, identify additional assets that may be taken as collateral for a loan, identify the ownership of various assets, provide a more detailed picture of how the applicant manages finances, and quantify the claim that current liabilities (debts) have on assets. The credit investigator will compare the debts listed on the personal financial statement with those on the credit report to identify possible sources of additional information. The investigator also can alert the lender to problems or opportunities related to the loan.

PERSONAL TAX RETURNS

Lenders may require tax returns for any number of reasons, such as for large loan requests, self-employed individuals, or additional support. In fact, the tax return is the only reliable way to verify income for a self-employed person. Exhibits 8.4-C through 8.4-F on the next four pages are based on information provided for Frank Dunten, the person whose name appears on the application in exhibits 8.4-A and 8.4-B.

personal financial statement—A document that provides expanded information about the applicant's financial situation.

Did You Know ...

Under certain circumstances, consumers may be eligible for a free or reduced-cost credit report:
• The Fair Credit Reporting Act entitles every consumer to one free disclosure from each consumer reporting agency every 12 months.
• Applicants are entitled to a free credit report if a loan application is declined because of information on the credit report.
• Consumers are entitled to one free credit report a year if they certify in writing that they are unemployed and plan to look for a job within 60 days, they are on welfare, or their report is inaccurate because of fraud.
• The state where a consumer resides may offer a free or reduced-price personal credit report.

Exhibit 8.4A   Sample Loan Application

Requested Loan Amount $ 4,000.   Term _____

Purpose of Loan Furniture

Application Taken By: ____ Phone   ____ Mail   ____ Interview

Application # _____

Branch# _____   Employee ID# _____

Please Tell Us About Yourself

Full Name Frank A. Dunten	Time At Job: 13 Years Months
Address 3171 Dunkirk Lane	Business Phone 219-824-3273
City South Bend State IN Zip 46311	Job Title/Position Laboratory Manager
Home Phone 219-824-6310	Gross Monthly Income $ 7,500.
Soc. Sec.# 314-29-3354 Birth Date 11-23-63	Previous Employer
Number of Dependents (Excluding Yourself) 0	Time At Job: Years Months
Time At Address: 9 Years Months	Additional Monthly Income* $
Nearest Relative Stephen Dunten Phone # 812-373-4510	Source of Additional Income
Employer Name The Dental Shop	

*Income from alimony, child support, or separate maintenance need not be revealed if you will not use it for repaying this oblication.

Tell Us About Your Co-Applicant (If Co-Applicant is not your spouse, Co-Applicant must complete a separate application.)

Full Name Katherine L. Dunten	Business Phone 219-361-2836
Address 3171 Dunkirk Lane	Job Title/Position Social Worker
City South Bend State IN Zip 46311	Gross Monthly Income $ 1,800.
Home Phone 219-842-6310	Previous Employer
Soc. Sec. # 312-68-7325 Birth Date 10-15-64	Time At Job: Years Months
Time At Address: 9 Years Months	Additional Monthly Income* $
Employer Name St. Joe County	Source of Aditional Income
Time At Job: 7 Years Months	

*Income from alimony, child support, or separate maintenance need not be revealed if you will not use it for repaying this obligation.

Tell Us About Your Finances

Applicant's Financial Information:	Co-Applicant's Financial Information:
Checking Account: 123456	Checking Account:
Bank 1st Bank Balance $ 15,000	Bank Same Balance $
Savings Account:	Savings Account:
Bank 1st Bank Balance $ 11,000	Bank Balance $
Other Account: Balance $	Other Account: Balance $

Rent	Monthly Payment $			
Mortgage	Monthly Payment $ 1,075	Balance $ 79,000	Value of Home $ 179,000	
Second Mortgage:	Yes No	(If Yes) Balance $	Monthly Payment $	

Financial Obligations (Please list type and dollar amount, and alimony/child support, if applicable.)

1. 1st Bank VISA	$ 1,500	3.	$
2. 2nd Bank Auto	$ 8,000	4.	$

If You Wish To Secure Your Loan, Please Tell Us About Your Collateral:

Auto Boat	Savings Account Certificate of Deposit
New Used	Bank Account # Balance $
Year, Make, Model	Stocks
Special Options	Name # of Shares
Cash Price $	
Vehicle ID #	

Signatures Frank A. Dunten   Katherine L. Dunten

I, meaning applicant who signs below, authorize "The Bank" ("you") to make credit inquiries about me and authorize anyone to furnish requested information to you. All information and this application is your property, whether or not credit is extended. You may disclose any information relating to this application or loan account to any applicant for or proposed guarantor of this loan. Everything I have told you in this application is true, complete, and correct. I will use my loan only for lawful purposes. This application, and any additional sheets attached, lists all debts and obligations I have, including those on which I am jointly obligated.

Applicant *Frank A. Dunten*	Co-Applicant *Katherine L. Dunten*
Signature Date	Signature Date

Exhibit 8.4B   Sample Personal Financial Statement

Name: Frank A. Dunten	Soc. Sec. No.: 314-29-3354	Annual Income: $90,000
Home Address: 3171 Dunkirk Lane	Home Telephone No.: 219-824-6310	
City: South Bend	State: IN	Zip Code: 46311

ASSETS (EXCLUDING YOUR BUSINESS)	Check if Jointly Owned	LIABILITIES (EXCLUDING YOUR BUSINESS)	
Cash on Hand and in Banks (personal only)	26,000 ☒	Notes Payable to Banks - Secured - Sch. D	
Readily Marketable Securities - Sch. A	15,000 ☒	Notes Payable to Banks - Unsecured - Sch. D	
Non-Readily Marketable Securities - Sch. A	☐	Notes Payable to Others	
Accounts, Notes, and Mortgages Receivable	☐	Accounts and Bills Due	
Residential Real Estate - Sch. B	179,000 ☒	Tax Payable	
Real Estate Investments - Sch. B	☐	Real Estate Mortgages Payable - Sch. B	79,000
Automobiles and Personal Property	41,000 ☒	Life Insurance Loans - Sch. C	
Cash Surrender Value of Life Insurance	1,500 ☐	Other Debts - Please Itemize VISA	1,500
IRA, Keough, profit sharing & Ret. Accts.	575,000 ☐	Automobile	8,000
Other Assets - please itemize	☐		
Antiques	12,000 ☐		
	☐	Total Liabilities	88,500
	☐	Net Worth (total assets - total liabilities)	761,000
Total Assets	849,500 ☐	Total Liabilities and Net Worth	849,500

If any joint assets, complete the following:	Joint owner name: Katherine	Soc. Sec. No.: 312-68-7325

SCHEDULE A - All securities (attach additional sheet if necessary)

No. of shares (stock) or face value (bonds)	Description	Owner(s)	Where Held	Current Market Valu	Pledge (if yes #)
READILY MARKETABLE SECURITIES (Including U.S. Governments and Municipals) (Statements may be substituted as an attachment)					
2100	OMNI Fund	J.T.	Broker	10,000	
100	IBM	J.T.	Broker	3,500	
100	Ohio Power	J.T.	Broker	1,500	
NON-READILY MARKETABLE SECURITIES (closely held, thinly traded, or restricted stock)					

SCHEDULE B - Personal Residence & Real Estate Investments, Mortgage Debt (000's)

Property Address	Legal Owners	% of Ownership	Purchase Yr. Price	Present Market Value	Present Loan Balance	Loan Maturity Date	Monthly Payment	Financial Institution
3171 Dunkirk	J.T.	100	04 135,000	179,000	79,000	2012	1,075	1st Bank

SCHEDULE C - Insurance - Life Insurance

Insurance Co.	Face Amount of Policy	Type of Policy	Owner of Policy	Beneficiary	Cash Surrender Value	Amount Borrowed
AETNA	200,000	Whole	Frank	Katherine	1,500	-0-

SCHEDULE D - Notes payable & installment loans (auto, credit cards, line of credit, home equity, education, department stores)

Due to	Type of Loan	Amount of Loan	Secured Yes No	Collateral	Interest Rate	Maturity	Unpaid Balance	Monthly Payment
1st Bank	VISA	10,000	☐ ☒		12.0		1,500	100
2nd Bank	Auto		☒ ☐	05 Ford	9.0		8,000	275

Your Signature:	Date:

Personal financial statements provide information on

- the consumer's liquidity
- additional assets for collateral
- asset ownership
- the consumer's management of finances
- ratio of assets to liabilities

Like the personal financial statement, tax returns provide more details about the applicant's financial situation and behavior. Because income and expenses may vary significantly from any given year to another, banks may require two or three recent tax returns. The applicant should provide all supporting schedules as well. These schedules provide important information for verification and decision-making.

WARNING SIGNS

In addition to red flags (see exhibit 8.3), credit investigators and lenders always should be alert for negative or unverifiable information. Gaps in information should prompt an extensive investigation. Common warning signs are information inconsistent with the applicant's age or income level, and aggressive or anxious behavior.

Gaps in Information

The credit investigator gives the lender as complete a picture of the applicant as possible within the given time constraints, noting gaps in information and any difficulties in obtaining acceptable forms of verification. The lender then decides whether to send the consumer a Notice of Incomplete Application or a Notice of Adverse Action—either must be sent within 30 days of the date of the application.

Information Inconsistent with Applicant's Age

An individual's age and life cycle stage should correlate to the information that is on the credit application. Indeed, lenders rely on the fact that most people are likely to exhibit the same behavioral patterns in the future as they have in the past, and that as they grow older, people move toward greater stability, higher income, and asset accumulation.

Variations from these norms may be acceptable, but they still warrant closer investigation and possibly an explanation from the consumer. It is unusual, for example, for a 40-year-old to claim to have no credit experience, or for a 30-year-old to claim five different addresses in the previous year.

Aggressive or Anxious Applicant

Many people have behavior patterns that emphasize getting their way by using manipulative or aggressive behavior. The danger is that a lender may be intimidated and may compromise the investigation process, sometimes with disastrous results.

Consumers who are themselves intimidated by the lending process present a similar dilemma. Although few consumers relish applying for a loan, most go through the process well. A skilled interviewer can make an anxious applicant comfortable; but an excessively anxious applicant actually may be hiding something.

Yet putting personal behavior factors on a red flag list is risky at best. Shy people may avoid eye contact; people experienced in borrowing but nervous about their chances of getting a loan may appear

Situation

During a loan interview with Bernard, a middle-aged applicant, Francine notices that he appears very nervous and pauses for long periods before answering questions. This is especially true when Francine asks Bernard why there is little information in his credit history. The rest of his application looks fine, and Francine is inclined to think that Bernard is just intimidated by the interview situation.

What else could this behavior signal?

Exhibit 8.4C   Sample 1040 Statement

Form **1040**

Department of the Treasury—Internal Revenue Service

U.S. Individual Income Tax Return 2008   (99)   IRS Use Only—Do not write or staple in this space.

For the year Jan. 1–Dec. 31, 2008, or other tax year beginning , 2008, ending , 20	OMB No. 1545-0074

Label

(See instructions on page 14.)

Use the IRS label.
Otherwise, please print or type.

	Your first name and initial	Last name	Your social security number
L A B E L	FRANK A.	DUNTEN	314 : 29 : 3354
	If a joint return, spouse's first name and initial	Last name	Spouse's social security number
H E R E	KATHERINE L.	DUNTEN	312 : 68 : 7325

Home address (number and street). If you have a P.O. box, see page 14.   Apt. no.

3171 DUNKIRK LANE

▲ You **must** enter your SSN(s) above. ▲

City, town or post office, state, and ZIP code. If you have a foreign address, see page 14.

SOUTH BEND, INDIANA, 40311

Checking a box below will not change your tax or refund.

Presidential Election Campaign ▶ Check here if you, or your spouse if filing jointly, want $3 to go to this fund (see page 14) ▶   ☐ **You** ☐ **Spouse**

Filing Status

Check only one box.

1 ☐ Single
2 ☑ Married filing jointly (even if only one had income)
3 ☐ Married filing separately. Enter spouse's SSN above and full name here. ▶
4 ☐ Head of household (with qualifying person). (See page 15.) If the qualifying person is a child but not your dependent, enter this child's name here. ▶
5 ☐ Qualifying widow(er) with dependent child (see page 16)

Exemptions

If more than four dependents, see page 17.

6a ☑ **Yourself.** If someone can claim you as a dependent, **do not** check box 6a . . . . .
b ☑ **Spouse** . . . .

c Dependents:		(2) Dependent's social security number	(3) Dependent's relationship to you	(4) ✓ if qualifying child for child tax credit (see page 17)
(1) First name Last name				
		:		☐
		:		☐
		:		☐
		:		☐

Boxes checked on 6a and 6b
No. of children on 6c who:
• lived with you
• did not live with you due to divorce or separation (see page 18)
Dependents on 6c not entered above

d Total number of exemptions claimed . . . .

Add numbers on lines above ▶ **2**

Income

Attach Form(s) W-2 here. Also attach Forms W-2G and 1099-R if tax was withheld.

If you did not get a W-2, see page 21.

Enclose, but do not attach, any payment. Also, please use **Form 1040-V.**

7	Wages, salaries, tips, etc. Attach Form(s) W-2	**7**	111,600 00
8a	**Taxable** interest. Attach Schedule B if required	**8a**	200 00
b	Tax-exempt interest. **Do not** include on line 8a . . .	**8b**	
9a	Ordinary dividends. Attach Schedule B if required	**9a**	368 00
b	Qualified dividends (see page 21)	**9b**	
10	Taxable refunds, credits, or offsets of state and local income taxes (see page 22) . .	**10**	
11	Alimony received	**11**	
12	Business income or (loss). Attach Schedule C or C-EZ	**12**	
13	Capital gain or (loss). Attach Schedule D if required. If not required, check here ▶ ☐	**13**	
14	Other gains or (losses). Attach Form 4797	**14**	
15a	IRA distributions . .	**15a**	b Taxable amount (see page 23)	**15b**	
16a	Pensions and annuities	**16a**	b Taxable amount (see page 24)	**16b**	
17	Rental real estate, royalties, partnerships, S corporations, trusts, etc. Attach Schedule E	**17**	
18	Farm income or (loss). Attach Schedule F	**18**	
19	Unemployment compensation	**19**	
20a	Social security benefits	**20a**	b Taxable amount (see page 26)	**20b**	
21	Other income. List type and amount (see page 28)	**21**	
22	Add the amounts in the far right column for lines 7 through 21. This is your **total income** ▶	**22**	112,168 00

Adjusted Gross Income

23	Educator expenses (see page 28)	**23**	
24	Certain business expenses of reservists, performing artists, and fee-basis government officials. Attach Form 2106 or 2106-EZ	**24**	
25	Health savings account deduction. Attach Form 8889 .	**25**	
26	Moving expenses. Attach Form 3903	**26**	
27	One-half of self-employment tax. Attach Schedule SE . .	**27**	
28	Self-employed SEP, SIMPLE, and qualified plans . .	**28**	
29	Self-employed health insurance deduction (see page 29) .	**29**	
30	Penalty on early withdrawal of savings	**30**	
31a	Alimony paid b Recipient's SSN ▶	**31a**	
32	IRA deduction (see page 30)	**32**	
33	Student loan interest deduction (see page 33) . . .	**33**	
34	Tuition and fees deduction. Attach Form 8917	**34**	
35	Domestic production activities deduction. Attach Form 8903	**35**	
36	Add lines 23 through 31a and 32 through 35	**36**	
37	Subtract line 36 from line 22. This is your **adjusted gross income** . . . . . ▶	**37**	112,168 00

For Disclosure, Privacy Act, and Paperwork Reduction Act Notice, see page 88.   Cat. No. 11320B   Form **1040** (2008)

Exhibit 8.4C Sample 1040 Statement—*continued*

Form 1040 (2008)   Page **2**

Tax and Credits	38	Amount from line 37 (adjusted gross income)	38	112,168	00

39a Check { ☐ **You** were born before January 2, 1944,   ☐ Blind. } **Total boxes**
if: { ☐ **Spouse** was born before January 2, 1944, ☐ Blind. } checked ▶ **39a** ☐

b If your spouse itemizes on a separate return or you were a dual-status alien, see page 34 and check here ▶ **39b** ☐

c Check if standard deduction includes real estate taxes or disaster loss (see page 34) ▶ **39c** ☐

Standard Deduction for—

• People who checked any box on line 39a, 39b, or 39c **or** who can be claimed as a dependent, see page 34.

• All others:

Single or Married filing separately, $5,450

Married filing jointly or Qualifying widow(er), $10,900

Head of household, $8,000

40	**Itemized deductions** (from Schedule A) **or** your **standard deduction** (see left margin) .	40	19,401	00
41	Subtract line 40 from line 38	41	92,707	00
42	If line 38 is over $119,975, or you provided housing to a Midwestern displaced individual, see page 36. Otherwise, multiply $3,500 by the total number of exemptions claimed on line 6d	42	6,400	00
43	**Taxable income.** Subtract line 42 from line 41. If line 42 is more than line 41, enter -0-	43	86,367	00
44	**Tax** (see page 36). Check if any tax is from: **a** ☐ Form(s) 8814 **b** ☐ Form 4972 .	44	0	00
45	**Alternative minimum tax** (see page 39). Attach Form 6251	45	0	00
46	Add lines 44 and 45 . . . . ▶	46	0	00

47	Foreign tax credit. Attach Form 1116 if required	47	
48	Credit for child and dependent care expenses. Attach Form 2441	48	
49	Credit for the elderly or the disabled. Attach Schedule R . .	49	
50	Education credits. Attach Form 8863	50	
51	Retirement savings contributions credit. Attach Form 8880 .	51	
52	Child tax credit (see page 42). Attach Form 8901 if required .	52	
53	Credits from Form: **a** ☐ 8396 **b** ☐ 8839 **c** ☐ 5695	53	
54	Other credits from Form: **a** ☐ 3800 **b** ☐ 8801 **c** ☐	54	

55	Add lines 47 through 54. These are your **total credits**	55	0	00
56	Subtract line 55 from line 46. If line 55 is more than line 46, enter -0- . . ▶	56	0	00

Other Taxes	57	Self-employment tax. Attach Schedule SE	57	
	58	Unreported social security and Medicare tax from Form: **a** ☐ 4137 **b** ☐ 8919	58	
	59	Additional tax on IRAs, other qualified retirement plans, etc. Attach Form 5329 if required .	59	
	60	Additional taxes: **a** ☐ AEIC payments **b** ☐ Household employment taxes. Attach Schedule H	60	
	61	Add lines 56 through 60. This is your **total tax** . . . . ▶	61	0	00

Payments

If you have a qualifying child, attach Schedule EIC.

62	Federal income tax withheld from Forms W-2 and 1099 . .	62	6,995	00
63	2008 estimated tax payments and amount applied from 2007 return	63	1,500	00
64a	**Earned income credit (EIC)**	64a		
b	Nontaxable combat pay election 64b			
65	Excess social security and tier 1 RRTA tax withheld (see page 61)	65		
66	Additional child tax credit. Attach Form 8812	66		
67	Amount paid with request for extension to file (see page 61)	67		
68	Credits from Form: **a** ☐ 2439 **b** ☐ 4136 **c** ☐ 8801 **d** ☐ 8885	68		
69	First-time homebuyer credit. Attach Form 5405	69		
70	Recovery rebate credit (see worksheet on pages 62 and 63) .	70		

71	Add lines 62 through 70. These are your **total payments** . . . . . ▶	71	8,495	00

Refund	72	If line 71 is more than line 61, subtract line 61 from line 71. This is the amount you **overpaid**	72	8,495	00

Direct deposit? See page 63 and fill in 73b, 73c, and 73d, or Form 8888.

73a	Amount of line 72 you want **refunded to you.** If Form 8888 is attached, check here ▶ ☐	73a	8,495	00

▶ b Routing number [_ _ _ _ _ _ _ _ _] ▶ **c** Type: ☐ Checking ☐ Savings

▶ d Account number [_ _ _ _ _ _ _ _ _ _ _ _ _ _ _ _ _]

74 Amount of line 72 you want **applied to your 2009 estimated tax** ▶ | 74 |

Amount You Owe	75	**Amount you owe.** Subtract line 71 from line 61. For details on how to pay, see page 65 ▶	75	0	00
	76	Estimated tax penalty (see page 65)	76		

Third Party Designee

Do you want to allow another person to discuss this return with the IRS (see page 66)? ☐ **Yes.** Complete the following. ☐ **No**

Designee's name ▶ _____   Phone no. ▶ (____)   Personal identification number (PIN) ▶ [_ _ _ _ _]

Sign Here

Joint return? See page 15.

Keep a copy for your records.

Under penalties of perjury, I declare that I have examined this return and accompanying schedules and statements, and to the best of my knowledge and belief, they are true, correct, and complete. Declaration of preparer (other than taxpayer) is based on all information of which preparer has any knowledge.

Your signature	Date	Your occupation	Daytime phone number
		LABORATORY MANAGER	(219) 824-5555
Spouse's signature. If a joint return, **both** must sign.	Date	Spouse's occupation	
		SOCIAL WORKER	

Paid Preparer's Use Only

Preparer's signature ▶	Date	Check if self-employed ☐	Preparer's SSN or PTIN
Firm's name (or yours if self-employed), address, and ZIP code ▶		EIN	
		Phone no. (____)	

Form **1040** (2008)

✿ *Printed on recycled paper*

Exhibit 8.4D   Sample Schedule A

SCHEDULES A&B
(Form 1040)

Department of the Treasury
Internal Revenue Service   (99)

Schedule A—Itemized Deductions

(Schedule B is on back)

▶ **Attach to Form 1040.**   ▶ **See Instructions for Schedules A&B (Form 1040).**

OMB No. 1545-0074

2008

Attachment
Sequence No. **07**

Name(s) shown on Form 1040

Your social security number

Medical and Dental Expenses	**Caution.** Do not include expenses reimbursed or paid by others.						
	1	Medical and dental expenses (see page A-1)	1				
	2	Enter amount from Form 1040, line 38 [2]					
	3	Multiply line 2 by 7.5% (.075)	3				
	4	Subtract line 3 from line 1. If line 3 is more than line 1, enter -0-.			4		
Taxes You Paid (See page A-2.)	5	State and local **(check only one box):**					
		a ☐ Income taxes, **or**	5	5,025	00		
		b ☐ General sales taxes					
	6	Real estate taxes (see page A-5)	6	1,650	00		
	7	Personal property taxes	7				
	8	Other taxes. List type and amount ▶ _____	8	5,000	00		
	9	Add lines 5 through 8			9	11,675	00
Interest You Paid (See page A-5.)	10	Home mortgage interest and points reported to you on Form 1098	10				
	11	Home mortgage interest not reported to you on Form 1098. If paid to the person from whom you bought the home, see page A-6 and show that person's name, identifying no., and address ▶					
Note. Personal interest is not deductible.		_____	11				
	12	Points not reported to you on Form 1098. See page A-6 for special rules.	12				
	13	Qualified mortgage insurance premiums (see page A-6)	13				
	14	Investment interest. Attach Form 4952 if required. (See page A-6.)	14				
	15	Add lines 10 through 14			15	6,926	00
Gifts to Charity	16	Gifts by cash or check. If you made any gift of $250 or more, see page A-7	16	375	00		
If you made a gift and got a benefit for it, see page A-7.	17	Other than by cash or check. If any gift of $250 or more, see page A-8. You **must** attach Form 8283 if over $500	17	425	00		
	18	Carryover from prior year	18				
	19	Add lines 16 through 18			19	800	00
Casualty and Theft Losses	20	Casualty or theft loss(es). Attach Form 4684. (See page A-8.)			20	0	00
Job Expenses and Certain Miscellaneous Deductions (See page A-9.)	21	Unreimbursed employee expenses—job travel, union dues, job education, etc. Attach Form 2106 or 2106-EZ if required. (See page A-9.) ▶	21				
	22	Tax preparation fees	22				
	23	Other expenses—investment, safe deposit box, etc. List type and amount ▶ _____	23				
	24	Add lines 21 through 23	24				
	25	Enter amount from Form 1040, line 38 [25]					
	26	Multiply line 25 by 2% (.02)	26				
	27	Subtract line 26 from line 24. If line 26 is more than line 24, enter -0-			27	0	00
Other Miscellaneous Deductions	28	Other—from list on page A-10. List type and amount ▶ _____			28	0	00
Total Itemized Deductions	29	Is Form 1040, line 38, over $159,950 (over $79,975 if married filing separately)? ☐ **No.** Your deduction is not limited. Add the amounts in the far right column for lines 4 through 28. Also, enter this amount on Form 1040, line 40. ☐ **Yes.** Your deduction may be limited. See page A-10 for the amount to enter.	} ▶		29	19,401	00
	30	If you elect to itemize deductions even though they are less than your standard deduction, check here . . . . ▶ ☐					

For Paperwork Reduction Act Notice, see Form 1040 instructions.   Cat. No. 11330X   Schedule A (Form 1040) 2008

Exhibit 8.4E   Sample Schedule B

OMB No. 1545-0074   Page **2**

Name(s) shown on Form 1040. Do not enter name and social security number if shown on other side.

Your social security number

Schedule B—Interest and Ordinary Dividends

Attachment
Sequence No. **08**

			Amount	
Part I **Interest** (See page B-1 and the instructions for Form 1040, line 8a.)	**1**	List name of payer. If any interest is from a seller-financed mortgage and the buyer used the property as a personal residence, see page B-1 and list this interest first. Also, show that buyer's social security number and address ▶		
		FIRST BANK	200	00
			1	
Note. If you received a Form 1099-INT, Form 1099-OID, or substitute statement from a brokerage firm, list the firm's name as the payer and enter the total interest shown on that form.	**2**	Add the amounts on line 1	**2**	200	00
	3	Excludable interest on series EE and I U.S. savings bonds issued after 1989. Attach Form 8815	**3**	
	4	Subtract line 3 from line 2. Enter the result here and on Form 1040, line 8a ▶	**4**	200	00

Note. If line 4 is over $1,500, you must complete Part III.

			Amount	
Part II **Ordinary Dividends** (See page B-1 and the instructions for Form 1040, line 9a.)	**5**	List name of payer ▶		
		OMNI FUND	100	00
		IBM	200	00
		OHIO POWER	68	00
			5	
Note. If you received a Form 1099-DIV or substitute statement from a brokerage firm, list the firm's name as the payer and enter the ordinary dividends shown on that form.				
	6	Add the amounts on line 5. Enter the total here and on Form 1040, line 9a . ▶	**6**	368	00

Note. If line 6 is over $1,500, you must complete Part III.

		Yes	No
Part III **Foreign Accounts and Trusts** (See page B-2.)	You must complete this part if you **(a)** had over $1,500 of taxable interest or ordinary dividends; or **(b)** had a foreign account; or **(c)** received a distribution from, or were a grantor of, or a transferor to, a foreign trust.		
	7a At any time during 2008, did you have an interest in or a signature or other authority over a financial account in a foreign country, such as a bank account, securities account, or other financial account? See page B-2 for exceptions and filing requirements for Form TD F 90-22.1.		
	b If "Yes," enter the name of the foreign country ▶		
	8 During 2008, did you receive a distribution from, or were you the grantor of, or transferor to, a foreign trust? If "Yes," you may have to file Form 3520. See page B-2		

For Paperwork Reduction Act Notice, see Form 1040 instructions.

Schedule B (Form 1040) 2008

Exhibit 8.4F   Credit Report for Frank Dunten

INFORMATIVE RESEARCH

File #	222-2222	Page 1 of 1
Lender:	AnytownBank	
Address:	124 48th St.	
Attn:	Sue Lee	
Rec'd:	6/11/09	
Compl'd:	6/12/09	
Rev:	6/20/09	

323 First Street
South Bend, Indiana 46310
219-824-2000

Borrower	Dunten, Frank A.
Coborrower	Dunten, Katherine L.
Address	3171 Dunkirk Lane
City, State, Zip	South Bend, IN 46311

REPOSITORIES   **CHARGES**

Global Reports   Conv. Report $55

Borrower		**Coborrower**	
Social Security #	314-29-3354	Social Security #	312-68-7325
Employer	The Dental Shop	Employer	St. Joe County
Position	Laboratory Manager	Position	Social Worker
Since	10/96	Since	12/00
Income	$90,000	Income	$21,600

Marital Status	**Additional Names**	**Number of Dependents**
Married	None disclosed	0

Previous Employment and Residence History

B Prior	American Dental Widgets – Asst. manager – 4 years
C Prior	BBB Dental Services – Technician – 2 years

Residence History	**Address**	**Length**
Present	See above	9 years
Prior	600 Second Street, Louisville, IN	2 years

Source	Credit Opened	Status Date	Type	Amount/ Line	Credit Balance	Status
1st Bank	09/00	04/06	Visa	$10,000	$1,500	Curr. Acct.
1st Bank	05/04	05/09	Mortgage/ Property	125,000	79,000	
2nd Bank	06/05	05/09	Install. Automobile	28,000	8,000	Curr. Acct.
BBNA	09/00	05/09	Visa	1,500	875	Curr. Acct.
Home Depot	11/05	05/09	Rev.	1,000	250	Curr. Acct.
Sears	09/97	05/09	Rev.	2,000	200	Curr. Was 90, 01/99
Friendly Savings	08/03	10/04	Install.	2,500	0	Paid, was 30, 2X
Bank Okla.	01/00	05/09	Visa	1,000	0	Curr. Acct
Signet student loan	08/00	05/09	Install.	10,000 $50/mo.	0	A/A

Inquiries	J. Chicago Bank 5/09 No open account		
(Last 90 days)	J. Fiat Finance	4/09	No open account

Public Records

Source/Type	Date	Liability	ECOA/ Court Location	Paid	Docket/Attorney
Z1234567					

evasive or display other signs of uneasiness. These actions should not be construed as signs of a credit problem. Lenders must stick to facts and avoid personal prejudices.

OPEN-END LOAN PRODUCT CONSIDERATIONS

The growth of open-end credit products has added some new twists to credit investigation, among them prescreening and account monitoring.

Prescreening

In a prescreened loan solicitation program, consumers are not aware that their names have been passed through a prescreening process, the bank does not know the names of those consumers who fail to pass the prescreening, and the information is not reported publicly on credit files. A consumer reporting agency compares all potential applicants in its files with the bank's defined credit requirements. The bank receives only the names and addresses of consumers who meet the bank's requirements. Only they are mailed a credit offer. Consumers may notify consumer reporting agencies not to provide their information to lenders for prescreening purposes. Exhibit 8.5 illustrates the prescreening process.

Account Monitoring

To monitor its accounts, the bank may compare files for its current loan customers with consumer reporting agency files, using bank-defined criteria. Consumers who no longer meet the bank's requirements may be subject to further screening. Usually, the bank receives a file of the credit reports of consumers who did not meet the criteria. A credit analyst examines each report and, depending on the circumstances, may continue the investigation. Once all required data are assembled, the lender may

- continue the account on its present terms
- block the line of credit from further use
- reduce the credit limit

If the lender blocks the line of credit or reduces the credit limit, the consumer must be notified immediately.

Monitoring accounts is an important part of the bank's effort to manage its loan portfolios. Although state laws may modify these general procedures or require specific legal disclosures, account monitoring is a responsible approach to protecting the integrity and quality of the bank's loan assets.

LAWS AND REGULATIONS

The primary law applying to credit investigation activities is the Fair Credit Reporting Act (FCRA).

Exhibit 8.5   Prescreen and Preapproval Process

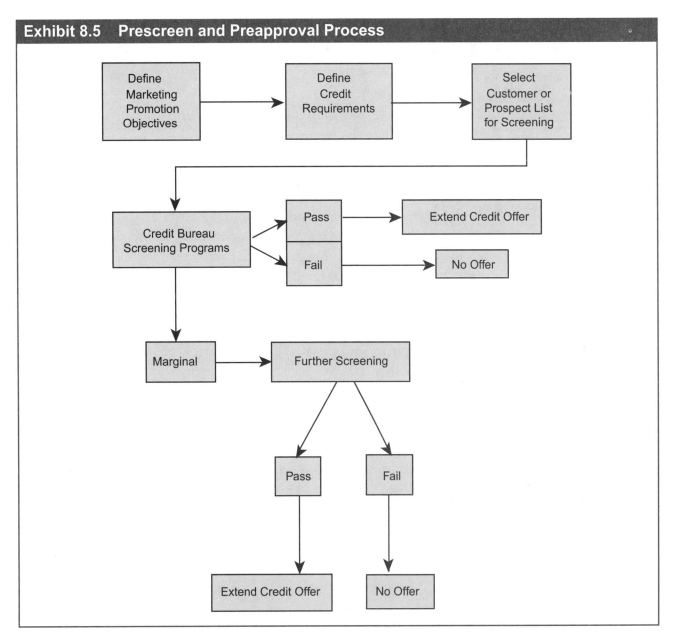

FAIR CREDIT REPORTING ACT

Enacted in 1971, the Fair Credit Reporting Act primarily governs how consumer reporting agencies report consumer credit. These agencies issue standard reports, known as **credit reports**. However, FCRA also affects users of the reports, such as financial institutions.

The FCRA has four primary objectives:

- establish acceptable purposes for which a credit report may be obtained

- define consumers' rights related to credit reports, especially giving consumers the right to request and receive their reports and a procedure to follow for correcting inaccurate information

credit report—Information that consumer reporting agencies communicate by written, oral, or other methods about a consumer's creditworthiness, credit standing, credit capacity, character, general reputation, personal characteristics, or mode of living. *Also known as* consumer report.

Situation

When applying for a loan with ABC Bank, Nick Adams provided information about his accounts with LMN Bank. Several months later Nick applies for a new job and gives ABC Bank as a reference.

If it answers the request, is ABC Bank a consumer reporting agency?

- require adverse action notices for decisions to deny an application that is based on information from a credit report
- define the responsibilities of consumer reporting agencies

Banks as Furnishers of Information

The information in a credit report, gathered by reporting agencies from banks and other creditors, can be passed on to third parties that have a legitimate business need for it. If a bank furnishes a consumer's credit history to another institution, it is considered to be a consumer reporting agency and is required to abide by the FCRA rules for agencies. However, if the bank only issues information from its own records about its own experience with the consumer, the bank is only a user of credit information and has fewer FCRA responsibilities.

Banks as Users of Information

Because banks prefer to avoid being considered reporting agencies, most FCRA provisions apply to banks as *users* of credit reports, as when lenders request a report because they have received an application or are monitoring an account.

adverse action—A creditor's decision to deny a consumer's request for credit; reduce an existing credit line (except for delinquency); or change the terms, rate, or amount of a credit request. Such actions require that the consumer be advised in writing of the reasons for the adverse action.

Banks have responsibilities as users: If a bank obtains a credit report and the report contributes to an **adverse action**, it must disclose the source and nature of the adverse information to the consumer within 30 days of the application date. Banks must disclose the name, address, and toll-free telephone number of the furnisher. They also must disclose when the information was obtained and used in the adverse decision. This disclosure must state that the consumer reporting agency did not make the decision and is not able to provide the reasons for the adverse action.

Consumers have the right to contact the consumer reporting agency that furnished the report to obtain a copy of their report and have erroneous information corrected.

FACT ACT

The Fair and Accurate Credit Transactions Act (FACT Act) of 2003 amended the FCRA to

- prevent identity theft related to credit
- improve accuracy in credit reporting
- increase privacy protections for consumers by ensuring proper disposal of records and placing restrictions on information sharing
- require more disclosures to consumers, such as credit scores and notifications of negative credit reports

- prohibit creditors from obtaining or using medical information in credit decisions, with certain exceptions

- restrict a consumer reporting agency's ability to disclose medical information

- give consumers more control over the type and number of marketing solicitations they receive

All bank regulators and the Federal Trade Commission have adopted final rules to implement the FACT Act. The Federal Reserve Board has two regulations that address it: FRS Regulation V, Fair Credit Reporting, covers the majority of FACT Act requirements. Regulation FF, Obtaining and Using Medical Information in Connection with Credit, specifies some exceptions to the restrictions on the use of medical information in credit decisions. A FACT Act requirement not covered by either regulation requires lenders to disclose credit scores to applicants for mortgage loans.

Identity Theft and Privacy Concerns

The FACT Act requires banks to implement an identity theft red flag program and to take steps to prevent identity theft, which is a crime. The program, approved by the bank's board of directors, must include a system for detecting red flags, responding to the alerts, and mitigating any damage to the consumer. Banks must report address discrepancies to consumer reporting agencies and verify address changes when new credit or debit card requests are received. Exhibit 8.3 lists identity theft red flags to which banks must respond.

The FACT Act requires banks that provide negative credit information to a consumer reporting agency to notify the consumer (whether borrower, cosigner, or guarantor) in writing of the action. The consumer notice must be sent before or no more than 30 days after the negative information is sent to the consumer reporting agency. FRS Regulation V offers two model notices banks may use.

Other privacy-related requirements of the FACT Act include the requirement to dispose of consumer information when the bank no longer needs it. It also requires that when a bank wants to share consumer credit-related information with an affiliate for marketing purposes, it must give the consumer notice and an opportunity to opt out.

Medical Information

The FACT Act prohibits creditors from obtaining or using **medical information** in credit decisions except as permitted by regulatory exemptions, and it restricts the ability of reporting agencies to disclose medical information. It also restricts the sharing of medical and related information with affiliates. In general, a creditor may not obtain or use a consumer's medical information to determine eligibility or continued eligibility for credit unless it is the type of financial information ordinarily used in making a credit decision; it is unsolicited, or it

Identity theft is a crime involving the possession of identifying information not lawfully issued for that person's use or the attempt to access the financial resources of another person by using illegally obtained information.

Regulations Implementing the FACT Act

Federal Reserve:	12 CFR 222, FRS Regulation V; 12 CFR 232, FRS Regulation FF
OCC:	12 CFR 41
FDIC:	12 CFR 334
OTS:	12 CFR 571

medical information— Under the FACT Act, which amended the Fair Credit Reporting Act, information, oral or recorded in any form, created by or derived from a health care provider or the consumer, that relates to the past, present, or future physical, mental, or behavioral health or condition of an individual; the provision of health care; or payment for health care.

Situation

Ben Hudson is applying for a loan from AnyCity bank. The loan application form provides a space where Ben may note other information or special circumstances. This space is for information that he would like the creditor to consider in evaluating the loan application. Ben notes that he has a pacemaker that needs annual checkups.

Can AnyCity Bank use this information?

forbearance—The act of refraining from legal action when a loan is in arrears (as when the delinquency is due to medical reasons), usually granted when a borrower satisfactorily brings payment up to date.

falls within one of the specific exceptions the regulators permit. Some exceptions to the rule are

- financial information routinely used in credit decisions (such as the dollar amount of a debt to a hospital), as long as it is used no less favorably than nonmedical information

- legal, contractual, and safety and soundness concerns, such as whether a consumer legally is capable of entering into a contract or, at the consumer's request, whether the consumer qualifies for a special credit program or credit-related assistance program that has medically related criteria

- verification of how the loan proceeds will be used when the purpose is to finance medical products or services

- whether a **forbearance** practice or program triggered by a medical condition or event applies

SUMMARY

- Thorough investigations help banks make sound credit decisions and limit open-end credit use by applicants who are having financial difficulties. A lender initiates the credit investigation after formal application is made for a new loan or to analyze risk on an existing account.

- The primary objectives of credit investigation are to verify that application data are accurate and complete; conduct the investigation in an efficient, cost-effective manner; identify negative trends or potential problems that may affect the consumer's creditworthiness; and acquire enough information to make a sound credit decision. The basic steps in a credit investigation are to review the application for information that warrants immediate rejection; check bank files to determine the applicant's account history; obtain a credit agency report; contact employers and creditors for references; and verify the value of any collateral securing the loan.

- The information the investigator needs depends on the type, size, and risk of the loan. Most investigations review the applicant's credit history, income, employment, and residence and the value of the collateral. In evaluating credit history, the lender wants to know from whom applicants have borrowed, what type of accounts they have used and still have available, how long the accounts have been open, how the accounts have been paid, current obligations, and potential credit exposure.

- Credit history is available from the application, the bank's own files, other financial institutions, consumer reporting agencies, and public records. Income, a principal indicator of the applicant's capacity to repay the loan, is investigated for source, reliability, frequency, and probable continuity over the term of the loan. To verify income, credit investigators may contact employers directly or rely on information from pay stubs, W-2 forms, tax returns, legal documents, and direct payroll deposits. The major elements of employment to investigate are type of job, time on the job, employer's business and stability, and applicant's employment history. Residence information can evidence an applicant's stability and character. Investigators seek information on type of residence, time at residence, and previous residence.

- Investigators must determine the value and ownership of collateral offered to secure a loan. For purchase-money loans the bill of sale, invoice, or purchase order should reveal the actual selling price, the amount and composition of any down payment, and a complete description of the item being purchased. Investigators also check public records and valuation guidebooks and obtain appraisals. Documents like deeds, titles, or bills of sale can establish ownership.

- Consumer reporting agencies and the applicant's personal financial statements and tax returns offer the most comprehensive information. Credit reports contain information gathered from lenders and public files, consumer identifying information, trade lines, inquiries, and public record and collection information, such as judgments, liens, and bankruptcy. Personal financial statements give details on the consumer's assets, liabilities, and net worth.

- In addition to the red flags that may arise during the credit investigation, particularly on the credit report, investigators need to watch for other warning signs of potential problems: gaps in information, information inconsistent with the applicant's age, and the applicant's behavior during the loan interview, such as being aggressive or too anxious.

- Prescreening and account monitoring are credit investigation techniques used particularly for open-end loan products. Prescreening compares consumer reporting agency information on potential applicants with the bank's defined credit requirements. The bank receives only the names and addresses of consumers who meet the requirements. For account monitoring, the bank compares files on its current loan customers with consumer reporting agency files using bank-defined criteria. Consumers who no longer meet the bank's requirements are subject to further screening, and a determination is made whether to continue the account, block it from use, or reduce the credit limit.

- The Fair Credit Reporting Act (FCRA) is directed primarily at consumer credit reports and applies primarily to consumer reporting agencies, although banks may occasionally fall within its purview. Its objectives are to establish acceptable purposes for which a credit report may be obtained; define rights related to credit reports, with emphasis on consumers' rights to their reports and to a procedure for correcting information; set requirements for reporting to consumers adverse credit decisions resulting from credit report information; and define the responsibilities of a consumer reporting agency.

• When banks pass along information about a customer's account with another institution, they become furnishers of consumer information and thus fall under the FCRA. However, most banks are simply users of credit reports; they must abide only by the rules on notifying consumers about negative information in credit reports that result in an adverse action. Consumers have the right to order free credit reports once every 12 months as well as when they are notified by a bank that they have been denied credit.

• The Fair and Accurate Credit Transactions Act (FACT Act) amends FCRA to prevent identity theft, improve accuracy, better protect privacy, and require more disclosures to consumers, including credit scores and notifications of negative credit reports. The FACT Act also prohibits creditors from obtaining or using medical information in credit decisions, with certain exceptions; restricts consumer reporting agencies from disclosing medical information; and gives consumers more control over the type and number of marketing solicitations they receive.

• Each bank regulator has its own regulations to implement the FACT Act. The primary Federal Reserve regulation that addresses it is FRS Regulation V. FRS Regulation FF lists circumstances under which banks may obtain and use unsolicited medical information.

Learning Check

SELF-CHECK AND REVIEW

1. What are the objectives of credit investigation?

2. Why might a credit investigation begin by referring to bank files instead of credit reports or public records?

3. What are two drawbacks to using W-2 forms or tax returns to verify income data?

4. What information is available on a personal financial statement? How may a credit investigator use the information?

5. What are red flags for potential credit problems and how are they used? Give two examples.

6. What is account monitoring and how does it apply to open-end credit?

7. Under what circumstance could a bank become a furnisher of consumer information—a consumer reporting agency—as defined by the Fair Credit Reporting Act?

8. What is at least one circumstance in which a bank may obtain and use a consumer's medical information, according to the FACT Act?

ADDITIONAL RESOURCES

Resources

ABA Bank Compliance Magazine, Washington: American Bankers Association, periodical.

American Bankers Association, **www.aba.com**.

Analyzing Financial Statements, Washington: American Bankers Association, 2007.

Annual Credit report, www.annualcreditreport.com.

BUC International Corp., www.buc.com.

Credit Repair: How to Help Yourself, FTC Facts for Consumers.
www.ftc.gov/bcp/edu/pubs/consumer/credit/cre13.shtm.

Don't Be an Online Victim: How to Guard Against Internet Thieves and Electronic Scams, Federal Deposit Insurance Corporation,
www.fdic.gov/consumers/consumer/guard.

Equifax, www.equifax.com.

Experian, www.experian.com.

Identity Theft: Outsmarting the Crooks, DVD, U.S. Treasury Department, available through Federal Citizens Information Center, www.pueblo.gsa.gov.

Interagency Interpretive Guidance on Customer Identification Program Requirements Under Section 326 of the USA PATRIOT Act, FAQs: Final CIP Rule, www.fincen.gov/faqsfinalciprule.

Kelly Blue Book, www.bb.com.

National Automobile Dealers Association (vehicle valuation information), www.nada.org.

National Foundation for Credit Counseling, www.nfcc.org.

OCC Fair Credit Reporting Exam Procedures, OCC 2008-28, Office of the Comptroller of the Currency, www.occ.treas.gov/ftp/bulletin/2008-28a.pdf.

Reference Guide to Regulatory Compliance, Washington: American Bankers Association, updated annually.

The Beige Book, Summary of Commentary on Current Economic Conditions by Federal Reserve District, Federal Reserve Board,
www.federalreserve.gov/FOMC/BeigeBook/2008.

TradeMotorcycles, www.Trademotorcycles.com.

TransUnion, www.transunion.com.

U.C.C. Article 9—Secured Transactions; Sales of Accounts and Chattel Paper, Part 4, www.law.cornell.edu/ucc/9/overview.html.

Wage and Tax Statement, W-2 Form, www.irs.gov/pub/irs-pdf/fw2.pdf.

Wall Street Journal, www.wsj.com

Yahoo Autos, www.Yahooautos.com.

Your Access to Free Credit Reports, Federal Trade Commission,.
www.ftc.gov/bcp/edu/pubs/consumer/credit/cre34.shtm.

Your Credit Report, What It Says About You, Federal Reserve Bank of San Francisco, www.frbsf.org/publications/consumer/creditreport.html.

APPENDIX III

Sample Credit Report (print image format)

```
GOi duncan,elizabeth*2 9932,woodbine,chicago,il,60068*3 555,e,jackson,st,cleveland,oh,44123*5 002-02-2222**

                              TRANSUNION CREDIT REPORT
<FOR>       <SUB NAME>        <MKT SUB>     <INFILE>      <DATE>        <TIME>
(I) D248    ABC DEPT STORE    06 CH         4/79          5/20/08       09:36CT

<SUBJECT>                                          <SSN>          <BIRTH DATE>
DUNCAN, ELIZABETH                                  111-11-1111    2/55
<ALSO KNOWN AS>                                                   <TELEPHONE>
COOK, ELIZABETH                                                   (555)555-5555

<CURRENT ADDRESS>                                                 <DATE RPTD>
9932 WOODBINE, #9B, CHICAGO, IL. 60068                            1/06
<FORMER ADDRESS>
10 N. CAMINO, OAKLAND, CA. 94583                                  4/02
8500 N. WESTERN AV. CHICAGO, IL 60645

<CURRENT EMPLOYER AND ADDRESS>       <POSITION>    <VERF>   <RPTD>   <HIRE>
ABC HOTELS                           CONCIERGE
ANYTOWN, IL.                                       5/08     5/08     3/02
------------------------------------------------------------------------
S P E C I A L   M E S S A G E S
***ID MISMATCH ALERT:      PREVIOUS INPUT ADDRESS DOES NOT MATCH FILE ADDRESS(ES)***
***HIGH RISK FRAUD ALERT:   INPUT SSN NOT ISSUED BY SOCIAL SECURITY ADMINISTRATION***
***SSN YEAR OF ISSUANCE:   FILE SSN ISSUED: 1957-1960; STATE ISSUED: IL;
                           EST. AGE OBTAINED: 4-8***
***IDENTITY MANAGER VERIFICATION
  FRAUD MODEL SCORE: 200     ID SCORE: 900     SCORE FACTOR CODES: 345, 678, 901
  INPUT PHONE NUMBER AND ADDRESS DO NOT MATCH***
***OFAC NAME SCREEN: CLEAR***
***CONSUMER STATEMENT: SEE END RPT***
------------------------------------------------------------------------
M O D E L   P R O F I L E          * * * A L E R T * * *
***VANTAGESCORE ALERT:         SCORE +590: TK, 52, RF, 10 SCORECARD: 02 ***
***TRANSUNION BANKRUPTCY MODEL:   SCORE +533: 24, 07, 15, 08 ***
C R E D I T   S U M M A R Y               * * * T O T A L   F I L E   H I S T O R Y
PR=2  COL=1   NEG=1 HSTNEG=2-8 TRD=4  RVL=2   INST=1 MTG=1 OPN=0   INQ=4
              HIGH CRED   CRED LIM   BALANCE   PAST DUE  MNTHLY PAY AVAILABLE
REVOLVING:    $10.1K      $18.2K     $5.4K               $225       71%
INSTALLMENT:  $16.9K                 $12.9K    $1128     $282
MORTGAGE      $232.5K                $173.2K             $1470
TOTALS:       $259.5K     $18.2K     $191.5K   $1128     $1977
------------------------------------------------------------------------
P U B L I C   R E C O R D S
SOURCE        DATE       LIAB     ECOA      ASSETS    PAID     DOCKET#
TYPE                              COURT LOC                    ATTORNEY
Z 4932059     10/06R              C                            06B38521
CHAPTER 7 BANKRUPTCY                                           D. WINSLOW

ZP5027011     1/06R      $3128    I                   6/06     06M987654
PAID CIVIL JUDGMENT                                            WILLIAMS
------------------------------------------------------------------------
C O L L E C T I O N S
SUBNAME       SUBCODE     ECOA     OPENED    CLOSED   $PLACED   CREDITOR   MOP
ACCOUNT#                           VERIFIED           BALANCE   REMARKS
ADVANCED COL  Y 999C004   I        5/03      5/03F    $2500     ABC BANK   09P
12345                              4/08A              $1000
------------------------------------------------------------------------
T R A D E S
SUBNAME       SUBCODE    OPENED    HIGHCRED  TERMS     MAXDELQ   PAYPAT    1-12   MOP
ACCOUNT#                 VERIFIED  CREDLIM   PASTDUE   AMT-MOP   PAYPAT    13-24

ECOA   COLLATRL/LOANTYPE CLSD/PD   BALANCE   REMARKS                 MO   30/60/90

ABC BK        B 6781001  8/06      $16.9K    60M282    1/08      445543211111     I05
9876543210               5/08A               $1128     $1410 05  11111111
I    AUTOMOBILE                    $12.9K    *CONTACT SUBSCRIBER   20   1/  1/  5

ABC RETAILER  D 1234567  12/05     $9.6K     MIN200    2/06      111111111111     R01
1234567890               5/08A     $16.7K              $230 02   111111111111
I    /CREDITCARD                   $5.2K                         29   1/  0/  0

ABC MORTGAGE  Q 1111111  11/02     $232.5K   360M1470            111111111111     M01
1112223333               5/08A                                  111111111111
C    /PROPERTY                     $173.2K                       48   0/  0/  0

ABC DEPARTMENT D 7654321 12/07     $500      MIN25               11111            R01
123123123123             5/08A     $1500
I    /CREDITCARD                   $150                          5   0/  0/  0
------------------------------------------------------------------------
I N Q U I R I E S
DATE      SUBCODE        SUBNAME              DATE      SUBCODE       SUBNAME
5/20/08   DCH248         ABC DEPT STORE       3/07/08   BPH9999(EAS)  TEST BANK
2/20/08   ASD1234(CAL)   MAIN ST AUTO         1/01/08   DNY777(EAS)   123 RETAILER
------------------------------------------------------------------------
C O N S U M E R   S T A T E M E N T
#HK#EFCRA EXTENDED FRAUD ALERT: ACTION MAY BE REQUIRED UNDER FCRA BEFORE OPENING OR
MODIFYING AN ACCOUNT.
------------------------------------------------------------------------
I N Q U I R Y   A N A L Y S I S
DATE      SUBCODE        SUBNAME
03/07/08  B 9999         TEST BANK
DUNCAN, ELIZABETH     (773) 123-4567
9932 WOODBINE, CHICAGO, IL 60693

02/20/08  A 1234         MAIN ST AUTO
DUNCAN, ELIZABETH     (773) 555-1234
9932 WOODBINE, CHICAGO, IL 60693
10 N. CAMINO, OAKLAND, CA 94583
EMPLOYER: GRAND HOTEL
------------------------------------------------------------------------
C R E D I T   R E P O R T   S E R V I C E D   B Y :
TRANSUNION               800-888-4213
P.O. BOX 1000, CHESTER, PA  19022
CONSUMER DISCLOSURES CAN BE OBTAINED ONLINE THROUGH TRANSUNION AT:
  HTTP://WWW.TRANSUNION.COM/DIRECT
------------------------------------------------------------------------
                       END OF TRANSUNION REPORT
```

This sample report is intended for educational purposes and cannot be used for testing. The actual Credit Report you receive will be customized to meet your specific request.

NOTE: Fields with dollar amounts will display:
K=thousands
M=millions

Note: The "TransUnion Credit Report User Guide" or portions thereof, TransUnion and the "T" logo are registered or unregistered copyrighted works, service marks or trademarks of TransUnion LLC. All Rights Reserved.

Credit Report Codes

ECOA (Equal Credit Opportunity Act) Inquiry and Account Designators

CODE	DESCRIPTION
A	Authorized user of shared account
C	Joint contractual liability
I	Individual account for sole use of customer
M	Account for which subject is liable but co-signer has liability if the maker defaults
P	Participant in shared account which cannot be distinguished as C or A
S	Account for which subject is co-signer and becomes liable if maker defaults
T	Relationship with account terminated
U	Undesignated
X	Deceased

Date Indicators

CODE	DESCRIPTION
A	Automated
C	Closed
D	Declined
F	Repossessed/Written Off/Collection
I	Indirect
M	Manually Frozen
N	No Record
P	Paid Out
R	Reported
S	Slow Answering
T	Temporarily Frozen
V	Verified
X	No Reply

MOP (Current Manner of Payment)

CODE	DESCRIPTION
00	Not rated, too new to rate, or approved but not used
01	Pays as agreed
02	30–59 days past the due date
03	60–89 days past the due date
04	90–119 days past the due date
05	120 days or more past the due date
07	Paying or paid under Wage Earner Plan or similar arrangement
08	Repossession
8A	Voluntary repossession
8D	Legal repossession
8P	Paying or paid account with MOP 08
8R	Repossession; redeemed
09	Charged off to bad debt
9B	Collection account
9P	Paying or paid account with MOP 09 or 9B
UC	Unclassified
UR	Unrated

Type of Account

CODE	DESCRIPTION
O	Open Account (30, 60 or 90 days)
R	Revolving or Option
I	Installment
M	Mortgage
C	Check credit (line of credit)

KOB (Kind of Business Classifications)

CODE	DESCRIPTION
A	Automotive
B	Banks and Savings and Loan Institutions
C	Clothing
D	Department, Variety and Other Retail
E	Educational Organizations and Employment Services Companies
F	Finance, Personal
G	Groceries
H	Home Furnishings
I	Insurance
J	Jewelry, Cameras and Computers
K	Contractors
L	Lumber, Building Material and Hardware
M	Medical and Related Health
N	Credit Card and Travel/Entertainment Companies
O	Oil Companies
P	Personal Services Other Than Medical
Q	Credit Unions and Finance Companies Other Than Personal Finance Companies
R	Real Estate and Public Accommodations
S	Sporting Goods
T	Farm and Garden Supplies
U	Utilities and Fuel
V	Government
W	Wholesale
X	Advertising
Y	Collection
Z	Miscellaneous

Note: The "TransUnion Credit Report User Guide" or portions thereof, TransUnion and the "T" logo are registered or unregistered copyrighted works, service marks or trademarks of TransUnion LLC. All Rights Reserved.

Public records

```
P U B L I C   R E C O R D S
SOURCE           DATE      LIAB     ECOA        ASSETS    PAID    DOCKET#
TYPE                                COURT LOC                     ATTORNEY
Z 4932059        10/06R             C                            06B38521
CHAPTER 7 BANKRUPTCY                                             D. WINSLOW

ZP5027011        1/06R     $3128    I                     6/06   06M987654
PAID CIVIL JUDGMENT                                              WILLIAMS
```

Public record information is maintained on a consumer's file in compliance with the Fair Credit Reporting Act (FCRA). This information is obtained from county, state and federal courts, and includes civil judgments, state tax liens, federal tax liens, and bankruptcies. The length of time each record is held on TransUnion's database varies by the type of record.

Typical retention periods (may vary by state)

Civil judgments	Seven years
Unpaid tax liens	Indefinite
Paid tax liens	Seven years from date paid
Chapter 7, 11 or 12 bankruptcies	Ten years
Chapter 13 bankruptcy filings	Ten years
Chapter 13 bankruptcy dismissal or discharges	Seven years
Bankruptcies voluntarily dismissed	Seven years

Collections

```
C O L L E C T I O N S
SUBNAME          SUBCODE   ECOA     OPENED      CLOSED    $PLACED   CREDITOR    MOP
ACCOUNT#                            VERIFIED              BALANCE   REMARKS
ADVANCED COL     Y 999C004  I       5/03        5/03F     $2500     ABC BANK    09P
12345                              4/08A                  $1000
```

Identifies consumer accounts that have been placed with a professional debt-collecting firm. Collection information includes the name of the collection agency providing information, consumer's account number with the collection agency and TransUnion-assigned reporting subscriber number (all collection agency subcodes begin with a "Y").

Also included are the Equal Credit Opportunity Act (ECOA) designator¨, date the amount was charged off by the original creditor, date the information was verified along with an indicator code¨, date the item was turned over to a collection agency (shown as date opened). Also included are original dollar amount of collection, the balance owed as of date verified or closed, name of the original creditor, and an explanation of current account status as reported by the collection agency.

¨¨ See the Credit Report Codes page of this brochure for more details.

Note: The "TransUnion Credit Report User Guide" or portions thereof, TransUnion and the "T" logo are registered or unregistered copyrighted works, service marks or trademarks of TransUnion LLC. All Rights Reserved.

Credit Report Fields

Subscriber-provided input and information

```
GOi duncan,elizabeth*2 9932,woodbine,chicago,il,60068*3 555,e,jackson,st,cleveland,oh,44123*5 002-02-2222**
                              TRANSUNION CREDIT REPORT
<FOR>     <SUB NAME>          <MKT SUB>      <INFILE>      <DATE>        <TIME>
(I) D248  ABC DEPT STORE      06 CH          4/79          5/20/08       09:36CT
```

The actual consumer information you entered to locate the file from TransUnion will be displayed at the top of the print image format report. On every TransUnion Credit Report the inquiring subscriber's TransUnion-assigned code, name, geographic area where the file resides within the TransUnion system, date the file was created, and inquiry date and time (Central Standard Time) are displayed.

Consumer demographic information

```
<SUBJECT>                                              <SSN>           <BIRTH DATE>
DUNCAN, ELIZABETH                                      111-11-1111     2/55
<ALSO KNOWN AS>                                                        <TELEPHONE>
COOK, ELIZABETH                                                        (555)555-5555

<CURRENT ADDRESS>                                                      <DATE RPTD>
9932 WOODBINE, #9B. CHICAGO, IL. 60068                                 1/06
<FORMER ADDRESS>
10 N. CAMINO, OAKLAND, CA. 94583                                       4/02
8500 N. WESTERN AV. CHICAGO, IL 60645

<CURRENT EMPLOYER AND ADDRESS>        <POSITION>    <VERF>    <RPTD>    <HIRE>
ABC HOTELS                            CONCIERGE
ANYTOWN, IL.                                        5/08      5/08      3/02
```

Helps verify consumer identification by providing:

- Names reported by data furnishers
- Current address and date it was first reported
- Up to two previous addresses and the date initially reported on first previous address
- Social Security number (SSN) if available

- Date of birth if available
- Telephone number or Phone Append (optional)
- Employment if available (including most current and one previous position, date employment was verified, reported and/or hired)

Special messages

```
S P E C I A L   M E S S A G E S
***ID MISMATCH ALERT:       PREVIOUS INPUT ADDRESS DOES NOT MATCH FILE ADDRESS(ES)***
***HIGH RISK FRAUD ALERT:   INPUT SSN NOT ISSUED BY SOCIAL SECURITY ADMINISTRATION***
***SSN YEAR OF ISSUANCE:    FILE SSN ISSUED: 1957-1960: STATE ISSUED: IL:
                            EST. AGE OBTAINED: 4-8***
***IDENTITY MANAGER VERIFICATION
   FRAUD MODEL SCORE: 200    ID SCORE: 900    SCORE FACTOR CODES: 345, 678, 901
   INPUT PHONE NUMBER AND ADDRESS DO NOT MATCH***
***OFAC NAME SCREEN: CLEAR***
***CONSUMER STATEMENT: SEE END RPT***
```

Highlights specific credit file conditions that may include:

- Presence of consumer statement
- No subject found

Some optional products may also appear.

ID MISMATCH ALERT messages (optional) appear when the input address, SSN or surname does not match what is on file; when a minimum of four inquiries have been made against the file within the last 60 days; or when an invalid ZIP code is entered.

HIGH RISK FRAUD ALERT messages (optional) appear if address, SSN or phone number have been used in suspected fraudulent activity; if the information on an application is inappropriate, such as a commercial or institutional address; or if the SSN has not been issued by the Social Security Administration or is that of a deceased person as reported by the Social Security Administration.

SSN YEAR OF ISSUANCE (optional) provides state, year/range of years and age of consumer when SSN was issued.

IDENTITY MANAGER VERIFICATION℠ (optional) combines sophisticated data analytics and multisourced databases to verify and validate consumer provided information, detect suspicious information, and identify potentially fraudulent transactions and/or accounts. Fraud messages are generated to alert subscribers of suspicious data. And, an identity/fraud score is provided which assesses the level of risk associated with the account. The ID Score® from ID Analytics® is available as an option for an additional lift in fraud detection.

OFAC NAME SCREEN (optional) is designed to screen an applicant's name against an enhanced U.S. Treasury Department's Office of Foreign Assets Control (OFAC) database of specially designated nationals (SDNs), drug traffickers and money launderers.

Note: The "TransUnion Credit Report User Guide" or portions thereof, TransUnion and the "T" logo are registered or unregistered copyrighted works, service marks or trademarks of TransUnion LLC. All Rights Reserved.

Model profile (optional)

```
M O D E L   P R O F I L E               * * * A L E R T * * *
***VANTAGESCORE ALERT:           SCORE  +590: TK, 52, RF, 10 SCORECARD: 02 ***
***TRANSUNION BANKRUPTCY MODEL:  SCORE  +533: 24, 07, 15, 08 ***
```

Displays empirically derived scores to help predict a consumer's future credit performance. Other available scores predict likelihood of bankruptcy, project recovery dollars, predict insurance risk, etc. Risk score factors are displayed numerically or in text, and are displayed in order based on their relative impact on the final score.

ALERT appears after Model Profile heading when Manner of Payment (MOP) is 7 or greater, or when a negative public record or a collection is present on the file.

Credit summary (optional)

```
C R E D I T   S U M M A R Y                    * * * T O T A L   F I L E   H I S T O R Y
PR=2  COL=1      NEG=1  HSTNEG=2-8  TRD=4  RVL=2  INST=1  MTG=1  OPN=0   INQ=4
                 HIGH CRED   CRED LIM   BALANCE   PAST DUE  MNTHLY PAY AVAILABLE
REVOLVING:       $10.1K      $18.2K     $5.4K               $225       71%
INSTALLMENT:     $16.9K                 $12.9K    $1128     $282
MORTGAGE         $232.5K                $173.2K             $1470
TOTALS:          $259.5K     $18.2K     $191.5K   $1128     $1977
```

Provides a "snapshot" of activity on the consumer's credit report.

- Available as an option covering either total file history or 12-month file history.
- "Total File History" or "12-Month History" is in the upper right hand corner of the credit summary corresponding to the option chosen.

From left to right, headers in the first row read as follows:

PR: Total number of public records

COL: Total number of collection accounts transferred to a third-party collection agency. These accounts are identified with a Kind of Business (KOB) code of "Y".

NEG: Total number of negative accounts (derogatory) with a current Manner of Payment (MOP) of 2 or greater.

HSTNEG: There are two separate pieces of information in this field. Both relate to historical negative information on a tradeline. Historical negative information is defined as any Manner of Payment (MOP) of 2 or greater, occurring in any month (excluding current month). The first half of this field describes the number of tradelines which have historical negative information and the second half describes the number of occurrences.

TRD: Total number of trades. TRD value is the sum of RVL, INST, MTG and OPN values.

RVL: Total number of revolving and/or check credit accounts (account types "R" and "C")

INST: Total number of installment accounts (account type "I")

MTG: Total number of mortgage accounts (account type "M")

OPN: Total number of open accounts (account type "O")

INQ: Total number of inquiries

From left to right, headers on the second row read as follows:

HIGH CRED: Highest amount ever owed on an account

CRED LIM: Maximum credit amount approved by credit grantor

BALANCE: Balance owed as of the date verified

PAST DUE: Amount past due as of the date verified or closed

MNTHLY PAY: Subscriber-reported monthly payment from the "TERMS" field on the account

AVAILABLE: Percent of credit available for revolving, check credit and open accounts. Field is calculated by subtracting balance from credit limit divided by credit limit.

TOTALS: Totals for second row headers are included for: Revolving, Installment and Mortgage Accounts (Open Accounts and Accounts Closed with a Balance are not shown on sample report)

Note: The "TransUnion Credit Report User Guide" or portions thereof, TransUnion and the "T" logo are registered or unregistered copyrighted works, service marks or trademarks of TransUnion LLC. All Rights Reserved.

Trades

```
T R A D E S
SUBNAME           SUBCODE    OPENED      HIGHCRED    TERMS        MAXDELQ     PAYPAT      1-12       MOP
ACCOUNT#                     VERIFIED    CREDLIM     PASTDUE      AMT-MOP     PAYPAT      13-24
ECOA  COLLATRL/LOANTYPE      CLSD/PD     BALANCE     REMARKS                    MO      30/60/90

ABC BK            B 6781001   8/06       $16.9K      60M282       1/08        445543211111           I05
9876543210                    5/08A                 $1128        $1410 05    11111111
I     AUTOMOBILE                         $12.9K      •CONTACT SUBSCRIBER        20    1/  1/  5

ABC RETAILER      D 1234567   12/05      $9.6K       MIN200       2/06        111111111111           R01
1234567890                    5/08A      $16.7K                   $230 02     111111111111
I     /CREDITCARD                        $5.2K                                  29    1/  0/  0

ABC MORTGAGE      Q 1111111   11/02      $232.5K     360M1470                 111111111111           M01
1112223333                    5/08A                                          111111111111
C     /PROPERTY                          $173.2K                                48    0/  0/  0

ABC DEPARTMENT    D 7654321   12/07      $500        MIN25                    11111                  R01
123123123123                  5/08A      $1500
I     /CREDITCARD                        $150                                   5    0/  0/  0
```

Provides a historical and current record of the consumer's buying and payment activities.

• Trades are available sorted by most derogatory, followed by date verified or vice-versa.

• Payment pattern is available displaying either 12 or 24 months.

Trade information includes the following:

SUBNAME: Abbreviated name of credit grantor/data furnisher with whom consumer has an account

ACCOUNT#: Consumer's account number with the credit grantor (for consumer protection reasons, partial or truncated account numbers are displayed within the tradelines)

ECOA: ECOA is a code representing the ownership designation on the account**

SUBCODE: Credit grantor's Kind of Business (KOB) designator and TransUnion-assigned reporting subscriber number**

COLLATRL/LOANTYPE: Collateral for an installment loan, or the type of loan

OPENED: Date the account was opened

VERIFIED: Date of last update on the account**

CLSD/PD: Date the account was closed or paid**

HIGHCRED: Highest amount ever owed by the consumer on that account

CREDLIM: Maximum amount of credit approved by credit grantor

BALANCE: Balance owed as of date verified or closed

TERMS: Minimum required payment or number of payments, payment frequency and dollar amount agreed upon

PASTDUE: Amount past due as of date verified or closed

REMARKS: If applicable, this field is used by data furnishers to further explain a special condition related to this account

MAXDELQ: Date on which the maximum level of delinquency for that account occurred

AMT-MOP: Dollar amount of consumer's maximum delinquency and the Manner of Payment (MOP) rating at the time

PAYPAT: The subject's payment pattern with his/her actual rating or Manner of Payment (MOP) over a period of time. Depending on which option a customer chooses either 24 months or 12 months of information will be shown. The default setting is 24 months. The first position on the left of the first row corresponds to the account status of the previously verified month. This will not correspond to the Manner of Payment (MOP) field, which represents the most recently reported account status, usually the current month on open or active trades. Each subsequent position to the right corresponds to one month further back in time.

In the first example below, the first half of the PAYPAT field is 445543211111. The first position indicates the information reported one month prior to verified date (MOP=4):

Manner of Payment (MOP)

One month ago	MOP = 4
Two months ago	MOP = 4
Three months ago	MOP = 5
Four months ago	MOP = 5 Etc.

MO 30/60/90: The four parts of this field summarize the reported delinquency on the account. The first column represents the number of months being summarized, up to 48 months. The second, third, and fourth columns equal the number of times the subject has been 30, 60, or 90 days delinquent, respectively.

When a tradeline is reported as "charged-off" (MOP 07 or greater), the payment pattern is removed.

In the first example, this field equals 20 1/ 1/5. This means that 20 months of data was reviewed. The subject was 30 days past due one time, 60 days past due one time, and 90 or more days past due five times.

MOP: Type of Account (R, I, M, O, C) and Manner of Payment (MOP) code at which the account is currently reported**

** See the Credit Report Codes page of this brochure for more details.

Note: The "TransUnion Credit Report User Guide" or portions thereof, TransUnion and the "T" logo are registered or unregistered copyrighted works, service marks or trademarks of TransUnion LLC. All Rights Reserved.

Inquiries

```
INQUIRIES
DATE      SUBCODE        SUBNAME            DATE       SUBCODE          SUBNAME
5/20/08   DCH248         ABC DEPT STORE     3/07/08    BPH9999(EAS)     TEST BANK
2/20/08   ASD1234(CAL)   MAIN ST AUTO       1/01/08    DNY777(EAS)      123 RETAILER
```

Displays which companies viewed the consumer's credit file over the last two years. Includes date the inquiry occurred, and the inquiring subscriber's TransUnion-assigned member number and name.

• Available in a one- or two-column display

• If two columns are requested, inquiries are displayed either left to right or top to bottom, by date

Consumer statement

```
CONSUMER STATEMENT
#HK#EFCRA EXTENDED FRAUD ALERT: ACTION MAY BE REQUIRED UNDER FCRA BEFORE OPENING OR
MODIFYING AN ACCOUNT.
```

Contains an explanation of facts or conditions affecting the credit file as requested by the consumer. This section may also include statements to protect consumers against fraud.

Inquiry analysis (optional)

```
INQUIRY ANALYSIS
DATE      SUBCODE        SUBNAME
03/07/08  B 9999         TEST BANK
DUNCAN, ELIZABETH    (773) 123-4567
9932 WOODBINE, CHICAGO, IL 60693

02/20/08  A 1234         MAIN ST AUTO
DUNCAN, ELIZABETH    (773) 555-1234
9932 WOODBINE, CHICAGO, IL 60693
10 N. CAMINO, OAKLAND, CA 94583
EMPLOYER: GRAND HOTEL
```

Returns the contact information provided by the consumer when applying for credit within the previous 90 days.
Information returned will include the consumer's name and current address, and potentially the consumer's previous address, telephone number, and employment.

Credit report serviced by

```
CREDIT REPORT SERVICED BY:
TRANSUNION               800-888-4213
P.O. BOX 1000, CHESTER, PA  19022
CONSUMER DISCLOSURES CAN BE OBTAINED ONLINE THROUGH TRANSUNION AT:
  HTTP://WWW.TRANSUNION.COM/DIRECT
```

This information should be used to provide contact information to consumers in the event of an adverse action.

Note: The "TransUnion Credit Report User Guide" or portions thereof, TransUnion and the "T" logo are registered or unregistered copyrighted works, service marks or trademarks of TransUnion LLC. All Rights Reserved.

Credit Evaluation and Decision Making

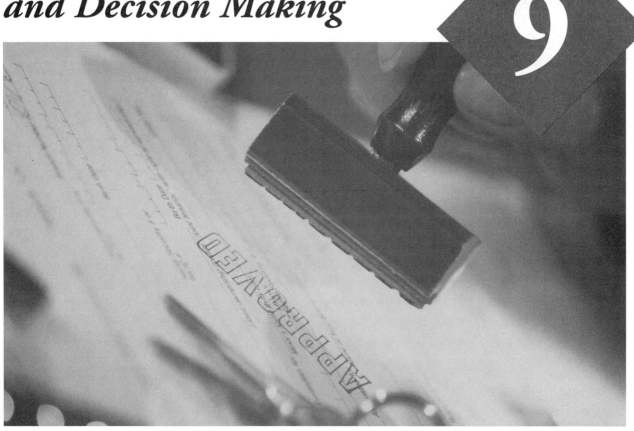

9

Learning Objectives

After completing this chapter, you should be able to

- discuss the objectives of the credit evaluation and decision-making process
- explain the five Cs used in credit evaluation
- explain credit-scoring systems and their possible benefits to banks
- describe the judgmental decision-making process
- explain the objectives for notifying consumers that their applications have been declined
- describe the Equal Credit Opportunity Act requirements for loan evaluation and decisions, credit scoring, and notifications to consumers
- define the terms that appear in bold type in the text

Introduction

Consumer lending managers often debate whether loan decision-making is an art or a science. Those who view it as an art emphasize the judgmental process and a disciplined approach to training lenders in how to evaluate loan applications. Those who view it as a science emphasize mathematics-based credit decision systems and focus more on training lenders to sell and build customer relationships. Most banks recognize the merits of both and use a combined approach.

Credit Evaluation and Decision-Making Objectives

- Make the best loan for the consumer and the bank.
- Ensure compliance with the law and bank policy.
- Retain the consumer's goodwill.
- Ensure that the credit risk is acceptable.

EVALUATION AND DECISION-MAKING OBJECTIVES

Consistent credit evaluation and sound decision-making are essential to the success of any consumer lending operation. In the evaluation process, the lender analyzes the application, the consumer credit report, and other data to reach a decision consistent with the bank's definition of an acceptable risk.

The primary objectives of the credit evaluation and decision-making process are to make the best loan for the consumer and the bank, ensure compliance with the law and bank policy, retain the consumer's goodwill, and ensure the credit risk is acceptable.

MAKE THE BEST LOAN

Making the best loan for the consumer and the bank highlights the importance of thoughtful analysis and financial counseling in the consumer lending process. Lenders are not mere order-takers who analyze loan applications only as requested by the consumer. Rather, they are active financial advisers who examine the consumer's application and structure the loan that best responds to both the consumer's and the bank's interests.

Exhibit 9.1 illustrates an application for a home-improvement loan for $5,000. The lender could evaluate the application as requested, granting the consumers a closed-end loan for 36 months would serve their current borrowing need and would be profitable for the bank. In this illustration, however, the lender has an opportunity to offer them a home equity line of credit (HELOC) or perhaps a closed-end second mortgage loan based on the equity in their home. Either of these products might offer greater benefits to the consumers and the bank.

Exhibit 9.1 Application for a Joint Loan

Requested Loan Amount $ __5,000__   Term __36 months__

Purpose of Loan __Home Improvement__

Application Taken By: __X__ Phone ____ Mail ____ Interview

Application # ____

Branch# ____   Employee ID# ____

Please Tell Us About Yourself

Full Name __Alan R. Johnson__

Address __1301 Main Street__

City __Indianapolis__   State __IN__   Zip __46220__

Home Phone __317-223-3900__

Soc. Sec.# __387-49-5831__   Birth Date __02-24-62__

Number of Dependents (Excluding Yourself) ____

Time At Address: ____ Years   ____ Months

Nearest Relative __Robert Johnson__ Phone # __914-356-1201__

Employer Name __Ford Motor Company__

Time At Job: __21__   Years   __3__   Months

Business Phone __317-686-1345__

Job Title/Position   __Design Engineer__

Gross Monthly Income $ __6,600__

Previous Employer   __General Motors__

Time At Job: __3__   Years   __6__   Months

Additional Monthly Income* $ ____

Source of Additional Income ____

*Income from alimony, child support, or separate maintenance need not be revealed if you will not use it for repaying this oblication.

Tell Us About Your Co-Applicant (If Co-Applicant is not your spouse, Co-Applicant must complete a separate application.)

Full Name __Sally L. Johnson__

Address __1301 Main Street__

City __Indianapolis__   State __IN__   Zip __46220__

Home Phone __317-223-3900__

Soc. Sec. # __304-49-3231__   Birth Date __3-27-62__

Time At Address: __12__ Years   __6__ Months

Employer Name __St. Vincents Hospital__

Time At Job: __20__   Years   __3__   Months

Business Phone __317-237-4515__

Job Title/Position __R.N. C.V. Intensive care__

Gross Monthly Income $ __3,500__

Previous Employer __School__

Time At Job: __3__   Years   ____ Months

Additional Monthly Income* $ ____

Source of Aditional Income ____

*Income from alimony, child support, or separate maintenance need not be revealed if you will not use it for repaying this obligation.

Tell Us About Your Finances

Applicant's Financial Information:

Checking Account:

Bank __Bank Two__   Balance $ __1,475.00__

Savings Account:

Bank __Bank Two__   Balance $ __20,000__

Other Account: Balance $ __3,000__

Co-Applicant's Financial Information:

Checking Account:

Bank ____   Balance $ ____

Savings Account

Bank ____   Balance $ ____

Other Account   Balance $ ____

Rent	Monthly Payment $			
Mortgage	Monthly Payment $ __1,312__	Balance $ __96,000__	Value of Home $ __395,000__	
Second Mortgage:	Yes	No __X__	(If Yes) Balance $	Monthly Payment $

Financial Obligations (Please list type and dollar amount, and alimony/child support, if applicable.)

1. __Bank United Auto__ $ __2,500/150__   3. __VISA-Bank Two__ $ __6,000/500__

2. __Beneficial Bank Auto__ $ __12,500/275__   4. ____ $

If You Wish To Secure Your Loan, Please Tell Us About Your Collateral:

Auto ____   Boat ____

New ____   Used ____

Year, Make, Model ____

Special Options ____

Cash Price $ ____

Vehicle ID # ____

Savings Account ____   Certificate of Deposit ____

Bank ____   Account # ____   Balance $ ____

Stocks ____

Name ____   # of Shares ____

Signatures

I, meaning applicant who signs below, authorize "The Bank" ("you") to make credit inquiries about me and authorize anyone to furnish requested information to you. All information and this application is your property, whether or not credit is extended. You may disclose any information relating to this application or loan account to any applicant for or proposed guarantor of this loan. Everything I have told you in this application is true, complete, and correct. I will use my loan only for lawful purposes. This application, and any additional sheets attached, lists all debts and obligations I have, including those on which I am jointly obligated.

Applicant ____   Co-Applicant ____

Signature   Date   Signature   Date

Did You Know ...

The FDIC publishes money-management how-to guides for senior citizens and their families and for young adults. Banks may make the information in the guides available to consumers by reprinting or linking to the material or making copies of the guides that include their own names, logos, special messages, and self-mailing information. The ABA Education Foundation also offers extensive money management resources.

Consumer benefits

- more extensive home improvements for the same monthly payment
- current, possibly higher-rate, loans paid off, thereby reducing monthly payments and interest
- possibly a lower rate and longer term on the secured loan
- a possible tax deduction for interest payments
- a line of credit that allows access to loan funds without the consumer having to reapply and pay new origination costs

Bank benefits

- a secured loan
- a better relationship with the consumer, possibly with cross-selling opportunities
- an opportunity to sell a larger loan at a good rate of return
- operational efficiencies, particularly on future borrowings against the line of credit

To make the best loan for the consumer and the bank, the lender first qualifies the consumer for the loan as requested and then analyzes the application for alternative loan structures that might meet the consumer's needs. The lender also may offer additional products and services.

COMPLY WITH REGULATIONS AND BANK POLICY

Credit decisions should be made within regulatory guidelines. Violations can result in penalties for the bank. All the laws that have been discussed thus far affect consumers directly or indirectly. Compliance with such laws as the Equal Credit Opportunity Act (ECOA), the Truth in Lending Act (TILA), the Fair

Credit Reporting Act (FCRA), the Community Reinvestment Act (CRA), and the Gramm-Leach-Bliley Act (GLBA), to name a few, is essential to protect both bank and consumer.

Standardized loan policies that provide a sound framework on which consumer lenders can base consistent and timely lending decisions facilitate compliance with these laws. Making good decisions sometimes requires a flexible bank loan policy. If an applicant fails to pass the bank's credit-scoring program, for example, but can secure a loan with a savings account, the lender could be authorized to make an exception to the policy that all loans must exceed a specified minimum score. However, lenders should make exceptions only when they still comply with fair lending laws such as the ECOA. When exceptions are made, the reasons should be documented.

RETAIN THE CONSUMER'S GOODWILL

Offering something of value with convenient access goes a long way toward fostering consumer goodwill. During the credit evaluation and decision-making phase, goodwill is maintained by emphasizing convenience and value.

One convenience for applicants is a quick loan decision. This presents a dilemma for lenders who must balance speed with sound credit decision-making. Consumers have come to expect quick decisions for many types of loans, and competitive pressure sometimes requires lenders to decide on loans within minutes of receiving the applications. On-the-spot credit decision-making systems facilitate this process.

Although some product applications, such as those for overdraft lines of credit, have fewer time constraints than most loans, many marketing programs still offer instant credit approval and access. The consumer's desire for a quick decision has changed the lending process.

The need to respond quickly should not overshadow the need for sound credit decision-making practices. Many tools for credit decision-making can accommodate the vast number of loan requests. Some loan requests may take longer to process, but lenders should take the time and not take any of the shortcuts that inevitably compromise the quality of the loan decision and the loan.

ENSURE THAT THE RISK IS ACCEPTABLE

Consumer loan decisions are based on the law of probability, which recognizes that a certain percentage of loans will not be paid off. Thus, loan policies and decision-making systems seek to identify risk factors and reject applications where the risk is excessive. Which loans will perform satisfactorily is always uncertain, but degrees of risk can be quantified. All banks set an acceptable level of credit risk, which is expressed in the loan policy.

Lenders rely heavily on financial information in determining the credit risk of a loan request. They analyze basic information about the consumer's current financial condition and credit history, as revealed by the application, credit report, and credit investigation. Detailed analyses of personal financial statements and tax returns typically are required on larger loans, such as those for airplanes, boats, and business purposes.

Other factors also help predict an applicant's credit risk, including past behavior patterns, family lifecycle, and likely ability to handle future financial emergencies.

Factors Contributing to Credit Risk

- past behavior
- family lifecycle
- ability to handle financial emergencies

Past Behavior

Behavioral research shows that people tend to follow certain patterns throughout their lives. The best predictor of future behavior is past behavior. Consumer lenders therefore can assume that applicants who have been responsible about handling credit obligations in the past probably will continue to be responsible.

judgmental decision-making process—
The process used to make credit decisions that relies primarily on the knowledge and experience of the lender, guided by standard loan policies.

five Cs of credit—A method of evaluating creditworthiness in terms of the consumer's character, capacity, capital, collateral, and conditions.

character—One of the five Cs of credit: it assesses the consumer's willingness and desire to repay a loan on time.

Family Lifecycle

Individuals and families normally follow well-defined lifecycle patterns, which generally include steadily rising income, greater stability, and predictable credit use. Supported by documented studies, lifecycle patterns help lenders make loan decisions with the knowledge that consumers will continue to behave similarly.

Handling Future Financial Emergencies

Not all people consistently follow normal lifecycle trends. Life-altering events can devastate a family's financial position and reverse past behavior patterns. For the past few decades, consumers have been saving less and less, so that today many people are not financially prepared for such emergencies as divorce, death, serious illness, or job loss. Less massive financial emergencies, such as a major home or auto repair, also may change a consumer's ability to meet loan commitments. Many situations may cause an otherwise good loan to go bad and lead to serious delinquency or even bankruptcy. These factors are considered when determining an applicant's credit risk.

THE JUDGMENTAL APPROACH

The two basic systems for making credit decisions are judgmental and credit scoring. A variation, credit scoring supplemented with judgmental factors, also is prevalent. These systems involve weighing information on the application to determine if the applicant will be an acceptable credit risk.

With **judgmental decision-making,** lenders use their knowledge and experience to evaluate both financial and nonfinancial variables to determine the consumer's creditworthiness. In doing so, lenders refer to the **five Cs of credit**: character, capacity, capital, collateral, and conditions.

CHARACTER

Character addresses the questions: What type of person are we dealing with? Will the consumer be willing to repay a loan? To answer, the lender must analyze the applicant's job and residence stability, personal characteristics, and credit history to discern behavior patterns. Although many lenders consider this the most important factor in granting a loan, character is difficult to measure precisely.

Stability

The applicant's residence and occupation give insight into stability. Assessing stability is important because consumer loans are made for extended periods. The lender must be reasonably sure that the consumer will continue to be employed during the term of the

---

Situation

Allen Lee is reviewing loan applications from three consumers. Applicant 1, Amy, who is 22 years old, has lived in the same community all her life. She has rented her own apartment for one year, during which time she has worked in corporate sales. She had previously been a college student. Applicant 2, Charles, is 40. Two years ago, he switched jobs after working for another company for nine years as a business manager. He is buying a home in the community he has lived in for 14 years. Applicant 3, Wesley, is 33. He has been at his present job as a store clerk for six months, after working for one year at a different store. He is new to the community, where he has been renting an apartment for four months.

How does Allen Lee determine the probability that each of these applicants will repay a loan?

---

loan, will continue to have regular income to service the debt, and can be found if problems arise.

Applicants whose backgrounds reveal career instability, with many job or occupation changes and frequent changes in residence, may pose problems. Today, lenders must bear in mind that, due to changes in the economy over a number of years, individuals may have several jobs and careers throughout their lives, so this is not always a sign of instability. It is important to use judgment when evaluating job stability. Although renting is considered less stable than home ownership, not all renters are high credit risks. Knowing how much weight to give stability factors, such as time in one location, is essential when assessing character.

Personal Characteristics

Type of job and personal reputation also reveal information about a consumer's character. Personal reputation may be very important when the lender knows the applicant, but the lender must be careful about making credit decisions based on personal knowledge. A consumer's reputation has to be evaluated and balanced with objective, tangible credit criteria so that credit decisions are sound and legally defensible.

Many studies demonstrate a correlation between job type and credit risk. Certain occupations provide higher incomes, greater employment security, and greater job mobility. Other occupations have inconsistent employment, high delinquency rates, and short job tenures. Lenders using judgmental systems often create lists of problem occupations based on recent experiences or local economic conditions and carefully verify all information before granting credit.

Credit History

Another measure of character is the applicant's credit history. An analysis of credit history takes into account the consumer's credit rating or payment history, types of credit the consumer has used, sources of credit, the dates accounts are opened and closed, other account activity, the amount of debt, and credit use patterns.

Exhibit 9.2 (page 241) illustrates a simplified credit report. It highlights only the most important information; an actual credit report is more detailed. The credit report reveals much about the applicant.

Credit rating or payment history. In the sample, a credit rating such as "Current" (an open account in good standing) or "Paid-Sat." (a closed account paid satisfactorily) is considered positive. However, the applicant also has several accounts that have not been paid satisfactorily: Mega Bank, "Cur was 90"; Sears, "Cur was 60"; Lords Jewelry, "Cur was 30"; and Macy's, "Cur was 120." These ratings indicate that, although the account is now current, there have been slow payments in the past. Thus, the payment history is mixed. Some lenders might decline this applicant based on the late-paid accounts. Others would continue to examine the report closely.

Credit Report Abbreviations

Cur: current, an open account in good standing

Paid-Sat: a closed account paid satisfactorily

Cur was 60, or 90, or 120: current now but slow payments in the past by these numbers of days

Credit History Factors

- credit rating or payment history
- types of credit used
- sources of credit
- dates accounts are opened and closed
- other account activity
- amount of debt
- credit use patterns

pyramid debt—Debt resulting from the borrowing of funds in rapid succession without first repaying previous loans. The additional debt is used to meet previous loan obligations and erodes the borrower's financial position.

Types of credit used. Fourteen of the applicant's accounts are open-end or revolving loan accounts, including the credit cards. Two accounts are automobile loans and one was an installment loan from Household Finance. The American Express account is a travel and entertainment (T&E) card, which calls for payment in full each month. This applicant has had experience with a variety of credit types.

Sources of credit. The applicant in exhibit 9.2 has borrowed from a variety of sources, including banks, retailers, and finance companies.

Dates opened and closed and other activity. Dates identify recent credit activity and define the length of credit experience. Recent credit activity is evident in the "Date Opened" column. Assuming the credit report was taken in May 2009, the applicant in exhibit 9.2 has not opened any accounts in the past year. A credit history that shows a number of recent activities could indicate that the applicant is taking on a significant amount of debt quickly. Recent debt may mean the applicant will be unable to adjust cash flow to properly handle new debt, resulting in **pyramid debt**. Over the years, banks have charged off a high percentage of loans that deteriorated in the first year after the loan was made.

Dates of inquiry also are important to the lender. An inquiry shows that the applicant has applied for credit from the lender listed. The sample credit report, exhibit 9.2, indicates that the applicant has submitted three applications for credit cards within the last month. The lender will want to determine the status of those applications. Prescreening and monitoring activity are not listed as inquiries on the credit report. Multiple inquiries on an applicant's credit report are considered in context. If, for example, the applicant filled out a loan application at an automobile dealership, the dealer may have shotgunned the loan to six or more banks and finance companies, resulting in multiple inquiries.

The credit report indicates the date a specific status was given. In evaluating the delinquent ratings on the sample credit report it is important to note that the delinquencies reported by Mega Bank, Sears, Lords Jewelry, and Macy's were all reported in October 2003. Later, each account was reported as current, and all accounts remain open. This indicates the applicant has had no significant credit problems recently. Although the lender may ask what caused the problem in 2003, many lenders feel that subsequent history and other information are more important to decision-making.

Level of debt. The level of debt is considered as much for its potential as for its current amount. Although the applicant in exhibit 9.2 has used $17,970 from his credit lines, he has the opportunity to use these lines up to $46,800.

Credit-use patterns. Analyzing credit-use patterns—open-end credit accounts in particular—is done by looking at the total amount of open-end credit lines available and the amount owed on those accounts. In our example, the applicant is a heavy user of three credit lines: Bank United, Beneficial, and Macy's. Most of the other lines are not used at all.

How the applicant uses credit may affect the final loan decision. Suppose an applicant had balances on most revolving credit accounts, and was applying for

Exhibit 9.2 Sample Credit Report

(REPORT DATE: MAY 2006)

CREDITOR	STATUS & DATE	DATE OPENED	CREDIT LINE OR ACCOUNT TYPE	LOAN AMOUNT $	BALANCE $
Chase	Current 5-09	4-04	Open-end	2,000	0
Bank United	Paid-Sat. 5-09	3-03	Auto	10,000	2,500
Beneficial Bank	Paid-Sat. 5-09	7-02	Auto	24,000	12,500
Bank America	Current 5-09	3-03	Visa	2,000	0
United Bank	Current 5-09	4-98	Mastercard	2,600	2,570
Mega Bank	Cur was 90 10/03	4-98	Open-end	2,000	0
Beneficial Bank	Current 5-09	3-01	Open-end	16,000	12,500
Union Trust	Current 5-09	7-02	Open-end	7,500	0
Sears	Cur was 60 10/03	9-97	Open-end	1,300	0
Bloomingdale's	Current 5-09	1-02	Open-end	800	0
Lords Jewelry	Cur was 30 10/03	9-99	Open-end	1,000	0
Macy's	Cur was 120 10/03	10Y	Open-end	2,500	2,400
Johnson's	Current 5-09	10Y	Open-end	800	0
Dept. store	Current 5-09	10Y	Open-end	300	0
Bank Two	Current 5-09	10Y	Visa	6,000	500
HFC	Paid-Sat. 5-09	6-97	Note	4,900	0
Dept. store	Current 5-09	10Y	Open-end	2,000	0
Amer. Exp.	Current	6-04	T&E		
Turnkey Bank	Inquiry	4-09	Visa		
Bank Three	Inquiry	4-09	MasterCard		
Bank America	Inquiry	4-09	Visa		

a loan to consolidate the account balances. The lender's priority would be to protect the bank's interest in case the applicant begins using the revolving accounts again after making the new loan.

The banker's ability to objectively analyze mixed references and arrive at sound credit decisions is critical to controlling risk within the consumer loan portfolio. Lenders often confront credit reports that contain a mixture of references, and perhaps a few red flags that warn of credit problems.

Exhibit 9.3 (next page) is the credit report of a heavy user of open-end credit. This applicant has established many such accounts, and virtually everyone is near or over the credit limit. A clear pattern of making purchases using credit cards is difficult to change; if offered another line of credit, this person would most likely accept the offer and use the account fully.

Warning Signs of Overextended Credit

- paying only the minimum payment month after month
- being out of cash constantly
- being late on important payments, such as rent or mortgage
- taking longer and longer to pay off balances
- borrowing from one lender to pay another

Exhibit 9.3 Sample Credit Report for a Heavy User of Revolving Credit

(REPORT DATE: MAY 2009)

CREDITOR	STATUS & DATE	DATE OPENED	ACCOUNT TYPE	CREDIT LINE OR LOAN AMT.	BALANCE
Your Bank	Current 5-09	11-05	Open-end	$2,000	$1,885
New Bank	Current 5-09	11-05	Open-end	2,000	1,953
Citibank	Current 5-09	9-05	Visa	1,500	1,443
JC Penney	Current 5-09	10Y	Open-end	1,700	1,496
Dial Finance	Current 5-09	10Y	Open-end	1,300	1,139
Sears	Current 5-09	10Y	Open-end	3,100	3,073
Nordstroms	Current 5-09	10Y	Open-end	3,000	1.947
Citicorp	Current 5-09	6-01	Mastercard	1,000	986
Security Pac	Current 5-09	6-03	Note	4,100	2,843
Finance Amer.	Current 5-09	3-04	Note	1,600	277
Gateway 2000	Current 5-09	3-01	Open-end	1,900	1,507
Firestone	Current 5-09	6-99	Open-end	900	884
GECC	Current 5-09	4-00	Visa	1,000	1,029
Beneficial	Current 5-09	5-01	Visa	3,200	3,356
Total				$28,300	$23,818

capacity—One of the five Cs of credit; it measures the applicant's ability to repay the loan when it is due.

debt-to-income ratio— A measure of a consumer's creditworthiness computed by dividing the dollar amount of monthly loan payments by the gross or net monthly income.

To measure capacity, evaluate consumer's

- income
- cash flow and ability to repay debt and expenses
- marketability (ability to change jobs)

CAPACITY

Capacity addresses the question: Does the applicant have the ability to repay the loan and handle the proposed new debt? Measuring capacity involves evaluating the applicant's income, cash flow, and ability to repay debt and other expenses, and determining the applicant's marketability or ability to change jobs.

Income

Many banks have minimum income requirements to qualify for loans. They also establish **debt-to-income ratios** to further measure the applicant's ability to repay the loan. A high monthly income is no assurance that an applicant can handle debt—most people increase their spending as their income goes up. Occasionally, high-income consumers are less able to meet cash demands than those with modest incomes. Lenders therefore analyze income in relation to expenses.

The types of income that add up to an applicant's total income are specified in bank policy and the law. The Equal Credit Opportunity Act requires lenders to count income from part-time jobs the same as income from full-time employment, and to include income from alimony, child support, and public assistance payments if the applicant so requests. To ensure consistency, bank policy specifies how to treat other types of income—for example, income from investments and from less predictable and consistent sources, such as commissions and bonuses.

A person's capacity to handle credit obligations may change if the applicant will reach retirement age during the term of the loan. Retirement can mean a change in income and lifestyle, and lenders consider this when evaluating future capacity to handle debt. A lender determines likely postretirement income before reaching a loan decision.

Another important income question is whether the debt-to-income ratio uses net or gross income. Either can be used, depending on the bank's lending strategy. Banks usually publish the allowable debt-to-income ratio in their loan policy.

The example below demonstrates how maximum monthly debt payments would differ, given the same debt-to-income ratio, for gross and net income.

	Gross Income	**Net**
	$5,000	$4,000
Debt-to-income ratio	35%	35%
Maximum monthly debt payments	$1,750	$1,400

To be more conservative, the bank that uses gross income might lower its debt-to-income ratio to 28 percent, for a maximum monthly debt payment of $1,400.

Ability to Repay: Cash Flow

To measure the applicant's **cash flow** and ability to repay, the lender should determine total monthly income and total debt payments, including the payment that will be required on the new loan. To determine the ratio, the lender totals the minimum monthly debt payments, including the payment on the proposed loan, and then divides that amount by the consumer's monthly income.

If the proposed loan falls within the debt-to-income ratio the bank's loan policy considers acceptable, the loan evaluation may continue. Exhibit 9.4 lists the amount of monthly debt payments that borrowers could have at various income levels based on 35 percent and 40 percent debt-to-income ratios.

Did You Know ...

The debt-to-income ratio went from 70% in the 1990s to 100% in 2000 to 140% in 2008. It is expected that debt service ratios will decline in coming years.

Source: Forbes, January 8, 2009

cash flow—The amount of money available to an individual to cover debts and discretionary expenditures, a factor in capacity.

Exhibit 9.4	Debt-to-Income Ratio Table		
		MAXIMUM MONTHLY DEBT SERVICE	
GROSS ANNUAL INCOME	**MONTHLY INCOME**	**35%**	**40%**
$20,000	$1,667	$ 583	$ 667
25,000	2,083	729	833
30,000	2,500	875	1,000
40,000	3,333	1,167	1,333
50,000	4,167	1,458	1,667
60,000	5,000	1,750	2,000
70,000	5,833	2,042	2,333
80,000	6,667	2,333	2,667
90,000	7,500	2,625	3,000
100,000	8,333	2,917	3,333

The lender uses the debt-to-income table to structure a loan that an applicant can afford. For example, an applicant with a gross annual income of $40,000 can afford $1,167 in monthly debt payments at the 35 percent debt-to-income ratio level. The following example shows an applicant who already exceeds the maximum. This applicant has a debt-to-income ratio of more than 40 percent.

Mortgage	$ 400
Auto loan	250
Finance company loan	175
Visa	75
MasterCard	50
Store account	50
Bank loan	200
New loan	150
Total monthly payments	$1,350
Monthly income	$3,333
Debt-to-income ratio	40.50%

If the applicant's debt-to-income ratio exceeds bank policy, the lender may decline the loan. The lender also may suggest restructuring the debts and consolidating some loans with the new loan so that the applicant may meet the bank's requirements.

Mortgage	$400
Auto loan	250
New loan/second mortgage	325
Total monthly payments	$975
Monthly income	$3,333
Debt-to-income ratio	29.25%

A sales-oriented lender will structure the best loan for the applicant and the bank. A loan that would have been declined now can be made. The original loan request would have brought monthly payments to $1,350 and would have been declined. The optional debt structure, including paying off some previous loans and extending the new loan for a longer term, results in monthly payments of $975 and brings the loan request in line with the bank's debt-to-income policy.

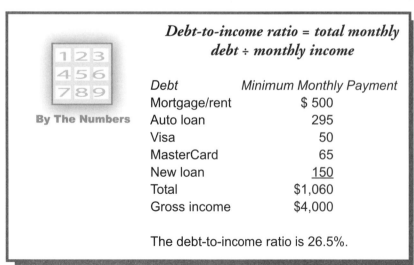

By The Numbers

Debt-to-income ratio = total monthly debt ÷ monthly income

Debt	Minimum Monthly Payment
Mortgage/rent	$ 500
Auto loan	295
Visa	50
MasterCard	65
New loan	150
Total	$1,060
Gross income	$4,000

The debt-to-income ratio is 26.5%.

Ability to Repay: Other Factors

Several other factors are considered in evaluating an applicant's ability to repay debt. Among them are potential debt, variable rate debt, and overextension.

Potential debt. Measuring capacity is more difficult with revolving credit programs. The applicant in exhibit 9.2 has $17,970 in open-end credit account balances as of the date of the credit report but also has access to the $28,830 still available on the credit lines. Available balances, which the consumer can easily access, represent **potential debt**, which the consumer controls.

Banks have a variety of policies about how to treat potential debt when evaluating an applicant's ability to repay debt.

Assume the applicant will fully use the credit lines.
This is the most conservative approach. The lender calculates an assumed monthly payment obligation based on a minimum monthly payment factor, multiplied by the potential debt amount. The risk is that many creditworthy applicants are declined because of high potential-debt factors based on the bank's debt-to-income policy.

Assume the applicant will not use the credit lines.
This assumption is the most liberal approach, and it is based on the laws of probability. The risk is that consumers may draw down potential debt and then be unable to handle monthly obligations.

Assume a certain percentage of potential debt will be used.
To the amount of potential debt, a minimum monthly payment percentage is applied. The result is the new minimum monthly payment requirement. The approach recognizes that the consumer will draw on existing credit lines. The risk is that the consumer will not do so, and a creditworthy loan would be denied.

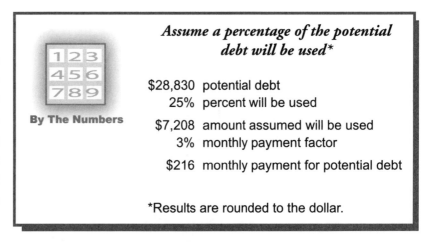

By The Numbers

Assume a percentage of the potential debt will be used*

$28,830	potential debt
25%	percent will be used
$7,208	amount assumed will be used
3%	monthly payment factor
$216	monthly payment for potential debt

*Results are rounded to the dollar.

Variable-rate debt. Since the 1990s many banks have increased their variable-rate portfolios. Variable rates help stabilize net interest margins by preserving the spread between the bank's cost of funds and the interest rates consumers are charged on loans.

On the other hand, variable rates may increase the credit risk of some accounts. A change in the rate also may change the consumer's monthly payment. A rise in the interest rate may mean higher monthly payments, possibly driving the consumer's debt-to-income ratio from acceptable to unacceptable. Thus, when interest rates are rising, consumers with variable rates on loans have difficulty making payments even when they do not have other debt.

Factors in Ability to Repay
- cash flow
- potential debt
- variable-rate debt
- overextension

potential debt—The difference between a consumer's current balances on revolving credit accounts and the total of all credit limits.

negative amortization— An increase in the unpaid balance of a loan resulting from adding unpaid interest to the principal. It occurs when the minimum monthly payment is no longer sufficient to cover the interest due. It is mainly a risk with variable rate, closed-end loans.

capital—One of the five Cs of credit; it is the net value of a consumer's assets.

liquid asset—An asset that is readily convertible to cash to meet short-term cash needs, Examples are bank accounts, stocks, bonds, or cash value of a life insurance policy.

Sample Debt Level Policy Statements

- "Total loan balances, including first mortgage loans, may not exceed the borrower's gross annual income."
- "Total loan balances, plus unused revolving credit lines (potential debt), but excluding first mortgage loans, may not exceed the borrower's gross annual income."

Rate increases on variable-rate loans result in higher monthly interest payments, sometimes causing **negative amortization**. When the shortfall added to the loan balance exceeds the collateral's value, the credit risk increases and impairs the bank's position.

Overextended consumers. Another consideration is the total amount of debt in relation to the applicant's income. It is possible for consumers to accumulate high debts relative to their income and still meet the bank's debt-to-income requirements. At some point, however, the consumer becomes overextended, taking on too much debt in relation to income. The trend toward longer repayment terms for closed-end loans and lower minimum monthly payments on open-end credit keeps monthly payments at levels that many consumers find attractive. Although monthly payments may be low, aggregate loan balances can be substantial. To address this concern, many bank loan policies set a maximum for allowable debt.

Regardless of policy, the bank should have a consistent standard for measuring capacity. Consumers have trouble handling debts when their income declines or their debt increases beyond a certain point. Cash flow problems lead first to slow payments, and then in serious cases, to losses and bankruptcies.

Marketability

An individual's marketability—ability to change jobs—requires a qualitative assessment rather than a quantitative measure of capacity. The applicant's type of job, education, employer, and current income all affect the assessment. This measure normally does not have a significant effect on credit decisions unless it appears that the employee's current employment may be changing.

CAPITAL

Lenders need to know if applicants have sufficient **capital** and liquidity to repay the bank if unfavorable situations arise. The lender analyzes the relationship between the consumer's assets and liabilities and the ability of the consumer to convert the assets into cash. The personal financial statement (see exhibit 9.5) most often is required on large or specialized loan requests (boats, airplanes, business-related loans) where capital is a critical concern. The statement must be signed, dated, and reviewed for accuracy. It is then analyzed as part of the credit investigation, evaluation, and decision-making processes.

The personal financial statement is used to measure current liquid assets and unsecured debt, identify assets available to secure or repay loans, define ownership of assets, itemize sources of income, list fixed expenses, and identify contingent liabilities and business interests.

Liquid Assets

A consumer's capital may consist of **liquid assets** and tangible assets. As the first line of defense against unexpected financial emergencies, liquid assets help meet short-term declines in income or increases in expenses, such as medical emergencies, funeral expenses, and accidents that result in a loss of income.

Exhibit 9.5   Personal Financial Statement

Name: Alan R. Johnson		Soc. Sec. No.: 387-49-5831	Annual Income: $179,200

Home Address: 1301 Main Street	Home Telephone No.: 317-223-3900

City: Indianapolis	State: IN	Zip Code: 46220

ASSETS (EXCLUDING YOUR BUSINESS)	Check if Jointly Owned	LIABILITIES (EXCLUDING YOUR BUSINESS)	
Cash on Hand and in Banks (personal only)	25,000 ☐	Notes Payable to Banks - Secured - Sch. D	12,500
Readily Marketable Securities - Sch. A	32,000 ☒	Notes Payable to Banks - Unsecured - Sch. D	2,500
Non-Readily Marketable Securities - Sch. A	☐	Notes Payable to Others	
Accounts, Notes, and Mortgages Receivable	☐	Accounts and Bills Due	
Residential Real Estate - Sch. B	395,000 ☒	Tax Payable	
Real Estate Investments - Sch. B	☐	Real Estate Mortgages Payable - Sch. B	96,000
Automobiles and Personal Property	80,000 ☒	Life Insurance Loans - Sch. C	
Cash Surrender Value of Life Insurance	1,000 ☐	Other Debts - Please Itemize	
IRA, Keough, profit sharing & Ret. Accts.	550,000 ☐	Open-end credit	17,970
Other Assets - please itemize	☐		
Antiques	10,000 ☒		
	☐	Total Liabilities	128,970
	☐	Net Worth (total assets - total liabilities)	964,030
Total Assets	1,093,000 ☐	Total Liabilities and Net Worth	1,093,000

If any joint assets, complete the following:	Joint owner name: Sally	Soc. Sec. No.: **304-49-3231**

SCHEDULE A - All securities (attach additional sheet if necessary)

No. of shares (stock) or face value (bonds)	Description	Owner(s)	Where Held	Current Market Value	Pledge (if yes #)

READILY MARKETABLE SECURITIES (Including U.S. Governments and Municipals) (Statements may be substituted as an attachment)

571	Ford MTC	H&W	Broker	32,000	N

NON-READILY MARKETABLE SECURITIES (closely held, thinly traded, or restricted stock)

SCHEDULE B - Personal Residence & Real Estate Investments, Mortgage Debt (000's)

Property Address	Legal Owners	% of Ownership	Purchase Yr. Price	Present Market Value	Present Loan Balance	Loan Maturity Date	Monthly Payment	Financial Institution
1301 Main St.	Both	100	91 145,000	395,000	96,000	2012	1,312	Bank Two

SCHEDULE C - Insurance - Life Insurance

Insurance Co.	Face Amount of Policy	Type of Policy	Owner of Policy	Beneficiary	Cash Surrender Value	Amount Borrowed
AETNA	100,000	Whole	Sally	Sally	1,000	-0-

SCHEDULE D - Notes payable & installment loans (auto, credit cards, line of credit, home equity, education, department stores)

Due to	Type of Loan	Amount of Loan	Secured Yes No	Collateral	Interest Rate	Maturity	Unpaid Balance	Monthly Payment
Bank United	Auto		☒ ☐	95 Auto	8.5		2,500	150
Beneficial	Auto		☒ ☐	97 Auto	8.5		12,500	275

Your Signature:	Date:

Alan Johnson has $58,000 in assets that fit this category ($25,000 in cash, $32,000 in readily marketable securities, and $1,000 cash value of life insurance). There is a significant amount of liquidity to meet current cash needs.

Tangible Assets

Equity in a home, a **tangible asset**, is a substantial portion of **net worth** for many consumers. For homeowners, equity is the difference between the market value of the home and the amount owed on mortgages. The Johnson home is valued at $395,000, with a mortgage of $96,000. Therefore, the Johnsons have $299,000 in equity in their home. For the lender, the equity represents a source of capital and potential collateral for a loan, which accounts for the widespread popularity of home equity and second mortgage loans.

Automobiles, boats, recreational vehicles (RVs), and other assets may give the consumer additional capacity. Although the value in these assets could provide some protection for lenders, it depends on their age, model, market demand, and condition, and the amount of debt they already secure. Because these assets usually depreciate, the value already may have deteriorated significantly. Proceeds from the sale of depreciating-value assets may not be enough to cover the current loan balance, much less other debts.

Art collections and antiques rarely are considered in a loan evaluation. The problems of appraising, obtaining a lien, repossessing, and selling these types of assets makes it difficult, if not impossible, for collectibles to be considered liquid.

Debt Structure

A personal financial statement also offers insight into the consumer's debt structure. One way to determine the equity position of consumers is to look at their debts in relation to their assets or to their net worth. This is a way to measure a consumer's **leverage**. The Johnsons' net worth of $964,030 reflects their assets of $1,093,000 minus their liabilities of $128,970.

Young consumers often are highly leveraged; their debts nearly equal or exceed their assets, and their net worth is small or nonexistent. Net worth increases over time, if the consumer practices sound financial management. When debts exceed the value of the assets, the consumer is insolvent, and **insolvency** usually leads to bankruptcy.

The importance of capital in evaluating consumer credit requests has increased along with the availability of open-end credit programs. The accessibility of an open-end line of credit exposes the bank to loss over a much longer period than a closed-end loan. In addition, many open-end accounts are unsecured. Therefore, in analyzing requests for large open-end lines of credit, and when reconfirming a line of credit after account monitoring, lenders often require updated financial statements. Some banks require consumers to submit financial statements at regular intervals so the bank can identify adverse trends or marketing opportunities.

Another reason for using analytical tools to evaluate capital is the size of consumer loans. The consumer's capital is a critical concern for closed-end loans for

---

tangible asset—Property and goods in a physical form that can be touched or seen, such as an automobile or a plot of land. The asset is not liquid but may provide more protection against serious financial problems.

net worth—Assets minus liabilities. The amount by which the value of assets exceeds liabilities.

leverage—A measure of the consumer's financial strength that relates debt to assets or to net worth.

insolvency—The inability to pay debts when due; negative net worth.

boats, airplanes, and second mortgages, which can be for many thousands of dollars. As loan size increases, the credit analysis becomes more detailed.

COLLATERAL

When considering a loan request, lenders may ask whether there is **collateral**—a readily available secondary source of repayment. As a secondary source of repayment, collateral should not replace a loan decision based on sound lending criteria. In many cases, the goods being purchased become the collateral for the loan. Forms of collateral often accepted on consumer loans are personal residences, savings accounts, and stocks or bonds. The analysis of collateral differs from the analysis of capital in general. The lender evaluates a specific asset pledged as collateral to secure the loan.

The consumer's recurring income is the primary source of repayment on consumer loans. When something happens to diminish that income, the bank looks first to capital, such as liquid assets, and then to the collateral pledged on the loan to supply the funds needed to pay off the balance.

It is not necessary or possible to secure every loan. Sound unsecured lending is part of virtually every successful consumer lending program. Lenders primarily rely on the consumer's character and capacity when making consumer loans, but they acknowledge the legitimate role of collateral in reducing risk. Nevertheless, the larger the loan, the more important the collateral becomes.

Collateral protects the bank when it can be sold for more than the cost of repossession, but often the forced sale of collateral results in a loss or deficiency balance: money is still owed to the bank after the proceeds of the sale have been applied to the account. For example:

Amount owed on loan	$7,500
Repossession expenses	+ 350
Repossessed car sold at auction	−5,000
Amount applied to loan	$4,650
Deficiency balance	$2,850

Bank loan policies usually define what is acceptable as collateral. Lenders should not make a loan simply because there is collateral to secure the loan. The borrower's capacity as measured, for example, by the debt-to-income ratio is a much better indicator of whether the loan will be repaid. All too often banks take a loss or incur expenses in trying to collect loans from consumers who should not have been granted a loan in the first place. Although collateral may reduce risk and strengthen the loan, it does not replace the primary requirements of character, credit, and the capacity to handle the debt.

Situation

Julie and her husband have owned their home for several years. Until now, they have worked near each other and needed only one car to commute. They finished making loan payments on their car several months ago and have no additional debt. Recently, Julie's office relocated to another part of town, which meant they had to purchase a second car. After reviewing her application for a car loan, the bank tells Julie that she qualifies for a loan with no down payment required. This surprises Julie, who remembers having to come up with a 20 percent down payment when they financed their first car four years ago.

How can the bank lend Julie the full purchase price of the car, even though the value of the car will soon be less than the amount of the loan?

collateral—One of the five Cs of credit: an asset pledged by a borrower to a lender to guarantee a loan. The asset becomes the property of the lender if the borrower fails to repay the loan.

Collateral Evaluation

- Identify collateral.
- Value the collateral.
- Assess value behavior—depreciating, appreciating, stable, or fluctuating?
- Determine ease of repossession.
- Determine marketability.
- Identify owners.

CONDITIONS

conditions—One of the five Cs of credit: external variables that affect the risk of the loan, such as the economy, social and political environment, government regulations, competition, or changes in the bank's goals and objectives.

Conditions are such factors as changes in the economy, social and political environment, laws, and competition, and changes in the bank's goals and objectives. Consider these examples:

Changes in the economy	A lender receives an application from a consumer who works for a firm that recently announced a plant closing and employee layoff.
Social or political environment	The local union is planning a job action because of a contract dispute. The lender has applications from a number of union members.
Laws and regulations	A lender receives an application from someone who is an alien with a temporary visa.
Competition	The bank down the street has a special loan promotion.
Changes in the bank's goals and objectives	Because the local economic forecast calls for growing unemployment and declining residential property values in the region, the bank has decided to promote small business loans rather than credit cards.

Often, only individual loan requests are affected by outside conditions; in other cases, the bank may alter its loan policy so that all consumers are affected equally. When making any policy change, the bank should consider whether the change would affect protected classes disproportionately. For example, if the bank decides not to make small loans and institutes a minimum loan amount, this action might affect women and members of racial minorities disproportionately.

In the late 1990s, many lenders reduced credit requirements in an attempt to gain a greater share of weak loan demand. Beginning in 2000, there was a trend that favored the promotion of HELOCs with teaser rates, no fees, interest rebates, and loan-to-value ratios of 100 percent. In late 2007 and through 2008 the housing and credit markets weakened to the point that the number of liberal HELOC programs decreased substantially.

This fluctuation indicates that changes in the external environment often are reflected in changes to a bank's loan policy. New government regulations must become an immediate part of the loan policy, but changes in the social environment usually tend to take longer to be reflected in lending practices.

MAKING A JUDGMENTAL DECISION

In a judgmental system, the final credit decision rests on a lender's analysis of an applicant's strengths and weaknesses. By reviewing data from the application, personal financial statement, and credit report, a lender can construct a chart of the consumer's strengths and weaknesses and evaluate the trade-offs (see exhibit 9.6). The lender then reviews the bank's loan policy to see whether the loan would comply with all requirements. The biggest concern is the debt-to-income ratio. No loan should be granted when capacity is not established.

A consumer-oriented lender will recognize the potential to strengthen the loan, perhaps by offering a HELOC or a closed-end second mortgage. The lender would thus be able to secure the loan with sound collateral and could suggest debt consolidation to pay off other credit balances. Doing so would reduce monthly debt payments substantially and still give the consumer the amount requested for home improvements.

During the decision-making process, the lender is looking for ways to make the loan, not turn it down, and for ways to make the loan request more effective for both the consumer and the bank.

Questions on Capacity
- How does the bank treat potential debt in its policy?
- What is the probability that this consumer will use more potential debt?
- Can the loan be structured to offset potential debt weaknesses?

Exhibit 9.6 The Five C's of Credit —Sample Elements

Strengths	Weaknesses
Character	
Buying home	
Length of residence	
Type of job – professional	Time on current job
Previous job – long-term	
Spouse co-signing	Spouse's time on job
Pays bills on time	
Credit	
Most accounts paid satisfactorily	Some slow payment
Extensive credit history	Recent inquiries
	High potential open-end debt
Capacity	
Debt-to-income ratio – 25% of gross	Debt-to-income ratio with 25% of potential debt and payment factor of 3%
($1,737 ÷ $10,100 = 17.20%)	($1,737 + 216 = $1,953 1,953 ÷ 10,100 = 19.34%)
Collateral	
	Unsecured loan request
Capital	
Collateral – mortgage balance = home equity	($395,000 – $96,000 = $299,000)
Net worth	$964,030
Liquidity (investments, savings)	$ 58,000
Conditions	
New customer acquisition	Not currently a bank customer
	Strike potential at Ford

CREDIT SCORING

Credit-scoring systems, developed from large bases of actual credit experiences, are based on the assumption that credit risk can be quantified scientifically by using the law of probability.

credit scoring—A valid and empirically derived statistical analysis used to evaluate an applicant's creditworthiness.

Credit scoring may not be for every bank. Some banks are too small to justify the expense of a credit-scoring system. However, vendors offering credit-scoring systems now sell affordable personal computer software programs that extend the benefits of credit scoring to banks of almost every size. Since 2008, some banks have been operating in an economic environment where the judgmental system is necessary to make a sound loan decision.

Often banks are satisfied with their judgmental system. As long as the results align with management's portfolio objectives, there may be little need or motivation to change. Other banks, particularly large branch-banking systems, have much to gain by using credit scoring. In fact, some banks have managed to automate the process to the point where it is possible for consumers to type an application on a personal computer and the system then scores the request, giving conditional approval on the spot.

CREDIT SCORE VARIABLES

Credit scoring quantifies the pluses and minuses of the judgmental system (see exhibit 9.7). Key credit variables are identified and numerically weighted to calculate the probability that the consumer will repay the loan. These variables are based on selected application data and the historical experience of hundreds of thousands of consumer loans. Sophisticated mathematical analysis is used to define the risk on a given application. Credit scores can be obtained from the bank's own credit-scoring system or from a third party, such as a consumer reporting agency.

Did You Know ...

"The average interest rate as of Nov. 24, 2008, for a $300,000, 30-year fixed mortgage in Massachusetts is 5.652 percent for those with a score in the 760-850 range compared to 9.931 percent for those with a score in the 500-579 range. This difference in interest rates means higher monthly payments of $885 dollars for those with a FICO score between 500 and 579."

Source: Boston Globe, January 8, 2009.

To comply with the law, lenders should carefully select the variables in credit-scoring models. They should not use variables that may discriminate on a prohibited basis as defined in fair lending laws like the Equal Credit Opportunity Act. Instead, they should consider factors that determine creditworthiness. Bank regulators have expressed concern about weighing variables such as whether the applicant rents or owns a home and has personal finance company references. For any variable a bank uses, there must be a well-documented relationship to creditworthiness.

Similarly, banks establish policies and procedures for credit-scoring overrides (high- or low-end), including who may make these decisions and what constitutes an override (exception). If the bank approves a loan application for an applicant with a credit score that is lower than what the bank's loan policy requires, the exception is a "low-side" override. If the bank decides to deny an application to an applicant with a credit score that meets the minimum, the exception is a "high-side" override. Overrides occur when the bank decides that another characteristic of the applicant takes precedence over the criteria that compose the credit score. Overrides, like other exceptions, should be documented in accordance with loan policy.

Exhibit 9.7   Hypothetical Credit-Scoring System

Applicant Characteristics	Points
Checking and savings account ownership	
Checking and savings	36
Checking only	32
Savings only	26
None	10
Residence/status	
Own/buying	34
Rent	15
Live with parents/relatives	20
Other	5
Time with present employer	
15 years or more	27
12 to 15 years	26
3 to 12 years	14
1 month to 3 years	12
Less than 1 month	5
Student	3
Retired	35
Unemployed with income	–3
Time at current address	
Under 1 year	0
1 to 5 years	8
5 to 10 years	12
Over 10 years	20

Application Score

Credit reporting scoring
Credit references

	Points
All references good (3 or more)	20
At least 2 good references and no negatives	15
No references	0
Some minor derogatory references	–5
Major derogatory information – judgments, repossessions, bankruptcy	–15
Credit inquiries (last 6 months)	
None	8
1 to 3	2
More than 3	–5
Credit Report Score	
None	0
200 – 450	–10
451 – 600	–5
601 – 750	20
751+	35

Variables in a Credit Score

- payment history (35%)
- debt and potential debt (30%)
- length of credit history (15%)
- new credit (10%)
- other factors, such as types of credit (10%)

Source: "Your Credit Scores," Fair Isaac, Inc.

Did You Know ...

The three major consumer credit-reporting agencies—Equifax, Experian, and TransUnion—jointly provide a credit-scoring system intended to simplify the loan process for lenders and borrowers. With VantageScore, a single methodology is used to create consumer credit scores for all three agencies. Score variance among consumer reporting agencies is attributed to data differences within the consumer credit files and not to the scoring model or data interpretation.

In order to meet ECOA requirements, a credit scoring system must be statistically sound. Most reputable vendors of credit scoring systems rigorously test their programs to ensure they comply with federal fair lending requirements. Banks that develop their own systems also should do such testing.

CREDIT SCORES AND THE Cs OF CREDIT

Scoring systems use the same logic as do judgmental systems. The five Cs of credit are analyzed to identify the combination of variables that best predicts credit risk. Variables that do not improve the statistical predictability of credit scores are removed from the scoring program. Today, most score cards have only eight to twelve variables, but depending on the need, others may have hundreds.

Each variable is assigned a specific point value, which is based on information given by the applicant and obtained from the credit report. Because each type of loan is unique, the bank may use different score cards for different product lines. The process results in a decision-making system similar to that shown in exhibit 9.7.

After the bank reviews the application and credit history, the results are given a credit score. If the applicant does not achieve the minimum score defined in the bank's policy, the bank usually declines the loan or investigates further. For a consumer who meets the minimum scoring requirement, the lender then verifies income and employment and calculates the debt-to-income ratio.

Credit-scoring systems have helped lenders, economists, and demographers understand consumer purchasing and credit use behavior. Today, most consumers have credit scores in the range of 650 to 799 (see exhibit 9.8).

CREDIT SCORING ADVANTAGES

The credit-scoring approach offers the advantages of increased management control, reduced loan-processing costs and time, a more legally defensible system, easier training for new lenders, and facilitation of data-gathering. Due to these improvements, the loan portfolio improves along with the lending process.

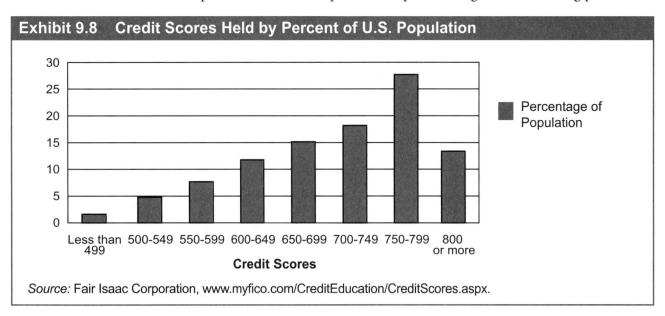

Exhibit 9.8   Credit Scores Held by Percent of U.S. Population

Source: Fair Isaac Corporation, www.myfico.com/CreditEducation/CreditScores.aspx.

Increased Management Control

An effective credit-scoring system ensures consistent decision-making. All loans that comply with the bank's loan policy and meet the scoring requirements are approved; loans not meeting those requirements are declined. The bank may raise or lower credit requirements simply by adjusting the minimum acceptable score. The bank also may override the credit score thresholds, but this would be an exception to policy.

Reduced Loan-Processing Costs

A bank may terminate a loan request if the applicant fails to meet the minimum requirements. Because the bank need not conduct further investigations, additional loan processing costs are avoided.

Reduced Time

Automated credit-scoring systems substantially reduce the time it takes to reach a credit decision. They also make it easier for banks to centralize decision-making.

More Legally Defensible System

The Equal Credit Opportunity Act recognizes statistically valid credit-scoring systems as acceptable. They help lenders make consistent decisions and control the variables used in arriving at a final decision, so there is less opportunity to discriminate unfairly.

Many lenders now rely on credit scores, either exclusively or in combination with judgmental factors, in deciding whether to approve a loan application and to set credit limits, interest rates, and other terms of loans. Some institutions apply different processing according to an applicant's credit score. All these credit-score-based underwriting practices may be examined by bank regulators for evidence of discrimination.

Easier Training for New Lenders

Banks with large lending staffs often are challenged to keep lenders' skills polished. Credit scoring makes it easier to train new lenders to make consistent decisions. It shifts the role of the lender from one who evaluates credit risk to one who markets loans and is responsible for structuring them and selling other bank services.

Facilitates Data-Gathering

Good system design allows the bank to monitor the loan portfolio to ensure that the system is functioning properly. Therefore, management is better able to monitor trends for the entire portfolio or, if desired, for smaller portfolio units, such as branch offices or product categories.

Advantages
- increased management control
- reduced loan processing costs
- reduced time
- more legally defensible
- easier training of new lenders
- easier data-gathering

Disadvantages
- may not include all credit risk factors
- may not easily customize for bank
- order-taking replaces relationship-building

CREDIT SCORING DISADVANTAGES

Credit scoring systems have demonstrated many advantages for lenders, but there are also disadvantages to automated systems that bankers must recognize.

Exclusion of Some Risk Factors

Most credit scoring systems do not take into account all credit risk factors. They may not incorporate the debt-to-income ratio, for example. Off-the-shelf credit scoring models may not give the same emphasis to the credit risk factors that are most important to a particular bank.

Possible Lost Loan Opportunities

Many lenders use the quantitative credit scoring system models provided by consumer reporting agencies, and some use the credit score as the sole factor to determine loan approval. Such practices may lead to the denial of a potentially good loan request. The credit scoring models simply do not detect circumstances that could improve the request and the loan decision. A trained lender who interviews the applicant and analyzes the loan request can detect these quality factors.

Lenders Replaced by Application Takers

Another result of overreliance on credit scoring systems, especially with centralized loan processing, is the reduced employment of skilled consumer lenders. The trend toward using credit-scoring systems, coupled with policies that prohibit overrides, has meant that trained and skilled lenders leave for other employment. The application takers remain, and banks often lose loan opportunities.

CREDIT SCORING WITH JUDGMENTAL ELEMENTS

Most banks use both credit-scoring systems and judgmental variables to reach final decisions. A bank may grant senior lenders authority to make exceptions, allowing them to decline loan requests although credit-scoring requirements were met or approve loans that are below the minimum score. Exceptions must be documented, monitored, and controlled to preserve scoring-system integrity.

Another judgmental feature used to supplement credit scoring is the debt-to-income ratio. A bank may decline the loan request of an applicant who meets many of the bank's scoring requirements but does not meet the loan policy ratio.

A lender may review a declined credit-scored loan to ensure that it "makes sense." On occasion, the credit-scoring system may decline a loan because of insufficient duration of employment or residence when the applicant has just moved to a new home or taken a better job. Additional well-documented information may justify an exception to override a loan declined due to credit scoring.

Situation

Ernesto and Maria met in law school and married soon after graduation. They each brought substantial student loan debt to the marriage. A large portion of their paychecks as law clerks will go toward paying off the student loans for the next few years. They want to buy furniture and pay for a vacation in Hawaii but do not have enough money. Hoping they will qualify, they apply for a personal loan from their local bank. When the letter arrives telling them their request was declined, it includes a personal note from Mr. Hamata, their banker. Mr. Hamata is offering to meet with Ernesto and Maria to talk about handling their debt and building their credit.

What does Mr. Hamata gain from helping this couple?

DECLINING A LOAN

The percentage of loan applications declined varies by bank and loan product. On average, up to 50 percent of all loan applications are declined. To ensure compliance with the Fair Credit Reporting Act and the Equal Credit Opportunity Act, banks document the reasons for adverse credit decisions.

RETAIN THE CONSUMER'S GOODWILL

When communicating an adverse action, such as a declined loan request, the loan officer strives to retain the consumer's goodwill.

Now that so many loan processing options are technology-based, the application process has become much less personal. Although new application options meet consumer goals for quicker loan decisions, they also reduce, and in fact may remove, opportunities for lenders and consumers to establish rapport. To preserve goodwill when a loan is declined, lenders may offer financial counseling. The offer of assistance usually is appreciated. Consumers who are aware of the factors the lender considers in evaluating creditworthiness may take steps to qualify for credit in the future.

Many loans are declined because a consumer is overextended on credit accounts and simply does not have the income to support additional debt. In these cases, a lender may suggest ways the consumer can get debt under control and reduce monthly payments to an acceptable level.

Although many consumers suspect they may not qualify for a loan, they still apply. What they may not know is how to correct the problem. The consumer's lack of knowledge gives the lending officer an opportunity to provide valuable counseling so that the consumer leaves with a positive impression of the bank.

LEGAL AND REGULATORY COMPLIANCE

The law requires that lenders notify consumers whose loan application is declined within 30 days from the time the completed application is made. The notice, prepared in accordance with the Equal Credit Opportunity Act, communicates the reasons for the adverse decision or tells the applicant how to obtain the reasons.

EQUAL CREDIT OPPORTUNITY ACT

Implemented by FRS Regulation B, ECOA forbids discrimination in credit transactions for specified reasons ("prohibited bases"). This rule is meant to protect applicants from credit decisions based on characteristics other than creditworthiness.

EVALUATION CRITERIA

Under ECOA, a lender may use any information it receives about an applicant from whatever source when deciding whether to extend credit, but the information may not be used to discriminate on a prohibited basis.

Generally, FRS Regulation B forbids lenders from seeking information about an applicant's sex, race, religion, color, or national origin. The application form, however, may use optional courtesy titles such as Ms., Mrs., Mr., or Miss. Family planning, birth control practices, the ability to bear children, and child-rearing intentions cannot be discussed with any applicant. A lender cannot ask about an applicant's dependents other than the number for purposes of evaluating capacity to repay the debt.

Age

The lender may ask about age only to establish legal capacity to enter into a contract or for another related element of creditworthiness, such as stability of income. If the applicant is 62 or older, age may be a factor used in favor of the applicant.

Marital Status

A lender may ask about marital status if the applicant is relying on income from alimony, child support, or separate maintenance payments to establish creditworthiness. The bank may request marital status when the applicant lives in a community property state or is pledging collateral that is located in a community property state. Only the terms married, unmarried, and separated may be used. The application must note that information about alimony, child support, or separate maintenance is not required, unless the applicant is relying on it to confirm capacity to repay.

Income Source

Under ECOA, the lender must inform the applicant that income from alimony, child support, or separate maintenance does not have to be disclosed unless the applicant wants such information to be considered in the loan decision. If the applicant wants such income considered in the evaluation, the lender must do so, but the lender also has the right to consider reliability of the income. The lender may review the court decree ordering payment, the payment history, available procedures to compel payment, and the creditworthiness of the party paying the income.

A lender may ask whether any part of an applicant's income comes from public assistance. Although public assistance income cannot be discounted, the lender may consider whether it will continue.

Lenders must give part-time income the same consideration as full-time income. An applicant with qualifying income from part-time employment cannot be evaluated differently from one earning the same amount in a full-time job.

ECOA requires lenders to review all accounts for which an applicant has contractual liability. If the applicant provides information that the credit history, such as a credit report, is incorrect, the lender must consider it.

CREDIT SCORING

ECOA recognizes that many banks legitimately use credit-scoring systems to evaluate credit risk. FRS Regulation B gives guidelines for building the systems, selecting the criteria, and maintaining the system. To be statistically sound, each proprietary scoring system must use actual data from the bank's loan accounts. The items on the scorecard and the values assigned must be consistent with recognized statistical procedures. All credit-scoring systems must be monitored periodically to validate how accurately they predict a consumer's ability to repay.

NOTIFICATIONS

ECOA requires notifications for approved and denied loan requests and for appraisal information.

Approvals

After evaluating the applicant's creditworthiness, the lender must notify the applicant of the decision within 30 days of receipt of the completed application. On approval of the application, the lender may grant credit by written, oral, or implied notice of approval.

Denials

When a lender refuses to grant credit to an applicant for the requested term and amount, the loan is declined, which is an adverse action. A lender who is willing to make a different loan must make a counteroffer to the applicant suggesting the alternative. Both decisions—to decline a loan request or to make a counteroffer—are covered by FRS Regulation B's adverse action provisions. If the consumer accepts the counteroffer, no special disclosures are needed. However, if the counteroffer is not accepted, the lender must send an adverse action notice to the consumer.

FRS Regulation B states that lenders must notify applicants in writing of an adverse action within 30 days of receiving a completed application or taking adverse action on an existing account, such as lowering the limit or terminating a line of credit. If a counteroffer is not accepted, lenders have up to 90 days to send a formal adverse action notice. Exhibit 9.9 (next page) illustrates the timing of the Notice of Adverse Action.

FRS Regulation B prescribes the content of the adverse action notice and has draft model forms lenders may use. A sample Notice of Adverse Action is shown in exhibit 9.10 (page 261). The notice must include

- a statement of the action taken, such as a denied loan request
- the name and address of the federal agency regulating the creditor

> ## *Situation*
>
> Paola Ponti requested a loan to purchase a boat. She asked for $20,000 at 7.5 percent for six years. The lender, Tom Chase, decided that, considering Ms. Ponti's income and credit history, the best offer he could make was $15,000 at 8.30 percent for five years. Tom wrote a letter, setting forth the terms of the counteroffer. The letter was mailed on June 25. Ms. Ponti received the letter and began to search other banks for the loan on the terms she wanted.
>
> *Does Tom Chase have any other responsibility to Ms. Ponti?*

Exhibit 9.9 Adverse Action Flow Chart

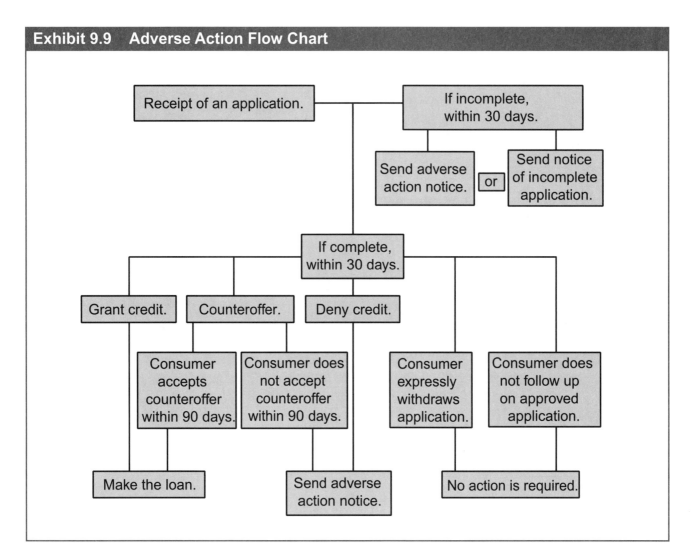

- a paragraph summarizing ECOA's purpose and scope
- a statement informing the applicant of the reasons for credit denial or a statement that the reasons for denial may be obtained from the lender.

The purpose of the adverse action provisions in ECOA is to allow consumers to understand why their application failed to qualify for a loan. Knowing the reasons for a loan denial allows consumers to correct problems or to understand why they do not qualify.

APPRAISAL NOTICES

ECOA requires lenders to notify applicants that they may request a copy of an appraisal on any loan to be secured by a one- to four-family dwelling. The notice is not needed, if the lender routinely provides copies of appraisals to applicants or if applicants are not required to pay for appraisals. Otherwise, the appraisal notice must be given within 30 days of receipt of the application.

Exhibit 9.10 Notice of Adverse Action

Notice of Adverse Action

1. Date: _____

2. Applicant's Name: _____

3. Description of Account, Transaction, or Requested Credit: _____

4. Description of Action Taken: _____

5. Part I – PRINCIPAL REASON(S) FOR CREDIT DENIAL, TERMINATION, OR OTHER ACTION TAKEN CONCERNING CREDIT. This section must be completed in all instances.

a. _ Insufficient number of credit references provided
b. _ Unable to verify credit references
c. _ Temporary or irregular employment
d. _ Unable to verify employment
e. _ Length of employment
f. _ Income insufficient for amount of credit requested
g. _ Excessive obligations in relation to income
h. _ Unable to verify income
i. _ Length of residence
j. _ Temporary residence

k. _ Unable to verify residence
l. _ No credit line
m. _ Limited credit experience
n. _ Poor credit performance with us
o. _ Delinquent past or present credit obligation with others
p. _ Garnishment, attachment, foreclosure, repossession, collection action, or judgment
q. _ Bankruptcy
r. _ Value or type of collateral not sufficient
s. _ Other, specify: _____

6. Part II—DISCLOSURE OF USE OF INFORMATION OBTAINED FROM AN OUTSIDE SORUCE. This section should be completed if the credit decision was based in whole or in part on information that has been obtained from an outside source.

• Our credit decision was based in whole or in part on information obtained in a report from the consumer reporting agency listed below. You have a right under the Fair Credit Reporting Act to know the information contained in your credit file at the consumer reporting agency. The reporting agency played no part in our decision and is unable to supply specific reasons why we have denied credit to you. You also have a right to a free copy of your report from the reporting agency, if you request it no later than 60 days after you receive this notice. In addition, if you find that any information contained in the report you receive is inaccurate or incomplete, you have the right to dispute the matter with the reporting agency.

• Name: _____

• Address: _____

• Toll-free telephone number: _____

• Our credit decision was based in whole or in part on information obtained from an outside source other than a consumer reporting agency. Under the Fair Credit Reporting Act, you have the right to make a written request, no later than 60 days after you receive this notice, for disclosure of the nature of the information.

If you have any questions regarding this notice, you should contact:

• Creditor's name: _____

• Creditor's address: _____

• Creditor's toll-free telephone number: _____

NOTICE: The federal Equal Credit Opportunity Act prohibits creditors from discriminating against credit applicants on the basis of race, color, religion, national origin, sex, marital status, age (provided the applicant has the capacity to enter into a binding contract); because all or part of the applicant's income derives from any public assistance program; or because the applicant has in good faith exercised any right under the Consumer Credit Protection Act. The federal agency that administers compliance with this law concerning this creditor is (name and address as specified by the agency).

SUMMARY

- The primary objectives of the credit evaluation and decision-making stage are to make the best loan for the consumer and the bank, ensure compliance with regulations and bank policy, retain the consumer's goodwill, and ensure that the credit risk is acceptable.

- Consumer lenders rely on financial information in determining the loan's credit risk. Information sources for the credit investigation are the application, personal financial statements, tax returns, and credit reports. Credit evaluation weighs trade-offs and balances key decision variables. Sound lending policies that stipulate acceptable credit characteristics help to guide decision-making and ensure consistency and conformity to policy.

- Judgmental and credit-scoring systems are used to evaluate the information gathered on the application and verified by the credit investigation, thus enabling the lender to reach a final credit decision. In a credit evaluation, lenders are guided by the five Cs of credit: character, capacity, capital, collateral, and conditions. For most consumer loan requests, the primary emphasis is on the applicant's character, credit, and capacity.

- Analysis of character looks at such factors as stability (age, residence, time at residence, and job or career); credit history; credit rating or payment history; types and sources of credit used; dates accounts are opened, closed, or active; debt levels; credit use patterns; and the consumer's personal characteristics. For capacity, lenders analyze cash flow, debt-to-income ratio, potential debt, variable rate accounts (particularly for negative amortization), and the consumer's marketability (ability to change jobs). Capital measures the net value of a consumer's assets. It generally is evaluated by analyzing the personal financial statement to identify assets (liquid and tangible), liabilities, net worth, and the potential for repaying the loan from sources other than regular income. Collateral is considered an available secondary source of repayment to secure, and thus strengthen, the loan. Conditions are reviewed as factors that could change and affect the consumer's ability to repay the loan.

- In a judgmental system, the final credit decision rests with the lender's analysis of an applicant's strengths and weaknesses. During the decision-making process, the lender is looking for ways to make the loan, not turn it down, and for ways to strengthen the loan request for both the consumer and the bank.

- Credit-scoring systems, developed from large databases of actual credit experiences, are based on the assumption that credit risk can be quantified. Credit scoring quantifies the factors used in the judgmental system, such as the five Cs of credit. Key credit variables are identified and then numerically weighted to calculate the probability that the consumer will repay the loan. After the bank reviews the application and credit history, the resulting information is given a credit score. If the applicant does not achieve the minimum score defined in the bank's policy, the loan usually is declined but may be investigated further. Advantages of credit scoring are increased management control, reduced loan-processing costs, reduced time to decision, a more legally defensible system, easier training for new lenders, and facilitation of data-gathering for the loan decision. Disadvantages of using credit scoring systems are that many models do not consider all elements of risk, banks may rely upon quantitative models only, and banks may replace lenders with application takers and thereby miss lending opportunities.

- Many banks combine credit-scoring systems with elements of the judgmental evaluation system. Exceptions may be made to the credit-scored decision or the loan may be restructured. Scoring systems must comply with the bank's loan policy, and exceptions usually require senior officer approval. Exceptions are documented, monitored, and controlled to preserve scoring-system integrity.

- A loan decision must be made within 30 days of receipt of the application. If the lender makes a counteroffer, the decision must be made 90 days after the counteroffer is communicated to the consumer. If the loan is declined, the lender seeks to retain the consumer's goodwill while complying with the law, such as the Equal Credit Opportunity Act (ECOA), implemented by FRS Regulation B.

- ECOA is an important law that governs the process of loan evaluation and decision-making. This law protects consumers from credit decisions based on prohibited characteristics rather than on creditworthiness. FRS Regulation B prohibits lenders from seeking information about an applicant's sex, race, religion, color, or national origin. Birth control practices, family planning, ability to bear children, and child-rearing intentions cannot be discussed. A lender cannot ask about dependents other than the number for purposes of evaluating capacity. Among other factors, the regulation gives rules on questions related to age, marital status, and income sources.

- ECOA gives rules on the use of credit-scoring systems to ensure that they are objective, including a requirement that credit-scoring systems be monitored and validated periodically. ECOA also mandates notifications to consumers about appraisals and the loan decision, including approvals, counteroffers, and adverse actions, such as a declined loan request. Timing and content are prescribed and model notices are given. When appraisals are required for collateral that is a one- to four-family dwelling, consumers must be notified about how to obtain copies of the appraisals.

Learning Check

SELF-CHECK AND REVIEW

1. What does making the best loan for the consumer and the bank mean?

2. What proven assumption about human behavior helps the lender predict a loan's credit risk?

3. What are the five Cs of credit? Give an example of the information the lender reviews for each.

4. How important are the consumer's assets to the evaluation of creditworthiness?

5. What benefits does a credit-scoring system offer?

6. How do banks combine the effectiveness of the judgmental and the credit-scoring approaches to credit evaluation and making loan decisions?

7. What are the bank's primary objectives in handling an adverse action?

8. What notifications does the Equal Credit Opportunity Act require lenders to make in evaluating and deciding whether to make a loan?

Resources

ADDITIONAL RESOURCES

"2009 Will Be Very, Very Bleak," Nouriel Roubini, *Forbes*, January 8, 2009, www.forbes.com.

ABA Bank Compliance Magazine, Washington: American Bankers Association, periodical.

ABA Education Foundation, www.aba.com/Consumer+Connection.

American Bankers Association, **www.aba.com**.

Banking and Finance Terminology, Washington: American Bankers Association, 2005.

Fair Lending Implications of Credit Scoring Systems, Supervisory Insights, Federal Deposit Insurance Corporation, www.fdic.gov/regulations/examinations/supervisory/insights/sisum05/si_summer05.pdf.

Fiscal Fitness for Older Americans: Stretching Your Savings and Shaping Up Your Financial Strategies, Federal Deposit Insurance Corporation, iwww.fdic.gov/consumers/consumer/news/cnfall05.

Interagency Fair Lending Examination Procedures, revised August 2004, www.fdic.gov/consumers/community/fairlend.pdf.

"Knowing Your FICO Credit Score," Andrew Chan, *Boston Globe*, January 8, 2009, www.boston.com.

Law and Banking, Washington: American Bankers Association, 2008.

National Foundation for Consumer Credit, www.nfcc.org.

Reference Guide to Regulatory Compliance, Washington: American Bankers Association, annual publication.

"Taking Control of Your Finances: A Special Guide for Young Adults," *FDIC Consumer News*, Federal Deposit Insurance Corporation, www.fdic.gov/consumers/consumer/news/cnspr05.

"Your Credit Score," Fair Isaac, Inc. brochure, www.fairisaac.com.

Loan Pricing
and Profitability

Learning Objectives

After completing this chapter, you should be able to

- explain the major factors affecting consumer loan pricing
- discuss the categories used to analyze bank costs in making loans
- describe methods used to calculate loan profitability
- explain regulations on lending limits, debt cancellation contracts, and debt suspension agreements
- define the terms that appear in bold type in the text.

Introduction

Managing a profitable consumer lending portfolio is challenging. The number of products and competition for consumers keep increasing. The variety in products, rate structures, and other loan features challenge bankers to determine the cost of loans accurately, price loans appropriately, and keep lending profitable.

Factors influencing pricing vary widely and come from different sources. The economic and regulatory environment, competition, changes in consumer demand, and the bank's business strategy create the structure that determines consumer loan pricing. Banks analyze the cost of making loans and the margin between cost and income, and then adjust pricing as needed.

Like so many other processes in banking, pricing loans is both a technical activity and an art. Mindful of their role in the community and the need for the bank to remain stable and profitable, bankers apply artful vision to their technical skills when pricing products to serve both consumers and banks. The Galaxy Bank Financial Case Study that is an appendix to this chapter illustrates the pricing decisions banks make.

THE COST TO BORROW

In addition to returning the principal amount of money borrowed, consumers pay for the use of the money, which provides earnings for the bank. The biggest charge is interest, but credit insurance and other miscellaneous charges also influence the total amount a consumer pays for a loan.

CALCULATING INTEREST

Lenders rarely are required to calculate interest manually. Computer programs allow them to determine the financial terms for a loan. Nevertheless, it is important for lenders to understand the elements incorporated into interest calculations: principal, rate, time, and frequency.

By The Numbers

Calculating Interest on a 30-day Single-Payment Loan

Principal:	$1,000
Rate:	12% simple interest
Time:	30 days
Frequency:	Single payment

Principal x Rate x Time = Interest

(interest based on 365 days)

At the end of 30 days, the consumer would pay $1,009.86.

Banks calculate the interest earned on the loan by using the basic formula:

Principal x Rate x Time = Interest

Principal	The amount of money loaned to the consumer, before fees or interest
Rate	The interest rate that applies to the loan
Time	The proposed loan term, the length of time the money will be used
Frequency	The timing of loan payments, such as monthly, quarterly, or at the end of a specified term

INTEREST RATES

Consumer loan rates may be grouped into three categories based on their function. Within each are two variations.

Category	*Variations*
Interest or total finance charges	• simple interest rate • annual percentage rate (APR)
Externally determined rates	• usury rate • index rate
Stable and flexible rates	• fixed rate • variable rate

Rates for Calculating Interest or Total Finance Charge

Simple interest. To calculate simple interest, an interest rate is applied to the loan's **average daily balance** outstanding during a specific period. **Simple interest** generally is expressed as an annual rate, such as 12 percent, although on open-end credit accounts it also may be shown as a daily periodic rate. For example, if the simple interest rate is 12 percent, the daily periodic rate is 12 percent divided by 365 (days in a year), so the daily rate is 0.032877 percent (some states stipulate use of 360 days in this formula).

Annual percentage rate (APR). The APR is not an interest rate; it is the total cost of borrowing, including not only interest but also other finance charges, expressed as a percentage. The APR is intended to allow fair comparison of the cost of consumer credit and to provide a common language for describing loan costs to consumers.

The Truth in Lending Act (TILA), implemented by FRS Regulation Z, details, formulas that banks must use to calculate the APR for a variety of loans. The annual percentage rate will differ from the simple interest rate if the

average daily balance—
The sum of daily loan balances in a billing cycle divided by the number of days in the cycle.

simple interest—Interest computed by applying a daily periodic interest rate to the amount of principal outstanding.

By The Numbers

Calculating Simple Interest for a Billing Period

Average daily loan balance:	$1,294.89
Billing cycle :	29 days
Daily periodic rate:	.032876

Average daily loan balance x Days in billing cycle x Daily periodic rate

$ 1,294.89 x29 days = $37,551.81 x .032876 = $12.35 interest

loan includes fees that are part of the finance charge. For example, if the bank charges points or loan fees, the simple interest rate on a loan may be 12 percent but the APR could be 12.25 percent, depending on what the other charges are. The finance charge is equal to the interest plus any other charges deemed by TILA to be part of the cost of credit.

Externally Determined Rates

The usury rate is an externally determined rate set by state law. The index rate is usually determined by an entity outside the bank.

Usury rate. Many states have set maximum **usury rates** for certain types of loans made by lenders operating in the state. However, application of a usury law may depend on where a bank is headquartered. Usury rates sometimes are referred to as ceiling rates.

Index rate. **Indexes** used by banks include the prime rate, the U.S. Treasury bill rate, and the London Interbank Offered Rate (LIBOR). The prime rate as reported in the *Wall Street Journal* is widely quoted as an indicator of interest rates in general. For example, a bank may price its variable-rate lines of credit at prime rate plus 8 percent. If the prime rate reported in the *Wall Street Journal* is 6 percent, the variable rate for the consumer would be 14 percent (6 percent plus 8 percent).

An external index—one not controlled by the bank—is easier to defend against criticism than an internal index. Many state laws stipulate that resident banks must use an external index. Ideally, the index selected should track the behavior of the bank's cost of funds. Because consumers need to accept and understand the index, banks should choose one that is readily available and understandable.

Fixed and Variable Rates

Unlike a **fixed rate**, a variable rate will change in response to changes in the index rate as defined in the loan agreement.

Because they cannot adjust to changes in market interest rates, fixed-rate loan portfolios expose lenders to higher interest-rate risk. Because variable-rate loans do adjust to changes in market interest rates, they have less interest-rate risk.

Most consumer loan portfolios contain a mix of fixed- and variable-rate loans. Fixed-rate loans tend to be high-yield products, such as some credit card and most check overdraft programs and traditional closed-end products, such as automobile loans. Variable rates are more common on open-end credit accounts, boat loans, and home equity loans and lines of credit. Mixed portfolios give lenders a base for meeting consumer demands for credit while optimizing profits.

Fixed rate. Applying a fixed interest rate on a closed-end loan means that the consumer will have the same monthly payment as long as the account is repaid satisfactorily, although minor adjustments may be required in the final monthly payment to reflect early or late payments received. Consumers who make payments after scheduled due dates may be required to pay additional finance charges.

---

usury rate—The maximum interest rate permitted by state law that legally may be charged on a loan, usually set by type of loan.

index rate—A benchmark rate, such as the prime or the 90-day U.S. Treasury bill rate, used to determine the variable-interest rate in effect at any given time.

fixed-rate loan—A loan with an interest rate that remains the same over the life of the loan.

Factors in Pricing Variable-Rate Loans

- selecting an index rate
- determining pricing strategy
- determining marketing strategy
- determining frequency of pricing changes
- selecting rate floors and caps
- evaluating the effect on credit and collateral risk

Many homeowners consider a home equity loan to consolidate debt, but not every homeowner should do so. The Federal Reserve urges homeowners to consider these options first:

- Talk with creditors or with representatives of nonprofit or other reputable credit or budget counseling organizations to work out a plan that reduces bill payments to a more manageable level.

- Contact a local social service agency, community or religious group, and local or state housing agencies about programs that help consumers, including the elderly and those with disabilities, with energy bills, home repairs, or other emergency needs.

- Contact a local housing counseling agency to discuss credit support needs. The U.S. Department of Housing and Urban Development has a toll-free number and Web site with center listings.

- Before making any decisions, talk with someone, other than the lender or broker offering the loan, who is knowledgeable and trustworthy.

- If a loan is the best choice, comparison shop by talking with several lenders, including at least one bank, savings and loan, or credit union, in your community.

Source: Federal Reserve Board of Governors, www.federalreserve.gov.

On open-end credit accounts, the creditor cannot change the fixed rate without the consumer's consent. In these cases, consumers usually avoid rate increases on fixed-rate, open-end accounts by paying off the loan or by not using the account after receiving a **change in terms notice**.

Variable rate. By using a variable rate, lenders may pass on to consumers changes in the cost of funds and thereby retain their net interest margins and reduce interest-rate risk. The variable interest rate is tied to a preselected index. As the index rate changes, either up or down, so does the variable rate. Increases may be passed on to the consumer in higher monthly payments, by increasing the number of required payments, or by a larger final payment. Decreases may result in lower monthly payments, fewer monthly payments, or a smaller final payment.

Pricing Variable-Rate Loans

Many factors are considered when variable-rate loans are priced. It is necessary to select an index, decide on a pricing and marketing strategy relative to variable-rate loans, determine how often prices will change, select rate floors and caps, and evaluate the effect of these decisions on credit and collateral risk.

Selecting an index. Many banks use the **prime rate** as published in the *Wall Street Journal*, a U.S. Treasury bill rate, or **LIBOR** as their index.

Pricing and marketing strategy. One strategy for marketing variable-rate closed-end loans is to offer them side by side with fixed-rate loans, with the variable-rate loan priced slightly lower. This gives the consumer an incentive to take the variable rate with its initial lower monthly payment. The interest rate gap between fixed and variable rates tends to narrow as rates rise and widen as they fall.

change in terms notice— A written notice required by the Truth in Lending Act, implemented by FRS Regulation Z, for open-end credit accounts when, for example, terms required in the initial disclosure table are changed or the required minimum periodic payment is increased. It must be mailed to the consumer before the effective change date; generally, 15 days in advance for home-secured credit lines and 45 days for unsecured credit lines.

prime rate—An index rate from which a bank may compute a variable rate of interest for a loan contract. For consumer variable-rate loans, many banks use the prime rate as published in the *Wall Street Journal*.

London Interbank Offered Rate (LIBOR)— An international money market interest rate that represents the average rate offered by banks for interbank placements of Eurodollars.

Frequency of pricing changes. Variable interest rates on loans may change monthly, quarterly, or less often. Some banks use less frequent adjustment periods so as to position their product advantageously in the market. Less frequent adjustments may help bank yields when rates decline but hurt them when rates rise.

Rate floors and caps. Banks use rate floors and caps (ceilings) to balance interest-rate risk with credit and collateral risk. A rate cap protects the consumer from higher monthly payments or negative amortization, but it limits the bank's ability to pass on total interest rate risk to the consumer. Rate floors, on the other hand, protect the bank's yield when prices are falling and help preserve a yield objective.

Evaluating the effect on credit and collateral risk. Increases in the monthly payments resulting from rate increases can affect the consumer's debt-to-income ratio and ability to repay the loan. The credit risk on the loan thus becomes higher. Collateral risk threatens if the loan term is extended—depreciating-value collateral will be worth less at the new maturity date. When the value of the collateral declines further than originally contemplated, the loan's collateral risk is higher (see exhibit 10.1).

PAYMENT PROTECTION

Payment protection for consumers can be provided through two sets of arrangements—credit insurance and debt cancellation or suspension agreements.

Credit Insurance

Credit insurance often is sold as part of a consumer loan transaction. Banks traditionally partnered with insurance companies to offer this protection but the Gramm-Leach-Bliley Act (GLBA) now allows banks to offer customers this

payment protection—
Products that are sold in conjunction with loans so that the loan can be paid if the borrower dies, is injured or disabled, or loses his or her income source. There are two types: credit insurance and debt protection contracts.

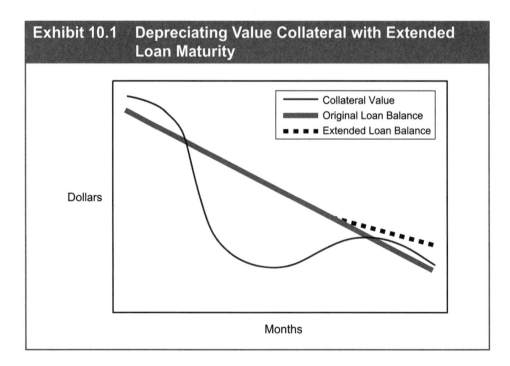

Exhibit 10.1 Depreciating Value Collateral with Extended Loan Maturity

— Collateral Value
— Original Loan Balance
■ ■ ■ Extended Loan Balance

Dollars

Months

and other types of insurance through their own insurance subsidiaries. However, the GLBA also prohibits banks from requiring credit life insurance as a condition of making a consumer loan, and banks cannot require that credit life insurance be purchased from its affiliate.

Credit life insurance generally will pay off the balance due on the loan if an insured consumer dies. This relieves the family and the estate of the financial burden. Credit life insurance for a single policy covers the primary consumer; for a joint policy, it covers the primary consumer and the spouse (or in some states other co-consumers). Credit accident, health and disability, and loss-of-income insurance will make the monthly payments on a loan until the insured returns to gainful employment, subject to the policy terms. This insurance relieves the family of a financial burden during periods of reduced income and preserves the consumer's credit standing.

Insurance coverage increases the amount financed because the lender loans the consumer the amount of the insurance premium. This in turn increases the finance charge, the monthly payment, and the total cost of the loan. Here is the payment computation for a $4,500 loan for 36 months at a 5 percent rate without and with credit insurance.

Types of Credit Insurance

- credit life
- credit accident
- credit health
- credit disability
- credit loss-of-income

	No Credit Insurance	With Credit Insurance
Loan amount	$4,500.00	$4,500.00
Life insurance	0	90.66
Accident and health insurance	0	206.54
Finance charge	355.26	378.70
Total loan payment	4,855.26	5,175.90
Monthly payment	$ 13.87	$ 143.78

Debt Cancellation and Debt Suspension

Debt cancellation contracts (DCC) and debt suspension agreements (DSA) are products similar to credit insurance. The consumer pays the lender a fee for these services at the time a loan agreement is executed. A debt cancellation contract provides that all or part of the consumer's obligation on a loan will be canceled pending certain events. For example, if the consumer dies, the loan may be canceled rather than having to be paid by the consumer's estate. A debt suspension agreement suspends the debt for a time, such as while the consumer is disabled or unemployed.

DCCs and DSAs differ from credit insurance. They are not subject to state insurance regulation, because lenders, not insurance companies, sell them. The lender, not an insurer, receives the fee from the DCC or DSA sale, assumes the risk, and is obligated to cover any claims.

Situation

Recently, Jenny Wu's father died and she decided to ask her mother to live with her. About five years ago, Jenny bought a small house with an attached garage and she would like to convert the garage into a living area for her mother. She knows how much the conversion will cost and how much she and her mother can jointly pay each month to repay a loan. Jenny's banker gives her several loan options. She notices that if she takes a four-year instead of a two-year loan, the payments will be well within her budget. Even though she will end up paying more for the loan overall by extending the term, it is important to Jenny that the loan payments are affordable.

Are other consumers similarly influenced by the monthly payment?

Did You Know ...

There are three big money challenges most consumers have during their lifetime and banks can help consumers prepare and finance for all of them. They are
- buying a home
- paying for college
- preparing for retirement

LOAN TERMS

The term of the loan also can have a significant effect on the consumer's loan cost. Exhibit 10.2 shows the effect that increasing the term of the loan has on the monthly payment and total cost of a $5,000 loan at 8 percent. As the term increases, the monthly payment decreases, although the total cost increases. Extending the loan from two to three years results in a $69.46 reduction in the monthly payment and a $213.29 increase in the total cost of the loan, from $5,427.27 to $5,640.56.

The importance of the monthly payment to a consumer should not be underestimated. In fact, many consumers make their borrowing decisions based more on the affordability of the monthly payment than on the interest rate on the loan. The size of the monthly payment is an important variable in evaluating credit risk and measuring the consumer's ability to repay the loan.

Structuring the loan term and the monthly payment to fit the consumer's capacity is important for both lender and consumer. Lenders structure repayment terms to optimize the consumer's ability to repay and control risk for the bank.

Terms (maturities) on closed-end loans generally are set by bank policy based on the type of collateral securing the loan. On the other hand, except for home equity lines of credit (HELOCs), open-end lines of credit often have no set maturity. Instead, the bank establishes a monthly payment based on repayment of a specified percentage of the outstanding balance, such as 5 percent for many credit cards or 1 percent for many HELOCs.

The actual percentages depend on product design and bank policy: the lower the required minimum monthly payment percentage, the longer the anticipated payback term. Reduced monthly payments will increase the amount of cash the consumer has available to spend on other debts. When consumers borrow against lines of credit, however, account balances must be paid off in full before the account can be closed.

Exhibit 10.2 Effect of Loan Term on Monthly Payments

For a $5,000 loan at 8.0%

LOAN TERM (IN MONTHS)	MONTHLY PAYMENT	CONSUMER'S TOTAL INTEREST COST
12	$434.94	$ 219.31
24	$226.14	$ 427.27
36	$156.68	$ 640.56
48	$122.06	$ 859.12
60	$101.38	$1,082.94

LOAN PRICING

The regulatory environment; the competitive environment; economic conditions; and the bank's own costs, profit objectives, strategies, and financial condition affect loan pricing decisions. Other factors, such as the consumer's credit risk and collateral, also factor into the loan pricing decision.

REGULATORY ENVIRONMENT

The regulatory environment has a significant influence on the prices of loans because state laws govern the interest rates and fees lenders may charge for many consumer loans. There is considerable rate variation from state to state, and many states have abolished rate limits altogether. Moreover, banks with offices in different states may use the rates allowed by the state in which they are chartered.

The interest rates permitted by state laws influence the kind of loan products banks will offer, the availability of credit, and the credit risk banks will accept. Like other businesses, banks offer products from which they may earn a fair return on their investment. For example when the cost of deposits goes up, the bank cannot raise fixed interest rates on loans to preserve its profit margin. Federal law does not regulate the interest rates charged on consumer loans, but periodically legislators consider imposing national maximum interest rates on consumer credit products. Credit card programs have been the targets of review in the past, particularly when the spread between the rate charged on fixed-rate credit card programs and the rates for variable-rate money market instruments widens. One solution has been for banks to use variable-rate pricing for credit card plans.

COMPETITIVE ENVIRONMENT

Competition for consumer loans is intense as new participants enter the market and banks expand lending operations beyond their traditional market areas. Competitors' rates are monitored and factored into pricing decisions.

Lenders use different methods to monitor competitor prices and products. They may follow media advertisements, shop the competition by telephone, and question employees about loan pricing elsewhere. Because it is impossible to monitor all competitors constantly, many bankers focus on those that are price leaders by virtue of their market share or their aggressive marketing. Banks have to be creative to remain competitive while maintaining their credit standards.

The competitive environment is probably the most important single factor in setting interest rates on consumer loans. If its interest rates are too far above the market, the bank will be unable to attract a significant number of credit-worthy consumers. If the interest rates are too low relative to competitors, the bank most likely is sacrificing profit unnecessarily.

Situation

Elise would like to finance a new bedroom set. She finds what she is looking for at a furniture store that advertises "90 days same as cash" to finance purchases. The prospect of not having to make payments for the first few months is very appealing to Elise. She is on a tight budget and has to keep her monthly payments under a certain amount. Elise decides to speak to a loan officer at her bank to find out if the bank can make a similar offer.

How can the bank compete with this type of offer?

Loan Pricing Factors

- legal environment
- competitive environment
- general economic conditions
- bank's costs, profit objectives, strategies, and financial condition

Sample Charges Included in the Finance Charge

- interest
- amount payable under add-on or discount system of charges
- service, transaction, activity, or carrying charges
- points, loan fees, assumption fees, finders' fees
- premiums for guarantees or insurance to protect the creditor against default
- charges imposed on the creditor for purchasing or accepting the credit
- premiums or fees for credit life, accident, health, or loss-of-income insurance
- premiums or fees for insurance against loss of or damage to property
- discounts for the purpose of inducing payment, other than use of credit
- debt cancellation fees

Did You Know ...

Many banks charge a processing or origination fee for automobile, home improvement, mobile home, and recreational vehicle loans.

ECONOMIC CONDITIONS

Economic conditions also affect pricing decisions. Deposit interest rates, demand for credit, and conditions in the bank's market area are reflected in consumer loan pricing.

Fluctuations in deposit interest rates affect the bank's cost of funds. As the cost of deposits and other bank liabilities change, so do the costs of consumer loans. Rising deposit interest rates mean a rise in the cost of funding the loan portfolio. The bank may react by raising interest rates, as is automatic for variable-rate loans, or it may elect to hold rates steady. Raising rates on new loans helps preserve profit margins; holding rates at the current level narrows short-term profit margins but may result in a higher market share if competitors raise their rates. Declines in market rates generally result in price reductions, which tend to stimulate demand for consumer loans.

Demand for consumer loans influences pricing decisions. Several indexes are monitored to assess the relative strength of demand, among them measures of retail sales, consumer buying intentions and confidence, and direct measures of lending activity itself. All things being equal, loan prices tend to rise or stabilize when demand is strong and decline when demand softens.

Economic conditions in the bank's market area influence demand and thus loan pricing. High unemployment and low retail sales, for example, lower demand for loans—an incentive to reduce rates.

THE BANK'S INTERNAL ENVIRONMENT

The bank's costs, objectives, and strategies—its internal environment—affect its loan pricing. Because objectives and strategies generally are set at the product line level, pricing varies from product to product. If the bank has aggressive growth plans for a product, it may price at the low end of the market's interest rate range. If growth goals are modest, and other goals, such as increased profitability, are more important, the pricing may be more toward the upper end.

A bank's financial condition influences its loan pricing. In an increasingly competitive, deregulated environment, banks that deliver loan products at the lowest cost have a competitive advantage. Low-cost providers are better able to price their loans at the lower end of the market range and still achieve the desired profit margin.

OTHER FACTORS

Going beyond interest rates, other product elements are important in loan pricing, including the annual percentage rate, monthly payment, credit insurance charges, fees charged, and the time value of money. Each element is an opportunity to increase income and compete in the marketplace.

Although the process of pricing loan products varies, some practices are common. Many lenders price loans based on the type of loan and the collateral securing it. Exhibit 10.3 illustrates a sample pricing strategy based on the risk

Exhibit 10.3   Sample Pricing Schedules

		LTV 81–90%	LTV 91–100%
Variations based on collateral value			
Home equity loan	60 months	6.25%	6.75%
	120	7.00	7.50
	180	7.75	8.25
Variations based on loan term			
New automobile loan	36 months	6.00%	
	48	6.25	
	60	6.50	
Variations based on size of loan			
New boat loan	$5,000–$24,999	7.99%	
	$25,000 and up	8.75	
Unsecured loan	Up to $3,499	8.00	
	$3,500 and up	8.25	
Variations based on credit risk			
Credit score	650–675 points	8.75%	
	676–699	8.00	
	700–739	7.50	

Typical Loan Fees

- late charges
- overlimit fees
- returned check charges
- application fees
- minimum finance charges
- annual account fees
- credit report fees
- processing or origination fees

associated with various collateral types, as well as the loan term, credit risk, and loan amount.

Collateral   There is a risk that collateral will change in value, especially for fluctuating- and depreciating-value collateral.

Term   Risk and operational costs increase as the loan term increases, thus justifying a higher rate.

Loan size   Larger loans offer some operational efficiencies that can justify lower rates.

Credit risk   Consumers with less credit risk are rewarded with lower rates.

Time Value of Money

The concept of the **time value of money** is simply that a dollar received today is worth more than a dollar received in the future; and a dollar to be received in the future is worth less than a dollar received today. Money received today is worth more because it can be invested and earn interest.

Lenders consider the time value of money when pricing loans and managing loan portfolios. A single sum of money or a series of payments or receipts promised in the future can convert to an equivalent value today. There are two important aspects to understanding the concept: **present value** and **future value**. If a payment is made today, its present value is equal to the amount of the payment. If a payment will be made later, its future value is the size of the payment being made in the future, and thus its present value would be less by an amount determined by the interest rate.

time value of money— The expected value of the income earned on a loan based on the value of money today (present value) or its expected value in the future (future value).

present value—The value today of payments that will be received in the future.

future value—The value tomorrow of money lent today.

Did You Know ...

The 2008 Study of Consumer Payment Preferences found that 63 percent of all consumer purchases are made using electronic payment methods, including bill payment. The share of paper-based payments in total bill payments shrank from 55 percent in 2005 to 38 percent in 2008.

Source: Hitachi Consulting, October 6, 2008, www.hitachiconsulting.com.

Exhibit 10.4   Time Value of Money: Present and Future Value

$$PV = FV_n \div (1 + I)^n$$

PV = present value
n = number of periods when the payment occurs
FV_n = future value after *n* periods
i = interest rate per period

$$FV = PV (1 + i)^n$$

Present value for a single-payment loan[1]

FV = $108
n = 1
i = 8.0%
$PV = 108 \div (1 + .08)^1$
PV = $100

Future value for a single-payment loan
PV = $100
n = 1
i = 8%
$FV = \$100 (1 + .08)^1$
FV = $108

Exhibit 10.4 illustrates the calculation for present value and future value. Using the formula, it is possible to determine any one variable, if the other two are known. For example, future value can be determined if present value and the interest rate are known.

When they lend to consumers, banks in essence are investing money, and the return is the income they derive from the loan. A more complicated version of the formula shown in exhibit 10.4 may be used to determine the size of each payment when there are multiple payments, and to consider other risks, such as inflation risk. However, because these formulas are quite complex, the calculations normally are done on a computer. Nevertheless, the questions are the same: If the money is loaned today to a consumer at a specified interest rate, what will it be worth tomorrow? What is the future value?

Lenders know that the value of a payment received one year from now is lower than the value of the same loan payment received today. Applying the formula for present value shown in exhibit 10.4 will give the lender a better understanding of what that value is likely to be.

Knowing the time value of money is important to lenders who are considering future payments to determine which loans will have more value. This information is important to structuring loan terms and pricing the loan profitably.

LOAN PROFITABILITY

The profitability of consumer loans underlies all cost and pricing decisions. Many factors, especially the loan's cost to the bank, determine the profitability of the consumer loan portfolio.

THE BANK'S COST

To be profitable, a loan must generate more in income than it costs to acquire and service. Banks continually refine their accounting and control systems to identify and allocate costs. Among the production cost categories banks analyze to determine loan portfolio profitability are acquisition costs, maintenance and liquidation costs, loan loss cost, and the cost of funds.

Acquisition Costs

Acquisition costs are all the expenses incurred in generating loan applications, processing them through to a decision, and documenting approved loans and adverse actions. They include advertising and sales promotion, personnel costs for handling loan applications at all stages of the lending process, legal expenses, credit-scoring program expenses, miscellaneous supply costs, and communications costs.

As acquisition costs rise over time, banks work to improve operating efficiency by such means as automated systems; targeting marketing efforts better; and directing loan business to more cost-efficient products, such as open-end lines of credit, which eliminate the need to go through the full application and documentation process each time the consumer wants to borrow. Operational efficiencies also have been achieved by automating portions of the lending process and selling larger loans. Automated application tracking systems, credit scoring, and document preparation are practices that help control costs and improve performance.

Maintenance and Liquidation Costs

Maintenance and liquidation costs occur after the loan is made. They include sending out coupon books and billing statements, processing payments, and servicing, collecting, and recovering loans.

Major maintenance and liquidation costs are for personnel, computer hardware and software, and related communication costs, including keeping the database current and preparing reports.

One of the first priorities of automation is to reduce maintenance and liquidation costs. One example is having consumers make payments by automated debits from their bank accounts to increase efficiency and reduce late payments. Many banks offer lower rates to consumers who use this feature. Today, banks continue to search for efficiencies in all areas of the loan process: accounting, documentation, customer service, and collection and recovery.

Loan Loss Costs

Loan loss costs, expressed as a rate, represent the bank's loss experience on its consumer loans over time. Loans charged to the bank's loss reserve are an expense because they are assets that the bank may not recover. Although the **loan-loss rate** varies among banks, it usually follows a fairly consistent pattern and range. Loan losses tend to fluctuate with general economic conditions, the extent of the risk the bank is willing to take, and the mix of consumer loans within the portfolio. Credit cards typically have higher loan-loss rates than HELOCs.

Cost of Funds

The final factor is, perhaps, the most important. Cost of funds represents the price the bank must pay for the money it lends to consumers. Banks typically draw upon three sources to fund loans: their capital, cash, and deposits.

acquisition cost—The total cost associated with making a loan. It includes costs for marketing, taking applications, interviewing applicants, investigating the credit risk, gathering and processing documents, and making the credit decision.

maintenance and liquidation cost—The cost of collecting payments and servicing open loan accounts, including overhead expenses such as rent and utilities, salaries for loan processors and customer service representatives, coupon books, office supplies, and computer expenditures.

loan-loss rate—A measure of a lender's previous experience with bad loans computed by dividing the dollar amount of total losses by the dollar amount of total loans outstanding.

Increased competition in banking can have a significant effect on the cost of these funds. Sources command varying rates for funds based on availability and demand for the funds. Unpredictable fluctuations in the cost of funds can make loans unprofitable or erode profit margins. Although consumer loan managers have some control over operational expenses for lending, they have no control over the cost of funds.

Fluctuations in the cost of funds affect not only loan pricing but also the bank's product strategy, credit policies, and sometimes growth objectives. Banks must plan for fluctuations, because the cost of funds is the largest single expense item for most loans. They seek to minimize the risk inherent in these fluctuations by expanding the use of variable-rate loans and refining their asset and liability management programs.

Average and Marginal Cost Analysis

There are two primary methods for analyzing loan costs: the **average cost** basis and the marginal cost basis. The average cost basis is calculated by dividing the consumer credit department's total expenses by the number of accounts in the loan portfolio. By putting more accounts on the books without adding to fixed costs, a bank can reduce its average cost. If the bank must add staff and office equipment to handle additional volume, the average cost may increase instead.

The variable costs associated with each additional loan also are known as **marginal costs**. The standard is that when income from a loan would exceed the marginal cost for its acquisition and maintenance, the loan should be made. Thus, if it would cost $100 to make and the income earned would be $101, the loan should be made. Although the standard seems relatively simple, it is difficult to implement.

EVALUATING LOAN PROFITABILITY

Banks are businesses that must generate an acceptable profit for their shareholders. They are skilled at evaluating the profitability both of their entire portfolio and of individual products and accounts. The profitability of individual accounts can be evaluated and applied more broadly to loan pricing and policies.

Loan Term

Exhibit 10.5 shows the effect that loan term has on loan profitability. Net income changes as a result of the change in term. Although acquisition costs do not change with the term, maintenance costs increase because more payments must be processed. The cost of funds also increases because the loan is outstanding for a longer period. The loan-loss rate is based on the size and type of loan, so in this case it does not change. It is more profitable to extend the term of the loan.

average cost—The cost of lending spread over the entire loan portfolio so that every loan is allocated an equal share of the total cost; the total cost of lending divided by the total number of loans in the portfolio.

marginal cost—The additional cost attributable to the production of each additional loan.

Risks in Banking

- strategic
- reputation
- credit
- interest rate
- liquidity
- price
- foreign exchange
- transaction compliance

Exhibit 10.5 Profitability Analysis—Effect of Loan Term

COST CATEGORY	$5,000 LOAN AT 12.0%	
	12-MONTH LOAN	**36-MONTH LOAN**
Cost to make a loan	$196.00	$196.00
Cost to collect payments	$ 66.00	$198.00
Cost of funds at 1.7%	$ 85.00	$255.00
Loan loss rate 1.0%	$ 50.00	$ 50.00
Total costs	$397.00	$699.00
Finance charge	$330.93	$978.60
Net income	**($66.07)**	**$279.60**
Monthly payment	$444.24	$166.08

Did You Know ...

The monthly cost-of-funds index (COFI) reflecting the weighted-average interest rate paid by 11th Federal Home Loan Bank District savings institutions for savings and checking accounts was 2.455 percent as of January 2009, a drop of 1.515 points from the 3.970 rate of January 2008. The San Francisco District Bank covers Arizona, California, and Nevada. The COFI is an index used by many banks to set rates for variable-rate loans. Loan rates tied to COFI usually change more slowly than those tied to market interest rates.

Source: Federal Home Loan Bank San Francisco, www.fhlbsf.com/cofi/monthly/monthly.asp

Interest Rate

Increasing the rate on a loan also has a positive effect (see exhibit 10.6). An increase of 150 basis points in the rate, from 7.5 percent to 9.0 percent, increases income by $338.91 over the term of the loan. This example illustrates the effect of a rate increase on the profitability of an individual loan, not the loan portfolio. Fixed-rate loans have greater interest rate risk than variable-rate loans. If the bank's cost of funds rises, the net interest margin on a fixed-rate loan will be reduced. If the cost of funds declines, the net interest margin will increase. Banks use a variety of funding strategies to reduce risk on fixed-rate portfolios, generally matching loans with liabilities that also have fixed rates and similar maturity patterns.

Breakeven Analysis

Breakeven analysis is a tool for setting policy for minimum loan size, pricing, and term combinations and for determining where improvements can be made for cost efficiency. The breakeven point is where total fixed and variable costs

Exhibit 10.6 Profitability Analysis—Rate Effect

COST CATEGORY	$10,000 LOAN—48 MONTHS	
	Interest Rate 7.5%	**Interest Rate 9.0%**
Cost to make a loan	$ 196.00	$ 196.00
Cost to collect payments	$ 264.00	$ 264.00
Cost of funds at 1.7 %	$ 170.00	$ 170.00
Loan loss rate 1.0%	$ 100.00	$ 100.00
Total costs	$ 730.00	$ 730.00
Finance charge	$1,605.92	$1,944.83
Net income	**$ 875.92**	**$1,214.83**
Monthly payment	$ 241.79	$ 248.85

Situation

To pay their tuition Jodi and Franco each took out a $10,000 simple-interest loan from the same bank and with the same terms. Franco makes his monthly payments three or four days before the payment is due and pays a little more than the required amount. Jodi caught a glimpse of Franco's monthly statement lying on his desk and was surprised that his interest payment was less than her payment. She immediately called the bank to find out why.

What did she find out?

exactly equal the income earned from a loan, a product line, or a loan portfolio. Because costs such as cost of funds, loan loss reserve, and costs to collect payment will vary depending on factors such as loan amount, term, and product line, the analysis can be as complex and diverse as the data included. Usually averages for the variable costs are used to simplify the analysis.

Exhibit 10.7 compares the cost factors of two banks using the same rate and term to illustrate the resulting differences in the break even loan amounts.

Timing of Payments

Simple-interest calculations are used on open-end credit accounts, variable-rate loans, and many closed-end loans. A simple-interest loan calculation is based on the date that payments actually are received. As illustrated in exhibit 10.8, if payments on an account with a balance of $10,000 and a rate of 6 percent were received on different dates each month, the amount of interest would vary. Sample figures are shown in exhibit 10.8.

Consumers may reduce interest costs on simple-interest loans by paying before the scheduled due date. On the other hand, the bank will realize higher interest income on late payments. Consumers also may reduce interest costs on simple-interest loans by paying more than the minimum monthly payment, because the additional payment is applied to the unpaid principal balance.

Exhibit 10.7   Breakeven Analysis for Loan Amount

	BANK A	BANK B
Breakeven loan amount	$5,266.64	$4,297.50
Cost to make a loan	175.00	150.00
Cost of funds*	212.50	202.50
Loan loss reserve*	125.00	105.00
Cost to collect payments*	330.00	230.00
Total costs	$842.50	$687.50
Interest Rate	6.0%	6.0%
Term	60 months	60 months
Monthly payment amount	$101.82	$83.08
Total amount of payment	$6,109.14	$4,985.00
Finance charge	$842.50	$687.50

*Cost of funds, a variable that relates to the loan amount and term, is set at an average amount for each bank in this illustration. Loan loss reserve, also referred to as loan loss rate, varies depending on loan type and term. Cost to collect payments varies with loan term.

Exhibit 10.8 Interest Accrual on Simple-Interest Loans		
$10,000 balance at 6.0%		
DATE PAYMENT RECEIVED	**NUMBER OF DAYS BALANCE OPEN**	**INTEREST**
5 days before due date	25	$41.09
On due date	30	$49.31
5 days after due date	35	$57.53

PRODUCT LINE PROFITABILITY

Each consumer loan product has unique profitability characteristics. These characteristics reflect varying risks, cost structures, and interest rates. Banks may construct a profitability analysis for consumer loan products, as shown in exhibit 10.9. Credit cards have high gross yields and many fee income sources to offset high operating costs and loan loss expenses. Auto loans have much lower yields but also may have lower operating expenses and loan losses. Home equity loans generally offer even lower operating expenses and losses and a yield that often is higher than that for auto loans.

Indirect loans present different profitability considerations because the bank generally must pay a dealer a percentage of the finance charge. Besides offering a financial incentive, the bank may have to compensate the dealer for handling the application and loan closing. Two examples of dealer earnings on typical retail contracts are illustrated in exhibit 10.10 (next page).

LAWS AND REGULATIONS

Bankers must constantly address risk. That is why one of the key functional areas in banking is asset and liability management. Legal lending limits set by bank regulators address concerns about asset and liability management and bank financial stability. A risk that lenders have with every loan is repayment—

Did You Know ...

The net worth of American households fell in the fourth quarter of 2008 by the largest amount since the Federal Reserve began tracking the statistic in 1951. Household net worth fell 9 percent from the reported level in the third quarter and marked the sixth consecutive quarter drop, to $51.48 trillion from the previous high of $64.36 trillion in the second quarter of 2007.

Source: Associated Press, March 12, 2009.

Exhibit 10.9 Product Line Profitability			
	BANKCARD %	**AUTO LOAN %**	**HOME EQUITY %**
Portfolio yield	14.00	6.75	6.50
Cost of funds	−5.00	−3.00	−3.00
Net yield	9.00	3.75	3.50
Other income	3.00	1.25	0.75
Operating expenses	−4.00	−3.00	−2.00
Loan losses	−3.00	−0.50	−0.10
Net pretax yield	5.00	1.50	2.15

Exhibit 10.10   Bank Income on Two Dealer Contracts

EXAMPLE 1: WITHOUT DEALER RESERVE

Amount financed – term 36 months	$15,100.00
Bank buy rate	5.50%
Consumer rate	6.50%
Total finance charge @ 6.50%	$1,560.75
Bank interest retention	$1,314.51
Dealer interest participation	$ 246.24

EXAMPLE 2: WITH DEALER RESERVE

Amount financed – term 48 months	$19,500.00
Bank buy rate	6.00%
Consumer rate	6.75%
Total finance charge @ 6.75%	$2,805.32
Bank interest retention	$2,481.99
Dealer interest participation	$ 323.33
Dealer reserve	$ 323.33

The dealer also can increase the income on a retail transaction by selling credit life, accident and health (A&H) insurance, and warranty policies. In example 2, if the dealer sold all of these policies, the income would increase as follows:

SOURCE	PREMIUM	DEALER INCOME	
Life insurance	$ 559.65	$184.68	33.0% commission
A&H insurance	$1,423.49	$469.75	33.0% commission
Warranty policy	$ 885.00	$435.00	Excess over $450.00 cost to dealer
Total fee income =		$1,089.43	
+ dealer reserve =		$ 3,23.33	
Total dealer income		$1,412.76	

the credit risk. Credit insurance and products such as the debt cancellation contract (DCC) and debt suspension agreement (DSA) address this risk, and regulators have rules for these products.

LEGAL LENDING LIMITS

Diversity in the loan portfolio is important for bank stability. Loans are made using depositors' funds. Too much concentration in one borrower, group of borrowers, or industry creates risk on the deposit (liability) side of the bank ledger as well as the loan (asset) side. To ensure quality asset management, the government regulates bank **legal lending limits**. These limits apply to the total lending relationship with a borrower, not just an individual loan. Regulated lending limits are meant to reduce loan concentrations, promote diversification in a bank's asset mix, and allow equitable access to banking services.

The Garn-St Germain Depository Institutions Act of 1982 instituted lending limits to promote bank safety and soundness. The federal government imposes lending limits on national banks through the Office of the Comptroller of the Currency (OCC) and on national savings associations through the Office of Thrift Supervision (OTS). State governments impose lending limits on state banks. Often bank boards of directors set their own more restrictive lending limits (for example, 50 percent of the regulatory lending limit).

legal lending limit—
The maximum amount of money a bank may legally lend to a single borrower or combination of financially related borrowers, expressed as a percentage of the bank's capital and surplus.

National banks and federal savings associations may make loans and extend credit of up to 15 percent of their unimpaired capital and surplus to a single borrower or up to 25 percent if the loan is secured by readily marketable collateral and the bank has a perfected security interest.

Lending limits are calculated at the end of each quarter when the Consolidated Report of Condition and Income (Call Report) is submitted or when there is a change in a capital category. This is also the effective date of the regulatory lending limit used.

Some loans are exempted from the general lending limits and have their own rules, such as loans made to other financial institutions. In certain instances, special rules allow national banks and federal savings associations to lend additional amounts to a single borrower.

Combining Rules

In some cases, the rules require that loans to different borrowers be combined for calculation, such as when the loan proceeds benefit another party. For example, a bank may lend $100,000 to a chief executive officer, who then transfers the proceeds to his corporation for use as working capital. Although the loan was made to the CEO, it must be combined with other loans the bank has made to the corporation.

Nonconforming Loans

A loan that is within the bank's lending limit at the time it is made may later exceed it and become **nonconforming**. This may happen when the bank's capital has declined, lowering its lending limits. It also may happen when business borrowers merge or form a common enterprise, when banks merge, when the lending limit or capital rules change, or when collateral securing loans declines in value. In these instances, the loan is nonconforming but is not considered to be out of compliance with the lending limit rules. The bank may not lend any additional funds to the borrower, but it is not in violation of the law.

nonconforming loan— A loan with terms that fall outside the regulatory guidelines for loans of that type.

DEBT CANCELLATION CONTRACTS AND DEBT SUSPENSION AGREEMENTS

Debt cancellation contracts and debt suspension agreements incur risk. If the event stipulated in the contract occurs, the lender must pay off the loan or assume the payments. In the past, consumers have misunderstood the product terms and made complaints and lawsuits. In response, the Office of the Comptroller of the Currency issued a final rule in 2002 governing DCC and DSA sales and disclosure practices for national banks. The rule prohibits or limits certain practices by national banks in connection with the sale of these products.

Tying	DCC and DSA contracts are optional. Lenders cannot require customers to purchase a DCC or DSA to receive a loan or to obtain better terms, such as a lower interest rate.
Contract modification	Lenders cannot modify contract terms unless the modification is favorable and there is no charge to the customer, or the customer is given advance notice of the change and reasonable opportunity to cancel the contract without charge.
Unfavorable pricing	A DCC or DSA fee may be paid in a single payment (lump sum) only if the customer has been offered an installment contract. An installment contract may not be priced to discourage a customer from choosing it.
	A DCC or DSA fee may not be paid as a lump sum if the underlying loan is for a residential (one- to four-family) mortgage.
No-refund feature	For lump-sum contracts without a refund feature, the bank must offer the option to purchase a contract that allows a refund of the unearned fee if the customer terminates the contract or prepays the loan.

Two disclosures, a short form and a long form, are required in connection with the sale of a DCC or DSA. Both must include a statement that the product is optional. The short-form disclosure is provided to the consumer early in the loan sale and may be either oral or in writing (see exhibit 10.11).

The long-form disclosure must have an explanation of the DCC or DSA, the cost, the refund policy, eligibility requirements, conditions, and exclusions. It must be in writing and given to the customer before the DCC or DSA is purchased. The customer must acknowledge receipt of this disclosure and agree to the purchase. The OCC offers model disclosures that a bank may adapt. The disclosures must be "conspicuous, simple, direct, and readily understandable."

SUMMARY

- The consumer's loan costs comprise factors other than the actual interest rate and the principal amount borrowed. The factors that affect the loan cost to the customer are the interest rate type, the annual percentage rate, the term, and whether the loan has payment protection.
- Interest rates may be fixed or variable. The most typical fixed rate is simple interest. Most closed-end loans use fixed rates. Variable rates usually are based on an outside index, such as a U.S. Treasury bill rate, LIBOR, or the prime rate. A popular index is the prime rate as published in the

Exhibit 10.11 DCC Short Form Disclosure Sample

ANYNATIONAL BANK DEBT CANCELLATION DISCLOSURE

This product is optional: Your purchase of Anynational Bank Debt Cancellation is optional. Whether or not you purchase it will not affect your application for credit or the terms of any existing credit agreement you have with the bank.

Lump sum payment of fee: You may choose to pay the fee in a single lump sum or in monthly payments. Adding the lump sum of the fee to the amount you borrow will increase the cost of Anynational Bank Debt Cancellation.

Refunds: You may choose Anynational Bank Debt Cancellation with or without a refund provision. Prices of refund and no-refund products are likely to differ.

Anynational Bank Debt Cancellation with refund feature: You may cancel Anynational Bank Debt Cancellation at any time and receive a refund.

We will give you additional information before you are required to pay for Anynational Bank Debt Cancellation. This information will include a copy of the contract containing the terms of Anynational Bank Debt Cancellation.

There are eligibility requirements, conditions, and exclusions that could prevent you from receiving benefits under Anynational Bank Debt Cancellation.

You should read the contract carefully for a full explanation of the terms of Anynational Bank Debt Cancellation.

Source: 12 CFR 37, Debt Cancellation Contracts and Debt Suspension Agreements.

Wall Street Journal. For variable-rate loans, many banks assign ceiling and floor rates. State governments set usury (ceiling) rates, the top rates banks can assign to loans.

- Consumers may purchase payment protection to pay their loans when they die or are disabled or unemployed. There are two basic forms. Credit insurance (credit life, credit accident and health, and credit loss-of-income insurance) is provided through an insurance company selected by the bank. The premiums are included in the loan and paid with the regular loan payments. Debt cancellation contracts (DCC) and debt suspension agreements (DSA) are bank products that the customer purchases separately. With credit insurance, the insurer assumes the risk on the outstanding loan payment. With a DCC or DSA, the bank assumes the risk.

- Loan terms affect pricing. Extended loan terms increase credit risk— the risk that the loan will not be paid—as may the collateral, because its value may have depreciated by the time it might be needed to recoup the outstanding loan amount. To offset this risk, banks often charge higher rates on longer-term closed-end loans. Most variable-rate open-end products do not have maturities but instead have minimum monthly percentage payment rates ranging from 1 percent to 5 percent of the outstanding balance.

- The regulatory environment, competition, economic conditions, and the bank's objectives, strategies, and financial condition affect loan pricing. The interest rate structures permitted by state laws influence the kinds of loan products banks offer, the availability of credit, and the credit risk that banks will accept. Banks consider competitor rates when they price loans. However, maintaining credit standards is important to banks, and to regulators.

- Economic changes influence pricing, particularly changes in the cost of funds. Deposits, cash, and capital are the three sources of funding for loans; the interest paid on deposits is important in determining loan prices. The bank's own costs, objectives, and strategies will influence pricing decisions. If profitability is the main goal, a bank may price for surges in loan volume. Low-cost providers are better able to price their loans at the lower end of the market's interest rate range and still achieve profit margin objectives. The loan price is influenced by the annual percentage rate (APR), monthly payment, credit insurance charges, fee structure, type of loan and collateral, and the bank's analysis of the time value of money.

- The profitability of consumer loans is affected by the bank's pricing policies and practices and the cost structure of its operation. Consumer credit costs fall into four categories: acquisition expenses, maintenance and liquidation costs, loan losses, and the cost of funds. The last is the largest single expense and the one over which consumer loan managers have the least control. Loan costs are analyzed using either an average or a marginal cost approach. Banks evaluate the profitability of the whole portfolio and of individual loans. They use breakeven analysis to evaluate factors such as loan term, interest rate, and timing of payments.

- Risk is constantly changing. That is why one of the key functional areas in banking is asset and liability management. Lending limits set by bank regulators address concerns about asset and liability management and bank financial stability. Another risk the lender faces with every loan is that it will not be repaid—the credit risk. Credit insurance and products like debt cancellation contracts (DCC) and debt suspension agreements (DSA) address this risk, and regulators have issued rules for these products.

Learning Check

SELF-CHECK and REVIEW

1. What are the differences between fixed- and variable-rate loans? What implications do these differences have for profitability?

2. Why is the amount of the monthly payment on a consumer loan such an important factor when a loan is structured? How can the lender adjust a loan to lower the payment without lowering the principal or rate?

3. What factors are taken into consideration when setting the price for consumer loans? Which single factor is the most important? Why?

4. List the cost categories for consumer loans. What is the trend of costs in each category?

5. Why does a profitability analysis need to consider the product lines? Give some examples of differences by product line.

6. What are legal lending limits and why do regulators set lending limits?

7. What are debt cancellation contracts (DCCs) and debt suspension agreements (DSAs)? How does the Office of the Comptroller of the Currency (OCC) regulate them for national banks?

ADDITIONAL RESOURCES

Resources

2008 Study of Consumer Payment Preferences, BAI and Hitachi Consulting, www.hitachiconsulting.com/files/pdfRepository/AR_ConsumerPayments_Allen Fox_JanFeb09_Final.pdf.

American Bankers Association, **www.aba.com**.

BankRate Monitor, www.bankrate.com.

Consumer Credit Delinquency Bulletin, Washington: American Bankers Association, 2009.

Debt Cancellation Contracts and Debt Suspension Agreements, 12CFR37, Office of the Comptroller of the Currency, www.occ.gov/fr/cfrparts/12cfr37.htm.

Economic Statistics from the Federal Reserve, www.stls.frb.org/fred/index.html.

Electronic Payments Now Account for Majority of Consumer Payments, Hitachi Consulting, Oct. 6, 2008, www.hitachiconsulting.com/newsDetails.cfm?EID=269.

FDIC Bank Data, www.fdic.gov/bank/index.html.

Fed Reports Record Fall in Household Net Worth, Martin Crutsinger, Associated Press, March 12, 2009.

Financial Calculators, ABA Education Foundation Consumer Connection, www.aba.com/aba/static/calculators.htm.

OnLine Strategies for Internet Banking, www.onlinebankingreport.com.

Putting Your Home on the Line Is Risky Business, Federal Reserve Board of Governors, www.federalreserve.gov/pubs/riskyhomeloans/default.htm.

APPENDIX IV

Galaxy Bank Financial Case Study

Bob Burke has been CEO at Galaxy Bank for about six months. He came to Galaxy from a solid East Coast superregional bank and looked at this opportunity in the Midwest as a chance to return to his roots in banking. Before accepting his new position, he had briefed himself thoroughly and was well aware of the challenges Galaxy faces going forward.

Bob's experience has made him a consumer retail expert, and Galaxy has been primarily a retail organization. Galaxy has recently become a more significant player in the commercial market, but at the expense of the retail side of the business.

Bob is now facing his first real test. Dave Winthrop has been head of the consumer lending division at Galaxy for over 25 years and has just submitted a letter announcing his retirement. Bob admires the job Dave has done at Galaxy, but he also knows that Dave has not kept the division current with technology or innovation in the consumer credit world.

Bob must select Dave's successor. Should he stay within the ranks of Galaxy or go outside for the right candidate? The first choice would seem to be Frank Dole, Dave's right-hand man for the last 10 years, but Bob doesn't know whether Frank has become another Dave, which would mean he would not be able to move the division up to the next level.

Long before Bob could contact Frank to make an assessment, Frank contacted him. Frank sent a memo to Bob outlining what he thought were the strengths of the division and the bank. The memo helped Bob make the decision to give Frank the opportunity to run the division. Frank's memo identified the very issues Bob had identified as challenges facing the division. The memo also set out what Frank thought would be the solutions. These are some of the conclusions that Frank reported in his memo to Bob:

- A combination of new products could increase the contribution of consumer credit to the bank's prosperity. Frank will be looking for further market penetration with new products and more efficient delivery methods.

- Some people-intensive functions need to be re-engineered for greater operating efficiencies and profitability. The current consumer loan application system, which is about 10 years old, probably needs to be upgraded.

- Frank recognizes that the success of his ideas and efforts will require the support of senior management.

- He also recognizes that his personal income opportunities are tied directly to achieving objectives.

- He is not willing to accept large loan losses even when profit objectives are achieved by improving performance in other areas of the business. He equates the bank's reputation for safety and soundness with low-percentage delinquencies and dollar charge-offs.

- He wants to explore and keep up with the latest technology Galaxy could employ so that it becomes an industry leader instead of a follower.

Frank's memo made some major points about Galaxy as a whole:

- Galaxy is a bank holding company with total assets more than $5 billion, more than 3,300 employees, and 120 offices in its domicile, a Midwestern state that is still economically strong. Its total assets have grown approximately 24 percent over the past two years, and income has increased by 31 percent.

- Like all major financial institutions in its region, Galaxy faces heavy competition in all its lines of business, from local banks as well as regional and national institutions. The bank is aggressively managed and focuses first on soundness, then on bottom-line profitability within the soundness constraint. Galaxy singles out retail lending as the area where it can outperform its competition.

The memo also summarized Galaxy's major credit product lines.

Galaxy Bank Statement of Condition
(as of December 31, 20XX)

	Current Year	Previous Year	Two Years Previous
Assets			
Cash and due from banks	$424,668	$394,776	$389,474
Interest-earning deposits in other banks	39,305	145,732	107,508
Investments in securities	974,930	931,281	518,950
Securities in trading account	1,002	42,179	45,658
Funds sold, including repurchase agreements	146,780	37,053	66,726
Loans and leases	3,390,692	3,132,642	2,560,376
Reserves against loan losses (-)	81,745	59,729	41,863
Net loans	3,308,947	3,072,913	2,518,513
Other assets	180,982	185,130	227,017
Total assets	$5,076,614	$4,809,064	$3,873,846
Liabilities			
Deposits	$3,603,902	$3,437,357	$2,796,066
Funds purchased and repurchase agreements	542,088	650,042	515,229
Short-term debt	188,089	179,487	99,332
Long-term debt	170,962	101,423	93,524
Other liabilities	138,944	179,156	203,354
Stockholder equity	322,802	281,127	246,395
Total liabilities and stockholder equity	$4,966,787	$4,828,592	$3,953,900

Summary of Loan Data Year-end Loans Outstanding ($000)

	Current Year	Previous Year	Two Years Previous
Commercial	$1,056,575	$1,094,320	$919,315
Construction	208,153	165,602	122,265
Residential mortgage	734,425	594,361	477,015
Bankcard	419,346	406,807	205,933
Other consumer	848,462	703,273	552,823
Foreign	192,604	211,983	252,996
Leases	123,631	102,042	58,770
Charge-offs, less recoveries			
Commercial	1,544	5,565	4,451
Construction	—	1,337	634
Residential mortgage	18	191	238
Bankcard	20,691	12,926	2,219
Other consumer	4,502	4,129	1,591
Foreign	4,887	2,241	1,702
Leases	175	(63)	80

Retail Credit Loans Outstanding
(Year-end totals—$000)

	Current Year	Previous Year	Two Years Previous	Three Years Previous
Home equity lines	$137,000	$67,000	$31,000	$15,000
Unsecured lines	18,000	14,600	14,200	14,500
Indirect auto	308,000	290,000	242,000	198,000
Marine	106,000	75,000	43,000	40,000
Other direct installment	101,000	126,000	124,000	73,000
Mobile home indirect*	180,000	131,000	99,000	92,000
Credit cards**	419,000	407,000	206,000	132,000
Total retail	$1,269,000	$1,110,600	$759,200	$564,500

* Through separate subsidiary of holding company.
** Through credit card subsidiary of holding company.

Summary of Operating Data
(Year-end totals—$000)

	Current Year	Previous Year	Two Years Previous
Interest income			
Loans	$358,608	$318,025	$287,549
Funds	4,582	6,722	8,901
Deposits at other banks	5,541	11,722	15,042
Securities	70,019	52,755	44,264
Total interest income	438,750	389,224	355,756
Interest expense			
Deposits	165,780	146,981	145,321
Short-term borrowing	43,983	43,984	49,967
Long-term debt	15,902	12,245	10,581
Total interest expense	225,665	203,210	205,869
Net interest income	213,085	186,014	149,887
Less provision for loan losses	53,834	44,137	15,061
Net	159,251	141,877	134,826
Noninterest income	84,953	79,419	56,463
Noninterest expense			
Personnel costs	92,391	84,642	78,827
Occupancy expense	21,106	18,987	16,694
Equipment	19,001	18,887	16,896
Other	56,986	59,989	42,551
Total noninterest expense	189,484	182,505	154,968
Net income before taxes	54,720	38,791	36,321
Income taxes	14,821	7,243	8,722
Net Income	$39,899	$31,548	$27,599

AMERICAN **BANKERS** ASSOCIATION

HOME EQUITY LINES OF CREDIT (HELOCs)

Galaxy was one of the last major banks in its marketplace to offer a home equity product to consumers. Frank felt it was Dave Winthrop's philosophy to let the other banks "test" a product in the market; Galaxy would wait and see if the product was appropriate for the bank, given management's aversion to risk. This line of thinking proved faulty when Galaxy had to play serious catch-up as consumer acceptance of the product soared.

The features of the Galaxy HELOC were:

- no closing costs
- loan-to-value (LTV) ratio amounts of the first and second mortgage not to exceed 85 percent of the appraised value of the home
- minimum monthly payments of 1.75 percent of the average daily balance
- no investment properties or second homes would be taken as collateral

Galaxy's loans outstanding grew steadily, and the company has experienced minimal losses since it first offered the HELOC program. Delinquencies average between 0.5 percent and 0.75 percent. An analysis revealed line use to be lower than the industry average.

	Galaxy	Industry Average
Percentages of:		
Dollar line use	36%	55%
Accounts active	62%	76%

The free closing-cost plan significantly affected profitability because the bank absorbed an average of $285 for each line booked. This led the bank to switch from "no closing cost" to a "closing cost rebate" plan in which the customer initially paid costs but received a rebate if the amount of interest paid on the line equaled or exceeded the closing costs during the first 12 months.

The HELOC product also suffered because customers paid off and closed their lines during the boom in refinancing first mortgages. Homeowners with high-rate mortgages rushed to refinance as fixed rates fell to the lowest level in years. They often rolled up their outstanding consumer loan balances, including HELOCs and credit card balances, into the new mortgage. Outstanding balances fell $7 million that year, and some of the more active users consolidated their accounts.

For the past year income as a percentage of average loans outstanding was as follows:

Home Equity Line Pro Forma Statement

Income

Interest	9.25%
Other	0.15
Total income	9.40%

Less

Operating expenses	1.50%
Loan loss provision	0.25
Cost of funds	5.50%
Total costs	7.25%
Net pretax yield	2.15%

Galaxy Bank Financial Case Study

Competition

Home equity loans continue to dominate consumer credit advertising and sales promotion efforts among Galaxy's major competitors, as the following demonstrates.

	Galaxy	**Major Bank**	**Super Regional Bank**	**Money Center Bank**
Rate	Prime+2%	Prime+2%	Prime+1%	Prime
Minimum payment	1.75%	1.95%	Interest only	Interest only
LTV ratio	85%	90%	100%	100%
Second homes	No	No	Yes	Yes
Closing costs	Rebated	None	Rebated	1 point

A number of banks currently offer introductory-rate specials, such as 5.9 percent for the first year or a 7.9 percent fixed rate for three years, then conversion to a variable rate. Major Bank allows customers to convert their balances to a fixed-rate closed-end loan at any time. Galaxy and Super Regional offer closing cost rebates, and Major Bank offers "no closing cost" plans.

Super Regional Bank offers several different plans, including a lower rate prime + 1 percent for lines over $50,000. It also will go to 100 percent LTV for preferred customers.

To build their portfolios, a number of competitors use targeted direct mail and customer credit offers. One common theme is for customers to use the line to pay off high-interest-rate credit card balances as well as college expenses or automobile purchases. Other banks successfully retain customers by aggressively working to subordinate their HELOC lines when customers refinance first-mortgage loans.

Questions:
1. What is the reason for Galaxy's success to date in this product line? Is the approach likely to continue to be successful?
2. Because market share for this product is very important, what can the bank do to increase sales?
3. What can Galaxy do to increase use of current HELOCs? Are new marketing efforts needed?

INDIRECT AUTOMOBILE LOANS

This market is fiercely competitive, with the bulk of the business controlled by finance subsidiaries of a domestic automaker. Several midsized local banks ($750 million to $2 billion) maintain steady volume and outstanding growth through long-established relationships with key dealers. The portfolios of large banks are concentrated in foreign automobile dealerships.

With improvements in the economy, competition has intensified. As a result, the market has seen the following trends:

- aggressive pricing that further erodes already low margins
- dealer and market pressure to handle marginal business, resulting in higher delinquencies and the anticipation of higher losses
- loan policies that allow advances to 100 percent of the selling price and maturities beyond 60 months on higher-priced vehicles, further increasing risk

For the last decade, Galaxy has been inconsistent in its approach to this market. It withdrew almost entirely during a recent recession, keeping relationships with only a few selected dealerships. When the economy stabilized, the bank re-entered the market and has achieved significant growth in recent years. However, its profit on this product line has eroded despite portfolio growth.

New Indirect Auto Plan
(all non-recourse)

	Galaxy	MFC	Money Center Bank	Super Regional Bank	Local Bank
Retail plan dealer rate	8.25%	8.25%	7.90%	7.90%	7.75%
Maximum customer rate	Dealer rate + 5%	No cap	No cap	Dealer rate + 5%	No cap
Reserves paid	As earned	Up front	Up front	Up front	Up front
Maximum maturity	60 mos.	60 mos.	60 mos. 72 mos.$20K	60 mos.	60 mos. 72 mos..$18k
Wholesale plan dealer rate	Prime +.5%	Prime + .25%	Prime + .25%	Prime	Prime

Indirect Auto Loan Portfolio Pro Forma Statement

Income	Current Year	Previous Year
Interest	9.95%	10.50%
Other income	0.55	0.50
Total Income	10.50%	11.00%
Less		
Operating expenses	3.50%	3.15%
Provision for losses	1.75	1.35
Cost of funds	5.00	5.50
Total costs	10.25%	10.00%
Net pretax	0.25%	1.00%

(Entire portfolio is on a fixed rate.)

Questions:

1. What is Galaxy doing wrong? Why do the midsized banks seem to be more successful? Why would out-of-state banks be interested in getting into this market?

2. Should Galaxy exit this product line? Would doing so adversely affect other aspects of its emphasis on relationship banking?

3. What alternatives are available to Galaxy as a substitute for this product line if it decides to exit?

MARINE PORTFOLIO

The strong marine market in the bank's area has three distinct segments, each showing solid growth potential:

- small powerboats (under 25 feet), used primarily for recreation on rivers and lakes (average loan: $20,000)

- large powerboats (over 25 feet), used primarily for recreation or charter fishing (average loan: $75,000, some as high as $1 million)

- sailboats (20 feet and over), used primarily for recreation (average loan: $40,000)

Most marine dealers are relatively unsophisticated in controlling retail sales and selling credit-related products, such as insurance. Many use marine service companies, brokers, to handle sales of financial services, although small-powerboat dealers typically try to set up direct loan referral networks with local bank branches.

Brokers usually contract with a number of financial institutions to provide services to their dealers. They negotiate standard rates, terms, and other loan features. They get loan applications from dealers and try to place them with a lender. When applications come back to them, the choice of lender depends primarily on the buy rate the lender offers and the strength of the broker-lender relationship. If a loan is approved, the broker handles all the paperwork and sends it to the lender for payment. Banks try to build marine business through reputable brokers who do business with the dealers and the market segments they seek. Some brokers have multistate operations, which allow banks to expand their geographic area. Brokers tend to be highly rate-sensitive.

Historically, Galaxy took a rather conservative approach to this market because management was uncomfortable with the large average loan size and long maturity (12–15 years) of these loans. In recent years, in reevaluating all its markets the bank has concluded that this line offers good growth potential. Galaxy now has a competitive plan for marine loans, although it relies almost exclusively on two brokers.

Marine Loan Portfolio Pro Forma Statement

	Large Boats	Small Boats
Income		
Interest	10.25%	14.50%
Other income	0.35	0.25
Total income	10.60%	14.75%
Less		
Operating expenses	1.25%	4.00%
Provision for losses	0.55	1.75
Cost of funds	6.50	6.50
Total costs	8.30%	12.25%
Net pretax yield	2.30%	2.50%

Many boat owners have converted their variable-rate or higher fixed-rate boat loans to lower fixed-rate loans. Galaxy competed aggressively to get a share of this business, and its portfolio grew nicely as a result.

A relatively small number of banks are active in the marine market. Competition for large-boat loans comes primarily from superregional and money center banks. Smaller banks compete directly for small-boat loans.

Questions:

1. Can the bank attract new marine brokers and still manage its relationships with current brokers? If yes, how can Galaxy do this?

2. What will happen to this product line if there is a significant recession? What is likely to happen to the current portfolio? What would happen to demand for new marine loans?

CREDIT CARDS

The credit card market is very competitive. Creditworthy people receive several new product offerings monthly from financial institutions nationwide. Galaxy moved its credit card operations to Delaware several years ago to take advantage of that state's attractive lending laws. Since then it has aggressively expanded this business via direct mail and telemarketing programs to potential prospects throughout the United States. In the 1990s, credit cards contributed 25–35 percent of the holding company's annual profits, despite loss and delinquency rates above its targets. Over the past year the loan-loss rate reached 4.5 percent, leading management to demand tighter credit policies.

The highly automated credit card operation is apparently efficient. The bank uses credit-scoring systems for decision making on new accounts and preapproved credit offers; behavioral scoring models are used for prospect screening, overlimit advance requests, delinquency monitoring, and card renewal.

In recent years, Galaxy has fine-tuned its credit card program to emphasize affinity group programs, premium cards, and a secured credit card plan. Also, reacting to what management concluded were unacceptably high loss and delinquency levels— even though its portfolio was performing above industry profit norms— Galaxy raised credit requirements sharply on new accounts and renewals and stopped all new promotions until portfolio quality reached acceptable levels.

Competitive plans are shown in the following table:

	Galaxy	*Super Regional Bank*	*Money Center Bank*
Standard card			
Fixed rate	19.79%	18.50%	19.85%
Variable rate	N/A	Prime + 8%	Prime + 8%
Annual fee	$15	$18	$20
Premium card			
Fixed rate	14.00%	14.50%	14.00%
Variable rate	N/A	P + 4%	P + 4%
Annual fee	$35	$40	$50

Although these terms represent the standard rates offered, the market has been flooded with special offers and customized marketing plans. For example:

- Super Regional Bank became one of the dominant banks in the country offering affinity plans. Group members customarily are offered "no annual fee for the first year" and slightly lower rates. Value-added options are generally part of the package.

- Money Center Bank has an almost unlimited variety of credit card plans. In fact, the majority of its customers are not on its standard plan. This bank recently teamed up with major airlines and gasoline companies to offer value-added features, such as frequent flier mileage credits.

- Other competitors also are attacking the market with offers. Companies like American Express are hitting Galaxy's market with a wide variety of credit offerings.

Galaxy has been slow to expand the variety of its card options, choosing to stay with a standard plan for each product category (standard and premium cards). It believed that slow expansion would make the product easier to sell. The following are the results from Galaxy's credit card portfolio during the most recent year:

Credit Card Portfolio Pro Forma Statement

Income	
Interest	17.50%
Annual fees	1.50
Other fees	2.00
Total income	21.00%
Less	
Operating expenses	5.25%
Loan loss provision	4.50
Cost of funds	6.50
Total costs	16.25%
Net pretax yield	4.75%

Questions:

1. What should Galaxy do about its credit card products? Are there new marketing programs that it can use to build market share successfully and have a higher profile for this product line?

2. Can Galaxy continue to be a viable player in a market increasingly dominated by major national players?

3. Is the credit card market nearing the complete saturation point? Might the product begin to lose market share to debit cards and other types of transactional products?

DIRECT CONSUMER LOANS

Galaxy offers direct loans statewide through its 120 branch offices. Each branch has a monthly target for new consumer loan sales. Incentive compensation is available to branch "platform" personnel for each application that results in a booked loan. Meeting the loan objectives is taken into account in the branch manager's performance evaluation. The emphasis given to loan production tends to vary as management priorities shift. Because the bank is flush with deposits, the importance of generating loan volume has become a very high priority.

Galaxy has emphasized building its sales culture. It expended significant effort on cross-selling and building broad customer relationships, promoting credit cards, debit cards, automobile loans, HELOCs, and depository services. The bank trained branch personnel to sell investment products, and managers are expected to pass the test for a Series 6 license. In addition to the emphasis on selling, branch personnel still are responsible for customer service, transaction processing, and the day-to-day operations of the branch.

Two years ago, Galaxy installed an automated loan processing system (ALPS), with all lending authority vested in the central consumer credit department. Branches take loan applications and enter the data in the ALPS, the application is credit-scored, and the system makes the final decision. The credit department reviews the decisions and must in any case approve all HELOCs and any loan more than $20,000. A decision to decline a loan may be reversed; if the branch makes an appeal, the regional manager grants an override.

The ALPS system seems to be a mixed blessing. On the positive side it offers faster credit decisions (five minutes or less is possible); improved cross-selling—the system automatically qualifies applicants for credit cards or a line of credit; and better control of delinquency and loan losses. On the negative side, many loan opportunities are lost. Branch personnel no longer seemed to have a feel for lending — many missed opportunities to generate loan applications; bankers rarely used the override process; being removed from direct contact with the consumer, lenders are losing touch with the market; and approval rates even for good customers declined, when credit-score requirements tightened in response to a local recession. The credit requirements did not change quickly when the economy rebounded.

Galaxy offers a full range of standardized consumer credit products. Only HELOCs have variable rates, and the leasing program is just beginning to grow. The bank's loan policies have the usual menu of maximum advance and term provisions for closed-end loans, which are competitive with all but the most aggressive competitors. Standardized rates vary only by product type, such as automobile, boat, and unsecured loans.

The direct lending results are mixed. HELOCs and direct marine loans show good growth. Other direct loan types, including the bank's unsecured lines of credit, either have declined in loans outstanding or show only marginal growth. The bank does not emphasize its check overdraft line-of-credit or professional line-of-credit products.

Delinquencies on direct loans and the bank's revolving credit products, other than credit cards, are about half the industry average. Loan losses have improved significantly, except in the credit card portfolio, where they remain steady at a level equal to the industry average, and in the indirect auto portfolio, where losses continue.

Questions:

1. What types of objectives should branch personnel establish for consumer credit products? What consumer credit training should branch personnel receive? How can Galaxy motivate its employees to generate more consumer loans? What actions should the bank take to stimulate volume?

2. What should Galaxy do about its credit decision-making process?

INTERNET BANKING

Galaxy has done little to move into the world of e-commerce. The extent of its exposure is mostly ATMs. The superregional and money center banks all have interactive Web sites, although local community banks have made about as much progress as Galaxy. Galaxy plans to build an interactive Web site.

Questions:

1. What market research would help Galaxy determine its approach to online banking?

2. At a minimum, what should Galaxy do with online banking?

3. Should Galaxy create a fully interactive Web site with loan capabilities and other bank services?

4. Is Galaxy too late getting into the Internet market to go online now? If not, how can the bank use its late position to its advantage?

See Answers to *Galaxy Bank Financial Case Study* that starts on page 413 for answers to the questions.

Selling and
Loan Structuring

11

Learning Objectives

After completing this chapter, you should be able to

- differentiate between operations-driven and market-driven bank sales strategies
- describe the requirements of a sales-oriented bank and the sales skills a banker needs
- describe the elements of the selling process
- explain how loan structuring helps banks achieve their objectives
- discuss loan structuring variables and options
- discuss the Home Ownership and Equity Protection Act and Truth in Lending provisions for higher-priced mortgage loans
- define the terms that appear in bold type in the text

Introduction

"Pretend that every single person you meet has a sign around his or her neck that says, 'Make me feel important.' Not only will you succeed in sales, you will succeed in life." Mary Kay Ash, founder of Mary Kay Cosmetics.

What is true for the world of fashion and retail is true for financial services businesses like banking. Usually customers know, for the most part, what their lending needs are and some of the benefits they want to experience, but they may not know the products that will help them achieve satisfaction. The job of the banker is to understand the customer's needs and find product and service solutions for them.

Loan structuring is the most effective tool lenders have to achieve their sales goals. Techniques like consultative selling will elicit the information they need for loan structuring. When lenders use effective personal selling skills, they make customers feel appreciated.

MARKET-DRIVEN SELLING

Banking has changed its approach in response to evolving social, economic, regulatory, and internal business environments. To remain competitive, banks have improved the delivery of their products and services. With competition for financial services from many nontraditional sources, banks are challenged to gain market share.

The standard sales strategy in banking had been to seek a competitive advantage based on convenient branch locations, pricing differentials, and service quality. Banks were operations-driven, creating products that suited only their own needs. Bankers were primarily **order-takers**. Although these activities are still important, they are not the only components of a bank's sales strategy.

Today banks are market-driven, working first to determine customers' needs and then identifying the products and services they have to satisfy those needs. Using market analysis, market segmentation, and target marketing, banks are adept at promoting products that customers want as well as need. Those banks that do this most effectively are more profitable and have more satisfied customers. Order-taking by bankers in direct lending transactions is being replaced by market-driven techniques of consultative selling and cross-selling.

order-taking—A passive process in which bank employees give the consumer the product exactly as requested without trying to identify the consumer's real needs.

CONSULTATIVE SELLING

Order-taking is a passive sales approach; **consultative selling** is active. Much like a doctor taking a patient's medical history before deciding on the proper course of treatment, with this approach bankers determine the customer's financial status, needs, and goals, and then suggest product and service solutions. When a consultative sales approach is part of bank strategy, it usually increases loan volume and profitability, loan quality is better, and customers are more satisfied and loyal.

Consultative selling is becoming ingrained in bank sales culture: many lenders do not even realize they are **selling**. This is a big step in the right direction for bankers, who in the past considered themselves simply as lenders or customer service representatives. Many who felt uncomfortable or unqualified to take on the role of "salesperson" are now finding consultative selling to be a natural extension of the customer service they have long provided. Customers look to their bankers for guidance with their banking needs. Consultative selling is a useful way for bankers to address this opportunity.

CROSS-SELLING

By expanding the customer relationship into areas beyond the loan product, **cross-selling** takes consultative selling one step further. Cross-selling opportunities are abundant throughout the lending process. The completed loan application gives lenders access to information that can help them assess the customer's needs for other products and services, such as checking and savings accounts, investment programs, or insurance plans. The ability to cross-sell can expand account relationships, enhance customer loyalty and retention, and increase bank profits.

However, cross-selling and consultative selling alone cannot guarantee success for banks. These tools are most effective when they are part of a bank-wide sales culture that is truly market-driven.

THE SALES-ORIENTED BANK

Bank sales do not function in a vacuum. Truly sales-oriented and successful banks nurture effective sales skills among the staff and create approaches that follow the phases of the sales cycle.

ESTABLISHING A SALES CULTURE

To be effective, a sales-oriented strategy must be woven into the fabric of the bank's daily activities. For optimum success, management must constantly reinforce the sales culture. Establishing a sales culture involves building and honing selling skills, motivating employees to sell, supporting the sales force, and staying focused on the customer.

---

consultative selling— Selling bank products and services by working with the customer to identify the best solution for the customer's financial need.

selling—The process of persuading the consumer to buy the product or service offered by the bank.

cross-selling—The practice of promoting financial services and products in addition to those already used by the customer.

sales culture—A company-wide effort to focus bank employees on the need to take every opportunity to sell the bank's services.

Consumer Financial Services Needs

- *methods of exchange*: products that enable consumers to make purchases
- *storage and accumulation of wealth*: products that enable consumers to save money and achieve financial growth
- *purchasing power*: products that enable consumers to borrow money and pay over time
- *security or safety net*: products that give consumers financial protection

Situation

Tony Blanco and his family are facing another cold winter in their older home, whose doors and windows leak cold air into the house. Tony has decided that this is the year to replace the doors and windows. He knows exactly how much that will cost. Using a loan calculator he found on the Internet, he knows the payments he can afford on a $5,000 closed-end loan.

Tony presents this information to his bank's loan officer, Arnold Carson, expecting to apply for a specific loan. Arnold reviews Tony's application and asks a few questions. He learns that Tony has children who will be going to college and that Tony has some low-yielding savings accounts at another bank. Arnold suggests a different type of loan, a home equity line of credit, which Tony had not considered. Tony agrees that this alternate suggestion is a much better solution for his needs. Arnold then discusses with Tony some other deposit and service solutions at the bank, including a higher-yielding savings account and a debit card to access the funds.

Why did not Arnold just fill Tony's initial request? What type of sales approach did Arnold use?

Communication Skills

- listening
- reading body language
- understanding voice tone and inflection
- careful questioning

Building and honing selling skills

Bankers with basic selling skills continuously practice and improve. Training and practice sharpen their ability to identify needs, handle concerns, provide solutions, and close sales.

Motivating employees to sell

Sales-oriented businesses constantly motivate their employees to sell. They use both nonmonetary incentives, such as recognition awards, sales rallies, and leader boards, and monetary rewards tied to sales goals. Motivational approaches should, however, be directed to meeting customer needs, not pushing products to meet goals.

Supporting the sales force

The sales and service culture extends to every department in the bank. The support areas need to deliver quality service across the board. The quality of service to internal customers (coworkers) is as important as service to external customers. One touches the other.

Staying focused on the customer

The sales staff should have the tools, systems, and authority to sell effectively. Excessive tracking, filing, and monitoring are deterrents to focusing on the primary goal, which is serving the customer.

EFFECTIVE SELLING SKILLS

Successful selling requires an ability to communicate effectively, a focus on selling, the ability to self-motivate, an enjoyment of the sales challenge, and a desire to help customers. The process of helping customers involves establishing rapport, identifying needs, understanding product solutions and matching them to customers' needs, handling concerns, and closing the sale.

Effective Communication

When "communication" is mentioned, the first thing that comes to mind is talking. However, talking is not the only part of effective communication—bankers who think they can convince customers to purchase a financial service product by simply talking to them about it are missing an important opportunity. Effective communication also includes the ability to listen, read body language, and understand voice tone and inflection—in other words, to receive and correctly interpret the signals sent by the customer rather than just sending oral information.

Bankers become trusted advisors by listening and asking open-ended questions to gain an understanding of the customer's needs.

Self-Motivation and Focus

A banker who is able to stay focused on selling, who realizes that the goal of selling is to provide guidance for customers who are seeking it, will be successful. The sales manager can do only so much to motivate the sales force. Self-motivation and focusing on what is important to the customer and for the bank are necessary selling abilities.

Enjoying the Challenge

A successful salesperson approaches the sales opportunity as a positive challenge rather than an unavoidable task. Bankers learn to take pride in their accomplishments and to enjoy the opportunities that selling presents.

Establishing Rapport

The importance of the banker-customer relationship cannot be overemphasized. Establishing rapport with customers is essential for a positive lending experience and is necessary to put the customer at ease. When customers feel free to reveal more about their financial needs, the banker is in a better position to match products and services to those needs. Building rapport with the customer throughout the sales process enhances the banker's credibility and the customer's trust. These factors improve the banker-customer relationship and encourage the customer to return to the bank for more services.

Identifying Needs

Identifying a customer's financial needs is easier when each transaction is viewed as part of a total relationship rather than as a simple loan or information request. Sales cultures thrive in an atmosphere where lenders focus on identifying and meeting all the customer's financial needs.

Understanding Product Solutions

It is not enough to understand the customer's financial needs. Bankers must be thoroughly familiar with the **features** and **benefits** of their products and know how each customer need can be met. Features of a home equity product may include no closing costs, a low interest rate, and a substantial line of credit, for example, but a benefit to the customer may be the tax deductibility of interest paid. Together the combined features and benefits satisfy the customer's need. The banker who can effectively present product features and benefits as solutions to customers is truly selling.

Overcoming Concerns

Another essential skill is the ability to overcome a customer's concerns. A banker with this skill is able to recognize a concern raised by a customer as an opportunity. Often it is the customer's way of asking for more information or clarification. In response to an expressed concern, the salesperson may empathize

Did You Know ...

A good listener is someone who looks interested in what is being said, does not interrupt or appear hurried, gives full attention to the speaker, and makes the speaker feel that what is being said is important.

feature—A specific characteristic that describes the product, such as no closing costs for a home equity line of credit.

benefit—The value that the product or service feature gives to customers, such as to make money, save money, save time, provide convenience, or provide security.

- Empathize with the customer.
- Clarify any misunderstanding.
- Offer solutions.
- Promise to get back with an answer.
- Follow through on commitments.

Elements of Effective Selling

- communicating effectively
- self-motivation
- focusing on selling
- enjoying the sales challenge
- liking to help customers
- establishing rapport with customers
- identifying customer needs
- understanding product solutions
- matching products to customer needs
- overcoming customer concerns
- closing the sale well

with the customer, clarify any misunderstanding, offer a solution, or promise to get back to the customer with more information—and then follow through.

Closing the Sale

Closing the sale is not a single event at the end of the process. The closing is a process completed incrementally throughout the discussion as the consumer and the banker reach agreement on the consumer's financial needs and the best solution. The final step in closing a sale is to ask the customer, "What do you want to do?"

A prudent salesperson follows up with the customer after the closing. Because customers may have second thoughts about their financial decisions, a call from the banker can be reassuring.

THE SELLING PROCESS

The delivery channels opened by technology have changed the way banks sell products and services. Whereas technology has enhanced and facilitated many aspects of the lending process, one of the unintended consequences has been that fewer customers have personal contact with their bankers. Bankers must personalize customer contacts—even electronic ones—so as to maintain the banker-customer relationship.

Many customers still forgo the convenience afforded by technology for the personal service provided by bankers. However, most customers want more: They want the benefit of both faster, more accessible service and their banker's help and expertise. In these days of electronic communication, it is important for bankers to make the most of each personal contact, providing information, guidance, and product solutions to help customers satisfy their financial needs.

At any given time, customers are ready, willing, and able to purchase consumer loan products. The challenge for banks is to market products in a way that will attract consumers who need loan products and meet the credit requirements.

The sales effort begins with an understanding of the consumer's purchasing cycle. Exhibit 11.1 shows that the cycle for any product or service has four basic stages. Understanding and responding to each is important for successful selling.

Needs Recognition

The process begins when the consumer needs to borrow. A consumer's need for a loan is derived from the desire to satisfy some other need that cannot be purchased with cash. For example, when the consumer's automobile has high mileage or has had numerous repairs, the consumer may decide it is time to purchase another and finance the purchase. Most consumers do not need to buy a luxury automobile for basic transportation, but a luxury automobile may satisfy other needs, such as a desire for a certain image. Bankers who can identify the consumer's motivation for the purchase will be able to make an intelligent decision about the types of loans to offer.

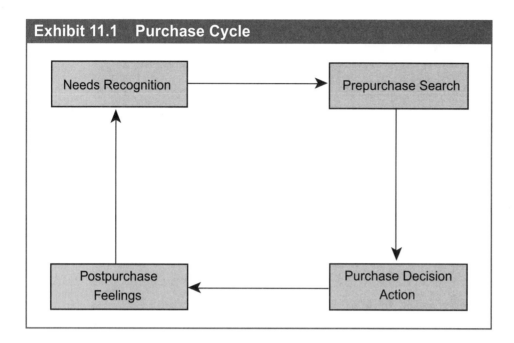

Exhibit 11.1   Purchase Cycle

- Needs Recognition → Prepurchase Search
- Prepurchase Search → Purchase Decision Action
- Purchase Decision Action → Postpurchase Feelings
- Postpurchase Feelings → Needs Recognition

Prepurchase Search

The search for a loan begins when the consumer needs funds to buy goods or services. This process may be brief or it may be extensive, depending on the consumer and the relative importance of the decision. Some consumers search no further than a dealer's finance and insurance office. Others turn to the Internet. Some people respond readily to a direct-mail offer or a newspaper advertisement. Still other consumers do **comparison-shopping**: they get information from their own bank and other financial institutions before applying for a loan. Many will stay with their primary bank, particularly if they have established a good relationship with their banker.

The prepurchase search is highly individual. What is important to consumers varies. Bankers need to identify the factors in the decision-making process that are most important to each customer and tailor the sales effort accordingly.

Purchase Decision

Prepurchase activity generally culminates in a purchase. If the bank's loan products are convenient and supported by exceptional service, customers may purchase them even when the bank does not offer the lowest available rate. Skilled salespeople also can control sales and minimize customer comparison shopping for credit by identifying the customer's needs early and offering tailored product solutions.

Matching needs to bank products and services helps the banker build credibility and trust with customers. Indeed, many bankers have loyal customers who trust their advice and seek their services even when competitors offer better prices on similar products. The lender who has built rapport with the customer is likely to win that customer's business. Exceptional rapport also leads to referrals, adding to growth potential.

The period between the time the loan application is taken and the loan decision is made is a sales opportunity. This period is unique to loan sales. In

comparison-shopping—
To shop for the best product choice by comparing the prices and features of products from competing providers.

Did You Know ...

• Selling is making a promise, and service is delivering on the promise.
• Relationship selling fits the world of banking services better than transactional selling.
• Your most important sale in life is to sell yourself to yourself.

other types of retail sales, the customer makes a decision to buy and presents the necessary form of payment, and the transaction is concluded. With loan products, the customer waits for the bank—the seller—to make a decision. That is why this decision should be made as quickly as possible. While the loan decision-making process continues, however, the banker can use the information on the application to identify other sales opportunities.

Postpurchase Feelings

Customers often feel anxious after a purchase that entails a relationship, as in banking, or has a significant cost. Doubting the wisdom of the purchase after the fact is commonly referred to as buyer's remorse. The customer is reassessing whether the alternatives that were not selected might have been better choices. Following up after the purchase reassures the customer and helps to relieve insecurity. Some banks send thank-you notes to new customers or call to thank them for their business.

When they are satisfied with their loans and the loan process is handled efficiently and professionally, customers probably will return to the bank the next time they need a loan or another financial service. They also will be receptive to cross-selling efforts. On the other hand, when they had an unpleasant experience applying for a loan, found the rate too high, decided the product did not perform as expected, or have another negative experience during repayment of the loan, they will be less receptive to, or even reject, future selling efforts.

LOAN STRUCTURING

loan structuring—The process of analyzing an applicant's debts and recommending a new loan with different features that better meets the needs of both consumer and bank.

Loan structuring gives lenders their best opportunity to sell effectively and achieve bank sales objectives. Variables for different product lines will influence lender loan-structuring choices to make the best loan for the customer and the bank.

MEETING SALES OBJECTIVES

Although they may vary, bank sales objectives in lending typically are to make the best loan for the customer, actively sell loans and not passively take orders, optimize bank earnings by selling other bank products, retain customers, and minimize credit and interest rate risk.

Making the Best Loan

The concept of making the best loan for both the customer and the bank embodies most of the lending objectives. The customer is looking for a loan product that meets specific needs, is priced fairly, is convenient, and offers high-quality service. The bank wants to earn an acceptable yield on its investment, limit its risk, and build strong customer relationships. Finding the best way to structure the loan ensures that it is the best loan for both customer and bank. With this objective, banks adopt procedures that include analyzing alternative

Bank Lending Sales Objectives

• Make the best loan.
• Sell, do not just take orders.
• Optimize bank earnings by cross-selling other products.
• Retain the customer.
• Minimize credit and interest rate risk.

loan structures for most applications. The structuring process varies with the type of loan product requested, how the application is received, and how the bank processes applications.

Selling, Not Order-Taking

Just taking the customer's order or loan request is not acceptable in a bank that has a sales culture. Just taking orders conflicts with the objective of making the best loan for the customer and the bank. Loan structuring is an integral part of consultative selling because it considers the customer's total financial picture and immediate and long-term needs.

Optimizing Bank Earnings by Cross-selling

Appropriate loan structuring helps bankers recognize cross-selling opportunities that might have been missed in an order-taking environment. They suggest related products, such as automatic payment, offering to reduce the interest rate if the loan payments are debited automatically from the customer's account at the bank.

Retaining the Customer

One of the most important assets any bank has is its base of customers. Building and retaining a customer base is critical to the success of any retail business. Customer retention is enhanced when the bank consistently delivers high-quality service and sells products that meet customer needs. An appropriately structured loan is an integral part of a long-term customer relationship. A customer who is satisfied with the loan's terms will be more inclined to use the bank for other financial solutions.

Did You Know ...

Minimizing Credit and Interest Rate Risk

Sound loan structuring goes hand-in-hand with properly controlling credit and interest rate risks. Training and sound decision-making and lending policies also are necessary. Well-structured bill consolidation loans, for example, reduce the customer's monthly payments and improve cash flow so those payments can be made more easily. Some bill consolidation loans may be unsecured with little risk; others may be secured by collateral. The collateral usually reduces the risk, so the bank can offer lower interest rates, longer maturities, and lower monthly payments. Offering variable-rate options for certain loan terms will lower interest rate risk for the bank and may benefit customers who can manage fluctuating payments or extended loan maturities. Yet some customers may prefer the consistency of a fixed-rate option. Not all loan features work well for all customers.

Much of the lending process is automated, including new cross-selling systems that produce loan-structuring possibilities driven by loan policy and procedures and a package of bank products tailored for the individual customer. Such technology frees the lender to focus on consultative selling.

LOAN STRUCTURING BY PRODUCT LINE

A bank that embraces loan structuring has a variety of opportunities, depending on the product line and delivery channel.

Direct Lending

Direct lending offers the bank the best opportunity for significant loan structuring and cross-selling other bank services. Bankers with effective selling skills can identify customer needs, decide which products offer attractive benefits, and present those benefits by using an effective sales approach. Direct contact allows the lender to obtain better information and respond to the customer's concerns.

Indirect Lending

Indirect lending offers few opportunities for bank employees to structure loans or cross-sell other bank products. However, it brings new customers to the bank, and many banks take that opportunity to actively cross-sell products once these customers are established. Structuring a loan through indirect lending is restricted to adjusting the loan's terms as requested by the dealer. The bank may ask for a larger down payment, modify the **term** of the loan, approve a lower loan amount, require cosigners, or limit the amount of the monthly payment. After the loan is made, the bank may cross-sell other services through direct mail and telemarketing and expand its customer base for future relationship-building.

The bank's influence in structuring loans is based on its arrangement with the dealers. The banker may instruct the dealer to make credit-related sales, such as credit insurance or warranty policies that are appropriate to the customer's creditworthiness and ability to pay. If the customer cannot comfortably handle the debt load including the new loan, the banker may restructure the loan to bring it within the bank's standards. For example, if the new loan would result in a debt-to-income ratio of 45 percent, and the bank's policy standard is 40 percent, the terms may be adjusted to bring the loan into compliance with loan policy.

Indirect lending is valuable because the bank can generate loan volume quickly and efficiently. Nevertheless, there is less chance to sell the best loan for the customer and the bank. Regardless of how good the relationship with the dealer is, bankers have less control over loan structuring in indirect lending than they do with direct lending, so unless there is an opportunity to meet with the customer, the lender is less able to do anything about the customer's other debt obligations.

Open-End Credit

The ability to structure loans and to cross-sell to open-end credit applicants varies depending on the product and how the application is generated. Loan structuring is a good strategy for selling home equity lines of credit (HELOCs) and large unsecured line-of-credit products. HELOCs are large enough to allow customers to consolidate debts and to gain other advantages, such as lower rates, lower monthly payments, and perhaps a tax deduction.

term—The period between the commencement and the termination of a debt or contract.

Did You Know ...

In the competitive marketplace, banks differentiate themselves by shaping customer experience. One strategy for bankers is to take the fiduciary role to heart and be an advocate for customers. "Customers naturally want to put their money in an institution that they believe is looking out for them."

Source: ABA Community Banker, October 2008.

The one area open to loan structuring on credit card and check overdraft plans is the credit limit. For credit cards, loan structuring may include offers of more prestigious premium-card products. In practice, lenders may influence the sale of these products only when the customer applies on a direct basis and not in response to a direct-mail offer. Nevertheless, there are other cross-selling opportunities for open-end accounts. The monthly billing statement is a convenient vehicle for cross-selling and may be used to supplement other direct-mail and telemarketing efforts.

The credit limit for an open-end credit account affects the value of the account to the customer. Higher credit limits encourage use of the account. For example, a $2,000 classic card limits card use, because the credit limit is practical only for smaller purchases and short-term cash flow requirements. A $5,000 premium card, on the other hand, allows the customer to purchase higher-ticket items and may alleviate concerns about going over the limit and being embarrassed at the time of purchase.

The close relationship between the credit line limit and account usage is reflected in the lending practices of market-driven banks. Some credit card lenders establish the highest practical limit at the outset and encourage customers to use the credit line to pay off other credit card balances. Other banks issuing credit cards set low-to-moderate initial credit limits, and then steadily increase the limit for creditworthy customers. Customers are informed of their new limits, but no action is required of them unless they prefer to decline the new limits and close their accounts. Adjusting credit limits is a form of loan structuring, because the bank attempts to increase the account value for the customer to encourage use of the account and ultimately build profitability.

Loan structuring and cross-selling efforts are enhanced when open-end applications are generated through direct personal contact or by telephone. Direct contact gives the banker greater flexibility in obtaining information and tailoring the sales approach to the customer. The banker can fulfill the objective to sell "the best loan for the customer and the bank." Ultimately, this may mean the banker will offer a closed-end or open-end loan that is different from the one the customer initially requested.

LOAN STRUCTURING VARIABLES

The loan structuring options available to lender and customer are influenced by the customer's needs, pricing (fixed or variable rate), schedule of interest rates, type of loan (open-end or closed-end), amount of the loan, term of the loan, collateral, control of loan proceeds, automated loan payments, and payment protection.

Consumer Needs

The customer's financial management needs determine the loan structuring and cross-selling effort. Discerning these needs and matching them with the most appropriate products determines the success of the selling effort.

Did You Know ...

Recommended techniques when taking applications are to
- Smile and greet the customer.
- Use the customer's formal name.
- Set the customer at ease.
- Create a comfortable environment.
- Use a conversational approach.
- Use open-end and closed-end questions.
- Practice active listening.
- Close the interview politely.

Loan-structuring Variables

- the consumer's needs
- pricing (fixed or variable rate)
- schedule of interest rates
- type of loan (open-end or closed-end)
- amount of loan
- term of loan
- collateral
- control of loan proceeds
- automated loan payments
- payment protection

Pricing

Banks offer both fixed- and variable-rate options on some loan products so that customers may choose the pricing approach they prefer. When market rates are high, customers generally choose variable rates, hoping they will decline. When market rates are low, customers prefer fixed rates. When both options are available, customers usually choose the one that offers the lowest monthly payment at the time.

The bank's loan policy may not give the customer a pricing option for all loan types. For example, the bank may not want to offer fixed rates on loans with a maturity of more than five years or to make any variable-rate loans with maturities of 36 months or less. These policy decisions are based on factors like the competitive environment, risk, the bank's asset and liability management strategy, and state lending laws.

Interest Rate Schedule

The schedule of interest rates and loan products may direct the sales effort to the best loan for the customer and the bank. The bank may offer lower rates to creditworthy customers or on loan products that carry less risk. For example, collateral on a loan reduces the risk factor because part or all of the loan amount can be collected, if necessary, by selling the collateral. A customer with an excellent credit report has established character by demonstrating willingness and ability to repay debt. In both instances, to establish a profitable relationship the bank may benefit by offering the customer the advantage of a reduced interest rate.

Type of Loan

The type of loan offered to customers is important to banks. In part, the decision may be based on the loan products the bank wishes to promote, but it usually is driven by the objective of meeting the customer's financial needs. Loan structuring involves consultative selling and cross-selling. Where a different type of loan will enhance the likelihood that the credit request will be approved or provides other financial solutions, the customer is informed of the other choice. For example, a customer applying for a closed-end home equity loan may benefit in the long run by having a home equity line of credit that can be used as needed.

Loan Amount

The size of the loan advance or credit limit affects profitability. Generally, banks encourage their staff to look for ways to sell larger loans to qualified borrowers. One common practice is to set minimum loan sizes that are high enough to make each loan profitable. For example, a bank may set a minimum loan size of $2,000 for closed-end loans and $1,000 for a check-credit plan. Assuming a larger loan cannot be sold, smaller loan requests would be directed toward open-end products where they can be handled more cost-efficiently.

A sample advertisement for a home equity loan demonstrates how one bank handles the loan-size variable. This bank indicates that loans below a certain minimum may carry a higher interest rate.

The disclosed variable APR is based on the prime rate as published by the *Wall Street Journal*; it is currently 4.0% as of 01/16/09, and assumes a 240-month term on a second mortgage. The disclosed APR assumes that you qualify for and accept a loan of $75,000 or more. If you qualify for a loan of less than $75,000, your APR may be higher.

Exhibit 11.2 illustrates how increasing the size of the loan affects interest income, which underscores the importance of selling each qualified customer the largest loan that is appropriate. The ability to increase loan size improves consumer loan productivity, because larger loan volume amounts are going through the system for fewer loans. It also increases profitability, because many costs are fixed regardless of the size of the loan, such as the cost to investigate an automobile loan application.

Before a customer considers a larger loan, the banker explains the benefits. The benefits may include a reduction in total monthly payments as a result of paying off other obligations, reduced interest rates on some debts, a lower monthly payment as the size and term of the loan increase, or tax advantages associated with certain types of loans, such as home equity lines of credit.

Situation

Bernard Stevens has requested a $5,000 unsecured line of credit to be used to consolidate a number of open accounts he has with other banks. Of his three open lines of credit, the balance on two is up to the limit and the third is over the limit. Bernard has a good credit history and each of the accounts is rated "as agreed." If the bank makes the loan, however, there is always the risk that Bernard will resume borrowing on the other accounts after paying off the current balances with the new loan, and then would be unable to handle the added debt burden.

What should the lender do?

Loan Term

The loan term is a consideration in structuring a closed-end loan. The term directly affects the monthly payment, which is a concern for many customers. Some bankers argue that the amount of the monthly payment is as important as, or more important than, the annual percentage rate (APR) when selling a loan. However, stretching the maturity can increase the bank's risk exposure, particularly on unsecured loans and loans with declining-value collateral, such as automobiles. Risk exposure should be discussed in the bank's loan policies and procedures.

Exhibit 11.2   Loan Size Relative to Interest Income— Closed-End Loans

LOAN AMOUNT $	TERM (MONTHS)	INTEREST RATE %	INTEREST INCOME $
1,000	12	7.75	42.48
2,000	12	7.75	84.94
3,500	12	7.75	148.67
2,000	36	8.00	256.21
3,500	36	8.00	448.38
5,000	36	7.50	599.10
5,000	48	7.50	802.97
7,500	48	7.50	1,204.44
10,000	48	8.00	1,718.19

Collateral Values

- *stable-value collateral:* assets pledged for a loan that have a definite value that is maintained throughout the loan term, such as certificates of deposit
- *appreciating-value collateral:* assets pledged for a loan that increase in value over time, such as real estate
- *fluctuating-value collateral:* assets pledged for a loan that rise and fall in value over time, such as stocks and bonds
- *depreciating-value collateral:* assets pledged for a loan that decline in value over time, such as most automobiles

Small differences in interest rates have little effect on monthly payments, but lengthening the loan term can lower payments significantly. Exhibit 11.3 illustrates how to compete against low interest rates by offering longer maturities. The monthly payment on a long-term loan may be less than a lower-interest-rate loan offered by a competitor. The lower monthly payment allows the banker to present options to price-sensitive customers and brings the loan within reach of a broader market.

Offering longer terms allows bankers to sell higher rates to offset the risk and potentially accrue more interest income. A loan may cost slightly more per month but the bank's service may be worth the additional cost. Notice the difference that a longer term with an interest rate change makes on the $5,000 loan in exhibit 11.3.

Collateral

The availability of collateral is important to loan structuring. Normally, the more security the collateral offers the bank, the lower the interest rate the bank can offer. Stable or appreciating-value collateral usually qualifies customers for lower rates than depreciating or fluctuating-value collateral.

Selling the customer a loan secured by real estate rather than an unsecured loan reduces the bank's risk and allows for larger loan amounts, lower rates, and longer terms. Both the bank and the customer benefit if the loan can be secured by collateral.

However, the lender must exercise care when considering collateral value. Collateral should not be used to justify selling a larger loan to a customer who is not creditworthy. The prudent banker requests collateral to strengthen those loans that do not qualify for outright approval.

LOAN AMOUNT $	TERM (MONTHS)	INTEREST RATE %	CONSUMER'S MONTHLY PAYMENT $	BANK'S TOTAL INTEREST INCOME $
2,000	12	6.00	172.14	65.60
2,000	24	6.00	88.65	127.39
2,000	36	6.25	61.08	198.55
5,000	24	6.25	222.17	332.00
5,000	36	6.50	153.25	516.79
5,000	48	6.75	119.16	719.34
15,000	36	7.25	464.88	1,735.45
15,000	48	7.50	362.69	2,408.84
15,000	60	7.75	302.30	3,141.30

Exhibit 11.3 Term, Rate, and Monthly Payment Comparisons

Control of Loan Proceeds

When lending directly to the customer, the banker has more control of how the loan proceeds are used and can structure the loan knowing that the proceeds will be used as intended. Controlling loan proceeds is particularly important when the banker is making a marginal or a bill consolidation loan. In direct lending, the lender may require that certain obligations be paid off directly by the bank. In this case, the bank, not the customer, prepares individual checks for each payee.

Automated Loan Payments

Banks have an opportunity both to improve convenience and to increase earnings on loans by encouraging customers to establish automatic debits for loan payments. On average, costs for loan payments are much higher when the payments are collected in the conventional way, by mail or through branch operations, than when they are collected electronically by automatic debits to a customer's deposit account. Automated loan payment improves earnings, ensures that payments are made on time, and eliminates paper transactions. It also gives customers a safe and convenient way to make loan payments.

Exhibit 11.4 (next page) demonstrates the potential for loan structuring that is available for many consumer loan requests. It presents options that offer significant benefits for the customer and the bank without compromising loan quality.

Payment Protection

Payment protection is another important consideration in structuring and selling consumer credit products. The sale of credit life, credit accident and health, and credit loss of income insurance enhances the bank's profits and protects both customer and banker. Many banks offer alternative payment protection products. Whereas insurers sell credit insurance products, debt cancellation contracts (DCCs) and debt suspension agreements (DSAs) are bank fee-based products paid for separately from the loan. Some banks offer credit insurance as well as DCCs and DSAs.

With both credit insurance and DCC or DSA payment protection products, the bank benefits by reducing delinquencies and losses associated with a borrower's death, disability, or temporary loss of income. It is good practice to offer credit insurance to all signers on the loan. This is particularly important when there is a guarantor, or when both incomes on co-applicant loans are required to repay the loan.

Situation

To reduce monthly debt payments to a manageable level, Theresa Schwenke wants to consolidate four closed-end loans. The new loan would reduce her monthly debt obligations by $150 and would satisfy the bank's debt-to-income ratio policy. Melissa Parks, the lender, approves Theresa's loan request. However, rather than giving all the proceeds directly to her, Melissa sends individual checks directly to each of Theresa's creditors to pay off the other debts.

Why did Melissa do this?

Exhibit 11.4   Loan Structuring

Ms. Brown wants to borrow $5,000 for home improvements and she currently has the following debts:

	MONTHLY PAYMENT	BALANCE	RATE	TERM
Automobile	$250	$2,800	6.25%	36 months
Bank credit card	50	1,000	15.00	Open-end
Bank installment loan	75	500	8.00	24 months
Department store credit card	15	200	13.00	Open-end
Total	$390	$4,500		

Option A: Offer a $5,000 new loan, 24-month term at 8.0% APR.

	MONTHLY PAYMENT	BALANCE	RATE	TERM	INTEREST INCOME
New loan	$226.14	$5,000	8.0%	24 months	$427.27
+Existing debt	390.00	4,500			
Total	$616.14	$9,500			

Option B: Consolidate existing loans with the new loan for total of $9,500 and a 36-month term at 7.75% APR.

	MONTHLY PAYMENT	BALANCE	RATE	TERM	INTEREST INCOME
Consolidated loan	$296.60	$9,500	7.75%	36 months	$1,177.64

Option B would benefit the customer because it would

- Reduce monthly debt payments by $93.40 (from current $390.00 to $296.60).
- Reduce the rate paid on some of the loans outstanding.
- Give the customer a lower rate on the new money than she would have on a smaller separate loan.

Option B would benefit the bank because it would

- Create a new loan with an interest income gain of $1,177.64.
- Enhance the relationship with the customer.

Payment Protection

Credit insurance is an insurer's product. DCC and DSA are bank fee-based products.

Although the bank cannot require the consumer to buy credit insurance sold by the bank or one of its affiliates, it may require that the consumer purchase credit insurance from an unrelated company as a condition of loan approval; however, doing so would make the insurance premium a finance charge.

Exhibit 11.5 shows the effect that credit insurance plans have on the cost of closed-end consumer loans. The first line shows the monthly payment and finance charge if the borrower does not buy credit insurance. The second line shows

Exhibit 11.5   Credit Insurance Sales: Effect on Loan Payments and Bank Income

LIFE PREMIUM	DISABILITY PREMIUM	MONTHLY PAYMENTS	FINANCE CHARGE
$3,000 loan, 36 months, 7.0% APR			
No insurance	No insurance	$92.65	$334.73
$35.39	Not included	$93.63	$338.72
$35.39	$107.31	$97.10	$350.78
$10,000 loan, 60 months, 7.0% APR			
No insurance	No insurance	$198.05	$1,880.75
$202.15	Not included	$202.06	$1,918.79
$202.15	$469.63	$211.55	$2,008.87

these items plus the cost of the credit life insurance premium, assuming the customer purchases life insurance only. The third line shows the amount of each item, assuming the customer purchases both credit life and disability insurance.

LAWS AND REGULATIONS

Many of the laws and regulations discussed in earlier chapters apply to loan structuring and sales. For example, bank lending limits may affect the maximum amount that any one borrower may obtain from a lender, and rules on subprime lending protect consumers from loan structuring abuses. Another law, the Home Ownership and Equity Protection Act, protects consumers from abusive structuring practices for loans secured by real estate.

HOME OWNERSHIP AND EQUITY PROTECTION ACT

The Truth in Lending Act (TILA) mandates additional disclosures for reverse mortgages and mortgages with high interest rates or fees. The Home Ownership and Equity Protection Act (HOEPA) requires these disclosures.

HOEPA was enacted in response to consumer complaints about unfair and deceptive home equity lending practices, such as offering the elderly and minorities high-cost home-secured credit with high upfront fees, and setting repayment amounts and schedules based on the equity in the home rather than the consumer's ability to repay. When homeowners had difficulty repaying the debt, they were encouraged to refinance the loan and thus incur more high fees that cannot be repaid. In some cases, borrowers lost their homes.

HOEPA loan: This is a high-interest-rate or high-fee real estate-secured loan that the Home Ownership and Equity Protection Act subjects to additional federal disclosure requirements.

Coverage

It is important to note that not all loans are covered by HOEPA. Loans to purchase a borrower's principal dwelling, reverse mortgages, and home equity lines of credit are not covered.

HOEPA does cover the following loans:

- a first-lien loan with an annual percentage rate that is more than eight percentage points above the interest rates on U.S. Treasury securities of comparable maturity

- a second-mortgage loan with an annual percentage rate that is more than ten percentage points above the interest rates on U.S. Treasury securities of comparable maturity

- a loan where the total fees and points the consumer must pay at or before closing exceed the greater of a flat amount or a percentage of the total loan amount that is established annually by the Federal Reserve Board. Credit insurance premiums are counted as fees.

For comparison purposes, the lender must reference yields from the Federal Reserve's H.15 release as of the 15th day of the month immediately preceding the month in which the application was received.

Disclosure Requirements

HOEPA disclosures primarily apply to refinancing and closed-end home equity loans. Lenders must provide a disclosure notice at least three business days before the loan is closed that tells the customer

Loan completion not required	The loan need not be completed, even if the customer has received the loan application and required disclosures.
Customer could lose residence	Because the lender will have a mortgage on the customer's home, the customer could lose the residence and any money invested in it, if payments are not made.
Costs	The APR, the regular payment amount and any balloon payments, the loan amount, and any amount borrowed for credit insurance premiums must be stated. For variable-rate loans lenders must disclose that the rate and monthly payment may increase, and what the maximum monthly payment amount will be.

Prohibited Practices

HOEPA bans a variety of abusive lending practices. For high-rate high-fee loans, it prohibits

- making a loan without considering the borrower's ability to repay and verifying the applicant's income and assets

- refinancing another HOEPA loan within the first 12 months of origination unless the new loan is in the borrower's best interest
- **balloon payments** for loans with less than five-year terms
- negative amortization, where smaller monthly payments do not fully pay off the principal and in fact cause it to increase
- default interest rates that are higher than pre-default interest rates
- a repayment schedule that consolidates more than two periodic payments to be paid in advance from the proceeds of the loan
- most prepayment penalties
- a due-on-demand clause, unless the customer commits **fraud** or **material misrepresentation** in connection with the loan, fails to repay the loan as agreed, or acts in a way that adversely affects the lender's security interest

HIGHER-PRICED MORTGAGE LOANS

In 2008 the Federal Reserve added another category of protected loans to FRS Regulation Z, Truth in Lending, called higher-priced mortgage loans. A higher-priced home loan is one that has high costs or fees or an interest rate that is higher than that for the average loan of that type at the time it is made. The Federal Reserve publishes the average prime offer rate on its Web site. If a loan secured by the borrower's principal dwelling has an interest rate that is 1.5 percentage points above the prime offer rate and is secured by a first lien or is 3.5 percentage points above the prime offer rate and secured by a subordinate lien, it is a higher-priced mortgage loan. Loans to finance the construction or purchase of a principal dwelling and temporary loans are not included in the definition of higher-priced home mortgage loans.

Higher-priced mortgage loans are subject to some of the same restrictions as HOEPA loans, including the prohibition on prepayment penalties and the requirement to consider the borrower's ability to repay. Lenders also must require escrow accounts for taxes and insurance on these loans.[1]

balloon payment loan—A loan where the regular payments do not fully pay off the principal balance and a lump sum payment of more than twice the amount of the regular payment is required.

fraud—An intentional misrepresentation made by one person to another who, believing the misrepresentation, takes some action and suffers a loss of property or a right to the first person.

material misrepresentation—In law, the crime of misstating relevant and significant facts in a legal document, such as a loan application or contract, in order to obtain money, goods, or benefits from another party.

SUMMARY

- Banks are changing the way they market and sell their products and services. In the old model, banks were operations-driven, creating products that suited the bank's needs, building branches, and competing on price and service quality. Although these activities are still important, they are not the only components of a bank sales strategy. Today banks are market-driven, with an emphasis on first determining customers' needs and then identifying or creating products and services to satisfy those needs.

- To be a truly sales-oriented institution, banks must build a sales culture, nurture effective sales skills in the staff, and create approaches that mirror the activities of the purchase cycle. Creating a sales culture as it relates to consumer loan structuring and selling involves building and honing selling skills, motivating employees to sell, supporting the sales force, and staying focused on the customer. In place of mere order-taking, bankers use a consultative sales approach and cross-sell other bank services whenever possible.

- Effective selling is based on two-way communication that includes listening, reading body language, understanding voice tone and inflection, and asking well-thought-out questions. Loan interviewers should be self-motivated with a focus on what is important to the customer and the bank, enjoy challenges, know how to establish rapport with the customer, identify customer financial needs, understand product solutions, handle and overcome customer concerns, and be able to close the sale.

- The purchase cycle for any product or service has four stages: needs recognition, prepurchase search, purchase decision, and dealing with postpurchase feelings. For bankers the loan structuring and selling objectives are to make the best loan for the customer and the bank, not order-taking but selling loans, optimizing bank earnings by selling other products, retaining the customer, and minimizing credit and interest rate risk.

- A bank that embraces loan structuring has to deal with a variety of issues, depending on the product. Direct lending affords the best opportunity for significant loan structuring and cross-selling other bank services. Indirect lending does not provide many opportunities at the time of application: loan structuring is restricted to adjusting the terms of the loan as requested by the dealer; other services may be sold after the loan is made. For open-end applications, the ability to structure a loan and the opportunity to cross-sell vary depending on the product and how the application is generated. Marketing techniques such as direct mail preclude cross-selling and loan structuring. However, banks may cross-sell other credit card programs to current customers and they may increase credit limits.

- The loan-structuring options available will be influenced by the customer's needs, fixed- or variable-rate pricing, the schedule of interest rates, whether the loan is open-end or closed-end, the loan amount, the term of the loan, the collateral, control of loan proceeds, use of automated loan payments, and credit insurance protection choices.

- The Home Ownership and Equity Protection Act (HOEPA), which revised the Truth in Lending Act (TILA), and is implemented by FRS Regulation Z. HOEPA bans a variety of practices, such as balloon payments for loans with less than five-year terms, and requires early disclosures of the loan's costs and the fact that the consumer could lose the residence. The lender is required to determine the borrower's ability to repay the loan based on income and assets, not collateral value. HOEPA restricts terms on closed-end home loans with interest rates that are higher than the average, known as higher-priced mortgage loans, and requires that the lender establish escrow accounts for taxes and insurance.

END NOTE

[1] Truth in Lending requirements for higher-priced mortgage loans also are discussed in chapter 7.

SELF-CHECK AND REVIEW

Learning Check

1. What is meant by a market-driven approach to selling?

2. What is the distinction between consultative selling and cross-selling? Give an example of each.

3. What are the steps necessary to establish a sales culture? Briefly explain each.

4. What are the stages of the purchase cycle to which bankers respond? Give an example of how each influences the consumer lending process.

5. What sales objectives does loan structuring help banks achieve, and how?

6. Why does direct lending offer the bank the best opportunity for significant loan structuring and cross-selling other bank services?

7. What factors influence the loan-structuring options lenders have?

8. What is the purpose of the Home Owners Equity Protection Act? What loan types are covered by the act that revised FRS Regulation Z, Truth in Lending? What loan types are not covered?

ADDITIONAL RESOURCES

Resources

ABA Bank Marketing Magazine, Washington: American Bankers Association, periodical.

American Bankers Association, **www.aba.com**.

ABA Banking Journal Community Bank Competitiveness Survey, 2008, www.ababj.com.

"Creating Customer Experiences" by Bridget Trask, Community Banker, American Bankers Association, October 2008.

Law and Banking, Washington: American Bankers Association, 2008.

Marketing Financial Services, Washington: American Bankers Association, 2009.

Reference Guide to Regulatory Compliance, Washington: American Bankers Association, annual publication.

Understanding Bank Products, Washington: American Bankers Association, 2008.

Loan Documentation and Closing

Learning Objectives

After completing this chapter, you should be able to

- identify objectives for loan documentation and the closing process
- discuss documentation requirements for different types of loans
- explain how to create a security interest in collateral through attachment and perfection
- explain the loan closing process and the marketing opportunities it offers
- discuss the responsibilities of the loan review function
- describe the process and requirements for flood disaster protection
- define the terms that appear in bold type in the text

Introduction

The consumer lending process starts, continues, and ends with the customer. Based on an understanding of the market and customer needs, bankers craft products, services, policies, and processes to serve customers better. Loan applications are generated, reviewed, investigated, evaluated, and approved or declined, and loans are priced, structured, and documented. At every stage, the customer is the focus; although lenders must also keep in mind that the bank needs to earn a return, mitigate risk, and comply with the law and bank policies.

Loan documentation is the process of preparing loan papers, obtaining necessary signatures, examining executed documents for accuracy, and recording collateral documents with the proper authorities. The loan closing is the part of the documentation process in which the customer signs the loan papers, becoming obligated to the bank, and directly or indirectly receives the loan proceeds.

The documentation and closing process, like all previous stages, is centered on both customer and bank. Managing this process competently, with dedication to accuracy, completeness, and compliance, protects both parties and fosters the customer-banker relationship.

DOCUMENTATION AND CLOSING OBJECTIVES

loan documentation— The process of completing all the papers necessary to secure the lender's interest and to comply with the law.

loan closing—The process in which all required loan documents are signed and funds are disbursed to the borrower.

loss payee—The party that would have first claim on the proceeds of funds disbursed in payment of an insurance claim.

Proper documentation is essential for banks to protect their investment and to ensure that customers understand the loan products they have selected. Failure to properly document and close loans can leave banks exposed to lawsuits, loan losses, and costly penalties for violating regulations.

The major objectives for **loan documentation** and **loan closing** are to complete all documents required by state and federal law; prepare them efficiently, accurately, and professionally; comply with the law and bank loan policy; ensure that the customer understands the loan's terms; create a positive image for the bank; and use the opportunity to cross-sell and ask for referrals.

COMPLETING THE DOCUMENTS

Most bank loan policies and procedure manuals detail how to prepare documents for each type of loan. Procedures explain the requirements for loan applications, loan note and disclosure statements, security agreements, the insurance **loss payee** letter, and title or other ownership documents.

The lender is responsible for preparing these documents and having them properly signed at closing. Generally, lenders rely on forms and other standardized documents designed by vendors or legal counsel that when properly executed comply with the law. The bank's compliance officer or legal counsel reviews vendor-created documents to ensure they comply with federal and state regulations. Lenders ensure the documents are executed properly—all sections are complete, all numbers are accurate, the math is correct, the description of collateral (such as model and serial number) is correct, all necessary signatures are obtained, and the signers' identities have been verified.

Depending on the complexity of the transaction, the loan closing actually may take place with a closing agent, who may be an independent agent or an employee of an escrow or title company or law firm. The selection of the closing agent is critical for the bank because, as the bank's representative, the agent must be professional and courteous.

Accurate document preparation is essential to quality service, efficient operation of the consumer lending department, and compliance with the law. Properly completed forms flow through the system without delay and without expensive special handling. Documentation errors disrupt normal workflow and add time and expense to the process. Errors also require extra time for consumers to make corrections or sign amended documents and may undermine their confidence in the bank. Undetected documentation errors, moreover, may expose the bank to legal and credit risk.

Lender Documentation Responsibilities

- All necessary sections are completed.
- Numbers are accurate.
- Math is correct.
- Collateral description is correct.
- All necessary signatures are present.
- Signers' identities have been verified.

EFFICIENT AND ACCURATE DOCUMENT PREPARATION

Most banks use automated document preparation systems to ensure efficient, accurate, and professional completion of loan documents. Using automated systems allows banks to reap the benefits of

- faster document preparation
- the ability to add or correct information up to the last minute
- more accurate documents with no common calculation errors
- confidence that all required documents are prepared
- enhanced service that helps build customer relationships

Automated systems, however, do not replace careful review of all loan documents before closing. Lenders should use documentation checklists to guide review of all documents for completeness and accuracy.

COMPLIANCE WITH THE LAW AND LOAN POLICY

Complete and accurate documents are necessary to comply with regulations, which often specify not only the documents required but also, for example, the order in which documents are presented and signed. FRS Regulation Z, which

promissory note—A written document in which one party (the maker) agrees to pay a certain sum of money to another party (the payee) or to his or her order on demand or at a determinable future date. It is the customer's promise to pay back a loan according to the conditions detailed in the loan agreement.

truth-in-lending disclosure statement—The document that contains all required federal truth-in-lending disclosures, such as the annual percentage rate and finance charges. It is typically part of the promissory note for closed-end loans and of the terms of agreement for open-end loans, such as credit cards.

Did You Know ...

There is an old saying in lending that still rings true today: "A loan well made is half collected."

implements the Truth in Lending Act (TILA), requires lenders to present federal disclosures to consumers before they become obligated on the loan. How the disclosure is made varies with the type of loan. Lenders violate this regulation, for example, if customers sign **promissory notes** before they have received the truth-in-lending disclosure form.

The lender is responsible for guiding the borrower through the loan documents in the correct order at closing. To facilitate compliance with the TILA, for many loans the **disclosure statement** is combined with the promissory note. Consumers must receive their own copy of the required disclosures before they actually sign a loan contract.

MAKING SURE THE CUSTOMER UNDERSTANDS THE TERMS

Ensuring that customers understand the loan terms, the process, and their rights and obligations as borrowers is another important objective. Although customers should be aware of the loan requirements, they usually are informed about the documents and process only at closing. Lenders should thoroughly understand all documents, especially the small-print details, so that they can confidently explain them to customers. Banks may revise documents; it is important that lenders routinely review them for changes or updates. The customer needs to understand

Interest rates	• the method of calculating simple interest
	• how variable-rate features affect the loan: whether rate changes are reflected in changes to the monthly payment, the loan term, or both
Payments	• when payments are due
	• where payments are made
	• how payments are to be made, such as by coupon book or automatic bill payment
	• the importance of making payments on time to preserve a good credit rating
	• how late payments affect the loan cost, such as by incurring late payment fees
	• how payments of more than the minimum required monthly payment are handled and how they affect future payments
Access	• how to access the line of credit and any restrictions, such as minimum check amount
Who to contact	• who to contact, perhaps a relationship banker or the customer service department, with problems or questions, such as the payment due date

Customers who understand loan features from the outset are more likely to comply with the terms. By ensuring that they are informed, lenders minimize the number of loans that become delinquent. A sound loan decision and a well-executed closing can prevent problems in the future. Both the customer and the bank benefit when the customer understands the terms and the process. Customers are less likely to have questions later if they understand these factors.

CREATING THE BEST IMAGE FOR THE BANK

The customer is more likely to form a positive image of the bank if documents are prepared completely and accurately and the closing is handled in an organized, professional, and customer-friendly way. The satisfied customer is likely to use other bank services and thus initiate a long-term positive relationship with the bank.

Convenience is another way to create a positive image for the bank. For loan applications taken over the Internet, some lenders deliver documents in person with a notary public to witness the customer's signature so that customers do not have to come to the bank. Some banks deliver the proceeds of the loan along with the documents.

SELLING OTHER BANK SERVICES AND ASKING FOR REFERRALS

Throughout the lending process (see exhibit 12.1, next page), there are many opportunities to sell bank products. The loan closing is an excellent opportunity for lenders to sell other services and build the customer relationship. Customers usually are pleased to have a loan, and a closing that is handled well enhances their impression of the bank. This makes it easier for the lender to cross-sell other financial services that may meet the customer's needs. In fact, because it is a face-to-face meeting, the loan closing is one of the best opportunities to cross-sell. At a minimum, customers may be given product literature, and if time permits, the lender can discuss the benefits of other products with the customer.

Follow-up phone calls made a few days after loan closing offer another opportunity to cross-sell bank products and services. In these calls lenders thank customers for their business, offer to answer questions, and perhaps ask for referrals. Many lenders send thank you notes with their business cards, asking customers to tell a friend if they are satisfied with the service.

TYPES OF DOCUMENTATION

The forms required to document a consumer lending transaction vary with the type of loan and the collateral securing it. Documentation checklists often are part of the bank's policy

Did You Know ...

Insurance Business Adds Value for Banks
Ninety-six percent of banks currently distributing insurance products believe that their insurance businesses add value for bank shareholders. Nearly 40 percent say it adds "significant" value.

Source: The 2008 Study of Banks in Insurance, American Bankers Association and Reagan Consulting.

Situation

Andrea has been approved for the personal loan she applied for at her local bank. This morning she is meeting with the lender to sign the final papers and receive the funds. She is taken to a conference room where a loan folder has been prepared for her. Joseph, the lender, goes through the documents in the folder, explains the contents of each, and makes sure Andrea understands all documents before asking her to sign. Andrea is grateful for the opportunity to ask some questions about repayment conditions. Finally, Joseph offers Andrea a check for the loan proceeds. Noting that Andrea does not have a checking or savings account with his bank, Joseph suggests she might want to open a deposit account from which she can withdraw the loan proceeds as needed.

How did Andrea feel after this experience?

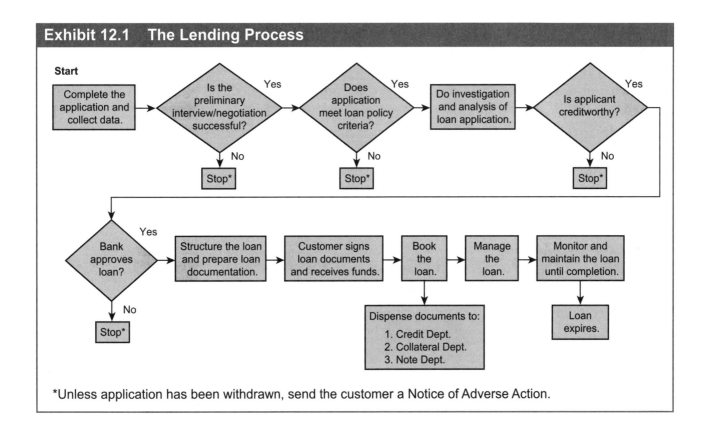

Exhibit 12.1   The Lending Process

Start

Complete the application and collect data. → Is the preliminary interview/negotiation successful? — Yes → Does application meet loan policy criteria? — Yes → Do investigation and analysis of loan application. → Is applicant creditworthy? — Yes

Is the preliminary interview/negotiation successful? — No → Stop*

Does application meet loan policy criteria? — No → Stop*

Is applicant creditworthy? — No → Stop*

Bank approves loan? — Yes → Structure the loan and prepare loan documentation. → Customer signs loan documents and receives funds. → Book the loan. → Manage the loan. → Monitor and maintain the loan until completion.

Bank approves loan? — No → Stop*

Book the loan. → Dispense documents to:
1. Credit Dept.
2. Collateral Dept.
3. Note Dept.

Monitor and maintain the loan until completion. → Loan expires.

*Unless application has been withdrawn, send the customer a Notice of Adverse Action.

---

manual as a reference for lenders. Loans secured by real estate require more documentation than unsecured loans, which require only the application, the truth-in-lending disclosure statement, and the promissory note. Regardless of the type of loan, though, banks institute controls to ensure that all documentation is complete and accurate.

The following are examples of documentation requirements for specific types of loans (see also exhibit 12.2).

FIXED-RATE CLOSED-END LOANS

Except for **mortgage** loans, documentation for fixed-rate closed-end accounts can be handled at the time the loan is made. Although follow-up is required to ensure documents are obtained from the appropriate agency for perfecting **liens**, there are no other documentation or disclosure requirements except for insurance renewals. The loan policy specifies the types of documentation needed to close each type of fixed-rate closed-end loan, whether made directly or indirectly.

Several of these documents may be combined into a single form, and there are variations by bank and by state.

Direct lending automobile loan

- credit application
- truth-in-lending disclosure statement
- insurance sales disclosure for credit life and credit accident and health insurance
- promissory note, which may contain the truth-in-lending disclosure

mortgage—A legal document, the requirements for which vary by state, in which a borrower gives the lender a lien on property as security for repayment of the loan.

lien—A legal claim or attachment on public record against property as a security interest for the payment of an obligation. It reflects the guaranteed right of a lender or investor to specific property in case the loan defaults. Under UCC Article 9, this also is known as a security interest.

Exhibit 12.2   Documentation Required for Certain Loan Products

TYPE OF LOAN	POSSIBLE DOCUMENTATION REQUIRED*
Fixed-rate closed-end	Loan application Credit report Copy of pay stub, IRS wage and tax statement (W-2 form), or personal tax return Results of any direct investigation to verify address and employment Truth-in-lending disclosure statement Promissory note Security agreement Insurance policy Motor vehicle title Privacy notice
Indirect auto	Loan application Credit report Closed-end installment sales contract Agreement to insure Credit insurance and warranty policies Motor vehicle title
Variable-rate	Loan application Credit report Copy of pay stub, IRS wage and tax statement (W-2 form), or personal tax return Results of any direct investigation to verify address and employment Variable-rate promissory note Variable-rate disclosure notice Privacy notice Notices of any rate changes
Home equity line of credit	Loan application Copy of pay stub, IRS wage and tax statement (W-2 form), or personal tax return Results of any direct investigation to verify address and employment Promissory note with disclosures of credit Mortgage agreement (deed of trust) Insurance binder Title search Appraisal Flood determination Proof of flood insurance, if needed Notice of right to receive an appraisal report Notice of right to rescind Privacy notice Truth-in-lending disclosure statement Insurance sales disclosure, if needed Flood insurance disclosure, if needed Monthly periodic statement
Open-end credit	Loan application Credit report Credit acceptance form Open-end credit agreement with disclosures Privacy notice Monthly periodic statement

*The lender may require additional documents.

- security agreement
- insurance policy or agreement to insure, which verifies that the collateral is covered by insurance and the bank is named as loss payee; proceeds may be used to repair collateral to restore its value or to reduce, or pay off, the loan balance
- motor vehicle title, which identifies the legal owner of the vehicle
- privacy notice

Indirect lending automobile loan

- loan application
- closed-end installment sales contract, which often combines the federal and state disclosures with the security agreement and note
- agreement to insure
- copies of any credit insurance and warranty policies, which are usually submitted with the loan documents
- motor vehicle title

VARIABLE-RATE LOANS

Unlike fixed-rate closed-end loans, variable-rate loans require continuing disclosures to the customer after the loan has been consummated. Generally, the lender must notify customers of changes in the loan rate and how these will affect the loan payments (higher, lower, or unchanged) and the remaining term (extended, shortened, or no change). Such notifications usually are part of the monthly statement sent to the client.

In addition to standard documentation, variable-rate loans have their own promissory note that contains, for example, disclosures about notification of rate changes and changes to payment amounts.

A home equity line of credit (HELOC) typically has a variable rate and is secured by the customer's residence. The security interest is facilitated through a mortgage on the property. Typical documentation for the HELOC would be

- promissory note (with initial disclosures)
- mortgage (**deed of trust**)
- **insurance binder**
- **title search**
- appraisal
- flood determination
- proof of flood insurance, if necessary
- notice of right to rescind
- insurance sales disclosure

deed of trust—A sealed instrument in writing, duly executed and delivered, that transfers property to a trustee. It is used in some states instead of a mortgage. The borrower transfers property to a trustee for the benefit of the lender, and it is conveyed back to the borrower when the loan is paid back.

insurance binder—The written evidence that an insurance company or its agent has agreed to provide temporary hazard or title insurance coverage. It is valid only for a specified time, after which it must be replaced by a permanent policy.

title search—A review of public records to disclose past and current facts (chain of title) about the ownership of a piece of real estate.

OPEN-END LOAN ACCOUNTS

The bank's loan policy specifies the documents required for open-end lines of credit—unsecured check overdraft and professional line of credit programs and credit card programs. These typically are

Credit application	Usually, a consumer application or an abbreviated application used for preapproved and prescreened credit offers
Open-end credit agreement	Sets forth the contract for the account and includes the truth-in-lending disclosures; although not always signed, usually the consumer must receive the agreement before using the account.

All consumer open-end account programs must provide periodic disclosures to account holders. Lenders also may make legally approved changes to the terms of their open-end loan programs. They may reduce the minimum monthly payment or lower the rates; they also may add fees, such as for being over the limit or paying late or for annual membership.

Changes of terms on HELOCs are limited. The APR may change if the rate is tied to an index that is outside the lender's control. Other terms can change if the customer agrees or the change benefits the customer. To change a loan term, the bank generally sends the customer a Notice of Change in Terms.

The ability to change the terms of line of credit agreements without having to redocument the credit enables lenders to enhance these products. Customers who do not want to accept the new provisions may pay outstanding balances and close their accounts. Exhibit 12.3 (next page) summarizes the periodic statements and notices associated with open-end credit.

Situation

Paul receives a Notice of Change in Terms with his credit card bill. The notice outlines three changes to his account: his minimum monthly payment is being reduced to $15 and the annual percentage rate on the account is being reduced to 12 percent, but there will now be a $30 fee if he exceeds his credit limit. Paul is pleased with the first two changes and, although the third change represents an increase in fees, he is not concerned because he does not expect to go over his credit limit.

Does Paul need to do anything to accept these changes to his account?

ESTABLISHING A SECURITY INTEREST

The Uniform Commercial Code (UCC), drafted in response to the need for uniformity in handling commercial transactions, also applies to consumer loans. The UCC is a model code that individual states can choose to adopt. Because states can amend the uniform text, specific provisions may vary by state.

Of particular importance to consumer lenders is UCC Article 9, which governs most loans secured by personal property. Article 9 states that two steps are necessary to give a lender the right to take the collateral if the borrower defaults. Lenders must take great care to meet all the conditions for attachment and perfection. If they do not, their security interest in the collateral could be compromised and the loan would no longer be secured.

Exhibit 12.3   Sample Open-end Credit Statements and Notifications

STATEMENT OR NOTIFICATION	TIMING	CONTENTS	LAW AND REGULATION
Periodic statements	End of each billing cycle 14 days before payment due date	Transaction details Billing error instructions Other pertinent information	Truth in Lending (TILA), FRS Regulation Z
Annual statement of billing rights	Annually, or short version in periodic statement	Instructions for error resolution or other account inquiries Credit card purchase protections	Truth in Lending (TILA), FRS Regulation Z
Change in terms disclosure	Before the effective date; generally 15 days for home secured credit lines and 45 days for unsecured credit lines	Changed terms to the table in the initial disclosure Increase in required minimum periodic rate	Truth in Lending (TILA), FRS Regulation Z
Change in credit card insurance provider	Not less than 30 days before change Within 30 days after change	Increases in rate Decreases in coverage Cancellation option Name and address of new provider Copy of new policy Cancellation option	Truth in Lending (TILA), FRS Regulation Z
Checks to access credit card accounts	Must be provided with the checks	Promotional rates Fees and charges	Truth in Lending (TILA), FRS Regulation Z
Renewal disclosure for charge or credit card account	30 days or one billing cycle before cycle in which charge will appear	Fee for renewal Open-end account disclosures Termination instructions to avoid fee	Truth in Lending (TILA), FRS Regulation Z
Response to written request for information on residential real estate loans	Acknowledge within 20 business days of request Action within 60 business days	Error resolution process Lender may not report delinquency for payment in dispute	Real Estate Settlement Procedures Act (RESPA)/ HUD Regulation X

security agreement—A document that precisely describes the collateral and sets forth the rights and responsibilities of each party relative to the collateral. Signed by the borrower and other owners of the property, it establishes a lender's right to take possession of loan collateral if the borrower defaults.

CREATING A VALID LIEN—ATTACHMENT

A lender making a secured loan covered by the UCC must create a valid lien, called a security interest. This attachment gives the bank the legal right to take possession of collateral if a customer fails to repay the loan. Attachment often is accomplished by having the customer execute a **security agreement** that creates or provides for a security interest. Because the UCC filing rules may vary, actual state procedures should be verified.

Under the UCC, the security agreement document must be in writing, provide for a security interest, be authenticated by the debtor, and describe the collateral. If persons other than the debtor own the collateral, they must consent in writing to pledge the collateral to secure the loan.

Debtors must authenticate the security agreement. That is, they must sign it, accept it by adopting a symbol, or process their acceptance through encryption. Encryption allows security agreements to be authenticated electronically, which facilitates loans being made through the Internet.

The security agreement stipulates creditor and debtor rights and duties regarding the collateral. To create a valid security interest, the person granting the security interest—usually the borrower—must have an ownership interest in the collateral.

GIVING NOTICE—PERFECTION

Once the borrower signs the security agreement and creates a valid lien, the bank must perfect the lien so that other potential creditors can learn of the bank's interest in the property and the bank will have first claim on the collateral if the debtor defaults. A lien may be perfected in a variety of ways, depending on the property used as collateral, the local laws where the property is located, and the customer's place of residence. Usually the lien is perfected by filing a financing statement.

A perfected interest in collateral provides a **secondary source of repayment** as long as the bank properly attaches and perfects its interest so that it does not become subordinate to other properly filed interests.

Financing Statement

The financing statement used to file notice of a security agreement on property that is serving as collateral may include some nontitle items. It must contain the name of the customer and the name of the bank filing the statement. Although a complete description of the collateral is not necessary, any description should coincide with the security agreement. State governments generally have accepted the financing statement in the Uniform Commercial Code (UCC). Financing statements are filed with the government unit prescribed in state law, usually in a central state office, but it also may be necessary to file in the county where the debtor lives.

Most state automobile title laws are similar, but laws on title to other types of vehicles vary. In addition, FRS Regulation AA, Unfair or Deceptive Acts or Practices, and many state laws protect a consumer's household goods. Therefore, a lender cannot **attach** a security interest to most household goods unless the goods were purchased using proceeds from the loan. In this case, the lender would have a purchase-money **security interest**, which is allowed by law. In a purchase-money security interest, the goods purchased become the collateral for the loan. To avoid errors in the **perfection** process, banks must know the requirements in every state where they conduct business.

secondary source of repayment—Another source of funds to help the bank recover its investment should the customer be unable to repay the loan for any reason, for example, a guarantor, a cosigner, or collateral.

attachment—The process by which property owned by a debtor is pledged to a secured party, which obtains a right to the property. *Also known as* establishing a valid lien.

security interest—A claim to property that secures repayment of a debt by allowing the creditor to take the property, sell it, and retain the proceeds, up to the amount of indebtedness, if the debt has not been repaid as promised.

perfection—The process by which a secured party protects its security interest from third parties by possession, certificate of title, control, or filing or recording documentation of the security interest in local or state public records.

Situation

Abraham and Kari Nichols are financing the purchase of a new auto. The loan for the auto, which will serve as collateral, will be in Abraham's name alone, but the auto title is in Kari's name. When completing the documents for the loan, Iwona, the lender, requires both Abraham and Kari to sign the security agreement. Abraham questions this because, with only his name on the note, he will be solely responsible for repayment.

Why are both signatures required?

Special Requirements

Exhibit 12.4 lists common perfection methods for various types of collateral. Lenders need to know both federal and state requirements for some types of collateral, such as aircraft and boats.

Aircraft	The Federal Aviation Act specifies the documentation requirements. The security agreement must be recorded with the Federal Aviation Administration (FAA) so that the aircraft cannot be sold without the bank's loan being paid first. This is particularly important because of the large dollar value of these loans.
Boats	The Ship Mortgage Act provides for federal documentation of vessels weighing five tons or more and those that operate in international waters or in states that enforce Coast Guard requirements. Federal documentation takes priority over state titles or UCC filings.

Because Coast Guard documentation is relatively complex and can take months to record, many banks outsource the process to documentation companies. Meanwhile, they record their lien using a financing statement or a state title.

POSSESSION OF COLLATERAL

Most collateral for consumer loan transactions remains in the possession of the consumer and is available for the consumer's use, subject to any limitations in the security agreement. Automobiles, boats, and recreational vehicles, referred

---

Exhibit 12.4 Methods of Perfecting a Security Interest

TYPE OF COLLATERAL	HOW PERFECTED*
Airplanes	File against Federal Aviation Administration title
Automobiles	File with State Bureau of Motor Vehicles
Boats	State title, financing statement, Coast Guard Ship Mortgage Act documentation
Consumer goods	Financing statement, purchase-money security agreement
Mobile homes	Title or mortgage, financing statement
Recreational vehicles	Title, financing statement
Real estate	Mortgage/deed of trust
Certificate of deposit	Control of item
Life insurance policy	Policy assignment

*These methods may vary by state by state.

to as **nonpossessory collateral**, are examples. Collateral like savings accounts and stock that is held or controlled by the bank is referred to as **possessory collateral**. Certain obligations are associated with the borrower's possessing and using the collateral; violating them can affect the terms and status of the loan. Some security agreements require the customer to keep the collateral in a specified location. Before a boat may be moved from its home state to another, for example, the customer is obligated to obtain the lender's approval. Failure to notify the lender is a breach of contract and can be a condition for **default**. Both lender and customer should fully understand all requirements in the security agreement.

LOAN CLOSING

The loan closing is the final step in the process of documenting a new loan. At this point, the correctly prepared documents are presented to the customer for review and signature.

Direct loans usually are closed at the branch, unless the customer's convenience suggests another location. Indirect loans usually are closed at the dealer's business site. Open-end lines of credit may be closed by mail or at the bank's offices. If the loans are complex or out of the bank's usual service area, they may be closed by an attorney or a service company that represents the bank.

An efficient closing helps control costs and creates a positive impression of the bank. The closing also offers significant marketing opportunities for the bank. Among other things, it can lay the foundation for a future loan and for cross-selling other bank services.

LOAN REVIEW

Although the loan technically is complete at the time of closing, the bank still must monitor it to ensure that documents required throughout the life of the loan are sent and received. To handle this responsibility, many banks have established a formal loan review function within the loan operations department. Banks often use post-closing checklists to follow up on items that still may be pending.

The loan review function examines the documents to ensure they are accurate, complete, and in compliance with the law and bank loan policies. Loan review also monitors long-term documentation and loan status. Sophisticated computer programs have enhanced the bank's ability to control risk by tracking, for example, loan exceptions, insurance, and UCC filing expirations. The bank defines what the program monitors and what information is transmitted to the related reporting system.

Some review tasks are performed before the loan is **booked** on the bank's loan application system. Others require follow-up after it is booked. The loan review function helps to

nonpossessory collateral—Collateral for a consumer loan that remains in the possession of the consumer, such as an automobile, boat, or airplane.

possessory collateral—Collateral held by the lender, such as savings accounts and stock.

default—Failure to comply with any of the terms of a loan agreement.

book—To enter a loan on the records of the lender.

ensure that the loan complies with the law. Staff review documents for accuracy, completeness, and adherence to bank lending policy; resolve documentation errors; expedite the booking of new loans; record and report on documentation problems and lender performance; and track follow-up for lien and insurance documents.

ENSURE COMPLIANCE WITH THE LAW

The loan review function usually is responsible for ensuring each loan complies with state and federal regulations. Failure to do so can result in an enforcement action, such as a fine or lawsuit against the bank. The Financial Institutions Reform, Recovery, and Enforcement Act (FIRREA) sets fines for violations of most federal banking statutes and regulations. For example, violations of credit underwriting or loan documentation standards are subject to FIRREA civil money penalties. Violations of the Home Mortgage Disclosure, Truth in Lending, and other laws may be subject to FIRREA penalties. Individual laws also may carry their own penalties, such as the truth-in-lending requirement to refund money if the rescission notice is not given or if an annual percentage rate (APR) is understated.

EXAMINE DOCUMENTS AND RESOLVE ERRORS

Loan reviewers examine the documents after closing for completeness, such as proper signatures, disclosures, and rescission periods.

The loan review function is responsible for correcting any errors. Even when the bank obtains all the documents it needs to properly perfect liens, errors may occur. The state motor vehicle department may overlook the bank's lien and issue a title to the customer. A dealer may add another name to the title, causing a problem if state law requires all owners on the title to sign the security agreement. Detected early, such errors can be resolved.

EXPEDITE BOOKING NEW LOANS

In an efficient lending program, loans are booked quickly, new loan information is accurate and complete, and essential information is stored correctly for retrieval. A sophisticated customer information system (CIS) improves the efficiency and quality of the booking process. If already part of a CIS, the customer's information is verified and the loan is booked quickly. The new account information is added to the CIS, linking the loan account with other services the customer may have. New technology, such as **imaging** software, further expedites loan booking.

When borrowers sign an electronic signature pad to execute the loan documents, banks do not use paper documentation. Electronic documents are uploaded to the bank's documentation system and stored. Borrowers may choose to have printed copies of the documents or the electronic documents may be sent to them by e-mail.

imaging—A process that captures information from, for example, a loan document or check and stores it digitally.

RECORD AND REPORT

Reports that are generated after the loan review process can strengthen the bank's consumer lending operation in many ways. They can detect, for example, if an individual loan officer regularly makes documentation errors. Management may resolve this kind of problem with additional training. Likewise, if the loan review identifies a dealer who has problems preparing contracts or resolving contract errors, the bank may decide either to remedy the problem with additional training or end the relationship.

Risk ratings on consumer loan products also are monitored to assess credit quality. The information is used to establish the bank's loan loss provision and manage consumer loan portfolios.

OBTAIN LIEN AND INSURANCE DOCUMENTS

Lien and insurance follow-up is essential for a bank to ensure that collateralized loans are secured properly. Checklists of all necessary forms and records are used to track, for example, the source, such as the state motor vehicle department or an insurance company. Monthly reports enable the loan review function to follow up when documents are late in arriving. If the state motor vehicle department normally sends the bank its lien notification within 30 days, the bank would follow up on those not received after 30 days.

LAWS AND REGULATIONS

Disclosures and documentation are a requirement of most business transactions, particularly in banking. Protecting consumers' rights and the safety and soundness of banks is a responsibility of government regulators. Almost all the laws and regulations discussed so far have disclosure, documentation, and reporting requirements. The Gramm-Leach-Bliley Act (GLBA) requires banks to make disclosures when selling or soliciting insurance sales. Another requirement, often in the news due to hurricanes and flooding in various parts of the country, addresses flood disaster protection. Still other regulations protect consumers by prohibiting banks from using unfair terms in loan agreements or unfairly taking a security interest in household goods.

INSURANCE SALES DISCLOSURES

GLBA requires lenders to make certain disclosures to consumers at the time of application and at closing when the lender cross-sells any insurance product, such as credit life insurance. These disclosures must be made orally and in writing. They inform the consumer that the purchase of insurance or the purchase of the product from the lender is not a condition of obtaining the loan. A noncoercion disclosure statement must be included. It states that the lender cannot prohibit the consumer from purchasing credit insurance from another provider.[1]

Did You Know ...

In many states the financing statement for boats used as collateral must be filed in both the borrower's county of residence and the county where the boat will be stored if that is different from the borrower's county of residence.

FLOOD DISASTER PROTECTION

Floods can damage or destroy individual homes and whole communities. Although private flood insurance policies can be costly, without insurance homeowners risk mortgage default for damage due to a flood. Recognizing the problem, the federal government created the National Flood Insurance Program (NFIP) under the Flood Disaster Protection Act of 1973 (FDPA). The program provides flood insurance to property owners in communities that participate in the program.

When a loan will be secured by improved real estate, a bank must determine whether the property is in a **special flood hazard area** (SFHA) designated by the Federal Emergency Management Agency (FEMA). If it is, the bank must determine whether the community where the property is located participates in the NFIP by consulting FEMA flood hazard maps or by hiring a flood determination expert to do so. A flood determination usually is ordered at the same time as the appraisal and must be documented on a standard FEMA form before closing. The bank is required to retain evidence that it has determined the flood status of loans on improved property.

Loans secured by improved real property in an SFHA within a participating community must have flood insurance. The requirement covers construction loans and properties like condominiums and mobile homes as well as commercial, farm, and agricultural buildings. Borrowers of qualifying loans must be notified "within a reasonable time before the completion of the loan" so that they have time to obtain the insurance.

Before loan closing, the lender must receive a written acknowledgement of disclosure of the flood insurance status from the customer. The insurance amount must be equal to the lowest of the amounts of the loan principal, the value of the appraised improved property, or the maximum insurance limit. The bank must monitor insurance throughout the loan term and notify the customer should coverage lapse; if the insurance is not renewed within 45 days, the bank must **force place** the insurance.

UNFAIR OR DECEPTIVE ACTS OR PRACTICES

FRS Regulation AA, commonly known as the Credit Practices Rule, prohibits lenders from using certain unfair or deceptive clauses in consumer loan contracts, including provisions in which the consumer by confessing judgment waives the right to a court proceeding in the case of default, or waives the right under state law that exempts property from seizure. The regulation also forbids taking a security interest on the consumer's **household goods**, unless it is a purchase-money security interest. The bank must ensure that its contracts have no prohibited clauses and that its procedures prevent taking prohibited types of collateral.[2]

special flood hazard area—Land in the flood plane within a community that has at least a 1 percent chance of flooding in any given year, as designated by the Director of FEMA.

force place—The process by which a lender purchases insurance for the borrower, usually hazard or flood insurance, on real property used to secure a loan. The premium is added to the principal of the loan. The borrower must pay all premium costs before the lender's lien on the property will be released.

household goods — Under FRS Regulation AA, Unfair or Deceptive Acts or Practices, a consumer's and the consumer's dependents' personal possessions. Not included are works of art, antiques, or jewelry other than a wedding ring.

SUMMARY

- The loan documentation and closing process is important for a sound consumer loan portfolio. The major objectives for loan documentation and closing are to: complete all required legal documents; prepare documents efficiently, accurately, and professionally; comply with regulations and bank policy; ensure the customer understands the loan's terms; create a positive image for the bank; cross-sell other bank products; and ask for referrals.

- The forms required to document a consumer lending transaction vary with the type of loan and any collateral. Loans secured by real estate require the most documentation. Unsecured closed-end loans require simply the application, the truth-in-lending disclosure statement, and the promissory note. Regardless of the type of loan, the bank will have controls to ensure that documentation is complete and accurate.

- Loan documents must be accurate and complete to establish bank and consumer rights under the loan agreement. When a loan is to be secured by collateral, the bank must perfect a security interest in the collateral. This requires an understanding of state law on perfecting liens and any special documentation requirements for collateral such as real estate, aircraft, and boats.

- The loan closing offers the lender an opportunity to create a positive image for the bank, to ensure that the consumer fully understands the loan product, and to sell other bank services. An efficient loan closing also helps to control costs.

- The loan review function in the loan operations department ensures that the loan complies with the law; examines completed documents for accuracy, completeness, and adherence to bank lending policy; resolves documentation errors; expedites the booking of new loans; records and reports management information about documentation problems and lender performance; and follows up for necessary lien and insurance documents. It also is responsible for following up on securing collateral and reporting to management.

- The Gramm-Leach-Bliley Act (GLBA) requires lenders to make disclosures when selling or soliciting insurance sales. It also requires banks selling insurance products to give consumers non-coercion notices. Banks must determine whether any improved real property taken as collateral is in a special flood hazard zone, and if so require flood insurance. FRS Regulation AA, commonly known as the Credit Practices Rule, prohibits lenders from using unfair terms in loan agreements or unfairly taking a security interest in household goods.

END NOTES

[1] Payment protection also is discussed in chapter 10.

[2] FRS Regulation AA, commonly known as the Credit Practices Rule, is discussed in detail in chapter 3.

Learning Check

SELF-CHECK AND REVIEW

1. What are the objectives of the loan documentation and closing process?

2. How does the documentation required for fixed-rate, closed-end loans differ from that for variable-rate loans?

3. Under UCC Article 9 what two steps are necessary to give the lender the right to take the collateral if the borrower defaults? Why is it important for banks to follow these steps?

4. What happens if the bank does not properly perfect its security interest on collateral pledged for a loan?

5. Why is it important to create a positive image for the bank during a loan closing? Give at least two reasons.

6. What is the purpose of loan review? What benefits does it offer the bank?

7. What is the process for ensuring that a loan secured by real estate, such as a home equity loan, has flood disaster protection, if needed?

Resources

ADDITIONAL RESOURCES

2008 Study of Banks in Insurance, American Bankers Insurance Association and Reagan Consulting, www.aba.com/ABIA/ABIAMarketplace.htm

ABA Bank Compliance Magazine, Washington: American Bankers Association, periodical.

American Bankers Association, **www.aba.com**.

Federal Aviation Administration (FAA), www.faa.gov.

Federal Aviation Administration Aircraft Registration Branch, AFS-750 PO Box 25504, Oklahoma City, OK 73125-0504.

Federal Emergency Management Agency (FEMA), www.fema.gov.

Federal Financial Institutions Examination Council, reports on HMDA and CRA ratings, www.ffiec.gov.

Law and Banking, Washington: American Bankers Association, 2008.

"Merchant Vessels of the United States" (CG408), list of U.S. merchant and recreational vessels documented under the laws of the United States, National Technical Information Services (NTIS), Springfield, VA, www.ntis.gov.

Reference Guide to Regulatory Compliance, Washington: American Bankers
    Association, updated annually.

Uniform Commercial Code (UCC), www.law.cornell.edu/ucc.

U.S. Coast Guard, www.uscg.mil.

*When Your Home Is on the Line: What You Should Know About Home Equity
    Lines of Credit*, www.federalreserve.gov/Pubs/HomeLine.

Collection and Recovery

Learning Objectives

After completing this chapter, you should be able to

- explain the objectives, activities, and organization of the collection and recovery functions
- discuss factors contributing to consumer loan delinquencies
- describe the stages and strategies of the collection cycle
- explain the consumer protections afforded by the Fair Debt Collection Practices Act and the Servicemembers Civil Relief Act
- define Bankruptcy Code Chapter 7 and Chapter 13 and the changes made by the Bankruptcy Abuse Prevention and Consumer Protection Act
- define the terms that appear in bold type in the text

Introduction

"Debt, grinding debt, whose iron face the widow, the orphan, and the sons of genius fear and hate; debt, which consumes so much time, which so cripples and disheartens a great spirit with cares that seem so base, is a preceptor whose lessons cannot be forgone, and is needed most by those who suffer from it most."
(Ralph Waldo Emerson, 1803–1882)

One would expect Emerson to have such a grim view on debt: Life was much more precarious in the nineteenth century. Consumers did not have the vast array of manageable consumer loan products and the legal protections now afforded to them by both federal and state law.

Managing debt is the primary responsibility of borrowers and lenders. However, the government and the agencies that oversee the safety and soundness of important commercial enterprises, such as banks, have an interest as well. When borrowers and lenders manage debt well, the wheels of commerce function efficiently and the economy benefits. When they do not, the unfortunate results ripple throughout the economy and touch everyone. Such events were illustrated in the financial crisis of 2008 that resulted in large numbers of foreclosures, the demise of long-standing financial corporations, a spike in unemployment, and a world recession. [1]

By lending funds to consumers and businesses, banks enhance commercial activity. As businesses with fiduciary responsibility to their depositors and investors, banks also protect assets and earnings by monitoring their contracts with borrowers, collecting outstanding debts, and recovering outstanding losses.

OBJECTIVES OF COLLECTION AND RECOVERY

collection function— The bank area primarily responsible for following up on past due accounts.

recovery function— The bank area responsible for collecting whatever repayment is possible on a charged-off loan.

Loan collection and recovery are essential to consumer loan operations. The **collection function** of the bank collects payments from consumers who are delinquent—those who make payments later than their contractual due date. The **recovery function** collects money still owed on accounts after the bank has charged them off as a loss. These functions help preserve the quality of the consumer loan portfolio and avoid unnecessary loss of revenue.

The primary objectives of the collection and recovery functions are to keep loan delinquencies and losses within acceptable limits, generate recoveries at desired levels, counsel customers who are having difficulty handling debt, ensure consistency with bank objectives, and manage their own costs effectively. These objectives are determined by the loan policies that guide banks in assessing loan quality and evaluating the performance of the collection and recovery functions as well as the lending function.

KEEP DELINQUENCY LEVELS ACCEPTABLE

The collection function contacts customers who are behind in their payments (delinquent), but whose loans are still active, to arrange for payment on the amount due. For each type of product in the loan portfolio, management decides what **delinquency rates** are acceptable. Generally, the delinquency objective is defined as a maximum percentage of the portfolio that can be in default, such as "1.5 percent delinquency rate for direct closed-end loans."

Management strives for lower delinquency rates; higher rates indicate problems that may require adjustments to the lending program. A portfolio delinquency objective of less than 1 percent is regarded as conservative; an objective of more than 3 percent is aggressive or liberal.

Both internal and external factors can affect delinquencies, the rates of which tend to vary with the type of loan, the season, and economic conditions generally.

Type of Loan

Of the six types of loans listed in exhibit 13.1, unsecured loans (credit card, revolving, and personal loans) have the highest delinquency rates. Secured loans usually have the lowest, because customers tend to make these payments first to avoid the risk of losing their homes, vehicles, or other valuable property.

delinquency rate—
The percentage of either dollar amount or number of loan accounts that is past due by 30 days or more. *Also known as* delinquency percentage or delinquency ratio.

Exhibit 13.1 Consumer Credit Delinquency Percent Delinquent—National Averages						
TYPE OF LOAN	**JULY %**		**AUGUST %**		**SEPTEMBER %**	
	#	$	#	$	#	$
Unsecured, closed-end	2.63	2.63	2.74	2.68	2.79	2.80
Automobile—direct	1.64	1.47	1.79	1.59	1.75	1.54
Automobile—indirect	3.13	2.76	3.29	2.90	3.5	3.06
Home equity, closed-end	2.50	2.13	2.60	2.33	2.65	2.49
Credit cards	4.04	4.34	4.18	4.49	4.28	4.74
Home equity, open-ended	1.07	1.62	1.11	1.68	1.16	1.74

Source: ABA Consumer Credit Delinquency Bulletin, 3rd Quarter 2008. Percentages based on total number of accounts and total of outstanding balances.

Situation

Donna started a new job this year. Her salary gives her enough money to cover her living expenses, make her monthly auto payment, and allow for some savings. For the first time, she feels she can use her credit card to buy nice Christmas gifts for family and friends. She knows that her income will allow her to pay for the purchases over a few months. When Donna gets her first post-Christmas credit card bill, however, she realizes that the interest rate on her credit card is higher than the interest rate on her auto loan. She decides to use her auto payment money to pay off her credit card and skip a month on her auto payment. She is concerned when a "past due" notice arrives in the mail.

Is the lender really worried that she will not pay off her loan?

charge-off—The amount of principal and interest on a loan that is written off the bank's books when the bank no longer expects to be able to collect it.

benchmark—A standard or rule to which other items or processes can be compared.

Seasonal Factors

There are seasonal delinquency patterns in every bank's market area. Many banks experience rising delinquencies in the fourth quarter of the year, when heavy retail buying for the holiday season puts a strain on family budgets.

Economic Conditions

Defaults and losses usually increase during recessionary or stagnant economic cycles when more people are unemployed, or when inflation outstrips income. The delinquency rate tends to fall when interest rates are lower, because consumers are refinancing higher-rate debt with new lower-rate loans. Ideally, banks respond proactively to expected economic changes. They tighten credit standards before a recession begins, for example, rather than chase rising delinquencies as the economy declines.

KEEP LOAN LOSS LEVELS ACCEPTABLE

The objective of recovery is to keep loan losses within acceptable limits. Management may set loan-loss objectives either for the total portfolio or by individual product. The difference between gross loss and net loss is the amount recovered from consumers through the recovery process after loans have been **charged off**. A significant difference represents a large recovery for the bank. Exhibit 13.2 illustrates the variation in losses for different loan products as reported by the Federal Reserve for the commercial banking industry.

Loan losses tend to follow patterns that track the economy, rising during recessionary periods and falling when the economy is stronger. Loan losses increased, for example, in the late 1980s, early 1990s, late 2000, and 2008. Charge-off rates tend to move in unison with delinquency rates; thus, a higher delinquency rate normally means higher losses.

GENERATE LOSS RECOVERIES

If the collection function is unsuccessful in securing payment on a delinquent loan, the loan is charged off as a loss to the bank, but the bank still makes recovery efforts. The amount of money collected from customers whose accounts have been charged off is a **benchmark** for measuring both the performance of the recovery function and total portfolio quality. Banks benefit by recovering losses because, once loans are charged off the books, the money recovered goes directly to net income.

COUNSEL CUSTOMERS EXPERIENCING DIFFICULTY

Although it is important to set quantifiable goals for the collection and recovery functions, it is also important to recognize the qualitative aspects of loan collection. Successful collectors usually are good salespeople and good financial counselors.

Exhibit 13.2 Residential and Consumer Credit Charge-Offs Commercial Banks, 4th Quarter 2008

TYPE OF LOAN	TOTAL OUTSTANDING[1] (BILLIONS OF DOLLARS)	DOLLARS CHARGED OFF[2] %	AMOUNT CHARGED OFF (BILLIONS OF DOLLARS)
Residential real estate			
Revolving home equity	592.00		
Other residential	1,496.60		
Total	**2,088.60**	1.62%	**33.84**
Consumer credit cards and other revolving credit lines	403.10	6.30%	25.40
Consumer credit —other	891.80	2.91%	25.95
Total	**1,294.90**		**51.35**

[1] Federal Reserve Statistical Release H-8, February 13, 2009, "Assets and Liabilities of Commercial Banks in the United States," not seasonally adjusted, www.federalreserve.gov/releases/h8/20090213.

[2] Federal Reserve *Charge off and Delinquency Rates on Loans and Leases at Commercial Banks*, 4th quarter 2008, www.federalreserve.gov/releases/chargeoff/delallnsa.htm.
Residential real estate loans include loans secured by one- to four-family properties, including home equity lines of credit, booked in domestic offices only. Charge-offs, which are the value of loans removed from the books and charged against loss reserves, are measured net of recoveries as a percentage of average loans and annualized.

They must "sell" customers on making payments and can counsel consumers on how to manage their finances to achieve a workable repayment schedule. This is true especially when they are collecting unsecured loan payments. Collectors must try to retain customer goodwill despite the difficult relationship situation. Their sales and counseling skills can contribute over time to lower losses and delinquencies.

Not surprisingly, many collectors go on to have very successful careers in other areas of the bank. Collecting payments requires a special ability to work with people. This ability transfers to other areas, especially sales. Many banks now include collections in their management training programs and view successful collectors as management prospects.

ENSURE CONSISTENCY WITH BANK OBJECTIVES

Many banks set loan delinquency and loss objectives in conjunction with other product line objectives. For example, if a bank is embarking on an aggressive marketing program to promote its credit cards and is liberalizing its lending policies, it must plan for higher delinquencies and losses and may want to budget more resources for collection. It is unlikely that a bank can liberalize its lending standards without lowering the quality of its assets.

Did You Know ...

Each bank must maintain an Allowance for Loan and Lease Losses (ALLL) liability account that is adequate to offset the estimated credit losses associated with the loan and lease portfolio (the loans and leases that the bank has the intent and ability to hold for the foreseeable future or until maturity or payoff).

The collections and recovery functions follow policies put in place by senior management, including the asset and liability committee (ALCO), and approved by the bank board of directors. Although a bank's ALCO focuses on loan and deposit pricing and net interest margin, it also monitors portfolio quality for delinquencies, charge-offs, losses, and recoveries. Monitoring provides information to support management and ALCO recommendations for policies on loan product and pricing strategy.

MANAGE COLLECTION AND RECOVERY COSTS

The final objective is to accomplish collection and recovery as cost-efficiently as possible. Automated collection systems help to keep costs under control and improve efficiency and productivity. Automated dialing machines linked to online terminals enhance collection results by maximizing contact with delinquent customers. Another cost-efficient technique is flextime scheduling that matches collection staff schedules with times when customers can be reached, usually 5:00 p.m. to 9:00 p.m.

At the individual loan level, collectors compare the expected costs of each collection technique with the potential for recovery: The collector who spends $250 repossessing an automobile worth the same amount has wasted time and effort without reducing the loan's outstanding balance. Similarly, it is difficult to justify the cost of attempting to recover a $250 loss from a customer who has left the market area and has no job or assets. It might be better to target higher-value accounts with more potential for recovery.

Collection procedures are structured to keep costs low. Low-cost, computer-generated notices, automatically sent to all past-due accounts, help reduce the number of delinquencies before expensive personal contacts are needed.

Banks periodically outsource some accounts, or even their entire collection portfolio, to collection agencies. To be cost-efficient they also may outsource repossession of vehicles.

Objectives for Collections and Recovery

- Keep delinquencies within acceptable limits.
- Keep loan losses within acceptable limits.
- Generate loss recoveries at desired levels.
- Counsel customers who are having difficulty handling debt.
- Ensure consistency with bank objectives.
- Manage the collection and recovery functions cost-effectively.

CAUSES OF DELINQUENCY

To appreciate the challenges of the collection process, it is helpful to understand what causes customers to default. Some customers simply abuse credit and feel no obligation to pay their debts, but most delinquencies are caused by unexpected events that change the consumer's income or debt situation, economic downturns, excessive debt, poor money management skills, and marital problems. Others are caused by the consumer's carelessness, changing attitudes toward credit, irresponsible lending, fraud or intentional default, substance abuse, and gambling.

UNEXPECTED CHANGES IN FINANCIAL SITUATION

Unexpected problems that lead to either a decrease in income or an increase in expenses are a major cause of delinquency. Examples are illness or physical disability, job layoff or termination, unplanned major expenses, or death. These changes may alter the customer's ability to repay a loan for a short or a long period. Careful examination of the facts is necessary to determine the best possible remedy for each problem loan.

ECONOMIC DOWNTURN

A downturn in economic conditions—local, regional, or national—will affect the business environment, resulting in job losses and layoffs. Consumers who are victims of economic downturns will have difficulty meeting loan obligations, so delinquency rates will rise. That is why employment rates in the community affect the quality of consumer loan portfolios.

EXCESSIVE DEBT

In recent years, consumers have increased their debt, which in many cases has reduced their capacity to pay. When debts become too large for their income, consumers cannot make loan payments when they are due. At best, the consumer may be able to make only minimum monthly payments and eventually may need to choose which loans to repay.

When financial problems arise, most consumers have a priority order for loan repayments:

- mortgage or rent
- other primary residence–secured loans, such as a home equity line of credit
- automobile loan
- other secured loan, such as for a recreational vehicle
- credit card account
- unsecured closed-end loan
- unsecured open-end line of credit other than a credit card

This priority order of repayment helps explain why delinquency objectives and collection experiences vary by type of product.

POOR MONEY MANAGEMENT

Poor money management is revealed in many ways. Failure to plan for financial emergencies, establish a reasonable budget, and organize finances, or a lack of self-control when purchasing goods—all contribute to financial problems. Lenders may detect poor financial management by examining the consumer's credit history and capacity when the loan request is investigated and evaluated. In many cases, however, problems do not appear until after a loan closes.

Causes of Delinquency

- unexpected changes in the consumer's income or debt situation
- economic downturns
- excessive debt
- poor money management skills
- marital and other family problems
- carelessness and changing attitudes toward credit
- irresponsible lending
- fraud or intentional default
- substance abuse and gambling

MARITAL PROBLEMS

Marital breakups often leave both parties scrambling to manage their debts. An income and debt structure that was in balance when the couple was one financial unit may be disrupted after the marriage ends. Some marital breakups reduce income or increase debts to the point where they are unmanageable. One of the parties may deny responsibility for the debts.

CARELESSNESS AND CHANGING ATTITUDES

Carelessness leads to some delinquencies. Those who can pay but are not strongly motivated to pay, on time are simply casual about repaying debts. Such consumers have credit histories with delinquencies for which there is no financial reason. Carelessness is evidence that the consumer fails to attend to financial responsibilities. It reflects poor character.

Carelessness also represents a changing attitude toward financial responsibilities and personal debt management. Many consumers are casual in their commitment to honor debt obligations and feel they have nothing to lose by defaulting on a loan. This behavior has resulted in increased numbers of bankruptcies and the enactment of the Bankruptcy Abuse Prevention and Consumer Protection Act of 2005, by which Congress meant to change consumer debt-management behavior.

IRRESPONSIBLE LENDING

Occasionally, a loan in default should never have been made. A lender may have failed to follow the bank's policies or to investigate adequately the consumer's credit history. A common factor is pressure to achieve bank growth goals, which can lead to rationalizing bad credit decisions. The result may be loans with chronic collection problems or losses. Predatory lending practices and poorly underwritten loans are examples of irresponsible lending. Although they sometimes may be legal, they are not in the best interest of the customer or the bank.

FRAUD OR INTENTIONAL DEFAULT

Fraud or intentional default is a deliberate attempt to avoid repaying an obligation. Most fraud is uncovered by the collection function after an account already has been booked and the culprit has the bank's money. When detected, these loans typically are removed from the main collection process and given to a specialist, such as the bank's chief security officer or a law enforcement agency.

SUBSTANCE ABUSE AND GAMBLING

Some consumers have difficulties that drain family resources and may reduce their ability to earn a living, such as substance abuse or a gambling addiction. People in crisis rarely place a high priority on repaying debts. Delinquencies resulting from such crises present special challenges for collectors.

THE COLLECTION AND RECOVERY FUNCTIONS

The collection function encourages consumers in the early stages of delinquency to make their payments. When those efforts become futile, the loan is charged off the bank's books and referred to the recovery function. The organization, objectives, and strategies of these two functions differ.

THE COLLECTION FUNCTION

The collection function's goals are to keep delinquencies and losses to acceptable levels, get accounts current as quickly as possible, and retain customer goodwill. The approach taken usually reflects the bank's strategy, organizational structure, and size. In a centralized operation, collection specialists devote their full attention to resolving delinquency problems. Because they acquire considerable expertise, these specialists become highly efficient and effective in handling delinquency problems. The centralized approach also leaves lenders free to grow new business using up-front risk control tools, such as credit scoring.

In a decentralized environment, lenders and other employees handle collection tasks in addition to their other duties. Some banks prefer the decentralized approach because when they must collect loans they have approved, lenders learn to use more discretion in making lending decisions; moreover, lenders who are familiar with a delinquent customer may be more effective in collecting payment.

Whether centralized or decentralized, the collection process must function efficiently. The essentials of a collections operation are

- early identification of delinquent accounts

- an automated system to spot delinquencies early

- a means of obtaining information so that collectors can work intelligently with delinquent customers

- a system for tracking customer contacts and monitoring repayment promises

- isolation of serious loan problems for the attention of specialized collectors

RECOVERY OPERATIONS

Because the recovery function is concerned solely with collecting money that has been charged off to loan loss, it operates differently from the collection function. For example, the recovery function will search for assets to attach through a lien, with the consent of the customer; the recovery specialist appeals to the customer's goodwill to sell some assets and use the proceeds to pay off the loan.

Did You Know ...

In the collection of debt, there is a good way and a bad way to ask questions of the customer in order to obtain information.

Bad way: "When are you going to make the payment?" or "When am I going to get my money?" This approach is aggressive, with a negative tone.

Good way: "Mr. Jones, I notice that the payment on your auto loan is past due. Can you tell me if you are having a problem and when you will be able to make the payment?" This approach is customer-oriented and conveys empathy.

Sometimes accounts are referred to attorneys and collection agencies. These experts either charge a flat fee or work on a commission, keeping a percentage of the amount collected, usually up to half. The bank must monitor the performance and methods of outside collection agencies and attorneys to ensure recovery efforts are legal and meet bank goals.

The recovery specialist, whether a bank employee or an outside agent, first attempts to work directly with the customer to arrange for repayment of the debt. The specialist will sometimes settle for a lump sum that may be less than the balance owed, such as accepting $750 for a $1,000 debt if the smaller amount is paid by a certain date. However, recovery specialists generally try to recover the full amount owed.

If repayment cannot be arranged, the recovery specialist next attempts to locate any assets the customer has that might be claimed to settle the debt. The initial credit application can be helpful here, particularly if it includes a personal financial statement, tax returns, or similar information, such as the location of bank accounts. The search for assets is directed to tangible property, such as automobiles, houses, and boats; financial holdings, such as checking and savings accounts, stocks, and bonds; and sources of income. Any of these may provide the secondary resources needed to collect a bad debt.

Once assets are located, collection is pursued through direct contact and legal action, which together can persuade customers to settle their debts, even after the loan is charged off.

As with collection, the cost of recovery must be balanced against the potential gain. It does not make sense to spend time and money on accounts when chances of recovery are slim or when the balance owed is small—better to target the accounts that offer the best chance of recovery and the highest possible dollar value.

THE COLLECTION CYCLE

The vast majority of consumer loan customers make their payments on time. Of those who do default, the majority pay within 15 days of the due date. Those who do not pay within that time are the focus of most collection activity.

There are four stages in the **collection cycle**: early stage, personal contact, serious delinquency, and charge-off. Exhibit 13.3 illustrates the stages in the cycle for a typical closed-end loan. Open-end accounts, which generally have a longer cycle, are not charged off until 180 days after they become due.

Exhibit 13.4 illustrates the distribution of accounts at each stage of the collection cycle. The percentage of accounts entering the process may seem high, but payment often is made before the bank takes any action. Most borrowers respond to notices and the imposition of late charges, paying their accounts before or soon after the 15-day past-due point. Thus, by the time collectors are involved, delinquent accounts have been reduced to a manageable number.

collection cycle—The stages of and processes for handling delinquent accounts from the first date of delinquency through charge-off.

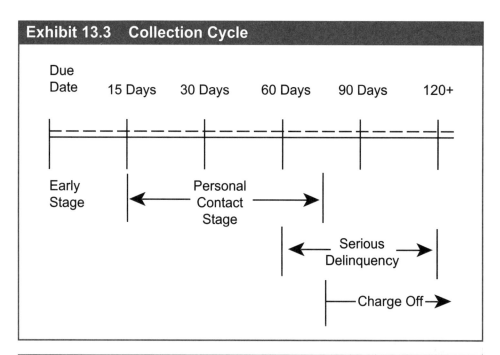

Exhibit 13.3 Collection Cycle

Due Date | 15 Days | 30 Days | 60 Days | 90 Days | 120+

Early Stage

Personal Contact Stage

Serious Delinquency

Charge Off

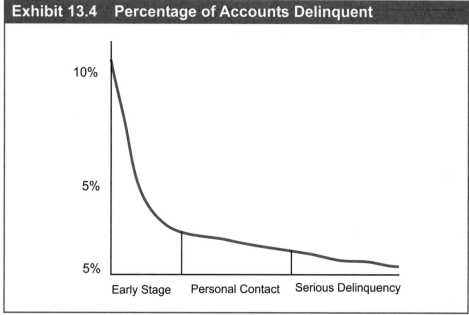

Exhibit 13.4 Percentage of Accounts Delinquent

10%

5%

5%

Early Stage   Personal Contact   Serious Delinquency

EARLY STAGE

Most accounts in default one day or more do not pose a significant problem. The primary objective in the early stage is to collect as many past-due accounts as possible before the problem becomes serious. The early stage of collection, which is automated, requires little personal involvement and is less costly than the other stages.

Letters, reminder notices, late charges, simple interest, and due-date adjustments are collection tools used at the early stage. A simple, inexpensive reminder notice, usually the first formal action, brings in many payments. The notice may be very low key, and may even have a sales-oriented message.

Tools of Early Stage Collection

- letters
- reminder notices
- late charges
- raising the simple interest rate
- due-date adjustments

Personal Contact Stage
Collection Remedies

- payment collection plan
- loan extension
- loan refinancing
- new loan
- insurance claim
- right of setoff
- consumer credit counseling

Delinquency notices on closed-end accounts typically are mailed 10 days after the due date. For an open-end account, the billing statement usually carries a notice to the customer that the payment is past due.

Late charges imposed generally 10 to 15 days after the payment due date are another incentive for customers to make payments on time. Changes in simple interest also encourage on-time payment. Customers who understand that late payments will cost more because of interest charges and other penalties are predisposed to make payments as soon as possible.

Due-date adjustments often are effective on closed-end loans when the due date coincides with a monthly shortfall in customer cash flow. If the customer is paying twice a month, for example, and the loan payment is due at the same time as the mortgage payment, the customer may have difficulty making both payments from the same paycheck. By changing the due date, the bank reduces its costs, and the customer avoids late notices and late charges. This problem is not severe for open-end accounts because customers often have a grace period of about 25 days in which to make payments and can plan the payments to match their cash flow.

PERSONAL CONTACT STAGE

The collection effort is more intensive when an account is more than 15 days past due. At this point, a collector personally contacts the customer to try to resolve the problem in an acceptable manner. The personal contact continues until the delinquency is resolved, by bringing the account current, paying it off, refinancing it, or charging it off.

Telephone calls and letters are the primary methods of communicating with customers in the personal contact stage of the collection cycle. Talking with the customer generally is preferable to sending letters because more information can be obtained and the collector has the opportunity to work with the customer.

At this stage, problem-solving is an important collection practice. The collector identifies the reasons for the late payments and then determines how and when the payment can be made. The key is to identify the problem and find the best solution. Some problems are temporary, others are chronic, but assessing the nature and depth of the problems is important to determining and offering viable solutions. Typical remedies are a payment collection arrangement, loan extension, loan refinancing, a new loan, an insurance claim, right of setoff, and consumer credit counseling.

Payment Collection

Collectors resolve the majority of delinquencies by having the customer make the delinquent payment by an agreed date. Collectors attempt to establish exactly when the customer will be able to make the past-due payment; why the payment will be made on that date (perhaps because

> ### *Situation*
>
> Carlton's loan payment is 20 days past due. When Tracy, the bank's collector, calls him, Carlton says he will make his payment on Friday. When she asks, "Why Friday?" Carlton says that he gets paid on Friday. Tracy then asks, "How will you be making your payment?" to which Carlton replies that he will bring the payment to the Main Street branch.
>
> *Why did Tracy ask these questions?*

it is payday); and how the payment will be made, such as by personal delivery to the bank or by mail.

Loan Extensions

A loan **extension** is another collection remedy. This approach allows the customer to postpone or skip a payment. On a closed-end loan, the bank may postpone payment until the end of the loan's term, usually increasing the term by one month. For example, the customer may skip a June payment and resume regular payments in July. For open-end lines of credit, when customers miss a payment they are charged a fee or additional interest for an extension.

Granting an extension is an appropriate collection remedy when the customer misses one or two payments but is expected to resume normal payments and make up the delinquent payments. For example, a customer who is laid off temporarily due to a short-term plant closing may not be able to meet all debt obligations. After the layoff, the customer may be able to make payments on time but cannot make up the delinquent payment. Granting an extension resolves the delinquency and preserves customer goodwill.

Extensions are controlled by the manager of the collection function but they are monitored by management, because collectors who are looking for easy ways to reduce the number of past-due accounts may use extensions too liberally, a practice that may hide serious delinquency problems. In addition, bank regulators take a dim view of liberal extension policies that may undermine portfolio safety and soundness.

Refinancing

An appropriate collection remedy if the customer is facing a cash flow squeeze and needs to reduce debt payments is **refinancing**. Refinancing reduces the customer's monthly payment, extends the number of payments, and may allow the bank to add collateral to the loan. This solution works well when a customer has changed jobs and has less income and therefore a higher debt-to-income ratio. Assuming the customer has a good credit history and the bank is able to reduce the monthly payments, refinancing may be the best collection remedy.

New Loan

Assuming the cause of the delinquency was a short-term problem that is being resolved and that the customer has no other credit issues, such as an excessive debt-to-income ratio, a new loan is a workable solution to some collection problems. Not only does it resolve many minor delinquency problems, it positively affects loan volume and customer relations. Debt consolidation loans can reduce both payments and interest rates for a customer.

Insurance Claims

Some delinquencies are resolved by filing accident and health credit-insurance claims. If the customer is delinquent because he or she has been out of work

extension—A delinquency remedy that allows the customer to defer loan payments for a specified time, such as 30 days. For a closed-end loan, the account is brought up to date and the missed payments are added to the term of the loan, extending the maturity. *Also known as* re-aging an account.

refinance—The rewriting of a closed-end loan to reduce monthly payments or change interest rates or other terms. It is a collection remedy.

Situation

Betty Adams is 21 days late with her loan payment. In response to collector Steven's call, Betty apologizes and says she will make the payment today. She explains that she had to pay for auto repairs, which is becoming a more common occurrence for her old automobile. Steven responds by telling Betty about the bank's new auto rates, which are very low right now. He encourages Betty to consider purchasing a new automobile so she will not have to keep pouring money into the old auto.

Why would the collector suggest a new loan to Betty Adams?

right of setoff—A provision in loan contracts that allows the lender to use funds deposited in the borrower's accounts for payment of delinquent loans.

skip tracing—The process of locating debtors who have stopped making loan payments and cannot be located through their last known address or employer.

due to illness or injury, the collector will check for credit disability insurance. If the customer has the insurance, the collector may arrange to have a claim form processed. Potential credit-life insurance claims are pursued in a similar manner. To preserve goodwill in these circumstances, it is important for collectors to act on claims with discretion and sensitivity.

Right of Setoff

Some loan contracts give the bank the **right of setoff**. If state law allows, setoff enables the bank to withdraw funds the consumer has on deposit with the bank to make delinquent payments or pay the loan in full. Because the right of setoff has other repercussions for the customer's relationship with the bank, it is used only as a last resort. To avoid creating overdrafts, the customer is notified immediately when this action is taken. Credit card issuers, however, cannot offset delinquent credit card accounts against deposits.

Consumer Credit Counseling

Another remedy is to refer customers to a qualified credit counseling agency that assists consumers who are deeply in debt. Counselors work with the customer and the bank to devise a repayment schedule in order to avoid serious problems, such as bankruptcy. The bank must be sure the counseling services it works with are reputable.

SERIOUS DELINQUENCY

Many collection functions let less experienced collectors handle accounts that are only 16 to 30 days past due and give more experienced collectors responsibility for seriously delinquent accounts. Generally, the longer a loan is in default, the more time and skill are required to resolve the problem.

The serious delinquency stage may occur at any time, depending on the customer's circumstances. However, most collectors feel that any account more than 60 days in default is a serious problem. Serious delinquencies most often arise when customers declare bankruptcy; move in an effort to hide from creditors; die, leaving behind uninsured debt; or simply lose all regard for their responsibilities. These events may occur at any stage of the collection cycle, sometimes even before a customer is delinquent.

Third-party experts who specialize in **skip tracing**, fraud, or bankruptcy cases may handle seriously delinquent accounts requiring special attention. These trained personnel have the time and knowledge to handle the accounts effectively, freeing the bank to address more routine collection activities. Serious delinquency cases, such as fraud and bankruptcy cases, require time-consuming and structured follow-up.

Banks often enlist agencies that specialize in repossessing collateral, which is a sometimes dangerous and usually unpleasant task. They may hire attorneys and collection agencies to handle customers who are not responding to the bank's collection staff. A letter or a personal call from an attorney often has more effect on the delinquent customer than the efforts of the bank's collectors. Collection remedies for seriously delinquent accounts include repossession and collection lawsuits resulting in judgments, foreclosure, and wage garnishment.

Repossession

When the consumer is uncooperative and the bank stands to recover some or all of its investment, **repossession** of collateral is an appropriate collection remedy. Most states have laws that govern a consumer's rights when a creditor seeks to repossess collateral. The consumer usually has the right to redeem the collateral by paying the balance in full plus all expenses. If the consumer does not redeem the collateral, the bank may sell it and apply the proceeds to the loan balance. The customer usually remains liable for any balance owed after the sale.

Collection Lawsuits

Another option is to sue. If the bank establishes its claim and proves the consumer is liable for the balance due on the account, it will be granted a judgment. The judgment allows the bank to place a claim against the assets of the consumer.

Foreclosure

Because of the consequences of **foreclosure**, state laws regulate the procedures used. Proceeds from the sale of property are generally distributed based on the order of claim: First mortgages are paid in full first, then second and subsequent mortgages, and lastly **judgments**. If the proceeds cover all debts and expenses, any excess must go to the consumer. This also is true for the sale of repossessed merchandise. Variations in state law can affect the distribution process.

Wage Garnishments

Some states allow creditors to use **wage garnishment** to recover debts. A garnishment requires the consumer's employer to send a certain percentage of the employee's wages directly to the lender until the debt is paid in full. This is a forceful incentive for consumers to work out their delinquency problems before they become serious.

CHARGE-OFFS

Although charging off accounts as a loss is the final stage in the loan collection cycle, it is not the end of the bank's efforts to collect. The collection manager reviews all accounts to be charged off during the month in order to check on the progress of the collection effort, evaluate alternatives to charge-offs, and inform management of the dollar amount of loans scheduled for charge-off. Managers may recognize some account losses even though the accounts may not be at the required charge-off point. A loan may be charged off as a loss when the collateral has been sold and there is no hope for recovery, even when the account is less than 120 days past due.

Collection Remedies for Seriously Delinquent Accounts

- repossession
- collection suits resulting in judgments
- foreclosure
- wage garnishment

---

repossession—The act of taking possession of property or goods given as security on a loan when the borrower has defaulted.

foreclosure—A legal procedure that allows a creditor to sell real estate held as collateral on a loan if the borrower defaults.

judgment—A sum due for payment or collection as a result of a court order.

wage garnishment—A court order that requires an employer to withhold a portion of an employee's wages to pay a creditor. *Also known as* wage attachment.

By The Numbers

Calculating Loan Loss

New loan volume x Loan loss rate
= Loan loss reserve account increase

$1,000 X 1.0% = $10

For every $1,000 of new loan volume,
$10 is added to the loan loss reserve account.

Did You Know ...

Bankruptcy laws predate U.S. law. The first English bankruptcy law was enacted in 1570 in the reign of Henry VIII. Early American bankruptcy laws were patterned after the English law.

Bankruptcy Code— The federal law that governs legal proceedings for those who are no longer able to pay their debts.

When an account is charged off, steps are taken to report the loss to consumer reporting agencies and plan for future recovery efforts. The collector who has been working on the account may have some guidance that will help the recovery function move quickly and efficiently.

Accounts recognized as losses are charged against the bank's loan-loss reserve account (see exhibit 13.5): As each new loan is made, a percentage of the dollar volume is set aside or added to the loan-loss reserve account based on the bank's loss experience and other factors. The balance in the loan loss account declines as individual loan accounts are charged off. The loan-loss reserve account is a reduction in loans receivable on the bank's balance sheet.

BANKRUPTCY

Bankruptcy is a significant problem for banks, individual consumers, and society. Unfortunately, the problem is growing. Recently there have been more than one million consumer bankruptcies a year in the United States (see exhibit 13.6).

The magnitude of the problem is great. Each year a large percentage of credit card losses are due to bankruptcy. Deeply in debt and unable or unwilling to pay debts when due, borrowers may resort to filing for bankruptcy. Although it is an event to be avoided, borrowers sometimes find it necessary to seek the protection of the bankruptcy laws, often due to circumstances beyond their control, such as medical emergencies.

Federal and state bankruptcy laws were enacted to eliminate the destructive aspects of earlier, more punitive practices, such as debtors' prisons. The intent was to rehabilitate debtors and at the same time treat creditors fairly. Subsequent legislation has attempted to balance these two objectives.

The **Bankruptcy Code** provides options for consumers. Chapter 7, Liquidation, and Chapter 13, Adjustment of Debts of an Individual with Regular Income, are the two types of bankruptcy most commonly used by consumers. Chapter 11,

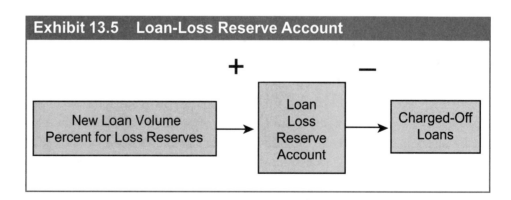

Exhibit 13.5   Loan-Loss Reserve Account

Exhibit 13.6 Nonbusiness Bankruptcy Petitions

	TOTAL	CHAPTER 7	CHAPTER 11	CHAPTER 13
1980	287,463	215,460	471	71,532
1985	341,189	237,610	2,976	100,603
1990	718,107	506,940	2,501	208,666
1995	874,642	597,048	1,369	276,225
2000	1,217,972	838,885	687	378,400
2001	1,452,030	1,031,493	783	419,750
2002	1,539,111	1,087,602	984	450,516
2003	1,625,208	1,156,274	930	467,999
2004	1,563,145	1,117,766	946	444,428
2005	1,748,421	1,322,888	861	424,667
2006	617,232	360,890	5,163	251,179
2007	850,488	519,364	6,353	324,771
2008	1,042,609	679,982	8,799	353,828

Source: Administrative Office of the U.S. Courts.

Reorganization, applies mainly to corporations but also to individuals with large incomes or debts. Chapter 12, Adjustment of Debts of a Family Farmer with Regular Income, applies to family farmers whose gross income is at least 50 percent farm-dependent and whose debts are at least 50 percent farm-related.

CHAPTER 7, LIQUIDATION

Liquidation under Chapter 7 is the most common type of bankruptcy proceeding. In this process, all of a debtor's assets are collected and converted to cash, which is distributed among the creditors according to the type and amount of their claims. Then the debtor is **discharged** from indebtedness.

Generally, a debtor with income above the state median is not allowed to file a Chapter 7 bankruptcy. If a debtor does not meet the income test, the filing is likely to be dismissed or converted to a Chapter 13 procedure, unless proven special circumstances prevent the debtor from paying legally specified amounts over a five-year period. A person filing under Chapter 7 must **reaffirm** or **redeem** a secured loan or surrender the property within a specified period after the filing. State laws allow consumers to exempt many assets from distribution to creditors.

The bankruptcy law allows consumers to redeem some property for personal, family, or household use. Secured creditors are protected only up to the value of the collateral as determined by the court. Thus, if the bank has an automobile loan with a balance of $10,000 but the auto's value is determined to be $6,000, the debtor could pay $6,000 and keep the automobile, and the bank would likely take a $4,000 nonrecoverable loss. Unsecured creditors are likely to suffer a total loss of the loan balance.

discharge—Under the Bankruptcy Code, the release from the legal obligation to pay certain debts.

reaffirmation—Upon consent of the creditor with a secured interest, a bankrupt debtor may keep personal property pledged as collateral by promising to repay the underlying debt, even when the debt is greater than the value of the collateral.

redemption—The right of the bankrupt debtor to recover collateral abandoned by the bankruptcy court trustee by paying either the remaining amount owed or the value of the collateral.

Situation

First National Bank has a valid security interest in Barry Hanover's automobile, which Barry bought as transportation for his family. Barry failed to make his payments and his loan was charged off. First National's recovery specialist repossessed the automobile. Barry filed for a Chapter 7 bankruptcy. The debt that the auto secures is $15,000 and the auto is worth $12,000.

What can Barry do to get the automobile back?

automatic stay—
The Bankruptcy Code requirement that once a bankruptcy petition is filed, creditors must halt any recovery efforts except through the bankruptcy court.

proof of claim—A document filed by the creditor during bankruptcy proceedings that identifies both the creditor and the amount the creditor asserts is owed by the debtor.

Voluntary and Involuntary Liquidation

Chapter 7 liquidation petitions may be voluntary or involuntary. In a voluntary liquidation, the debtor files the bankruptcy petition. When creditors file the petition against the debtor, the involuntary liquidation ensures that the debtor's assets are distributed according to Bankruptcy Code priorities.

To initiate a voluntary liquidation, the debtor files a petition with the clerk of a federal bankruptcy court. The petition has a

- schedule (list) of the debtor's assets and debts
- statement of the debtor's financial affairs with questions answered by the debtor
- schedule of the debtor's current income and expenses
- list of the debtor's creditors to be notified

When the petition is filed, the bankruptcy court places an **automatic stay** against further debt collection: Once notified of the proceedings, creditors must halt any efforts to obtain payment directly from the debtor or to foreclose or sell collateral. The creditor must go through the bankruptcy court and file a **proof of claim**.

CHAPTER 13, ADJUSTMENT OF DEBTS

This chapter, also known as a "wage-earner plan," is an alternative for consumers who sincerely want to repay debts but are unable to do so. The goals of Chapter 13 debtor rehabilitation are to conserve assets and restore the debtor to solvency. Chapter 13 is the bankruptcy proceeding usually required of debtors with income in excess of the state median income. The bankruptcy court ultimately will approve a plan, usually providing for lower monthly payments, to enable the consumer to repay obligations from future income. Consumers may seek total discharge from specific debts.

BANKRUPTCY AND BANKS

A bank may be able to recover money loaned to a bankrupt consumer by filing a proof of claim and petitioning the court for recovery of its investment, such as through sale of collateral that may secure the loan. However, if the loan is unsecured and the consumer has few or no assets, the bank may not recover any amounts owed.

Banks often fight bankruptcy filings when they believe customers have misrepresented their financial condition or filed a false financial statement. The court may agree to release collateral to secured lenders, allowing them to repossess and sell the goods in order to recover all or a portion of the loan balance. The court also may establish a repayment plan under Chapter 13, which restructures debts so that creditors are reimbursed over time.

LAWS AND REGULATIONS

Three important laws that affect collections and recovery are the Fair Debt Collection Practices Act of 1978, the Servicemembers Civil Relief Act of 2003, and the Bankruptcy Abuse Prevention and Consumer Protection Act of 2005, which amended the Bankruptcy Code.

FAIR DEBT COLLECTION PRACTICES ACT

Consumer complaints about abusive debt collection methods brought this issue to the attention of Congress. The result was the passage of the Fair Debt Collection Practices Act (FDCPA) in 1978.

There are no federal banking agency regulations implementing the law. The Federal Trade Commission enforces the act for nondepository institutions because the law applies to independent **debt collectors**, not to banks collecting from their own customers.

Nevertheless, the FDCPA provisions set a standard for appropriate practices for a bank's direct collection function as well as any collection efforts outsourced to third parties, including subsidiaries. The act is the basis for many state laws dealing with collection practices. The three main purposes of the Fair Debt Collection Practices Act are to

- ensure that debt collectors treat consumers fairly
- give consumers certain rights
- eliminate abusive, deceptive, and unfair practices

When a consumer fails to make a payment when it is due, the bank tries to protect its interests and recover its investment. This is not a critical concern when the consumer's problem is minor, such as forgetting to make the payment, or is easily resolved and temporary. The issue becomes far more difficult when it is clear the consumer no longer can or will make payments.

Before the act was passed, some collectors and collection agencies engaged in abusive collection practices. The FDCPA addresses abusive practices such as harassment, abuse, false or misleading representations, unfair practices, validation of debts, legal actions by debt collectors, and debt collection forms.

Prohibited Practices

The FDCPA prohibits harassment, oppression, or abuse; false representations; unfair practices; and making threats.

Harassment, oppression, or abuse	There can be no obscene or profane language, advertising of consumers' debts, or repeated telephone calls to annoy consumers. For example, collection calls can be made only between 8:00 a.m. and 9:00 p.m.

debt collector—As defined by the Fair Debt Collection Practices Act, a person who collects or attempts to collect debts owed by a borrower to a third party.

Did You Know ...

Consumer reporting agencies and credit-scoring providers have bankruptcy predictor models and scoring systems. These systems help screen out consumers with high potential for declaring bankruptcy, thus allowing banks to block those consumers from credit card offers and to block current credit lines.

False representations	Collection practices must be honest. Dishonest practices include implying that the caller is an attorney or a representative of a government agency or that the consumer has committed a crime and faces arrest, or misrepresenting the amount or terms of the debt.
Unfair practices	Collectors cannot use postcards; discuss customers' debts with neighbors, friends, or other third parties; require customers to accept collect calls or pay for mail or telegrams; or deposit postdated checks before the date on the check.
Threats	Collectors cannot threaten any action to cure a default that is not provided for in the loan contract or otherwise legally permitted; nor can they threaten actions they will not take.

Other prohibited practices are using or threatening violence, stalking, concealing identity, and misusing government documents.

Although they may not be bound by the requirements of the FDCPA, banks follow its legal principles because the law makes good business sense. Many state laws that govern debt collection practices also apply to banks collecting their own debts. Sound debt collection practices enable the collector to resolve delinquent obligations without delay while preserving the customer's goodwill.

SERVICEMEMBERS CIVIL RELIEF ACT

Active-duty military, and reservists and members of the National Guard called to active duty, are eligible for protection from civil actions under the Service-

members Civil Relief Act (SCRA) of 2003, which replaced the Soldiers' and Sailors' Civil Relief Act enacted in 1918. Coverage starts on the date active-duty orders are received. Dependents of the military also are covered in certain situations. Civil matters covered by the law are lease agreements, lawsuits, loan obligations, and insurance contracts.

When servicemembers are covered by the SCRA, lenders are subject to limitations on interest rates charged and on the fulfillment of lease, mortgage, and installment contract obligations.

Interest Rate Cap

A servicemember who is called to active duty may ask to have the interest rate on credit card accounts, consumer loans, or mortgages capped at 6 percent for the duration of the military obligation. This rule applies only to debts of the servicemember or spouse incurred before the call to active duty. Any debts made afterward are not covered. The bank can require that the servicemember provide a written request and a copy of the military orders. It must then reduce the interest rate as of the first day of active duty. The portion of the original interest debt more than 6 percent is forgiven permanently, and the monthly payment must be reduced by the amount of interest saved during the period.

Leases and Installment Loans

SCRA applies to residential leases, automobile leases, mortgages, and installment loans. Automobile leases and installment loans are considered consumer loan products.

Automobile Leases

Servicemembers who signed automobile leases before the call to active duty may terminate the leases while on active duty for periods of 180 days or more. Members who sign automobile leases while on active duty may terminate leases if their orders are for a permanent change of station outside the continental United States or they are deployed for 180 days or longer.

When a lease is terminated, the lessor may not charge an early lease termination fee. However, the lessee is obligated to pay taxes, summonses, title and registration fees, and other lessee liabilities according to lease terms, including charges for excess wear, use, and mileage.

Installment Loans

The lender cannot repossess property securing an installment loan while the servicemember is on active duty if the member has made at least one payment before going on duty. In addition, the contract cannot be terminated for breach without a court order.

Obligation Enforcement

During or within six months after military service, a servicemember or dependent may apply to a court for relief of any debt or liability incurred by either before the active-duty service. The court may grant stays of enforcement during which no fine or penalty can accrue.

BANKRUPTCY ABUSE PREVENTION AND CONSUMER PROTECTION ACT

The first bankruptcy law in U.S. history that had any permanence was the Bankruptcy Act of 1898. This law was in effect until 1978, when the Bankruptcy Reform Act, which implemented the Bankruptcy Code, replaced it. The Bankruptcy Code was more debtor-friendly than the previous law and had a stronger consumer rehabilitation chapter (Chapter 13) than ever before. The 1978 law remained fairly untouched until 2005, at which time Congress amended the law to better balance the interests of creditors and debtors.

Did You Know ...

Even famous people have faced bankruptcy in the past. For example:
• Mark Twain (Samuel Langhorne Clemens), 1835–1910, American author
• Henry John Heinz, 1844–1919, condiment manufacturer
• Milton Snavely Hershey, 1857–1945, founder of Hershey's Chocolate
• Henry Ford, 1863–1947, automobile manufacturer

The Bankruptcy Abuse Prevention and Consumer Protection Act of 2005 (see exhibit 13.7) sets out an objective needs-based bankruptcy test that determines whether debtors can afford to repay some or all of their debts. This change corrects a Bankruptcy Code flaw that had made Chapter 7 liquidation proceedings available to debtors who could afford repayment.

Now, more bankruptcy filers who are capable of repaying a significant portion of their debts must do so under **Chapter 13**, Adjustment of Debts of an Individual with Regular Income. The needs test creates a presumption that debtors can repay their debts if they earn more than the median income in their state, which in 2007 was a national average of over $62,000 for a family,[2] and they have at least $100 per month remaining after deducting living expenses and priority payments like taxes, alimony, and child support.

Special circumstances, such as a sudden loss of income or an extraordinary medical expense, still are taken into account; those affected may file for a **Chapter 7** liquidation.

Prospective petitioners for bankruptcy must receive credit counseling from a United States Trustee–approved agency within the 180-day period before filing for bankruptcy to learn about their options. Debtors must complete a financial literacy course in order to be discharged from bankruptcy.

Women and children are protected better now than in the past. The law gives priority in bankruptcy proceedings to child support and alimony payments and firms up enforcement of those obligations. Furthermore, a debtor's ability to run up significant debt just before filing for bankruptcy is limited. Exhibit 13.8 outlines sample provisions of the 2005 bankruptcy law.

Chapter 13—The Bankruptcy Code provisions for the adjustment of debts of an individual with regular income. The debtor is allowed to "reorganize" the debt and make partial or full repayment over a court-approved period. Chapter 13 often is referred to as the "wage-earner" plan.

Chapter 7—The Bankruptcy Code provisions for the court-administered liquidation of the debtor's nonexempt assets to pay creditors. Upon repayment, the debtor is relieved of the financial obligations.

Exhibit 13.7 U.S. Bankruptcy Laws Timeline	
1800	Debtors could not seek relief. Creditors could seize property.
1841	Debtors could file bankruptcy petitions for relief. Introduces concept of "fresh start."
1867–1878	Third federal statute followed by efforts for uniform state laws.
1898–1978	National Bankruptcy Act, amended in 1938 to allow for straight bankruptcy (asset liquidation).
1978	Bankruptcy Reform Act created the U.S. Bankruptcy Code. The Code covers both liquidation (straight bankruptcy) and debtor rehabilitation. Revised in 1994 and in 2005.
1994	Bankruptcy Reform Act attempted to remedy perceived abuses of the system and to crack down on fraud, reduce administrative and legal costs, expedite bankruptcy proceedings, and help lenders obtain more equitable recoveries.
2005	Bankruptcy Abuse Prevention and Consumer Protection Act. Among other requirements, debtors must take a means test before filing for straight bankruptcy (liquidation).

- Makes it more difficult for debtors to file a Chapter 7 petition by implementing a means test.
- Increases the time period before filing when a debtor cannot discharge debts.
- Decreases the amount of debt incurred shortly before a bankruptcy filing that is assumed to be abusive and therefore not dischargeable.
- Prevents debtors from using a state's real estate exemption laws unless they have lived in the state for at least two years. Debtors may not use more than $125,000 of state real property exemptions unless they have lived in the state for at least 40 months.
- Makes debt to pay state and local taxes nondischargeable.
- Makes any judgment, order, or settlement for securities fraud nondischargeable.
- Increases the length of Chapter 13 plans to five years.
- Requires debtors to submit federal tax returns before the first creditors' meeting.
- Bars the discharge of education loans.
- Requires debtor's attorneys to certify that they have investigated the debtor's circumstances and the filing is well-grounded.
- Requires debtors to get debt counseling and take financial management classes.
- Gives domestic support obligations priority.
- Requires payments to continue for secured loans.
- Prohibits cramdowns of car loans made within two and one-half years of filing and cramdowns of other loans made within one year of filing.
- Defines the value of secured claims as the replacement value of the property.
- Allows a secured creditor to retain its lien until the bankruptcy is discharged or the debt is paid.
- Requires a Chapter 7 debtor to reaffirm or redeem a secured loan or surrender the property within 45 days of filing.
- Requires lenders to give new disclosures and include certain Truth in Lending Act disclosures with credit card solicitations.

SUMMARY

- The collection and recovery functions are essential to the success of a consumer loan operation. Well-trained and motivated collectors make the difference between retrieving a bank asset and writing off an account as a loss. The primary objectives for the collection and recovery functions are to keep delinquencies and loan losses within acceptable limits, generate loss recoveries at desired levels, counsel customers who are having difficulty handling debt, ensure consistency with bank objectives, and manage collection and recovery functions cost-effectively.

- There may be many causes for delinquency that change the consumer's income or debt situation, such as unexpected changes in personal finances, economic downturns, excessive debt, poor money management, marital problems, carelessness and changing attitudes toward credit, irresponsible lending, fraud or intentional default, and substance abuse and gambling.

- Collection functions may be either centralized or decentralized. In either case, they follow precise procedures to collect payments. The collection function's goals are to keep delinquencies and losses at acceptable levels, get accounts current as quickly as possible, and retain customer goodwill to the extent possible.

- The recovery function is less structured than the collection function. Its job is to recover as much of the bank's investment as possible. Money recovered on charged-off accounts can improve the bank's loan loss record and contribute to profitability. Both the collection and recovery functions may be outsourced to collection agencies or other recovery specialists.

- The collection cycle consists of the early stage, personal contact stage, serious delinquency stage, and charge-off stage. Different methods and remedies are used for each. For the early stage, letters, reminder notices, late charges, applying the simple interest rate, and due-date adjustments are used. Personal contact stage remedies include payment extensions, loan refinancing, a new loan, insurance claims, right of setoff, and consumer credit counseling. Remedies for serious delinquency include repossession, collection lawsuits resulting in judgments, foreclosure, and wage garnishment. If all else fails, the account is charged off as a loss. At any point, consumers may file for bankruptcy protection under Bankruptcy Code Chapter 7, Liquidation; Chapter 13, Adjustment of Debts of an Individual with Regular Income; or, for individuals with large incomes or debt, Chapter 11, Reorganization.

- The Fair Debt Collection Practices Act is directed at independent debt collection agencies, but it forms the standard for bank collection practices. The purposes of the law are to ensure that collectors treat consumers fairly, define consumer rights, and eliminate abusive, deceptive, and unfair practices.

- When borrowers are covered by the Servicemembers Civil Relief Act (SCRA), there are limits on the interest rates lenders may charge and on the fulfillment of lease, mortgage, and installment contract obligations.

- The Bankruptcy Abuse Prevention and Consumer Protection Act of 2005 makes it more difficult for higher-income debtors to file Chapter 7 petitions and narrows some pro-debtor provisions of previous law. For example, it provides an objective needs-based bankruptcy test that determines whether debtors can afford to repay some or all of their debts.

END NOTES

[1]For more discussion about the financial crisis of 2008, read chapter 1 and the consumer resources available on the Web sites of the American Bankers Association, U.S. Department of the Treasury, Federal Reserve, Federal Deposit Insurance Corporation, Office of the Comptroller of

the Currency, Office of Thrift Supervision, Securities and Exchange Commission, and the U.S. Bankruptcy Court.

[2]State Median Income, U.S. Census Bureau, www.census.gov/hhes/www/income/statemedfaminc.html.

SELF-CHECK AND REVIEW

Learning Check

1. What are some common objectives for the bank collection function? Why might different objectives be set for different loan products?

2. What are some loan collection practices that are illegal under the Fair Debt Collection Practices Act?

3. What are some causes of consumer loan delinquencies? Is it possible to predict any of these at the time the loan is made?

4. What is an advantage of the decentralized approach to loan collection in a bank? What are the advantages of the centralized approach?

5. What are the stages of the collection cycle? What are some of the characteristics of each stage?

6. What is the purpose of the loan recovery function? How does it differ from the collection function?

7. What is the difference between Chapter 7 and Chapter 13 of the Bankruptcy Code? What major change did the Bankruptcy Abuse Prevention and Consumer Protection Act make to the code?

8. What is the objective of the Servicemembers Civil Relief Act (SCRA)?

ADDITIONAL RESOURCES

Resources

ABA Bank Compliance Magazine, Washington: American Bankers Association, periodical.

American Bankers Association, **www.aba.com**.

American Bankruptcy Institute, www.abiworld.org.

Bankruptcy Abuse Prevention and Consumer Protection Act of 2005, S-256, http://frwebgate.access.gpo.gov/cgibin/getdoc.cgi?dbname=109_cong_public_laws&docid=f:publ008.109.pdf.

Bankruptcy Code, www4.law.cornell.edu/uscode/11.

Consumer Credit Delinquency Bulletin Survey Report, Washington: American Bankers Association, quarterly publication.

FedStats, www.fedstats.gov.

Federal Deposit Insurance Corporation, www.fdic.gov.

Federal Citizen Information Center, Resources for Personal Finance Management, www.pueblo.gsa.gov.

Federal Reserve, www.federalreserve.gov.

Federal Reserve Education, Resources for Consumer Credit Information, www.federalreserveeducation.org/fred.

Federal Trade Commission (FTC), Consumer Information, www.ftc.gov/ftc/consumer.htm.

Law and Banking, Washington: American Bankers Association, 2008.

National Foundation for Credit Counseling (NFCC), www.nfcc.org.

Office of the Comptroller of the Currency, www.occ.gov.

Office of Thrift Supervision, www.ots.treas.gov.

Reference Guide to Regulatory Compliance, Washington: American Bankers Association, annual publication.

Securities and Exchange Commission, www.sec.gov.

U.S. Bankruptcy Courts, www.uscourts.gov/bankruptcycourts.

U.S. Census Bureau, www.census.gov.

U.S. Courts, www.uscourts.gov.

U.S. Department of the Treasury, www.treas.gov.

Answers to Situations and Self-Check and Review Questions

CHAPTER 1
INTRODUCTION TO CONSUMER LENDING

Situations

1. The Rileys own a small business selling garden plants. ABC Bank has long financed their plant inventory. The business has been successful, and when the Rileys purchased their home five years ago, ABC Bank provided the mortgage loan. When the Rileys wanted to buy furniture and did not want to use their savings to pay for it, they applied for a credit card from ABC Bank. Later, when they wanted to build an addition to their home, they obtained a home equity loan from ABC Bank.

   Are all these loans the same?

   Although all the Riley loans are from the same bank, they are categorized differently. The inventory loan is a commercial loan, the mortgage loan is a residential or real estate loan, and the home equity loan and credit cards are consumer loans.

2. Jacob, a farmer in colonial America, has just moved his family. With winter approaching, he is in a hurry to buy a larger cast-iron wood-burning stove so that the family remains warm and healthy. Because he does not yet have a crop to sell for cash, he must take out a loan to pay for the stove. Jacob turns to an unscrupulous "lender," who lends him the money at an exorbitant rate of interest. The loan is due in full, interest included, after the fall harvest. Jacob knows that if he has no money to repay the loan, the lender will use harsh tactics to collect. He is afraid for himself and his family but feels he has no choice and must take the risk.

   Could this happen today?

   Unfortunately, in some areas, nonbank lenders are able to charge very high interest rates. The rates may be legal, depending on the state laws governing the business and the type of loan. For market-driven banks, keeping rates low enough to attract consumers but high enough to maintain profitable loan portfolios requires loan products that are as diverse as the market.

3. The Thompsons, a dual-income couple that is doing fairly well, have been investing in mutual funds through a nonbank financial institution. They also have a variety of insurance products they bought from an insurance agent. The Thompsons use their bank for savings and checking accounts, a mortgage loan, and most recently a home

equity loan. In a casual conversation with their lender, Paul Baselton, they expressed frustration over having their financial business so fragmented. They were surprised when Paul referred them to a financial planner in the bank to discuss consolidating all their financial activities.

When did banks become true full-service providers?

When the Gramm-Leach-Bliley Act of 1999 (the Financial Modernization Act) was passed, banks became able to offer products they had previously been restricted from offering, such as insurance and securities trading.

4. As a busy lender, Matt barely has time for lunch, let alone attend another four-hour compliance training program; but the notice on his desk does not give him a choice. He will have to be in the training room at 9:00 A.M. on Thursday morning. What could have changed in the six months since his last compliance training session? Then he remembers how valuable that last session was—how he learned procedures for resolving customer inquiries.

In what ways do Matt, his customers, and his bank benefit from regular compliance training?

Compliance training ensures that lenders learn how to give the consumer the best service possible within the law. Regulations are often amended. Regulatory and bank auditing examinations can raise issues that have not been covered by the bank previously. Regular compliance training ensures prudent and legal lending practices. By keeping up with compliance issues, Matt can better serve bank customers.

Self-Check and Review

1. *What is consumer lending? What types of loans made to consumers are not included in this definition? Why not?*

   Consumer lending covers all credit extended to consumers for buying goods and services. The definition generally does not cover residential or purchase-money (first mortgage) loans or leasing transactions, because these are specialized, are handled usually by different areas in a bank or affiliate, and are regulated by different laws. However, the consumer lending area may manage some leases, such as vehicle leases, and it usually handles home equity loans and lines of credit.

2. *What effect did the consumer movement in the 1960s and 1970s have on the consumer lending industry?*

   The consumer movement in the 1960s and 1970s precipitated enactment of a number of laws that protect consumers and make credit widely available.

   The Truth in Lending Act, which is part of the Consumer Protection Act of 1968, sounded the opening bell for laws to increase and unify consumer disclosures. The laws of this period also allowed lenders to introduce credit products for diverse groups of consumers.

3. *What short- and long-term effects did deregulation of the banking industry during the 1980s through early 2000s have on bank consumer lending programs?*

Deregulation of bank deposit pricing and products in the 1980s jolted the consumer lending market. Rising deposit costs squeezed net interest margins and led to restraints on consumer borrowing. Only after states enacted laws lowering or eliminating rate caps and enabling banks to offer other credit products, such as home equity lines of credit, were banks able to grow their loan portfolios.

When consumer spending began to grow rapidly in the late 1990s as the real estate market opened up, competition became intense. Market growth and competition influenced the use of nontraditional and risky loan products and securitization of loans to sell to investors. Nonbank financial institutions had a significant role in this market. The result was that subprime lending grew quickly, and was uncontrolled for the most part. When real estate prices dropped in 2007, risky loans began to default far faster than anticipated. Large institutional investors holding securitized investments in such real estate loans suffered from the defaults, and some folded. The negative effects rippled throughout the financial industry and the entire economy.

4. *What are the four basic consumer financial management needs? Which specifically apply to consumer lending?*

The four basic consumer financial management needs are

- a method of exchange
- a means of preserving and accumulating wealth
- a way to increase purchasing power
- assurance of security and safety

The need to increase purchasing power is addressed specifically by consumer lending.

5. *How has technology changed the way banks compete for consumer loans?*

Technological advances have created alternative ways to deliver consumer lending products. Debit cards, credit cards, and stored value cards are becoming the access devices of choice for many convenience-seeking consumers. Furthermore, Internet banking has increased the opportunities to deliver credit services to customers and for customers to make purchases.

6. *How are banking laws made and implemented? What are the primary federal agencies that regulate banks?*

Congress enacts federal laws; state legislatures enact state laws. Federal laws affecting consumer lending primarily address consumer protection concerns, such as keeping the public informed through required disclosures and ensuring access to credit. State banking laws address permissible types of loans and interest rates, fees, and maturities; add-on products, such as credit insurance; and contract terms, such as warranties. State laws also address unfair credit practices.

Government regulators interpret the laws and then issue regulations to guide the banks under their supervision. Although the regulators enforce bank compliance by, among other sanctions, taking administrative actions on lesser violations, courts may ultimately render decisions on whether the law has been violated.

Among the federal regulators that supervise banks are the Office of the Comptroller of the Currency (OCC), the Federal Reserve, the Federal Deposit Insurance Corporation (FDIC), and the Office of Thrift Supervision (OTS).

7. *What is the functional regulation system? What is the source of this concept?*

The functional regulation system is a principle incorporated into the Gramm-Leach-Bliley Act that assigns certain banking activities to the authority of federal and state regulators other than the principal bank regulators. For example, bank affiliates selling securities are under the authority of the Securities and Exchange Commission (SEC).

8. *What are the purposes of the Equal Credit Opportunity Act (ECOA) and Truth in Lending Act (TILA)? Name the bases on which a provider of credit may not discriminate.*

ECOA is an antidiscrimination law passed in response to repeated denial of credit to applicants based on factors other than their ability to repay. ECOA prohibits lenders from treating one borrower or prospective borrower more or less favorably than another in any aspect of a credit transaction. ECOA specifically prohibits discrimination on the basis of the applicant's race; color; religion; national origin; age; sex; marital status; income from alimony, child support, separate maintenance payments, or public assistance; or exercise of rights under the Consumer Credit Protection Act. Age and marital information may be obtained only when this information affects a loan's legality or is a pertinent element of creditworthiness.

TILA protects consumers by requiring credit providers to make uniform and detailed disclosures of credit terms. It emphasizes disclosures that allow consumers to determine the cost associated with a credit transaction and to compare rates and other credit costs to make informed decisions.

9. *What should be the primary objectives of most bank consumer lending compliance programs?*

Objectives of most bank consumer lending compliance programs are to

* improve customer service by having procedures in place to resolve inquiries and problems efficiently
* increase bank efficiency by standardizing some tasks and providing clear direction about actions to be taken in certain situations
* ensure compliance with regulations
* avoid costly penalties and litigation resulting from violations of a regulation

CHAPTER 2 THE CONSUMER LENDING MARKET

Situations

1. When Ellen graduated from college, she received gifts of money from friends and relatives. She has enough now for the down payment on a new automobile and plans on financing the balance. Ellen assumes that, once she finds the auto she wants to purchase, she will have to go to her bank for a loan. This is her first auto purchase, and she does not know the dealer offers financing.

   How can the dealer do that?

   The automobile dealer has an arrangement with a bank to provide financing to qualified buyers. It also has a relationship with the captive finance company for the automobile manufacturer. Ellen will complete her loan application at the dealership, which will then forward the application electronically to several banks and the captive for a quick decision.

2. John and Susan Miller both turned 35 in 2009. John recently was promoted and Susan re-entered the work force after their youngest child started school. After the lean years of living on only John's income and the expenses associated with starting a family, John and Susan were anxious to experience a few of life's luxuries. With confidence that their combined monthly income could absorb some debt payment for the next few years, John and Susan took out a loan to fund a vacation, a new automobile, and new living room furniture.

   Is this typical behavior?

   John and Susan exemplify the family growth period of the consumer life cycle. Incomes rise along with financial responsibilities, such as the number of children. With more stable jobs and credit history, households often borrow to meet obligations or to improve their lifestyle.

3. Ahmed is a teacher. He takes care of most of his financial business through the credit union, which is available only to school-system employees. Although he has other choices, the credit union offers the most competitive rates on savings, loans, and other products. Several years ago Ahmed received in the mail a credit-card solicitation from the captive finance company of a major automobile manufacturer. By using this card, he could earn credit toward the purchase of a new automobile. Knowing the time was not far off when he would need an automobile, Ahmed applied for the card. He used this card almost exclusively for his card-based transactions. When he was ready to purchase his automobile, he went to the dealer and discovered that he also could finance the automobile purchase through the manufacturer's captive finance company at an even lower rate than his credit union's auto loan rate offer.

   Could Ahmed have gotten these services from a bank?

   Ahmed demonstrates that consumers can take care of most of their financial needs without going near a bank. Although he could have gone to a bank, he was able to get a lower-interest auto loan from the captive finance company. Bankers are aware that consumers can shop elsewhere.

4. Roberto is Spanish; English is his second language. He lives in a community that is predominantly Spanish-speaking. When he went to his bank, EFG Bank, to inquire about a personal loan and asked to speak to a loan officer, the customer service representative told him, in an unfriendly tone of voice, that no one was available. She handed him a brochure, printed in English, and told him to read it and call back with any questions. She did not offer to make an appointment for him, although this is a common practice at EFG Bank.

Because Roberto did not understand the brochure fully, he went across the street to XYZ Bank, which advertised Spanish language assistance. The XYZ customer service representative did not speak Spanish either, but she found a loan officer who did. Roberto applied and received his loan. He also transferred his deposit accounts, totaling $50,000, to XYZ Bank.
What form of discrimination does this situation exemplify?

This is an example of disparate impact. The customer service representative's treatment discouraged Roberto from applying for a loan at EFG Bank. He asked to speak to a loan officer and was not given that opportunity; nor was an appointment offered.

Self-Check and Review

1. *What is the difference between loan volume and loans outstanding? Why are these numbers important?*

Loans outstanding refers to the total dollar amount of money owed as credit obligations in any one portfolio; loan volume is the amount of new money borrowed by consumers during a specific period, such as one month. These two figures are used to measure the size of the bank's share of the consumer lending market.

2. *What is the difference between closed-end and open-end loans? Referring to exhibits 2.1 and 2.3, what has been the trend of closed-end and open-end loans over time?*

A closed-end loan is a fixed amount of credit for a specific purpose established at the beginning of the transaction. It is repaid in regular installments during a predetermined term.

An open-end loan, or revolving line of credit, is for a specified amount of credit to be made available for use at the consumer's discretion. Repayment is a minimum amount or a percentage specified in the contract.

Since revolving lines of credit were introduced in the late twentieth century, they have grown to be a significant percentage of total loans outstanding.

3. *What is the difference between direct and indirect lending? What are some examples of each?*

Loans made through direct lending are made directly by the bank to the consumer. Loans made through indirect lending involve a third party that transfers the bank's credit to the customer. Examples of direct lending are a customer obtaining a personal loan from a banker in a local branch or applying for a home equity line of credit on a bank's secure Internet Web site. Examples of indirect lending are a customer obtaining a bank-financed auto loan from a dealership or a bank-financed home improvement loan from a contractor.

4. *What are the most important factors determining the position of a product in the product life cycle?*

The most important factor is the extent to which the product meets the consumer's needs. Other factors are the availability of the product, how long it has been on the market, sales efforts, and alternative products.

5. *What are the five stages in the consumer financial needs life cycle? Which products are most appropriate for each stage?*

The stages in the consumer financial needs life cycle are early development, family growth, midlife, empty nest, and retirement. Early development is characterized by low income and high borrowing. Family growth is characterized by more stable jobs and incomes rising along with financial responsibilities. Midlife typically means high household expenses, including college education fees. The empty nest period shifts from borrowing to investing as income exceeds obligations. With retirement, loan demand is at its lowest because retirees live on pensions and investment income. Typical products appropriate to each stage are

Early development:	low-cost checking
Family growth:	mortgage
Midlife:	home equity lines of credit
Empty nest:	loans for investment purposes
Retirement:	estate planning

6. *What advantages and disadvantages do commercial banks have in the consumer lending market?*

The primary advantages banks have are a positive image with consumers, a large base of retail consumers, a convenient branch distribution system, and expanding use of the Internet and other electronic means to deliver products and services. Among the disadvantages are that the Internet and other electronic resources have leveled the playing field for competitors as consumers seek speed, convenience, and alternative ways to access credit. Competitors have made themselves accepted in a number of niche markets.

7. *Why do captive finance companies offer credit to their customers? How has their share of the credit market fared?*

The primary reason captive finance companies offer credit to consumers is to increase the sale of goods and services to their customers; having credit available brings their products within reach of the average consumer. Captive finance companies, such as those owned by automobile manufacturers, increased their market share in the late twentieth century and became formidable competitors in the financial services market.

8. *Which type of discrimination is each of the following according to the fair lending laws?*
   a. a bank loan policy that unsecured credit is not to be extended to single women because they generally have only one source of income

   b. a policy that loans will not be made below a certain amount, when there is no objective business reason for that policy

   c. a statement by a loan officer to a disabled applicant that the bank does not like to make construction loans to persons with physical handicaps

   d. quotation of more favorable conditions for a loan for a Caucasian male than an African-American male with the same credit rating

   a. overt discrimination
   b. disparate impact
   c. overt discrimination
   d. disparate treatment

9. *What are some examples of accommodations for customers with disabilities under Americans with Disabilities Act?*
   The following are accommodations that banks have instituted:
   * printing bank documents in large type
   * having documents transcribed onto audiotape
   * having employees read documents to customers who have impaired eyesight
   * allowing service animals in the bank
   * allowing a disabled customer to complete transactions at a desk if a bank does not have a wheelchair-accessible teller window
   * allowing a customer to sign documents using a drive-up window
   * installing ramps
   * making curb cuts in sidewalks
   * rearranging tables, chairs, display racks, and other furniture
   * installing flashing alarm lights
   * widening doors
   * installing text telephone (TTY) services
   * putting Braille instructions on ATMs

CHAPTER 3 DIRECT LENDING

Situations

1. The Rodriguezes have chosen a contractor to remodel their kitchen. The contractor will finance the new kitchen on what appear to be reasonable terms. On the way home from the contractor's office, they stop at their bank branch to cash a check. While talking to Gina, a teller they have known for years, they mention their plans. Gina suggests they talk to Hannah Katz, the loan officer, to compare the costs of a

bank loan with the loan offered by the contractor. After discussing loan options with Hannah, they decide to apply. Hannah takes their application, and after pressing several keys on the computer, tells the Rodriguezes they will have their answer in a few minutes.

How can this be done so fast?

With automation, lenders have immediate access to internal bank files for customer information, credit reports, and other information critical to the loan decision. Armed with the information provided by the applicant and these additional verifications, lenders can make a credit decision quickly. If Hannah had not been able to do this, the Rodriguezes might have gone back to the contractor for financing.

2. Loan officer Hannah Katz knows the Rodriguezes. They are long-time customers and visit the branch often to make deposits and open savings accounts for their children. The information on their loan application, along with bank files and credit history reports that Hannah requested electronically, suggest that the Rodriguezes may have other options. Hannah notes that they own their home and have several outstanding loans in addition to their mortgage. She demonstrates that, by taking out a home equity loan, the Rodriguezes can pay off all existing debt, pay for the new kitchen, and reduce their overall monthly payments.

Should Hannah Katz suggest this option to the Rodriguezes or should she process their original request for a personal loan?

She should suggest it. The Rodriguezes will benefit from an option they had not considered. By suggesting a home equity loan to consolidate loan payments or more flexibility in the use of loan proceeds and to finance the new kitchen, Hannah can save the couple money and simplify their monthly payments.

3. Colum O'Neill takes out a four-year loan for $18,000 to buy a $20,000 automobile. After a year, Colum stops making payments and defaults on the loan, leaving a principal balance of $13,500. The bank takes possession of the collateral, the automobile, and turns it over to an agent for sale. The agent sells the automobile for the market value of $12,000. After paying the agent's fees and other costs associated with the default, the bank receives $11,000 for the automobile.

How much is the bank losing?

In addition to the interest payments, the bank may have lost $2,500 on the loan principal. Assuming that Colum has not filed for bankruptcy, the bank may attempt to collect from him the now unsecured amount of $2,500. The potential for loss on the principal that is associated with depreciating value collateral is a risk the bank assumed.

4. Raji Turner is a loan officer in a small community bank. One of his more affluent customers has submitted a loan application for $25,000 to buy a valuable oil painting. The loan will be secured by the painting. To his knowledge, this is the first time a customer has asked to use art as collateral. His bank does not have experience in

valuing art, and he wonders whether its use as collateral is consistent with bank loan policy.

What steps should Raji take to determine whether this loan should be made?

Raji should
* evaluate the entire financial picture of his customer
* determine why the customer wishes to pledge the art as collateral
* determine how to establish the value of the painting
* research the bank's loan policy to determine if the painting is acceptable collateral and what the loan-to-value ratio would be
* see if another solution—perhaps a home equity line of credit or even a personal unsecured line of credit—might better serve his customer 's needs

5. John Matsuda has always dreamed of buying a sporty two-seater. Now that the children have grown and the family budget is less strained, he has found the model automobile of his dreams. Instead of raiding the family savings, he plans to take out a loan with the automobile as collateral, make monthly payments, and own the automobile within three years. Ashanti Daniels is the loan officer who has accepted John's application.

What type of collateral value has John offered to secure the loan?

If the sports automobile is a current standard model, it is depreciating value collateral. If it is a classic sports automobile, it may be appreciating value collateral. Nevertheless, Ashanti knows that collateral is a secondary source for repayment; her first consideration is John's creditworthiness.

Self-Check and Review

1. *What is the difference between centralized and decentralized approaches to organizing the direct lending function?*

   Large banks typically have a centralized direct lending function in which applications are accepted at branches or through other retail sources and are forwarded, usually electronically, to a centralized credit approval area. The credit decision and loan documents are returned to the branch. Small banks may use a decentralized approach in which each branch may be responsible for attracting loan applications, making decisions, closing loans, and even collecting payments or handling delinquencies. Because this type of system is expensive, many banks are switching to a centralized approach or using advances in technology to combine the two approaches.

2. *What are the advantages and disadvantages of direct lending for the bank? How are banks reducing the effect of the disadvantages?*

   Advantages to the bank include
   * a high level of control over the loan process
   * personal contact with the consumer
   * loan structuring and cross-selling opportunities
   * ensuring compliance with laws and regulations and bank policy

Disadvantages include the cost of administering direct lending programs and inability to make the most of the lending situation's opportunities.

Today banks are meeting these challenges through cost-saving measures, such as automating or centralizing much of the loan process; using open-end credit products to reduce the costs of handling future borrowing needs; and using alternative methods to take applications, such as telephone and direct mail, supermarket branches, and the Internet. Banks are training their lenders in product knowledge and sales skills so that they may offer other bank services to loan customers.

3. *What are the advantages and disadvantages of direct lending for the consumer? What can banks do to limit the disadvantages?*

Consumers benefit from direct lending through increased financial counseling and the lower costs associated with flexible loan structuring.

The main disadvantage is the possible inconvenience of meeting with the lender in a branch. Banks are meeting this challenge by offering easier ways to apply for loans, such as through a Web site, and using technology, such as e-mail, to keep in personal touch with the consumer during the loan process.

4. *What are four categories of collateral value for secured loans? How does each affect credit risk?*

Depreciating value collateral (automobiles, boats, recreational vehicles, or airplanes). The greatest risk is that the value of the collateral declines faster than the loan balance. Collateral that is mobile can be moved easily and is therefore difficult to retrieve.

Fluctuating value collateral (stocks, bonds, and other financial instruments). The value of this type of property can change drastically. When banks rely on this type of collateral they usually retain the right to require additional collateral or only lend for a percentage of the value. If the value declines, the bank would require the customer to pay down the loan balance or provide additional collateral to readjust the loan margin requirements.

Stable value collateral (typically items like savings accounts and certificates of deposits). The loans have minimal risk if the collateral and the loans are properly documented and if the bank has procedures to protect the collateral, which is usually in the lender's possession.

Appreciating value collateral (real estate and classic automobiles). Because it is generally assumed that the value of personal residential real estate will increase over time, the collateral risk on such loans usually is low. However, lenders are aware that residential real estate may lose value in response to general economic declines or changes in a market area. Such negative events may cause unexpected collateral risk.

5. *What intangible factors does unsecured lending depend on?*

Unsecured lending depends on the trustworthiness, honesty, and integrity—the character—of the customer. Although character is the foundation for all consumer credit activities, it is especially important for unsecured loans. The creditworthiness of the customer is highly important, as is effective risk management of the loan relationship.

6. *Why do federally guaranteed loans usually have the least risk for banks? List some popular guaranteed loan programs.*

Loans made under such loan programs are guaranteed against default up to a certain high percentage of the loan amount by agencies of the federal government. Banks are reimbursed for losses due to borrower nonpayment. Examples are the Federal Family Education Loan (FFEL) Program and USDA Rural Development, Housing and Urban Development (HUD), and Small Business Administration (SBA) loans.

7. *What federal law protects cosigners on a loan agreement? What is the bank required to do? What other protections are included in this law?*

The Credit Practices Rule, implemented by the Federal Reserve as FRS Regulation AA, Unfair or Deceptive Acts or Practices, protects cosigners. Banks must provide with or on the loan agreement a notice of the cosigner's liability to pay the loan if the borrower defaults.

The rule also protects consumers from such practices as pyramiding late charges and incorporating unfair clauses in loan agreements, such as confessions of judgment, waivers of exemption, assignment of wages, and security interests in household goods (unless it is a purchase money loan).

CHAPTER 4 INDIRECT LENDING

Situations

1. The Krandalls have retired. They want to buy an RV so they can see the country in comfort. They have found the perfect RV at a local dealership and met with the dealer to arrange financing. They would like to put 10 percent down and have a four-year term on the loan. The dealer has them complete an application, asks a few questions, and faxes the information to several banks.

    Fifteen minutes later, the dealer receives one bank's reply and says he can make the loan if the Krandalls either make a slightly larger down payment or increase the term to five years. According to the bank, the Krandalls' income cannot quite support the monthly payments for the loan requested but could support a loan with a slight change in terms.

    Who sent the fax that promoted the counteroffer of different terms?

    One of the banks that received the application sent the counteroffer. Because the couple's income is insufficient, this bank was unable to make the loan under the requested terms. However, if the monthly payments can be reduced with a slight change in the amount of the down payment or the term of the loan, the bank can make the loan.

    Where a large number of loans are received through indirect lending or because of terms in the dealer agreement, such customization through counteroffers may not be possible. Instead, the dealer may seek another bank that is willing to accept the terms the couple requests.

Once the loan is approved, the consumer signs the loan contract, subject to the terms of approval, and the contract is sold to the lender.

2. John Rossini works for a Ford dealership. Alice Field is shopping for a Taurus. She would like the high-end model with leather seats, moon roof, and other amenities, but it is beyond her budget. Alice settles on a base model, trades in her current automobile, and asks for a 36-month loan for the balance. John works out some figures. He explains to Alice that by extending the loan term to 48 months, she can buy the more expensive model while keeping her payments the same as for the cheaper model on a 36-month term.

How do the dealer and the consumer both benefit from this offer?

John, the dealer, is able to show Alice, the consumer, that she can afford the automobile she really wants by extending her monthly payments over a longer term. Alice must now decide whether the upgraded automobile is worth the additional amount that she will pay by extending her payments.

3. Sally has a new job with a high monthly income and prospects for continued advancement. She wants to buy a new auto but does not have enough in her savings account for a down payment. Because she is upwardly mobile, she plans to get a new auto every two years. Frank, the dealer, suggests she might be interested in leasing instead of buying. Frank refers Sally to the dealer's leasing agent for more information.

How is the bank involved in this leasing arrangement between Frank, the dealer, and Sally, the consumer?

In addition to offering floorplan lines of credit to the dealer and having a dealer agreement for consumer sales contracts for the dealer's sales, the bank may underwrite the dealer's leasing program. Sally, the consumer, may find that leasing is a good option for her. The lease agreement is another option financed by the bank.

Self-Check and Review

1. *In what ways may a bank reduce its risk on a loan made through indirect lending?*
   A bank may reduce its risk by carefully screening and selecting dealers; maintaining the bank's credit standards for individual loans; and having the dealer assume some risk (dealer recourse) on individual transactions. Recourse options include full recourse, repurchase recourse, limited recourse, and nonrecourse (no liability).

2. *At what point in the indirect lending process does the bank have direct contact with the consumer?*
   The bank usually does not have any contact with the consumer until the bank records the loan, disburses the proceeds to the dealer, and sends billing statements to the consumer. With the consumer now a customer, the bank may begin direct contact to expand the relationship.

3. *How does dealer recourse reduce a bank's risk on a loan made through indirect lending? Why have nonrecourse arrangements become more common?*

Dealer recourse reduces the risk by having the dealer accept some responsibility for loan performance. In these arrangements, the bank has recourse to the dealer to recover all or a portion of any loss it may suffer on a retail loan, although in recent years there has been a trend to the nonrecourse option due to competitive pressures. This trend has increased the risk to banks.

4. *How do dealers benefit financially from indirect lending, other than being able to make the sale? Explain.*

Dealers usually are paid a portion of the finance charge on the loan as well as income from the sale of credit-related insurance and of any related warranty service policies. Thus, in addition to the profit made on the sale of the goods or services, the dealer does generate additional income from such loans.

5. *Why may a loan to purchase a new auto through indirect lending not be the best loan alternative for a consumer*

The loan made through indirect lending must stand on its own merits. The lender is not able to review the consumer's financial situation and offer a different type of loan or restructure the loan. In addition, consumers may be pressured to buy in an indirect lending arrangement. Such pressure may prevent them from shopping for the best price on the goods and for the best loan terms.

6. *What is leasing? Explain how banks can offer leases on either a direct or an indirect basis.*

In leasing, one party, the lessor (which may be the bank) owns the collateral being leased and rents it to the consumer, the lessee, for a specified period and monthly payment. Banks may offer leasing programs directly, by offering the consumer the lease itself, or indirectly, by underwriting a leasing company that offers the lease to the consumer.

7. *What is a floorplan line of credit and how does it enhance a dealer relationship?*

A floorplan line of credit is a commercial credit line in which the bank finances the dealer's inventory. When the goods are sold, the bank is repaid. It is sometimes called inventory financing or a wholesale line of credit program. This financial relationship enhances the possibility of obtaining other business from a dealer, perhaps giving the bank first priority on the dealer's consumer loans.

8. *What does FRS Regulation O address and why should it be considered when a bank establishes a dealer relationship?*

FRS Regulation O applies to credit extended by a bank to an insider, such as an executive officer, a director, or a principal shareholder.

Banks need to be sure that when establishing dealer relationships they determine whether the dealer is a related interest of a bank insider. Many insider loans are subject to approval by the board of directors and to the bank's lending rules.

9. *What change to the UCC Article 3 holder-in-due-course concept did the Federal Trade Commission (FTC) make in situations such as bank purchases of promissory notes from dealers and subsequent responsibilities to consumers?*

The FTC rule requires that a purchaser of a consumer credit contract for the sale of goods continue to be subject to claims the consumer has against the original seller—such as a claim against warranties or a claim that the goods are defective.

Consumer credit contracts that are sold by a retailer, such as an automobile dealer, to a financial institution, must contain a legend that states the rule and the consumer's rights.

Chapter 5
Open-End, Revolving Credit Products

Situations

1. Alan Fredricks is starting college in the fall. His parents have some savings for his tuition but only enough to cover about half the cost. They also have some credit card debt that they carry over from month to month and they have another year to pay on an automobile loan. They are thinking about taking out a new loan to cover the rest of the tuition. Their banker, Tom Wilson, recommends that they consider a home equity line of credit and describes the features and benefits. The credit line is appealing to the Fredricks because they are not exactly sure how much they will need.

   How does a HELOC benefit the Fredricks and the bank?

   The loan, secured by their home, can be used to pay off current debt at a lower interest rate, and the interest the Fredericks pay on it may be tax deductible. They also can use the loan to pay their son's college tuition or other expenses. They are pleased with the feature that allows them to use as much of the credit line as they need.

   The bank also benefits. Home equity line of credit customers usually are creditworthy. The accounts have higher levels use and lower levels of delinquency and loss.

2. When Alan Fredricks gets to college, he immediately opens a checking account at the local bank. He applies for and receives a debit card tied to his new account. Like all students at his college, Alan also gets a University Express card. This card can be used like a check for many purposes, including paying for books, food, and laundry—providing he has enough money on the card. When Alan runs out of money on his University Express card, he can replenish it.

   What kind of card is this?

   The University Express card is a stored-value card, also known as a smart card.

3. Janice has had the same credit card for several years. Hoping to find a better deal, she decided to compare the terms of her card to other plans. For the next month, Janice saves the credit card solicitations that arrive in the mail. Each states that she has been preapproved for credit and needs only to return an enclosed form. By the end

of the month, Janice has received six or seven of these notices. She can now compare the costs and features of these cards with each other and with her current card.

How did all these banks find Janice?

Prospect names obtained from a variety of sources are run through consumer reporting agency programs to identify consumers who generally meet the bank's credit criteria. In addition, the bank may purchase a customized prospect list from consumer reporting agencies by providing its specific criteria, such as for credit history and geographical location. Using prescreening techniques, banks can weed out obvious high-risk consumers, select others for preapproval, and investigate still others further. Consumers like Janice who pass this screening receive a preapproved credit offering.

Self-Check and Review

1. *Why have open-end credit products had the highest rate of growth of any form of consumer credit in recent years?*

   Open-end credit products have grown rapidly because lenders have made them widely available and because consumers have accepted them. Lenders favor open-end credit products because they increase profits, are efficient, expand the bank's market beyond the branch network, and have strong demand. Consumers have embraced open-end credit because the credit lines offer more control over borrowing, a high level of flexibility and convenience, and, in the case of home equity lines of credit, often lower monthly payments, lower rates, and access to large amounts of credit.

2. *What are four different types of open-end credit products? Describe each.*

   Credit cards. Private label retailer, national, and international credit cards (Visa and Mastercard) allow consumers to purchase goods and services at participating retail locations, and travel and entertainment cards (American Express and Diners Club) can be used like credit cards except that balances must be paid in full when billed. There are also special-value cards, such as affinity, cobranded, and reward cards.

   Check overdraft lines of credits. These credit lines automatically advance funds up to their credit limits to cover amounts that exceed customers' checking account balances. Banks also provide customers with special checks that allow them to directly access the credit portion of the account.

   Unsecured lines of credit. These accounts are stand-alone lines of credit that normally are marketed to groups with above-average credit characteristics. These unsecured lines of credit usually have higher credit limits than check overdraft lines. The customer usually accesses the account with special checks.

   Secured lines of credit. These accounts, such as home equity lines of credit, usually are stand-alone accounts. They generally have much higher credit limits and allow for access in a number of ways, such as through special checks and, in some states, by credit card.

3. *What is the difference between a check or debit card and a stored-value card?*

A check, or debit, card transaction draws funds directly from the consumer's checking account. If a check overdraft line of credit is attached to the account, a credit balance may be created when the deposit account is overdrawn. A check, or debit, card can be used repeatedly to access the checking account.

With stored-value cards, a monetary value is preloaded on the card. Consumers make purchases much as they would with a credit or debit card, and the value on the card is reduced with each transaction. Once the value is used up, some cards are discarded; others may be reloaded with value.

4. *What is a preapproved open-end credit offer? Why do banks make such offers?*

In a preapproved credit offer, the lender makes a commitment to extend a specified amount of credit based on a prescreening credit investigation and receipt of a properly executed acceptance agreement. In the prescreening, prospect names obtained from a variety of sources are run through special credit reporting agency programs to identify consumers who meet the bank's criteria. The selected consumers are offered the opportunity to obtain credit.

Prescreening allows lenders to weed out obvious high-risk consumers, select some to be preapproved, and investigate others further. This approach often is used for marketing credit cards to get higher response rates.

5. *In today's consumer credit environment, what primary advantages do home equity lines of credit offer to banks? To consumers?*

Banks may attract consumers who have better than average credit characteristics and secure the loan with collateral that is generally sound. Banks also enjoy the operational efficiencies of open-end credit products that have large credit lines and longer pay-off periods.

Because the credit line is larger, the HELOC can replace or consolidate most of a consumer's outstanding credit. It also can be used for major expenses, such as college tuition, home improvements, and automobile purchases. Potentially, the interest paid on a home equity line of credit is tax deductible. HELOCs generally have lower interest rates than other lines of credit or credit cards.

6. *What are the types of income a bank may derive from a credit card program? Which is the most important?*

There are four major possible sources of income from a credit card program:

* Finance charges represent the interest and other charges consumers pay on outstanding balances. They are the largest and most important source of income for most credit card programs.

* Interchange fees are charged by credit card companies and issuers who process transactions through the credit card network. They may be either a source of income or an expense to the bank.

* Merchant discount fees are charged to merchants for processing their credit transactions.

- Annual membership and transaction-related fees depend on the particular card a consumer carries. Annual fees, overlimit fees, cash advance fees, credit insurance premiums, and late charges are common fees charged to consumers on credit card programs.

7. *What protections for consumers are provided in the Fair Credit Reporting Act as revised by the FACT Act?*

    Financial institutions and credit reporting agencies are required to implement systems to detect identity theft red flags and alert consumers when their personal information has been stolen or their credit records are damaged due to fraudulent transactions.

8. *What are some protections the TILA gives against unauthorized use of open-end credit?*
    Credit cards may be issued to consumers only in response to an application or request or as a renewal of a previously issued card. A customer's liability for unauthorized use of a credit card is either $50 or the amount of credit obtained with the card before the customer notifies the issuer of the unauthorized use, whichever is less. The card issuer must give customers notice of the potential liability and the process for reporting any unauthorized use.

Chapter 6
Formulating a Consumer Loan Policy

Situations

1. Elton works for State National Bank. He and his wife are remodeling their home and Elton inquires about his bank's home equity loan program. Other State National Bank employees have applied for loans, and there is a special loan officer who handles their requests. Elton meets with this loan officer and receives a document that outlines the bank's policy for loans to employees.

    How will Elton's loan request be handled compared with other customers of State National Bank?

    Elton's loan request will be reviewed by his bank's employee loan committee but will still be subject to the conditions specified in the loan policy.

2. A customer of TBF Bank loan officer David Mertz is seeking a $50,000 unsecured consumer loan. Because David's individual lending authority is only $25,000 for this type of loan, he cannot make the decision to grant the loan on his own. He calls on Ethyl Rich, whose lending authority is also $25,000, to review the application jointly with him.
    Can they make the loan decision together?

    It depends on whether TBF's loan policy permits aggregation of authority. If TBF Bank allows its loan officers to combine their lending authority to make consumer loans and together David and Ethyl have enough authority to authorize this loan, they can make the decision.

3. Danny is a good friend of Marty Paulson, a loan officer at ABC Bank. Danny is unable to get an auto loan due to his negative credit history. Marty has known Danny for a long time and is aware of how his recent divorce changed his financial situation. He also knows that Danny has a new job that pays well. Marty decides to loan Danny enough money from his personal funds at a low rate of interest.

Could Marty's personal loan to Danny be considered an unethical transaction?

A bank that values integrity requires that all financial transactions withstand scrutiny. Personal loans to customers, by which an employee profits, can create perceptions of wrongdoing that damage the bank's or the employee's reputation. To avoid this problem, bank employees should not borrow from nor lend to customers, vendors, or other employees without written approval from bank management.

4. Maria Alonso is a loan officer. On Thursday morning, the chairman of the loan committee calls her into a meeting. The loan policy has been revised to refine the policy on maintaining consumer financial privacy. The chairman explains the change to all the loan officers. Maria asks several questions, as do some of the other loan officers. By the end of the meeting, she is confident that she understands the policy. Later that day, Maria receives an updated consumer loan policy and procedures manual with a cover memo highlighting the changes and additions. She also receives an e-mail from the bank's president emphasizing the importance of the change.

Why is this much communication regarding changes to the loan policy important?

Because Maria has received information from a variety of sources about the privacy policy change, including the consumer loan policy and procedures manual, and has had her questions answered, she now knows what she needs to do to comply with the policy. The e-mail message from the bank's president also draws attention to the policy change.

Self-Check and Review

1. *Why is loan policy creation a dynamic rather than a static process?*
   Policies reflect and evolve with the bank's strategy and objectives. They are responses to rapidly changing external environments—competitive, economic, regulatory, and sociodemographic. As the bank introduces new products and enters new markets or geographic areas, its policies should be reviewed and amended to reflect new risks.

2. *In what way does a formal lending policy help curb regulatory violations?*
   Sound credit policies help reduce the opportunity for employees to willfully or unknowingly violate regulations. Combined with sound review procedures, they help identify inadvertent compliance violations and ensure timely correction of errors. By clearly setting out the guidelines, the policy statement helps lenders to structure loans in a way that is consistent with policy and complies with regulations. Loans that cannot be made in conformity with policy should be rejected; those that comply should be made.

3. *What is lending authority and how is it granted?*
    Lending authority identifies the amounts individual or groups of loan officers can make without referring the loan to the loan committee. The power to grant lending authority is vested with the board of directors. The directors are responsible for setting lending limits for each lender or loan committee and for monitoring their performance.

4. *How does the loan policy help lenders judge an applicant's character?*
    Loan policy helps a lender judge an applicant's character by setting standards for interpreting credit history. The policy usually focuses on those factors in the applicant's credit history that lead to automatic rejection of the application; however, it also specifies circumstances in which exceptions may be made.

5. *Why does the loan policy need to clarify how "debt" and "income" are calculated for use in the debt-to-income ratio?*
    The amount of money that may be loaned to any one applicant and the credit risk to the bank are determined by the debt-to-income ratio. These numbers change depending on how each term is defined. For example, open-end loan debt may be calculated against the current balance outstanding or the full credit limit. Income may be calculated against the borrower's gross monthly income or net income. Banks that are trying to reduce their risk exposure may want to use a more restricted definition of debt or income. Having debt and income well defined also helps keep lending practices fair and consistent.

6. *What information would help the following ambiguous loan policy statements become clear and unambiguous?*

    > *Statement 1: Do not make loans to applicants who have been at their address less than one year, unless there are offsetting positive attributes.*

    > *Statement 2: Decline loan requests from applicants who have major derogatory credit histories.*

    Statement 1. Banks might define positive attributes as time on job and at current residence, profession, minimum debt level, down payment amount, and excellent credit history. For example, some banks may state that applicants with less than one year at their current residence should list a previous residence where they lived for a longer period.

    Statement 2. Banks might define derogatory credit history to include a history of bankruptcy, repossessions, charge-offs, and tax liens. "Derogatory credit history" also can be quantified by using credit scores.

7. *Why does the federal government restrict purpose loans?*
    A purpose loan is a loan backed by securities and used for purchasing securities or for carrying securities (maintaining, reducing, or retiring debt incurred for obtaining securities). Because of past unsound business practices, such as those that preceded the 1929 market crash and ushered in the Great Depression, the government regulates margin requirements on purpose loans to curb securities speculation and help stabilize the securities market.

CHAPTER 7 GENERATING LOAN APPLICATIONS

Situations

1. Nina wants to purchase a used auto from a neighbor. She must come up with the money quickly or the neighbor will sell it to someone else. She immediately calls several banks in her area. One requires her to come to the bank during business hours, complete an application, and wait three days for a response. At a second, she can apply at a loan terminal in the bank lobby and have her response in 24 hours. The third bank directs Nina to its Web site, where she can submit an application online this evening from her home computer and get her response in the morning at the latest.

   At which bank is Nina likely to choose to apply for her loan? Why?

   For Nina convenience and a prompt response are priorities. She probably will apply at the bank that offers the quickest response. The third bank with the Web site application probably will be her choice.

2. The Kangs moved into their new home five years ago. Not wanting to wait to furnish the house, they financed their furniture purchases with credit cards and personal loans. They thought they could handle the payments but miscalculated how much the interest charges would be over time. Just when they were wondering what options were available to them, they received a phone call from the bank that holds their mortgage. The pleasant voice on the other end described a home equity line of credit with no closing costs and a much lower interest rate than they are paying on their credit cards.

   How did this banker know they were looking for a new plan?

   Using a Marketing Customer Information File (MCIF) the bank probably conducted a search to select customers for loan applications. The banker who made the call received a list for telemarketing. By handling the call well, the banker may produce good will for the bank. It certainly worked for the Kangs, who were very receptive to the offer of a home equity line of credit.

3. Dora Blanca, who is 22, applied for her first loan to cover the cost of college. She was very nervous about meeting with the loan officer, Ms. Johnson. When Ms. Johnson came out to the lobby to greet Dora, she smiled and shook Dora's hand. Ms. Johnson's small talk about the weather on the way to her office helped put Dora at ease, and she welcomed the offer of a cup of coffee. She also was flattered that Ms. Johnson called her "Ms. Blanca." It made her feel respected. Dora soon relaxed as the interview became more like a conversation with a friend than a trip to the principal's office.

   Why is Dora's experience no longer a unique customer experience? What did Ms. Johnson do to encourage the relationship with Dora?

   In today's competitive market, bankers know that the customer comes first. Ms. Johnson has been trained to put Dora at ease by shaking her hand, using her name, and being hospitable by offering her coffee. The experience most likely will result in a successful loan interview.

4. Ryan wants to refurbish for his elderly in-laws an apartment that is on top of the garage attached to his home. He has a deposit account at Meadow Lark Bank. One evening, he reviewed the bank's Web site for loan information. Then he decided to check other banks in his community. When he calls Adams Mill Bank, customer service representative Tracy answers the phone. Ryan asks Tracy about the bank's rate on home improvement loans.

What should Tracy do?

Tracy should ask Ryan to tell her more about his loan need, especially the purpose and the amount, explaining that the bank has different loan products that might be suitable. Then she should quote the rates on those products, which would probably be a home improvement loan or a home equity loan or line of credit. She should provide examples of loan terms and repayment examples.

Tracy should not discourage Ryan from applying, but she should state that the branch loan officer will review all factors in the application before making a decision. She may mention such items as the possibility of tax advantages for home equity loans and the potential for refinancing other loans secured by his home.

Self-Check and Review

1. *What are the five primary objectives of the loan application process? Describe each objective.*

The five primary objectives are to

- *Generate a flow of applications.* To meet its objectives for loans outstanding, volume, portfolio diversification, asset quantity and quality, and profitability, the bank must have a continuous flow of applications from which to make loans.

- *Get information for a decision.* The bank must ensure that the application and any loan interview capture enough information so that the lender can make a well-informed decision. How much information is needed depends on the loan request, the amount, any collateral, and the loan risk.

- *Comply with the law.* Banks and lenders must ensure that in generating applications they adhere to the laws governing marketing efforts and applications for different products and loan interviews.

- *Provide a timely response.* Although different products have different timing requirements, the guiding principle should be to reach a decision and communicate it as rapidly as possible.

- *Secure applicant goodwill.* Marketing efforts should reach potential borrowers, offer something of value, and create enough interest that consumers respond. The application process should be convenient and pleasant.

2. *Does the type of loan and delivery channel have any effect on the effort to generate loans? Discuss in terms of direct lending, indirect lending, and open-end loan products.*

Yes, different techniques are used to promote different types of loans. Because direct lending products are generated through bank branches, the selling efforts of branch personnel are an important aspect of the program. The bank may advertise home equity loans, special low-rate auto loans, or even a general loan sale. Once consumers contact the branch for information, it is up to the branch personnel to help them apply.

The bank attracts indirect loan applications by carefully selecting dealers and building good business relationships with them. It then facilitates application generation by offering loan products that are competitive with those of the dealers' other loan sources.

The type of open-end product desired will affect the choice of marketing effort. Credit cards, home equity lines of credit, and unsecured lines of credit usually are marketed through direct mail with follow-up calls or e-mail to maximize response. Applications for these products also may be received through other channels.

3. *What are the elements of a consumer loan marketing program? Give examples of how marketing techniques are used to optimize results.*

Successful marketing programs define objectives, select target markets, select promotion channels, implement the promotion, and measure the results. For example:

Select market segments: Identify the characteristics of consumers most likely to use the product or be receptive to purchasing it now. This might be done by using the bank's Marketing Customer Information File (MCIF) and matching the characteristics identified against the market to find prospects. The five principal segmentation alternatives are geographic, demographic, psychographic, volume, and benefit.

Select the promotion channel: In addition to general media advertising, such as television, radio, billboards, and posters, banks also use direct mail, telemarketing, e-mail marketing, bank Web sites, banker incentives, and consumer incentives, such as special offers. To reach consumer segments with a targeted message, banks send mailings that tailor the message to a particular segment and perhaps plan follow-up calls.

4. *What are some techniques that may make the in-person loan application process successful?*

Techniques that may make the in-person loan application process successful for both the consumer and the lender are

- smiling and greeting the customer
- using the customer's name
- setting the customer at ease
- creating a comfortable environment
- using a conversational approach

- using open-end and closed-end questions
- practicing active listening
- closing the interview politely after explaining the lending process

5. *What advantages do electronic (including the Internet), telephone, and mail-in applications have over traditional in-person applications? What are some challenges for lenders taking loan applications in person and through other channels?*

Electronic, telephone, and mail-in applications may be handled by a centralized unit, such as a central banking center, that is more efficient because it has trained specialists to handle the applications. These types of applications are more convenient ways to apply, take less time to complete, and do not require a special trip to the lender's office.

One challenge may be getting complete information from mail-in or electronic forms. Another is increased competition. This is especially true for the Internet, where information and applications can be obtained easily from other lenders.

Establishing identity and averting application fraud and identity theft is a challenge for alternative delivery channels, because the consumer is not in the presence of the lender so verification cannot be immediate.

Determining when an inquiry is an application can be a regulatory compliance challenge with all delivery systems, except perhaps direct mail applications and those completed on the bank's Web site. To comply with the Equal Credit Opportunity Act, banks need to be careful not to either wander into an unintentional application situation or discourage a consumer from applying. Most bankers encourage consumers to apply when the inquiries extend beyond interest rate quotations, basic product features, or general bank procedures.

6. *What is an established business relationship, and may banks use telemarketing to promote products and services to their own customers?*

An established business relationship is one where the consumer has conducted a financial transaction with the bank within the 18 months immediately preceding a telemarketing call, or the consumer has inquired about or applied for a product or service offered by the bank within the 3 months immediately preceding the call. Banks may telemarket to their own customers without checking the National Do Not Call Registry, though the established business relationship does not usually extend to affiliates. However, if customers ask to be placed on the bank's own do-not-call list, no calls can be made to them.

CHAPTER 8 CREDIT INVESTIGATION

Situations

1. Chip, 28, is a software developer for a new high-tech company. He has worked for four companies since he graduated from college at 21. Although this is typical in the high-technology arena, his father is concerned that being a job-hopper on paper will keep Chip from getting the consumer loan he is seeking.

   Will changing jobs so often prevent Chip from getting a loan?

For young people like Chip who work in fields like the high-technology industry, frequent job transfers are common. Changing jobs may indicate Chip's ability rather than instability.

2. Brenda is conducting a credit investigation on Carlene Smith, who has applied for a $20,000 personal loan. Smith wants to convert a room in her home to a children's playroom. The money will be used for shelving, carpeting, furniture, and lighting. Because of a policy of confidentiality, Smith's employer will verify that she works for the company but will not verify current income or earnings history. Without this verification, Brenda cannot approve the loan.

   What should Brenda do?

   Many employers are reluctant to provide direct verification or will verify only that someone is employed. In these cases, lenders must rely on indirect sources to verify income. Brenda should ask for Ms. Smith's pay stub to verify income. She also might ask for copies of her tax returns.

3. During a loan interview with Bernard, a middle-aged applicant, Francine notices that he appears very nervous and pauses for long periods before answering questions. This is especially true when Francine asks Bernard why there is little information in his credit history. The rest of his application looks fine, and Francine is inclined to think that Bernard is just intimidated by the interview situation.

   What else could this behavior signal?

   As an anxious applicant, Bernard may indeed be simply intimidated and may have good reason for his lack of credit history. However, the situation raises a concern (red flag) that Francine should investigate further.

4. When applying for a loan with ABC Bank, Nick Adams provided information about his accounts with LMN Bank. Several months later Nick applies for a new job and gives ABC Bank as a reference.

   If it answers the request, is ABC Bank a consumer reporting agency?

   If the information given is solely about Nick's accounts with ABC Bank, the bank is not subject to Fair Credit Reporting Act requirements for furnishers of consumer information. However, if the bank also passes along information gathered from LMN Bank during the credit investigation, it is acting as a consumer reporting agency and must adhere to FCRA requirements.

5. Ben Hudson is applying for a loan from AnyCity bank. The loan application form provides a space where Ben may note other information or special circumstances. This space is for information that he would like the creditor to consider in evaluating the loan application. Ben notes that he has a pacemaker that needs annual checkups.

   Can AnyCity Bank use this information?

   Yes, the bank can use the information. This is an example of obtaining and using medical information at the request of the consumer. The bank may use the information Ben provided voluntarily on the loan application. Doing so is consistent with practices for safety and soundness. The bank also may disregard it.

Self-Check and Review

1. *What are the objectives of credit investigation?*
   The primary objectives of the credit investigation process are to
   - verify that the data supplied on the application are accurate and complete
   - conduct an efficient and cost-effective investigation
   - identify negative trends or potential problems that may affect creditworthiness
   - acquire enough information to make a sound credit decision

2. *Why might a credit investigation begin by referring to bank files instead of credit reports or public records?*
   The bank's records are the least expensive and least time-consuming source of information. If the bank's previous experience with the consumer has not been satisfactory, it will not be necessary to investigate any further. If its experience has been satisfactory and the files contain helpful information, the investigation can proceed more efficiently.

3. *What are two drawbacks to using W-2 forms or tax returns to verify income data?*
   W-2s and tax returns provide information only about the consumer's past income; they may no longer accurately reflect current income. Although historical information may be helpful to some credit decisions, it is usually desirable to verify current income.

   Another problem with W-2s and tax returns is their reliability. It is possible for someone to make up fraudulent forms for verification of income and employment. Thus, this information should be confirmed from other sources.

4. *What information is available on a personal financial statement? How may a credit investigator use the information?*
   The personal financial statement contains a complete listing of the applicant's assets, liabilities, and net worth. It captures more detailed information than the application about equity in various assets, structure of debts, and the relative liquidity of the applicant. The investigator will compare the debts listed on the statement with those on the credit report to identify possible sources of additional information. The investigator also can alert the lender to problems or opportunities related to the loan.

5. *What are red flags for potential credit problems and how are they used? Give two examples.*
   Credit-quality red flags are items of information recorded on a credit application or discovered during the investigation that signal the need for special attention and further investigation. A red flag alerts the credit investigator to seek more information or to insist on direct instead of indirect sources to verify data. Common credit-quality red flags are the following (see exhibit 8.3 for more examples):
   - All credit history is less than 12 months old.
   - Applicants over 21 have no credit history.
   - There are many recent inquiries or applications for credit from other lenders.
   - All credit references are with unknown or small companies.

6. *What is account monitoring and how does it apply to open-end credit?*
   For account monitoring, the bank compares files on its current loan accounts with consumer reporting agency files, using bank-defined criteria. Consumers who no longer meet the bank's requirements are subject to further screening. Once all required data are assembled, the lender may choose to continue the account on its present terms, block it from further use, or reduce the credit limit.

7. *Under what circumstance could a bank become a furnisher of consumer information—a consumer reporting agency—as defined by the Fair Credit Reporting Act?*
   When a bank passes along information about a customer's account with another institution, it has furnished information and must comply with the requirements for consumer reporting agencies.

8. *What is at least one circumstance in which a bank may obtain and use a consumer's medical information, according to the FACT Act?*
   In general, a creditor may not obtain or use a consumer's medical information in determining the consumer's eligibility or continued eligibility for credit unless it is the type of financial information ordinarily used in making a credit decision; it is unsolicited; or it falls within one of the specific exceptions permitted by bank regulators. For example, the dollar amount of a debt to a hospital may be taken into account, as long as it is used no less favorably than nonmedical information.

CHAPTER 9
CREDIT EVALUATION AND DECISION MAKING

Situations

1. Allen Lee is reviewing loan applications from three consumers. Applicant 1, Amy, who is 22 years old, has lived in the same community all her life. She has rented her own apartment for one year, during which time she has worked in corporate sales. She had previously been a college student. Applicant 2, Charles, is 40. Two years ago, he switched jobs after working for another company for nine years as a business manager. He is buying a home in the community he has lived in for 14 years. Applicant 3, Wesley, is 33. He has been at his present job as a store clerk for six months, after working for one year at a different store. He is new to the community, where he has been renting an apartment for four months.

   How does Allen Lee determine the probability that each of these applicants will repay a loan?

   Knowing how much weight to give the time-in-one-location factor is essential when using stability to assess character. Applicant 1, Amy, is a recent college graduate; therefore she would not be expected to exhibit long-term stability. Charles, applicant 2, at age 40 has been at his present job for only two years but has a history of job stability and is buying a home in a community he has lived in for years. He is still employed. For Wesley, the 33-year-old applicant 3, lack of stability might be a negative factor.

2. Julie and her husband have owned their home for several years. Until now, they have worked near each other and needed only one car to commute. They finished making loan payments on their car several months ago and have no additional debt. Recently, Julie's office relocated to another part of town, which meant they had to purchase a second car. After reviewing her application for a car loan, the bank tells Julie that she qualifies for a loan with no down payment required. This surprises Julie, who remembers having to come up with a 20 percent down payment when they financed their first car four years ago.

   How can the bank lend Julie the full purchase price of the car, even though the value of the car will soon be less than the amount of the loan?

   Although collateral is a means of strengthening a loan, it is not a substitute for other credit requirements. This philosophy is evident in 100 percent automobile financing programs, such as the one that attracted Julie. Less emphasis is placed on equity and collateral, and more on the borrower's character and ability to pay. Julie's application revealed, among other things, job stability, homeownership, and the ability to handle prior debt.

3. Ernesto and Maria met in law school and married soon after graduation. They each brought substantial student loan debt to the marriage. A large portion of their paychecks as law clerks will go toward paying off the student loans for the next few years. They want to buy furniture and pay for a vacation in Hawaii but do not have enough money. Hoping they will qualify, they apply for a personal loan from their local bank. When the letter arrives telling them their request was declined, it includes a personal note from Mr. Hamata, their banker. Mr. Hamata is offering to meet with Ernesto and Maria to talk about handling their debt and building their credit.

   What does Mr. Hamata gain from helping this couple?

   A consumer's lack of knowledge about handling debt gives the lender an opportunity to provide financial counseling and send the consumer away with a positive impression of the bank. The letter informing them that their request was declined disappointed Ernesto and Maria. They were grateful, however, for Mr. Hamata's suggestion that they come to the bank to talk about how to manage their debt. They intend to make that appointment and will likely turn out to be committed long-term customers.

4. Paola Ponti requested a loan to purchase a boat. She asked for $20,000 at 7.5 percent for six years. The lender, Tom Chase, decided that, considering Ms. Ponti's income and credit history, the best offer he could make was $15,000 at 8.30 percent for five years. Tom wrote a letter, setting forth the terms of the counteroffer. The letter was mailed on June 25. Ms. Ponti received the letter and began to search other banks for the loan on the terms she wanted.

   Does Tom Chase have any other responsibility to Ms. Ponti?

   Yes, Tom must send a Notice of Adverse Action because Ms. Ponti did not accept the counteroffer. A lender must send this notice within 90 days after notifying the applicant of a counteroffer, if the applicant does not accept or use the offered credit.

Self-Check and Review

1. *What does making the best loan for the consumer and the bank mean?*
    It means that the loan will be good for the borrower and it will be profitable for the bank. This process requires thoughtful analysis and financial counseling throughout the consumer lending process. Lenders are not mere order-takers who analyze applications solely at the request of the consumer. They are active financial advisers who work to structure the loan that best meets both the consumer's and the bank's interests.

2. *What proven assumption about human behavior helps the lender predict a loan's credit risk?*
    Behavioral research shows that people tend to follow certain patterns throughout their lives. The best predictor of future behavior is past behavior. Lenders therefore can assume that applicants who have been responsible about handling credit obligations in the past will continue to be responsible.

3. *What are the five Cs of credit? Give an example of the information the lender reviews for each.*
    The five Cs of credit are character, capacity, capital, collateral, and conditions.

    Character requires an assessment of the consumer's willingness to repay a loan on time. Analysis of character looks at factors such as stability (age, residence, time at residence, and job or career); credit history; credit rating or payment history; types and sources of credit used; dates accounts were opened, closed, or active; debt levels; credit use patterns; and the consumer's personal characteristics.

    Capacity measures the applicant's ability to repay the loan when it is due. To measure capacity, the analyst evaluates the consumer's income, ability to repay the loan (cash flow and debt-to-income ratio), and marketability (ability to change jobs).

    Capital measures the net value of a consumer's assets. This generally is evaluated by analyzing the consumer's personal financial statement to identify assets (liquid and tangible), liabilities, net worth, and the potential that the loan can be repaid from sources other than regular income.

    Collateral is an asset pledged by a borrower to a lender to guarantee a loan. Goods purchased with loan proceeds usually are used to secure consumer loans. Other forms of collateral often accepted on consumer loans are personal residences, savings accounts, and stocks or bonds.

    Conditions describe external variables that affect the risk on the loan, such as the economy, the social and political environment, changes in government regulation, competition, and changes in the bank's goals and objectives.

4. *How important are the consumer's assets to the evaluation of creditworthiness?*
    Assets provide evidence of additional sources for repaying a loan. For example, when there is established equity in the consumer's primary residence, the lender may offer a home equity line of credit so that the loan is secured by the home as collateral. Alternatively, simply knowing the applicant's equity in the home may reassure the lender that there is a secondary source of repayment. The

consumer's liquid assets (savings, checking, and investment accounts) should be available to protect the consumer's capacity—the ability to repay the loan on time.

5. *What benefits does a credit-scoring system offer?*

   Advantages of credit scoring are increased management control, reduced loan-processing costs, reduced time requirements, a more legally defensible system, easier training of new lenders, and facilitation of data-gathering for the loan decision.

6. *How do banks combine the effectiveness of the judgmental and the credit-scoring approaches to credit evaluation and making loan decisions?*

   In a judgmental system, the final credit decision rests with the lender's analysis of an applicant's strengths and weaknesses. During the decision-making process, the lender is looking for ways to make the loan, not turn it down, and for ways to strengthen the loan request for both the consumer and the bank.

   Combined with the credit scoring system, the judgmental approach allows the lender to seek opportunities to restructure the loan to the benefit of both borrower and bank. Overrides may be made to the credit-scored decision, or the loan may be restructured. Such exceptions must comply with the bank's loan policy and usually require senior officer approval. They are documented, monitored, and controlled to preserve the scoring system's integrity.

7. *What are the bank's primary objectives in handling an adverse action?*

   When informing the consumer of an adverse loan decision or other adverse action, the lender seeks to retain the consumer's goodwill and to comply with the law, such as the Equal Credit Opportunity Act (ECOA), implemented by FRS Regulation B.

8. *What notifications does the Equal Credit Opportunity Act require lenders to make in evaluating and deciding whether to make a loan?*

   ECOA requires lenders to notify consumers about appraisals and the loan decision, including approvals, counteroffers, and adverse actions (such as declining a loan). Timing and content are prescribed and model notices are provided.

CHAPTER 10 LOAN PRICING AND PROFITABILITY

Situations

1. Recently, Jenny Wu's father died and she decided to ask her mother to live with her. About five years ago, Jenny bought a small house with an attached garage and she would like to convert the garage into a living area for her mother. She knows how much the conversion will cost and how much she and her mother can jointly pay each month to repay a loan. Jenny's banker gives her several loan options. She notices that if she takes a four-year instead of a two-year loan, the payments will be well within her budget. Even though she will end up paying more for the loan overall by extending the term, it is important to Jenny that the loan payments are affordable.

   Are other consumers similarly influenced by the monthly payment?

   Many consumers are like Jenny. Most consumers are willing to pay more for a loan over a longer term, if the monthly payment is manageable.

2. Elise would like to finance a new bedroom set. She finds what she is looking for at a furniture store that advertises "90 days same as cash" to finance purchases. The prospect of not having to make payments for the first few months is very appealing to Elise. She is on a tight budget and has to keep her monthly payments under a certain amount. Elise decides to speak to a loan officer at her bank to find out if the bank can make a similar offer.

    How can the bank compete with this type of offer?

    Banks must employ creative measures to remain competitive while maintaining credit standards. The lender in this situation might present a payment structure that will cost Elise less over the term of the loan even if she must make payments in the first three months. With the loan from the furniture company, she eventually would have to pay interest going back to the first day of the loan, probably at a higher rate, and for a shorter loan term. This would make the monthly payments much higher than Elise anticipated, and probably higher than the payments for the bank loan.

3. To pay their tuition Jodi and Franco each took out a $10,000 simple-interest loan from the same bank and with the same terms. Franco makes his monthly payments three or four days before the payment is due and pays a little more than the required amount. Jodi caught a glimpse of Franco's monthly statement lying on his desk and was surprised that his interest payment was less than her payment. She immediately called the bank to find out why.

    What did she find out?

    Because Jodi waits until the last minute to make loan payments each month, she incurs higher interest costs than Franco. Franco pays early and he pays extra on the principal balance, lowering the overall amount for the loan.

Self-Check and Review

1. *What are the differences between fixed- and variable-rate loans? What implications do these differences have for profitability?*
    Fixed-rate loans have rates that do not change during the term of the loan. The interest rate on a variable-rate loan may change based on the movement of a stated index, such as the prime rate.

    Fixed-rate loans carry greater interest-rate risk for the bank than variable-rate loans. If the bank's cost of funds rises, the net interest margin on a fixed-rate loan will be reduced. If the cost of funds declines, the net interest margin will be greater. Banks use a variety of funding strategies to help reduce risk on fixed-rate portfolios, generally matching the loans with liabilities that also have fixed rates and similar maturity patterns.

    Variable-rate loans are designed to maintain a relatively stable net interest margin throughout the life of the loan, thereby reducing, if not eliminating, interest-rate risk and preserving a predictable profit margin. However, these loans do have credit risk. If the rates rise too high too quickly and the loan allows for monthly payment increases, the consumer's debt-to-income ratio will rise as well, to the point where it may become impossible for the consumer to repay the loan.

If the loan term is extended, collateral risk may threaten; depreciating value collateral may be worth much less at the time of the new maturity date.

2. *Why is the amount of the monthly payment on a consumer loan such an important factor when a loan is structured? How can the lender adjust a loan to lower the payment without lowering the principal or rate?*

The monthly payment is often the most important element in selling a loan to a consumer. If the monthly payment is affordable and attractive compared with other options, the consumer is more likely to take the loan. On the other hand, if the monthly payment is too high, the consumer may not meet the bank's requirements for debt-to-income ratio or may decide not to take the loan.

The monthly payment on a loan may be reduced simply by extending the term of the loan, as by increasing it from 36 to 48 months, or by reducing the minimum monthly payment on a line-of-credit account, as from 5 percent to 3 percent of the balance. In either case, the consumer's payment amount will decrease without any change in the principal balance portion.

3. *What factors are taken into consideration when setting the price for consumer loans? Which single factor is the most important? Why?*

Four major factors affect loan pricing:

- The law sets the maximum rates that may be charged on various types of loans.
- The competitive environment consists of the rates competitors offer the public.
- Economic conditions may cause fluctuations in market interest rates, including those for deposits, which vary with market conditions.
- The bank's internal environment refers to its costs, objectives, strategies, and financial condition.

Of these, the competitive environment is probably the most important single factor in establishing consumer credit rates. If its interest rates are too far above the market, the bank will be unable to attract loan business. If they are too low relative to competitors, the bank most likely is sacrificing profit.

4. *List the cost categories for consumer loans. What is the trend of costs in each category?*

The cost categories for consumer installment loans are

- ***Acquisition costs.*** These are the costs of making a loan, including all expenses incurred in generating loan applications, processing them through to a decision, and documenting that they have been approved or declined. These costs have risen steadily over the years, causing banks to improve operating efficiency by such means as automated systems; target marketing; and by directing loan business to more cost-efficient products, such as open-end lines of credit.

- ***Maintenance and liquidation costs.*** This category covers the expenses of servicing accounts once the loan has been made, such as for coupon books and billing statements, payment processing, and collection and recovery processes. To hold these costs within a narrow range, efficiencies have been achieved through automation, such as preauthorized automated payments.

- *Loan-loss costs.* This factor, expressed as a loan-loss rate, reflects a bank's ability to control the credit risk in its portfolio. Variations in the loan-loss rate often are associated with trends in economic conditions, rising as the economy declines and falling during stable economic periods. There can be differences between banks and types of loan products. Credit cards typically have significantly higher loan-loss rates than home equity loans, for example.

- *Cost of funds.* The cost of funds varies over time with changes in market interest rates and each bank's funding process. Banks have sought to minimize the risk inherent in these fluctuations by expanding their use of variable-rate loans and refining their asset and liability management programs.

5. *Why does a profitability analysis need to consider the product lines? Give some examples of differences by product line.*

   For different products, the degree of risk, cost structure, and interest rate vary. Each product line is assessed to determine its contribution to bank profits. Credit cards, for example, have high gross yields and many fee income sources to offset their high operating and loan-loss costs. Auto loans have lower yields but also usually lower operating expenses and loan losses. Home equity loans offer even lower operating expenses and losses and a yield that is often higher than that for auto loans.

6. *What are legal lending limits and why do regulators set lending limits?*

   Applied to a bank's portfolio, legal lending limits refer to the total lending amount that may be extended to any one borrower, group, or industry. Regulators impose legal lending limits to promote bank safety and soundness by encouraging diversification of bank assets and to promote equitable access to banking services.

7. *What are debt cancellation contracts (DCCs) and debt suspension agreements (DSAs)? How does the Office of the Comptroller of the Currency (OCC) regulate them for national banks?*

   DCCs and DSAs are bank products similar to credit insurance. However, with credit insurance the insurer provides the product and takes the risk. The premium is added to the loan payment. DCCs and DSAs are contracts, separate from the loan agreement, that are purchased at the time the loan is obtained; the bank owns the contract and assumes the risk. A DCC may provide, for example, that if the customer dies, the loan is canceled rather than having to be paid by the customer's estate. A DSA suspends the consumer's debt pending certain conditions, such as a return to health if disabled or to employment if unemployed.

   The OCC's rule on DCCs and DSAs prohibits or limits certain practices by national banks in connection with the sale of these products, including tying, contract modification, unfavorable pricing, and no-refund features. Two disclosures must be given to the consumer. The short form, given when the consumer applies for the loan, stipulates that the product is optional. The long form is given when the loan closes and the customer must affirm in writing that the notice was received. This notice describes the DCC or DSA, the fee amount, refund policy, eligibility requirements, conditions, and exclusions.

CHAPTER 11 SELLING AND LOAN STRUCTURING

Situations

1. Tony Blanco and his family are facing another cold winter in their older home, whose doors and windows leak cold air into the house. Tony has decided that this is the year to replace the doors and windows. He knows exactly how much that will cost. Using a loan calculator he found on the Internet, he knows the payments he can afford on a $5,000 closed-end loan.

   Tony presents this information to his bank's loan officer, Arnold Carson, expecting to apply for a specific loan. Arnold reviews Tony's application and asks a few questions. He learns that Tony has children who will be going to college and that Tony has some low-yielding savings accounts at another bank. Arnold suggests a different type of loan, a home equity line of credit, which Tony had not considered. Tony agrees that this alternate suggestion is a much better solution for his needs. Arnold then discusses with Tony some other deposit and service solutions at the bank, including a higher-yielding savings account and a debit card to access the funds.

   Why did not Arnold just fill Tony's initial request? What type of sales approach did Arnold use?

   Arnold's bank has an established sales culture. Lenders see opportunities to build the banker-customer relationship. Bankers cannot be mere order-takers. They use consultative selling and cross-selling techniques to determine the customer's needs, structure the best loan for the customer, and cross-sell other bank products and services.

   Using consultative selling skills, Arnold reviewed Tony's total debt structure, financial position, and immediate and long-term needs. He then considered other relevant issues, such as the number and ages of Tony's children and other outstanding debt.

   Instead of simply filling the order for a $5,000 loan, Arnold recommended a home equity line of credit for a higher amount that will cover the cost of the current need (replacing doors and windows) and also provide for future borrowing (meeting college expenses).

   Using cross-selling skills, Arnold recommended that Tony consolidate several smaller low-yielding savings accounts into a higher-yielding account and get a debit card to access funds.

2. Bernard Stevens has requested a $5,000 unsecured line of credit to be used to consolidate a number of open accounts he has with other banks. Of his three open lines of credit, the balance on two is up to the limit and the third is over the limit. Bernard has a good credit history and each of the accounts is rated "as agreed." If the bank makes the loan, however, there is always the risk that Bernard will resume borrowing on the other accounts after paying off the current balances with the new loan, and then would be unable to handle the added debt burden.

   What should the lender do?

   Many bankers are reluctant to grant an additional open-end line of credit under these circumstances. Some bank policies prohibit loans to consumers who have more than a specified number of open-end loan accounts. The lender may be able to structure a closed-end loan that would limit Bernard's access to further debt without reapplying. The lender also may require that Bernard close the other accounts and that the bank send the final payments directly to the other lenders.

3. To reduce monthly debt payments to a manageable level, Theresa Schwenke wants to consolidate four closed-end loans. The new loan would reduce her monthly debt obligations by $150 and would satisfy the bank's debt-to-income ratio policy. Melissa Parks, the lender, approves Theresa's loan request. However, rather than giving all the proceeds directly to her, Melissa sends individual checks directly to each of Theresa's creditors to pay off the other debts.

Why did Melissa do this?

The lender wants to be sure the loans are paid off. Otherwise, Theresa's debt-to-income ratio could increase, creating an even greater strain on her budget and weakening the bank's loan. To avoid this possibility, Melissa ensures separate checks are made out to each creditor, and no new funds are given to Theresa. Melissa also cautions Theresa on the perils of continuing to add debt before the consolidation loan is repaid and provides her with literature from the ABA Education Foundation on managing credit and the Get Smart About Credit program.

Self-Check and Review

1. *What is meant by a market-driven approach to selling?*
   The market-driven approach emphasizes first determining a customer's needs and then identifying or creating products and services to satisfy those needs. This is in contrast to an operations-driven approach, which emphasizes offering products that primarily are beneficial to the bank.

2. *What is the distinction between consultative selling and cross-selling? Give an example of each.*
   In consultative selling, the lender considers an applicant's total financial picture when determining how best to handle a loan request—for example, suggesting a home equity loan in place of an unsecured consumer loan. Cross-selling identifies related products and services that might be of value to the customer—for example, automatic debit of loan payments.

3. *What are the steps necessary to establish a sales culture? Briefly explain each.*
   The steps necessary to establish a sales culture are
   - *Hone selling skills.* Once they have basic skills and an interest in sales, bankers must continuously train and practice to improve their selling skills.

   - *Motivate staff to sell.* By using techniques like monetary and nonmonetary rewards, sales- oriented businesses constantly seek to motivate their employees to sell.

- **Support the sales culture.** The entire bank must be committed to meeting customer expectations and to quality service. The quality of internal service to coworkers is as important as service to customers of the bank.

- **Stay focused on the customer.** The sales force is supported by tools, systems, and people whose objective is to let salespeople do what they do best with a minimum of distraction and stay focused on the customer.

4. *What are the stages of the purchase cycle to which bankers respond? Give an example of how each influences the consumer lending process.*
   - **Needs recognition.** Consumers must first recognize the need to borrow money before they actually seek out loan information. The demand for consumer loans usually is driven by a consumer's desire to purchase goods and services that cannot be paid for out of current income.

   - **Prepurchase search.** Once a borrowing need is recognized, consumers will seek information about how that need might be met. Some consumers use comparison shopping, calling different financial institutions for the lowest rate or the quickest credit approval. Others simply call a trusted banker.

   - **Purchase decision.** Once consumers have satisfied their need for information, they will select a loan source and agree on a particular loan arrangement. Because they generally want to resolve borrowing needs quickly, consumers do not accept unnecessary or cumbersome delays.

   - **Postpurchase feelings.** Consumers will have a general impression of the lending process and their acceptance of the loan. If the process is handled well and the best possible loan arrangement made, the opportunity for future business is enhanced. If the process is handled poorly, or if the consumer is not happy with the loan, it will be very difficult to attract future business.

5. *What sales objectives does loan structuring help banks achieve, and how?*
   Loan structuring helps bankers achieve sales objectives of
   - **Making the best loan for the customer and the bank.** For example, using the variables of interest rates, loan term, monthly payment, and collateral, the lender can structure a loan that is affordable for the customer and profitable for the bank.

   - **Selling, not order-taking.** Using consultative selling skills, the lender can structure a loan suitable for the customer and help the customer meet longer-term financial needs.

   - **Optimizing bank earnings.** Through consultative selling and cross-selling, the banker can use the information on applications to discover other financial needs and provide solutions for the customer. This, in turn, helps grow bank assets and earnings.

   - **Retaining customers.** A properly structured loan enhances the customer's experience with the bank so that the customer will be more inclined to return to the bank for solutions to other financial needs.

- ***Minimizing credit and interest rate risk.*** Well-structured loans can help the bank minimize the credit risk that otherwise might exist with a given customer or loan request. By balancing options of pricing (fixed or variable interest rates), term, amount, and collateral, the lender can determine the right match for customer and bank.

6. *Why does direct lending offer the bank the best opportunity for significant loan structuring and cross-selling other bank services?*

Direct lending offers the most opportunity for loan structuring because the banker meets the consumer and can offer loan alternatives. This flexibility is not available for indirect lending, because the consumer is interacting with a third party, the dealer, and the transaction generally is confined to the purchase of particular goods and services. Similarly, if the consumer responds to a specific product offering, such as a direct mail credit card offer, the bank only provides that particular product. However, in all cases, the bank may market its broader lending and retail banking services to those customers later.

7. *What factors influence the loan-structuring options lenders have?*

Loan-structuring options are influenced by

- consumer needs
- pricing: fixed or variable interest rates
- schedule of interest rates
- type of loan: open-end or closed-end
- amount of the loan
- term of the loan
- collateral
- control of loan proceeds
- automated loan payments
- payment protection products

8. *What is the purpose of the Home Owners Equity Protection Act? What loan types are covered by the act that revised FRS Regulation Z, Truth in Lending? What loan types are not covered?*

HOEPA bans a variety of practices, such as balloon payments for loans with less than five-year terms, and it requires early disclosures of the loan's costs and the fact that the consumer could lose the residence. The lender is required to determine the borrower's ability to repay the loan based on income and assets, not the collateral value. The following loan types are covered by HOEPA:

- a first-lien loan with an annual percentage rate that is more than eight percentage points above the interest rates on U.S. Treasury securities of comparable maturity
- a second-mortgage loan with an annual percentage rate that is more than ten percentage points above the interest rates on U.S. Treasury securities of comparable maturity

- a loan where the total fees and points the consumer must pay at or before closing exceed the greater of a flat amount or a percentage of the total loan amount that is established annually by the Federal Reserve Board. Credit insurance premiums are counted as fees.

Loan types not covered are loans to purchase a borrower's principal dwelling, reverse mortgages, and open-end credit loans (home equity lines of credit).

CHAPTER 12
LOAN DOCUMENTATION AND CLOSING

Situations

1. Andrea has been approved for the personal loan she applied for at her local bank. This morning she is meeting with the lender to sign the final papers and receive the funds. She is taken to a conference room where a loan folder has been prepared for her. Joseph, the lender, goes through the documents in the folder, explains the contents of each, and makes sure Andrea understands all documents before asking her to sign. Andrea is grateful for the opportunity to ask some questions about repayment conditions. Finally, Joseph offers Andrea a check for the loan proceeds. Noting that Andrea does not have a checking or savings account with his bank, Joseph suggests she might want to open a deposit account from which she can withdraw the loan proceeds as needed.

    How did Andrea feel after this experience?

    A satisfied loan customer is likely to use other bank services and enter into a positive long-term relationship with the bank. A good experience with a loan closing makes it easier for bankers to cross-sell other services that meet customer needs.

    Andrea's positive experience at the loan closing will make her receptive to the deposit account Joseph has suggested.

2. Paul receives a Notice of Change in Terms with his credit card bill. The notice outlines three changes to his account: his minimum monthly payment is being reduced to $15 and the annual percentage rate on the account is being reduced to 12 percent, but there will now be a $30 fee if he exceeds his credit limit. Paul is pleased with the first two changes and, although the third change represents an increase in fees, he is not concerned because he does not expect to go over his credit limit.

    Does Paul need to do anything to accept these changes to his account?

    Paul just needs to continue using the account. If he does not accept the terms, he will need to pay any outstanding balance and close the account.

3. Abraham and Kari Nichols are financing the purchase of a new auto. The loan for the auto, which will serve as collateral, will be in Abraham's name alone, but the auto title is in Kari's name. When completing the documents for the loan, Iwona, the lender, requires both Abraham and Kari to sign the security agreement. Abraham questions this because, with only his name on the note, he will be solely responsible for repayment.

Why are both signatures required?

The security agreement stipulates the creditor's and the debtor's rights and duties related to collateral. To create a security interest, the debtor must execute the security agreement. Because Kari also owns the automobile, she must agree to pledge her property. She must authenticate the security agreement so that the bank can obtain a valid lien, even though Abraham will be the only signer on the promissory note.

Self-Check and Review

1. *What are the objectives of the loan documentation and closing process?*
   The objectives of the loan documentation and closing process are to

   * complete all documents required by state and federal law

   * prepare loan documents efficiently, accurately, and professionally

   * comply with the law and the bank's loan policy

   * ensure that the consumer understands the loan's terms

   * create a positive image for the bank

   * use the opportunity to sell other bank products

2. *How does the documentation required for fixed-rate, closed-end loans differ from that for variable-rate loans?*
   All documentation for fixed-rate, closed-end accounts is handled at the time the loan is made, at closing. Variable-rate loans require continuing disclosures to the consumer after the loan has been made. Generally, the lender is required to notify consumers of changes in the loan rate and the effect they will have on payments (higher, lower, or unchanged) and the remaining loan term (extended, shortened, or the same).

3. *Under UCC Article 9 what two steps are necessary to give the lender the right to take the collateral if the borrower defaults? Why is it important for banks to follow these steps?*
   The first step is attachment, to create a valid lien that establishes the lender's legal right to the property. This is done by executing a security agreement. The second step is perfection, to notify others of the bank's security interest in the collateral. Lenders must take great care to meet all the conditions for creating a lien and perfecting a security interest. Any error could compromise the process; if that happens, the loan would be unsecured, and the bank could not take possession of the property if the borrower defaults.

4. *What happens if the bank does not properly perfect its security interest on collateral pledged for a loan?*
   If the bank does not properly perfect its security interest, it may find itself in an unsecured position, or its claim may be subordinated to a lien for a loan that actually was made later. For example, if the bank failed to perfect its lien on an automobile title, the consumer could take the title to another lender and borrow against it. If the second institution properly recorded a lien, its claim would have priority.

5. *Why is it important to create a positive image for the bank during a loan closing? Give at least two reasons.*

The loan closing can affect the bank's future relationship with the customer. If the closing is handled well, the customer will be receptive to future sales efforts and more likely to consider the bank for future business. A good closing also can help eliminate any problems or confusion that could arise in handling the credit obligation.

6. *What is the purpose of loan review? What benefits does it offer the bank?*

Loan review

- ensures that the loan fully complies with the law

- examines completed documents for accuracy, completeness, and adherence to the bank's loan policy

- resolves documentation errors

- expedites the booking of new loans

- reports on documentation problems and lender performance

- ensures that all necessary lien and insurance documents have been obtained

7. *What is the process for ensuring that a loan secured by real estate, such as a home equity loan, has flood disaster protection, if needed?*

When a loan will be secured by improved real estate, the bank must determine whether the property is in a special flood hazard area designated by FEMA. If it is, the bank must determine if the community participates in the National Flood Insurance Program. These determinations, documented on a standard FEMA form, must be completed before loan closing.

If the property is not in an SFHA, the bank documents this fact in the loan file by maintaining a copy of the determination on the approved FEMA form. If it is, and the community participates in the NFIP, the bank notifies the consumer that purchasing subsidized flood insurance is a requirement for the loan and before loan closing obtains from the consumer a written acknowledgement of flood disclosure status. When flood insurance is required, the bank must have proof of insurance at closing.

CHAPTER 13 COLLECTION AND RECOVERY

Situations

1. Donna started a new job this year. Her salary gives her enough money to cover her living expenses, make her monthly auto payment, and allow for some savings. For the first time, she feels she can use her credit card to buy nice Christmas gifts for family and friends. She knows that her income will allow her to pay for the purchases over a few months. When Donna gets her first post-Christmas credit card bill, however, she realizes that the interest rate on her credit card is higher than the interest rate on her auto loan. She decides to use her auto payment money to pay off her credit

card and skip a month on her auto payment. She is concerned when a "past due" notice arrives in the mail.

Is the lender really worried that she will not pay off her loan?

Many banks experience rising delinquencies during the fourth quarter of the year because heavy retail buying during the holiday season puts a strain on personal budgets. Donna normally makes her auto loan payments on time. Because she did not communicate with the bank about her need to skip a payment, the bank automatically sent a past-due notice. After a short period of delinquency because of holiday credit card bills, she can be expected to resume payments.

2. Carlton's loan payment is 20 days past due. When Tracy, the bank's collector, calls him, Carlton says he will make his payment on Friday. When she asks, "Why Friday?" Carlton says that he gets paid on Friday. Tracy then asks, "How will you be making your payment?" to which Carlton replies that he will bring the payment to the Main Street branch.

Why did Tracy ask these questions?

Collectors try to find out exactly when the consumer will be able to make the past-due payment, why the payment will be made on that date, and how the payment will be made. Because Tracy knows when and where Carlton will be making his payment, she can follow up immediately if the payment is not made then. A clearly defined payment arrangement is a commitment on the part of the customer, which improves the likelihood that it will happen.

3. Betty Adams is 21 days late with her loan payment. In response to collector Steven's call, Betty apologizes and says she will make the payment today. She explains that she had to pay for auto repairs, which is becoming a more common occurrence for her old automobile. Steven responds by telling Betty about the bank's new auto rates, which are very low right now. He encourages Betty to consider purchasing a new automobile so she will not have to keep pouring money into the old auto.

Why would the collector suggest a new loan to Betty Adams?

A new loan is a good solution for some collection problems. Not only does it resolve many minor delinquency problems, it positively affects loan volume and customer relations. The auto loan Steven offered to Betty is a good remedy for her, the customer, and for the bank.

4. First National Bank has a valid security interest in Barry Hanover's automobile, which Barry bought as transportation for his family. Barry failed to make his payments and his loan was charged off. First National's recovery specialist repossessed the automobile. Barry filed for a Chapter 7 bankruptcy. The debt that the auto secures is $15,000 and the auto is worth $12,000.

What can Barry Hanover do to get the automobile back?

By paying the bank $12,000, Barry can redeem the auto. The remaining $3,000 still owed is unsecured debt.

Self-Check and Review

1. *What are some common objectives for the bank collection function? Why might different objectives be set for different loan products?*

   Objectives set for the collection function are to

   - Keep delinquencies within acceptable limits.
   - Keep loan losses within acceptable limits.
   - Generate loss recoveries at desired levels.
   - Counsel customers who are having difficulty handling debt.
   - Ensure consistency with bank objectives.
   - Manage the collection and recovery functions cost-effectively.

   The delinquency and loss limits that are acceptable vary by product line, reflecting the different risks associated with each. For example, losses and delinquencies are normally higher on unsecured loans than on home equity lines of credit.

2. *What are some loan collection practices that are illegal under the Fair Debt Collection Practices Act?*

   The Fair Debt Collection Practices Act bans the following types of practices:

   - harassing, oppressing, or abusing any person
   - using false statements
   - acting unfairly in attempting to collect a debt

   The act prohibits repeatedly calling consumers, using obscene or profane language, advertising a consumer's debt, using postcards as a collection tool, telling third parties about a person's debts, and requiring consumers to accept collect telephone calls.

3. *What are some causes of consumer loan delinquencies? Is it possible to predict any of these at the time the loan is made?*

   The primary causes of delinquency are

   - unexpected health problems that change the consumer's income or debt situation
   - economic downturns
   - excessive debt
   - poor money management
   - marital problems
   - carelessness and changing attitudes toward credit use
   - irresponsible lending
   - fraud or intentional default
   - substance abuse and gambling

   Some of these problems may be uncovered during the credit investigation process—excessive debt and poor money management often are apparent on credit reports. However, many other problems cannot be identified at the time a loan is made, such as changes in an individual consumer's circumstances.

4. *What is an advantage of the decentralized approach to loan collection in a bank? What are the advantages of the centralized approach?*

   Some consumer loan managers believe the decentralized approach, in which lenders must collect their own loans, is better because it forces them to use more discretion in making credit decisions, and the lender may be more effective in collecting the loan.

   Advocates of the centralized approach argue that using collection specialists who work full time to collect delinquent accounts is more effective and efficient. The centralized approach also leaves lenders free to build new business using up-front risk control tools, such as credit scoring.

5. *What are the stages of the collection cycle? What are some of the characteristics of each stage?*

   The stages of the collection cycle are as follows:

   - *early stage* (up to 15 days past the due date). This stage is highly automated, requiring little personal involvement. The early stage uses reminder notices and late charges with little or no personal contact.

   - *personal contact stage* (16 days to charge off). Here collectors become involved with the account. Tools used for collection are mailed notices and telephone calls. Some remedies are payment extension, loan refinancing, a new loan, an insurance claim, right of setoff, and consumer credit counseling.

   - *serious delinquency stage* (60 days or more in default). A delinquency problem may be identified at any time; however, accounts usually are defined as seriously delinquent when they reach 60 days past due. The seriousness of the delinquency at this stage limits the types of collection remedies that may be used. Only the most experienced collectors usually handle this stage. Collection remedies for seriously delinquent accounts are repossession, lawsuits resulting in judgments, foreclosure, and wage garnishment.

   - *charge-off.* This is the point at which the bank recognizes the account as a loss, usually 65 to 120 days after default. Responsibility for handling the account now passes to the recovery function.

6. *What is the purpose of the loan recovery function? How does it differ from the collection function?*

   The recovery function is concerned with collecting as much of the money already charged against loss reserves as possible. The collection function works to collect payments, keep accounts current, or prevent losses; the recovery function determines the best way to recoup as much of a charged-off loan balance as possible in a reasonable time and for a reasonable cost. The recovery specialist may negotiate a settlement, pursue court action against the consumer's income or assets, or simply abandon any further collection effort.

7. *What is the difference between Chapter 7 and Chapter 13 of the Bankruptcy Code? What major change did the Bankruptcy Abuse Prevention and Consumer Protection Act make to the code?*

   In Chapter 7, Liquidation, all of a debtor's nonexempt assets are converted to cash, which is distributed among the creditors according to the type and amount of their claims. Then the debtor is discharged from indebtedness.

Chapter 13, Adjustment of Debts of an Individual with Regular Income, also known as the "wage-earner plan," is a rehabilitation plan to conserve the debtor's assets and restore him or her to solvency. The bankruptcy court must approve a plan, usually providing for lower monthly payments, to enable the consumer to repay obligations from future income.

The Bankruptcy Abuse Prevention and Consumer Protection Act of 2005 sets out an objective needs-based bankruptcy test that determines whether debtors can afford to repay some or all of their debts. This change corrects a Bankruptcy Code flaw that had made Chapter 7 liquidation proceedings available to debtors who can afford to repay debt. More bankruptcy filers who are capable of repaying a significant portion of their debts must now do so under Chapter 13.

8. *What is the objective of the Servicemembers Civil Relief Act (SCRA)?*
   SCRA provides debt relief for servicemembers and dependents when the members are called to active duty. For borrowers covered by the SCRA, there are limitations on the interest rates lenders can charge and on the fulfillment of lease, mortgage, and installment contract obligations.

Learning Check

Answers to Galaxy Bank Financial Case Study Questions

HOME EQUITY LINES OF CREDIT

1. *What is the reason for Galaxy's success to date in this product line? Is the same approach likely to continue to be successful?*

   Most of the success is due to a competitively priced and structured product and high consumer demand. Yes, the approach should continue to be successful; remaining competitive in product pricing and structure will be important for future success.

2. *Because market share for this product is very important, what can the bank do to increase sales?*

   Some alternatives are offering teaser rates, waiving fees completely, premiums or gifts, and an extensive marketing campaign through direct mail and advertising. The bank could also build strategic alliances with other businesses, such as home improvement "big box" retailers, local retailers, or general contractors, or align with established business customers to add value to the commercial banking relationship.

3. *What can Galaxy do to increase dollar use of current HELOCs? Are any new marketing efforts needed?*

   Again, Galaxy can offer premiums for dollar use, reduce rates, offer interest rebates, and initiate a direct contact campaign. Galaxy also can pull credit reports on current borrowers and target those with credit card balances to call to discuss consolidating their debt. Indirect lending borrowers with loans maturing in six months can be solicited for new automobile loans, using a HELOC to finance the purchase.

INDIRECT AUTOMOBILE LOANS

1. *What is Galaxy doing wrong? Why do the midsized banks appear to be successful with this product? Why would out-of-state banks be interested in getting into this market?*

   Galaxy is not competitive with its dealer rate, customer rate, and terms. The midsized institutions manage the process closely, and they maintain relationships with key dealers. Out-of-state banks use indirect lending as a way to build loan volume quickly and expand their geographic market.

2. *Should Galaxy exit this product line? Would doing so adversely affect other aspects of its emphasis on relationship banking?*

   Getting out of the product line is one alternative; however, Galaxy could try to enlarge its relationship with select dealers. By packaging the entire relationship, it might be profitable. There would be consequences if Galaxy exited improperly, such as loss of good will in the community and compromising its reputation with the dealers.

3. *What alternatives are available to Galaxy as substitutes for this product line if it decides to exit?*

   Galaxy could offer an online lending program, promote its direct lending function in the branch locations, and become more efficient at this than the competition. Galaxy could also introduce a leasing option that would compete with the dealers.

MARINE LENDING

1. *Can the bank attract new marine brokers and still manage its relationships with current brokers? If yes, how can Galaxy do this?*

   The bank certainly can build a more effective program, if it wants to keep this business. Creating some competitively priced and structured loans and offering dealers additional services are a few of ways to do that. It can establish an excellent marine financing program and build strong relationships with dealers. Bank personnel could attend boat and sports shows and offer the same program to dealers' customers as well as prospective dealers.

2. *What will happen to this product line if there is a significant recession? What is likely to happen to the current portfolio? What would happen to demand?*

   Most boats are considered luxury items, and a recession would have a negative effect on certain segments of this portfolio. Top-end luxury boats would be unaffected, but low-end pleasure craft would be. Demand for new boats definitely would be less.

CREDIT CARDS

1. *What should Galaxy do about its credit card products? Are there new marketing programs that it can use to build market share successfully and have a higher profile for this product line?*

   Galaxy can expand the product line with additional features and benefits. In fact, the marketplace dictates this expansion if the bank wants to increase market share. New marketing ideas include creating credit card products for different target markets and lifestyles and adding access features to ensure use in worldwide networks for international as well as local and national acceptance. Galaxy also might discuss the affinity card program with some large local or regional groups and think about cobranding with a large nonbank partner.

2. *Can Galaxy continue to be a viable player in a market increasingly dominated by major national players?*

Most banks are selling their portfolios to larger administrators, and Galaxy could consider this course of action.

3. *Is the credit card market nearing the saturation point? Might the product begin to lose market share to debit cards and other types of transactional products?*

The credit card business may experience some erosion in market share with the increase in debit cards and other transactional cards that serve multiple purposes. In addition, an aging population segment will move into another life-style category and will require less credit.

DIRECT CONSUMER LOANS

1. *What types of objectives should branch personnel establish for consumer credit products? What consumer credit training should branch personnel receive? How can Galaxy motivate its employees to generate more consumer loans? What specific actions should the bank take to stimulate volume?*

Objectives should be set for loan products, credit insurance and related products, and other bank services to be cross-sold to consumers. Branch personnel can be trained in relationship building, generating applications, cross-selling techniques, loan structuring, and loan closing. Incentive programs, properly managed, can motivate sales staff. The bank can offer rate specials supported by a marketing campaign.

2. *What should Galaxy do about its credit decision-making process?*

Galaxy should streamline the process and ensure that the credit-scoring system is valid and current. The bank should train lenders to be proficient relationship-builders and improve the credit score override process.

INTERNET BANKING

1. *What market research would help Galaxy determine its approach online banking?*

Galaxy should engage in competitive research, especially on historical perform-ance in other markets where banks have used the Internet for a longer period, and conduct community group leader surveys, bank customer surveys or polling, and focus groups. The bank also should research Internet providers to choose a provider and the level of support it needs.

2. *At a minimum, what should Galaxy do with online banking?*

   Galaxy should provide information about branches; employee or department contact addresses or phone numbers; lists of services and product descriptions; instructions on how to open accounts or apply for loans; simple loan applications that can be completed on the Web site or printed, completed, and returned by mail or to a branch.

3. *Should Galaxy create a fully interactive Web site with loan capabilities and other bank services?*

   Yes. Galaxy should have an interactive site that allows customers to do their banking in addition to applying for loans. Lending should be part of a complete relationship package that also includes services such as account access and bill payment services.

4. *Is Galaxy too late getting into the market to go online now? If not, how can the bank use its late position to its advantage?*

   Although late, it is important for Galaxy to have a Web site in order to remain competitive. Galaxy can build a 'personal touch' into the Internet program, so that bankers are consultative rather than just order processors. The bank can use the Internet for transactions, education, basic information, and personal account management. Branch personnel can certified as financial service advisors.

Glossary

access device A card, code, or other means of access to a consumer's account, or any combination thereof, that may be used by the consumer to initiate electronic funds transfers.

accommodation loan A loan that is approved even though it contains exceptions to the bank's stated loan policy, because making the loan benefits the bank in some other way.

account monitoring Analyzing the status and behavior pattern of current loan customers to guide decisions on whether to change or continue credit limits or to terminate lines of credit.

acquisition cost The total cost associated with making a loan. It includes costs for marketing, taking applications, interviewing applicants, investigating the credit risk, gathering and processing documents, and making the credit decision.

add-on *See* aftermarket product.

adverse action A creditor's decision to deny a consumer's request for credit, reduce an existing credit line (except for delinquency); or change the terms, rate, or amount of a credit request. Such actions require that the consumer be advised in writing of the reasons for the adverse action.

affiliated business arrangement An ownership interest of more than 1 percent in a business connected to a federally regulated mortgage transaction.

affinity card A card product offered by a bank in conjunction with a partner and targeted to a group of like-minded individuals brought together by a common interest, such as a profession, university affiliation, or cause.

aftermarket product An additional product added to a loan, such as credit insurance or warranty services. *Also known as* add-on.

Allowance for Loan and Lease Losses (ALLL) A liability account to offset estimated credit losses associated with the loan and lease portfolio (the loans and leases that the bank has the intent and ability to hold for the foreseeable future or until maturity or payoff).

amortization Periodic repayment of the principal amount due on a term loan until the entire balance is paid.

annual percentage rate (APR) The interest and other finance charges on a loan expressed as an annual rate.

applicant A person who requests or receives credit from a lender, including anyone who is to be contractually liable on the debt.

application An oral or written request for an extension of credit that is made according to the procedures established by a lender for the type of credit requested.

appraisal The valuation of property. The value determined on a specific date is known as the appraised value.

appreciating value collateral An asset pledged for a loan that increases in value over time, such as real estate.

arm's length basis A transaction that is conducted by parties freely and independently on market terms and conditions with each party acting in its own best interest without any preferential treatment or other special relationship.

assessment area Under the Community Reinvestment Act, the geographical area a bank designates as the community it will serve. Generally, this will be the area where the bank has branches, from which the bank receives most of its deposits, and in which the bank makes the majority of its loans.

asset and liability committee (ALCO) The bank committee that monitors the costs of deposits and the income from loans, reviews the matching of term and interest rates of deposits and loans, and otherwise manages the bank's assets and liabilities to maximize long-term wealth for bank shareholders.

assignment of wages Prohibited clauses in loan agreements whereby the customer agrees that the lender may obtain the customer's wages to pay a loan debt that is in default. Such clauses are illegal, unless revocable by the customer or applicable only to wages earned at time of contract.

attachment The process by which property owned by a debtor is pledged to a secured party, which obtains a right to the property. *Also known as* establishing a valid lien.

authentication Under Uniform Commercial Code Article 9, to sign or to execute or otherwise adopt a symbol or encrypt or similarly process a record in whole or in part, with the present intent of the authenticating person to identify the person and adopt or accept a record.

automatic stay The Bankruptcy Code requirement that once a bankruptcy petition is filed, creditors must halt any recovery efforts except through the bankruptcy court.

average cost The cost of lending spread over the entire loan portfolio so that every loan is allocated an equal share of the total cost; the total cost of lending divided by the total number of loans in the portfolio.

average daily balance The sum of daily loan balances in a billing cycle divided by the number of days in the cycle.

average prime offer rate A rate published by the Federal Reserve that represents the average of offer rates for the lowest-risk prime mortgages. It is used to set reporting thresholds for first-lien and subordinate lien loans and to require other lender actions, such as the establishment of escrow accounts.

balance sheet A detailed list of assets, liabilities, and owner's equity (net worth), showing a company's financial position at a specific time. Also known as a statement of condition.

balloon payment loan A loan where the regular payments do not fully pay off the principal balance and a lump sum payment of more than twice the amount of the regular payment is required.

Bankruptcy Code The federal law that governs legal proceedings for those who are no longer able to pay their debts.

benchmark A standard or rule to which other items or processes can be compared.

benefit The value that the product or service feature gives to customers, such as to make money, save money, save time, provide convenience, or provide security.

book To enter a loan on the records of the lender.

breach of contract The unexcused failure to perform an action promised in a contract.

breakeven point The point at which total fixed and variable costs exactly equal revenues.

buy rate The rate of interest a lender will charge a dealer of consumer goods or services for the purchase of retail contracts originated by the dealer. *Also known as* retention rate.

buyer's remorse The tension a customer may experience after making an expensive purchase. It is a time when the customer needs reassurance about the purchase decision. *Also known as* cognitive dissonance.

buying on margin The use of borrowed funds, plus some equity, to purchase assets such as securities. The difference between the amount of equity and the amount of the loan is the margin.

call loan *See* demand loan.

call report *See* consolidated report of condition and income.

CAMELS Acronym for the rating system, on a 1-to-5 scale, used by bank regulatory agencies to evaluate bank safety and soundness. It stands for measurements of capital adequacy, asset quality, management, earnings, liquidity, and sensitivity to market risk.

capacity One of the five Cs of credit; it measures the applicant's ability to repay the loan when it is due.

capital One of the five Cs of credit; it is the net value of a consumer's assets.

captive finance company A subsidiary of a large corporation the primary business of which is to perform credit operations and finance consumer purchases of the parent corporation's products.

cash flow The amount of money available to an individual to cover debts and discretionary expenditures, a factor in capacity.

cash selling price The actual price the consumer is paying for an item, including the full price plus any sales tax.

cash value The book or fair market value of an asset on the day it is sold.

change in terms notice A written notice required by the Truth in Lending Act, implemented by FRS Regulation Z, for open-end credit accounts when, for example, terms required in the initial disclosure table are changed or the required minimum periodic payment is increased. It must be mailed to the consumer before the effective change date; generally, 15 days in advance for home-secured credit lines and 45 days for unsecured credit lines.

Chapter 7 The Bankruptcy Code provisions for the court-administered liquidation of the debtor's nonexempt assets to pay creditors. Upon repayment, the debtor is relieved of the financial obligations.

Chapter 13 The Bankruptcy Code provisions for the adjustment of debts of an individual with regular income. The debtor is allowed to "reorganize" the debt and make partial or full repayment over a court-approved period. Chapter 13 often is referred to as the "wage-earner" plan.

character One of the five Cs of credit: it assesses the consumer's willingness and desire to repay a loan on time.

charge-off The amount of principal and interest on a loan that is written off the bank's books when the bank no longer expects to be able to collect it.

chattel mortgage A loan secured by a pledge of personal property.

closed-end loan A loan for a specific purpose and for a fixed amount that is established at the beginning of the transaction, to be repaid in one or more regular payments over a set term.

cobranded card A bankcard issued with a commercial partner, such as an airline, telephone company, or retailer, to promote loyalty through value-added incentives, such as discounts, rewards, and other consumer benefits.

code of conduct A formal set of guidelines that represents a company's policies for corporate responsibility and individual conduct.

Code of Federal Regulation (CFR) The codification of federal rules by title and chapter numbers so that rules can be referenced easily. The CFR has 50 titles. Title 12 applies federal agency rules that affect banks.

collateral One of the five Cs of credit: an asset pledged by a borrower to a lender to guarantee a loan. The asset becomes the property of the lender if the borrower fails to repay the loan.

collateral risk The financial risk to a bank that the value of collateral will not cover the principal balance on a loan.

collection cycle The stages of and processes for handling delinquent accounts from the first date of delinquency through charge-off.

collection function The bank area primarily responsible for following up on past due accounts.

comaker The person who by signing a promissory note with another person becomes jointly liable to pay. *See also* cosigner.

common stock One of the two major types of equity on which dividends are paid. This stock also carries voting privileges. Claim on corporate assets by owners of this stock are subordinate to those of bondholders, preferred stockholders, and general creditors. *See also* preferred stock.

comparison-shopping To shop for the best product choice by comparing the prices and features of products from competing providers.

compliance officer The bank employee charged with establishing controls to ensure compliance with banking regulations and bank policies.

conditions One of the five Cs of credit: external variables that affect the risk of the loan, such as the economy, social and political environments, government regulations, or competition, or changes in the bank's goals and objectives.

confession of judgment A clause in a loan agreement that allows a creditor to file a suit against a customer and take a judgment without notifying the customer. It is prohibited by the Credit Practices Rule.

conflict of interest An action taken by a person in an official capacity that may benefit that person personally to the detriment of the employer.

conservatorship A legal process in which a person or an entity is appointed to establish control and oversight of an individual's or company's legal and financial affairs. Beneficiary individuals are usually minors or have been declared incompetent by a court. Beneficiary companies are usually in financial distress and are held in conservatorship until they are sound and solvent. A conservatorship may be appointed by a court or through a statute. *Also known as* guardianship.

consolidated report of condition and income A sworn statement of a bank's financial condition as of a certain date, submitted in response to a demand from a supervisory agency or authority. *Also known as* call report.

consultative selling Selling bank products and services by working with the customer to identify the best solution for the customer's financial need.

consumer The person who buys and uses goods and services for family or personal use. In lending, the person ultimately responsible for repaying a consumer loan.

consumer credit Credit extended to consumers, either individually or jointly, primarily for buying goods and services for personal use.

consumer report *See* credit report.

consumer reporting agency An organization or company that assembles or evaluates the credit histories of consumers for purposes of furnishing credit report s to third parties. *Also known as* credit reporting agency, credit bureau.

consummation In lending, the time the consumer signs the loan contract and becomes liable on a credit transaction.

contingent liability A liability that may exist if a specific event occurs that is out of the control of the borrower or the lender.

controlled business arrangement An ownership interest of more than 1 percent in a business connected to a federally regulated mortgage transaction.

convenience user A credit account customer who uses the account and pays the balance in full each month, thereby avoiding finance charges.

cosigner A natural person who assumes liability for the obligation of another person without receiving goods, services, or money in return or, in the case of an open-end credit obligation, without receiving the contractual right to obtain extensions of credit on the account. A cosigner signs the promissory note or other evidence of debt.

cost of funds What the bank pays to secure the money it uses to lend, usually in terms of interest on deposits or funds borrowed from investors.

cramdown A Bankruptcy Code provision allowing a court to confirm a debtor's reorganization or debt adjustment plan although only one class of creditors may accept it. The court must find that the plan is fair and equitable to the creditors.

credit facility A lending structure made in a business, corporate, or government finance context. In the private sector, it is used usually in connection with equity financing. In the public sector examples are agency programs established to foster government sponsorship of private sector commercial activities.

credit insurance Insurance the borrower buys to assure payment of any outstanding credit balance in the event of death, disability, or loss of income source. It is provided by an insurance company that may be a partner with or an affiliate of the bank.

credit investigation The process of verifying information provided by a loan applicant to determine the applicant's ability to repay a loan.

credit limit The maximum allowable unpaid balance on open-end credit accounts, such as credit cards or lines of credit.

credit repair clinic A firm that advertises fee-based services to consumers for the purpose of improving credit ratings and resolving bad debts. Some clinics are illegitimate and have been involved in scams.

credit report Information that consumer reporting agencies communicate by written, oral, or other methods regarding a consumer's creditworthiness, credit standing, credit capacity, character, general reputation, personal characteristics, or mode of living. *Also known as* consumer report.

credit reporting agency *See* consumer reporting agency.

credit risk The probability, which exists with any loan that the debtor cannot or will not repay the debt.

credit scoring A valid and empirically derived statistical analysis used to evaluate an applicant's creditworthiness.

creditworthiness A borrower's ability and willingness to repay debt, usually assessed on the basis of the amount and quality of the borrower's assets and repayment history.

cross-selling The practice of promoting financial services and products in addition to those already used by the customer.

data mining Using specialized software to locate patterns and relationships within a database, such as locating customers with common interests.

dealer An individual or firm that buys, holds inventory, and resells goods or securities for profit.

dealer agreement A business contract that describes the rates, terms, and other requirements on which a bank will buy loans from a dealer.

dealer recourse The right of the bank to collect from the dealer full or partial payment of a loan on which a consumer defaults.

dealer reserve account A deposit reserve account set up by a bank containing the interest rate differential that accrues to dealers when they sell or discount installment loan contracts to a bank.

dealer trade A product exchange process whereby two dealers trade similar products, such as vehicles, without a monetary exchange. The trade typically is used when a consumer has located a desired high-ticket product at another dealership. This practice is prevalent in the automobile market.

debit card A plastic card similar to a credit card that enables a cardholder to withdraw cash or purchase goods or services, the cost of which is charged immediately to the cardholder's bank deposit account. It may be activated at point-of-sale terminals. Online settlement requires a personal identification number (PIN).

debt cancellation contract (DCC) A contract that provides for the cancellation of the consumer's obligation on a loan pending certain events, such as the consumer's death. This debt protection service is purchased separately from the loan and has a separate contract.

debt collector As defined by the Fair Debt Collection Practices Act, a person who collects or attempts to collect debts owed by a borrower to a third party.

debt suspension agreement A contract that provides for the suspension of the consumer's debt for a time, such as when the consumer is disabled or unemployed. This debt protection service is purchased separately from the loan and has a separate contract.

debt-to-income ratio A measure of a consumer's creditworthiness computed by dividing the dollar amount of monthly loan payments by the gross or net monthly income.

deed of trust A sealed instrument in writing, duly executed and delivered, that transfers property to a trustee. It is used in some states instead of a mortgage. The borrower transfers property to a trustee for the benefit of the lender, and it is conveyed back to the borrower when the loan is paid back.

default Failure to comply with any of the terms of a loan agreement.

delinquency rate The percentage of either dollar amount or number of loan accounts that is past due by 30 days or more. *Also* *known as* delinquency percentage or delinquency ratio.

demand loan A loan that has no specified maturity date but is due for payment on demand by the creditor or at the initiative of the borrower. Also known as call loan.

depreciating value collateral An asset pledged for a loan that declines in value over time, such as a standard automobile.

dictionary attack Generating e-mail addresses by combining names, letters, or numbers into multiple permutations.

direct lending Lending that is straight from bank to consumer.

direct verification A credit investigation procedure that involves direct contact with creditors, employers, and landlords to verify information on an application.

disability A physical or mental impairment that substantially limits one or more major life activities, a record of such impairment or being regarded as having such an impairment.

discharge Under the Bankruptcy Code, the release from the legal obligation to pay certain debts.

disclosure The notice that must be given to a consumer borrower pertaining to credit terms and other facts relevant to the loan.

discount The amount or percentage below the face or stated value at which securities are bought or sold; the opposite of premium.

disintermediation The flow of funds out of depository institutions, such as banks, and into alternative sources, such as mutual funds, that pay higher rates.

disparate impact A policy or practice applied to everyone but which has the effect of discriminating because of a disproportionate negative affect on a group

of persons. It does not require an intent to discriminate.

disparate treatment The handling of people or classes of people differently based on a prohibited basis. It does not require proof of actual intent to discriminate.

double financing The fraudulent practice in which a dealer applies for and receives loans for the same consumer from two different sources.

down payment A partial payment made at the time of purchase, with the balance to be paid later; the consumer's initial investment in the goods.

earnings statement *See* profit-and-loss statement.

electronic application An application for a bank service or product that is completed and sent through a fax machine or over the Internet.

encryption A process of transforming plain (readable) text into cipher (unreadable) text for security or privacy. It allows customers to authenticate security agreements electronically and facilitates loans being made over the Internet.

equity The interest or value an owner has in the property less the amounts of liens on it.

equity stripping Requiring and financing so many fees that the borrower's equity in the property is substantially lessened.

established business relationship A relationship where the consumer has conducted a financial transaction with a company, such as a bank, within the 18 months immediately preceding a telemarketing call, or the consumer has inquired about, or applied for, a product or service offered by the company within the 3 months immediately preceding a telemarketing call.

ethics Principles of conduct and judgment that affect business practices.

exception Part of the loan policy that details what policies can be waived and under what circumstances.

extension A delinquency remedy that allows the customer to defer loan payments for a specified time, such as 30 days. For a closed-end loan, the account is brought up to date and the missed payments are added to the term of the loan, extending the maturity. Also known as re-aging an account.

feature A specific characteristic that describes the product, such as no closing costs for a home equity line of credit.

Fed funds rate *See* federal funds rate.

Federal Financial Institutions Examination Council (FFIEC) A group comprised of representatives of U.S. financial agencies, including the Federal Deposit Insurance Corporation, the Federal Home Loan Bank Board, Federal Reserve Board, National Credit Union Administration, and Office of the Comptroller of the Currency.

federal funds rate The interest rate charged on short-term loans made by one bank to another through the Federal Reserve System. Also known as the Fed funds rate.

Federal Reserve discount rate The interest rate charged by the Federal Reserve to member banks for loans from its reserves made to banks to finance temporary liquidity, and seasonal or emergency needs.

finance charge The borrower's cost for a loan in dollars and cents. It includes any charge payable directly or indirectly by the consumer and imposed directly or indirectly by the creditor as an incident to or a condition of the extension of credit. It does not include any charge of a type payable in a comparable cash transaction.

financing statement A document that contains basic information about certain collateral pledged by a borrower on a loan. It is filed in local or state public records.

five Cs of credit A method of evaluating creditworthiness in terms of the consumer's character, capacity, capital, collateral, and conditions.

fixed-rate loan A loan with an interest rate that remains the same over the life of the loan.

floorplan line of credit A commercial line of credit in which the bank finances the dealer's inventory. When the goods are sold, the bank is repaid. *Also known as* inventory financing, wholesale line of credit program.

fluctuating value collateral An asset pledged for a loan that rises and falls in value over time, such as a share of stock.

forbearance The act of refraining from legal action when a loan is in arrears (as when the delinquency is due to medical reasons), usually granted when a borrower satisfactorily brings payment up to date.

force place The process by which a lender purchases insurance for the borrower, usually hazard or flood insurance, on real property used to secure a loan. The premium is added to the principal of the loan. The borrower must pay all premium costs before the lender's lien on the property will be released.

foreclosure A legal procedure that allows a creditor to sell real estate held as collateral on a loan if the borrower defaults.

fraud An intentional misrepresentation made by one person to another who, believing the misrepresentation, takes some action and suffers a loss of property or a right to the first person.

functional regulation system A regulatory principle incorporated in the Gramm-Leach-Bliley Act that places certain authorized banking activities under the authority of federal and state regulators other than the principal federal bank regulators.

future value The value tomorrow of money lent today.

garnishment *See* wage garnishment.

good faith estimate The disclosure statement provided to an applicant for a mortgage loan within three business days of the application. It describes the proposed loan, the types and amounts of charges payable at the closing of the loan, and the tolerances within which each category of closing costs may change before closing.

grace period The period during which no interest accrues on a credit card; the time between the date a credit card transaction is posted to a cardholder's account and the date when the payment is due.

guarantor A natural person who agrees to assume the debt of another by executing a guaranty agreement. The agreement can be specific to one loan or it may cover all debts of the principal borrower.

harvesting Using computer programs that search public areas on the Internet to compile lists of e-mail addresses from Web sites, newsgroups, chat rooms, and other online destinations for the purpose of sending e-mail communications to the captured addresses.

HOEPA loan A high-interest-rate or high-fee real estate-secured loan that the Home Ownership and Equity Protection Act subjects to additional federal disclosure requirements.

holder in due course A purchaser of a negotiable instrument, such as a check or a promissory note, that buys the instrument in good faith, for value, and without knowledge of any claims or defenses the maker has against the original holder.

household goods Under FRS Regulation AA, Unfair or Deceptive Acts or Practices, a consumer's and the consumer's dependents' personal possessions. Not included are works of art, antiques, or jewelry other than a wedding ring.

identity theft A crime involving the possession of identifying information not belonging to the person using it, or the attempt to access the financial resources of another person by using illegally obtained identifying information.

imaging A process that captures information from, for example, a loan document or check and stores it digitally.

income statement *See* profit and loss statement.

index rate A benchmark rate, such as the prime or the 90-day U.S. Treasury bill rate, used to determine the variable-interest rate in effect at any given time.

indirect lending A lending program in which a third party, such as a retailer, arranges the financing for the borrower and by prior arrangement sells the loan to the bank.

inquiry A notation on a credit report that indicates the applicant has applied for credit from a specific organization or that an updated report was ordered.

insider As defined by FRS Regulation O, an executive officer, director, or principal shareholder, and any related interest of such a person.

insolvency The inability to pay debts when due; a negative net worth.

installment loan A loan repaid in two or more periodic payments of fixed amounts.

insurance binder The written evidence that an insurance company or its agent has agreed to provide temporary hazard or title insurance coverage. It is valid only for a specified time, after which it must be replaced by a permanent policy.

inventory financing *See* floorplan lines of credit.

judgment A sum due for payment or collection as a result of a court order.

judgmental decision-making process The process used to make credit decisions that relies primarily on the knowledge and experience of the lender, guided by standard loan policies.

lease A contractual arrangement through which the owner of property, such as automobiles or equipment, rents the property to someone else.

leasing A financing program in which a lessor (a bank or dealer) agrees to allow the use of the collateral (goods to be leased) by a lessee (the consumer renting the goods) for a specified period and monthly payment.

legal lending limit The maximum amount of money a bank may legally lend to a single borrower or combination of financially related borrowers, expressed as a percentage of the bank's capital and surplus.

lending authority The maximum dollar amount of a loan that an individual lender or group of loan officers can make without referring the loan to the bank's loan committee.

lessee One who rents and uses property or goods owned by someone else.

lessor The owner of property or goods rented to someone else.

leverage A measure of the consumer's financial strength that relates debt to assets, or to net worth.

LIBOR *See* London Interbank Offered Rate.

lien A legal claim or attachment on public record against property as a security interest for the payment of an obligation. It reflects the guaranteed right of a lender or investor to specific property in case the loan defaults. Under UCC Article 9, this also is known as a security interest.

liquid asset An asset that is readily convertible to cash to meet short-term cash needs. Examples are bank accounts, stocks, bonds, or cash value of a life-insurance policy.

liquidity The speed and ease with which an asset may be converted to cash without loss in value.

loan application fraud The attempt by criminals to use loan applications to obtain bank funds dishonestly, such as by using another person's identity.

loan closing The process in which all required loan documents are signed and funds are disbursed to the borrower.

loan consummation The time at which the consumer signs the loan contract and becomes liable on a credit transaction.

loan documentation The process of completing all the papers necessary to secure the lender's interest and to comply with the law.

loan flipping Frequent refinancing with no benefit to the borrower.

loan-loss rate A measure of a lender's previous experience with bad loans computed by dividing the dollar amount of total losses by the dollar amount of total loans outstanding.

loan loss reserve An amount set aside to cover undetermined losses from borrowers likely to default on their loans. The amount is built from deductions to net income and funds counted in the bank's capital.

loan policy A written statement of the goals, guidelines, standards, and procedures for lending set forth by the board of directors and executive officers. It helps employees make decisions at every stage of the lending process.

loan review The function of examining loan documents to ensure accuracy, completeness, and conformity with bank loan policies and regulatory requirements. It also monitors long-term documentation and loan status.

loan structuring The process of analyzing an applicant's debts and recommending a new loan with different features that better meets the needs of both consumer and bank.

loan-to-value ratio (LTV) The ratio used to calculate the maximum amount a consumer can borrow based on an appraised value of the collateral and the maximum percentage of this value that the bank will lend.

loan volume The number and dollar amounts of new loans made or advanced during a period, such as a month or year.

loans outstanding Interest-earning assets that represent the total amount of money owed to a bank from its borrowers.

London Interbank Offered Rate (LIBOR) An international money market interest rate that represents the average rate offered by banks for interbank placements of Eurodollars.

loss payee The party that would have first claim on the proceeds of funds disbursed in payment of an insurance claim.

low-quality asset An asset that examiners so classify, is on a nonaccrual status, is more than 30 days past due, or has been rene-gotiated due to the borrower's deteriorating financial condition.

maintenance and liquidation cost The cost of collecting payments and servicing open loan accounts, including overhead expenses such as rent and utilities, salaries for loan processors and customer service representatives, coupon books, office supplies, and computer expenditures.

margin The difference or spread between the market value of securities used as collateral for a loan and the amount of loan granted.

marginal cost The additional cost attributable to the production of each additional loan.

marginal loan A loan considered to be a borderline credit risk.

market segmentation The process of dividing the market into relatively homogeneous groups to more effectively market products and services.

marketing customer information file (MCIF) An internal bank database containing detailed demographic information about customers and prospects.

material misrepresentation In law, the crime of misstating relevant and significant facts in a legal document, such as a loan application or contract, in order to obtain money, goods, or benefits from another party.

medical information Under the FACT Act, which amended the Fair Credit Reporting Act, information, oral or recorded, in any form, created by or derived from a health care provider or the consumer, that relates to the past, present, or future physical, mental, or behavioral health or condition of an individual, the provision of health care, or the payment for provision of health care.

Morris Plan bank A financial institution of the type established in 1910 by Arthur J. Morris to make small and medium-sized unsecured loans to consumers who could secure two cosigners. Because most banks at that time made loans only to businesses, Morris Plan banks were among of the earliest institutions to provide consumer credit.

mortgage A legal document, the requirements for which vary by state, in which a borrower gives the lender a lien on property as security for repayment of the loan.

mortgage-backed security (MBS) A security that represents an undivided interest in a pool of mortgages. An MBS commonly is referred to as a "pass-through" certificate because the principal and interest of the underlying loans are passed through to investors. The interest rate on the security is lower than the interest rate on the underlying loans to cover payment of servicing and guaranty fees.

negative amortization An increase in the unpaid balance of a loan resulting from adding unpaid interest to the loan principal. It occurs when the minimum monthly payment is no longer sufficient to cover the interest due. It is mainly a risk with variable-rate, closed-end loans.

net interest margin (NIM) The difference between the percentage yield on the loan portfolio and the cost of funds to the lender.

net worth Assets minus liabilities. The amount by which the value of assets exceeds liabilities.

netting The process of valuing the payment obligations for both sides of a transaction and having the party that pays more transfer only the difference to the other.

nonconforming loan A loan with terms that fall outside the regulatory guidelines for loans of that type.

nonpossessory collateral Collateral for a consumer loan that remains in the possession of the consumer, such as an automobile, boat, or airplane.

Notice of Right to Rescind The notice that establishes the right of a customer to cancel a contract or legally binding agreement within a specified period, usually three business days after signing the contract. This right is available for consumer credit agreements that give the creditor a security interest in the consumer's primary residence. If after that period the consumer has not canceled the contract, the loan proceeds are disbursed.

open-end loan A specified amount of credit available for use at the customer's discretion; repayment ranges from interest only through minimum stated amounts to a percentage specified in the contract.

operating statement *See* profit-and-loss statement.

order-taking A passive process in which bank employees give the consumer the product exactly as requested without trying to identify the consumer's real needs.

override In reference to a credit score, when the decision to make or deny an application does not conform to the bank's stated policy on the minimum qualifying credit score. A "high-side override" occurs when an applicant with a credit score that meets the bank's policy is denied for another reason. A "low-side override" occurs when an applicant with a credit score below the minimum is approved for another reason.

overt discrimination Blatant and open discrimination against an individual or a class of persons, such as by expressing a preference for illegal discriminatory activities, even if the lender never acts on the statement.

participation An interest in a loan acquired by a third party, such as another lender or group of lenders, from the lender that originates and services the loan.

payment protection Products that are sold in conjunction with loans so that the loan can be paid if the borrower dies, is injured or disabled, or loses his or her income source. There are two types: credit insurance and debt protection contracts.

payroll card A plastic stored-value card allowing an employee to access earned wages by using the card like a deposit account debit card. It can be used at participating automatic teller machines and point-of-sale terminals. Usually, the employer establishes a single deposit account in its own name, which will hold the funds for all participating employees. Some programs establish separate accounts for the employees.

perfection The process by which a secured party protects its security interest from third parties by possession, certificate of title, control, or filing or recording documentation of the security interest in local or state public records.

periodic rate The rate that the creditor applies to the account balance for a day, week, month, or other subdivision of a year. For example, for an APR of 18 percent, the periodic monthly rate is 1.5 percent (18 divided by 12).

personal financial statement A document that provides expanded information about the applicant's financial situation.

personal tax return The tax form individuals file with federal and state agencies.

phishing The illegal transmission of e-mail disguised as coming from a legitimate business that asks recipients for confidential information or invites recipients to visit an illegitimate Internet Web site.

possessory collateral Collateral held by the lender, such as savings accounts and stock.

potential debt The difference between a consumer's current balances on revolving credit accounts and the total of all credit limits.

preapproved credit offer An offer in which the lender makes a commitment to extend a specified amount of credit based on a preliminary credit analysis and receipt of a properly executed acceptance agreement. *Also known as* preselected credit offer.

preferred stock One of the two major types of equity securities that is first in line to receive dividend payments; the dividend rate is fixed at the time of issuance. If a corporation is liquidated, the stockholders are given access to company assets ahead of common stockholders. The stockholders usually do not have voting rights in the company. *See also* common stock.

premium The amount or percentage above the face or stated value at which securities are bought or sold; the opposite of discount.

prescreening The practice of examining consumer credit reports to identify individuals who meet certain requirements in order to offer them credit opportunities.

preselected credit offer *See* preapproved credit offer.

present value The value today of payments that will be received in the future.

pretext calling The practice of obtaining consumer account information over the telephone by fraudulent means, such as by pretending to be the account holder or authorized signer on the account.

prime rate An index rate from which a bank may compute a variable rate of interest for a loan contract. For consumer variable-rate loans, many banks use the prime rate as published in the *Wall Street Journal.*

principal 1) The actual amount of a loan, exclusive of interest charges. 2) The individual with primary ownership or management control of a business.

privacy notice A notice the law requires to be given to customers explaining a bank's policies and practices related to disclosure of nonpublic personal information.

procedures manual A written statement of how tasks are to be accomplished within the bank to comply with bank policy.

product life cycle The successive stages of a product's sales and profits. The four stages, which vary in length from product to product, are introduction (low sales and losses likely), growth (sales growth and profit gains), maturity (slower sales and reduced profits), and decline.

profit-and-loss statement A financial statement that shows a summary of a company's income and expenses for a specific period. Also known as income statement, earnings statement, operating statement.

prohibited basis Under the Equal Credit Opportunity Act, a characteristic of the applicant that cannot be considered when a creditor makes a decision on a consumer credit application.

promissory note A written document in which one party (the maker) agrees to pay a certain sum of money to another party (the payee) or to his or her order on demand or at a determinable future date. It is the customer's promise to pay back a loan according to the conditions detailed in the loan agreement.

promotion channel A method a bank uses to communicate with consumers, such as advertising, direct mail, and direct selling.

proof of claim A document filed by the creditor during bankruptcy proceedings that identifies both the creditor and the amount the creditor asserts is owed by the debtor.

purchase-money mortgage A loan the proceeds of which are used to purchase real property, which also secures the loan.

purchase-money secured loan A loan the proceeds of which are used to purchase the goods securing the loan.

purpose loan A loan backed by securities and used for purchasing securities or for carrying securities (maintaining, reducing, or retiring debt incurred for obtaining securities).

pyramid debt Debt resulting from the borrowing of funds in rapid succession without first repaying previous loans. The additional debt is used to meet previous loan obligations and erodes the borrower's financial position.

pyramiding late charges The accumulation of charges by assessing a late charge against an amount that includes an unpaid late charge; the practice is prohibited by the Credit Practices Rule.

reaffirmation Upon consent of the creditor with a secured interest, a bankrupt debtor may keep personal property pledged as collateral by promising to repay the underlying debt, even when the debt is greater than the value of the collateral.

re-aging an account *See* extension.

reasonable accommodation Under the Americans with Disabilities Act, an accommodation of a disabled person's limitations that can be made without undue financial hardship to the business making the accommodation.

recovery function The bank area responsible for collecting whatever repayment is possible on a charged-off loan.

redemption The right of the bankrupt debtor to recover collateral abandoned by the bankruptcy court trustee by paying either the remaining amount owed or the value of the collateral.

red flag An indicator that something is wrong. Examples include information uncovered during a credit investigation that appears suspicious or requires further action to verify, or an indicator during the credit process or in the bank's record systems that there has been an incident of identity theft.

redlining An illegal practice in which certain areas of a community are eliminated from eligibility for mortgages or other loans, either intentionally or unintentionally, allegedly because the geographic area is considered a poor investment risk. In effect, a red line is drawn around the eliminated area on a map.

refinance The rewriting a closed-end loan to reduce monthly payments or change interest rates or other terms of the loan. It is a collection remedy.

regulatory agency A government entity responsible for interpreting legislation and formulating and enforcing regulations.

related interest As defined by FRS Regulation O, an entity controlled by an insider, such as an executive officer, director, or principal shareholder.

relaying Sending e-mails through a computer or network without permission; for example, by taking advantage of open relays.

repossession The act of taking possession of property or goods given as security on a loan when the borrower has defaulted.

reputation risk The risk that negative publicity will affect the bank in a damaging way, such as by making it difficult to attract or retain customers or to raise capital; causing a loss of revenue; or leading to litigation.

residual value The estimated value of an asset at the conclusion of a lease agreement.

retention rate *See* buy rate.

reverse mortgage A mortgage agreement whereby the homeowner borrows against the home's equity and receives tax-free payments until the principal and interest reach the credit limit of the equity. Upon the owner's decision to move or death, the home is sold. The lender has priority claim to the proceeds of the sale, and any remaining equity would go to the homeowner or the estate. This is a special-purpose loan; it is not suited for everyone.

right of rescission The right of a customer to cancel a legally binding agreement within a specified period, such as three days after a contract is signed. This right is available for consumer credit agreements that give the creditor a security interest in the consumer's primary residence for a purpose other than to purchase the home.

right of setoff A provision in loan contracts that allows the lender to use funds deposited in the customer's accounts for payment of delinquent loans.

risk-based loan *See* subprime lending.

sales culture A company-wide effort to focus bank employees on the need to take every opportunity to sell the bank's services.

scripting With regard to illegal spam activity, the use of scripts or other automated ways to register for multiple e-mail or user accounts in order to send commercial e-mail. Script languages are computer languages that were initially used only for simple and repeated actions.

secondary source of repayment Another source of funds to help the bank recover its investment should the customer be unable to repay the loan for any reason, for example, a guarantor, a cosigner, or collateral.

secured loan A loan for which an asset (collateral) has been pledged as a source of debt repayment if the borrower defaults.

securitization The packaging of loans as a unit to be sold to outside investors. The loans are no longer assets of the bank, although the bank may continue to service them for investors.

security agreement A document that precisely describes the collateral and sets forth the rights and responsibilities of each party relative to the collateral. Signed by the borrower and other owners of the property, it establishes a lender's right to take possession of loan collateral if the borrower defaults.

security interest A claim to property that secures repayment of a debt by allowing the creditor to take the property, sell it, and retain the proceeds, up to the amount of indebtedness, if the debt has not been repaid as promised. *See also* lien.

selling The process of persuading the consumer to buy the product or service offered by the bank.

shotgunning The practice by which a dealer sends a loan application by fax or other electronic means to a number of lenders at one time.

simple interest Interest computed by applying a daily periodic interest rate to the amount of principal outstanding.

skip tracing The process of locating debtors who have stopped making loan payments and cannot be located through their last known address or employer.

spam Unwanted e-mail messages, intended to sell something, that clog e-mail inboxes.

special flood hazard area Land in the flood plane within a community that has at least a 1 percent chance of flooding in any given year, as designated by the Director of FEMA.

special value card A category of credit cards that includes affinity, cobranded, and reward cards. These cards have features that are especially important to the consumer.

stable value collateral An asset pledged for a loan that has a definite value throughout the loan term, such as a certificate of deposit.

statement of condition *See* balance sheet.

stored-value card A prepaid plastic wallet-size card that stores a predetermined amount of money to be used for purchases or specific transactions, such as telephone calls or public transit fares. As the card is used, the amount is deducted from the card until the balance is depleted. Some cards, also known as smart cards, may be replenished with a new balance.

straw purchaser A lending scenario where one party's name and credit strength are used by another person to borrow money and receive the benefit of the financed goods.

subprime lending The lending to borrowers who do not qualify for prime rates or conventional loans. Because of the higher risk, these loans have higher interest rates and fees than other loans.

tangible asset Property and goods in a physical form that can be touched or seen, such as an automobile or a plot of land. The asset is not liquid but may provide more protection against serious financial problems.

term The period between the commencement and the termination of a debt or contract.

time value of money The expected value of the income earned on a loan based on the value of money today (present value) or its expected value in the future (future value).

title search A review of public records to disclose past and current facts (chain of title) about the ownership of a piece of real estate.

trade line Detailed information about credit accounts found on a credit report, including the name of the creditor, type of loan, loan amount, account balance, payment terms, cosigners, and the consumer's payment history.

travel and entertainment (T&E) card A transaction card that serves as an alternative to cash and personal checks. American Express and Diners Club are examples.

triggering term A phrase or figure used in advertising that will require regulatory disclosures. For example, the following terms require further disclosure on closed-end credit: payment period, payment amount, down payment amount, and finance charge.

truth-in-lending disclosure statement The document that contains all required federal truth-in-lending disclosures, such as the annual percentage rate and finance charges. It is typically part of the promissory note for closed-end loans and of the terms of agreement for open-end loans, such as credit cards.

unauthorized use The use of a credit or debit card by a person other than the cardholder when such person does not have actual, implied, or apparent authority to use the card and from which use the cardholder receives no benefit.

underwrite To analyze credit quality and determine whether the bank should assume the risk of making a loan. The term also is used in the insurance and securities industries.

Uniform Commercial Code (UCC) A set of laws adopted by states to govern commercial and financial transactions between parties. Many states add their own amendments to the basic code.

Uniform Commercial Code Article 3, Negotiable Instruments The law that provides the definitions of a negotiable item that turns a piece of paper into an item that can be exchanged for cash or used as payment of goods and services. It governs the rights and duties of parties to a negotiable instrument.

unsecured line of credit A line of credit not secured by collateral. The borrower may use the available credit, repay the loan, and withdraw again. *Also known as* unsecured revolving line of credit.

unsecured loan A loan for which no collateral is offered or required.

usury Charging interest rates that are higher than the law allows on money borrowed.

usury rate The maximum interest rate permitted by state law that legally may be charged on a loan, usually set by type of loan.

variable-rate loan A loan with an interest rate that may fluctuate. The rate usually is tied to an index that reflects changes in the market rates of interest. A fluctuation in the interest rate causes changes in either the payments or the loan term. Limits may be placed on how much the interest rate or the payments will vary.

wage garnishment A court order that requires an employer to withhold a portion of an employee's wages to pay a creditor. *Also known as* wage attachment.

waiver of exemption A clause in a loan agreement in which a customer waives property exemption rights provided under state law. It is prohibited by the Credit Practices Rule.

warrant A certificate attached to a new securities issue that gives a shareholder the right to buy a certain number of shares of stock at a specified price within a certain period.

warranty A guarantee made by a seller of the quality or suitability of the product or service for sale. It is often required for loans secured by used vehicles.

wholesale line of credit *See* floorplan line of credit.

A to Z Index

A

access device, 111, 113
accommodation loan, 8
account monitoring, 194, 216, 248
acquisition cost, 279
active listening, 178, 179
add-on, *See* aftermarket product
adverse action, 259, 260
   flow chart, 260
   notice, 261
advertising, Truth in Lending Act and, 168
affiliate, 4, 153, 219, 273
   business arrangement, 186, 187
   transactions with, 153
affiliated business arrangement, 186, 187
affinity card, 104-106
aftermarket product, 80
age
   in credit evaluation, 258
   in credit investigation, 197, 203, 206, 210
agriculture
   business program, 64
   Community Facilities Loan Program, 64
   Rural Development Loans, 63, 64
   Single-Family Housing Guaranteed Loan, 64
   U.S. Department of (USDA), 63, 64
aircraft, as collateral, 334
Alighieri, Dante, 6
allowance for loan and lease losses (ALLL), 68
American Express, 104, 112, 240
Americans with Disabilities Act (ADA), 47
amortization, 33
   negative, 246, 272
annual percentage rate (APR), 19, 123, 170, 181-182, 269-270, 276, 289, 313, 318, 336
annual fee, 104, 114
applicant, 16
   asking questions, 178-179
   capacity, 200-202, 205, 207, 242-245
   capital, 246
   character, 62, 197-204, 210, 238-246, 252
   cosigner and, 62
   creditworthiness, 53, 117, 146, 147, 150, 152, 196-199, 238-246, 252, 254
   disabled, 47
   disclosure or notice to, 186, 187, 219, 259-260
   ECOA protection, 16, 236, 257-260
   fair lending law, 46-47
   free credit report, 207
   HMDA data, 45
   HOEPA, 318
   identity of, 181, 206
   obtaining goodwill of, 166, 169, 178, 237
   prescreened, 216
   risk, 84, 194, 237, 238, 246
application process, objectives, 166-169
applications
   direct mail, 55, 180
   distinguished from inquiry, 181-182
   electronic, 157, 177, 180
   generating, 166, 169, 176
   in-person, 177-179, 180
   sources, 170, 171
   telephone, 177, 180
   verifying accuracy and completeness, 145, 195, 324, 325, 336
appraisal
   fraud, 61
   notices, 260
appreciating value collateral, 60-61, 314
arm's-length basis, 153
Ash, Mary Kay, 302
assessment area, 44, 45
asset and liability committee (ALCO), 142, 348
asset
   liquid, 246-247, 249

low-quality, 153
intangible, 62
tangible, 246, 248
assignment of wages, 66, 67
attachment, 323, 331, 332-333
creating, 332-333
attitudes, carelessness and changing, as cause of
delinquency, 348, 350
authentication, 333
automated collection system, 348
automated loan payments in structuring, 311, 315
automobile loan policy, 148, 149
automated loan support system, 55
automated teller machine (ATM), 39, 111
automatic stay, 360
automobile dealer financing, 35
automobile lease, 90
average cost, 280
average daily balance, 269
average prime offer rate, 185

B

balance sheet, 32, 116, 358
balloon payment loan, 318
bank code of conduct, contents of, 139-147
banker incentives, 174, 176
bank files, 196, 197, 198
checking, for applicant's account history, 197
in credit history, 196
Banking Act (1933), 6, 153
Banking Act (1935), 6
bankruptcy
banks and, 360
Chapter 7, Liquidation, 358, 359-360, 364
Chapter 11, Reorganization, 358, 356
Chapter 12, Adjustment of Debts of Family Farmer
with Regular Income, 358
Chapter 13, Adjustment of Debts of an Individual with
Regular Income, 358, 359, 360, 363, 364
collection cycle, 356
predictor model, 117, 205
prohibited practices, 361-362
Bankruptcy Abuse Prevention and Consumer Protection
Act (2005), 350, 361, 363-364
Bankruptcy Act, 363
Bankruptcy Reform Act (1994), 363
banks
asking for referrals, 324, 327
bankruptcy and, 360
creating best image for, 327
direct lending and, 54-55

ensuring consistency with objectives of, 345, 347-348
as furnishers of information, 218
as information users, 218
internal environment of, 276
loan profitability and costs of, 280-282
as market driven, 302-303, 311
open-end credit and, 113-118
optimizing earnings by selling other products, 308
perspective on indirect lending, 81-86
sales-oriented, 303-308
selling services of, 327
Bear Stearns, 9
Bernanke, Ben S., 9, 10
benchmark, 346
benefit
segmentation of, 173
boats, as collateral, 57, 205, 334
bond, 42
book, 326, 335
boomers, 39
breach of contract, 335
breakeven analysis, loan profitability and, 281-282
breakeven point, 78, 281
business programs (BP), 64
buy rate, 77, 80, 84, 86, 98
buyer's remorse, 308
buying on margin, 5

C

call loan, *See* demand loan
call report, *See* consolidated report of condition and income
caller identification, 188
CAMELS, 138
capacity, 61, 103, 147-148, 198-199, 242-246, 248, 249,
251, 258, 274, 349
decision-making systems and, 147-148
capital, 122, 138, 153, 238, 246-249, 279, 285
captive finance company, 35, 42, 56, 76, 84, 89
cash flow, 107, 119, 240, 242, 243-244, 246, 309, 311,
354, 355
cash selling price, 204
cash value, 59, 204, 248
centralized functions, 53, 54, 80, 81, 116, 256, 351
certificate of deposit, as collateral, 59
change in terms notice, 271, 331
Chapter 7, Liquidation, 358, 359-360, 364
Chapter 11, Reorganization, 358, 356
Chapter 12, Adjustment of Debts of Family Farmer
with Regular Income, 358
Chapter 13, Adjustment of Debts of an Individual with
Regular Income, 358, 359, 360, 363, 364

character, 62, 147, 150, 198, 203, 238-241, 249, 312, 350
   credit history and, 147, 198, 239-241
charge-off, 145-146, 346, 352, 357-358
   in loan policy, 146
chattel mortgage, 4
check card, 111-112
check overdraft line of credit, 107-108
Civil Rights Act, 46
Clemens, Samuel, 363
closed-end credit, 3, 33, 34, 142, 185
closed-end loan, 33, 36, 57, 61-62, 107, 119, 194, 234,
      246, 248, 251, 270, 282, 313, 238-330
   consolidation, 119
   delinquency, 345, 349, 352, 354, 355
   disclosure, 183-184
   open-end, versus, 108, 113, 115, 148, 167
   questions, 178-179
closing costs, 111, 168, 186-187, 305
Coast Guard, 334
cobranded card, 103, 106, 107, 112
code of conduct, 139
Code of Federal Regulations, 15
collateral
   aircraft, 334
   appreciating-value, 60-61, 314
   boat, 57, 205, 334
   in credit information, 204-205
   depreciating value, 11, 57-59, 272, 277
   fluctuating value, 57, 59, 108, 314
   identification of, 205
   in loan structuring, 314
   nonpossessory, 335
   ownership of, 204-205, 333
   possession of, 57, 332, 334-335
   possessory, 335
   stable-value, 57, 59-60, 314
   collateral risk, 52, 57, 58, 59, 60, 138, 147, 204,
      271, 272
   collateral value, 58, 59
   types of, 57, 85, 148, 334, 338
   verifying, 197
collection costs, managing, 348
collection cycle, 352-358
   charge-off, 357-358
   early stage, 352-354
   personal contact stage, 354-356
   serious delinquency, 356-357
collection function, 344, 345, 346, 350, 351, 355, 361
collection information, public record and, 205, 207
collection in loan policy, 145-146
collector, *See* debt collector

comaker, *See* cosigner
combining rules, 285
communication
   effective, 304-305
   in loan policy, 151
   skills, 56, 304
community development loans under CRA, 45
Community Facilities Loan Program, 64
Community Reinvestment Act (CRA), 15, 20, 42, 43,
      44-45, 47, 134, 136, 141, 168, 236
   posting of notice, 44
   public file, 44-45
comparison shopping, 181, 307
competitive environment, 41-43, 275, 312
Competitive Equality Banking Act, 153
computer software control tools, 117
compliance, 152, 156, 166, 168, 179, 181, 234, 236,
      257, 285
   ensuring legal, 166, 168, 236, 257
   programs, 152
compliance and loan review in loan policy, 140, 145
compliance officer, 145
compliance risk, 144
Comptroller of the Currency, *See* Office of the
      Comptroller of the Currency
conditions, *See* external conditions
confession of judgment, 66
conflict of interest, 139, 147
conservatorship, 65
consolidated report of condition and income, 285
consultative selling, 302, 303, 309, 312
consumer
   benefits and challenges, open-end credit and, 118-121
   consumption, 7, 8, 36
   defined, 2
   demand for credit, 8, 36, 40, 43, 276
   direct lending and, 55-57
   financial management needs, 12-13, 248, 311, 349
   financial needs life cycle, 36, 38-39
   identifying information for, 205, 206
   maintaining goodwill of, 107, 169, 178, 234, 237,
      257, 347, 351, 355, 362
   payment priorities, 117
   perspective of indirect lending, 88-89
consumer credit
   closed-end, 3, 21, 33, 34, 142, 185
   counseling on, 354, 356
   defined, 2-4
   history, 205, 218, 237, 238, 239-241, 349, 350, 355
   open-end, 3
   restraint program for, 7, 8

secured, 3, 57, 61, 103, 107, 108-111, 115

types, 3

unsecured, 3, 8, 21, 33, 57, 58, 61, 62, 103, 108, 115, 174, 248, 310

Consumer Credit Protection Act, 2, 16

Consumer Credit Restraint Program, 7, 8

consumer goodwill, 107, 169, 178, 234, 237, 257, 347, 351, 355, 362

retaining, 237, 257

consumer incentive programs, 176

Consumer Leasing Act, 94, 96

consumer loan application, *See* applications

consumer loan policy

authority in, 143

charge-off, 146

collection, 145-146

compliance and review, 145

components of, 139-140

corporate responsibility and ethics, 141, 146-147

credit criteria, 144

defined, 134-139

documentation, 144-145

geographic limits of market area, 141

insiders and employees in, 143

need for, 136

objectives of, 40

pricing guidelines, 141-142

statement of bank's objectives, 140

types desired, 142

consumer payment priorities, 117

consumer protection, telemarketing and, 187-188

consumer report, *See* credit report

consumer reporting agency, 19, 113, 174, 187, 195, 204, 205-207, 216, 218, 219, 252

consummation, 36, 183, 185

contingent liability, 83

controlled business arrangement, 187

disclosure of, 186, 187

Controlling the Assault of Non-solicited Pornography and Marketing Act (CAN-SPAM Act), 175, 182, 188

convenience user, 114, 127

corporate responsibility and ethics in loan policy, 134, 140, 146-147

cosigner, 62, 85, 197, 219

cost of funds, 7, 84, 141, 245, 270, 271, 276, 279-280, 281, 282

creative loan structuring, 56

credit

in early colonies, 4-5

sources of, 35, 55, 239, 240

types, 46, 107, 239, 240

credit-agency report, *See* credit report

credit card

affinity, 104-106

cobranded, 103, 106, 107, 112

international, 103, 104

national, 104

registration plan, 114

retail private label, 103-104

reward, 106, 107

risks to earnings or capital in lending, 122

special value, 103, 107

travel and entertainment, 103, 104, 140

unauthorized use, 102, 126

credit criteria in loan policy, 144, 147-148

credit evaluation and decision-making objectives, 234-238

credit history, factors in, 239-241

credit information

banks as users of, 218

collateral in, 204-205

credit history, 198-199

employment in, 201-203

history in, 198-199

income in, 199-201

residence in, 203-204

sources of, 205-216

credit insurance, 80, 89, 114, 184, 268, 272-273, 284, 310, 315, 316, 330, 337, 355

credit investigation

defined, 194-198

information verified in, 196

objectives of, 195-196

process of, 196-198

credit limit, 207, 216, 241, 311, 312

on overdraft lines of credit, 107, 108

Credit Practices Trade Regulation Rule, 66-67

credit rating or payment history, 239, 326

credit repair clinic, 199

credit reporting agency, *See* consumer reporting agency

credit report, 146, 206, 207, 216, 234, 237, 239, 240, 245, 312

abbreviations in, 239

free report for consumer, 207

red flags on, 196

stored-value card, 112

See also Fair Credit Reporting Act

credit risk, 52, 54, 84-85, 102, 148, 194, 199, 202, 203, 239, 272, 274, 275, 277, 284, 325

CAMELS and, 138

credit scoring and, 252-256

ECOA and, 259

factors contributing to, 237-238, 256
    lender requirements, 88, 116, 117, 142, 234, 237-238
    minimizing, 54, 57, 62-63, 138
    subprime lending and, 68
    variable rates and, 245-246
credit scoring, 62, 117, 144, 147, 205, 236, 238,
        252-256, 259, 279, 351
    advantages of, 254-255
    Cs of credit and, 254
    defined, 252-256
    with judgmental elements, 256
    variables in, 252-254
    vendors in, 117, 252, 254
credit union, 41, 42
credit-use patterns, 240-241
creditworthiness, 32, 53, 61, 62, 70, 195, 196, 238,
        252, 257, 258, 310
criteria, evaluation, 257-258
cross-selling, 4, 10, 54-55, 102, 171, 236, 302, 303,
        308, 309, 310, 311, 312, 335
Cs of credit, See Five Cs of Credit
customer identification program (CIP), 177
customers
    counseling those experiencing difficulty, 346-347
    optimizing retention of, 303, 309
    overcoming concerns, 305-306
    profitability of, 78

D

data mining, 173
dealer
    agreement, 79-80, 81, 83
    fraud, 85-86
    goods sold, type of, 79
    identifying, 79
    income, 87
    perspective on indirect lending, 86-87
    recourse of, 82-83, 84-88
    reserve account, 82, 86
    trade, 93
    unacceptable sales practices of, 85
debit card, 111-112, 219
debt cancellation contract (DCC), 273, 284, 285, 315
debt collector, 361
debt
    excessive, 348, 349, 355
    level of, 240
    potential, 116-117, 148, 245
    pyramid, 240
    structure of, 244, 248-249, 350
    variable-rate, 245-246

debt suspension agreement (DSA), 273, 284
debt-to-income ratio, 243, 310, 355
    bank policy, 103, 142, 144, 146, 148, 150, 246, 249
    capacity, 242-244, 251, 254
    credit scoring, 256
    exceptions, 152
    variable rate, 292
decentralized function, 53-54, 351
deceptive dealer practices, 89
decision-making system, 147-148, 237, 254
deed of trust, 330
default, 9, 61, 62, 67, 107, 335, 338, 345, 348, 350,
        352, 356, 362
delinquency
    causes of, 345-346, 348-350
    keeping levels acceptable, 176, 345-346
    rate of, 177, 345
delinquency notice, 353
demand loan, 3, 33, 59
demographic segmentation, 172
depreciating value collateral, 11, 57-59, 272, 277
Diners Club, 104
direct lending
    bank and, 54-55
    consumer and, 55-57
    decentralized approach, 53-54
    deciding factors, 53
    defined, 169-170, 310
    documentation for, 54
    loan structuring and, 54-55, 56
    organized, 53-54
direct mail
    applications, 55, 180
    marketing, 55, 115, 171, 174, 180, 307, 310, 311, 320
direct verification, 200, 204
disability, 47, 273, 315, 317, 349, 355
discharge, 359, 360
disclosure
    changes in terms, 124
    DCC notice, 285
    for closed-end credit, 183-184
    for open-end loan, 183-184
    truth in lending statement, 328, 337
    for variable-rate loan, 124
discrimination
    evidence of, 47
    overt, 47
disintermediation, 7
disparate impact, evidence of, 47
disparate treatment, evidence of, 47

documentation
    accurate, 60, 85, 145
    bank policy, 20, 137, 140
    collateral, 111, 204, 205, 331-335, 337, 338
    completion of, 324-325
    creditworthiness, 61, 147, 207
    efficient, 41, 54, 80, 115, 279, 325
    examination, 141, 187, 336
    exception, 142, 152, 236, 252, 256
    fixed-rate, closed-end loan, 328-330
    legal, 67, 68, 81, 90, 113, 177, 182, 187, 200-201, 256
    open-end loan, 113
    procedures manual, 151
    process, 36, 53, 80-82, 93, 103, 326, 335
    types of, 327-331
    variable-rate loan, 330
do-not-call list, 175, 182, 188
do-not-call rule, 188
do-not-mail list, 174, 175
double financing, 85
down payment, 77, 79, 138, 148, 150, 196, 204, 310
due-date adjustments, 353, 354

E

early stage collection, 352-354
earnings statement, *See* profit-and-loss statement
economic conditions, loan delinquency and, 346
economic environment, 36, 40, 116, 252
effective lending, 169
electronic application, 57, 177, 180
e-mail marketing, 174, 175
Emerson, Ralph Waldo, 344
employees, loans to, 143
employer verification, 200
    red flags from, 201
employment in credit information, 201-203
encryption, 333
Equal Credit Opportunity Act (ECOA), 2, 16, 46, 145,
    168, 170, 180, 182, 202, 236, 242, 252, 255,
    257-261
evaluation criteria, 257-258
Equifax, 254
equity, 109
equity stripping, 69
established business relationship, 188
ethical business conduct, 10, 134, 135, 139
ethics, 139, 140, 146-147
exception, 109, 147, 148, 152, 188, 196, 197, 236,
    252, 255, 256
excessive debt as cause of delinquency, 348, 349, 355
Experian, 254

extension loan, 354
extension of credit, Regulation O definition of, 94-95
external conditions, 5, 114, 116, 142, 202, 238, 239,
    250, 276, 279, 345, 346, 349

F

Fair and Accurate Credit Transactions Act (FACT Act),
    43, 120, 121-123, 218
Fair Credit Reporting Act (FCRA), 19, 22, 101, 121-123,
    181, 216, 217-219, 236, 257
Fair Debt Collection Practices Act (FDCPA), 361-362
Fair Housing Act (FHA), 46, 182
fair lending, 43, 45, 46, 135, 139, 142, 152, 168, 175,
    182, 236, 252, 254
    Joint Policy Statement, 47
Fannie Mae, *See* Federal National Mortgage Association
feature, 109, 111, 256, 279, 305
Fed funds rate, *See* federal funds rate
Federal Aviation Act, 334
federal box, 183, 184
Federal Communications Commission (FCC)
    telemarketing rules, 188
federal consolidation loan, 63
Federal Deposit Insurance Corporation (FDIC), 6, 13,
    15, 68, 135
    Money Smart program, 119
Federal Emergency Management Agency (FEMA), 338
Federal Family Education Loan (FFEL) Program, 63-64
Federal Financial Institutions Examination Council
    (FFIEC), 45
federal funds rate, 40
Federal Home Loan Mortgage Corporation (Freddie
    Mac), 65
federally guaranteed student loan programs, 63
Federal National Mortgage Association (Fannie Mae), 65
federal regulations, 14, 329, 336
Federal Reserve Act, 94, 153
    Sections 23A and 23 B, 153
Federal Reserve Board, 66, 219, 318
Federal Reserve discount rate, 40
Federal Reserve System (FRS), 15, 16
    Regulation B, Equal Credit Opportunity, 16, 18, 46,
        168, 182, 257-261
    Regulation C, Home Mortgage Disclosure, 15, 18,
        43, 45-46, 47, 168, 182, 336
    Regulation M, Consumer Leasing, 18, 75, 94, 96
    Regulation O, Loans to Executive Officers, Directors,
        and Principal Shareholders of Member Banks,
        75, 94-95, 143
    Regulation P, Privacy of Consumer Financial
        Information, 67-68

Regulation T, Credit by Brokers and Dealers, 18, 152

Regulation U, Credit by Banks and Persons Other than Brokers or Dealers for the Purpose of Purchasing or Carrying Margin Stocks, 18, 152, 153

Regulation V, Fair Credit Reporting, 18, 219, 222

Regulation W, Transactions Between Member Banks and Their Affiliates, 18, 153

Regulation X, Borrowers of Securities Credit, 16, 18, 168, 186

Regulation Z, Truth in Lending, 2, 16-19, 43, 121, 145, 168, 181, 182-185, 236, 269, 317, 326

Regulation AA, Unfair or Deceptive Acts or Practices, 18, 66, 333, 338

Regulation BB, Community Reinvestment, 15, 18, 168

Regulation FF, Obtaining and Using Medical Information in Connection with Credit, 219

Federal Trade Commission (FTC), 66, 94, 96, 219, 361

   telemarketing rules of, 187-188

fees, 14, 19, 68, 104, 114, 134, 176, 182, 183, 184, 185, 186, 250, 269, 270, 276, 317, 318, 326, 331, 363

   annual, 104, 114

   interchange, 114

   merchant discount, 114

finance charge, 19, 33, 87, 108, 123, 124, 182, 183, 269-270, 273, 283, 316

   charges included in, 183

finance company, 5, 35, 41, 42, 56, 76, 84, 89, 240, 252

financial counseling, 54, 56, 88-89, 98, 234, 257

financial crisis of 2008, 9-11, 35, 134

financial information, 102, 119, 120, 121, 219, 237

   safeguarding, 121, 122

Financial Institutions Reform, Recovery, and Enforcement Act (FIRREA), 133

Financial Institutions Regulatory and Interest Rate Control Act (FIRA), 94

financial situation, changes in, as cause of delinquency, 349

financing statement, 199, 333, 334

firm offer of credit, 121

Five Cs of credit, 147, 238-251, 254

   capacity, 242-246

   capital, 246-249

   character, 238-241

   collateral, 249

   conditions, 250

fixed-rate loan, 270-271, 281, 328-329, 330

   documentation for, 328-329

flood disaster protection, 337, 338

Flood Disaster Protection Act (FDPA), 338

floorplan financing, 89-90

fluctuating value collateral, 57, 59, 108, 314

force place, 338

Ford, Henry, 363

Ford Credit, 43

foreclosure, 60, 70, 357

foreign exchange risk, 137, 280

Franklin, Benjamin, 4

fraud, 118, 119, 120-121, 319, 365

   appraisal, 61

   as cause of delinquency, 348, 350, 356

   credit repair, 199

   dealer, 85-86

   detecting, 116

   identification, 206

   loan application, 179, 180, 181

   open-end credit and, 116, 181

   personal tax return, 200

Freddie Mac, *See* Federal Home Loan Mortgage Corporation

full recourse or recourse, 82

functional regulation system, 16

future value, 277-278

G

gambling as cause of delinquency, 348, 350

garnishment, *See* wage garnishment

Garn-St Germain Depository Institutions Act, 284

Generation X, 39

geographic influences on credit needs, 36, 40-41

geographic limits of market area in loan policy, 139, 141

geographic segmentation, 172

Ginnie Mae, *See* Government National Mortgage Association

Glass-Steagall Act, 6, 153

good faith estimate, 186-187

Government National Mortgage Association (Ginnie Mae), 65, 66

grace period, 124, 354

Gramm-Leach-Bliley Act, 13, 16, 67, 236, 272, 337

Great Depression, 5-6, 9, 134, 152, 153

guaranteed loan programs, 62-66

guarantor, 2, 62, 219, 315

H

Hearst, William Randolph, 166

Heinz, Henry John, 363

Hershey, Milton Snavely, 363

HOPEA, *See* Home Ownership and Equity Protection Act

holder in due course rule, 75, 94, 96

   holder notice, 96

holiday advice, 121
home equity line of credit (HELOC), 36, 108-110,
        111, 113, 149-150, 172, 173, 177, 182, 186,
        195, 234, 250, 251, 312, 330, 349
    benefits, 110
    documentation required for, 113
    loan structuring and, 312
home equity loan market, 111
Home Mortgage Disclosure Act (HMDA), 15, 43,
        45-46, 47, 168
Home Ownership and Equity Protection Act
        (HOEPA), 45, 317
    coverage, 318
    disclosure requirements, 318
    prohibited practices, 318
household goods, as collateral, 66, 67, 333, 338
Housing and Urban Development (HUD) loans, 16,
        63, 64-66, 186,
    Federal Home Loan Mortgage Corporation, 65
    Federal National Mortgage Association, 65
    Government National Mortgage Association, 65, 66
    loan programs of, 65-66
    Regulation X, 16, 168, 186
HUD-1 (or HUD-1A) settlement statement, 186, 187

I

identity theft, 19, 43, 118, 120, 121, 123, 181, 196,
        206, 218, 219
imaging, 175, 336
incentives, 174, 176, 304
    banker, 174, 176
    consumer, 176
income
    capacity and, 342-343
    in credit information, 199-200
    source of, in credit evaluation, 80, 199
    verifying, 318
income statement, *See* profit and loss statement
index rate, 269, 270, 271
indirect lending
    bank's perspective on, 81-86
    consumer's perspective on, 88-89
    dealer agreement, 79-80
    dealer's perspective on, 86-87
    defined, 35-36, 76-78
    establishing dealer relationship, 79
    future of, 93-94
    loan applications, 80-81
    loan structuring and, 310
    relationship of, 77-78
indirect lending automobile loan, 84

Industrial Revolution, 4
inflation, 40, 185, 276, 346
information
    acquiring, to support sound decision, 196
    banks as furnishers of, 218
    banks as users of, 218
    financial, 102, 119, 120, 121, 219, 237
    medical, 219
information technology, 53, 138
in-person application, 177-179, 180
inquiry, 170, 180, 181-182, 205, 207, 240
insider lending (FRS Regulation O), restrictions on,
        94-95
insider, 94-95, 140, 143, 147, 153
    loans to, 140, 143, 147
    transactions, Federal Reserve Act sections 23A and
        23B, 153
insolvency, 248
installment loan, 5, 138, 147, 207, 240, 363
insurance
    credit, 4, 80, 89, 114, 184, 268, 272-273, 276, 284,
        310, 315, 316, 318, 330, 337, 355
    national flood, 338
insurance binder, 330
insurance claim, 354
intentional default as cause of delinquency, 348, 350
Interagency Guidance on Nontraditional Mortgage
        Loans, 70
Interagency Guidance on Subprime Lending, 68
Interagency Policy Statement on Prescreening by
        Financial Institutions, 123
Interagency Statement on Meeting the Needs of
        Creditworthy Borrowers, 140
interchange fees, 114
interest
    accrual, 283
    calculating, 268-269, 326
    simple, 269, 270, 282, 326, 353, 354
interest rate cap, 362-363
interest rate risk, 137, 138, 270, 271, 272, 281, 308, 309
    minimizing, 309
interest rate schedule in loan structuring, 312
interest rates, 7, 14, 40, 42, 43, 46, 60, 62, 80, 83, 109,
        170, 181, 245, 255, 269-272, 275, 276, 281,
        309, 311, 312, 313, 314, 317, 318, 326, 346,
        355, 362
    loan profitability and, 281
international credit cards, 103, 104
Internet, 12, 39, 41, 42, 43, 45
    solicitation, 127
inventory financing, *See* floorplan financing

involuntary liquidation, 360
irresponsible lending, 348, 350

J

Japanese JCB card, 104
judgmental decision-making, 238, 250-251
judgmental elements, credit scoring with, 256
judgment, 66, 117, 357

L

late charge, 66, 184, 352, 354
lease, 4, 68, 90-92
    automobile, 90
    installment loan and, 92
    losses, *See* allowance for loan and lease losses
leasing, 90-91
    buying versus, 92
    Consumer Leasing Act, 96
    Servicemembers Civil Relief Act, 362-363
legal document, 113, 200
legal lending limit, 95, 284-285
lending
    direct, 35, 51-70
    indirect, 35, 42, 75-96
    irresponsible, as cause of delinquency, 348, 350
    retail banking and, 12, 13, 54
lending authority in loan policy, 140, 143
lessee, 90, 363
lessor, 90, 92, 363
leverage, 248
LIBOR, *See* London Interbank Offered Rate
lien, 61, 81, 82, 125, 145, 151, 199, 204, 248, 332-334,
        336, 337, 351
    first, 148, 185, 186, 318,
    obtaining documents, 328, 337
    subordinate, 185, 186,
    tax, 205, 207
    See also attachment, perfection.
life insurance policy, 334
limited recourse, 82
line of credit
    check overdraft, 107
    floorplan, 89-90
    home equity, 103, 108-111
    revolving, 13, 14, 33, 61, 101-127
    secured, 108
    unsecured, 108
liquid asset, 246-27, 249
liquidation, 70, 279, 359-360, 364
liquidity, 114, 116, 123, 138, 207, 246
liquidity risk, 123, 137, 138

listening, active, 178, 179
loan amount in structuring, 312-313
loan application fraud, 181
loan application register (LAR), 45
loan application, processing, 80-81
loan broker, 43
loan closing, 54, 80, 125, 135, 183, 186, 283, 324,
        335, 338
loan consummation, 36, 183
loan cost, 269, 274, 280, 326
    calculating interest, 268-269
    interest rate, 281
    payment protection, 206, 272-273
loan documentation, 144-145, 323-335, 337
    in loan policy, 144-145
loan extension, 354, 355
loan fees, typical, 277
loan flipping, 69
loan guarantees, 62-66
loan loss, 79, 82, 83, 145-146,
    calculating, 358
    cost of, 279
    keeping acceptable level of, 145, 237, 351
    rate of, 279
loan loss reserve, 32, 139
loan policy, *See* consumer loan policy
loan policy and credit criteria, 147-152
    capacity and decision-making system, 147
    character and credit history, 147
    collateral, 148
loan portfolio, 176, 177, 216, 241, 255, 270, 276, 277,
        278, 280, 344, 349
    diversification, 161, 284-285
    objectives, 78, 135, 138-139
loan pricing, 267-278
    bank's internal environment, 276
    competitive environment, 275
    economic conditions, 276
    regulatory environment, 275
loan proceeds, control of, in loan structuring, 311, 315
loan product considerations, 169-170
    direct lending, 169-170
    indirect lending, 170
    open-end products, 171
loan profitability, 278-288
    bank's cost, 278-280
    evaluating, 280-283
loan review, 335-337
loan shark, 5
loan standards in loan policy, 150-151

loan structuring, 166, 274, 308-317
  amount in, 312
  automated payments, 315
  collateral in, 314
  control of proceeds in, 315
  direct lending and, 310
  indirect lending in, 310
  interest rate schedule in, 312
  meeting sales objectives, 308-309
  open-end credit and, 310-311
  payment protection in, 315
  pricing in, 312
  by product line, 310
  term in, 313
  types of, 312
  variables in, 311-317
loan term, 124, 182
  loan profitability and, 280
  in structuring, 313-314
loan-to-value ratio (LTV), 109, 250
loan volume, 32, 36-43, 114, 139, 310, 313, 355
  increasing, 303
loans
  closed-end, *See* closed-end loan.
  cosigned, 62
  declining, 257
  delivery channel, 52, 166, 169, 306, 310
  expediting booking of new, 336
  to insiders and employees in loan policy, 143
  installment, 5, 33, 138, 142, 362, 363
  leases and installment, 363
  making the best, 89, 234, 308
  mortgage, 3, 4, 8, 9, 10, 36, 40, 42, 45, 65, 70, 109, 110, 180, 185, 186, 219, 317, 318, 328, 330, 334, 357, 362
  nonconforming, 285
  open-end, See open-end loan.
  outstanding, 32-35, 39, 65, 82, 109, 114, 118, 135
  personal, 61, 139, 345
  secured,57-61, 108, 144, 185, 204, 332, 334
  single-payment, 3
  type of, in loan structuring, 310, 312
  unsecured, 61-62, 103, 108, 115, 116, 124, 174, 248, 249, 309, 313, 331, 345, 347, 360
  variable-rate, 19, 124, 245-246, 270, 275, 280, 282, 309, 312, 326, 330
locate-to-order, 93
London Inter-Bank Offered Rate (LIBOR), 270, 271
loss payee letter, 324
loss recovery, generating, 346

low-quality asset, 153
loyalties, shifting, 84

M

maintenance and liquidation cost, 279
margin, 5, 59, 152-153
marginal cost, 141, 280
marginal loan, 84, 88, 146, 315
margin requirement, 152-153
marine loan policy, 149
marital problems as cause of delinquency, 350
marital status in credit evaluation, 16, 258
market
  area, 41, 79, 115, 116, 134, 136, 141, 168, 202, 275, 276, 346
  home equity loan, 111
  indirect lending, 35, 76, 84
market risk, 32, 138
market segmentation, 172-173, 302
  benefits, 173
  demographic, 172
  geographic, 172
  psychographic, 172
  volume, 173
marketability, 242, 246
market-driven selling, 302-303
marketing customer information file (MCIF), 173-174
marketing program, 53, 78, 88, 171-177
  defining objectives, 172
  implementing plan, 176
  measuring results, 177
  selecting promotion channels, 174-176
  selecting target markets, 172-173
MasterCard, 104, 112
material misrepresentation, 319
medical information, 219-220
merchant discount fees, 114
Merrill-Lynch, 11
millennials, 39
mobile homes, as collateral, 57, 186, 334, 338
money management, poor, as cause of delinquency, 349
Morris Plan bank, 5, 12
mortgage-backed security (MBS), 65, 66, 70
mortgage, *See also* loans, mortgage
  chattel, 4, 12
  higher-priced mortgage loan, 319
  reverse, 110-111, 317, 318
  second, 3, 142, 150, 234, 248, 251, 318
motivation, 304, 305, 306

N

National Bankruptcy Act, 364
national credit cards, 104
National Do Not Call Registry, 187, 188
National Flood Insurance Program (NFIP), 338
natural environment, 40-41
needs recognition, 306
negative amortization, 246, 272, 319
net interest margin (NIM), 7, 177, 245, 271, 281, 348
netting, 114
net worth, 207, 248
new loan, 355
nonbank institution, 7, 8, 35, 40, 41, 42, 115, 180, 181
nonconforming loan, 285
nonpossessory collateral, 335
nonrecourse or no liability, 82
Nordstrom Bank, 43
notice, giving, 333
notice of adverse action, 170, 210, 259
Notice of Right to Rescind, 125
notifications for loan requests, 46, 259-260
NYCE Payments Network, LLC, 111

O

obligation enforcement, 363
Office of the Comptroller of the Currency (OCC), 15,
        68, 137, 284, 285
    Advisory to national banks on brokered or purchased
        loans, 69
    Guidance for national banks on predatory lending, 69
    model disclosures for debt cancellation and debt
        suspension contracts, 286
    Rules for Debt Cancellation Contracts and Debt
        Suspension Agreements, 17
    Rules for Federal Pre-emption of State Law and the
        Agency's Powers, 70
    Rules for Lending Limits, 17
Office of Thrift Supervision (OTS), 15, 68, 284
open-end credit (loan), 34, 55, 56, 102-103, 103-121,
        123, 142, 145, 171, 174, 194, 198, 216, 240,
        241, 245, 246, 248, 269, 270, 271, 282,
        310-311, 331
    applicants, 113, 194, 310
    benefits to bank, 113-116
    challenges for bank, 116-118
    consumer benefits and challenges, 118-121
    disclosures for, 123
    documentation required for, 113
    features of, 102-103
    fraud and, 116, 118
    loan structuring and, 310-311

open-end credit products, 55, 103-112, 115, 116, 118,
        142, 216
    check overdraft line of credit, 107-108
    considerations in, 216
    credit card, 103-107
    secured line of credit, 108-111
    unsecured line of credit, 108
open-ended questions, 305
operational efficiency, 110, 114, 115-116, 135, 136-137,
        236, 277, 279
operational risk, 32
order taker, 302, 303, 309
overdraft
    payment to insiders, 95
    protection, 95
overdraft line of credit, 107
    benefits, 119, 237
    credit limit on, 107,108, 331
    debit card and, 111
    disclosure, 331
    overdraft protection versus, 107
    payday loan versus, 108
    variable rate, 270
overextended credit, warning signs of, 241, 246
override, 147, 252, 255, 256
overt discrimination, 47

P

Pareto, Vilfredo Federico Damaso, 171
Pareto principle, 171, 173
pay stub, 196, 197, 200, 203
payday loan, overdraft line of credit versus, 108
payment, 126, 269, 272-273, 282-283, 315-317, 354
    collection, 315-317 126
    protection in loan structuring, 315-317
    timing, 269, 282-283
payroll card, 112
perfection, 331, 333-334
periodic rate, 123, 124, 269
periodic statement disclosure, 124
Perkins loan, 63
personal characteristics in evaluating character, 16, 238,
        239
personal contact stage collection remedies, 354
personal finance company, 252
personal financial statement, 55, 207, 209, 210, 246,
        247, 248, 250, 352
personal loan, 61, 139, 142, 345
personal tax return, 200
PLUS loan, 63
portfolio liquidity, 116

possessory collateral, 335
postpurchase assessment, 308
potential debt, 116-117, 148, 245
preapproved credit offer, 113, 122, 167, 174
predatory practices, 69-70, 350
premium, 4, 103, 116, 311, 316, 317
prepurchase search, 307
prescreening, 113, 121-122, 194, 216, 240
preselected credit offer, *See* preapproved credit offer
present value, 277-278
pretext calling, 68
price risk, 138
pricing
   for profitability, 278-283
   guidelines in loan policy, 140, 141-142
   in loan structuring, 312
   variable-rate loan, 271-272
prime rate, 182, 185, 270, 271, 313
principal, 33, 66, 268, 269, 282, 338,
privacy
   notice, 67-68
   provision, 19, 66, 67-68
Privacy of Consumer Financial Information Act, 67
procedures manual, 151
product life cycle, 34-35
product line, 12, 79, 84, 103, 276, 282, 310-311, 347
   loan structuring by, 310-311
   profitability, 84, 282, 283
product solution, 304, 305, 306, 307
profit-and-loss statement, 32
profitability, 84
   declining, 84, 282-283
   loans, 78, 278-283
   product line, 84, 282, 283
prohibited basis, 16, 47, 140, 252, 257
prohibited practice, 318, 361-362
promissory note, 62, 96, 326, 328, 330
promotion channel, 174-176
   selection, 174-176
proof of claim, 360
psychographic segmentation, 172
public records
   collection information and, 207
   in credit history, 198, 199, 204
purchase cycle, 306-307
purchase decision, 307-308
purchase-money mortgage, 4
purchase-money secured loan, 204
purpose loan, 152-153
   regulation of, 152-153

pyramid debt, 240
pyramiding late charges, 245, 266, 272

R

re-aging an account, *See* extension
Real Estate Settlement Procedures Act (RESPA), 16,
   182, 186-187
recovery costs, managing, 348
recovery function, 344, 346, 351-352, 358
recreational vehicles, as collateral, 57, 334-335
red flag
   on credit applications, 81, 210
   on credit reports, 196, 241
   from employment and residence verification, 201
   identity theft, and, 121, 123, 181, 196, 206, 219
redemption, 359
redlining, 203
referrals, asking for, 327
refinance, 40, 102, 109, 185, 186, 317, 355
regulatory agency, 15-16, 46, 47
regulatory environment, 36, 41, 275
related interest, 95
repossession, 249, 348, 357
repurchase recourse, 82
reputation risk, 32, 138
rescission, 125, 336
residence in credit information, 203, 204
residual value, 90
retail private label credit cards, 103-104
retention rate, *See* buy rate
reverse mortgage, 110-111
revolving line of credit, 33
reward card, 106, 107
right of rescission, 19, 125, 183
right of setoff, 354, 356
risk,
   analysis of, 137, 194
   collateral, 52, 57, 58, 59, 60, 138, 147, 204, 271, 272
   compliance, 144
   credit, *See* credit risk
   environmental, 139
   foreign exchange, 137, 280
   interest rate, 137, 138, 270, 271, 272, 281, 308, 309
   investment, 203, 308
   liquidity, 123, 137, 138
   management, 59, 61, 68, 70, 84, 138
   market, 32, 138
   minimizing, 146
   operational, 32
   price, 138
   ratings, 337

reputation, 32, 138
strategic, 123, 137
strike of the pen, 33
systemic, 79
term 277
transaction, 138
to earnings or capital in lending, 122
risk-based loan, *See* subprime lending
Rural Development Loans, 64

S

safeguarding financial information, 121
Sage, Russell, Foundation, 5
sales
    closing, 901
    culture, establishing, 303-304
    strategies, 302
    See also selling
sales objectives, meeting, 308-309
sales-oriented bank, 303-308
Sallie Mae, 64
savings and loan crisis, 7, 8, 134
savings institutions, 14, 41, 42-43
seasonal delinquency patterns, 346
seasonal demand for credit, 40-41
secondary source of repayment, 249, 333
secured line of credit, 108-111
secured loan, 57-61, 185, 204, 236, 332, 349, 359
    purchase-money, 204
securities, 5, 6, 7, 16, 40, 59, 65, 66, 70, 152, 153, 248, 318
Securities and Exchange Act, 6
Securities and Exchange Commission, 6
securitization, 9, 116
security
    bank, 181, 350
    collateral, 314
    consumer, 13
    deposit, 97
    electronic, 180
    job, 6, 40, 239
    transaction, 43, 118
security agreement, 57, 145, 330, 332, 333, 334, 335, 336
security interest, 67, 125, 285, 330, 331, 332, 333, 337, 338
    establishing, 331
    in household goods, 67
selling, 81-82, 116, 169, 181, 302-308, 327
    consultative, 302, 303, 309, 312
    effective skills of, 304-306
    market-driven, 302-303

process of, 306-308
    See also sales
seriously delinquent accounts, collection remedies for, 356-357
Servicemembers Civil Relief Act (SCRA), 361, 362-363, 366
    automobile lease, 363
    installment loan, 363
    interest rate cap, 362-363
    lease and installment loan, 363
    obligation enforcement, 363
servicing disclosure statement, 186
settlement costs booklet, 186
Ship Mortgage Act, 334
shotgunning, 80
simple interest, 269, 270, 282, 326, 353, 354
Single-Family Housing Guaranteed Loan, 64
single-payment loans, 3, 268
skip tracing, 356
Small Business Administration (SBA) loan programs, 63, 66
smart card, 111, 112
Social Security number, 118, 206
sociodemographic environment, 36-39, 134
Soldiers' and Sailors' Civil Relief Act, 362
spam, 175
special flood hazard area (SFHA), 338
special value credit card, 103, 107
stability in reviewing character, 203, 238-239
stable value collateral, 314
Stafford loan, 63
STAR Systems, Inc., 111
State Farm Federal Savings Bank, 43
state regulation, 14, 325
statement of condition, *See* balance sheet
stock, 5, 59, 95, 152, 153, 335
stored-value card, 12, 112
strategic risk, 123, 137
straw purchaser, 85, 86
stroke-of-the-pen risk, 33
subprime lending, 9, 40, 66, 68, 317
substance abuse as cause of delinquency, 348, 350

T

tangible asset, 246, 248
technological development, tie-ins with, 115
technology, 4, 36, 41, 43, 52, 53, 57, 93, 118, 120, 137, 138, 151, 168, 171, 181, 194, 257, 306, 336
telemarketing, 174-175, 182, 187-188, 310, 311
    consumer protection and, 187-188

Telemarketing and Consumer Abuse Protection Act, 17, 187
telephone application, 80, 116, 169, 177, 180
Telephone Consumer Protection Act, 17, 187
term, 88, 124, 274, 277, 280-282, 310, 313-314, 330, 355
text message marketing, 174, 175
tie-in with technological development, 115
time value of money, 276, 277-278
timing of payments, loan profitability and, 182, 188
title search, 330
trade line, 205, 206-207
transaction risk, 138
Transactions with Affiliates Act, 152, 153-154
TransUnion, 225, 254
travel and entertainment (T&E) card, 103, 104, 140
triggering term, 184
truth in lending, 121, 123, 326, 336
 change in terms, 124
 disclosure statement, 125, 326, 328
 initial disclosures, 123-124
 payment disputes, 126
 periodic disclosures, 124
 right of rescission, 125
 unauthorized use, 126
 variable rate, 124
Truth in Lending Act (TILA), 2, 19, 43, 123-127, 145, 168, 181, 182-185, 236, 269, 317, 319, 326-328, 336
Twain, Mark, 262
tying, 286

U

unauthorized use, 102, 126
underwriting standards, 70, 140, 144, 167
unfair practices, 66, 183, 185, 361, 362
Uniform Commercial Code (UCC), 96, 331, 333
 Article 3, Negotiable Instruments, 96
Uniform Small Loan Law, 5
unsecured line of credit, 108, 117, 174, 310
unsecured loan, 61-62, 108, 313, 314, 328, 345
USA PATRIOT Act, 206
usury, 6
usury rate, 41, 269, 270

V

valid lien, creating, 332-333
valuation, 52, 61, 85, 204
 sources of information, 204
VantageScore, 254

variable-rate loan, 19, 124, 246, 270, 271-272, 280, 281, 282, 312, 318, 330
 disclosure, 124
 documentation for, 330
 documentation required for, 330
 pricing, 271-272, 312
variable rate, 182, 269, 270-272, 311, 312, 318, 330
vehicle, as collateral, 148
Visa, 10, 106, 112
volume segmentation, 173
voluntary liquidation, 360

W

W-2 form, 200
wage garnishment, 357
waiver of exemption, 66
warrant, 196, 210
warranty, 80, 89, 310, 330
wholesale line of credit, *See* floorplan line of credit
World War II (1941–1945), credit after, 6

AMERICAN **BANKERS** ASSOCIATION